D1713758

SYNTAX and SEMANTICS

VOLUME 5

SYNTAX and SEMANTICS

VOLUME 5

Japanese Generative Grammar

Edited by

MASAYOSHI SHIBATANI

University of Southern California
Los Angeles, California

ACADEMIC PRESS *New York San Francisco London*

A Subsidiary of Harcourt Brace Jovanovich, Publishers

ACADEMIC PRESS, INC.
111 Fifth Avenue, New York, New York 10003

United Kingdom Edition published by
ACADEMIC PRESS, INC. (LONDON) LTD.
24/28 Oval Road, London NW1

LIBRARY OF CONGRESS CATALOG CARD NUMBER: 72-9423

ISBN 0-12-785425-8

PRINTED IN THE UNITED STATES OF AMERICA

CONTENTS

Tense, Aspect, and Modality

MINORU NAKAU

Nominal Compounds

SEIICHI MAKINO

Honorifics

S. I. HARADA

LIST OF CONTRIBUTORS

Numbers in parentheses indicate the pages on which the authors' contributions begin.

S. I. HARADA (499), *Tokyo Metropolitan University, Tokyo, Japan*

IRWIN HOWARD (201), *Department of Linguistics, University of Hawaii, Honolulu, Hawaii*

KAZUKO INOUE (117), *Language Division, International Christian University, Tokyo, Japan*

LEWIS S. JOSEPHS (307), *Department of Linguistics, University of Hawaii, Honolulu, Hawaii*

SUSUMU KUNO (17), *Department of Linguistics, Harvard University, Cambridge, Massachusetts*

S.-Y. KURODA (1), *Department of Linguistics, University of California, San Diego, La Jolla, California*

JAMES D. MCCAWLEY (295), *Department of Linguistics, University of Chicago, Chicago, Illinois*

NORIKO AKATSUKA MCCAWLEY (51), *Department of Linguistics, University of Chicago, Chicago, Illinois*

NAOMI HANAOKA MCGLOIN (371), *Department of Far Eastern Languages and Literatures, University of Michigan, Ann Arbor, Michigan*

SEIICHI MAKINO (483), *Center for Asian Studies and Department of Linguistics, University of Illinois, Urbana, Illinois*

MINORU NAKAU (421), *Department of Literature and Linguistics, University of Tsukuba, Sakura-mura, Ibaraki-ken 300–31, Japan*

AGNES M. NIYEKAWA-HOWARD (201), *Department of East Asian Languages, University of Hawaii, Honolulu, Hawaii*

MASAYOSHI SHIBATANI (239), *Department of Linguistics, University of Southern California, Los Angeles, California*

PREFACE

The year 1975 marks the tenth year since the theory of generative grammar has been systematically applied to the Japanese language. Ever since pioneering dissertations such as Kuroda's "Generative grammatical studies in the Japanese language" (1965:MIT) were written in the generative framework a decade ago, research in the field has acquired both depth and breadth, which only investigations under a received paradigm permit.

The contributions of generative theory to the study of language need not be mentioned here, and this is not the place to discuss the nature of the theory. However, it is noteworthy that generative theory has provided the linguist with a new orientation toward language, and a framework that permits him to relate systematically under one cohesive system what appear to be unrelated, independent linguistic phenomena. In this regard, this volume presents research results radically different from those found in the traditional Japanese grammar book, for example, Tokieda's *Kokugo-gaku genron* (1941, Tokyo:Iwanami). Nowhere in the traditional grammar book can one find discussions systematically relating, for example, the phenomenon of reflexivization to so many grammatical constructions as some of the chapters in this volume do. Indeed, many of the chapters contained here amply demonstrate that various grammatical constructions are systematically related to each other to such an extent that one can readily appreciate how closely knit a system language is.

The present volume is also different from a few currently available books on Japanese written in the generative framework, for instance, Nakau's *Sentential complementation in Japanese* (1973, Tokyo: Kaitakusha). The depth and breadth current linguistic research demands make it almost impossible for any single person to conduct an in-depth study of a wide range of topics in a short period of time. Consequently, the currently available generative treatises either focus on a very limited number of closely related topics or deal with a wide range of topics rather superficially. Again, in none of these can one find such comprehensive, in-depth studies of topics ranging from negation to honorifics as found in this volume.

A third characteristic of the present volume lies in its presentation of perhaps the most rigorous applications of current theoretical apparati to various grammatical structures of a non-Indo-European language. A transformational approach and an interpretive approach to the same phenomenon of Japanese reflexivization are presented side by side with great rigor by N. McCawley and Inoue. A related discussion of reflexivization is also taken up and a further insight into the phenomenon is developed in the course of discussion of passivization by Howard and Niyekawa-Howard. The chapters by Harada, Kuno, Kuroda, J. McCawley, and McGloin present discussions of where unique grammatical structures of Japanese find their places in the grammatical tradition or in the total grammatical construct. On the other hand, the chapters by Josephs, Nakau, and Shibatani set the pace for detailed semantic descriptions without involving overly formal apparati. And, like many of the chapters, Makino's chapter examines the adequacy of the currently available theoretical devices—particularly those exploited in the analysis of nominal compounds. In short, the present volume is the first comprehensive illustration of how the detailed study of a non-Indo-European language can shed light on current theoretical problems and controversies.

Despite the fact that the present volume covers a wide range of topics with a great deal of comprehensiveness, there are many more important areas that have not been covered here. Research continues, and one may find the research results of the areas not covered here in professional journals such as *Papers in Japanese Linguistics*, published by the Japanese Linguistics Workshop, Department of Linguistics, University of Southern California.

The compilation of this volume has been made possible by the cooperation and assistance rendered to the editor by many. I first wish to thank those who contributed their work to the volume for their cooperation. I also would like to express my gratitude to the staff of Academic Press. Finally, my thanks go to my wife, Noriko, for her editorial assistance.

CONTENTS OF PREVIOUS VOLUMES

Volume 1

Volume 2

Volume 3

Volume 4

SUBJECT

S.-Y. KURODA

THE CONCEPT OF SUBJECT IN GRAMMAR

The concept of subject is certainly one of the oldest in the Western tradition of grammatical scholarship. In fact, it is not simply a concept in grammar; it has been fundamental in Western philosophy and logic since antiquity. 'Subject' can be a metaphysical, logical, or grammatical concept. In describing the conceptual ramifications of 'subject', we shall begin with metaphysics, go on to logic, and finally come to grammar, which is our main concern.

As a metaphysical concept, the subject is a unit of existence—whatever is assumed to exist as an individual entity.[1] A subject is that in which various properties are contained, those properties which can be affirmed of it as an entity. The entity as a subject may be identified by the properties that belong to it, and these properties may be considered as making up the notion of the entity as a subject. 'Subject', in this sense, overlaps the concept of 'substance'. What types of subjects one allows depends on, or rather, conversely, determines one's metaphysical beliefs. We will not be concerned with this metaphysical concept of subject in what follows.

[1]This sense of 'subject' corresponds to that specified as *sujet réel*, *sujet d'inhérence*, or *sujet métaphysique* in Lalande (1968:1068): 'Le sujet *réel*, c'est-à-dire, au sens aristotélicien, l'être individuel, oúsía prōtē, qui produit les actes ou en qui résident les qualités qu'on en affirme.'

The logical concept of subject may be derived conceptually from the metaphysical concept of subject. If the universe is assumed to consist of subjects in the metaphysical sense (each subsisting independently and endowed with its respective properties), then a primary unit of knowledge concerning the universe, that is, the content of a single judgment, must take the form of affirming or denying the attribution of some property to some subject. That to which a judgment affirms or denies the attribution of a property is called the subject of the judgment, and that which the judgment affirms or denies of the subject is called its predicate.[2] The proposition, i.e., the ideal content of a judgment, is then composed of two ideas, corresponding to the subject and the predicate of the judgment. Somewhat ambiguously, we may also call the 'subject idea' of the proposition the subject of the judgment. 'Traditional logic' is based on this conception of judgment, or proposition. The concept of subject as the subject of a judgment, or of a proposition, is, thus, a fundamental concept of traditional logic.

Modern formal logic, however, assumes that a proposition consists of a 'predicate' and a number of 'arguments' (and 'quantifiers', if some of the arguments are variables). The arguments are related to each other via the predicate, but none of them is assumed to have any particular role as the subject. Thus, the logical concept of subject is dispensed with in modern formal logic. In fact, it is considered as one of the basic achievements of modern logic that it has freed logic from the notion of subject, and, hence, also freed it from traditional metaphysics.

Let me again quote a passage that I have quoted elsewhere (Kuroda, 1972):

> According to most earlier logicians there could be no adequate representation of a judgement without a distinction between subject and predicate, but Frege rejects this dogma. There may indeed be a rhetorical difference between 'The Greeks defeated the Persians' and 'The Persians were defeated by the Greeks'; but the *conceptual content* of the two statements is the same, because either can be substituted for the other as a premiss without effect on the validity of our reasoning, and this is all we need consider when we try to make a language for the purpose he has in mind [Kneale and Kneale, 1962:479. By permission of Clarendon Press.].

According to traditional logic, one makes a judgment about a subject, either *the Greeks* or *the Persians*, in the case of the preceding examples. If the sub-

[2] 'Le jugement que nous faisons des choses, comme quand je dis; *la terre est ronde*, s'appelle proposition; et ainsi toute proposition enferme necessairement deux termes: l'vn appellé *sujet*, qui est ce dont on affirme, comme *terre*; et l'autre appellé *attribut*, qui est ce qu'on affirme, comme *ronde*: et de plus la liaison entre ces deux termes, *est* [Lancelot and Arnauld, 1660:28–29].'

ject is *the Greeks*, the property *defeated the Persians* is to be predicated of it; if the subject is *the Persians*, the property *was defeated by the Greeks* is to be predicated of it. According to modern logic, on the other hand, there is one and the same proposition underlying these two linguistic expressions, whereby the two terms *the Greeks* and *the Persians* are related by the predicate *defeated*; schematically, *defeated* (*the Greeks*, *the Persians*).

It might, however, be premature to conclude directly from the remarkable achievements of modern formal logic that traditional logic has been rendered totally insignificant. To be sure, insofar as logic is conceived as a pure science concerned with the formal relationships between premisses (assumptions) and their valid conclusions (logical consequences), modern formal logic has superseded traditional logic. And for this progress to have been achieved, it has been essential that modern formal logic discard the assumed subject–predicate structure of a proposition as irrelevant, and that it abstract from a proposition the relational structure of 'predicate'—that which is essential for the validity of reasoning. Logic, in this sense, is not concerned with judgments as psychological processes, or with propositions as psychologically real representations of the contents of judgments, in whatever sense. It remains neutral with respect to psychological accounts of human mental acts of judging. This is the basic attitude of 'standard' modern formal logic. It is with this deliberately neutral attitude toward psychological factors that modern formal logic has succeeded in studying the formal structure of reasoning far beyond the limits to which traditional logic was confined.

In contrast, traditional logic has quite a different attitude toward the basic objects of study. It begins with a view of judgment as a mental process. Putting aside for now the question of whether the analysis proposed by traditional logic is acceptable or not, one must admit, in comparing traditional logic and modern formal logic, that their different assumptions on the form of the basic unit of logic (judgment or proposition) need not be incompatible with each other. It is possible that, as a theory of the form of human judgment, the attitude of traditional logic is justified. Then, as a formal theory of logical deductions, modern formal logic may be said to have succeeded in removing irrelevant factors from the basic forms of propositions.

Among logicians, and also among linguists following suit, reaction against the indifference of 'standard' formal logic toward the theory of human judgment seems to have been gaining ground in recent years. Logicians and linguists have tried to develop a formal system of 'logical forms' for human language. Their attempt may be said to resurrect neglected aspects of traditional logic. However, with some notable earlier exceptions like Geach and Strawson, the traditional notion of subject–predicate structure does not seem to have attracted much attention from modern logicians of natural language.[3] Neither does there seem to be particularly active or conscious concern with the traditional notion of subject among linguists who are not involved in the 'natural logic' movement. To be sure, 'topic' and 'comment' (or 'theme' and 'rheme') are familiar terms in contemporary linguistics, and this dichotomy is reminiscent of the opposition subject–predicate. But in the current usage of linguists, the term TOPIC seems to refer to a notion to be defined 'in terms of contextual dispensability or predictability: the topic, or "subject of discourse" is described as that element which is GIVEN in the general situation or in some explicit question to which the speaker is replying ... [Lyons, 1968:335].' Such a notion of topic is, in my opinion, different from the traditional concept of subject. Such a notion is, in fact, conceptually independent of any claim one might make on the form (or forms) of judgments. Thus, the notion of topic defined as 'given' in terms of contextual dispensability or predictability is applicable even under the assumption that all judgments are of the form that modern formal logic suggests. Indeed, even if the sentence *The Greeks defeated the Persians* were expressed in the form *defeated* (*the Greeks*, *the Persians*), neither 'argument' being assigned the special status of subject, *the Greeks* might still be the topic, in the sense defined earlier, if *the Greeks* were a 'given' in the general situation of the discourse or, more specifically, when a question like 'What, then, did the Greeks do?' had been asked. We can say the same thing for *the Persians*.

Furthermore, a topic in the general sense under discussion may not even be a constituent of a sentence. We can easily conceive of a situation in which *the Greeks* and *the Persians* are equally 'given,' for example, after the question 'What, then, happened to the Greeks and the Persians?' In such a situation, the pair (*the Greeks*, *the Persians*) would have to be taken as the topic of the sentence *The Greeks defeated the Persians*, according to the general definition of 'topic'. And this conclusion must be independent of any claim on the form of judgment expressed by this sentence (whether it is in the subject–predicate form of traditional logic or in a form similar to the propositional form of modern logic).

If the traditional conception of judgment should prove to be correct (or

[3]Cf. Geach (1950), Strawson (1964). It is true that we can detect in the recent work of 'non-standard' formal logicians some formalisms that might be taken as modern, formalized versions of the traditional concept of subject. What I have in mind, in particular, is some uses of the abstraction operator by certain logicians who deal with natural languages, for example, by those who work in Montague grammar. But it is not obvious whether the proponents of such formalisms have intended, or even would allow, such an interpretation.

partially correct, as I will claim shortly), then there would exist, to be sure, a plausible conceptual connection between the notion of topic and the logical concept of subject. That is, it might be claimed that the subject of a judgment must be a topic in each contextual situation in which the judgment is made, provided that the notion of 'given' in the definition of topic is sufficiently refined.[4] But such a claim is simply a claim about a pragmatic property of 'subject', not a claim on the basis of which one might identify the notion of topic with the traditional, logical concept of subject.

To repeat, then, the traditional, logical concept of subject does not, at present, seem to be a focus of active attention either for logicians of natural language or for linguists.

But, after all, does the claim of traditional logic on the form of human judgment have any validity? Or does the formalization of propositions by modern formal logic faithfully reflect the form of human judgment in this regard? I am of the opinion that there are two different forms of judgments, one with the subject–predicate structure and the other without. Thus, it is claimed that traditional logic is partially correct, that is, correct to the extent that it recognizes the form of a judgment with subject–predicate structure, but that it is incorrect in that it assumes that all judgments are necessarily of this form.

I discussed in some detail this distinction between the two types of judgments in an earlier study, in which I called the subject–predicate form of judgment 'categorical' and the subjectless form 'thetic', borrowing these notions from the Brentano–Marty theory of judgment and extending their senses.

My opinion is based on linguistic facts concerning Japanese. I assume that two different forms of sentences that we can recognize in Japanese correspond to the two different forms of judgments. I shall illustrate this point with a few examples. Whether we can generalize our claim based on linguistic facts in Japanese to a universal claim on the forms of human judgments in general is, of course, a separate issue. As far as English is concerned, I believe that a distinction between sentences with subject–predicate structure and subjectless sentences is valid. (Of course, on the surface level sentences may be ambiguous with respect to this dichotomy.) But linguistic evidence for this claim would have to be much more complicated and subtle in English than in Japanese, and the demonstration that relates such evidence to the proposed conclusion would, inevitably, be more indirect and, hence, more interesting. I refer the reader to Pope (1972) for an attempt to demonstrate the distinction between categorical and thetic sentences in English.

[4]For a refinement of the notion of 'given', see Kuno (1973:39ff).

I shall now give a brief summary of the relevant facts in Japanese. The reader may refer to Kuroda (1972) for details. The characteristic of a categorical judgment is that it is expressed by a sentence with a sentence-initial *wa* phrase, which represents the subject of the judgment. On the other hand, a sentence without a sentence-initial *wa* phrase is assumed to express a thetic judgment.[5] Thus:

(1) *Inu-ga hasitte iru.*
'A/the dog(s) is/are running.'

(2) *Inu-ga neko-o oikake-te iru.*
'A/the dog(s) is/are chasing a/the cat(s).'

express thetic judgments, while:

(3) *Inu-wa hasiru.*
'Dogs/the dog(s) run(s).'

(4) *Inu-wa hasitte iru.*
'The dog(s) is/are running.'

(5) *Inu-wa neko-o oikakeru.*
'Dogs/the dog chase(s) (a/the) cat(s).'

(6) *Inu-wa neko-o oikake-te iru.*
'The dog(s) is/are chasing (a/the) cat(s).'

(7) *Neko-wa inu-ga oikake ru.*
'Cats/the cat(s) are/is chased by (a/the) dog(s).'

[5]Strictly speaking, however, the intended referent of 'sentence-initial *wa* phrase' may be neither in sentence-initial position nor a *wa* phrase in the real surface structure. For example, the particle *wa* may be deleted from the surface structure when some other particle, such as *sae* 'even', is attached to the same noun phrase as *wa*; or a non-*wa* phrase may be preposed when it is especially long:

(i) *Fido-sae neko-o oikakeru.*
'Even Fido chases cats.'

(ii) *Fido-sae neko-o oikakeru koto-o John-wa kataku sinzite iru.*
'John believes firmly that even Fido chases cats.'

Thus, the characterization 'sentence-initial *wa* phrase' must be given in some near-surface, but not quite surface, level.

(8) *Neko-wa inu-ga oikake-te iru.*
'The cat(s) is/are being chased by (a/the) dog(s).'

are categorical judgments; *inu-wa* represents the subject of a judgment in (3)–(6), and *neko-wa* represents the subject of a judgment in (7) and (8).

Notice that (3), (5), and (7) make generic statements, while the rest of the examples are sentences that make specific statements referring to specific events. Notice, also, that the noun *inu* bears the same grammatical relation to the verb in each of these sentences—namely, the relation 'subject-of', in the sense of Chomsky (1965) (this sense is different from the one we have been discussing)—and that, by definition, with this particular verb, *oikakeru*, the noun *inu* has the semantic function, 'the actor-of', in each sentence. Similarly, *neko* is the patient of the action *oikakeru*. But in (5) and (6), *inu* represents the subject of a judgment, while in (7) and (8), *neko* represents the subject of a judgment.

On what basis do I claim that a sentence with a sentence-initial *wa* phrase represents a judgment of the subject–predicate form? A piece of circumstantial evidence not based entirely on simple intuition might be cited. A sentence-initial *wa* phrase cannot be semantically indefinite specific. For details the reader may refer to Kuroda (1972), but I shall give a brief explanation here. A sentence like (2) can be used when the speaker perceives a scene in which a dog (which has not been in his attention) is chasing a cat. The noun *inu* has a particular referent, the dog in question. The speaker sees this object and perceives it as a dog. He uses the noun *inu* to refer to this particular object in question. In this referential act, the speaker is not interested in particular characteristics of the dog as an individual dog; he grasps it simply as an unmarked representative of the entities having the attribute 'dogness'. We call this use of a noun 'indefinite specific'. Now, assume that *inu* in the sentence-initial *wa* phrase of (6) is indefinite specific. Then the speaker must be attributing the action of chasing a cat (or cats) to an arbitrary representative of the class of entities that can be named by the particular property used to refer to this entity, namely, *inu*. In other words, the speaker would in effect have made a generic statement on the class of objects namable as 'dog'. But in fact, (6) cannot be taken as a generic statement. The *inu-wa* in (6) must refer to a definite dog (or dogs) whose identity has already been established in the speaker's consciousness.

But there is, admittedly, not much more that I can do to support the claim that a sentence with a sentence-initial *wa* phrase represents a judgment of the subject–predicate structure, while a sentence without a sentence-initial *wa* phrase represents a judgment without the subject–predicate structure, except appealing directly to native intuition. Sentences like (3)–(6) are felt to be about the dog or dogs, affirming whatever is stated by the rest of the sentences. Similarly, sentences like (7) and (8) are felt to be about the cat or cats, affirming whatever is said by the rest of the sentences. On the other hand, sentences without a sentence-initial *wa* phrase, like (1) and (2), do not give rise to such intuitive feeling about the 'subject of a judgment'. In particular, in a sentence with a transitive verb, like (2), there is intuitively no particular precedence of one noun phrase over the other. The sense of (2) does not change noticeably when one changes word order:

(9) *Neko-o inu-ga oikakete iru.*

Hence, one can at least claim that the contention that the sentence-initial *wa* phrase represents the subject of a judgment is compatible with the concept of subject conceived by traditional logicians. One can claim that the difference between the two structures exemplified by the pair (2) and (6), which are truth-functionally equivalent, can be accounted for by referring to the difference between the forms of judgments (propositions) assumed by traditional logic and those assumed by modern formal logic.

Now, notice that, by making the claim that sentence-initial *wa* phrases represent the subjects of judgments, we have, in effect, made a statement about a grammatical fact; having started from metaphysics and gone through logic, we have now arrived at grammar. For a characterization of something as a sentence-initial *wa* phrase is a syntactic characterization. Our claim relates this syntactic characterization to a logical characterization, to use traditional terminology, or to a semantic characterization, to use terminology more familiar to us. An entity syntactically characterized as a sentence-initial *wa* phrase has the semantic function of expressing the subject of a judgment. This is the meaning of our claim. Based on this claim, the grammatical concept of subject may now be formulated for Japanese. The sentence-initial *wa* phrase may be called the 'subject of a sentence'. The subject of a sentence represents the subject of the judgment that the sentence represents.

This is a grammatical concept of subject with respect to Japanese. Before making the grammatical concept of subject a general concept, let us settle a terminological problem. This grammatical concept of subject in Japanese and the concept we are about to define in a more general setting may be considered as a clarification of the grammatical concept of subject discussed in the original works of traditional grammar, such as the Port-Royal grammar. But in current linguistic terminology we have grammatical notions of subject other than this. We are familiar with the terms DEEP SUBJECT and SURFACE SUBJECT in transformational tradition. We are also aware of the distinction made by some earlier grammarians in terms of 'logical subject' and 'grammatical subject'.[6] These notions of subject are also grammatical notions. But they are conceptually different from the grammatical concept of subject we have been discussing, although they are by no means unrelated to this concept; in fact, the various concepts are entangled with each other rather hopelessly in the history of discussions on the ramifications of the notion of subject. I shall return to these other notions of subject and make some comments on them. At the moment, however, we need a term by which we can unambiguously refer to the grammatical concept of subject we have been discussing, in contradistinction to other grammatical notions of subject. For lack of a better choice, I shall call it 'L-subject'. The letter *L* hints at 'logic', but this concept is intended to be a concept in grammar, not in logic.

The definition of L-subject to be given now is too broad and vague to be of any specific use in the description of a specific language such as English. The aim of presenting a general definition is simply to give some idea of the conceptual status of the concept of L-subject in Japanese, which has a concrete manifestation as the sentence-initial *wa* phrase.

Assume that the following claim is made: A constituent of a sentence satisfying some syntactic characterization represents the subject of the judgment that this sentence represents, and, conversely, a judgment with a subject (a categorical judgment) is represented by a sentence containing a constituent satisfying this syntactic characterization. Then the L-subject of a sentence is defined as a constituent satisfying this syntactic characterization.

So if we replace 'some syntactic characterization' and 'this syntactic characterization' in the preceding paragraph with 'sentence-initial *wa* phrase', we obtain the definition of L-subject in Japanese.

I leave the term SYNTACTIC CHARACTERIZATION deliberately vague. 'Syntactic characterization' is a characterization one can give in terms of one's syntactic theory. Thus, the meaning of the term can vary according to the type of syntactic theory one assumes. It may not necessarily refer exclusively to some straightforward surface or near-surface characterization like 'to be a sentence-initial *wa* phrase'. This point will be illustrated in the next section, where we try to interpret the meaning of the term NOMINATIVE in the Port-Royal grammar. The Port-Royal grammar gives an 'underlying' characterization of L-subject, and furnishes us with interesting evidence that it recognizes the level of underlying structures. However, in my view the

[6]'... many linguists have drawn a distinction between the "grammatical" and "logical" subject of passive sentences; saying that in *Bill was killed by John* the "grammatical" subject is *Bill* and the "logical" (or underlying) subject *John* whereas in the corresponding active sentence *John killed Bill* the noun *John* is both the "grammatical" and the "logical" subject (and *Bill* the object) [Lyons, 1968:343].'

Port-Royal grammarians' conception of L-subject is mistaken, since it is based on their assumption that all judgments are of the subject-predicate form.

"NOMINATIVE" IN THE PORT-ROYAL GRAMMAR

The traditional concept of subject we have been dealing with originated in the scholarly tradition of speakers of Indo-European languages. But it turns out to be more difficult to see in the case of English, for example, than in the case of Japanese, whether (or to what extent) the traditional theory of subject is applicable. Let us now consider what traditional grammar says about subject. 'Traditional grammar' is an ambiguous term. To be historically exact, we should make our target specific and discuss, for example, the Port-Royal grammar. Indeed, the Port-Royal grammar exerted a decisive influence in the development of 'traditional grammar', and may be considered the origin of modern 'traditional grammar'. But let us start with what might be taken as a simplified, 'popular image' of traditional grammar, perhaps a straw man in the context of a serious attempt at analyzing the history of grammatical theory.

The position of the 'popular image' of traditional grammar may be stated in our terminology as follows: The surface subject is the L-subject. For our present purposes, we may agree to understand by surface subject that constituent of a sentence which determines the surface form of the verb, that is, the constituent with which the main verb agrees in number and person. Thus, *the Greeks* and *the Persians* are assumed to represent the subjects of the judgments represented by *The Greeks defeated the Persians* and *The Persians were defeated by the Greeks*, respectively.

The 'impersonal' construction, however, provides an obvious difficulty for this theory of subject. The problem of the 'impersonal' construction attracted a great deal of attention from philosophers and linguists in the late nineteenth century, in the declining days of traditional grammar, and contributed to the development of the Brentano–Marty theory of judgment. The Port-Royal grammarians were already aware of this problem, however. Thanks to Chomsky, we now know that the Port-Royal grammar is more sophisticated than people might have assumed traditional grammar to be (Chomsky, 1966, 1968). We see in it some signs of the distinction between surface structure and underlying structure. And in fact, the treatment of 'impersonal' sentences by the Port-Royal grammar gives us another example of its position on underlying structure.

The Port-Royal grammar does recognize that the surface subject of an impersonal sentence (i.e., in the case of French, the impersonal use of the pronoun *il*) cannot be the real subject. But it claims that 'our language', properly speaking, does not have impersonal sentences, which implies that 'impersonal' sentences, too, have subjects and, thus, do not constitute counterexamples to the claim that all sentences consist of subject and predicate. To quote:

> Par là on peut conclure ce semble, que nostre langue n'a point proprement d'impersonnels. Car quand nous disons, *il faut, il est permis, il me plaist*: cet *il* est là proprement vn relatif qui tient toûjours lieu du nominatif du verbe, lequel d'ordinaire vient aprés dans le regime; comme si je dis, *il me plaist de faire cela*, c'est à dire, *il de faire*, pour *l'action* ou *le mouvement de faire cela me plaist*, ou *est mon plaisir*. Et partant cet *il* que peu de personnes ont compris ce me semble, n'est qu'vne espece de pronom, pour *id*, cela, qui tient lieu du nominatif sous-entendu ou renfermé dans le sens, et le represente [Lancelot and Arnauld, 1664:124–125].

Also:

> Et l'on peut encore remarquer que les verbes des effets de la nature, comme *pluit*, *ningit*, *grandinat*, peuvent estre expliquez par ces mesmes principes en l'vne et en l'autre Langue. Comme *pluit* est proprement vn mot dans lequel pour abreger on a renfermé le sujet, l'affirmation et l'attribut, au lieu de *pluvia fit* ou *cadit*. Et quand nous disons *il pleut*, *il nege*, *il gresle*, etc. il est là pour le nominatif, c'est à dire, *pluie*, *nege*, *gresle*, etc. renfermé avec leur verbe substantif *est* ou *fait*: comme qui diroit, *il pluie est*, *il nege se fait*, pour *id quod dicitur pluvia est*, *id quod vocatur nix fit*, etc. [ibid. 125–126].

Note the use of the term NOMINATIF in these quotes. The sense of the term RELATIF in the first quote is not obvious, yet what the Port-Royal grammar intends to say about the 'impersonal' *il* is clear enough. *Il* stands for the 'nominative', which the Port-Royal grammar says comes after verb in the former examples and is contained in the verb in the latter examples. Here, then, 'nominative' does not mean what is in the nominative case in the surface structure (the surface subject). It might be intended to mean what, in a sense, SHOULD be in the position for the nominative case in a sentence and, in effect (in the modern terminology), what is to be taken as the underlying subject.

This concealed sense of 'underlying subject' in some uses of the term NOMINATIVE in the Port-Royal grammar is seen more clearly in its last chapter on syntax, 'De la Syntaxe ou Construction des mots ensemble':

> Mais il est bon de remarquer quelques maximes generales, qui sont de grand vsage dans toutes les Langues.
>
> La 1. qu'il n'y a jamais de Nominatif qui n'ait rapport à quelque verbe exprimé ou sous-entendu, parce que l'on ne parle pas seulement pour marquer ce que l'on conçoit, mais pour exprimer ce que l'on pense de ce que l'on conçoit, ce qui se marque par le verbe.

> La 2. qu'il n'y a point aussi de verbe qui n'ait son Nominatif exprimé ou sous-entendu, parce que le propre du Verbe estant d'affirmer, il faut qu'il y ait quelque chose dont on affirme, ce qui est le sujet ou le Nominatif du verbe, quoy que deuant les infinitifs il soit à l'accusatif, *scio Petrum esse doctum* [Lancelot and Arnauld, 1660:142–143].

Thus, it is claimed that (1) no 'nominative' is used without some verb, expressed or understood, because one does not speak only to mark what one conceives, but to express what one thinks about what one conceives, and (2) there is no verb without its 'nominative', expressed or understood, because, the role of the verb being that of affirming, there must be some entity of which the verb affirms, some property which entity, the Port-Royal grammar states, 'is the subject or the Nominative of the verb, although before the infinitives it is in accusative case, *scio Petrum esse doctum*'.

The last sentence seems particularly remarkable, since it, in effect, states that 'nominative is accusative before an infinitive'. Such a statement is a sheer contradiction if the term NOMINATIVE is understood exclusively as indicating a particular word form, that is, as a morphological notion belonging to the surface structure.

Thus, the term NOMINATIVE in the Port-Royal grammar refers ambiguously to the surface constituent characterized by nominative case in the morphological sense, and to the underlying constituent characterized as the real 'subject' of the sentence, i.e., the constituent assumed to represent the subject of the judgment expressed by the sentence.

It is significant, I believe, that the Port-Royal grammar used the syntactic term NOMINATIVE in the formulation of its claim that all sentences, including impersonals, have subjects. What is implicit in this formulation of the claim is the conception of an underlying representation as definable in terms of primitive notions such as 'nominative', which notions are also involved in the description of surface representations. Underlying representations have the constituent 'nominative' and parallel the structure of surface representations in this regard. Thus, on the one hand, it is recognized that surface structures do not necessarily correspond uniformly to the semantic structure of sentences; in the surface structures the nominative case does not necessarily represent the subject of a judgment, nor is the subject of a judgment necessarily represented by the nominative case. On the other hand, it is also assumed that the typical, or proper, function of the nominative case is to indicate the subject of a proposition. The underlying representation of a sentence is to be reconstructed on the basis of this assumption, when its surface structure is not proper and the surface nominative does not represent the subject of a judgment.

Thus, the ambiguous use of the term NOMINATIVE implies a syntactic theory that assumes two different levels of syntactic representations that share common formal characteristics. If, on the other hand, one is concerned solely with semantic interpretations, it suffices to state simply that the extraposed complement, for example, represents the subject of an impersonal sentence, without associating the semantic function of the logical subject with the syntactic notion of 'nominative'. As far as the form of the theory is concerned, then, the ambiguous use of the term NOMINATIVE in the Port-Royal grammar parallels the similar ambiguity of the term SUBJECT (deep or underlying versus surface subject) in transformational grammar. One might cite this situation as another piece of evidence supporting the claim that the Port-Royal grammar anticipated transformational grammar.

It must, however, be noted that the motivation for setting up the underlying nominative in the Port-Royal grammar is different from the motivation for recognizing deep subjects in transformational grammar. For example, transformational grammar assumes that a pair of active and passive sentences share the same deep subject; the deep subject bears the same grammatical relation, 'subject-of', to the verb in both the active and passive sentences, corresponding to a constant semantic function determined by the verb, for example, 'the actor-of'. The active–passive pair serves as a paradigmatic case for the distinction between deep and surface subject made by transformational grammarians (and indeed, it served the same role for the distinction between 'logical' and 'grammatical' subject made by some recent traditional grammarians, who anticipated transformational grammar in this respect). Passive sentences did not provide any immediate difficulty for the Port-Royal theory of 'subject'. The surface subject was identified with the subject of a judgment. In contrast, impersonal sentences provided the Port-Royal grammarians with a paradigmatic example for their theory of underlying representations, since these are obvious *prima facie* counterexamples to their theory of subject that they were challenged to overcome.

Because the motivations for a distinction between deep and surface subject differ in the Port-Royal grammar and transformational grammar, the extent to which this distinction manifests itself in the respective grammatical descriptions varies too. In fact, the real discrepancy between the underlying and surface nominatives in the Port-Royal grammar seems quite limited. In the examples quoted from the Port-Royal grammar, in which the underlying nominative is not the surface nominative, either the notion of surface nominative is irrelevant (in *scio Petrum esse doctum*, because there is no surface nominative), or the surface nominative is an 'impersonal' pronoun. No example represents the case in which (as with passive constructions) the surface subject is a constituent that bears a grammatical relation other than 'subject-of' with the verb in the underlying structure. Perhaps this situation reflects the substantial limitation on the use of the concept of underlying nominative in the Port-Royal grammar.

Thus, the theoretical significance of the concept of underlying 'nominative' in the Port-Royal grammar is not equatable with the concept of deep subject in transformational grammar.

In any event, it would be fair to summarize the Port-Royal position as follows. It distinguishes two levels of representations for sentences and, correspondingly, two concepts of subject (or nominative). The subject of a judgment is represented by the constituent that is the underlying nominative, i.e., that occupies the nominative position in the underlying representation. According to the conception of the Port-Royal grammar, then, the L-subject is the underlying nominative.

I am not concerned here with tracing, through the era of traditional grammar, the fate of the concept of L-subject in its subtler form in the Port-Royal grammar or in the simplistic form of the 'popular image' of traditional grammar. But the day of the L-subject in grammar was over by the time the influence of modern formal logic began to be felt in the intellectual community at large. We do not see a grammatical concept of subject corresponding to the logical concept of subject of a judgment in Bloomfield's *Language*, the Bible of American structuralism. Instead, we read statements like the following:

> In English we have two favorite sentence-forms. One consists of ACTOR–ACTION phrase—phrases whose structure is that of the actor–action construction: *John ran away. Who ran away? Did John run away?* The other consists of a command—an infinitive verb with or without modifiers: *Come! Be good!* [Bloomfield, *Language*, 1933:172. By permission of Holt, Rinehart, and Winston, Inc.].

Let us not be concerned with the appropriateness of the choice of the term ACTOR–ACTION. One could take it as merely a suggestive tag. It would be beside the point to attack Bloomfield by saying that the concept of 'actor–action' fails to characterize semantically what he intends to refer to by 'ACTOR–ACTION sentence form'. He may simply have wanted to give a name to what traditional grammar would call the subject–predicate sentence form without becoming entangled with the traditional concept of L-subject. This reluntance to use the traditional term was overcome in due course; twenty years later Gleason could write:

> [The subject–predicate sentence] is a construction which has as its immediate constituents a subject and a predicate. A subject is a nominal, a pronominal, certain types of phrases, or a clause. A predicate is a verbal or various larger constructions involving verbals. Neither of these descriptions is a definition. The defining characteristic is that subjects and predicates serve as immediate constituents in the formation of sentences. These definitions are both circular and inexact ... The important notion, however, is that sentences have a definable regularity of formation, and that this is expressible in terms of ICs [Gleason, 1956:137].

The term SUBJECT was restored, and the notion it represents is 'surface subject', without any ambiguity and without being associated with the concept of the subject of a judgment. The concept of L-subject had disappeared.

When transformational grammar followed structuralism, the notion of subject was again split into two, into deep subject and surface subject. Transformational grammar is now regarded as a modern version of traditional grammar or, more specifically, of the Port-Royal grammar. But as far as the theory of subject is concerned, it is not appropriate to assume that with transformational grammar we have returned to the Port-Royal grammar. The reason is simple. Transformational grammar is not based on, or associated with, the theory of judgment underlying the Port-Royal grammar. If a theory of grammar does not presuppose the theory of judgment according to which a judgment consists of subject and predicate, affirming or denying the predicate of the subject, then the concept of L-subject cannot be a theoretical concept in that theory. What reemerged in transformational grammar is the distinction between the concepts of underlying nominative and surface nominative of the Port-Royal grammar, realized as the distinction between deep and surface subject. But, as indicated earlier, the basic motivations for the distinctions in the two systems are not identical. In the Port-Royal grammar, the motivation is to accord a uniform grammatical expression to the subject of a judgment, that is to say, to establish the grammatical concept of L-subject as the underlying 'nominative'. In transformational grammar, the motivation for deep structure is to achieve a uniform syntactic expression for the grammatical relation 'subject-of' (as opposed to 'object-of', etc.). To the extent that these motivations are mutually compatible, the two grammatical theories yield identical descriptions. The cases in which the Port-Royal grammar sets up an underlying 'nominative' different from the surface 'nominative' are those in which transformational grammar would set up a deep subject different from the surface subject. From a formal point of view, it might appear that transformational grammar is an extension (generalization) of the Port-Royal grammar, as far as the particular aspect of grammar we are dealing with is concerned.

The Port-Royal grammarians, I believe, were mistaken in assuming that all sentences unambiguously represent judgments of the subject–predicate structure. From this mistaken assumption they proceeded to posit an underlying 'nominative' for impersonal sentences. But if there is any direct evidence for the subjectless structure of judgment in the grammatical structure of Indo-European languages, it is the structure of impersonal sentences. And in fact, impersonal sentences furnished a starting point for the movement against the 'traditional' theory of judgment in the nineteenth century, which culminated in the Brentano–Marty theory of judgment.

Thus, we have good evidence to show that the Port-Royal grammarians developed a prototype of transformational grammar, but for the wrong reasons, as far as this particular evidence is concerned. Such is the subtlety and irony of the historiography of grammatical theory.[7]

[7]There is another portion of the Port-Royal theory that might be interpreted as indicating that the Port-Royal theory relates the logical concept of subject to the notion of underlying subject. In fact, Chomsky refers to the treatment of 'implicit syllogisms' by the Port-Royal logic and apparently compares the Port-Royal logicians' reduction of implicit syllogisms to ordinary syllogisms with the transformationalist reduction of surface structures to underlying representations. To quote:

> Thus it is pointed out (pp. 206–207) [page reference by Chomsky to the English translation of the Port-Royal Logic by J. Dickoff and P. James] that the inference from *The divine law commands us to honor kings* and *Louis XIV is a king* to *the divine law commands us* to *honor Louis XIV* is obviously valid, though it does not exemplify any valid figure as it stands, superficially. By regarding *kings* as 'the subject of a sentence contained implicitly in the original sentence', using the passive transformation and otherwise decomposing the original sentence into its underlying propositional constituents, we can finally reduce the argument to the valid figure Barbara [Chomsky, *Cartesian linguistics*, 1966:44. By permission of Harper and Row.].

But this comparison has obvious difficulty. Assume that the 'underlying representation' is that in which the 'subject' of the first premiss of the figure Barbara is grammatically the subject of the sentence. Then we have to 'undo' the passive transformation to derive the 'surface structure', i.e., the sentence actually given as the first premiss in the implicit syllogism. This is contrary to the usual practice of transformational grammar, at least in the standard framework. In my opinion, the treatment of implicit syllogisms by the Port-Royal logic cannot be reinterpreted in terms of the transformational reduction of surface structures to their deep structures in the standard transformational framework, and, thus, cannot serve as good evidence to show that the Port-Royal grammar anticipated transformational theory, at least the standard type. In fact, the problem of implicit syllogisms is a problem that reveals the inadequacy of the unified theory of logic and grammar intended by the Port-Royal logicians and grammarians. But this is not the place to go into this question. (I have previously touched on this question; see Kuroda, 1969b.)

SUBJECT RAISING[1]

SUSUMU KUNO

INTRODUCTION

In English, there is a process, called subject raising, that takes the constituent subject out of the complement clause and makes it a constituent of the matrix clause. For example, observe the following pairs of sentences:

(1) a. *I expect that* ***Mary*** *will come.*
  b. *I expect* ***Mary*** *to come.*

(2) a. *That* ***Mary*** *will come is likely.*
  b. ***Mary*** *is likely to come.*

In (1a) and (2a), *Mary* is the subject of the object complement and the subject complement, respectively. On the other hand, in (1b) and (2b), it is the object and the subject, respectively, of the matrix sentence.[2] Subject raising is a common syntactic device in SVO languages, but its presence is not conspicuous in SOV languages.

[1]This is a revised version of a paper that originally appeared in *Papers in Japanese Linguistics*, 1972, **1**(1), 24–51. Research represented in the work has been supported by National Science Foundation Grants GS-2858 and GS-33263X to Harvard University.

[2]Chomsky (1973) claims that although *Mary* in (2b) is the subject of the main sentence, *Mary* in (1b) is still an element in the subordinate clause. There is, however, overwhelming evidence that *Mary to come* in (1b) does not constitute a subordinate clause (and, for that matter, is not even a constituent), and that *Mary* is the object of *expect* and, therefore, a constituent of the matrix clause. See Postal (1974) for details.

In a previous study (Kuno, 1974a), I attempted to account for the language universal that all VSO languages mark embedded clauses at clause-initial position, and that most SOV languages do so at clause-final position.[3] The explanation lies in the fact that from the point of view of speech perception, both center embedding (but not right embedding or left embedding) and juxtaposition of conjunctions of the same kind greatly reduce the intelligibility of sentences. From this point of view, it is easy to show that the clause-final positioning of conjunctions for VSO languages and their clause-initial positioning for SOV languages would guarantee center embedding and would often result in conjunction juxtaposition in case a subordinate clause contains another, smaller subordinate clause. On the other hand, if conjunctions are placed at clause-initial position in VSO languages and at clause-final position in SOV languages, conjunction juxtaposition will never arise, and center embedding will only in rare circumstances.[4]

[3]This generalization is related to three of Greenberg's (1963) Language Universals:

UNIVERSAL 3: *Languages with dominant VSO order are always prepositional.*
UNIVERSAL 4: *With overwhelmingly greater than chance frequency, languages with normal SOV order are postpositional.*
UNIVERSAL 12: *If a language has dominant order VSO in declarative sentences, it always puts interrogative words or phrases first in interrogative word questions; if it has dominant order SOV in declarative sentences, there is never such an invariant rule.*

[4]Consider hypothetical sentences corresponding to:

(i) a. *John says that he believes that the world is flat.*
b. *That that the world is flat is obvious is dubious.*

In VSO languages, these two statements will be realized as (ii) or (iii), depending on whether conjunctions are placed clause-initially or clause-finally:

(ii) VSO clause-initial.
a. *Says John **that** [believes he **that** [is-flat world]].*
b. *Is-dubious **that** [is-obvious **that** [is-flat world]].*

(iii) VSO clause-final.
a. *Says John [believes he [is-flat world] **that**] **that**.*
b. *Is-dubious [is-obvious [is-flat world] **that**] **that**.*

Note that (ii) involves neither self-embedding nor conjunction juxtaposition, while (iii) involves both. It is clear from this that it is better to mark embedded clauses at clause-initial position for VSO languages.

In SOV languages, (i) is realized as (iv) or (v), depending on whether conjunctions are placed clause-initially or clause-finally:

(iv) SOV clause-initial.
a. *John **that** [he **that** [world is-flat] believes] says.*
b. ***That** [**that** [world is-flat] is-obvious] is-dubious.*

Verb-medial languages (namely, SVO languages) have an ambivalent status—they are like SOV languages in that the subject appears to the left of the verb, but they are also like VSO languages in that the object appears to the right of the verb. Therefore, if they mark clause-initial boundaries, as in VSO languages, center embedding and conjunction juxtaposition will arise on the subject position; and if they mark clause-final boundaries, as in SOV languages, the same difficulty will arise on the object position. In actuality, most SVO languages have opted to mark clause-initial boundaries, thus giving a heavy handicap to subject complements. Hence, these languages yield sentences that are difficult to comprehend when the subject involves subordinate clauses. Among well-known examples of sentences of this type are:

(3) a. *That that the world is round is obvious is not certain.*
b. *The cheese the rat the cat chased ate was rotten.*

SVO languages that have the features of VSO languages (the clause-initial marking of embedded clauses and the postnominal positioning of relative clauses) make up for this handicap by using devices such as subject raising and extraposition. An example of subject raising from the subject complement has already been given in (2). The following is an instance of extraposition from the subject complement:

(4) a. ***That Mary will come*** *is likely.*
b. ***It*** *is likely* ***that Mary will come.***

From the preceding point of view, it is not surprising that SVO languages (e.g., English) that have subject raising from the object complement almost always have subject raising from the subject complement, but there are SVO languages that have subject raising only from the subject complement.[5,6] From the same point of view, it is not surprising that subject raising is not

---

(v) SOV clause-final.
a. *John [he [world is-flat]* ***that*** *believes]* ***that*** *says.*
b. *[[World is-flat]* ***that*** *is-obvious]* ***that*** *is-dubious.*

Both (iv.a) and (iv.b) involve self-embedding. Example (iv.b) also involves conjunction juxtaposition, and (iv.a) would also result in conjunction juxtaposition if *he* were deleted. On the other hand, (v.b) involves neither self-embedding nor conjunction juxtaposition. Example (v.a) contains self-embedding but no juxtaposition of conjunctions. Thus, it is clear that, for SOV languages, it is much better to mark clause-final boundaries than to mark clause-initial boundaries.

[5]In other words, in SVO languages, subject raising from the subject complement is much more common than subject raising from the object complement. This generalization, as far as I know, was first made by Arlene Berman (personal communication, 1969).

[6]French is an example of a language that has subject raising from the subject complement but not from the object complement, except in a few very restricted cases.

a common transformational device in SOV languages. Since SOV languages use clause-final conjunctions for both subject and object complements, as is dictated by the principle of economy on human temporary memory, there is no need for using a special device, such as subject raising or extraposition, to reduce the burden on the temporary memory.

There is another reason why subject raising is not common in SOV languages. Note in (2) that the predicate of the subject complement has been postposed to the position to the right of the matrix verb. It seems that this word order change is acceptable because English has the 'V + infinitive' construction independent of this rule. For example:

(5) a. *I want to go there.*
b. *I am glad to have met you.*

On the other hand, SOV languages do not allow the 'V + infinitive' pattern in general, with the infinitive following the main verb. Therefore, the predicate of the subject complement cannot be postposed to the right of the matrix verb. Thus, even if subject raising has applied to the pattern of (2), the constituent predicate would have to stay where it used to be, yielding a pattern that is not too different from the one before the application of the rule:

(6) a. [*Mary come-will*] *that likely-is.*
b. *Mary come-to likely-is.*

The same holds true for subject raising from the object complement in SOV languages.

What I have observed in the preceding paragraph should apply to the raising phenomenon from the object complement in SVO languages as well. Note that there is no word order change of meaningful elements between (1a) and (1b). Why is it, then, that English has some verbs that allow raising from the object complement? It seems that reducing the burden on the human temporary memory is not the only purpose of subject raising. Another purpose seems to be to make the constituent subject an element that is movable to the position usually reserved for the topic or the focus of the sentence. For example, observe the following sentences:

(7) a. ***Mary*** *is expected to come.*
b. ***Mary****, I expect to come, but* ***Bill****, I don't.*
c. *It is* ***Mary*** *that I expect to come.*
d. ***Who*** *do you expect to come?*

From the point of view just presented, it is not surprising that English, for example, has many verbs that do not allow subject raising from the object complement but allow it from the subject complement after passivization has been applied:[7]

(8) a. **They suppose* ***Mary*** *to have come.*
b. ***Mary*** *is supposed to have come.*

(9) a. **They say* ***Mary*** *to be rich.*
b. ***Mary*** *is said to be rich.*

If subject raising from the object complement in English exists at least partly for the purpose that I have described, in spite of the fact that there is no word order change effected by the transformation, then, there is no reason why SOV languages should not have the same transformation. There is one factor, however, that makes it difficult to prove that subject raising exists in SOV languages. That is, many SOV languages have a process, called verb raising, that takes the main verb of the embedded clause and attaches it to the matrix verb as the stem of the compound verb. For example, observe the following:

(10) *Koori ga toke-dasu.*
ice melt-begin
'Ice begins to melt.'

(11)

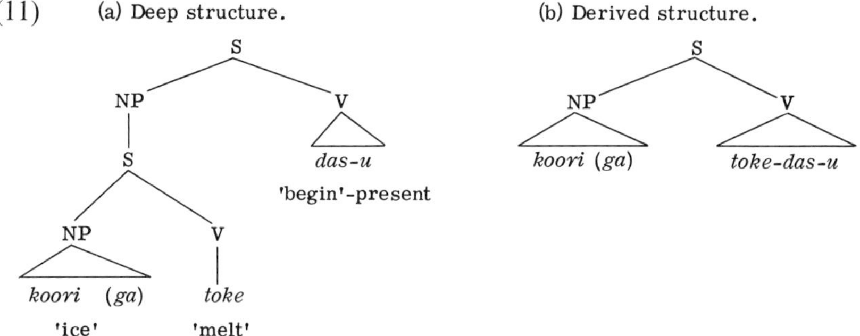

The verb stem *toke* 'melt' of the embedded clause is attached to the left of *das* 'begin' according to the general principle that all tenseless verbs must be attached to the left of the matrix verb. The derived form *toke-das* 'begin to melt' behaves as a single verb for all later transformations.[8] Now, since the predicate has disappeared, the subject complement loses its clausehood

[7]This fact was pointed out to me by Postal (personal communication, 1972). I believe that passivization precedes subject raising in rule ordering. See Kuno (1974b).

[8]See Shibatani (1973b) for arguments that this type of 'compound verb' must originate from the embedding structure.

owing to the tree-pruning convention, and the structure shown in (11b) results. Note that it is not necessary to have a special transformation for raising *koori* 'ice' out of the constituent clause.[9]

Similarly, observe the following examples of adversity passive in Japanese:

(12) *Taroo ga ame ni hur-are-ta.*
rain by fall-passive-past
'Taro was rained on. Taro was adversely affected by the rain falling.'

(13) 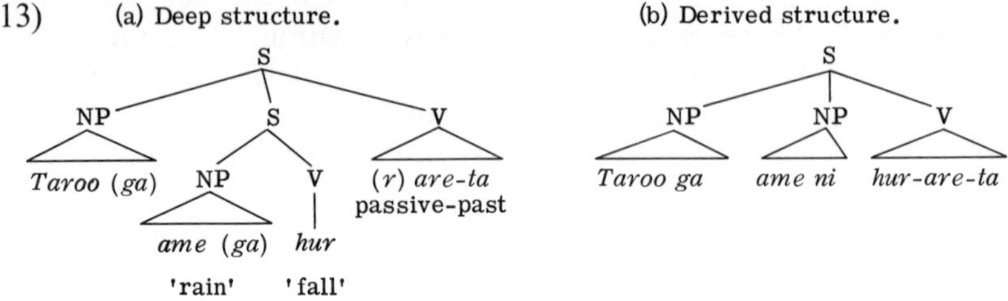

It is usually said that *ame*(*ga*) 'rain (nominative particle)' is raised from the constituent clause with *ni* attached to it. However, the raising of *hur* 'fall' by verb raising, which is needed for independent reasons, would cause the disappearance of the S node of the constituent clause, thus effectively causing the raising of *ame*. The attachment of *ni* to *ame* is needed, but the example does not show a need for subject raising.

There is yet another factor that makes it difficult to prove that subject raising exists in certain SOV languages. Observe the following examples from Japanese:

(14) *Taroo ga kuru koto ga kimatte imasu.*
come that determined is
'It is determined that Taro will come.'

[9]Assume that we had subject raising. After application of this rule to (11a) and subsequent application of tree-pruning rules, we would obtain the following intermediate structure:

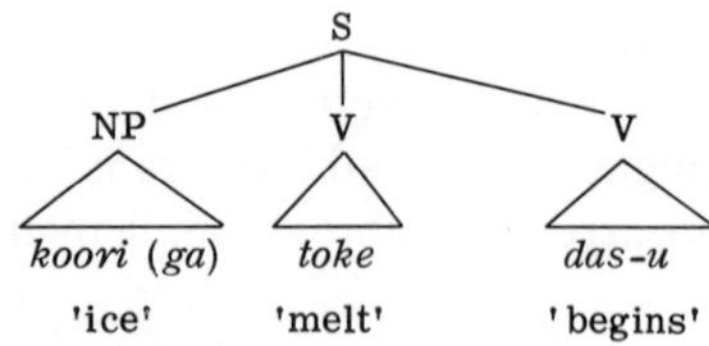

It is still necessary to have a rule that attaches *toke* to *das-u*. But this is exactly what verb raising is intended for, and if this transformation is applied to (11a), we will obtain (11b) without requiring subject raising.

The sentence seems to be ambiguous between the two interpretations shown in (15):

(15) a. [*Taroo ga kuru koto ga*] [*kimatte imasu*].
'It is determined that Taro will come.'
b. [*Taroo ga*] [*kuru koto ga kimatte imasu*].
'It is Taro for whom it is determined that he will come.'

What is crucial is the second interpretation. *Taroo ga* in this interpretation has the definite 'exhaustive listing' interpretation (namely, that of 'Taro and only Taro'), which is obligatory only for main clause subject NP-*ga* of stative predicates. However, this fact does not automatically lead to the conclusion that (15b) is derived from (15a) by raising the subject of the subject complement. This is because there is some likelihood that (15b) is derived from the deep structure corresponding to:

(16) $[\textit{Taroo}]_{\text{Theme/Focus}}[[\textit{Taroo (ga) kuru koto (ga)}]_{\text{NP}}$ $[\textit{kimatte imasu}]_{\text{VP}}]_{\text{S}}$

The sentence-initial noun phrase in (16) represents either the theme or the focus of the sentence, depending on whether *wa* or *ga* is attached to it. According to this analysis, (15b) is derived not by subject raising but by simply deleting the subject *Taroo ga* of the sentential subject under identity with the focus of the sentence.[10] Thus, for SOV languages that have special case markers for the theme and focus of sentences, whether patterns like (15b) involve subject raising or not depends on whether the theme and the focus exist as such in the deep structure or whether they are obtained by movement transformations and, in the latter case, whether what appears to be a case of subject raising is simply a part of a more general process of thematization and focalization. Needless to say, these are difficult questions, for which there are at present no clear-cut answers.

SUBJECT RAISING IN JAPANESE

In the previous section, I have shown why subject raising is not a common syntactic device in Japanese and other SOV languages, and why it is difficult to prove that the transformation exists in these languages. There is, however, one sentence pattern in Japanese that clearly shows that subject raising is involved. Observe the following sentence pairs:

(17) a. *Yamada wa* [***Tanaka ga*** *baka da*] *to omotte ita.*
fool is that thinking was
'Yamada thought that Tanaka was a fool.'

[10]See Kuno (1973: Chapters 2, 3, 21, 22) for some aspects of thematization and focalization.

b. *Yamada wa* ***Tanaka o*** *[baka da] to omotte ita.*
'Yamada thought Tanaka to be a fool.'

(18) a. *Yamada wa [**Tanaka ga** hannin da] to danteisita.*
culprit is that determined
'Yamada determined that Tanaka was the culprit.'
b. *Yamada wa* ***Tanaka o*** *[hannin da] to danteisita.*
'Yamada determined Tanaka to be the culprit.'

I will first give evidence that shows that, while the *Tanaka ga* of (17a) and (18a) is an element of the constituent clause, the *Tanaka o* of (17b) and (18b) is an element of the main clause.

Evidence for Subject Raising

CASE MARKER

First, the fact that *Tanaka* in (17b) and (18b) is marked with the accusative particle *o* gives strong evidence that it does not occupy the subject position of the embedded clause.

ADVERB PLACEMENT

Owing to the relatively free word order in Japanese, adverbs can be positioned in various places in the sentence. For example, observe the following:

(19) a. ***Orokanimo***, *Yamada wa sore o siranakatta.*
stupidly it knew-not
'Stupidly, Yamada did not know it.'
b. *Yamada wa,* ***orokanimo***, *sore o siranakatta.*
c. *Yamada wa sore o,* ***orokanimo***, *siranakatta.*

However, adverbs that are constituents of main clauses cannot be placed inside clauses that are embedded in the main clauses. Therefore, the following sentence is ungrammatical in the intended reading:

(20) **Yamada wa [Tanaka ga,* ***orokanimo***, *tensai de aru] koto*
stupidly genius is that
o siranakatta.
knew-not
'Stupidly, Yamada did not know that Tanaka was a genius.'

Let us examine how (17a) behaves with respect to the feature of adverb placement. Observe the following sentences:

(21) a. ***Orokanimo***, *Yamada wa [Tanaka ga tensai da] to*
Stupidly genius is that
omotte ita.
thinking was
'Stupidly, Yamada thought that Tanaka was a genius.'
b. *Yamada wa*, ***orokanimo***, *[Tanaka ga tensai da] to omotte ita.*
c. *Yamada wa [Tanaka ga tensai da] to*, ***orokanimo*** *omotte ita.*
d. **Yamada wa [Tanaka ga*, ***orokanimo***, *tensai da] to omotte ita.*

The grammaticality of (21a–c) and the ungrammaticality of (21d) is consistent with what we have observed before: namely, adverbs that modify the matrix verb cannot be placed inside subordinate clauses. The ungrammaticality of (21d) shows that *Tanaka ga tensai da* is an embedded clause.

Contrast the preceding with the following sentences:

(22) a. ***Orokanimo***, *Yamada wa Tanaka o tensai da to*
genius is that
omotte ita.
thinking was
b. *Yamada wa*, ***orokanimo***, *Tanaka o tensai da to omotte ita.*
c. *Yamada wa Tanaka o tensai da to*, ***orokanimo*** *omotte ita.*
d. *Yamada wa Tanaka o*, ***orokanimo***, *tensai da to omotte ita.*

The sentences of (22) are different from those of (21) only in that *Tanaka o* is used in the place of *Tanaka ga*. Note that (22d), with *orokanimo* between *Tanaka o* and *tensai da* 'is a genius', is a grammatical sentence. This fact stands in a marked contrast with the fact that (21d) is ungrammatical. This seems to show that *Tanaka o tensai da* does not form a subordinate clause, and that *Tanaka o* and *tensai da* are both constituents of the matrix clause. The same contrast is observable in the following pairs also:

(23) a. **Yamada wa Tanaka ga*, ***orokanimo***, *hannin da to*
stupidly culprit is that
danteisita.
determined
'Yamada determined stupidly that Tanaka was the culprit.'
b. *Yamada wa Tanaka o*, ***orokanimo***, *hannin da to danteisita.*

(24) a. **Yamada wa Tanaka ga* ***suguni*** *hannin da to suiteisita.*
immediately guessed
'Yamada guessed immediately that Tanaka was the culprit.'
b. *Yamada wa Tanaka o* ***suguni*** *hannin da to suiteisita.*

In case the nature of the main and constituent verbs are such that a given adverb can modify either of the two, ambiguity arises for the pattern of the (b) sentences in (23) and (24), but not for that of the (a) sentences:

(25) a. *Yamada wa Tanaka ga* ***mada*** *kodomo da to sinzite iru.*
still child is believing is
'Yamada believes that Tanaka is still a child.'
b. *Yamada wa Tanaka o* ***mada*** *kodomo da to sinzite iru.*
(i) 'Yamada believes that Tanaka is still a child.'
(ii) 'Yamada still believes that Tanaka is a child.'

WORD ORDER INVERSION

Nonsubject elements in the sentence can be preposed rather freely to the presubject position by the scrambling rule. However, it is not possible to prepose the subject of the embedded clause to the left of the matrix subject. Thus, although (26b) is grammatical, (27b) is ungrammatical in the intended reading:

(26) a. *Yamada wa Morita ni* ***Tanaka*** *o syookaisita.*
to introduced
'Yamada introduced Tanaka to Morita.'
b. ***Tanaka o***, *Yamada wa Morita ni syookaisita.*

(27) a. *Yamada wa [**Tanaka ga** tensai de aru] koto o siranakatta.*
genius is knew-not
'Yamada did not know that Tanaka was a genius.'
b. ****Tanaka ga***, *Yamada wa tensai de aru koto o siranakatta.*

Similarly, (28b) is ungrammatical:

(28) a. *Yamada wa* ***Tanaka ga*** *tensai da to omotte ita.*
genius is that thinking was
'Yamada thought that Tanaka was a genius.'
b. ****Tanaka ga***, *Yamada wa tensai da to omotte ita.*

On the other hand, note that (29b) is grammatical:

(29) a. *Yamada wa* ***Tanaka o*** *tensai da to omotte ita.*
b. ***Tanaka o***, *Yamada wa tensai da to omotte ita.*

It seems that this phenomenon can be accounted for most naturally by assuming that ***Tanaka ga*** in (28a) is a constituent of the embedded clause, but that ***Tanaka o*** in (29a) is a constituent in the matrix sentence.[11]

[11] This observation does not mean that Japanese does not have unbounded leftward movement rules. Observe, for example, the following:

(i) a. *Yamada wa [Tanaka ga* ***sono hon o*** *sutete simatta] to omotta.*
the book threw-away that thought

QUANTIFIER SCOPE

Observe the following sentence:

(30) ***Dareka*** *ga* ***minna*** *o mihatte ita.*
someone all watching was
'Someone was watching all.'

The predominant reading of this sentence is:

(31) a. There was someone who was watching all.

However, for some speakers it is not impossible to obtain the secondary reading, as shown in (31b), although this reading is very weak:

(31) b. For each person, there was someone who was watching him.

Similarly, (32) is ambiguous between (33a) and (33b), although this reading is extremely weak:

(32) ***Dareka*** *ga* ***minna*** *o aisite iru.*
someone all loving is

(33) a. There is someone who loves all.
b. For each person, there is someone who loves him.

Thus, it seems that the rule for interpreting two quantifiers Q1 and Q2 in a simplex sentence is:

(34) a. PREDOMINANT READING: *Interpret Q1, and then Q2.*
b. SECONDARY AND WEAK READING (possible only for some speakers): *Interpret Q2 first, and then Q1.*

When the second quantifier is in the subordinate clause, the secondary

---

'Yamada thought that Tanaka had thrown away the book.'
b. ***Sono hon o***, *Yamada wa [Tanaka ga ∅ sutete simatta] to omotta.*

(ii) a. *Kimi wa [Yamada ga* ***dare to*** *kekkonsita] to omoimasu ka?*
you who with married think
'Who do you think Yamada married?'
b. ***Dare to***, *kimi wa [Yamada ga ∅ kekkonsita] to omoimasu ka?*

It is not clear why (27b) and (28b) are ungrammatical, while (i.b) and (ii.b) (just given) are grammatical. The constraint might be that the subjects of the matrix and constituent clauses may not switch word order. Note that it would not do to say that NP-*wa* NP-*ga* cannot switch word order, because if both are in the same sentence it is possible to prepose NP-*ga*:

(iii) a. *Boku wa* ***Mary ga*** *dai-kirai da.*
much-hateful am
'I really dislike Mary.'
b. ***Mary ga*** *boku wa dai-kirai da.*
'I really dislike Mary.'

reading shown in (34b) is impossible for all speakers. For example:

(35) ***Dareka*** *ga* [***minna*** *ga sinda*] *koto o siranakatta.*
someone all died that knew-not

means only (36a). It is not possible to obtain the reading of (36b) for the sentence:

(36) a. There was someone who did not know that all had died.
b. For each person, there was someone who did not know that he had died.

Similarly, (37) means (38a) and not (38b):

(37) ***Dareka*** *ga* [***minna*** *ga baka da*] *to omotte iru.*
someone all fool is thinking is

(38) a. There is someone who thinks that all are stupid.
b. For each person, there is someone who thinks that he is stupid.

Now, consider (39):

(39) ***Dareka*** *ga* ***minna*** *o baka da to omotte iru.*

The predominant reading of this sentence is that of (38a). However, for some speakers it is not impossible to obtain the interpretation of (38b). This phenomenon can be accounted for most naturally, it seems, by assuming that the second quantifier, *minna* (*o*) 'all', in (39) is in the same S as the first quantifier, *dareka* 'someone'. Again, this assumption is consistent with the proposed analysis that (39) is derived from (37) by raising the constituent subject out of the embedded clause.

REFLEXIVIZATION

In Japanese, reflexivization is obligatory between the subject and the object of a verb, and optional between the subject of the matrix sentence and the subject of the constituent clause.[12] Thus, we have the following patterns:

(40) a. *Yamada*$_i$ *wa* ***zibun***$_i$ *o hihansita.*
self criticized
'Yamada criticized himself.'
b. **Yamada*$_i$ *wa* ***kare***$_i$ *o hihansita.*
him criticized

[12]Facts about reflexivization in Japanese are much more complex than this statement may imply. See Kuno (1972) and the chapters by N. McCawley and Inoue in this volume for details.

(41) a. *Yamada*$_i$ *wa* [***zibun***$_i$ *ga minna ni kiraw-are-te iru*] *koto ni*
self all by dislike-passive-ing is that
ki ga tuite i-nai.
realizing is-not
'Yamada does not realize that he is disliked by all.'
b. *Yamada*$_i$ *wa* [***kare***$_i$ *ga minna ni kiraw-are-te iru*] *koto ni*
ki ga tuite i-nai.

When the complement clause represents the internal feeling, or its external manifestation, of the referent of the matrix subject, it is better to use the reflexive pronoun *zibun*, but it is not impossible to use the nonreflexive pronoun:

(42) a. *Yamada*$_i$ *wa* [***zibun***$_i$ *ga tensai de aru*] *koto o sitte ita.*
self genius is that knew
'Yamada knew that he was a genius.'
b. ?*Yamada*$_i$ *wa* [***kare***$_i$ *ga tensai de aru*] *koto o sitte ita.*

Native speakers may disagree with our judgment on the degree of grammaticality of (42b), but I do not believe that therc is any disagreement with the judgment that (42b) is considerably better than (40b), which is totally ungrammatical.

Now, consider (43) and (44):

(43) a. *Yamada*$_i$ *wa* ***zibun***$_i$ *ga tensai da to omotte ita.*
self genius is that thinking was
'Yamada thought that he was a genius.'
b. ?*Yamada*$_i$ *wa* ***kare***$_i$ *ga tensai da to omotte ita.*
he

(44) a. *Yamada*$_i$ *wa* ***zibun***$_i$ *o tensai da to omotte ita.*
b. **Yamada*$_i$ *wa* ***kare***$_i$ *o tensai da to omotte ita.*

The contrast between (43b) and (44b) is parallel to that between (42b) and (40b). This phenomenon, too, can be accounted for most naturally by assuming that *zibun/kare ga* in (43) are in complement clauses, but that *zibun/kare o* in (44) are constituents of the matrix sentences.

Evidence against Equi-NP Analysis

In the preceding, I have shown that *Tanaka o* in (17b) is a constituent of the matrix clause:

(17) a. *Yamada wa* ***Tanaka ga*** *baka da to omotte ita.*
fool is that thinking was
b. *Yamada wa* ***Tanaka o*** *baka da to omotte ita.*

In order to show that it is really an instance of subject raising, I have to show that it is not an instance of equi-NP deletion applied to the deep structure of (45):

(45) [*Yamada wa Tanaka o* [*Tanaka ga baka da*] *to omotte ita*]

It is not easy to argue against the equi-NP analysis of (17b), just as it is not easy to argue against the equi-NP analysis of (1b) in English. As far as I know, there are only five arguments against the equi-NP analysis of (1b). First, observe the following sentence pairs:

(46) a. *I expected* ***the doctor*** *to examine Mary.*
b. *I expected* ***Mary*** *to be examined by the doctor.*

(47) a. *I persuaded* ***the doctor*** *to examine Mary.*
b. *I persuaded* ***Mary*** *to be examined by the doctor.*

Although (46a) and (46b) are synonymous, (47a) and (47b) are not. Thus, it would not do to assign the same deep structures to the *expect* and *persuade* patterns. Since *the doctor* and *Mary* in (47) represent the recipients of the persuasion, it is natural to have them as objects of the matrix clauses in the deep structure. On the other hand, on the assumption that passivization does not change basic meaning, the synonymity of (46a) and (46b) can be naturally accounted for by assuming that the deep structure did not have *the doctor* and *Mary* as matrix objects, but that they have been raised from the object complement by subject raising.

The second argument concerns sentences such as:

(48) a. *I expected* ***there*** *to be a riot.*
b. *I expected* ***it*** *to rain.*

The noun phrase objects of equi-NP verbs are animate, and they represent the recipients of the actions represented by the verbs. This semantically motivated generalization would be lost if (48a) and (48b) were to be derived from:

(49) a. *I expected* ***there*** [*there to be a riot*].
b. *I expected* ***it*** [*it rain*].

respectively. Note that:

(50) a. **I persuaded* ***there*** *to be a riot.*
b. **I persuaded* ***it*** *to rain.*

may both be marked as ungrammatical owing to this generalization.

More serious, however, is the status of dummy symbols such as *there* in the deep structure. All other indications are that *there* does not exist in the deep structure but is inserted by a transformation in the course of the derivation of the sentences. Hypothesizing a deep structure like (49a) clearly conflicts with this analysis.

The third argument involves expressions such as *make headway* and *keep tabs*. *Headway* can assume the meaning 'progress' only when it is used as the object of *make*. Similarly, *tabs* can be used in the sense of 'account, watch' only when it is used as the object of *keep*. Note that *headway* and *tabs* can appear in the pattern of (46b):

(51) a. *I expected some headway to be made.*
b. *I expected tabs to be kept on the suspects' activities.*

If these sentences were to be derived from deep structures of the pattern of (49), it would no longer be possible to make a simple statement on the coocurrence restrictions for *headway* and *tabs*. One would have to say that *headway* and *tabs* can be used in the specified interpretation only as the objects of *make* and *keep*, respectively, except that they can appear as objects of equi-NP verbs as long as the structural description of equi-NP deletion is met, and the rule is applied to delete the lower occurrence of these nouns. It is clear that this complex statement has been necessitated by the erroneous assumption that *expect* is an equi-NP type of verb.

The fourth argument involves the contrast in the degree of acceptability between (52b) and (53b):

(52) a. *Mary was persuaded by John to do it.*
b. (?)*Mary was persuaded to do it by John.*

(53) a. *Mary was expected by John to do it.*
b. **Mary was expected to do it by John.*

This phenomenon, which is observable in the speech of many (but not by any means all) speakers, can be automatically accounted for by assuming a subject-raising type of deep structure for *expect* and an equi-NP type of deep structure for *persuade*, and by assuming that passivization precedes subject raising. Since passivization places the *by* agentive at the end of the sentence, (52b) obtains after application of the rule to:

(54) *John persuaded Mary to do it.*

Example (52a) is derived from the structure corresponding to (52b) by applying heavy constituent shift and postposing the relatively heavy *to do it* over the light *by John*. On the other hand, in the course of the derivation of (53), if passivization applies before subject raising we will have, as an intermediate stage, the following structure:

(55) [[*For Mary to do it*] *was expected by John*].

This structure undergoes subject raising, which raises the constituent subject to the matrix subject position, and ***extraposes the rest of the constituent clause to sentence-final position***. Thus, application of this rule to (55) yields the structure corresponding to (53a). Example (53b) can be obtained only by illegally applying heavy constituent shift, thus postposing a light constituent (*by John*) over a heavy constituent (*to do it*).[13]

The fifth argument involves tough movement, which is a rule that derives the sentences (56b) and (57b) from the structure corresponding to the (a) sentences:

(56) a. *It is easy to talk with John.*
b. *John is easy to talk with.*

(57) a. *It is difficult to talk with John.*
b. *John is difficult to talk with.*

Berman (1973) has observed that tough movement may not move any noun phrase that has previously been moved by any other transformations or, otherwise stated, that tough movement may move a noun phrase only from its position in underlying structure. This constraint applies to noun phrases that have been moved by passivization, dative movement, *about* movement, or subject raising:

(58) a. *It is unpleasant to be kicked by John.* (passivization)
b. **John is unpleasant to be kicked by.*
c. cf. *A candle is difficult to study by.*

(59) a. *It is impossible to buy John presents.* (dative movement)
b. **John is impossible to buy presents.*
c. cf. *Presents are impossible to buy for John.*

(60) a. *It is difficult to talk about such things with John.* (*about* movement)
b. **John is difficult to talk about such things with.*
c. cf. *Such things are difficult to talk with John about.*

(61) a. *It is difficult to believe John to have made such a mistake.* (subject raising)
b. **John is difficult to believe to have made such a mistake.*
c. cf. *John is difficult to persuade to do anything.*

Note, in particular, that tough movement can apply to the object of *persuade* but not to the derived object of *believe*. Since Berman's generalization can be justified on the basis of (58), (59), and (60), it can be used as an argument for the subject-raising analysis of (61). Now, observe that *expect* behaves in the same way as *believe*:

[13]See Kuno (1974b) for a fuller discussion of this topic.

(62) a. *It is impossible to expect John to understand anything.*
b. **John is impossible to expect to understand anything.*

This fact also supports the hypothesis that *John* in (62a) did not start out as the object of *expect* in the deep structure, but has been placed in that position by some transformation (namely, subject raising).

The preceding five arguments, put together, give convincing evidence for the hypothesis that *expect* is not an equi-NP type of verb. Unfortunately, of these, only the argument concerning fixed expressions of the *make headway* type applies in Japanese. The pattern of (17b) is limited to cases that have either adjectives or 'nominal + copula' in the embedded clauses, so that it is not possible to contrast the active and passive versions to see whether they are synonymous or not. Similarly, since Japanese does not have dummy subjects such as *it* and *there*, the patterns of (48) do not exist. Since subject raising in Japanese does not place the rest of the constituent clause in sentence-final position, the contrast of the type that appeared between (52) and (53) is not observable in Japanese. Finally, tough movement in Japanese is difficult to apply to sentences that involve complement clauses, and it does not seem to discriminate between objects that started out as objects in the deep structure and objects that have resulted from raising.[14] Therefore, we have to look elsewhere for the evidence for subject raising and against equi-NP deletion in Japanese.

The Nature of the NP Object

First, observe the following examples of equi-NP verbs:

(63) a. *Yamada wa* ***Tanaka ni*** *[sore o site kureru] koto o kitaisite iru.*
to it do that expecting is
'Yamada expects of Tanaka that he will do it.'

[14]For example, both (i.b) and (ii.b) are equally unnatural:

(i) a. *Boku wa* ***Yamada ni*** *sore o suru koto o settokusi-ta.*
it do to persuade-past
'I persuaded Yamada to do it.'
b. ?*Yamada wa [nani o suru] koto mo settokusi-nikui.*
anything do to even persuade-hard-is
'Yamada is difficult to persuade to do anything.'

(ii) a. *Boku wa* ***Yamada o*** *supai da to danteisi-ta.*
I spy is determine-past
'I determined Yamada to be a spy.'
b. ?*Yamada wa [supai da] to danteisi-nikui.*
spy is conclude-hard-is
'Yamada is difficult to determine to be a spy.'

b. *Yamada wa* ***Tanaka ni*** *[sore o suru] koto o meizita.*
to it do that ordered
'Yamada ordered Tanaka to do it.'

c. *Yamada wa* ***Tanaka ni*** *[onaka ga suita] to itta.*
to belly empty-is that said
'Yamada told Tanaka that he was hungry.'

In all these sentences, *Tanaka* clearly represents the recipient of Yamada's expectation, order, and statement. This 'recipient' meaning is completely lacking in the *Tanaka o* of (17b). When inanimate objects appear in the pattern of (63), ungrammatical sentences result. On the other hand, the pattern of (17b) can involve inanimate objects without resulting in ungrammaticality:

(64) a. **Yamada wa* **sono hon ni** *[yoku ureru] koto o kitaisite iru.*
the book to well sell that expecting is
'Yamada hopes that the book will sell well.'

b. *Yamada wa* **sono hon o** *[tumaranai] to omotta.*
the book uninteresting-is that thought
'Yamada thought the book to be uninteresting.'

Case Marking

Second, observe that the objects in (63) are marked with *ni*, while the object in (17b) is marked with *o*. As far as I know, there are no equi-NP verbs whose object noun phrase is regularly marked with *o*.[15]

[15]This statement does not apply when verb raising is involved. Observe the following causative sentence:

(i) *Yamada wa kodomo* ***o*** *benkyoos-ase-ta.*
child study-made-past
'Yamada made the children study.'

I claim that (i) is derived from the underlying equi-NP structure:

(ii) *Yamada(wa) kodomo [kodomo(ga) benkyoos] sase-ta.*
child child study make-past

After equi-NP deletion and verb raising, with subsequent application of tree pruning, we obtain the structure corresponding to:

(iii) *Yamada(wa) kodomo benkyoos-ase-ta.*
child study-make-past

Now, since *kodomo* 'child' has come to occupy the position of the direct object of the compound causative *benkyoos-ase* 'make study', it is marked with the accusative particle *o*. This is why the deep structure noun phrase object *kodomo* of the equi-NP verb *sase* 'make' appears in the surface sentence with *o*, and not with *ni*. See Kuno (1973: Chapter 27, Section 6) and the chapter by Shibatani in this volume for details.

Masayoshi Shibatani (personal communication, 1974) has brought to my attention one class

PREPOSING OF THE OBJECT COMPLEMENT

It is possible to prepose the complement clause of (63) to the left of *Tanaka ni*, but it is not possible to prepose the complement clause of (17b) to the left of *Tanaka o*. Observe the following contrast:

(65) a. *Yamada wa* ***sore o site kureru koto o*** *Tanaka ni kitaisite iru.*
b. *Yamada wa* ***sore o suru koto o*** *Tanaka ni meizita.*
c. *Yamada wa* ***onaka ga suita to*** *Tanaka ni itta.*

(66) **Yamada wa* ***baka da to*** *Tanaka o omotte ita.*

I do not understand what prevents the application of the scrambling rule to (17b) to produce (66). Whatever the reason may turn out to be, the grammaticality of (65) and the ungrammaticality of (66) clearly indicates that we have here two different structures.

EQUI-NP DELETION

Equi-NP deletion is not obligatory for the equi-NP verbs of the (63) pattern. Although the following sentences are less natural than (63), they are, at worst, marginal, and are not completely ungrammatical:

(67) a. ?*Yamada wa Tanaka*$_i$ *ni* [***kare***$_i$ *ga sore o site kureru*] *koto o*
to he it do that
kitaisite iru.
expecting is
'Yamada expects of Tanaka that he will do it.'
b. ?*Yamada wa Tanaka*$_i$ *ni* [***kare***$_i$ *ga sore o suru*] *koto o meizita.*
to he it do that ordered
(Lit.) 'Yamada ordered Tanaka that he do it.'

On the other hand, it is totally impossible to use *kare ga* for (17b):

(68) **Yamada wa Tanaka*$_i$ *o* [***kare***$_i$ *ga baka da*] *to omotte ita.*
he fool is that thinking was
'Yamada thought of Tanaka that he was a fool.'

This phenomenon can be automatically explained if we assume that (17b) is

---

of possible equi-NP verbs that regularly take *o*. This class includes verbs such as *siiru* 'force', *kyooseisuru* 'coerce', and *sosonokasu* 'tempt', used as in (i).

(i) *Taroo wa iku yoo (ni) Ziroo* ***o*** *siita/kyooseisita/sosonokasita.*
'Taro forced/coerced/tempted Jiro to go.'

The verbs of this class, however, are slightly different from other equi-NP verbs such as *kitaisuru* 'expect' and *meireisuru* 'order' in that the complement sentence regularly appears before rather than after the matrix object noun.

derived, not from (45) by equi-NP deletion, but from (17a) by subject raising.

NOMINAL ADJECTIVES

In Japanese, there is a class of words called 'nominal adjectives'. They are adjectival in meaning, but they do not inflect. They share certain characteristics with nouns. For example, observe the following paradigms:

(69)

	Verbs	Adjectives	Nouns	Nominal adjectives
	'eat'	'red'	'book'	'quiet'
Present	*tabe-ru*	*aka-i*	*hon da*	*sizuka da*
Past	*tabe-ta*	*aka-katta*	*hon datta*	*sizuka datta*
Conditional	*tabe-tara*	*aka-kattara*	*hon dattara*	*sizuka dattara*
Gerundive	*tabe-te*	*aka-kute*	*hon de*	*sizuka de*

There are nominal adjectives that can be used in the (thematic) subject position. For example, compare (70) and (71)–(73):

(70) a. *Koko wa* ***sizuka*** *da.*
here quiet is
'It is quiet here.'

b. ****Sizuka ga*** *kono bessoo no biten desu.*[16]
quiet this summerhouse's merit is
'Quiet(ude) is this summerhouse's merit.'

(71) a. *Yamada wa* ***hutyuui*** *da.*
careless is
'Yamada is careless.'

b. ***Hutyuui*** *wa kega no moto da.*
carelessness injury's cause is
'Carelessness is a cause of injuries.'

(72) a. *Yamada wa* ***syooziki*** *da.*
honest is
'Yamada is honest.'

b. ***Syooziki*** {*wa* / *ga*} *saizyoo no bitoku da.*
honest best virtue is
'Honesty is the best virtue.'

[16]It is necessary to nominalize *sizuka* 'quiet' by adding a complementizer:

(i) ***Sizuka na koto*** *ga kono bessoo no biten desu.*
quiet is that this summer house 's merit is
'The fact that it is quiet is this summerhouse's merit.'

(73) a. *Yamada wa* ***kiyoo*** *da.*
adroit is
'Yamada is adroit.'
b. ***Kiyoo*** *wa bitoku de wa nai.*
adroit virtue is not
'Adroitness is not a virtue.'

As (70) shows, *sizuka* 'quiet' cannot be used in the (thematic) subject position, but, as (71)–(73) show, *hutyuui* 'careless', *syooziki* 'honest', and *kiyoo* 'adroit' can be used as (thematic) subjects of sentences.

Some of those nominal adjectives that can be used as subjects can also be used as objects, but others cannot. *Hutyuui* 'careless' belongs to the first category, *syooziki* 'honest' and *kiyoo* 'adroit' to the second:

(74) a. *Boku wa* ***hutyuui*** *o site-simatta.*
careless doing-ended-up
'I have done (something) careless.'
b. *Boku wa Yamada no* ***hutyuui*** *o hihansita.*
I 's careless criticized
'I criticized Yamada's carelessness.'

(75) a. **Boku wa* ***syooziki*** *o omonziru.*
I honest treasure
'I value honesty.'
b. **Boku wa Yamada no* ***syooziki*** *o sonkeisuru.*
's honest respect
'I respect Yamada's honesty.'

(76) a. **Boku wa* ***kiyoo*** *o omonzi-nai.*
I adroit treasure
'I don't value adroitness.'
b. **Boku wa Yamada no* ***kiyoo*** *o utagawa-nai.*[17]
I 's adroit doubt-not
'I don't doubt Yamada's adroitness.'

[17] It is necessary to nominalize *syooziki* 'honest' and *kiyoo* 'adroit' by adding a noun-forming suffix or a complementizer; for example:

(i) *Boku wa* ***syooziki-sa*** *o omonziru.*
I honesty value
'I value honesty.'

(ii) *Boku wa Yamada ga* ***kiyoo na koto*** *o utagawanai.*
I adroit is that doubt-not
'I don't doubt that Yamada is adroit.'

The fact that *hutyuui* 'careless, carelessness' can be used in the object position qualifies it as a full-fledged noun as well as a nominal adjective.

Thus, *syooziki* 'honest', *kiyoo* 'adroit', and other such nominal adjectives must be marked in the lexicon as those that can be used in the (thematic) subject position but not in the object position. Now, observe the following pairs of sentences:

(77) a. *Yamada wa* [***syooziki ga*** *saizyoo no bitoku da*]
honest best virtue is
to kangaete ita.
that thinking was
'Yamada thought that honesty was the best virtue.'

b. *Yamada wa* ***syooziki o*** [*saizyoo no bitoku da*]
to kangaete ita.

(78) a. *Yamada wa* [***kiyoo ga*** *bitoku de wa nai*] *to kangaete ita.*
adroit virtue is not that thinking was
'Yamada thought that adroitness was not a virtue.'

b. *Yamada wa* ***kiyoo o*** [*bitoku de wa nai*] *to kangaete ita.*

Note that (77b) and (78b) are grammatical. As far as I know, (17b) is the only pattern in which these nominal adjectives can appear in the object position. This phenomenon can be automatically accounted for if we assume that these sentences are derived by subject raising from the structure corresponding to (77a) and (78a). On the other hand, if we assume that they are derived from a deep structure like (45), the statement of the selectional restriction on *syooziki* 'honest', *kiyoo* 'adroit', and other such nominal adjectives would have to be made considerably more complex.

FOSSILIZED EXPRESSIONS

There are fossilized expressions that have the present tense form of a verb as the (thematic) subject of the sentence. For example, observe the following sentences:

(79) a. ***Nigeru*** $\begin{Bmatrix} \textit{wa} \\ \textit{ga} \end{Bmatrix}$ *saizyoo no saku da.*
run-away best strategy is
'To run away is the best strategy.'

b. ***Aisuru*** *wa wakare no hazime nari.*
love parting 's beginning is (archaic)
'To love is the beginning of a parting.'

Except in such fossilized expressions, the present tense form of a verb cannot be used as either subject or object. The following sentences are all ungrammatical:

(80) a. **Nigeru* *wa muzukasii.*
run-away difficult-is
'To run away is difficult.'
b. **Boku wa* ***nigeru o*** *keibetusi-nai.*
I run-away despise
'I don't look down on running away.'

(81) a. **Aisuru* *wa kantan da.*
love simple is
'To love is simple.'
b. **Hito o* ***aisuru o*** *wasureru na.*[18]
others love forget (imperative) not
'Don't forget to love others.'

Now, observe the following sentences:

(82) a. *Yamada wa [***nigeru ga*** *saizyoo no saku da] to omotta.*
run-away best strategy is that thought
'Yamada thought that to run away was the best strategy.'
b. *Yamada wa* ***nigeru o*** *[saizyoo no saku da] to omotta.*

(83) a. *Yamada wa [***aisuru*** *wa wakare no hazime (nari)] to kangaeta.*
love parting 's beginning is that thought
'Yamada thought that to love was the beginning of a parting.'
b. *Yamada wa* ***aisuru o*** *[wakare no hazime (nari)] to kangaeta.*

Examples (82a) and (83a) contain as embedded clauses (79a) and (79b). Examples (82b) and (83b) are awkward, but I think they are grammatical. Even those who regard them as marginal would agree that they are far better than (80b) and (81b). The subject-raising analysis offers a natural explanation for the grammaticality of (82b) and (83b). In spite of the fact that they involve otherwise unacceptable use of the present tense forms of verbs as objects, these sentences are grammatical because *nigeru o* 'to run away' and *aisuru o* 'to love' are derived objects (due to subject raising) and did not start out as underlying objects. On the other hand, if these sentences were to be derived from the equi-NP type of deep structure, a complex statement would be required to make sure that (80b) and (81b) are ruled out as ungrammatical and that (82b) and (83b) are accepted as grammatical sentences.

The preceding five arguments, put together, give convincing evidence for the subject-raising analysis, and against the equi-NP analysis, of the sentence pattern exemplified by (17b).

[18]It is necessary to nominalize *nigeru* 'run away' and *aisuru* 'love' by adding the complementizer *koto* 'to'.

A Peculiarity of Subject Raising in Japanese

In English, subject raising never applies to clauses whose main verbs are finite. Thus, although (84a) and (84b) are grammatical, (84c) and (84d) are not:

(84) a. *I expect Mary* ***to play*** *the piano.*
b. *I believe Mary* ***to be*** *honest.*
c. **I expect Mary that ∅* ***will play*** *the piano.*
d. **I believe Mary that ∅* ***is*** *honest.*

This characteristic is shared by most other languages that are known to have a rule of subject raising (see Postal, 1974:386).

The raising phenomenon in Japanese that we have been examining, on the other hand, involves clauses whose main verbs are finite. *Baka da* 'is a fool' in (17b) is in the present tense, and it is not possible to interpret it as an infinitive. I will give some arguments for this analysis:

1. Sentence-final particles, as is implied by their name, can ordinarily appear only at sentence-final position. They cannot appear after infinitives. Observe the following examples:

(85) a. *Yamada wa oyogu koto ga dekiru* ***yo/zo/no****.*
swim to can
'Yamada can swim.'
b. **Yamada wa oyogu* ***yo/zo/no*** *koto ga dekiru.*

Yo, *zo*, and *no* are sentence-final particles meaning, roughly, 'I am telling you'. They can appear after the finite verb *dekiru* 'can', as shown by the grammaticality of (85a), but not after the infinitive *oyogu* 'swim', as shown by the ungrammaticality of (85b). Now, note that some of the sentence-final particles can appear after the *baka da* of (17b):

(86) a. *Yamada wa Tanaka o baka da* ***zo*** *to omotta.*
b. *Yamada wa Tanaka o baka da* ***naa*** *to omotta.*

The yes–no question particle *ka* can appear in the same position:

(87) *Yamada wa Tanaka o baka* ***ka*** *to omotta.*[19]
'Yamada wondered if Tanaka was a fool.'

2. The constituent verb in (17b) is not restricted to the present tense. Future tense forms can also appear:

[19] *Da* 'is' is deleted obligatorily before the interrogative marker *ka* in main clauses and *to* clauses.

(88) a. *Yamada wa Tanaka o hannin* ***daroo*** *to suiteisita.*
culprit will-be guessed
'Yamada guessed that Tanaka would be the culprit.'
b. *Yamada wa Tanaka o hannin de wa* ***nakaroo*** *to suiteisita.*
culprit will-not-be that guessed
'Yamada guessed that Tanaka would not be the culprit.'

The use of past tense forms makes the pattern marginal, as shown in (89):

(89) ?*Yamada wa zibun o oroka na otoko* ***datta*** *to omotta.*
self stupid man was that thought
'Yamada thought that he had been a stupid man.'

However, the use of past tense forms in clear-cut cases of infinitives yields far less acceptable sentences:

(90) a. *Yamada wa* ***oyogu*** *koto ga dekita.*
swim to could
'Yamada could swim.'
b. ***Yamada wa* ***oyoida*** *koto ga dekita.*
swam to could

3. Various modals that represent the judgment of the referent of the subject of the main clause can appear in the pattern of (17b). Observe the following examples:

(91) a. *Yamada wa Tanaka o baka ni* ***tigainai*** *to omotta.*
fool must-be thought
'Yamada thought that Tanaka must be a fool.'
b. *Yamada wa Tanaka o baka* ***ka mo sire-nai*** *to omotta.*
fool might-be
'Yamada thought that Tanaka might be a fool.'
c. *Yamada wa Tanaka o baka de aru* ***hazu ga nai*** *to omotta.*
cannot
'Yamada thought that Tanaka couldn't be a fool.'

These forms can never appear as infinitives.

No-Koto Incorporation

In Japanese, when the object of feeling, thinking, and saying verbs is human, *no koto* '(someone)'s matter' appears optionally after the noun phrase for the human. Observe the following pairs of sentences:

(92) a. *Yamada wa Tanaka o nikunde iru.*
hating is
'Yamada hates Tanaka.'

b. *Yamada wa Tanaka* ***no koto*** *o nikunde iru.*

(93) a. *Yamada wa Hanako o aisite iru.*
loving is
'Yamada loves Hanako.'
b. *Yamada wa Hanako* ***no koto*** *o aisite iru.*

(94) a. *Yamada wa Hanako ga suki-rasii yo.*
fond-of seem
'Yamada seems to be fond of Hanako.'
b. *Yamada wa Hanako* ***no koto*** *ga suki-rasii yo.*

The (a) and (b) sentences are synonymous, although it seems that the (b) sentences are the more indirect way of saying what the (a) sentences say.

The appearance of *no koto* is limited to the object position of the feeling, thinking, and saying verbs. Examples (95b) and (96b) are ungrammatical because *musuko no koto* '(his) son's matter' in these sentences is not the object of such verbs:

(95) a. *Yamada wa [musuko ga baka na] koto o sira-nai.*
son fool is that know-not
'Yamada does not know that his son is a fool.'
b. **Yamada wa [musuko* ***no koto*** *ga baka na] koto o sira-nai.*

(96) a. *Yamada wa [musuko ga rikoo na] koto o zimansite iru.*
son clever is that bragging is
'Yamada is bragging of the fact that his son is bright.'
b. **Yamada wa [musuko* ***no koto*** *ga rikoo na] koto o zimansite iru.*

Observe, now, the following contrast:

(97) a. **Yamada wa musuko* ***no koto*** *ga baka da to omotte ita.*
son 's matter fool is thinking was
'Yamada thought that his son was a fool.'
b. *Yamada wa musuko* ***no koto*** *o baka da to omotte ita.*[20]

Example (97a) is ungrammatical, but (97b) is not. This phenomenon is consistent with the hypothesis that *Tanaka ga* in (17a) is a constituent in the embedded clause, but that *Tanaka o* in (17b) is the object of the matrix verb. However, in order to derive (97b) as a grammatical sentence, it is necessary to hypothesize that *no koto* is not in the deep structure for sentences like (92b), (93b), and (94b), but that it is added to the object of feeling, thinking, and saying verbs if it refers to a person. This optional

[20]I am indebted to Masayoshi Shibatani (personal communication, 1972) for calling the pattern of (97b) to my attention.

transformation applies after subject raising has applied to raise the constituent subject *musuko* '(his) son' of (97a) to the matrix object position.

SUBJECT RAISING AND PASSIVIZATION

In the foregoing, I have shown that (17b) is an instance of subject raising from the object complement. What kinds of verbs in Japanese can undergo subject raising? First, they must be verbs that take *to* clauses as their complements—namely, they must be verbs whose complements represent not abstract facts but indirect speech or internal feelings of the referents of their subjects. Among these verbs, those whose complements represent indirect speech are more likely not to be able to enter into the same pattern. Example (98) presents grammatical sentences and (99) ungrammatical ones. Note that the verbs in (98) are all thinking and feeling verbs, and that those in (99) are all saying verbs:

(98) a. *Yamada wa Tanaka o baka da to* ***sinzita****.*
fool is believed
'Yamada believed Tanaka to be a fool.'
b. *Yamada wa Tanaka o tensai da to* ***kantigaisita****.*
genius mistook
'Yamada mistook Tanaka for a genius.'
c. *Yamada wa Tanaka o hannin da to* ***kateisita****.*
culprit hypothesized
'Yamada hypothesized that Tanaka was the culprit.'
d. *Yamada wa Tanaka o hannin da to* ***omoikonda****.*
culprit believed-erroneously
'Yamada erroneously believed Tanaka to be the culprit.'

(99) a. **Yamada wa Tanaka o baka da to* ***itta****.*
fool said
'Yamada said that Tanaka was a fool.'
b. **Yamada wa sono hon o totemo omosiroi to* ***tutaeta****.*
the book very interesting reported
'Yamada reported that the book was very interesting.'
c. **Yamada wa Tanaka o baka da to* ***sitekisita****.*
fool pointed-out
'Yamada pointed out that Tanaka was a fool.'
d. **Yamada wa Tanaka o baka da to* ***nobeta****.*
stated
'Yamada stated that Tanaka was a fool.'

In English, subject raising can raise the constituent subject either into the main clause object position (without passivization) or into the subject position (after passivization). Observe the following sentences:

(100) a. *They expected* ***John*** *to come.* (raising into object position)
b. ***John*** *is expected to come.* (raising into subject position after passivization)

On the other hand, in Japanese it seems that the raised subject cannot appear in pure passive sentences. The (b) sentences in (101) and (102) clearly have the connotation of adversity passive:[21]

(101) a. *Yamada wa Tanaka o baka da to omotta.*
fool thought
'Yamada thought Tanaka to be a fool.'
b. *Tanaka wa Yamada ni baka da to omow-are-ta.*
by fool think-passive-past
'To Tanaka's chagrin, Yamada thought that he (= Tanaka) was a fool.'

(102) a. *Yamada wa Tanaka o tensai da to sinzita.*
genius believed
'Yamada believed Tanaka to be a genius.'
b. *Tanaka wa Yamada ni tensai da to sinzi-rare-ta.*
by genius believe-passive-past
'To Tanaka's chagrin, Yamada thought that he (= Tanaka) was a genius.'

The fact that (101b) and (102b) are instances of adversity passives can be shown by the ungrammaticality of (103b). Note that adversity passives (but not pure passives) require that the matrix subject be human or a higher animal:

(103) a. *Yamada wa sono hon o totemo omosiroi to omotta.*
the book very interesting thought
'Yamada thought that the book was very interesting.'
b. **Sono hon wa Yamada ni totemo omosiroi to*
the book by very interesting
omow-are-ta.
think-passive-past
'To the book's chagrin, Yamada thought that it was interesting.'

[21]See Kuno (1973: Chapter 25) and the chapter by Howard and Niyekawa-Howard in this volume for the derivation of pure and adversity passives.

I hypothesize that (101b) and (102b) are derived, not from (101a) and (102a), but from the following deep structures:

(104) a. *Tanaka(wa)* [*Yamada(ga)* [*Tanaka(ga) baka da*]$_S$
fool is
to omow]$_S$ *(r)are-ta.*
that think passive-past

b. *Tanaka(wa)* [*Yamada(ga)* [*Tanaka(ga) tensai da*]$_S$ *to*
genius
sinzi]$_S$ *rare-ta.*[22]
believe

Now, compare (101), (102), and (103) with the following sentences:

(105) a. *Tanaka wa baka da to omow-are-te iru.*
fool is think-passive-ing is
'Tanaka is thought to be a fool.'

[22]That *Tanaka o* in (101a) and (102a), in spite of the fact that it occupies the object position of the matrix sentences, cannot undergo pure passivization is consistent with at least one other phenomenon in Japanese. We have two causatives—*make* causative and *let* causative. (See the chapter by Shibatani in this volume for details).

(i) a. *Yamada wa Tanaka* ***o*** *benkyoos-ase-ta.* (*make* causative)
study-make-past
'Yamada made Tanaka study.'

b. *Yamada wa Tanaka* ***ni*** *benkyoos-ase-ta.* (*let* causative)
study-let-past

The behavior of these two causatives provides evidence that *make* causatives are derived from the deep structure that contains the noun phrase object in the matrix sentence (namely, by equi-NP deletion), while *let* causatives are derived from the deep structure that does not contain the noun phrase object (see Kuno, 1973: Chapter 27, Section 6 for evidence).

(ii) a. *Yamada(wa) Tanaka(o)* [*Tanaka(ga) benkyoosu*]$_S$ *sase-ta.* (*make*)
b. *Yamada(wa)* [*Tanaka(ga) benkyoosu*]$_S$ *sase-ta.* (*let*)

In other words, *Tanaka o* in (i.a) is the object of the matrix verb *(s)ase* 'make' all through the derivation of the sentence, while *Tanaka ni* in (i.b) has come to occupy the object position of the matrix verb *(s)ase* 'let' owing to verb raising applied to *benkyoosu* 'study' (and subsequent tree pruning).

Now, observe the following passive sentence:

(iii) *Tanaka wa Yamada ni benkyoos-ase-rare-ta.*
by study-cause-passive-ed
'Tanaka was made by Yamada to study.'

Example (iii) cannot mean that Tanaka was allowed (let) by Yamada to study. It is the passive of (i.a) but not of (i.b). The generalization seems to be that pure passivization does not apply to the object noun phrase that was not in the same position in the underlying structure. In other words, the rule does not apply to the object produced either by subject raising or verb raising (and subsequent tree pruning).

b. *Tanaka wa tensai da to sinzi-rare-te iru.*
genius believe-passive-ing is
'Tanaka is believed to be a genius.'

c. *Sono hon wa totemo omosiroi to omow-are-te iru.*
the book very interesting think-passive-ing is
'The book is thought to be very interesting.'

These sentences are grammatical as pure passives. This can be seen by the acceptability of (105c), whose subject is not human or a higher animal. Note that these sentences are different from (101b), (102b), and (103b) in that the matrix predicate gives a generic statement and does not represent a specific action.

I claim that the sentences of (105) are derived, not from the active pattern of (101a) and (102a), but from the very peculiar passive pattern shown in (106):

(106) a. [*Yamada ga Tanaka o korosita*] *to sinzi-rare-te iru.*
killed that believe-passive-ing is
'It is believed that Yamada killed Tanaka.'

b. [*Homer ga kono zyozisi o kaita*] *to omow-are-te iru.*
this epic wrote that think-passive-ing is
'It is thought that Homer wrote this epic.'

Examples (106a) and (106b) are pure passive sentences. I do not understand what status the *to* clauses have in these sentences because *to* clauses in general cannot be in the subject position. Whatever the analysis of these sentences might be, it is clear that they are grammatical in the interpretation in which *Yamada ga* and *Homer ga* are the subjects of the *to* clauses. Now, if (106a) and (106b) appear in the structures that have *Tanaka wa* and *Homer wa* as their themes, then pure passive sentences of the pattern of (105) will result:[23]

(107) a. [*Yamada-wa*]$_{\text{Theme}}$ [[$\underbrace{\textit{Yamada ga}}_{\emptyset}$ *Tanaka o korosita*]$_{\text{S}}$ *to sinzi-rare-te iru*]$_{\text{S}}$

b. [*Homer-wa*]$_{\text{Theme}}$ [[$\underbrace{\textit{Homer ga}}_{\emptyset}$ *kono zyozisi o kaita*]$_{\text{S}}$ *to omow-are-te iru*]$_{\text{S}}$

There are three interesting features about the pattern of (106). First, these

[23]Alternatively, one could argue that sentences of the pattern of (105) are derived from sentences of the pattern of (106) by applying subject raising into subject position. However, as mentioned earlier, the existence of the thematization and focalization processes in Japanese, as exemplified in (107), makes it difficult to argue convincingly that Japanese has subject raising into subject position.

sentences become ungrammatical if their matrix predicates represent non-generic actions. Observe the following:

(108) a. *[*Yamada ga Tanaka o korosita*] *to Hanako ni*
killed by
sinzi-rare-ta.
believe-passive-past
'It was believed by Hanako that Yamada killed Tanaka.'
b. *[*Homer ga kono zyozisi o kaita*] *to Yamada ni*
this epic wrote by
omow-are-ta.
think-passive-past
'It was thought by Yamada that Homer wrote this epic.'

This phenomenon explains why (101b) and (102b) cannot receive the pure passive interpretation: namely, their source sentences, which should be of the pattern of (108), are ungrammatical.

A second characteristic of (106) is that the predicate of the *to* clause is not limited to adjectives or 'nominal + copula'. In (106), we have the action verbs *korosi-ta* 'killed' and *kaita* 'wrote'. Recall that the pattern of (17b) is restricted to cases in which the constituent predicates are adjectives or 'nominal + copula':

(17) a. *Yamada wa* [***Tanaka ga*** *baka da*] *to omotte ita.*
'Yamada thought that Tanaka was a fool.'
b. *Yamada wa* ***Tanaka o*** *baka da to omotte ita.*

(109) a. *Yamada wa* [***Hanako ga*** *Tanaka o korosita*] *to sinzita.*
killed believed
'Yamada believed that Hanako killed Tanaka.'
b. **Yamada wa* ***Hanako o*** *Tanaka o korosita to sinzita.*

(110) a. *Yamada wa* [***Tanaka ga*** *Boston ni itte simatta*] *to omotta.*
to gone has thought
'Yamada thought that Tanaka had gone to Boston.'
b. **Yamada wa* ***Tanaka o*** *Boston ni itte simatta to omotta.*

If (105a–c) are derived, as I claim, from the pattern of (106), then it should be possible to have action verbs in the constituent predicate. This prediction is borne out by the following examples:

(111) a. *Yamada wa oozei no zyosei o* ***korosita*** *to*
many women killed
sinzi-rare-te iru.
believe-passive-ing is
'Yamada is believed to have killed many women.'

b. *Yamada wa Boston ni* ***itte simatta*** *to omow-are-te iru.*
to gone has think-passive-ing is
'Yamada is thought to have gone to Boston.'

The grammaticality of (111) shows that the sources of these sentences are not the patterns of (109b) and (110b), which are ungrammatical. Thus, it gives additional support to my hypothesis that the patterns of (101a) and (102a) are not the sources for the sentences of (105).

The third characteristic of the pattern of (106) is that verbs that cannot undergo subject raising can also enter into this pattern. Observe the following sentences:

(112) a. [*Yamada ga Tanaka o korosita*] *to iw-are-te iru.*
killed say-passive-ing is
'It is said that Yamada killed Tanaka.'

b. [*Homer ga kono zyozisi o kaita*] *to tutae-rare-te iru.*
this epic wrote report-passive-ing is
'It is said that Homer wrote this epic.'

Recall that saying verbs such as *iu* 'say' and *tutaeru* 'to report' cannot undergo subject raising, as shown by the ungrammaticality of (99).

If the sentences of (105) are derived, as I claim, from the pattern of (106), then it should be possible to obtain pure passive sentences of the pattern of (105) for these saying verbs, too. This prediction is borne out by the following:

(113) a. *Tanaka wa baka da to iw-are-te iru.*
fool is say-passive-ing is
'Tanaka is said to be a fool.'

b. *Yamada wa oozei no zyosei o korosita to*
many women killed
tutae-rare-te iru.
report-passive-ing is
'Yamada is reported to have killed many women.'

In case the matrix predicates of the pattern of (113) represent nongeneric actions, we obtain sentences of adversity passive connotation:

(114) a. *Tanaka wa Yamada ni baka da to iw-are-ta.*
by fool is say-passive-past
'To Tanaka's chagrin, Yamada said that he (= Tanaka) was a fool.'

b. *Tanaka wa Yamada ni tensai da to tutae-rare-ta.*
by genius is report-passive-past
'To Tanaka's chagrin, Yamada reported that he (= Tanaka) was a genius.'

c. **Kono hon wa Yamada ni omosiroku nai to iw-are-ta.*
this book by interesting not say-passive-past
'To this book's chagrin, Yamada said that it was not interesting.'

Note, in particular, the ungrammaticality of (114c).

On observing that the sentences of (99) are ungrammatical but that (113), (114a), and (114b) are grammatical, one might be tempted to make the generalization that in Japanese, as well as in English, there are verbs that can undergo subject raising on the condition that they will also undergo pure passivization. I have shown that this generalization, which would be interesting if true, cannot be maintained. This is because there is evidence to indicate that sentences derived by applying subject raising (in object position), even when they are grammatical, do not have corresponding pure passive sentences. I have shown that adversity passives involving feeling and saying verbs have nothing to do with the raised subject. I have also shown that pure passives involving generic statements are derived, not from subject-raised sentences, but from peculiar (probably subjectless) pure passive sentences of the pattern of (106), which are acceptable only when they represent generic statements.

REFLEXIVIZATION: A TRANSFORMATIONAL APPROACH[1]

NORIKO AKATSUKA McCAWLEY

INTRODUCTION

This is a study in the syntax and semantics of Japanese reflexivization. In Section 1, I show that Japanese reflexivization has two aspects, language specific and language independent. The former is the subject-antecedent condition and the latter the command condition. The domain of Japanese reflexivization is not confined to the simplex sentence, as is its English counterpart. It goes down into embedded sentences just like English pronominalization.

Section 2 treats backward reflexivization in emotive causatives in which the subject-antecedent condition appears to be violated. First, it is demonstrated that all of the current analyses of emotive causatives are far from adequate. Then it is shown that backward reflexivization in emotive causatives is actually part of a more general problem, namely, backward reflexivization in nonagentive causative constructions.

In Section 3, I claim that backward reflexivization is actually an instance of ordinary forward reflexivization in which the true antecedent has been

[1]This work consists of Chapters I, IV, V, and VI of my Ph.D. dissertation, "A study of Japanese reflexivization," University of Illinois, 1972. An extremely condensed version of Chapter III appeared as "On the treatment of Japanese passives," in P. M. Peranteau, J. N. Levi, and G. C. Phares (Eds.), *Papers from the Eighth Regional Meeting of the Chicago Linguistic Society* (Chicago: University of Chicago Department of Linguistics, 1972), pp. 259–270. Also, a revised version of Chapter IV appeared as "Emotive verbs in English and Japanese," *Studies in the Linguistic Sciences*, 1972, **2**(1), 1–15.

deleted in the course of the derivation. The subject-antecedent condition is claimed to be still operative here.

I have made the following assumptions throughout this study. First, case markers do not exist in the deep structure and are introduced by a transformation. The reader is referred to Kuroda (1965b) and Kuno (1973). Second, the VP node does not exist. Third, Japanese is an SOV language and English is an SVO language on both the deep and surface levels. In addition, I have ignored the topic marker *wa*, which occurs in many of the examples instead of the subject marker *ga*. The difference in meaning between sentences with *ga* and sentences with *wa* in its place is discussed with great insight in Kuno (1973).

1. BASIC CONDITIONS ON REFLEXIVIZATION

The Subject-Antecedent Condition[2]

Japanese reflexivization was first investigated by Kuroda (1965b) in the light of the treatment of English reflexivization by Lees and Klima (1963). Kuroda's conclusion was as follows:

> Referring back to the main subject, Reflexivization applies obligatorily on the main object and on the constituent object dominated by the main node VP, and optionally on the constituent subject. The applicability of Reflexivization is therefore much wider in Japanese than it is in English, where the condition is simply application within the simple sentence [Kuroda, 1965b:154].

He did not treat reflexivization when the reflexive is in neither subject position nor object position (e.g., reflexive possessives, reflexives before postpositions other than the subject marker or object marker). However, notice that his subject-antecedent condition is operative in those cases, too. Consider:

(1) *Satoo*$_i$ *wa Tanaka ni zibun*$_i$ *no syasin o miseta.*
self 's picture showed
'Sato$_i$ showed Tanaka$_j$ a picture of himself$_{i,*j}$.'

(2) *Satoo*$_i$ *wa Tanaka ni zibun*$_i$ *no koto ni tuite hanasita.*
self 's matter about talked
'Sato$_i$ talked to Tanaka$_j$ about himself$_{i,*j}$.'

[2]The term 'subject-antecedent' was introduced by Oyakawa (1973). The subject-antecedent condition is far from peculiar to Japanese. For example, Modern Greek, Swedish, Tamil, and Korean exhibit the same characteristic.

In (1) and (2) the English translation is ambiguous. *Himself* can refer back to both *Satoo* and *Tanaka*. However, Japanese *zibun* is not ambiguous. It can refer only to *Satoo*, the subject.

Next, observe the following sentences; literal translations follow:

(3) *Satoo*$_i$ *wa Tanaka*$_j$ *ga Hara ni zibun*$_{i,j}$ *ga suki na musume o*
self loves girl
syookaisita koto ni odoroita.
introduced that at surprised
'Sato$_i$ was surprised that Tanaka$_j$ introduced to Hara the girl self$_{i,j}$ loves.'

(4) *Satoo*$_i$ *wa Tanaka*$_j$ *ga Nakamura ni Hara*$_k$ *ga zibun*$_{i,j,k}$ *no ie de*
self 's house
koros-rare-ta koto o hanasite simatta no o satotta.
in kill-passive-past had talked that realized
'Sato$_i$ realized that Tanaka$_j$ had already told Nakamura that Hara$_k$ was killed in self$_{i,j,k}$'s house.'

Zibun in (3) and (4) is ambiguous. In (4), it can refer back to *Satoo*, *Tanaka*, and *Hara*. In (3), it can refer back to both *Satoo* and *Tanaka*. Note that *Tanaka* is not in the same simplex sentence as the reflexive, nor in the main sentence. Therefore, it is necessary to interpret Kuroda's subject-antecedent condition as saying that the reflexive refers back to the subject in the same simplex sentence or the subject in any higher sentence.

As pointed out by Kuroda, the domain of Japanese reflexivization is not confined to the simplex sentence. It acts like English simple pronominalization, going down into complement sentences, relative clauses, sentences in apposition, and adverbial clauses. Consider the following examples:

(5) *Mitiko*$_i$ *wa zibun*$_i$ *ga sukina seinen o yatto ryoosin ni*
self loves young man finally parents to
syookai sita.
introduced
'Michiko$_i$ finally introduced to her parents the young man whom self$_i$ loved.'

(6) *Mitiko*$_i$ *wa Hirosi ga zibun*$_i$ *o uragitta zizitu o wasure-nai.*
self betrayed fact forget-negative
'Michiko$_i$ does not forget the fact that Hiroshi betrayed self$_i$.'

(7) *Mitiko*$_i$ *wa zibun*$_i$ *ga Hirosi o korosita yume o mita.*
self killed dream saw
'Michiko$_i$ had a dream in which self$_i$ killed Hiroshi.'

(8) *Mitiko*$_i$ *wa zibun*$_i$ *no kamera to otooto no razio ga nusum-rare-ta*
self 's camera and younger brother's radio
koto o keisatu ni todoketa.
steal-passive-past that police to informed
'Michiko$_i$ reported to the police that self$_i$'s camera and her younger brother's radio were stolen.'

(9) *Mitiko*$_i$ *wa, zibun*$_i$ *ga minikui node, kanasinde iru.*
self ugly because sad is
'Michiko$_i$ is sad, because self$_i$ is ugly.'

(10) *Zibun*$_i$ *ga minikui node, Mitiko*$_i$ *wa kanasinde iru.*
self ugly because sad is
'Because self$_i$ is ugly, Michiko$_i$ is sad.'

Ross (1967) wants to extend his Complex NP Constraint and Coordinate Structure Constraint so that they can explain facts about feature-changing transformations as well as chopping transformations. These constraints are as follows:

(11) *The Complex NP Constraint: No element contained in a sentence dominated by a noun phrase with a lexical head noun may be moved out of that noun phrase by a transformation* [*Ross, 1967:127*].

(12) *The Coordinate Structure Constraint: In a coordinate structure, no conjunct may be moved, nor may any element contained in a conjunct be moved out of that conjunct* [*Ross, 1967:161*].

Like English pronominalization, Japanese reflexivization violates both of those constraints. Among the preceding examples, (5)–(7) are violations of the Complex NP Constraint. Example (8) is a violation of the Coordinate Structure Constraint. Examples (9) and (10) show that the reflexive can occur in an adverbial clause, and (10) also shows that the adverbial clause can also occur at the beginning of the sentence. Closer observation reveals that Japanese reflexivization is different from English simple pronominalization in that the reflexive always refers back to the subject, as in all of the examples just given.

Next we will consider apparent counterexamples to the subject-antecedent condition. Compare (13) with (14):

(13) *Hirosi*$_i$ *wa Mitiko ni zibun*$_i$ *no heya de eigo o osieta.*
self 's room in English taught
'Hiroshi$_i$ taught English to Michiko in self$_i$'s room.'

(14) *Hirosi*$_i$ *wa Mitiko*$_j$ *o zibun*$_{i,j}$ *no heya de benkyoo s-sase-ta.*
self 's room in study-make-past
'Hiroshi$_i$ made Michiko$_j$ study in self$_{i,j}$'s room.'

In (13) the reflexive refers only to *Hirosi*, the subject. However, (14) is ambiguous. The reflexive can refer both to *Hirosi* and to *Mitiko*. It seems as if the subject-antecedent condition is violated in (14). The ambiguity of (14), however, will be quite naturally explained if we assume that Japanese causative constructions are underlyingly complex, as proposed by Kuroda (1965a). Assume that the following two deep structures underlie (14):

(15) *Hirosi*$_i$ *wa* (*Mitiko*$_j$ *ga Mitiko*$_j$ *no heya de benkyoo s*)
Mitiko Mitiko 's room in study
sase-ta.
make-past
'Hiroshi$_i$ made (Michiko$_j$ study in Michiko$_j$'s room).'

(16) *Hirosi*$_i$ *wa* (*Mitiko*$_j$ *ga Hirosi*$_i$ *no heya de benkyoo s*)
Mitiko Hirosi 's room study
sase-ta.
make-past
'Hiroshi$_i$ made (Michiko$_j$ study in Hiroshi$_i$'s room).'

In (15), the following rules will apply:

1. Reflexivization. The application of reflexivization in the lower sentence changes *Mitiko* in *Mitiko no heya* 'Mitiko's room' into *zibun*.
2. Verb raising. *Benkyoo s* 'study' is combined with the higher verb *sase*, becoming *benkyoo s-sase*. Because of the tree-pruning convention (Ross, 1969), this operation has the effect of eliminating the lower S node and, thus, making the complement subject a constituent of the higher sentence.

Note that verb raising on the higher sentence must follow reflexivization on the lower sentence in (15). If verb raising on the higher sentence preceded reflexivization on the lower sentence, the latter would not be able to apply, since the antecedent *Mitiko* would no longer be a subject. On the basis of this fact plus some facts about passives, J. McCawley (1972b) has shown that verb raising, passivization, and reflexivization are in the cycle and apply in that order. In (16), the following rules will apply:

1. Reflexivization. The application of reflexivization in the higher sentence changes *Hirosi* in the lower sentence into *zibun*.
2. Verb raising as in (15).

The facts presented so far give no information about the sequence of those two steps; the results by J. McCawley cited earlier imply that verb raising must precede reflexivization in (16). So far, we have shown that reflexivization and verb raising are responsible for wiping out the difference between (15) and (16), yielding (14).

Let us consider another apparent counterexample to the subject-antecedent condition. Observe (17), which is ambiguous:

(17) *Hirosi*$_i$ *wa Mitiko*$_j$ *ni zibun*$_{i,j}$ *no heya de benkyoo suru*
self 's room in study
yoo ni itta.
told
'Hiroshi$_i$ told Michiko$_j$ to study in self$_{i,j}$'s room.'

Verbs like *iu* 'tell', *meirei suru* 'order', *tyuukoku suru* 'advise', etc., are subject to a deep structure constraint that their complement subject must be coreferential to their indirect object.[3] Thus, we assume that the following two deep structures underlie (17):

(18) *Hirosi*$_i$ *wa Mitiko*$_j$ *ni (Mitiko*$_j$ *ga Mitiko*$_j$ *no heya de*
Mitiko 's room in
benkyoo s) itta.
study told
'Hiroshi$_i$ told Michiko$_j$ (Mitiko$_j$ study Mitiko$_j$'s room).'

(19) *Hirosi*$_i$ *wa Mitiko*$_j$ *ni (Mitiko*$_j$ *ga Hirosi*$_i$ *no heya de*
Hirosi 's room in
benkyoo s) itta.
study told
'Hiroshi$_i$ told Michiko$_j$ (Mitiko$_j$ study Hirosi$_i$'s room).'

In (18), the following operations will be required:

1. Reflexivization. The application of reflexivization in the lower sentence changes *Mitiko* in *Mitiko no heya* 'Mitiko's room' into *zibun*.
2. Equi-NP deletion. The complement subject *Mitiko* deletes under the identity with the indirect object of the main sentence *Mitiko*.
3. Complementizer placement. The complementizer *yoo ni* is inserted after the object complement.

Note that equi-NP deletion and reflexivization are crucially ordered in (18). If the former preceded the latter, then the latter would not be able to apply. In (19), the following operations will be required:

[3]The theoretical importance of 'deep structure constraints' was first claimed by David Perlmutter (1971). Although I believe this is actually a semantic constraint rather than syntactic, I will not touch on that issue, since it has no direct consequences for the present discussion.

1. Reflexivization. The application of reflexivization in the higher sentence changes *Hirosi* in *Hirosi no heya* 'Hirosi's room' into *zibun.*
2. Equi-NP deletion as in (18).
3. Complementizer placement as in (18).

We have shown that reflexivization and equi-NP deletion wipe out the difference between (18) and (19), yielding (17). What is important here is that the true antecedent of the reflexive must be deleted by equi-NP deletion in the course of the derivation of (17) from (18). Therefore, *Mitiko* is not the true antecedent of the reflexive in (17).

The Command Condition

Consider the following examples:[4]

(20) a. *Hirosi*$_i$ *ga ima gesyuku site iru ie ni Hirosi*$_i$ *wa*
now board house in
moo gonen mo sunde iru.
already five years live
'In the house where Hiroshi$_i$ boards now Hiroshi$_i$ has been living as long as five years.'

b. *Zibun*$_i$ *ga ima gesyuku site iru ie ni Hirosi*$_i$ *wa*
self now board house in
moo gonen mo sunde iru.
already five years live
'In the house where self$_i$ boards now Hiroshi$_i$ has been living as long as five years.'

c. **Hirosi*$_i$ *ga ima gesyuku site iru ie ni zibun*$_i$ *wa*
now board house in self
moo gonen mo sunde iru.[5]
already five years live
'In the house where Hiroshi$_i$ boards now self$_i$ has been living as long as five years.'

(21) a. *Hirosi*$_i$ *ga ima gesyuku site iru ie ni Hirosi*$_i$ *ga*
now board house in
siranai hito ga hitori sunde iru.
know negative man one live

[4]I am indebted to Kuno (1971) for the revealing examples in (20).

[5]Example (20c) is grammatical if it means 'I have been living as long as five years in the house where Hiroshi boards now.' In this case, *zibun* is not a reflexive form but, rather, is being used as a first-person pronoun just like *watakusi, boku,* etc. As noted by Kuroda (1965a), this use of *zibun* is restricted to a very special class of male speakers, such as military people. I suspect, though, that female military personnel can also use this special first-person pronoun.

'In the house where Hiroshi_i boards now there lives a man whom Hiroshi_i does not know.'

b. *$\textit{Zibun}_i$ ga ima gesyuku site iru ie ni $\textit{Hirosi}_i$ ga siranai hito ga hitori sunde iru.*

'In the house where self_i boards now there lives a man whom Hiroshi_i does not know.'

c. *$\textit{Hirosi}_i$ ga ima gesyuku site iru ie ni $\textit{zibun}_i$ ga siranai hito ga hitori sunde iru.*

'In the house where Hiroshi_i boards now there lives a man whom self_i does not know.'

The preceding examples clearly indicate that the antecedent of the reflexive not only must be the subject but also must command the reflexive (cf. Langacker, 1969). In (20), although both occurrences of *Hirosi* are the subjects of the sentences, only the second occurrence of *Hirosi* commands the first occurrence of *Hirosi*. On the other hand, in (21) neither occurrence of *Hirosi* commands the other. Now, consider (22). We can correctly predict that neither the (b) nor the (c) form is grammatical: The (b) form does not satisfy the subject-antecedent condition, while the (c) form does not satisfy the command condition:

(22) a. *$\textit{Hirosi}_i$ ga ima gesyuku site iru ie ni $\textit{Hirosi}_i$ no*
now board house in Hirosi 's
tomodati ga hitori sunde iru.[6]
friend one live

'In the house where Hiroshi_i boards now there lives a friend of Hiroshi_i's.'

b. *$\textit{Zibun}_i$ ga ima gesyuku site iru ie ni $\textit{Hirosi}_i$ no tomodati ga hitori sunde iru.*

'In the house where self_i boards now there lives a friend of Hiroshi_i's.'

c. *$\textit{Hirosi}_i$ ga ima gesyuku site iru ie ni $\textit{zibun}_i$ no tomodati ga hitori sunde iru.*

'In the house where Hiroshi_i boards now there lives a friend of self_i's.'

Many rules of a particular language have two aspects, language specific and language independent. Japanese reflexivization is no exception. Just like many other instances of pronominalization in human languages, it also utilizes Langacker's notion of command in addition to the subject-antecedent condition, which certainly seems to be language specific.

[6]Examples (20a), (21a), and (22a) illustrate the common practice in Japanese of repeating the coreferential NP without applying either reflexivization or pronominalization.

Apparent Backward Reflexivization

(23) *Zibun$_i$ no sukina seinen o Mitiko$_i$ wa yatto ryoosin ni*
self love young man finally parents to
syookai sita.
introduced
'Michiko$_i$ finally introduced the young man who self$_i$ loved to her parents.'

(24) **Zibun$_i$ no sukina seinen wa Mitiko$_i$ o yatto ryoosin ni syookai sita.*
'The young man who self$_i$ loved introduced Michiko$_i$ to his parents.'

The subject-antecedent condition correctly predicts that only (23) is grammatical. In (23) *Mitiko* is the subject, whereas it is not in (24). Thus, (23) seems to be of no special interest to our analysis. However, I would like to show that the apparent backward reflexivization in (23) is due to NP scrambling, which has applied to a structure in which forward reflexivization has already applied. Scrambling would be roughly formulated as follows:[7]

(25) NP scrambling.

$$\begin{array}{ccccccc} X & - & \begin{Bmatrix} NP \\ ADV \end{Bmatrix} & - & \begin{Bmatrix} NP \\ ADV \end{Bmatrix} & - & Y \\ 1 & & 2 & & 3 & & 4 \\ 1 & & 3 & & 2 & & 4 \end{array} \quad \overset{\text{OPT}}{\Longrightarrow}$$

CONDITION 1: This rule is postcyclic.
CONDITION 2: This rule is upward-bound.

[7]I follow Ross' (1967) formulation of scrambling in Latin. Although it is obvious that the rule as it is, is far from satisfactory, I know of no better way to formulate it. I am not claiming here that all of the variants resulting from scrambling are synonymous in the very strict sense of the word. Although all of them do share the same proposition, certainly they differ as to such important factors as 'focus', 'contrast', etc. I suspect that this characteristic is shared by many, if not all, of the so-called 'optional' rules such as tough movement, raising, etc. One other very important function of Japanese scrambling is to enhance comprehensibility when the sentence involves multiple self-embedding. For example, compare:

(i) *(((Hara ga ga zibun no ie de korosareta) koto o Tanaka ga Nakamura ni*
self 's house in kill-passive-past
hanasite simatta) to Satoo wa omotta.)
had told that thought
'Sato thought that Tanaka had already told Nakamura that Hara was killed in self's house.'

(ii) ??*(Satoo wa (Tanaka ga (Hara ga zibun no ie de korosareta) koto o Nakamura ni hanasite simatta) to omotta).*

Example (ii) is very difficult to understand, since we have here three subjects in succession, while (i) is much easier to understand. For an insightful discussion of the related topic, the reader is referred to Kuno (1974c).

Consider the following sentence:

(26) *Mitiko*$_i$ *wa Hirosi ni zibun*$_i$ *no himitu o hanasita.*
self 's secret told
'Michiko$_i$ told Hiroshi self$_i$'s secret.'

By applying NP scrambling to (26), we get as many as six stylistic variants:

(27) a. *Mitiko wa Hirosi ni zibun no himitu o hanasita.*
1 2 3 4
b. *Mitiko wa zibun no himitu o Hirosi ni hanasita.*
1 3 2 4
c. *Hirosi ni Mitiko wa zibun no himitu o hanasita.*
2 1 3 4
d. *Hirosi ni zibun no himitu o Mitiko wa hanasita.*
2 3 1 4
e. *Zibun no himitu o Hirosi ni Mitiko wa hanasita.*
3 2 1 4
f. *Zibun no himitu o Mitiko wa Hirosi ni hanasita.*
3 1 2 4

Examples (27d), (27e), and (27f), then, are instances of apparent backward reflexivization. Scrambling also operates in embedded sentences. For example, (27a–f) can be very comfortably embedded in (28), yielding (29):

(28) *Keiko wa sore o sitta.*
it found out
'Keiko found it out.'

(29) a. *Keiko*$_i$ *wa Mitiko*$_j$ *ga Hirosi ni zibun*$_{i,j}$ *no himitu o hanasita koto o sitta.*
b. *Keiko*$_i$ *wa Hirosi ni Mitiko*$_j$ *ga zibun*$_{i,j}$ *no himitu o hanasita koto o sitta.*
c. *Keiko*$_i$ *wa Hirosi ni Mitiko*$_j$ *ga zibun*$_{i,j}$ *no himitu o hanasita koto o sitta.*
d. *Keiko*$_i$ *wa Hirosi ni zibun*$_{i,j}$ *no himitu o Mitiko*$_j$ *ga hanasita koto o sitta.*
e. *Keiko*$_i$ *wa zibun*$_{i,j}$ *no himitu o Hirosi ni Mitiko*$_j$ *ga hanasita koto o sitta.*
f. *Keiko*$_i$ *wa zibun*$_{i,j}$ *no himitu o Mitiko*$_j$ *ga Hirosi ni hanasita koto o sitta.*

In all of these examples, *zibun* is ambiguous, referring both to *Keiko* and to *Mitiko*. Therefore, (29d), (29e), and (29f) are also instances of apparent backward reflexivization.

Let us consider another example. Kuno (1972) has pointed out that when a proposition represented in the form 'X *ga* Y *to* V' is true, then propositions 'Y *ga* X *to* V', '(X *to* Y) *ga* V', and '(Y *to* X) *ga* V' are also true. His observation seems to be borne out by the following examples:

(30) a. *Hirosi ga Mitiko to kekkon sita.*
with got married
'Hiroshi got married to Michiko.'
b. *Mitiko ga Hirosi to kekkon sita.*
'Michiko got married to Hiroshi.'
c. *Hirosi to Mitiko ga kekkon sita.*
and
'Hiroshi and Michiko got married.'
d. *Mitiko to Hirosi ga kekkon sita.*
'Michiko and Hiroshi got married.'

However, compare (30) with (31). In (31), only the (a) form is grammatical:

(31) a. *Hirosi*$_i$ *ga zibun*$_i$ *ga suki na hito to kekkon sita.*
self love girl with got married
'Hiroshi$_i$ got married to a girl whom self$_i$ loved.'
b. **Zibun*$_i$ *ga suki na hito ga Hirosi*$_i$ *to kekkon sita.*
self love girl
'A girl whom self$_i$ loved got married with Hiroshi$_i$.'
c. **Hirosi*$_i$ *to zibun*$_i$ *ga suki na hito ga kekkon sita.*
and
'Hiroshi$_i$ and a girl whom self$_i$ loved got married.'
d. **Zibun*$_i$ *ga suki na hito to Hirosi*$_i$ *ga kekkon sita.*
'A girl whom self$_i$ loved and Hiroshi$_i$ got married.'

Notice that our subject-antecedent condition can correctly predict that only the (a) form is grammatical. Also, notice that if scrambling applies to (31a), (32) will be derived:

(32) *Zibun*$_i$ *ga suki na hito to Hirosi*$_i$ *ga kekkon sita.*
self love girl with
'With a girl whom self$_i$ loved Hiroshi$_i$ got married.'

Although (31d) and (32) are homophonous, their constituent structure is quite different; the former has a conjoined NP subject, but the latter has not. The fact that (32) does not have a conjoined NP subject is easily demonstrated. For example, compare (32) with (33):

(33) *Zibun*$_i$ *ga suki na hito to senzitu Hirosi*$_i$ *ga kekkon sita.*
the other day
'With a girl whom self$_i$ loved Hiroshi$_i$ got married the other day.'

If it were a conjoined NP subject, then it would be impossible to insert an adverb like *senzitu* 'the other day'. Example (33) is a perfectly good sentence. Also, consider (34):

(34) a. *Zibun$_i$ ga suki na hito to Hirosi$_i$ ga senzitu*
self love girl the other day
kekkon sita.
got married
'With a girl whom self$_i$ loved Hiroshi$_i$ got married the other day.'

b. **Senzitu kekkon sita no wa zibun$_i$ ga suki na hito to Hirosi$_i$ da.*
'It was a girl whom self$_i$ loved and Hiroshi$_i$ that got married the other day.'

If in fact *zibun ga suki na hito to Hirosi* were a conjoined NP, then (34b), which is a cleft sentence corresponding to (34a), would be grammatical. But (34b) is ungrammatical. These facts clearly indicate that sentences like (32), (33), and (34a) are further instances of apparent backward reflexivization due to scrambling.

I conjecture that in Japanese reflexivization always applies forward. However, the justification of this hypothesis is beyond the scope of this thesis. For example, consider (35):

(35) a. *Mitiko$_i$ wa, zibun$_i$ ga minikui node, kanasinde iru.*
self ugly because sad is
'Michiko$_i$ is sad, because self$_i$ is ugly.'

b. *Zibun$_i$ ga minikui node, Mitiko$_i$ wa kanasinde iru.*
self ugly because sad is
'Because self$_i$ is ugly, Michiko$_i$ is sad.'

In order to argue that (35a) is more basic and (35b) has been derived from (35a), we would have to present evidence that adverbial clauses originate after the subject in the deep structure in Japanese. At present, I have no good arguments for this, although I suspect that it is the case. Whether all instances of Japanese reflexivization are forward or not is itself an interesting question, but it is not at issue in the present study. Backward reflexivization becomes relevant only when it violates our conditions of reflexivization. In that sense, all instances of apparent backward reflexivization that I have discussed in this section are actually of no importance, for they all satisfy our conditions.

Summary

Our basic assumption concerning Japanese reflexivization is that *zibun* is not inserted as the lexical item at the underlying structure. We treat *zibun* as arising through a feature-changing transformation under linguistic coreferentiality between the two NPs. This rule makes the crucial use of variables (cf. Ross, 1967). It would be roughly formulated as follows:

(36) Reflexivization.

$$\begin{array}{ccccc} NP & - & X & - & NP \\ 1 & & 2 & - & 3 \end{array} \xrightarrow{\text{OBLIG}} 1 \quad 2 \quad \textit{zibun}$$

CONDITION 1: 1 = 3
CONDITION 2: 1 is a subject
CONDITION 3: 1 commands 3

2. EMOTIVE CAUSATIVES AND BACKWARD REFLEXIVIZATION

Counterexamples?

Consider the following examples:

(37) *Zibun*$_i$ *ga gan kamo sirenai koto ga Hirosi*$_i$ *o*
self cancer may have that
nayam-sase-ta
worried-make-past
'That self$_i$ might have cancer worried Hiroshi$_i$.'

(38) *Zibun*$_i$ *ga gan kamo sirenai to iu iyana yokan ga*
self cancer may have that awful presentiment
Hirosi$_i$ *o obie-sase-ta.*
frightened-make-past
'The awful presentiment that self$_i$ might have cancer frightened hiroshi$_i$.'

(39) *Zibun*$_i$ *nimo yotugi ga umareta koto ga Hideyosi*$_i$ *o*
self to heir born that
itaku yorokob-sase-ta.
very pleased-make-past
'That an heir was born to self$_i$ pleased Hideyoshi$_i$ very much.'

(40) *Koibito ga zibun*$_i$ *o uragitta koto ga Hirosi o*
girlfriend self betrayed that
hungai s-sase-ta.
furious-make-past
'That his girlfriend had betrayed self$_i$ made Hiroshi furious.'

(41) *Zibun*$_i$ *no ninki ga otidasita to iu uwasa ga Satoo-*
self's popularity drop began that rumor
syusyoo$_i$ *o iraira s-sase-te iru.*
Premier irritated-make gerund is
'The rumor that self$_i$'s popularity has started to drop irritates Premier Sato.'

In all of the preceding examples, the reflexive refers to the object of the higher sentence, violating one of our conditions of reflexivization, i.e., that the antecedent be the subject. Unless we can prove that this condition has been met at the time reflexivization applied, sentences like (37)–(41) will provide serious counterexamples to our generalization.

Note that (37)–(41) share two important properties: (1) The subject is nonagentive and (2) the predicate is formed from one of the special class of verbs denoting human emotion plus *sase*, which is homophonous to the causative morpheme *sase*. Henceforth, we will call this type of predicate constructions 'emotive causatives', although we have not yet demonstrated that *sase* in those sentences is, indeed, the causative morpheme *sase*. Also, we will call the class of verbs in question 'Ve'.

Thus far, at least two interesting analyses of emotive causatives have been proposed. One is a Japanese analog of G. Lakoff's Flip (1970a) or Postal's Psych Movement analysis (1970a), and the other is a causative analysis. I am going to show that both of them are far from adequate in several significant points and, especially, that they fail to provide well-motivated explanations for backward reflexivization in sentences like (37)–(41).

Arguments against Flip

Flip in Japanese

Backward reflexivization in emotive causatives was first noticed by me (Akatsuka, 1969). I then argued that Flip causes the reflexive to precede its antecedent. This approach seems to be quite attractive at first. For the native speaker of Japanese knows that the sentences (37)–(41) are essential paraphrases of (42)–(46), respectively. Consider:

(42) *Hirosi*$_i$ *wa zibun*$_i$ *ga gan kamo sirenai koto ni nayanda.*
self cancer may have that worried-past
'Hiroshi$_i$ was worried that self$_i$ might have cancer.'

(43) *Hirosi*$_i$ *wa zibun*$_i$ *ga gan kamo sirenai to iu iyana*
self cancer may have that awful
yakan ni obieta.
presentiment frightened-past
'Hiroshi$_i$ was frightened by the awful presentiment that self$_i$ might have cancer.'

(44) *Hideyosi*$_i$ *wa zibun*$_i$ *nimo yotugi ga umareta koto o itaku*
self to heir born that very
yorokonda.
pleased-past
'Hideyoshi$_i$ was very pleased that an heir was born to self$_i$.'

(45) *Hirosi*$_i$ *wa koibito ga zibun*$_i$ *o uragitta koto o/ni*
girlfriend self betrayed that
hungai sita.
furious-past
'Hiroshi$_i$ was furious that his girlfriend had betrayed self$_i$.'

(46) *Satoo-syusyoo*$_i$ *wa zibun*$_i$ *no ninki ga otidasita to iu*
Premier self 's popularity drop began that
uwasa ni iraira site iru.
rumor irritated is
'Premier Sato$_i$ is irritated at the rumor that self$_i$'s popularity has started to drop.'

According to this approach, Flip applies to sentences (42)–(46), interchanging the subject and the object. Although it sounds plausible, we would like to show that this analysis is quite superficial and that the solution for backward reflexivization must be of a more general nature.

Observe, first, that the interchange of the subject and the object is not all that Flip does. This rule has to introduce the morpheme *sase*, which is homophonous to the causative morpheme *sase*. Thus, this analysis makes the claim that *sase* in constructions like (37)–(41) is semantically vacuous and is totally unrelated to the causative morpheme *sase*. However, we will present five pieces of evidence that *sase* in emotive causative constructions is a causative morpheme. First, Karttunen (1970a) has pointed out that in affirmative assertions the causative sentence implies the factuality of its object complement. Thus, (47) implies (48):

(47) *Hirosi wa, Mitiko o nagutte, nak-sase-ta.*
hitting cry-make-past
'Hiroshi made Michiko cry by hitting her.'

(48) *Mitiko wa naita.*
cried
'Michiko cried.'

This property is shared by emotive causatives. For example, (37) implies (49):

(37) *Zibun*$_i$ *ga gan kamo sirenai koto ga Hirosi*$_i$ *o nayam-sase-ta.*
'That self$_i$ might have cancer worried Hiroshi.'

(49) *Hirosi wa nayanda.*
'Hiroshi was worried.'

Second, just like causative constructions, emotive causatives may take agentive subjects:

(50) *Mitiko wa takumi ni Hirosi o yorokob-sase-ta.*
cleverly pleased-make-past
'Michiko pleased Hiroshi cleverly.'

(51) *Mitiko wa waza to Hirosi o okor-sase-ta.*
purposely angry-make-past
'Michiko made Hiroshi angry purposely.'

Third, notice that nonagentive causatives always seem to have a paraphrase with a *node* 'because' clause sentence. Thus, for instance, (52) has (53) as a paraphrase:

(52) *Koibito ni uragir-rare-ta koto ga Hirosi ni ningen*
girlfriend by betray-passive-past that human
husin no nen o idak-sase-ta.
distrust notion conceive-make-past
'That he was betrayed by his girlfriend made Hiroshi think that humans are not to be trusted.'

(53) *Koibito ni uragir-rare-ta node, Hirosi wa ningen husin*
because
no nen o idaita.
'Hiroshi came to think that humans are not to be trusted because he was betrayed by his girlfriend.'

Just so, nonagentive emotive causatives have a paraphrase with a *node* 'because' clause sentence:

(54) *Koibito ni uragir-rare-ta koto ga Hirosi o*
girlfriend by betray-passive-past that
zetuboo s-sase-ta.
desperate-make-past
'That he was betrayed by his girlfriend made Hiroshi desperate.'

(55) *Koibito ni uragir-rare-ta node, Hirosi wa zetuboo sita.*
because became desperate
'Hiroshi became desperate, because he was betrayed by his girlfriend.'

Fourth, and most important, backward reflexivization takes place not just in nonagentive emotive causatives but in all nonagentive causatives. Consider:

(56) *Sinrai sikitte ita tuma ga zibun$_i$ o uragitta koto ga*
trusted wholeheartedly wife self betrayed that
Tanaka-si$_i$ ni ningen husin no nen o idak-sase-ta.
human distrust notion conceive-make-past
'That his wife whom he had trusted wholeheartedly betrayed self$_i$ made Mr. Tanaka$_i$ think that humans are not to be trusted.'

(57) *Zibun$_i$ ni ki ga aru to bakari omotte ita tonari no*
self loved only believed next door's
musume ga kyuu ni oyome ni itte simatta koto ga
daughter suddenly got married that
Taroo$_i$ ni situren nimo nita omoi o aziaw-sase-ta.
disappointed love like feeling taste-make-past
'That the neighbor's daughter got married suddenly who he had believed was in love with self$_i$ made Taro$_i$ experience the feeling just like that of disappointed love.'

(58) *Zibun$_i$ ga kasita pisutoru o nusumareta wakai keizi ga*
self lent pistol stolen young policeman
zisatu sita koto ga butyoo keizi$_i$ ni inoti no hakanasa o
suicide commit that police captain life 's transience
simizimi kangae-sase-ta.
seriously think-make-past
'The fact that the young policeman who had the pistol stolen which self$_i$ had lent him committed suicide made the police captain$_i$ think seriously about the transitoriness of human life.'

Notice that there is no source from which a Flip analysis could derive (56)–(58). Thus, according to the Flip analysis, backward reflexivization in emotive causatives and in nonagentive causatives would be totally unrelated, so an entirely different solution would have to be presented for the latter.

Fifth, backward reflexivization is blocked in agentive causatives as well as in agentive emotive causatives. Examples (59) and (60) are agentive causatives and (61) and (62) agentive emotive causatives:

(59) **Zibun$_i$ o nikunde iru yakuza ga tesita ni Tanaka-san$_i$ o*
self hate gangster follower
sanzan nagur-sase-ta.
much hit-make-past
'The gangster who hated self$_i$ made his followers hit Tanaka$_i$ repeatedly.'

(60) **Zibun*$_i$ *no syuusaiburi o netande iru zyuuyaku ga*
self 's brilliance jealous director
Satoo katyoo$_i$ *o hekiti e tennin s-sase-ta.*
manager remote place transfer-make-past
'The director who envied self$_i$'s brilliance transfered manager Sato$_i$ to the sticks.'

(61) **Zibun*$_i$ *o nikunde iru yakuza ga waza to Tanaka-san*$_i$ *o okor-sase-ta.*
angry-make-past
'The gangster who hated self$_i$ made Tanaka$_i$ angry purposely.'

(62) **Zibun*$_i$ *no syuusaiburi o netande iru zyuuyaku ga*
self 's brilliance jealous director
Satoo-katyoo$_i$ *o waza to komar-sase-ta.*
manager purposely bothered-make-past
'The director who was jealous of self$_i$'s brilliance purposely bothered manager Sato$_i$.'

If we accept the view that emotive causatives are genuine causatives, then it is no mystery at all that the two constructions have so many important properties in common. I will argue in the next chapter that it will be impossible to understand what is really going on in backward reflexivization in Japanese unless we realize the important role played by the nonagentive subject in causative constructions.

Next, notice that the Flip analysis fails to explain the derivation of agentive emotive causatives. Consider the following pairs of sentences:

(63) a. **Hahaoya wa Mitiko o/ni yorokonda.*
mother was pleased
'Michiko's mother was pleased with her.'
b. *Hahaoya wa Mitiko no kokorozukai o/ni yorokonda.*
's thoughtfulness was pleased
'Michiko's mother was pleased with her thoughtfulness.'

(64) a. **Hirosi wa Mitiko o/ni nayanda.*
was worried
'Hiroshi was worried about Michiko.'
b. *Hirosi wa Mitiko no kokorogawari nayanda.*
's change of mind was worried
'Hiroshi was worried about Michiko's change of mind.'

(65) a. **Mitiko wa Hirosi o/ni uresigatta.*
was happy
'Mitiko was happy about Hiroshi.'

b. *Mitiko wa Hirosi no osezi o/ni uresigatta.*
's flattery was happy
'Michiko was happy about Hiroshi's flattery.'

Note that Japanese Ve cannot take a human NP alone as its object, as the ungrammaticality of the (a) forms shows. Now, consider the following pairs of sentences:

(66) a. *Mitiko wa zyoozu ni hahaoya o yorokob-sase-ta.*
skillfully
'Michiko did a good job of pleasing her mother.'

b. *Mitiko no kokorozukai ga hahaoya o yorokob-sase-ta.*
's thoughtfulness mother pleased-make-past
'Michiko's thoughtfulness pleased her mother.'

(67) a. *Mitiko wa waza to Hirosi o nayam-sase-ta.*
purposely worried-make-past
'Michiko worried Hiroshi purposely.'

b. *Mitiko no kokorogawari ga Hirosi o nayam-sase-ta.*
's change of mind worried-make-past
'Michiko's change of mind worried Hiroshi.'

(68) a. *Hirosi wa zyoozu ni Mitiko o uresigar-sase-ta.*
skillfully happy-make-past
'Hiroshi did a good job of making Michiko happy.'

b. *Hirosi no osezi ga Mitiko o uresigar-sase-ta.*
's flattery happy-make-past
'Hiroshi's flattery made Michiko happy.'

The (a) forms in (66)–(68) have agentive subjects, and they are all perfectly grammatical. Now, it would be quite implausible to propose that they have been derived from the ungrammatical (a) forms in (63)–(65) by application of Flip.

One possible way out of this troublesome situation would be to hypothesize that the Japanese lexicon has many pairs of homophonous Ve's such as *yorokobu*$_1$, *yorokobu*$_2$, *nayamu*$_1$, *nayamu*$_2$, *uresigaru*$_1$, *uresigaru*$_2$, etc., and that only one member of each pair is a Flip verb. Note that this approach has several serious consequences. Among other things, the (a) forms in (66)–(68) would be true causative constructions. Then it would follow that Ve's that are embedded inside the causative construction are all intransitive verbs. Flip verbs must be transitive. Therefore, Japanese would have many pairs of transitive–intransitive Ve's. In a later discussion I will present several pieces of evidence that this treatment of Japanese Ve's must be incorrect.

In addition, the Flip analysis causes an ordering paradox, as noted by Harada (1971). Elsewhere I have established the ordering relation as in (69):[8]

(69) (Passivization
 (Reflexivization

in order to account for the fact that in the following pairs of sentences the reflexive refers only to the subject:

(70) a. *Tanaka$_i$ wa Satoo o zibun$_i$ no uti de korosita.*
 self 's house in killed
 'Tanaka$_i$ killed Sato in self$_i$'s house.'
 b. *Satoo$_i$ wa Tanaka ni zibun$_i$ no uti de koros-rare-ta.*
 self 's house in kill-passive
 'Sato$_i$ was killed by Tanaka in self$_i$'s house.'

Now, the Flip analysis claims that (71b) has been derived from (71a) by the application of reflexivization followed by Flip:

(71) a. *Tanaka$_i$ wa sinyuu ga Tanaka$_i$ o uragitta koto ni*
 close friend betrayed that
 gakkuri sita.
 disheartened
 'Tanaka$_i$ was disheartened that his close friend had betrayed Tanaka$_i$.'

[8]See N. McCawley (1972a, Chapter III). It is important to note that (70a) and (70b) are not synonymous. The passive form corresponding to (70a) is (i):

(i) *Satoo wa Tanaka$_i$ ni* {*Tanaka$_i$* / *kare$_i$*} *no uti de koros-ŗare-ta.*
 kare$_i$
 'Sato was killed by Tanaka$_i$ in {Tanaka$_i$'s / his$_i$} house.'

If *kare* 'he' is used, the sentence is ambiguous.
Now, (70a) would have a deep structure like (ii):

(ii) *Tanaka$_i$ wa Satoo o Tanaka$_i$ no uti de korosita.*
 'Tanaka$_i$ killed Sato in Tanaka$_i$'s house.'

If reflexivization preceded passivization, the following derivation would result:

(Reflexivization: (iii) = (70a) Tanaka$_i$ wa Satoo o zibun$_i$ no uti de korosita.
(Passivization: (iv) *Satoo wa Tanaka$_i$ ni zibun$_i$ no uti de koros-ŗare-ta.

Notice that (iv) is not acceptable. If, instead, passivization precedes reflexivization, we get the desired result:

(Passivization: (v) Satoo$_i$ wa Tanaka ni Satoo$_i$ no uti de koros-ŗare-ta.
(Reflexivization: (vi) = (70b) Satoo$_i$ wa Tanaka ni zibun$_i$ no uti de koros-ŗare-ta.

b. *Sinyuu ga zibun*$_i$ *o uragitta koto ga Tanaka*$_i$ *o gakkuri s-sase-ta.*
disheartened-make-past
'That his close friend had betrayed self$_i$ disheartened Tanaka$_i$.'

c. *Tanaka*$_i$ *wa sinyuu ga zibun*$_i$ *o uragitta koto ni gakkuri s-sase-rare-ta.*
disheartened-make-passive-past
'Tanaka$_i$ was made to be disheartened by the fact that his close friend had betrayed self$_i$.'

Compare (71b) and (71c). The latter is a passive version of the former.[9] Thus, the following ordering relation holds among the rules relevant to the derivation of the three sentences in (71):

(72) { Reflexivization
Flip
Passivization }

Note that (69) states that passivization must precede reflexivization, while (72) states that reflexivization must precede passivization. This ordering paradox can be avoided only if we either reject the Flip analysis or accept some alternative to strict ordering of syntactic rules, e.g., the extrinsic partial orderings proposed by Anderson (1970).

FLIP IN ENGLISH

Next I would like to discuss an English case. There is an analysis in English stating that a fairly large number of 'psychological' predicates such as *please*,

[9]There are good and bad passives of this sort. For example:

(i) *Tanaka*$_i$ *wa sinyuu ga zibun*$_i$ *o uragitta koto ni gakkari s-s̸ase-rare-ta.*
close friend betrayed that discouraged-make-passive-past
'Tanaka$_i$ was made to be discouraged by the fact that his close friend had betrayed self$_i$.'

(ii) *Tanaka*$_i$ *wa zibun*$_i$ *no musuko ga yatto daigaku ni haireta koto ni*
son finally university admitted
hotto s-s̸ase-rare-ta.
feel relieved-make-past
'Tanaka was made to feel relieved by the fact that his son finally was admitted to the university.'

(iii) **Tanaka*$_i$ *wa sinyuu ga zibun*$_i$ *o uragitta koto ni kanasim-s̸ase-rare-ta.*
sad-make passive-past
'Tanaka$_i$ was made to be sad by the fact that his close friend betrayed self$_i$.'

(iv) **Tanaka*$_i$ *wa zibun*$_i$ *no musuko ga yatto daigaku ni haireta koto ni yorokob-s̸ase-rare-ta.*
happy-make-passive-past
'Tanaka was made to be happy by the fact that his son finally was admitted to the university.'

amuse, *surprise*, *anger*, *frighten*, *worry*, *irritate*, etc., are marked in the lexicon as undergoing Flip obligatorily. Essentially, what I am going to claim is that these 'Flip verbs' are further decomposable as underlying causatives.

Observe the following pairs of sentences:

(73) a. *Alice cleverly amused Bíll.*
 b. *Alice amúsed Bill.*

(74) a. *Bill purposely surprised Álice.*
 b. *Bill surprísed Alice.*

Note that the (a) forms refer to an action performed by the subject of the sentence, while the (b) forms describe an emotional reaction to the subject of the sentence experienced by the object of the sentence. Lee (1971a, b) has observed that, quite interestingly, when the subject has the agentive reading the main stress falls on the object NP, but when the subject has the nonagentive reading it falls on the Flip verb itself. These examples clearly show that marking those 'psychological' verbs as 'Flip' in the lexicon does not work. For they can take both agentive and nonagentive subjects, as in the (a) and (b) forms. Obviously, Flip is not responsible for the derivation of the (a) forms. One could still maintain that English has many pairs of homophonous verbs such as $amuse_1$, $amuse_2$, $surprise_1$, $surprise_2$, etc., and that only one member of each pair is a Flip verb. This seems to be a plausible analysis, and the systematic difference in stress pattern in each pair also seems to support this approach. Now, observe the following:

(75) a. *Alice amúsed*$_1$ *hìm.* [ə myuzdhm] (by telling him jokes)
 b. *Alice amúsed*$_2$ *hi̊m.* [əmyuzdm]

(76) a. *Bill surprísed*$_1$ *hèr.*
 b. *Bill surprísed*$_2$ *he̊r.*

Quite interestingly, when the objects of 'Flip verbs' are in pronominal forms such as *him* or *her*, the difference in stress pattern disappears. And when the subject is nonagentive, as in the (b) forms, the /h/ is usually deleted. In the (a) forms, however, the /h/ remains. This observation is due to Berman and Szamosi (1972). Now, consider causative constructions like (77) and (78):

(77) *Alice made Bill happy.*

(78) *Bill made Alice sad.*

These sentences can be just as ambiguous as sentences like (73) and (74), although, unfortunately, the stress difference does not show up here. However, consider the following:

(79) a. *Alice made him happy.*
 b. *Alice made hi̊m happy.*

(80) a. *Bill made her sad.*
b. *Bill made he̊r sad.*

When the surface object is *him* or *her*, the semantic difference is paralleled by /h/ deletion, as in (75) and (76). What does this imply? It simply implies that English phonology is sensitive to semantic facts of sentences. Nobody will draw the absurd conclusion from (79) and (80) that *make* in (79a) and *make* in (79b) are different verbs or that *happy* in (80a) and *happy* in (80b) are different predicates, for example. Assume, on the other hand, that the 'Flip verbs' are underlyingly causatives and that their semantic representations are roughly something like (81):

(81)
amuse ≡ CAUSE + amused
surprise ≡ CAUSE + surprised
please ≡ CAUSE + pleased
(etc.)

We understand the abstract verb CAUSE as relating two states of affairs in such a way that because of the first state of affairs the second state of affairs becomes true. Then the real difference between $amuse_1$ and $amuse_2$ is simply the difference of the nature of the first state of affairs, whether an agent is involved in the first state of affairs or not. Therefore, it follows that the difference of deep structures between the (a) and (b) forms in (73) and (74) is parallel to that between the (a) and (b) forms in (79) and (80). It is no mystery at all to our analysis, therefore, that /h/ deletion behaves alike in 'Flip' constructions such as (75) and (76) and ordinary causative constructions such as (79) and (80). Also, notice that our analysis makes the prediction that predicates of human emotion such as *happy*, *unhappy*, *sad*, *sorry*, *angry*, *furious*, etc., will behave like *amused*, *surprised*, *pleased*, *scared*, *worried*, *disheartened*, etc. This prediction is verified by the following. Consider:

(82) *Bill was pleased that Alice passed the exam.*

(83) *Bill was happy that Alice passed the exam.*

(84) *Bill was aware that Alice passed the exam.*

Only (82) and (83) have a corresponding sentence modified with a *because* clause. Also note that the complement of the *because* clause is identical to the complement of *pleased* and *happy*:

(85) *Because Alice passed the exam, Bill was pleased.*

(86) *Because Alice passed the exam, Bill was happy.*

(87) **Because Alice passed the exam, Bill was aware.*

Also, notice that only (82) and (83) are semantically related to a causative construction whose subject is, again, identical with the complement of *happy* and *pleased*:

(88) *That Alice passed the exam pleased Bill.*

(89) *That Alice passed the exam made Bill happy.*

(90) **That Alice passed the exam made Bill aware.*

According to the Flip analysis, (82) and (83) have nothing significant in common. Also, notice that this analysis is in good agreement with our intuitive judgment that *amused*, *surprised*, *pleased*, etc., and *happy*, *sad*, *angry*, *desperate*, etc., constitute a semantically natural class that denotes human emotion and whose object NP denotes the cause of emotion.

Next, a nonagentive causative has a paraphrase with a *because* clause sentence, as is illustrated by (89) and (86). Likewise, every 'Flip' construction appears to have a corresponding *because* clause sentence, as shown by (88) and (85).

Finally, recall that in affirmative assertions the causative sentence implies that the proposition contained in the complement is true (Karttunen, 1970a). Likewise, (91) implies the factuality of (92):

(91) *Alice pleased Bill.*

(92) *Bill was pleased.*

Notice that this is true whether *Alice* in (91) is an agent or not.

For the reasons just presented, I would like to claim that the so-called 'Flip verbs' in English should be further decomposed into underlying causative constructions.

Arguments against Current Causative Analyses

Kuroda's Analysis

Kuroda (1965a) has proposed a causative analysis of emotive causatives. Details aside, the essential difference between the Flip approach and Kuroda's approach is the following. Kuroda also considered pairs of sentences such as (93) and (94) to be true paraphrases of each other. The examples are his:

(93) a. *Ongaku ga Taroo o tanosim-ȿase-ta.*
music amused-make-past
'Music amused Taro.'

b. *Taroo ga ongaku o tanosinda.*
was amused
'Taro was amused with music.'

(94) a. *Sono koto ga Taroo o nagek-s̸ase-ta.*
that fact grieved-make-past
'That fact grieved Taro.'
b. *Taroo ga sono koto o nageita.*
was grieved
'Taro was grieved at that fact.'

Instead of postulating that the (b) forms are the more basic and that the (a) forms are to be derived from the (b) forms by a transformation, Kuroda proposed that the (b) forms are embedded inside the (a) forms. Therefore, the deep structures for (93a) and (94a) are claimed to be something like the following:

(95) *Ongaku$_i$ ga (Taroo ga ongaku$_i$ o tanosim) sase-ta.*
music music amused make-past
'Music$_i$ made (Taro was amused with music).'

(96) *Sono koto$_i$ ga (Taroo ga sono koto$_i$ o nagek) sase-ta.*
that fact that fact grieved make-past
'That fact made (Taro was grieved at the fact).'

Notice that this analysis claims that Ve's like *tanosimu* 'amused' and *nageku* 'grieved' in (93) and (94) are underlyingly transitive verbs. Therefore, in order to get the desired sentences from (95) and (96) it is necessary to delete the complement objects that are coreferential to the main subjects. Kuroda postulated that there is a rule called recurrent object deletion in Japanese grammar. He then correctly pointed out that 'verbs which are subject to Recurrent-Object-Deletion are very restricted. Semantically, they share a characteristic feature in that they convey the emotional state of a human being [1965a:47].' However, he failed to realize the following fact: It is only when the main subject is not an agent that the complement object *must* coincide with this nonagent subject and, also, *must* be deleted.

Recall that the Flip analysis in both Japanese and English has failed to account for 'Flip' constructions whose subjects are agents. The same thing can be said about the recurrent object deletion approach. We have already shown that there are agentive emotive causatives as well as nonagentive causatives. For example, consider (61) and (62).

(97) *Taroo ga (zyoozu ni obekka o tukatte) Hanako o*
skillfully flattering
yorokob-s̸ase-ta.
pleased-make-past
'Taro pleased Hanaka (by flattering her skillfully).'

(98) *Taroo wa (waza to) Hanako o okor-s̸ase-ta.*
purposely angry-make-past
'Taro (purposely) angered Hanako.'

We have already shown that a Japanese Ve cannot take a human NP as its object. Thus, the following sentences are ungrammatical:

(99) **Hanako ga Taroo o/ni yorokonda.*
was pleased
'Hanako was pleased with Taro.'

(100) **Hanako ga Taroo o/ni okotta.*[10]
was angry
'Hanako was angry with Taro.'

Therefore, it will be totally implausible to say that the deep structures for (97) and (98) are something like the following:

(101) *Taroo$_i$ ga (*Hanako ga Taroo$_i$ o/ni yorokob) sase-ta.*
'Taro$_i$ made (Hanako was pleased with Taro$_i$).'

(102) *Taroo$_i$ ga (*Hanako ga Taroo$_i$ o/ni okor) sase-ta.*
'Taro$_i$ made (Hanako was angry with Taro$_i$).'

The only possible way to derive (97) and (98) would be to say that *yorokobu* and *okoru* in (97) and (98) are underlyingly intransitive. In that case, the deep structures for them would be something like the following:

(103) *Taroo ga (Hanako ga yorokob) sase-ta.*
'Taro made (Hanako was pleased).'

(104) *Taroo ga (Hanako ga okor) sase-ta.*
'Taro made (Hanako became angry).'

Now, it is very clear that Kuroda's recurrent object deletion approach to nonagentive emotive causatives has ended up claiming the same thing as the Flip analysis, i.e., that Japanese has transitive–intransitive pairs of Ve's.

CHOMSKY'S ANALYSIS

It is interesting to note that Chomsky (1970) has proposed an analysis of English emotive causatives that is exactly parallel to Kuroda's analysis. In order to explain the meaning relationship between (105) and (106), Chomsky proposed (107) to be a plausible deep structure for (106). The examples are his:

(105) *He was amused at the stories.*

(106) *The stories amused him.*

[10]The following sentence is grammatical. Here, *okoru* is synonymous with *sikaru* 'scold':

(i) *Hanako ga Taroo o okotta.*
'Hanako scolded Taro.'

(107) *The stories* (+cause) (*he was amused at the stories*).

In place of Kuroda's recurring object deletion, Chomsky proposed that 'the operation that erases the repeated noun phrase in the embedded proposition of (12) (=[107]) is of a sort found elsewhere, for example, in the derivation of such sentences as *John used the table to write on*, *John used the pen to write (with)*, *John used the wall to lean the table against*, etc., from *John used the table* (*John wrote on the table*), and so on [1970:25].' However, this claim is highly implausible, since, as pointed out by J. McCawley, the preposition is retained in *John used the table to write on* but is absent from (106). The following sentence is ungrammatical:

(108) **The stories amused him* ***at***.

Backward Reflexivization

Next I will show that a Kuroda–Chomsky type of analysis fails to account for the backward reflexivization we are concerned with. Consider the following example:

(109) *Zibun*$_i$ *ga gan de nakatta koto ga Hirosi*$_i$ *o*
self cancer negative-past that
yorokob-sase-ta.
'That self$_i$ did not have cancer pleased Hiroshi$_i$.'

According to recurrent object deletion analysis, (109) will have the deep structure roughly shown by the following tree configuration:

(110)

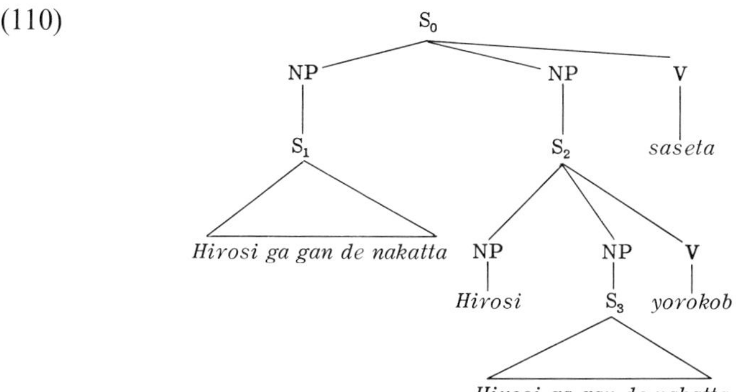

In the S_2 cycle, reflexivization applies, changing *Hirosi* in S_3 into *zibun*. Since recurrent object deletion could not apply any earlier than the S_0 cycle, when it applies, S_1 and S_3 will no longer be identical, since S_3, but not S_1, will have a reflexive subject. Moreover, reflexivization on the S_0 cycle could not reflexivize the subject of S_1 and thus make S_1 and S_3 identical, since at that point on the derivation *Hirosi* is not the subject. As a result, we would get an ill-formed sentence such as the following:

(111) **Hirosi*$_i$ *ga gan de nakatta koto ga Hirosi*$_i$ *ni zibun*$_i$ *ga gan de nakatta koto o yorokob-sase-ta.*
'That Hiroshi$_i$ did not have cancer made Hiroshi$_i$ happy that self$_i$ did not have cancer.'

Actually, even if we assume that recurrent object deletion applies in the S_0 cycle and deletes S_3 under less than full identity with S_1, our problem still remains. For there is no way to reflexivize the first occurrence of *Hirosi* in the derived sentence. Observe:

(112) *Hirosi*$_i$ *ga gan de nakatta koto ga Hirosi*$_i$ *o yorokob-sase-ta.*
'That Hiroshi$_i$ did not have cancer made Hiroshi$_i$ happy.'

Japanese pronominalization, including reflexivization, becomes optional under certain conditions that are not very clear to us. Because of this, (112) is not ungrammatical, although it is quite awkward. But the crucial point is that there is no way to get perfectly good sentences such as (109) in which the first occurrence of *Hirosi* is reflexivized:

(109) *Zibun*$_i$ *ga gan de nakatta koto ga Hirosi*$_i$ *o yorokob-sase-ta.*
'That self$_i$ did not have cancer made Hiroshi$_i$ happy.'

In summing up, we will be able to conclude that current analyses of emotive causatives are far from adequate in several significant ways, and in particular, they fail to provide a good explanation for the backward reflexivization phenomenon we are concerned with.

Ve as Underlyingly Intransitive

All of the current analyses we have discussed so far take it for granted that Ve's like *yorokobu* 'happy, pleased, overjoyed', *kanasimu* 'sad, unhappy', *nayamu* 'worried, annoyed', etc., are underlyingly transitive verbs. However, I would like to show that there are good reasons to doubt this assumption.

Notice, first, that ordinary transitive verbs are causativized without losing their object NPs. If they lose them, then the derived sentences are no longer grammatical, as shown in the following:

(113) a. *Hirosi wa Mitiko o nagutta.*
hit
'Hiroshi hit Michiko.'

b. *Satosi wa Hirosi ni Mitiko o nagur-~~s~~ase-ta*
hit-make-past
'Satoshi made Hiroshi hit Michiko.'

c. **Satosi wa Hirosi ni ∅ nagur-$ase-ta.*
'Satoshi made Hiroshi hit.'

(114) a. *Hahaoya wa kodomo o nagusameta.*
mother child consoled
'A mother consoled her child.'
b. *Titioya wa hahaoya ni kodomo o nagusame-sase-ta.*
father mother child console-make-past
'A father made a mother console their child.'
c. **Titioya wa hahaoya ni ∅ nagusame-sase-ta.*
'A father made a mother console.'

However, when Ve's are causativized, they obligatorily lose their object NPs. Otherwise, the derived sentences are ungrammatical. The same thing is true with English Ve's. Observe:

(115) a. *Tanaka wa otoko no ko no tanzyoo o yorokonda.*
baby boy 's birth pleased, happy
'Tanaka was pleased at the birth of a baby boy.'
b. **Satoo wa Tanaka ni otoko no ko no tanzyoo o yorokob-$ase-ta.*
pleased-make-past
*Sato pleased Tanaka at the birth of a baby boy.'
c. *Satoo wa Tanaka o ∅ yorokob-$ase-ta.*
'Sato pleased Tanaka.'

(116) a. *Tanaka*$_i$ *wa zibun*$_i$ *ga gan ni kakatta koto o kanasinda.*
self cancer have that
was sad
'Tanaka was sad that he had cancer.'
b. **Satoo wa Tanaka*$_i$ *ni zibun*$_i$ *ga gan ni kakatta koto o kanasim-sase-ta.*
sa sad-make-past
'*Sato made Tanaka$_i$ sad that he$_i$ had cancer.'
c. *Satoo wa Tanaka o ∅ kanasim-$ase-ta.*
'Sato made Tanaka sad.'

(117) a. *Syoonen*$_i$ *wa zibun*$_i$ *ga onna no ko ni moteru no ni odoroita.*
boy self girls with popular
surprised
'The boy was surprised that he was popular with girls.'

b. **Tomodati wa syoonen$_i$ ni zibun$_i$ ga onna no ko*
friend boy self girls
ni moteru no ni odorok-$ase-ta
with popular surprised-make-past
*'His friend surprised the boy$_i$ that he$_i$ was popular with girls.'

c. *Tomodati wa syoonen o ∅ odorok-$ase-ta.*
'His friend surprised the boy.'

(118) a. *Tanaka$_i$ wa koibito ga zibun$_i$ o uragitta koto*
girlfriend self betrayed that
o/ni hungai sita.
got angry
'Tanaka$_i$ got angry that his girlfriend had betrayed him$_i$.'

b. **Satoo wa Tanaka$_i$ ni koibito ga zibun$_i$ o uragitta koto o hungai s-$ase-ta.*
angry-make-past
*'Sato angered Tanaka$_i$ that his girlfriend had betrayed him$_i$.'

c. *Satoo wa Tanaka o ∅ hungai s-sase-ta.*
'Sato angered Tanaka.'

Second, note that the stative transitive verbs do not occur in causative constructions:[11]

(119) a. *Hanako wa yuurei ga mieta.*
ghost saw
'Hanako saw a ghost.'

b. **Taroo wa Hanako ni yuurei o mie-sase-ta*
ghost see-make-past
*'Taro made Hanako see a ghost.'

[11]English stative transitive verbs may occur in nonagentive causatives, but Japanese stative transitive verbs may not. Compare:

(i) *Biological inheritance makes sons resemble their mothers.*

(ii) **Seibutugakuzyoo no iden wa musuko o hahaoya ni ni-sase-ru.*
biological inheritance son mother resemble-make

The correct form for (ii) is (iii):

(iii) *Seibutugakuzyoo no iden no tame ni musuko wa hahaoya ni niru.*
because of
'Because of biological inheritance, sons resemble their mothers.'

(120) a. *Taroo wa Ziroo ni nite iru*
resemble is
'Taro resembles Jiro.'
b. **Hanako wa Taroo o Ziroo ni ni-sase-ta*
resemble-make-past
*'Hanako made Taro resemble Jiro.'

(121) a. *Taroo wa okane ga itta.*
money needed
'Taro needed some money.'
b. **Ziroo wa Taroo ni okane o ir-$ase-ta.*
money need-make-past
*'Jiro made Taro need some money.'

(122) a. *Tanaka-san wa eigo ga dekiru.*
English good at
'Tanaka has a good command of English.'
b. **Satoo-san wa Tanaka-san ni eigo o deki-sase-ta.*
good at-make-past
'*Sato made Tanaka have a good command of English.'

Therefore, one might argue that Ve's are stative transitive verbs. However, the deletion of the object does not change the ungrammaticality of the (b) forms. Observe:

(123) **Taroo wa Hanako ni $\emptyset$ mie-sase-ta.*
*'Taro made Hanako see $\emptyset$.'

(124) **Hanako wa Taroo o $\emptyset$ ni-sase-ta.*
*'Hanako made Taro resemble $\emptyset$.'

(125) **Ziroo wa Taroo ni $\emptyset$ ir-$ase-ta.*
*'Jiro made Taro need $\emptyset$.'

(126) **Satoo-san wa Tanaka-san ni $\emptyset$ deki-sase-ta.*
*'Sato made Tanaka have a good command of $\emptyset$.'

Thus, it is quite obvious that Ve's behave entirely differently from stative transitive verbs, too. Again, the same argument holds with English counterparts.

Third, every sentence with one of the emotive verbs in question is paraphrased by a sentence with a *node* 'because' clause. Consider:

(127) a. *Syoonen$_i$ wa zibun$_i$ ga onna no ko ni moteru*
self girls with popular
no o yorokonda.
that was pleased, happy
'The boy$_i$ was pleased that he$_i$ was popular with girls.'

b. *Zibun*$_i$ *ga onna no ko ni moteru node, syoonen*$_i$
self girls with popular because boy
wa yorokonda
was pleased, happy
'Because he$_i$ was popular with girls, the boy$_i$ was pleased.'

(128) a. *Syoonen*$_i$ *wa zibun*$_i$ *ga onna no ko ni motenai*
boy self girls with popular-negative
no o kanasinda.
that was sad
'The boy$_i$ was sad that he$_i$ was not popular with girls.'

b. *Zibun*$_i$ *ga onna no ko ni motenai node, syoonen*$_i$
self girls with popular-negative because
wa kanasinda.
was sad
'Because he$_i$ was not popular with girls, the boy$_i$ was sad.'

(129) a. *Syoonen*$_i$ *wa zibun*$_i$ *ga onna no ko ni motenai*
boy self girls with popular-negative
koto o/ni nayanda
that was worried
'The boy$_i$ was worried that he$_i$ was not popular with girls.'

b. *Zibun*$_i$ *ga onna no ko ni motenai node,*
self girls with popular-negative because
syoonen wa nayanda
boy was worried
'Because he$_i$ was not popular with girls, the boy$_i$ was worried.'

(130) a. *Tanaka wa koibito ga uragitta koto o/ni hungai sita.*
girlfriend betrayed that got angry
'Tanaka got angry that his girlfriend had betrayed him.'

b. *Koibito ga uragitta node, Tanaka wa hungai sita.*
girlfriend betrayed because got angry
'Because his girlfriend had betrayed him, Tanaka got angry.'

Note that the surface complement of *yorokobu* 'pleased', *kanasimu* 'sad', *nayamu* 'worried', and *hungai suru* 'angry' and the clause introduced by *node* 'because' in (127b)–(130b) are identical. This is very significant, for this kind of meaning relation does not hold in the case of ordinary transitive verbs.

For example, (131a)–(134a) are not paraphrased by (131b)–(134b):

(131) a. *Syoonen*$_i$ *wa zibun*$_i$ *ga onna no ko ni moteru koto o*
boy self girls with popular that
kakusin site iru.
certain is
'The boy$_i$ is certain that he$_i$ is popular with girls.'

b. **Zibun*$_i$ *ga onna no ko ni moteru node, syoonen*
self girls with popular because boy
wa kakusin site iru.
certain is
'*Because he$_i$ is popular with girls, the boy$_i$ is certain.'

(132) a. *Syoonen*$_i$ *wa zibun*$_i$ *ga onna no ko ni motenai*
boy self girls with popular-negative
koto o nattoku sita.
that persuaded
'The boy$_i$ was persuaded that he$_i$ was not popular with girls.'

b. **Zibun*$_i$ *ga onna no ko ni motenai node,*
self girls with popular-negative because
syoonen wa nattoku sita.
boy was persuaded
*'Because he$_i$ was not popular with girls, the boy$_i$ was persuaded.'

(133) a. *Syoonen*$_i$ *wa zibun*$_i$ *ga onna no ko ni motenai*
boy self girls with popular-negative
koto o mitometa.
that admitted
boy self girls with popular-negative
koto o mitometa.
that admitted
'The boy$_i$ admitted that he$_i$ was not popular with girls.'

b. **Zibun*$_i$ *ga onna no ko ni motenai node, syoonen*$_i$ *wa mitometa.*
*'Because he was not popular with girls, the boy admitted.'

(134) a. *Tanaka*$_i$ *was Satoo ga zibun*$_i$ *o matte iru koto*
self wait is that
o sukkari wasurete ita.
completely forget was
'Tanaka$_i$ had completely forgotten that Sato was waiting for him$_i$.'

b. **Satoo ga zibun*$_i$ *o matte iru node, Tanaka*$_i$ *wa sukkari wasurete ita.*
*'Because Sato was waiting for him$_i$, Tanaka had completely forgotten.'

Fourth, consider the (b) forms of (127)–(130) again:

(127) b. *Zibun*$_i$ *ga onna no ko ni moteru node, syoonen*$_i$ *wa yorokonda.*
'Because he$_i$ was popular with girls, the boy$_i$ was pleased.'

(128) b. *Zibun*$_i$ *ga onna no ko ni motenai node, syoonen*$_i$ *wa kanasinda.*
'Because he$_i$ was not popular with girls, the boy$_i$ was sad.'

(129) b. *Zibun*$_i$ *ga onna no ko ni motenai node, syoonen*$_i$ *wa nayanda.*
'Because he$_i$ was not popular with girls, the boy$_i$ was worried.'

(130) b. *Koibito ga uragitta node, Tanaka wa hungai sita.*
'Because his girlfriend had betrayed him, Tanaka got angry.'

Notice that the emotive verbs in these examples lack their objects. If in fact they are inherently transitive, why do they have no objects here? There must be a convincing account of what have happened to their objects. A possible analysis would be to say that ∅ pronominalization has taken place. Then the question is, What is the antecedent? Take the example of (127b). There are only two NPs in the *node* 'because' clause, *zibun* 'self' and *onna no ko* 'girls'. However, it is impossible to postulate that one of them is the missing object, since, as mentioned earlier in this chapter and elsewhere, Japanese Ve cannot take a human NP as object. One might propose that the missing object is not an NP but an entire proposition in the *node* clause. According to this proposal, the deep structure of (127b) would be roughly (135):

(135) *(Zibun*$_i$ *ga onna no ko ni moteru)*$_j$ *node, syoonen*$_i$ *wa (zibun*$_i$ *ga onna no ko ni moteru)*$_j$ *koto o yorokonda.*
'Because (he$_i$ was popular with girls)$_j$, the boy$_i$ was pleased that (he$_i$ was popular with girls)$_j$'.

However, this proposal is highly implausible for semantic reasons. We have already shown (in the third argument) that (127a) and (127b) are essential paraphrases of each other:

(127) a. *Syoonen*$_i$ *wa zibun*$_i$ *ga onna no ko ni moteru koto o yorokonda.*
'The boy$_i$ was pleased that he$_i$ was popular with girls.'
b. *Zibun*$_i$ *ga onna no ko ni moteru node, syoonen*$_i$ *wa yorokonda.*
'Because he$_i$ was popular with girls, the boy$_i$ was pleased.'

Notice that the proposition *zibun ga onna no ko ni moteru* 'he is popular with girls' is the cause of emotion denoted by the verb *yorokobu* 'pleased'. The preceding examples indicate that the cause of emotion can be stable either in the form of the direct object of emotive verbs or in the form of the complement of a *node* clause. We have already shown that there is no such complementary distribution in the case of the transitive verb constructions in (131)–(134). There is another fact to show that sentential pronominalization has nothing to do with the present issue. In English sentential pronominalization, the pronoun *it* is left behind. As the ungrammaticality of the (b) forms shows, ordinarily the pronoun *it* may not delete. Observe:

(136) a. *Although John was sick, he wasn't aware of it.*
b. **Although John was sick, he wasn't aware* ∅.

An entirely opposite situation holds in the case of English Ve's. The pronoun *it* must delete. Otherwise, the sentence is ungrammatical. Observe:

(137) a. **Because he was popular with girls, the boy was* {*happy* / *pleased*} *about it.*
b. *Because he was popular with girls, the boy was* {*happy* / *pleased*} ∅.

(138) a. **Because he was not popular with girls, the boy was* {*sad* / *unhappy* / *worried*} *about it.*
b. *Because he was not popular with girls, the boy was* {*sad* / *unhappy* / *worried*} ∅.

In the preceding discussion, I have shown that Ve's behave quite differently from transitive verbs in a number of significant ways. This leads us to hypothesize that Ve's are not underlyingly transitive. In the following section, I would like to discuss the consequences of this proposed hypothesis, showing that, indeed, this analysis makes correct predictions of many relations between syntactic facts and meaning, which otherwise would remain totally mysterious.

Causal Object Formation

We have seen in the preceding section that the following three sentences are essential paraphrases of each other, despite the difference in their surface structures:[12]

(139) a. *Hirosi wa haha ga gan de nakatta koto o yorokonda.*
mother cancer negative-past that happy
'Hiroshi was happy that his mother did not have cancer.'

b. *Haha ga gan de nakatta koto ga Hirosi o*
mother cancer negative-past that
yorokob-sase-ta.
happy-make-past
'That his mother did not have cancer made Hiroshi happy.'

c. *Haha ga gan de nakatta node, Hirosi wa yorokonda.*
mother cancer negative-past because happy
'Because his mother did not have cancer, Hiroshi was happy.'

This is quite significant, for this kind of close meaning relation does not hold among transitive verb constructions. For example, compare (140) with (139):

(140) a. *Hirosi wa haha ga gan de nakatta koto o sitta.*
mother cancer negative-past that found out
'Hiroshi found out that his mother did not have cancer.'

[12]For some reason that I do not quite understand, only two of these three sentences have negative counterparts:

(i) *Hirosi wa haha ga gan de nakatta koto o yorokobanakatta.*
happy-negative-past
'Hiroshi was not happy that his mother did not have cancer.'

(ii) *Haha ga gan de nakatta koto wa Hirosi o yorokobasenakatta.*
happy-make-negative-past
'That his mother did not have cancer did not make Hiroshi happy.'

(iii) **Haha ga gan de nakatta node, Hirosi wa yorokobanakatta.*
'Because his mother did not have cancer, Hiroshi was not happy.'

b. **Haha ga gan de nakatta koto ga Hirosi o*
mother cancer negative-past that
sir-sase-ta
find out-make-past
*'That his mother did not have cancer made Hiroshi find out.'

c. **Haha ga gan de nakatta node, Hirosi wa sitta.*
mother cancer negative-past because found out
*'Because his mother did not have cancer, Hiroshi found out.'

Adequate grammars of both Japanese and English will have to explain this fact on a principled basis. Recall that current analyses of Ve and emotive causatives can relate (139a) and (139b). However, they fail to explain how and why they are also related to (139c).

I have already concluded that sentences like (139b) are causative constructions. Now, I would like to propose that (139a) and (139c) are also underlyingly causative constructions. According to this proposal, all three sentences in (139) share the same deep structure, something like (141):

(141) *(haha ga gan de nakatta) (Hirosi ga yorokonda)* CAUSE
'(his mother did not have cancer) CAUSE (Hiroshi was happy)'

Example (141) may be roughly represented by (142):

(142)

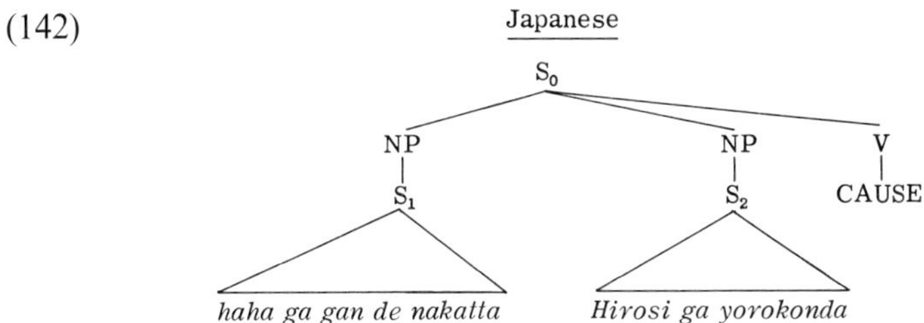

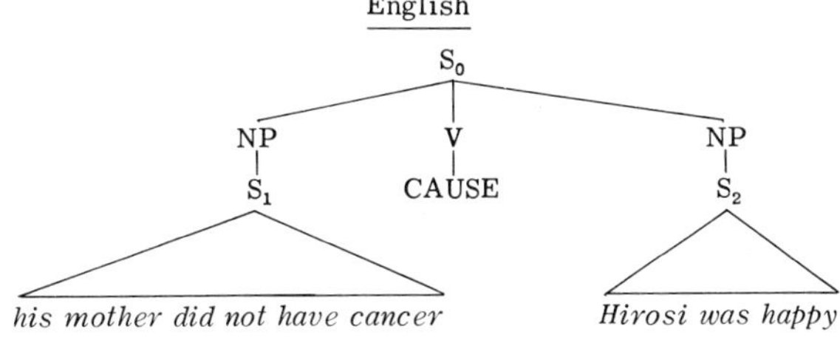

I have already maintained that the abstract verb CAUSE relates two states of affairs in such a way that because of the first state of affairs the second state of affairs becomes true. I would now like to propose that both Japanese and English have two transformations, i.e., causal object formation and *because* formation. Causal object formation takes the first argument of the abstract verb CAUSE and makes it a derived object of emotive verbs as in (139a). *Because* formation changes the tree configurations of (142) into something like the following:

(143)

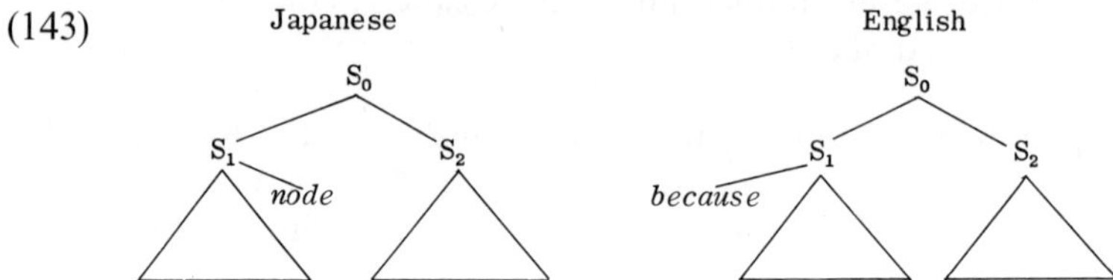

This operation will yield (139c). Example (139b) will result if verb raising applies in (142).

Notice that our analyses can explain why the object clause and the *node* clause, or *because* clause, are in complementary distribution in (139a) and (139c): They come from the same origin. Also, our analyses can explain why both Japanese and English Ve's in (139b) and (139c) do not have an object. Recall that Chomsky (1970) has proposed (145) as the deep structure of (144):

(144) *The stories amused him.*

(145) *The stories* (+ cause) *(he was amused at the stories).*

Our analyses predict that *he was amused at the stories* will not have a corresponding causative construction unless *at the stories* is deleted. This is a correct prediction. Observe:

(146) a. **Mary amused him at the stories.*
b. *Mary amused him* ∅

Also, our analyses predict that only the (b) form in the following example is well-formed:

(147) a. **Because of the stories$_i$, he was amused at them$_i$.*
b. *Because of the stories, he was amused* ∅.

For these reasons, I am quite skeptical about Chomsky's deep structure. I believe the phrase *at the stories* does not originate in the complement sentence, as he claims, and that it has been moved by causal object formation from the underlying subject position of the abstract verb CAUSE.

From this analysis it follows that the so-called 'pseudopassives' in English are different from true passives in that causal object formation has yielded the former but passivization has yielded the latter. This explains why the predicate of pseudopassives is stative and, therefore, the subject is non-agentive. Compare:

(148) a. *He was very amused at Alice.*
b. **He was very amused by Alice.*

(149) a. *He was very surprised at Alice.*
b. **He was very surprised by Alice.*

(150) a. *He was very scared at Alice.*
b. **He was very scared by Alice.*

The same predicates in the (a) sentences can take sentential objects:

(151) *He was very amused that Alice had declared her intention to marry a famous hippie.*

(152) *He was very surprised that Alice had failed the exam.*

(153) *He was very scared that he might be rejected by Alice.*

We have already demonstrated that the sentential objects of sentences of these types have been derived from the sentential complements of the underlying causative construction by causal object formation.

WRITTEN STYLE AND SPOKEN STYLE

Consider the following English causative sentences, which have nominalized subjects:

(154) *Alice's hitting Bill made him cry.*

(155) *Alice's forgetting to close the refrigerator caused the vegetables to rot.*

(156) *Alice's heating the metal for four hours liquefied it.*

Notice that there are no corresponding causative sentences in Japanese. The following are all unacceptable:

(157) **Arisu ga Biru o tataita koto ga kare o nak-$ase-ta.*
Alice Bill hitting he cry-make-past

(158) **Arisu ga reizooko o simewasureta koto ga yasai o*
Alice refrigerator forgetting vegetable
kusar-$ase-ta.
rot-make-past

(159) **Arisu ga sono kinzoku o yozikan atatameta koto ga*
Alice that metal four hours heating
sore o ekitai bi sita.
it liquid-become-make-past

In order to convey the same semantic content of each sentence, the Japanese speaker has to say the following, respectively:

(160) *Arisu ga Biru o tataita node, kare ga naita.*
'Because Alice hit Bill, he cried.'

(161) *Arisu ga reizooko o simewasureta node, yasai ga kusatta.*
'Because Alice forgot to close the refrigerator, the vegetables rotted.'

(162) *Arisu ga yozikan atatameta node, sono kinzoku wa ekitai ni natta.*
'Because Alice heated the metal for four hours, it turned to liquid.'

I would like to interpret this phenomenon as indirect evidence to show that, indeed, sentences like (160)–(162) are underlyingly causative constructions. Japanese has a general surface constraint that prevents nonanimate NPs from becoming the subjects of transitive verbs. So, for example, (163) is perfectly good, but (164) is not. Example (164) will be expressed as (165). Observe:

(163) *Taiboku ga taoreta.*
big tree fell down
'A big tree fell down.'

(164) **Taihuu ga taiboku o taosita.*
typhoon big tree overturned
'A typhoon overturned a big tree.'

(165) *Taiboku ga taihuu de taoreta.*
'A big tree was overturned in a typhoon.'

The ungrammaticality of (157)–(159) shows that this surface constraint is also applicable to derived transitive verbs such as *nak-$ase* 'make-cry', *kusar-$ase* 'cause-rot', etc.

Recall that the subject of a nonagentive causative construction is an abstract NP and, hence, nonanimate. If it is true that the surface constraint in question also applies to derived transitive verbs, then it will follow that nonagentive causative constructions themselves are ungrammatical in Japanese. I would like to show that, indeed, they are of marginal acceptability in spoken Japanese and are fully acceptable only in written Japanese. Compare the following pairs of nonagentive causative constructions:

(166) a. *Ano ko ga kyuu ni totemo kirei ni natta koto ga*
that girl suddenly very pretty became that
watasi o sukkari odorok-sase-ta.
me completely surprised-make-past
'That she had suddenly become very pretty completely surprised me.'

b. ??*Ano ko ga kyuu ni totemo kirei ni natta koto ga watasi o sukkari odorok-sase-ta* {*WA.* / *YO.*}

(167) a. *Nyuugaku siken ni mata otita koto ga uti no*
entrance examination again failed that our
musuko o sukkari gakkari s-sase-ta
son completely discouraged-make-past
'That he failed the entrance examination again completely discouraged our son.'

b. ??*Nyuugaku siken ni mata otita koto ga uti no musuko o sukkari gakkari s-sase-ta* {*WA.* / *YO.*}

(168) a. *Sinyuu ni uragir-rare-ta koto ga Mitiko ni*
close friend by betrayed that
dare mo sinyoo dekinai to omoikom-sase-ta
nobody trust cannot that believe-make-past
'That she had been betrayed by her close friend made Michiko believe that nobody can be trusted.'

b. ??*Sinyuu ni uragir-rare-ta koto ga Mitiko ni dare mo sinyoo dekinai to omoikom-sase-ta* {*YO.* / *WA.*}

The (a) forms are perfectly acceptable, but the (b) forms are not. Note that the only difference between them is that the latter are followed by sentence-final particles such as *YO* or *WA*. Those sentence-final particles only occur in spoken Japanese and never in written Japanese, except in quotation. Roughly speaking, the semantic content of those particles corresponds to the English expression 'I tell you'. Readers are referred to Uyeno (1971).

I would like to interpret the different behavior of nonagentive causatives in the written style and in the discourse style as follows: Some types of linguistic change take place under the influence of foreign languages. In syntax, they often appear first in the written style, perhaps under the influence of translation. Gradually, a number of professional writers participate in using a 'borrowed' construction, such as nonagentive causatives, violating a general surface constraint. Then, ordinary people start using it in written style. If this phenomenon penetrates into spoken Japanese, then eventually the suspension of this constraint for nonagentive causatives will result. At the present stage, however, it seems to be suspended only in the written style for many speakers of Japanese. Therefore, if the sentence is overtly marked as nonwritten in style, for example, by the addition of sentence-final particles, then it becomes of marginal acceptance, as in (166b)–(168b). Indeed, nonagentive causative constructions sound somewhat 'foreign' to many Japanese, and some people even reject them as 'non-Japanese sentences'. At any rate, they are definitely written Japanese.

For these reasons, grammatical though they are, sentences like (166a)–(168a) will hardly be produced in ordinary speech. Instead, the following sentences will be generated by the application of *because* formation and causal object formation to the underlying structure:

(169) *Ano ko ga kyuu ni totemo kirei ni natta node,*
that girl suddenly very pretty became because
(watasi wa) sukkari odoroita $\begin{Bmatrix} YO. \\ WA. \end{Bmatrix}$
I completely surprised
'I was completely surprised because she had suddenly become very pretty.'

(170) *(Watasi wa) ano ko ga kyuu ni totemo kirei ni natta*
koto ni sukkari odoroita $\begin{Bmatrix} YO. \\ WA. \end{Bmatrix}$
'I was completely surprised that she had suddenly become very pretty.'

(171) *Nyuugaku siken ni mata otita node, uti no musuko wa*
entrance examination again failed because our son
sukkari gakkari sita $\begin{Bmatrix} YO. \\ WA. \end{Bmatrix}$
discouraged
'Our son was completely discouraged because he had failed the entrance examination again.'

(172) *Sinyuu ni uragir-rare-ta node, Mitiko wa dare mo*
close friend betray-pass-past because nobody
sinyoo dekinai to omoikonda $\begin{Bmatrix} YO. \\ WA. \end{Bmatrix}$
trust cannot that believe

'Michiko came to believe that nobody can be trusted
because she was betrayed by her close friend.'

3. NONAGENTIVE CAUSATIVES AND BACKWARD REFLEXIVIZATION

On the Treatment of 'Counterexamples'

We have already seen that backward reflexivization takes place when the subject of the causative construction is nonagentive, as illustrated by (173) and (174):

(173) *Zibun*$_i$ *ga gan kamo sirenai koto ga Hirosi*$_i$ *o*
self cancer may have that
nayam-$\not{s}$*ase-ta.*
worried-make-past
'That self$_i$ might have cancer worried Hiroshi$_i$.'

(174) *Sinrai sikitte ita tuma ga zibun*$_i$ *ni somuita koto ga*
trusted wholeheartedly wife self betrayed that
Hirosi$_i$ *o zetuboo s-ase-ta.*
desperate-make-past
'That his wife who he had trusted wholeheartedly
betrayed self$_i$ made Hiroshi$_i$ desperate.'

Notice that one of the conditions on reflexivization, that the antecedent be the subject, is violated here, although the other condition, that the antecedent command the reflexive, is met. How are we to cope with this situation?

One possibility would be to revise the subject-antecedent condition as follows:

(175) *The antecedent must be the subject at some stage of derivation.*

Notice that *Hirosi* and *Tanaka-si* were the subjects before verb raising applied. However, this global derivational constraint must be rejected owing to the fact that agentive causatives do not allow backward reflexivization. Observe:

(176) **Zibun*$_i$ *o nikunde iru uwayaku ga sono hirasyain*$_i$ *o*
self hate boss the employee
waza to komar-$\not{s}$*ase-ta*
purposely bothered-make-past
'The boss who hated self$_i$ purposely bothered the
employee$_i$.'

(177) *$Zibun_i$ no syuusaiburi o netande iru uwayaku ga
self 's brilliance jealous is boss
$Tanaka\text{-}san_i$ o hekiti e tennin-\$ase-ta
remote place transfer-make-past
'The boss who was jealous of $self_i$'s brilliance
transferred $Tanaka_i$ to the sticks.'

In (176) and (177) *sono hirasyain* and *Tanaka-san* were the subjects before verb raising applied, and they do command the reflexive. And yet (176) and (177) are ungrammatical. Their ungrammaticality has nothing to do with the fact that the reflexive is inside a relative clause. For (178) and (179) are perfectly grammatical. Observe:

(178) *$Zibun_i$ o nikunde iru uwayaku no hidoi taido ga*
self hate is boss 's unreasonable behavior
sono $hirasyain_i$ o sukkari hungai s-\$ase-ta.
the employee completely angry-make-past
'The unreasonable behavior of his boss who hated $self_i$
completely enraged the $employee_i$.'

(179) *$Zibun_i$ no inoti o sukutte kureta oisya-san ga*
self 's life saved gave doctor
gan de nakunatta koto ga $Hirosi_i$ ni zinsei no
cancer died that to life 's
hiniku o kanzi-sase-ta.
irony feel-make-past
'That the doctor who had saved $self_i$'s life died of
cancer made $Hiroshi_i$ feel the irony of life.'

Thus, this fact clearly indicates that what is relevant to the grammaticality of (173)–(174) and (178)–(179) is that they are nonagentive causative constructions.

A possible solution would be to regard the backward relexivizations in question as genuine counterexamples to the subject-antecedent condition. In that case, we would have to add an extra condition, something like the following, to the grammar:

(180) *Backward reflexivization obligatorily takes place just in case one of the two coreferential NPs is in the same clause as a nonagentive subject that contains the other one.*

Indeed, there are some very interesting examples, such as (181)–(184), that seem to support this approach. Notice that backward reflexivization obligatorily takes place and that the subjects also are nonagentive:

(181) *Sinrai sikitte ita tuma ga zibun$_i$ ni somuita koto ga*
trusted wholeheartedly wife self betrayed that
Hirosi$_i$ o kanasimi de utinomesita
'That his wife whom he had trusted wholeheartedly betrayed self$_i$ overwhelmed Hiroshi$_i$ with sorrow.'

(182) *Zibun$_i$ ga gan de aru to iu sindan ga Mitiko$_i$ o*
self cancer is that diagnosis
zetuboo e oiyatta.
desperation drive away-past
'The diagnosis that self$_i$ had cancer drove Michiko$_i$ to desperation.'

(183) *Zibun$_i$ ga hisoka ni kooi o motte iru musume no*
self secretly in love is girl 's
yasasii hohoemi ga Hirosi ni koi no subarasisa o
gentle smile to love 's splendidness
osieta
taught
'The gentle smile of the girl whom self$_i$ had been secretly in love with taught Hiroshi how splendid love is.'

(184) *Koibito ga zibun$_i$ o konogoro zenzen deeto ni*
boyfriend self recently never date
sasotte kurenai koto ga Mitiko ni kare no
invite give-negative that to his
kokorogawari o sisasita
change of mind suggested
'That recently her boyfriend had never asked self$_i$ to go out suggested *to* Michiko$_i$ that he had changed.'

The major claim of this section, however, is that the preceding treatment of backward reflexivization must be wrong and should be rejected. Besides syntactic evidence to force me to take this position, there are reasons of a more general nature such as the following:

1. Adding an ad hoc condition something like (180), which is totally unrelated to other conditions of reflexivization, fails to capture any real generalization about Japanese reflexivization.
2. This approach does not explain why nonagentive constructions call for backward reflexivization.

3. The notion of 'agent' would have to be taken to be a primitive notion in the theory of grammar.
4. It would be a pure accident that backward reflexivization takes place in sentences like (181)–(184) as well as in nonagentive causative constructions.
5. While Japanese is a language that seems to be very reluctant to allow backward pronominalization, the reflexivization in question is unique in that backward application is not only allowed but OBLIGATORY.[13]

Therefore, it is reasonable to think that there is a deep-seated explanation for this phenomenon. This approach cannot supply that explanation.

My own treatment claims that the backward reflexivization in question is an instance of ordinary forward reflexivization in which the subject-antecedent condition is met but the antecedent is later deleted by a transformation. It is easy to find cases in which this happens. I have already given one such example (in Section 1). Another such example would be the following:

(185) *Zibun*$_i$ *no tuma ni uragir-ɾare-ta otoko*$_i$ *ga yo o*
self 's wife by betrayed-pass-past man world
hakanande, zisatu sita.
abandoning committed suicide
'The man$_i$ who had been betrayed by self$_i$'s wife lost his hopes in the world and committed suicide.'

Example (185) looks as if backward reflexivization has taken place. However, an earlier stage of (185) is (186):

[13]It is quite important to note that this is not at all an isolated fact about Japanese. For example, in English pronominalization, normally forward application is always allowed, while backward application is restricted by a command condition. However, mysteriously, nonagentive causative constructions call for obligatory backward application. Observe:

(i) *The mere thought of* $\left\{\begin{array}{l}\text{*}Harry_i\text{'s}\\ his_i\end{array}\right\}$ *kidnaped daughter depressed* $\left\{\begin{array}{l}\text{*}him_i.\\ Harry_i.\end{array}\right\}$

(ii) *The picture of* $\left\{\begin{array}{l}\text{*}Ann_i\text{'s}\\ her_i\end{array}\right\}$ *dead mother made* $\left\{\begin{array}{l}\text{*}her_i\\ Ann_i\end{array}\right\}$ *cry.*

Compare (i) and (ii) with (iii):

(iii) $\left\{\begin{array}{l}His_i\\ Harry_i\text{'s}\end{array}\right\}$ *mother came to see* $\left\{\begin{array}{l}Harry_i.\\ him_i.\end{array}\right\}$

Note that there are a lot of people who do not accept backward application in (iii), though everybody is quite happy with forward application.

(186) (*otoko*$_i$ *ga otoko*$_i$ *no tuma ni uragir-rare-ta) otoko*$_i$ *ga yo o hakanande, zisatu sita.*
'The man$_i$ (the man$_i$ was betrayed by the man$_i$'s wife) lost his hopes in the world and committed suicide.'

The true antecedent of the reflexive in (185) is the first occurrence of *otoko* in (186), but it is deleted by relative clause formation. Therefore, (185) is another instance of only apparent backward reflexivization.

The Necessity of Lexical Decomposition

Kuroda (personal communication, 1971) has made the interesting observation that backward reflexivization takes place in the following examples, even though the causative morpheme *sase* does not show up in the predicate position:

(187) *Zibun*$_i$ *ga Marii ni karakaw-ɾare-ta koto ga Zyon*$_i$ *o*
self Mary by made fun of that John
zetuboo e (to) oiyatta.
despair to drove
'That self$_i$ was made fun of by Mary drove John$_i$ to despair.'

(188) *Marii ga zibun*$_i$ *o hinan sita koto ga Zyon*$_i$ *o utinomesita.*
Mary self accused that John beat up
'That Mary accused self$_i$ bowled John$_i$ over.'

Therefore, he has concluded that backward reflexivization is not restricted to the causative construction and that sentences like (187) and (188) are genuine counterexamples to the subject-antecedent condition of reflexivization. I am going to show that *oiyaru* and *utinomesu* in (187) and (188) behave quite differently from *oiyaru* and *utinomesu* in their ordinary senses and that they share several important properties with emotive causative constructions.

Compare (187) with (189) and (190):

(189) *Hyakusyoo ga niwatori o torigoya no soto e (to) oiyatta.*
farmer chicken coop outside to drove
'The farmer drove the chickens out of the coop.'

(190) *Hyakusyoo ga ookami o konboo de utinomesita*
farmer wolf stick with beat up
'The farmer beat up the wolf with a stick.'

Now, let us examine the cooccurrence restriction of the *oiyaru* in (187) and that in (189). First, the former must always be preceded by the phrase *NP e* 'to NP'. The following sentence is ungrammatical:

(191) *$Zibun_i$ ga Marii ni karakaw-ɾare-ta koto ga $Zyon_i$ o ∅ oiyatta.
'That he was made fun of by Mary drove John away.'

This is not the case with the latter. The following sentence is perfectly grammatical:

(192) *Hyakusyoo ga niwatori o ∅ oiyatta.*
'The farmer drove the chickens away.'

Furthermore, the NPs in the NP *e* 'to NP' phrase are quite different in the two cases and, indeed, are mutually exclusive. In the case of *oiyaru* in Kuroda's example, they must be NPs that denote deep human sorrow. In my dialect, expressions of only mild sorrow or discomfort cannot occur in this position. Observe:

(193) *Koibito no uragiri ga Tanaka o zetuboo e oiyatta.*
girlfriend 's betrayal despair to drove
'The betrayal of his girlfriend drove Tanaka to despair.'

(194) ??*Koibito no uragiri ga Tanaka o hitan e oiyatta.*
grief
'The betrayal of his girlfriend drove Tanaka to grief.'

(195) *Kobibito no uragiri ga Tanaka o hitan no kiwami e*
grief's extremity
oiyatta.
'The betrayal of his girlfriend drove Tanaka to the depths of grief'

(196) ??*Koibito no uragiri ga Tanaka o kanasimi e oiyatta.*
sorrow
'The betrayal of his girlfriend drove Tanaka to sorrow.'

(197) *Koibito no uragiri ga Tanaka o kanasimi no kyokuti e*
sorrow 's extremity
oiyatta.
'The betrayal of his girlfriend drove Tanaka to the depths of sorrow.'

NPs that are associated with human happiness cannot occur. Observe:

(198) **Koibito no yasasii nagusame ga Tanaka o yorokobi e*
girlfriend's gentle consolation joy
oiyatta.
'The gentle consolation of his girlfriend drovc Tanaka to joy.'

(199) *$Zibun_i$ ga gan de nakatta koto ga $Tanaka_i$ o utyooten e
self cancer negative-past that rapture
oiyatta.
'That he_i did not have cancer drove $Tanaka_i$ to rapture.'

In the case of the other *oiyaru*, NPs that occur in NP *e* 'to NP' phrases are restricted to locative nouns such as *torigoya no soto* 'outside the coop', *hekiti* 'a remote place', etc.

Consider, next, the *utinomesu* pair. *Utinomesu* in Kuroda's example cannot cooccur with any instrumental phrase. The other *utinomesu* can. For example, observe the following:

(200) *$Zibun_i$ ga Marii ni karakaw-~~r~~are-ta koto ga $Zyon_i$ o
self Mary by made fun of that John
{*konboo* / *muti* / *tetuboo*} *de utinomesita.*
'That $self_i$ was made fun of by Mary bowled $John_i$ over
with {a stick. / a whip. / an iron stick.},

(201) *Hyakusyoo ga ookami o* {*konboo* / *muti* / *tetuboo*} *de utinomesita*
farmer wolf with beat up
'The farmer beat up the wolf with {a stick. / a whip. / an iron stick.}'

Actually, even when there is no instrumental phrase on the surface level, as in (202), it is implicitly understood that he has used something to perform the act of *utinomesu* 'beat up'.

(202) *Hyakusyoo ga ookami o ∅ utinomesita.*
'The farmer beat up the wolf ∅.'

In this sense, *utinomesu* in the ordinary sense of the word and an instrumental phrase are inseparably related.

Next I would like to show that Kuroda's *utinomesu* and *oiyaru* behave just like nonagentive emotive causatives in five important ways. First, the surface object of nonagentive emotive causatives must be a human NP because of the fact that the causativized verb is an emotive verb. Likewise, *utinomesu* and *oiyaru*, as used here, can take only human NPs as their objects. Observe that the following sentences are ungrammatical:

(203) **Zibun*$_i$ *ga koibito ni uragir-ɾare-ta koto ga Hirosi*$_i$ *no*
self girlfriend betray-passive-past that
sitai o utinomesita.
dead body beat up
'That self$_i$ was betrayed by his girlfriend bowled Hiroshi$_i$'s dead body over.'

(204) **Zibun*$_i$ *ga gan de aru to iu sindan ga sono inu*$_i$ *o*
self cancer have that diagnosis the dog
utinomesita.
beat up
'The diagnosis that self$_i$ had cancer bowled the dog over.'

(205) **Minna ga zibun*$_i$ *o baka ni site iru koto ga niwatori*$_i$
everybody self hold in contempt that chicken
o zetuboo e oiyatta.
despair drove
'That everybody made fool of self$_i$ drove the chicken to despair.'

(206) **Zibun*$_i$ *wa moo tasukaranai to iu zizitu ga sono neko*$_i$ *o*
self any longer heal-negative that fact the cat
kanasimi no kiwami e oiyatta.
sorrow extremety drove
'The fact that self$_i$ would not recover drove the cat to the depths of sorrow.'

This is not at all true with the other *utinomesu* and *oiyaru*, as is illustrated by (189) and (190) themselves:

(189) *Hyakusyoo ga niwatori o torigoya no soto e oiyatta.*
farmer chicken coop outside drove
'The farmer drove the chickens out of the coop.'

(190) *Hyakusyoo ga ookami o konboo de utinomesita.*
farmer wolf stick with beat up
'The farmer beat up the wolf with a stick.'

Second, notice that it is not the case that the object of emotive causatives can be just any human NP. It must refer to someone in the state of being capable of PERCEIVING the state of affairs expressed by the abstract surface subject. For example, compare the following pairs of sentences. The (b) forms are ungrammatical because the object NP fails to satisfy this requirement:

(207) a. *Zibun*$_i$ *no hitori musume ga yakuza ni yuukai s-*
self 's only daughter gangster by kidnap-

rare-ta to iu sirase ga Tanaka-san$_i$ *o gyooten s-*
passive-past report horrified-
$ase-ta
make-past
'The news that self$_i$'s only daughter had been kidnaped by gangsters horrified Tanaka$_i$.'

b. **Zibun*$_i$ *no hitori musume ga yakuza ni yuukai s-rare-ta to iu sirase ga nemurikokete iru Tanaka-san*$_i$ *o gyooten*
fast asleep
s-$ase-ta.
'The news that self$_i$'s only daughter had been kidnaped by gangsters horrified Tanaka, who was fast asleep.'

(208) a. *Koibito no yasasii sasayaki ga Hirosi o utyooten ni*
girlfriend's gentle whisper rapture to
s-$ase-ta
make-past
'The gentle whisper of his girlfriend enraptured Hiroshi.'

b. **Koibito no yasasii sasayaki ga tunbo no Hirosi o*
girlfriend's gentle whisper deaf
utyooten ni s-$ase-ta.
enraptured-make-past
'The gentle whisper of his girlfriend enraptured Hiroshi, who was deaf.'

The (b) forms in the following pairs are ungrammatical for the same reason:

(209) a. *Zibun*$_i$ *nó hitóri musuḿe ga yakuza ni koros-ɍare-ta to iu*
self 's only daughter gangster by kill-passive-past
sirase ga Tanaka-san$_i$ *o utinomesita*
news beat up
'The news that self$_i$'s only daughter had been killed by a gangster bowled Tanaka$_i$ over.'

b. **Zibun*$_i$ *no hitori musume ga yakuza ni koros-ɍare-ta to iu sirase ga nemurikokete iru Tanaka-san*$_i$ *o utinomesita.*
news fast asleep beat up
'The news that self$_i$'s only daughter had been killed by a gangster bowled Tanaka$_i$ over, who had fallen asleep.'

(210) a. *Koibito no uragiri ga Hirosi o zetuboo e oiyatta.*
girlfriend's betrayal despair to drove
'The betrayal of his girlfriend drove Hiroshi to despair.'

b. **Koibito no uragiri ga konsuizyootai no Hirosi o*
girlfriend's betrayal in a coma
zetuboo e oiyatta.
despair to drove
'The betrayal of his girlfriend drove Hiroshi, who was in a coma, to despair.'

Notice that this is not at all true with the other *utinomesu* and *oiyaru*. For example, the following example is perfectly grammatical:

(211) *Yakuza ga nemurikokete iru Tanaka-san o sanzan*
gangster fast asleep repeatedly
utinomesita.
beat up
'The gangsters beat up Tanaka repeatedly, who had fallen asleep.'

Third, recall that backward reflexivization is allowed both in nonagentive emotive causatives and in Kuroda's *utinomesu* and *oiyaru* sentences, which can take only nonagentive subjects. *Utinomesu* and *oiyaru* with agentive subjects do not allow backward reflexivization. Consider:

(212) **Zibun*$_i$ *o nikunde iru yakuza ga Tanaka-san*$_i$ *o sanzan*
self hate gangster repeatedly
utinomesita.
beat up
'The gangsters who hated self$_i$ beat up Tanaka$_i$ repeatedly.'

(213) **Zibun*$_i$ *no syuusaiburi o netande iru uwayaku ga waza to*
self brilliance jealous boss purposely
Tanaka-san$_i$ *o zetuboo e oiyatta.*
despair to drove
'His boss who had been jealous of self$_i$'s brilliance purposely drove Tanaka$_i$ to despair.'

Fourth, Lee (1970) has made the very important observation that a nonagentive subject of a causative construction in English can be a partial specification of the true subject. The same thing is true of Japanese. For example, compare the following two sentences:

(214) *Haha no tegami ga watasi o sukkari odorok-$\not{s}$ase-ta.*
mother's letter me completely surprised-make-past
'My mother's letter completely surprised me.'

(215) *Haha no tegami ga tukue no ue ni aru.*
mother's letter desk 's top at is
'My mother's letter is on the desk.'

Example (214) means that something about my mother's letter or some property of my mother's letter surprised me. For instance, (214) would be appropriate even to report that I was completely surprised because such a poor correspondent as my mother wrote to me. However, in (215) it is not the case that something about my mother's letter or some property of my mother's letter is on the desk. This partial nature of the subject is shared by Kuroda's *utinomesu* and *oiyaru.* The subjects of *utinomesu* and *oiyaru* in their literal senses do not have this property. Consider:

(216) *Haha no tegami ga Hirosi o utinomesita.*
mother's letter beat up
'His mother's letter bowled Hiroshi over.'

(217) *Haha ga Hirosi o utinomesita.*
'His mother beat up Hiroshi.'

(218) *Haha no tegami ga Hirosi o zetuboo e oiyatta*
despair to drove
'His mother's letter drove Hiroshi to despair.'

(219) *Haha ga Hirosi o heya no soto e oiyatta.*
mother room outside drove
'His mother drove Hiroshi out of the room.'

It is something about *haha no tegami* 'his mother's letter' that bowled Hiroshi over in (216), and likewise, it is something about *haha no tegami* that drove Hiroshi to despair in (218). On the other hand, in (217) and (219) it is not the case that something about *haha* 'his mother' beat up Hiroshi or drove Hiroshi out of the room.

Fifth, Kuroda's *utinomesu* and *oiyaru* are paraphrased by emotive causatives. For example, compare the following pairs of sentences. They seem to be nearly synonymous:

(220) a. *Zibun*$_{i}$ *ga Marii ni karakaw-~~r~~are-ta koto ga*
self Mary by make-fun of-passive-past
Zyon$_{i}$ *o zetuboo e oiyatta.*
John despair to drove
'That self$_{i}$ was made fun of by Mary drove John$_{i}$ to despair.'

b. *Zibun*$_{i}$ *ga Marii ni karakaw-~~r~~are-ta koto ga*
self Mary by make fun of-passive-past
Zyon$_{i}$ *o zetuboo s-~~s~~ase-ta*
John desperate-make-past
'That self$_{i}$ was made fun of by Mary made John$_{i}$ desperate.'

(221) a. *Marii ga zibun*$_i$ *o hinan sita koto ga*
Mary self accused that
Zyon$_i$ *o utinomesita*
John beat up
'That Mary accused self$_i$ bowled John$_i$ over.'
b. *Marii ga zibun*$_i$ *o hinan sita koto ga Zyon*$_i$ *o*
Mary self accused that John
gakkuri s-$ase-ta.
disheartened-make-past
'That Mary accused self$_i$ disheartened John$_i$.'

This is not the case with the other sense of *utinomesu* and *oiyaru*, as illustrated by the following examples.

(222) *Yakuza ga Tanaka-san o konboo de utinomesita.*
gangster stick beat up
'A gangster beat up Tanaka with a stick.'

(223) **Yakuza ga Tanaka-san o konboo de gakkuri s-$ase-ta.*
disheartened
'A gangster disheartened Tanaka with a stick.'

(224) *Hahaoya ga kodomotati o niwa e oiyatta.*
mother children garden to drove
'Mother drove her children into the garden.'

(225) **Hahaoya ga kodomotati o niwa e zetuboo s-$ase-ta*
desperate-make-past
'Mother made her children desperate into the garden.'

Examples (222) and (224) are not paraphrases of (223) and (225).

There is more than one way to treat the puzzling behavior of Kuroda's *utinomesu* and *oiyaru*. One might be satisfied, for example, with saying that *utinomesu*$_1$, *utinomesu*$_2$ and *oiyaru*$_1$, *oiyaru*$_2$ are homophonous. Notice, however, that just saying that much does not explain at all why one member of each pair acts like an emotive causative construction rather than an ordinary transitive verb or a passive construction, etc. On the other hand, if we assume that the *utinomesu* and *oiyaru* in question are underlyingly decomposable lexical items and that their underlying structures are roughly equivalent to emotive causative constructions such as in

(226) *zetuboo e oiyaru* ≡ *zetuboo s-$ase-ru*
'drive to despair' 'to make NP desperate'
utinomesu ≡ *kanzen ni gakkuri s-$ase-ru*
'beat up, bowl over' 'to make NP completely disheartened'

then everything will be very naturally accounted for. This causative analysis of Kuroda's *oiyaru* and *utinomesu* makes the claim that it is not an accident that backward reflexivization is allowed both in nonagentive causative constructions and in sentences with those verbs.

Kuno (personal communication, 1971) has found another interesting case. Observe the following examples, which are his:

(227) *Sono keiken wa Marii*$_i$ *ni zibun*$_i$ *ga baka de aru*
that experience Mary to self fool
koto o osieta
that taught
'That experience taught Mary$_i$ that self$_i$ was a fool.'

(228) *Zyon no zisatu wa Marii*$_i$ *ni-totte zibun*$_i$ *ga kare ni*
John 's suicide Mary to self him by
uragir-rare-ta koto o imisita
betray-passive-past that meant
'John's suicide meant to Mary$_i$ that self$_i$ had been betrayed by him.'

(229) *Kono zizitu wa Marii*$_i$ *ni dare mo zibun*$_i$ *o*
this fact Mary anyone self
aisite inai koto o sisasita
love negative that suggested
'This fact suggested to Mary$_i$ that no one loved self$_i$.'

In these examples, the reflexive does not refer to the subject of the main sentence but to the indirect object, *Marii*. Therefore, (227)–(229) seem to present another serious problem for the subject-antecedent condition of reflexivization.

Consider the following nonagentive causative constructions. Note that in (230)–(232), too, the reflexive does not refer to the subject but to the indirect object, *Marii*.

(230) *Sono keiken wa Marii*$_i$ *ni zibun*$_i$ *ga baka de aru*
that experience Mary to self fool
koto o sator-$\not{s}$*ase-ta.*
that realize-make-past
'That experience made Mary$_i$ realize that self$_i$ was a fool.'

(231) *Zyon no zisatu wa Marii*$_i$ *ni zibun*$_i$ *ga kare ni*
John 's suicide Mary to self him by
uragir-rare-ta to omoikom-$\not{s}$*ase-ta*
betray-passive-past that believe-make-past

'John's suicide made Mary$_i$ believe that self$_i$
had been betrayed by him.'

(232) *kono zizitu wa Marii$_i$ ni dare mo zibun$_i$ o aisite*
this fact Mary nobody self love
inai no kamo sirenai to kangae-\$ase-ta.
negative that possible that think-make-past
'That fact made Mary$_i$ think it may be that
nobody loved self$_i$.'

It is obvious, however, that (230)–(232) are not counterexamples to the subject-antecedent condition: *Marii* 'Mary' was the subject of *satoru* 'realize', *omoikomu* 'believe', and *kangaeru* 'think' before verb raising applied. Also, notice that Kuno's examples (227)–(229) and (230)–(232) are essentially paraphrases of each other. Assume, then, that *osieru* 'teach', sisasuru 'suggest', and *imisuru* 'mean' in (227)–(229) have underlying structures roughly equivalent to (233):

(233) *osieru* 'teach' ≡ CAUSE NP to realize S
imisuru 'mean' ≡ CAUSE NP to believe S
sisasuru 'suggest' ≡ CAUSE NP to believe that S is possible

This causative analysis of those verbs correctly predicts that if S contains an NP that is coreferential to NP, then that NP will be reflexivized, because NP is the subject of the complement verb and S is its object. In the following discussion, I will present several more facts that strongly argue for lexical decomposition of Kuno's verbs into nonagentive causative constructions.

First, observe that reflexivization itself behaves quite differently in the following pairs of sentences: The reflexive may refer to the object just in case the subject of *osieru* is nonagentive, as in the (b) forms. Compare:

(234) a. *Tanaka-daizin$_i$ ga Satoo-syusyoo$_j$ ni denwa de*
minister Premier phone over
zibun$_{i,*j}$ no ninki ga otidasita koto o osieta.
self 's popularity drop began that taught
'Minister Tanaka$_i$ informed Premier Sato$_j$ over
the phone that self$_{i,*j}$'s popularity had
started to drop.'

b. *Tanaka-daizin$_i$ no tegami ga Satoo-syusyoo$_j$ ni*
's letter
zibun$_{*i,j}$ no ninki ga otidasita koto o osieta
self 's popularity drop began that taught

'Minister Tanaka$_i$s letter taught Premier Sato$_j$
that self $_{i,j}$'s popularity had started to drop.'

(235) a. *Uwayaku$_i$ ga minna no mae de Tanaka-san$_j$ ni*
boss everybody in front of to
zibun$_{i,*j}$ no kangae ga matigatte ita koto
self 's thought wrong was that
o osieta
taught
'His boss$_i$ informed Tanaka$_j$ that self$_{i,*j}$ was
wrong in front of everybody.'

b. *Uwayaku$_i$ no taido ga Tanaka-san$_j$ ni zibun$_j$ no*
boss 's behavior self
kangae ga matigatte ita koto o osieta
thought wrong was that taught
'His boss$_i$'s behavior taught Tanaka$_j$ that
self$_{j,*i}$ was wrong.'

Any adequate grammar of Japanese has to explain this phenomenon on a principled basis. In my dialect, *sisasuru* 'suggest' and *imisuru* 'mean' cannot take agentive subjects, as in (236)–(237). Therefore, it is impossible to exhibit the same kind of contrast with them:

(236) **Uwayaku ga minna no mae de Tanaka-san ni zibun no*
boss everybody in front of self 's
kangae ga matigatte ita koto o sisasita
thought wrong was that suggested
'His boss suggested to Tanaka that he was wrong
in front of everybody.'

(237) **Uwayaku ga minna no mae de Tanaka-san ni zibun no*
kangae ga matigatte ita koto o imisita
'His boss meant to Tanaka that he was wrong in front
of everybody.'

Unless we assume that *osieru* in the (a) forms and *osieru* in the (b) forms are of different semantic structure and that the (b) forms are underlyingly causative constructions, it will be difficult to explain this peculiar behavior of reflexivization.

Next, three most important properties of nonagentive causative constructions are shared by Kuno's verbs. They are: (1) The object is a human NP; (2) that same human NP is in the state of being capable of perceiving the state of affairs expressed by the abstract subject; and (3) the subject can be a partial specification of the true subject. Recall that these properties are all shared by Kuroda's verbs, too. Consider the following examples:

(238) a. *Haha no namida ga Hirosi ni titi ga nakunatta*
mother's tears father died
koto o osieta.
that taught
'His mother's tears told Hiroshi that his father had died.'

b. *Hirosi wa inu no Taroo ni osuwari o osieta.*
dog sit-down taught
'Hiroshi taught Taro, the dog, to sit.'

c. **Haha no namida ga inu no Taroo ni titi ga*
mother's tears father die
nakunatta koto o osieta
died that taught
'His mother's tears told Taro, the dog, that his father had died.'

Note that (238c) is ungrammatical, while (238b) is perfectly good. Example (238a) becomes ungrammatical if *konsuizyootai no* 'in a coma' is added:

(239) **Haha no namida ga konsuizyootai no Hirosi ni*
mother's tears in a coma
titi ga nakunatta koto o osieta
father died that taught
'His mother's tears told Hiroshi, who was in a coma, that his father had died.'

Similarly, (240) becomes ungrammatical when *konsuizyootai no* 'in a coma' is added, as in (241):

(240) *Haha no namida ga Hirosi ni titi ga nakunatta koto*
Mother's tears father died that
o sator-ṡase-ta.
realize-make-past
'His mother's tears made Hiroshi realize that his father had died.'

(241) **Haha no namida ga konsuizyootai no Hirosi ni*
mother's tears in a coma
titi ga nakunatta koto o sator-ṡase-ta
father died that realize-make-past
'His mother's tears made Hiroshi, who was in a coma, realize that his father had died.'

Finally, in (238a) and (240) it is not the physical object *haha no namida* 'mother's tears' that told Hiroshi or caused Hiroshi to realize that his father had died. It is something about *haha no namida*. However, in (238b) it is not something about Hiroshi that taught Taro, the dog, to sit.

Third, backward reflexivization is obligatory in Kuno's verbs. Consider:

(242) *Zibun*$_i$ *no sinyuu ni uragir-rare-ta koto wa Hirosi*$_i$
self 's close friend betray-passive-past that
ni zinsei wa kibisii mono de aru koto o osieta
life harsh thing that taught
'That he was betrayed by self$_i$'s close friend taught Hiroshi$_i$ that life is a harsh thing.'

(243) *Zibun*$_i$ *no koibito ni sute-rare-ta koto wa Mitiko*
self 's boyfriend by desert-pass-past
ni-totte zibun$_i$ *no zinsei ga owatte simatta koto*
to self 's life over that
o imisita
meant
'That she was deserted by self$_i$'s boyfriend meant to Michiko$_i$ that self$_i$'s life was over.'

(244) *Konogoro Hirosi ga zibun*$_i$ *o zenzen deeto ni*
recently self never date
sasotte kurenai koto wa Mitiko$_i$ *ni kare ga*
ask give-negative that he
kokorogawari sita koto o sisasita
change mind that suggested
'That Hiroshi had never asked self$_i$ to go out recently suggested to Michiko$_i$ that he had changed'

If we assume that Kuno's verbs are underlyingly causative, then it is no mystery at all for our analysis that backward reflexivization is required with those verbs. For we already know that backward reflexivization is required in nonagentive causative constructions for some yet-to-be-determined reason.

From the preceding facts, I would like to conclude the following: The best way to account for why Kuno's verbs behave, in so many ways, just like nonagentive causative constructions both semantically and syntactically is to hypothesize that they are underlyingly nonagentive causative constructions. Note that this hypothesis makes the important claim that Japanese reflexivization is a prelexical transformation. Take *osieru* 'teach'. I claim that the metaphoric sense of *osieru* has an underlying structure something like the following:

(245) *osieru* $\equiv$ CAUSE NP to realize S

Then, if S contains an NP that is coreferential to an NP, it will be reflexivized before verb raising applies. Lexical insertion, of course, must follow verb raising. Therefore, reflexivization must be prelexical.

In this section, I have argued that both Kuroda's and Kuno's 'counter-examples' must be analyzed as underlyingly causative constructions and that it is not a pure accident that backward reflexivization is required both in nonagentive causatives and in constructions pointed out by Kuroda and kuno. The following section is an attempt to answer the question, Why is backward reflexivization required in nonagentive causative constructions?

Much Deeper Structure of Nonagentive Causatives

Lee's Observations

I have already mentioned Lee's important observation that nonagentive causatives have an abstract subject that can be a partial specification of the true subject. Let me quote his examples (1971b:175):

(246) *The painting flabbergasted Mary.*

(247) *The hammer broke the window.*

Example (246) means that something about the painting flabbergasted Mary. However, (247) does not mean that something about the hammer broke the window. I have shown (in the previous section) that this partial nature of the subject is equally shared by Japanese nonagentive causative sentences. Lee (1971a:93) has made another important observation, i.e., that *Mary* is presupposed to have perceived the lamp in the following sentence:

(248) *The lamp persuaded Mary that she was in Borneo (by having a peculiar shape).*

Compare his example with the following pair of sentences:

(249) a. *The lamp persuaded Mary, who was blind, that she was in Borneo by having a peculiar shape.*
b. **The lamp persuaded Mary, who was blind, that she was in Borneo by having a peculiar color.*

Why is (249a) grammatical while (249b) is not? Clearly, because her blindness does not prevent Mary from perceiving the shape of the lamp. On the other hand, her blindness does prevent her from perceiving the color of the lamp. These examples indicate that Lee's observation is correct. Consider Japanese sentences (250) and (251):

(250) a. *Sono ongaku ga Taroo o kandoo s-ȿase-ta.*
that music moved-make-past
'That music moved Taro.'

b. **Sono ongaku ga tunbo no Taroo o kandoo s-s̸ase-ta.*
deaf
'That music moved Taro, who is deaf.'

(251) a. *Sono e ga Hanako o kansin s-s̸ase-ta.*
that painting impressed-make-past
'That painting impressed Hanako.'
b. **Sono e ga mekura no Hanako o kansin s-s̸ase-ta*
blind
'That painting impressed Hanako, who is blind.'

The (b) forms are unacceptable for exactly the same reason as in the previous example. However, it is possible that some people might explain to Taro and Hanako 'something or some quality' about that music or that painting. That might possibly cause Taro and Hanako to come to be moved. Also, imagine that Taro is a musician like Beethoven, who could read the score despite the fact that he was deaf. In those cases, the (b) forms in (250) and (251) will become perfectly acceptable.

Unfortunately, Lee did not go a step further and ask why it is the case that the subject of nonagentive causatives can be a partial specification of the true subject and, also, why in the very same constructions the surface object is presupposed to have perceived the state of affairs expressed by the 'partial' subject. Recall that this is the very environment in which backward reflexivization is required in Japanese. I am going to show that, indeed, Lee's two observations are the crucial keys to understanding the mystery of Japanese reflexivization and, also, to understanding some interesting syntactic–semantic facts of English syntax.

Much Deeper Structure

In what follows I will discuss Japanese sentences and their English equivalents together. Each number is to be interpreted as referring to two sentences, one Japanese and one English.

In Section 2, I argued that both Japanese and English have a rule of causal object formation that takes the first argument of an abstract verb CAUSE and makes it a derived object of a Ve such as *yorokobu* 'happy, pleased', *kanasimu* 'unhappy, sad', etc. Thus, sentences like (252) and (253) were claimed to share a deep structure something like (254):

(252) *Haha ga gan de nakatta koto ga Hirosi o yorokob-sase-ta.*
mother cancer negative-past that happy-make-past
'That his mother did not have cancer made Hiroshi happy.'

(253) *Hirosi wa haha ga gan de nakatta koto o yorokonda.*
mother cancer negative-past that was happy
'Hiroshi was happy that his mother did not have cancer.'

(254)

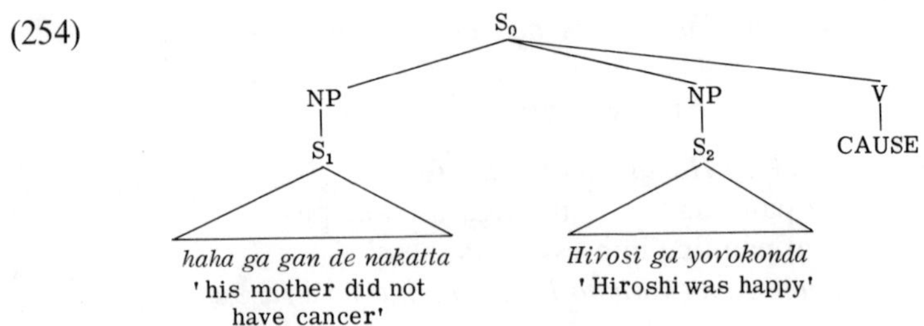

Now, consider (255):

(255) a. *Hirosi wa, haha ga gan de nakatta koto o sitte, yorokonda.*
'Hiroshi was happy to find out that his mother did not have cancer.'

b. *Hirosi wa, haha ga gan de nakatta koto o satotte, yorokonda.*
'Hiroshi was happy to realize that his mother did not have cancer.'

c. *Hirosi wa, haha ga gan de nakatta koto o kiite, yorokonda.*
'Hiroshi was happy to hear that his mother did not have cancer.'

d. *Hirosi wa, haha ga gan de nakatta koto o kikas-rare-te, yorokonda.*
'Hiroshi was happy to be informed that his mother did not have cancer.'

e. *Hirosi wa, haha ga gan de nakatta koto o hakken site, yorokonda.*
'Hiroshi was happy to discover that his mother did not have cancer.'

f. **Hirosi wa, haha ga gan de nakatta koto o soozoosite, yorokonda.*
'Hiroshi was happy to imagine that his mother did not have cancer.'

g. **Hirosi wa, haha ga gan de nakatta koto o kuusoo site, yorokonda.*
'Hiroshi was happy to dream that his mother did not have cancer.'

h. **Hirosi wa, haha ga gan de nakatta koto o hitei site, yorokonda.*
'Hiroshi was happy to deny that his mother did not have cancer.'

Observe that in (255) the subject of the subordinate sentence is *Hirosi*. By contrast, (256) is ungrammatical:

(256) **Hirosi wa, Mitiko ga haha ga gan de nakatta koto o satotte, yorokonda.*
Hiroshi was happy for Michiko to realize that his mother did not have cancer.'

Also, note that the verbs that can occur in constructions like (255) seem to be limited to verbs of experience/perception in some sense. Examples (255f–h) are ungrammatical.

These observations make me hypothesize that an earlier stage of (253) is really something like (257). Compare:

(253) *Hirosi wa haha ga gan de nakatta koto o yorokonda.*
'Hiroshi was happy that his mother did not have cancer.'

(257) *Hirosi wa, haha ga gan de nakatta koto o* __Ø__, *yorokonda.*
'Hiroshi was happy __Ø__ that his mother did not have cancer.'

That is, in (257) equi-NP deletion has deleted a higher subject *Hirosi*, as in (255), and another rule has deleted the abstract higher verb EXPERIENCE/PERCEIVE. After that, causal object formation has applied, making the leftover object complement of EXPERIENCE/PERCEIVE the derived object of Ve. According to this analysis, (253) would have a deep structure something like (258):

(258)

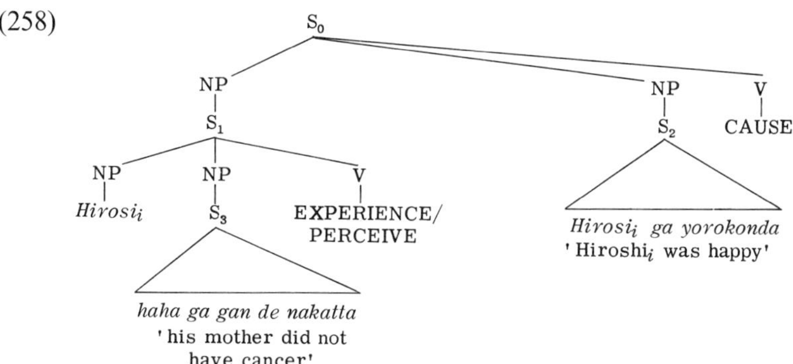

This analysis claims that it is not just the proposition *haha ga gan de nakatta* 'his mother did not have cancer' but Hiroshi's experiencing/perceiving of that proposition that caused Hiroshi to become happy. I maintain that sentences like (255) have the same underlying structure as in (258) except for the verb of S_1. Lee's example, (248), will be explained by a deep structure something like (259):

(259)

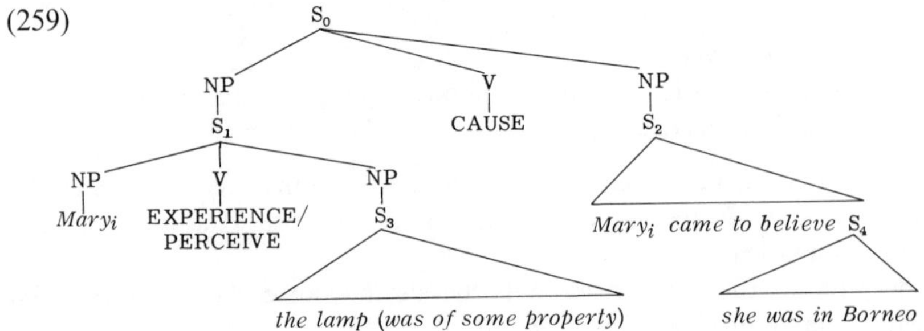

I would like to conclude that a nonagentive causative construction is a special case of causatives, i.e., that in which the subject of the subject complement and the object complement of the abstract verb CAUSE must be coreferential. Also, the verb of the subject complement must be limited to verbs of experience/perception in some sense. The subject of nonagentive causatives can be the abstract verb EXPERIENCE/PERCEIVE, which must undergo deletion, which may be followed by another deletion in S_3, leaving a mere trace of the true subject for CAUSE. This analysis can also explain why it is presupposed that the surface object of nonagentive causatives has perceived the state of affairs expressed by the partial subject.[14]

So far, I have shown that there are syntactic–semantic facts to suggest that the deep structure of nonagentive causatives must be something like (258) or (259). It is quite noteworthy that the same analysis predicts correctly that apparent backward reflexivization will be observable in nonagentive causatives in Japanese. For if S_3 in (258) contains *Hirosi*, an NP coreferential to the subject of S_1, it will be reflexivized in the S_1 cycle. After equi-object deletion, EXPERIENCE/PERCEIVE deletion, and verb raising in the S_0 cycle, a surface structure such as (260) will be derived:

[14]Oyakawa (personal communication, 1972) has pointed out that there are nonagentive constructions for which a different analysis must be given. For example:

(i) *Kisi-san no huninki ga Satoo-san o syusyoo no za ni tuk-sase-ta.*
's unpopularity premier seat take-make-past
'The unpopularity of Kisi put Sato in the office of premier.'

(ii) *Zinsin no taihai ga Rooma teikoku o metuboo s-ṣase-ta.*
moral deterioration Roman Empire fall -make-past
'Moral deterioration brought about the downfall of the Roman Empire.'

Note that in (i) and (ii) the nonagentive subject is not a partial specification but, rather, a nominalization of a proposition, and that the surface objects *Satoo-san* and *Rooma teikoku* are not presupposed to have perceived the state of affairs expressed by the surface subject.

(260) *Zibun$_i$ ga gan de nakatta koto ga Hirosi$_i$ o yorokob-sase-ta.*
self cancer negative-past that happy-make-past
'That self$_i$ did not have cancer made Hiroshi$_i$ happy.'

Thus, this analysis claims that *Hirosi* in (260) is not the true antecedent of the reflexive in the subject complement but that the true antecedent *Hirosi* has been deleted in the course of derivation. I maintain that a grammar has explanatory power only if it makes correct predictions of many relations between syntactic facts and meaning that otherwise would remain totally unaccounted for. So long as we treat backward reflexivization in nonagentive causatives as genuine backward reflexivization, it will be totally impossible to understand what is going on behind those interesting semantic–syntactic facts in Japanese.

4. CONCLUSION

This study began with a discussion of the basic condition of Japanese reflexivization, i.e., the subject-antecedent condition and the command condition, and ended with the claim that both of the conditions hold even in backward reflexivization in nonagentive causatives, in which it looks as if the subject-antecedent condition is violated. The subject-antecedent condition was formulated by Kuroda (1965b). Therefore, the natural question to ask would be, What is the difference between the present work and Kuroda's, or what is the contribution, if any, of the present work to the study of Japanese reflexivization and to the study of syntax in general. I would like to show that, indeed, the two works are quite different in that they make entirely different claims about the nature of grammar of human languages.

Kuroda's work was done within the *Aspects* conception of grammar (Chomsky, 1965), in which the domains of syntax and semantics were very clearly separated. The deep structure was assumed to be very close to the surface structure in those days. Therefore, it is quite certain that the backward reflexivization discussed in Sections 2 and 3 would have been treated as genuine counterexamples to the subject-antecedent condition and that an extra condition such as the following would have been added to the grammar of Japanese: Backward reflexivization obligatorily takes place just in case one of the two coreferential NPs is in the same clause as a nonagentive subject that contains the other one. I rejected that approach to backward reflexivization for several reasons. It is reasonable to think that there is a deep-seated reason for this phenomenon, and the 'aspects' approach evidently cannot provide one. I tried to show that it is far from pure accident that backward reflexivization is required in sentences with verbs like *utinomesu* 'beat up', *oiyaru* 'drive away', etc., just in case they have nonagentive subjects and are paraphrased by emotive causatives, and that those verbs must be analyzed as underlying causative constructions. This lexical decomposition hypothesis for those verbs led to the claim that reflexivization is a prelexical transformation. Finally, I proposed quite an abstract deep structure for nonagentive causatives and showed that this analysis correctly predicts that backward reflexivization is called for in nonagentive causatives. In short, this work makes the important claim that deep structures must be quite similar to semantic structures if one wants to capture the true generalization of Japanese reflexivization and other related syntactic facts in both Japanese and English. Of course, Kuroda (1965b) never made such a claim.

The research on reflexivization brought about several important consequences. Among other things, the following are of particular importance:

1. The Flip analysis of emotive verbs in Japanese and English was rejected in favor of a causative analysis. English 'Flip' verbs such as *amuse*, *please*, *surprise*, etc., were argued to be underlyingly causatives. Also, contrary to the Flip analysis, which treats them as underlyingly transitive, it was demonstrated that a class of emotive verbs in Japanese and English are underlyingly intransitive and that a transformation called causal object formation is responsible for the derivation of the surface objects of those verbs. Notice that the results of our analysis cast doubt on the Flip analysis of other verbs such as *seem*, *look*, *strike*, *remind*, etc., in English (Postal, 1970a, b) and *kowai*, *osorosii* 'frightening, horrifying', *wakaru* 'understand', etc., in Japanese (Akatsuka, 1971).
2. Deep structures for nonagentive causatives were proposed for Japanese and English. According to this analysis, a nonagentive causative construction is a special case of causative constructions, i.e., that in which the subjects of the subject complement and the object complement of the abstract verb CAUSE must be coreferential. Also, it was claimed that the verb of the subject complement is limited to verbs of experience/perception in some sense. Also, it can be the abstract verb EXPERIENCE/PERCEIVE that undergoes obligatory deletion. It was argued that those facts explain why the subject of nonagentive causatives can be partial and why it is presupposed that the surface object of nonagentive causatives has perceived the state of affairs expressed by the partial subject, as observed by Lee (1971a, b).

REFLEXIVIZATION: AN INTERPRETIVE APPROACH

KAZUKO INOUE

INTRODUCTION

The preceding chapter by Noriko A. McCawley is a good representative of the currently available works on Japanese reflexivization, which are by and large transformational in their approach. The work presented in this chapter is perhaps the first systematic attempt to approach the subject from the point of view of interpretive theory. It attempts first to bring to general attention certain limitations of the transformational approach, and then to formulate interpretive rules that take over the function of the hitherto-proposed transformational reflexivization rule. In the course of the discussion, subtle semantic effects of reflexive forms, which have been superficially dealt with so far, are considered; and, thus, the present study also attempts to show a direction for the refinements of syntactic and semantic study of Japanese reflexivization.

Section 1 is devoted to a summary of the past works on the subject. The differences between English and Japanese reflexives are brought up in this section. Section 2 contains semantic and syntactic arguments against transformational derivation of reflexives as well as the hypothesis of cyclic reflexivization. Section 3 introduces interpretation rules, with a detailed explanation of their applications. Finally, Section 4 gives a sketch of semantic factors that seem to contribute to the final adjustment of coreferential readings and determine the preferred antecedent for a reflexive form.

1. SUMMARY OF PAST WORKS ON THE REFLEXIVE *ZIBUN*

Conditions on Reflexivization

The standard reflexivization rule is formulated with the following conditions:[1]

1. Only higher animate nouns can be reflexivized.[2]
2. *Zibun* is used invariably, regardless of person, gender, and number.[3]
3. The antecedent must be the subject of a sentence (the subject-antecedent condition).
4. The antecedent must command the reflexive (the antecedent-command condition).[4]

Note, in addition, that it is not necessary for Japanese reflexivization to satisfy the condition that the antecedent and the reflexive be clausemates.[5]

Condition 1 excludes such sentences as the following:

[1] A similar list appears in Oyakawa (1973), but it differs from this in a few important points. Kuroda (1965a), Kuno (1972), and N. McCawley, among others, contributed to clarification of these conditions. For details of Conditions 3 and 4, cf. the chapter by N. McCawley in this volume.

[2] It may be said that *zitai* 'itself' is the reflexive form for inanimate nouns, but it is a bound form (unlike *zibun* or *ziko*) and very much limited in its use, appearing only immediately after nominals in the contrasitive sense. Therefore, it is omitted from this work. The following is one example of *zitai*:

Omae no kangae zitai ga hukenzen da.
your idea itself unsound be-non-past
'Your idea itself is unsound.'

[3] Actually, *zibun* is not the only reflexive form, as discussed later. We have plural forms of *zibun*, namely, *zibun-tati* 'selves' and *zibun-ra* ('selves'), but number agreement is not obligatory. When the antecedent is understood to be in the plural, *zibun-tati* or *zibun-ra* may be used, even if the antecedent is not marked for plurality:

(i) *Daihyoo$_i$ wa zibun-tati$_i$ no iken o matome-ta.*
representative their opinion summarize-past
'The representatives summarized their opinions.'

With the antecedent marked with plural formatives (*tati, ra, domo*), the use of the plural forms of the reflexive is preferred but not obligatory.

(ii) *Onna-domo$_i$ wa zibun-tati$_i$ no sigoto ni mutyuu ni nat-te-i-ru*
woman-folks their work in absorbed become-non-past
'The women are absorbed in their work.'

Thus, we should say that there is no obligatory number agreement.

[4] A node A "commands" another node B if (1) neither A nor B dominates the other and (2) the S node that most immediately dominates A also dominates B (Langacker, 1969:167).

[5] Noun phrases that command each other are clausemates. In other words, noun phrases in a simplex sentence are clausemates.

(1) **Syatyoo no kuruma ga zibun no syako ni hait-te i-ru.*
president's car self's garage in be non-past
'The president's car is in its own garage.'

Since *kuruma* in (1) is an inanimate noun, it cannot be reflexivized. It is often stated that only human nouns can be reflexivized, but nouns denoting higher animals are also given this possibility, especially in the case of pet animals, as shown by (2):

(2) *Inu wa zibun no ie o sit-te i-ru.*
dog self's house know-non-past
'Dogs know their houses.'

Condition 2 states that, contrary to the situation in English, there are no distinctions in Japanese reflexive forms according to person, gender, and number. Condition 3 is necessary to exclude such a coreferential relation as is indicated by the subscripts in (3):

(3) **Taroo ga Ziroo$_i$ ni zibun$_i$ no oitati o hanasi-ta.*
self's childhood tell-past
'Taro told Jiro$_i$ about self's$_i$ childhood.'

In (3), *zibun* must be uniquely interpreted as coreferential with *Taroo*. That is, owing to Condition 3, *Ziroo* does not qualify as the antecedent of *zibun*, since it is not the subject of the sentence.

Next, observe the unacceptability of the coreferential relation between *Taroo* and *zibun* in (4):

(4) **Taroo$_i$ ga kai ni der-are-nakat-ta no de zibun$_i$*[6] *wa Ziroo o*
meeting to go-can-not-past as, self
kawari ni yat-ta.
in his place send-past
'As Taro$_i$ could not go to the meeting, self$_i$ sent Jiro in his place.'

In (4), *Taroo* is the subject of the adverbial clause but does not command *zibun*. This is why it cannot be the antecedent of *zibun*. Example (5), in which *Taroo* and *zibun* switch their positions, is a perfect sentence, with the coreferential relation established between *Taroo* and *zibun*:

(5) *Zibun$_i$ ga kai ni der-are-nakat-ta no de Taroo$_i$ wa Ziroo o kawari ni yat-ta.*
'As he$_i$ could not go to the meeting, Taro$_i$ sent Jiro in his place.'

[6]In some dialects, *zibun* stands for the first person. Example (4) is grammatical if we interpret *zibun* in this sense. However, this particular use of *zibun* is not treated in this study.

Thus, Condition 4 is necessary to account for such sentences as (4) and (5). In (5), *zibun* and *Taroo* are not clausemates, which indicates that in Japanese the condition of clausemates is not necessary for reflexivization. However, reflexivization by a nonclausemate antecedent is not unconditional. Kuroda summarizes the condition as follows:

> *Zibun* in the object position of a constituent sentence may be anaphorically coreferential with the matrix subject if the constituent sentence is inside the matrix verb phrase. Thus, *zibun* can be anaphorically coreferential with the matrix subject, if it is, for example, the object of the verb phrase complement or of the noun phrase complement which is the matrix object. On the other hand, it cannot be so coreferential if it is the object of an adverbial clause.[7]

(6) [Kuroda 1965b (40)]
John wa Bill ga zibun o hometa koto o kiite yorokonda.[8]
self praise that hear-and glad be-past
'John was glad to hear that Bill had praised him/himself.'

In (6), the constituent sentence *Bill ga zibun o hometa koto* is the object of the matrix sentence. Therefore, *zibun* can be coreferential with the nonclausemate subject *John* as well as with the clausemate subject *Bill*. In (7), on the other hand, the constituent sentence [the boldfaced portion of (7)] is an adverbial phrase, so that *zibun* cannot be taken to be coreferential with *John*:

(7) ****John wa Bill ga zibun o hometa toki*** *Mary no soba ni i-ta.*
self praise when Mary 's side at be-past
'John was next to Mary, when Bill praised himself.'

This condition on adverbial clauses, however, holds only for the speaker-oriented style, i.e., the reportive style, as Kuroda (1973a:385) calls it.[9] Kuno (1972) has made a further observation on the restriction on the use of *zibun* in this context. According to him, *zibun* can be used only when the awareness of the subject is presupposed. For example, in (8), such awareness cannot be presupposed, so that the reading of coreferentiality between *John* and *zibun* is unacceptable:

[7]This condition was first stated by Kuroda (1965b). The quotation here is his own summary of this condition in Kuroda (1973a:385).

[8]When examples are cited from other sources, morphological segmentation and the English glosses are given as in the original forms, which very often differ from mine. Minimum modifications are made when they are necessary to prevent misunderstandings.

[9]Example (7) is unacceptable, according to Kuroda, if it is interpreted to be in the reportive style. As a sentence used in the nonreportive style, (7) is supposed to be acceptable. This should also be acceptable according to Kuno, because Kuno claims that the reflexive in this context can be coreferential with the matrix subject if the subject (in this case, *John*) is assumed to be aware of the event (in this case, 'being praised by Bill').

(8) **John*$_i$ *wa Bill ga zibun*$_i$ *o hometa toki Mary no soba de*
self praise when Mary 's side at
kizetu-si-te i-ta.
faint-state-past
'John$_i$ lay fainted next to Mary when Bill praised self$_i$.'

Kuno tries to solve this problem by the direct discourse analysis, positing the subject's direct speech, such as *Bill ga watasi o hometa toki* 'when Bill praised me'. Thus, both Kuroda and Kuno have made very important observations, clarifying the nature of this complex problem. It is obvious, however, that this must be studied further from various different angles.

Cyclicity and Reflexivization

Kuno (1973) argues that the simple passive in Japanese is derived from its active counterpart by movement transformations[10] similar to those employed to derive English passives from their active counterparts. The affective passive, on the other hand, is derived from a complement construction whose matrix subject is a human noun phrase.[11] His argument is basically as follows: First, there is a justification for positing complement construction for causative sentences. Namely, the ambiguity of *zibun* in such a causative sentence as (9) can be accounted for by assuming such a complement construction as (10) and the cyclic application of reflexivization:

(9) *Taroo*$_i$ *wa kodomo*$_j$ *o zibun*$_{ij}$ *no heya de benkyoo-s-ase-ta.*
self's room in study-do-cause-past
'Taro$_i$ made (or let) his child$_j$ to study in self's$_{ij}$ room.'

(10)[12]

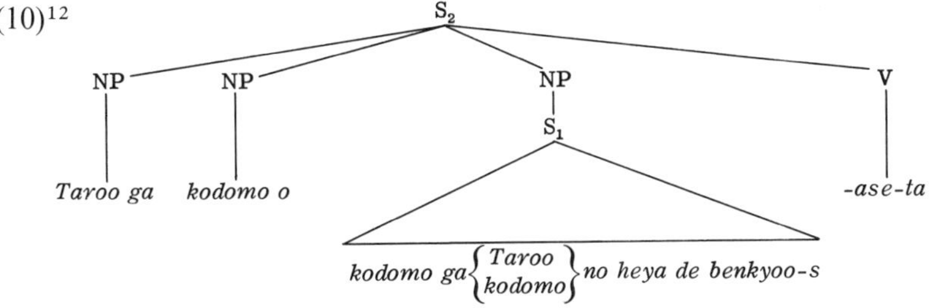

Zibun in (9) is ambiguously interpreted either as *Taroo* or *child*. If the

[10]Kuno assumes simple passivization to involve two movement transformations, subject postposing and object preposing.

[11]Cf. the chapter by Howard and Niyekawa-Howard in this volume for related discussion on Japanese passives.

[12]The tree structure assumed in Kuno (1973) is different from this, but the difference does not have a direct bearing on the point in question.

underlying structure in (10) and cyclic application of reflexivization are assumed, *zibun* can be derived on the basis of coreferentiality with *kodomo* on the first cycle, while *zibun* may have another derivation on the second cycle if the underlying NP is coreferential with *Taroo*.

Similarly, affective passives yield an ambiguous coreferential interpretation of *zibun*,[13] so that they must be assigned a similar underlying complement construction. Examples (11) and (12) are an affective passive and its underlying structure, respectively:

(11) *Taroo*$_i$ *wa tomodati*$_j$ *ni zibun*$_{ij}$ *no heya de sin-are-ta.*
friend by self's room in die-passive-past
'Taro's$_i$ friend$_j$ died in his$_{ij}$ room on him.'

(12)

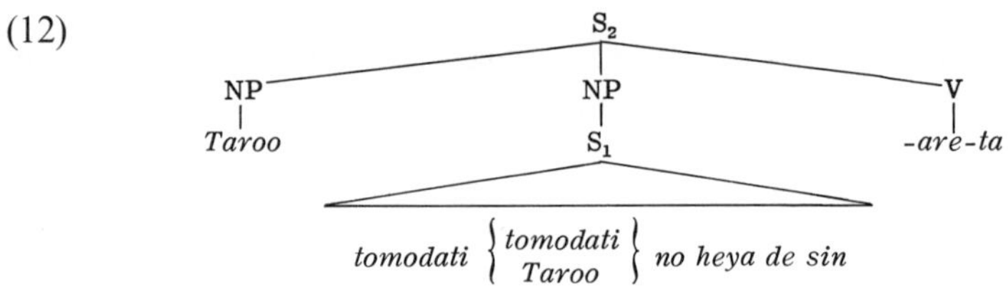

By assuming (12) as the underlying structure of (11), the ambiguity involved in (11) can be accounted for in exactly the same way as that of (9).

A simple passive, on the other hand, does not involve ambiguity, as is illustrated by (13):

(13) *Taroo*$_i$ *wa Ziroo ni zibun*$_i$ *no ofisu de batoo-s-are-ta.*
denounce-passive-past
'Taro$_i$ was denounced by Jiro in his$_i$ office.'[14]

If a complement construction similar to (12) is assumed for (13), it is also expected to receive ambiguous interpretation, which is not consistent with the fact just presented. Hence the assumption of the simplex underlying structure for simple passives. And by ordering passivization before reflexivization, we can account for the unique interpretation of *Taroo* as the antecedent of *zibun*, since *Ziroo* is no longer the subject of the sentence at the time of reflexivization.

N. McCawley (in this volume) takes up the cases of backward reflexivization. Examples (14) and (15) are relevant examples from her chapter:

[13]Some affective passives are unambiguously interpreted. This question is taken up in detail in Sections 3 and 4.

[14]There are quite a few speakers who give an ambiguous reading to this sentence, but there is agreement that the predominant reading is as indicated by indexes here.

(14) [McCawley's (109)]
Zibun$_i$ *ga gan de nakatta koto ga Hirosi*$_i$ *o yorokob-ase-ta.*
self cancer negative-past that happy-make-past
'That self$_i$ did not have cancer made Hiroshi$_i$ happy.'

(15) [McCawley's (182)]
Zibun$_i$ *ga gan de aru to iuu sindan ga Mitiko*$_i$ *o*
self cancer is that diagnosis
zetuboo e oiyat-ta.
desperation to drive away-past
'The diagnosis that self$_i$ had a cancer drove Michiko$_i$ to desperation.'

In these examples, the antecedents, *Hirosi* and *Mitiko*, do command *zibun*, but they do not meet the subject-antecedent condition. Considering the peculiarity of emotive causative sentences such as (14),[15] she posits as the underlying structure of (14) an abstract verb construction like (16):[16]

(16)

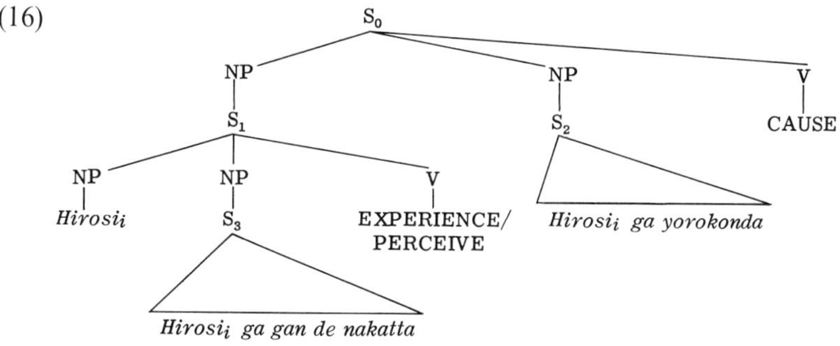

In (16), *Hirosi* under S_3 is reflexivized owing to its coreferentiality with the subject NP of S_1 on the S_1 cycle. On the S_0 cycle, *Hirosi* and the abstract verb under S_1 are deleted, and the verb *yorokonda* under S_2 is raised to the matrix verb position, deriving (14). Positing the underlying structure in (16) enabled McCawley to keep the subject-antecedent condition for reflexivization; that is, *Hirosi* under S_1 of (16) is the subject and qualifies to reflexivize *Hirosi* under S_3.

According to N. McCawley, verbs like *oiyaru*, *osieru*, and *utinomesu* in such emotive sentences as (15) are decomposable into emotive causative verb complexes, as in the following:

[15]Various characteristics of these sentences are also discussed in detail in Akatsuka (1971, 1972) and N. McCawley (1972a). What is relevant to our discussion is the relation of (14) to (18), and the fact that the object that follows the reflexive is the antecedent in (14).

[16]This is a slightly modified version of N. McCawley's (258).

osieru ≡ CAUSE NP to realize S
zetuboo e oiyaru ≡ *zetuboo s-sase-ru*
utinomesu ≡ *kanzen ni gakkari s-sase-ru*[17]

Thus, it is made possible to posit, for sentences with these verbs, underlying structures similar to (16).

It is, further, to be noted that (16) is assumed to underlie not only (14) but also sentences like (17) and (18):

(17) *Zibun$_i$ ga gan de nakatta node Hirosi$_i$ wa yorokon-da.*
as
'As self$_i$ did not have cancer, Hiroshi$_i$ was happy.'

(18) *Hirosi$_i$ wa zibun$_i$ ga gan de nakatta koto o yorokon-da.*
'Hiroshi$_i$ was happy that self$_i$ did not have cancer.'

'*Because* formation' and 'causal object formation' apply to (16), deriving (17) and (18), respectively. By doing this, McCawley claims, various syntactic peculiarities shared by the three constructions can be accounted for. For lack of space we cannot get into detailed discussion of her arguments.[18] However, a relevant observation in her discussion is that the objects of sentences like (14) and the subjects of sentences like (17) and (18) must be human noun phrases denoting perceivers or experiencers of events. This observation is formalized in terms of the abstract verb EXPERIENCE/PERCEIVE.

Kuno (1972) noted that N. McCawley's generalization has to be extended to account for such a contrast as is illustrated by (7) and (8). He maintains that this contrast is caused by the difference in the presupposition concerning awareness of the subject.

Thus, the three important works on Japanese reflexives coincide at least in one point, namely, the antecedent of the reflexive in such a sentence must be the experiencer of the event. Differences among them are seen first in their coverage of problems; that is, Kuroda and Kuno cover a wider variety of sentences, while N. McCawley limits herself to sentences with emotive verbs. Second, to account for such uses of the reflexive, Kuroda proposes the concept of a nonreportive (subject-oriented) style in which the use of the reflexive is less restricted than in the reportive (speaker-oriented) style; Kuno makes a proposal of the direct discourse analysis, and McCawley posits the abstract verb EXPERIENCE/PERCEIVE. In the present work, reflexives, *zibun*, *zisin*, *ziko*, etc., are assumed to be present in the deep structure, and coreferential relations of reflexives and their antecedents are determined by semantic interpretation rules. Together with the case Agent, the

[17]Cf. N. McCawley's (233) and (226).

[18]For an explanation of the mechanism employed in N. McCawley to derive (16), (17), and (18), readers are referred to her chapter in this volume.

Experiencer[19] may function as part of selectional restrictions on reflexives, and is called for in determining the preferred reading whenever an ambiguous reading is given to a sentence by the interpretation rules that operate on the basis of syntactic information (see Section 3).

2. THE CYCLIC PRINCIPLE AND REFLEXIVIZATION AS A TRANSFORMATION

As pointed out in Section 1, it has been proposed that Japanese reflexive *zibun* may be derived by a cyclic transformation. In this section I am going to present arguments against (a) transformational derivation of reflexives and (b) cyclic operation of both transformational and interpretive rules. The next two subsections contain semantic and syntactic arguments, respectively. These sections together present arguments against the cyclic reflexivization transformation. The arguments in the second subsection also function to refute the proposal for cyclic interpretation rules.

Reflexives as Lexical Items

I maintain, just as Helke (1971) does for English reflexive pronouns, that Japanese reflexives are not mere reflexes of their antecedents but carry their own semantic values. Not only are their semantic values felt intuitively, but also there is a substantial amount of evidence to support this intuition. First, some speakers, including myself, try to avoid as much as possible the use of *zibun*, one of the reflexives, in certain contexts, because we feel that its use has a rather direct effect of pointing to the expected self-consciousness of the event on the part of the referent of the coreferential noun, i.e., the antecedent, so that the use of *zibun* in inappropriate contexts create an impolite or impudent connotation. Take, for example, the following sentence used by Kuno (1972) and later taken up by Kuroda (1973b) for comment:

(19) [Kuno's (96a)]

John$_i$ *wa zibun*$_i$ *ga osie-te i-ru gakusei to kekkonsi-*
self teaching-is student with marry-
tagat-te i-ru yo.
wanting-is
'John wants to marry a student who he is teaching.'

[19]In this work, cases like Agent, Experiencer, Object, etc., are assumed to be semantic features carried by predicates. They are called 'semantic case features' or simply 'case features', and sometimes 'underlying cases' (see Inoue, 1972a, 1972b, 1973a, 1974a). OBJECT is used here to designate a semantic case feature assigned to a noun phrase that undergoes a change effected by a process verb. Thus, it corresponds to Gruber's Theme.

If we use *sensei* 'teacher' as the subject of (19) instead of *John*, we have to change the sentence into a polite style, as in (20), in which the boldface type indicates honorific markers added as a result of the change of the subject:

(20) *Sensei wa* ***go****-zibun ga osie-te i-****rassya****-ru gakusei to kekkon-si-tagat-te i-****rassya****-ru yo.*

The relevant point here is that even with this much honorification, some speakers, including myself, would hesitate to use this sentence, because it carries an accusatory tone to the effect that the teacher himself should be aware (i.e., directing to his own consciousness) that the student he wants to marry is his own student. Such hesitation is a reflection of the intuition that *zibun* has its own semantic value. Example (20′), without *go-zibun*, sounds quite appropriate to me. This indicates that what makes (20) inappropriate for some speakers is the use of *go-zibun*, and not the inappropriateness of the semantic content of the sentence:

(20′) *Sensei wa daigaku de osie-te i-rassya-ru gakusei to kekkon-si-tagat-te i-rassya-ru yo.*

The same intuition prompts us to use honorific *go-zibun* as a joke when addressing our superiors in nonserious situations:

(21) *Sensei wa* ***go****-zibun no kyoositu o* ***o****-wasure ni* ***nat****-ta*
teacher self classroom forget
no desu ka.
that be-polite-non-past question
'Did you forget your classroom?'

Arguing against Kuno's proposal, Kuroda (1973b) makes a comment on (19):

> For me, this sentence can be used in a situation where John wants to marry someone who I know he is teaching (perhaps in a large class at a multiuniversity) but who John himself does not realize that he is teaching, a situation that it seems to me is incompatible with the meaning to be assigned to (4) (in our (19)) in Kuno's analysis [p. 138].

Kuroda is correct in observing, in this context, the implication of awareness of the speaker of the fact, but the accusatory connotation pointed out earlier is due to the implication of the expected awareness of the subject.

Here is another example given by Kuroda to explain the use of *zibun* in the nonreportive style, i.e., subject-oriented speech:

(22) *John wa Bill ga zibun o ut-ta toki Mary no soba ni*
self hit-past time side at
tat-te i-ta.
standing was
'John was standing by Mary when Bill hit him.'

Kuroda (1973a) correctly points out that (22) would get the following reaction from a Japanese reader: '... The reader of the Japanese version would immediately adopt John's point of view in the first sentence. In particular, he would understand that when John was hit he must have been conscious of the fact—spontaneously if not reflectively—that he was standing by Mary [p. 386].' When it is changed to reportive style, *zibun* should be deleted or replaced by *kare* (he) (again Kuroda's observation).

The two interpretations, i.e., awareness of the speaker and/or the subject, are but a partial reflection of this complex problem. Furthermore, there are cases in which *zibun* appears optionally, as in (23) and (24):

(23) [Kuno, 1972: 182 (94a)]

a. *Taroo wa zibun ga komat-ta toki dake boku ni*
self in trouble time only I to
denwa-si-te ku-ru.
telephone
'Taro calls me up only when he is in trouble.'

b. *Taroo wa komat-ta toki dake boku ni denwa-si-te ku-ru.*

(24) a. *Zibun no kao o arai-nasai.*
self's face wash imperative
'Wash your own face!'

b. *Kao o arai-nasai.*
'Wash your face!'

Although there is no difference in acceptability between the (a) and (b) sentences, a semantic difference is felt, with (23a) involving the same implication as (19) and (22). Example (24a) implies the specific designation of one's own face. This use of *zibun* can be taken to be the contrastive use, but it is not very clear whether we can use this explanation for the use of *zibun* in (23a). At least this much seems clear to me; that is, *zibun* in a context like (23a) should not be omitted from our study as the contrastive use of the reflexive. The transformational theory, which accounts only for coreferential relations between the reflexive and its antecedent, is incapable of explaining such semantic differences between sentences with and without *zibun*.

We can solve this problem if we posit underlying reflexives with their own semantic contents. In this framework, acceptable and unacceptable uses of reflexives are due largely to conformity and nonconformity to selectional restrictions placed on reflexives by cooccurring elements. Stylistic distinctions also play a role in the selection of reflexives. Then we must have semantic interpretation rules to determine the coreferential relations. To do this, such rules will have to utilize syntactic information, such as the subjecthood and the command relation. After possible coreferential readings are decided, preferred readings are chosen by interpretation rules on the basis of case relations and other semantic factors (cf. Section 4).

Second, it should be pointed out that lexical items similar to *zibun* exist in Japanese, namely, *ziko* and *zisin*. The differentiations in the uses of *zibun*, *ziko*, and *zisin* depend largely on stylistic considerations. *Ziko* is used mostly in a formal style,[20] and *zisin* is appropriate with the honorific *go*, as explained before, and, thus, frequently used in an honorific style. The following is another such example:

(25) *Sensei ga go-zisin no hon o mot-te-ki-te kudasat-ta.*
teacher self 's book bring come give-honorific-past
'The teacher brought his own book (for me).'

Zisin is also used with proper nouns, for example, *Taroo-zisin*, *Yamada-san-zisin*. In such cases, *zisin* is used in nonhonorific contexts. *Zibun*, on the other hand, is more or less neutral as to stylistic distinctions.

Since all of these lexical items are reflexives, whose coreferentiality has to be identified, any transformational solution to this question meets a serious problem. The situation is similar to that obtaining between pronominalization and pronominal epithets.[21]

The third argument is concerned with the priority of Experiencer in the interpretation of antecedents of reflexives in certain contexts, which also seems to reflect their independent semantic value.

On the basis of the discussion in Section 1, let us assume, following Kuno (1971), that causatives and affective passives involve underlying complement structures, while the simple passives are derived from simplex sentences. Reflexivization is also tentatively assumed to be a cyclic transformation. Under these assumptions, we would predict that *zibun* in causatives is ambiguous concerning coreferentiality, as explained before. Causatives require unlike subjects for matrix and complement sentences, so that this is more or less a natural consequence. The following example shows that our prediction is correct:

(26) *Taroo*$_i$ *wa Ziroo*$_j$ *o zibun*$_{ij}$ *no kuruma de kaer-ase-ta.*
self's car in return-cause-past
'Taro$_i$ made (or let) Jiro$_j$ go home in self's$_{ij}$ car.'

Zibun in (26) is coreferential with either *Taroo* or *Ziroo*, as predicted. How-

[20] *Ziko* is most commonly used in formal scholarly writing. Martin has pointed out to me that *ziko* also appears in compounds like *ziko-hihan* 'self-criticism'. Other examples are *ziko-ken-o* 'self-hatred', *ziko-hon-i*, *ziko-syugi* 'egotism'.

[21] As is well known, it is impossible to derive pronominal epithets, such as 'that bastard', 'the poor fellow', etc., from underlying noun phrases, although their behaviors are similar to that of third-person pronouns.

ever, in some contexts the predicted ambiguity does not arise, at least in some dialects.[22] Observe the following:

(27) *Taroo wa Ziroo*$_i$ *ni zibun*$_i$ *no sippai o sator-ase-ta.*
self's failure realize-cause-past
'Taro made Jiro$_i$ realize his$_i$ failure.'

(28) *Taroo wa Ziroo*$_i$ *ni zibun*$_i$ *no sigoto o tanosim-ase-ta.*
self's work enjoy-cause-past
'Taro made Jiro$_i$ enjoy his$_i$ work.'

In (27) and (28), *zibun* is predominantly coreferential with the complement subjects. In the case of (29) and (30), on the other hand, the matrix subjects are given priority in the interpretation of antecedents:

(29) *Taroo*$_i$ *wa tuma o zibun*$_i$ *ga kat-ta kusuri de*
wife self buy-past medicine by
sin-ase-te simat-ta.[23]
die-cause-completive-past
'To his regret, Taro had his wife die because of the medicine he bought.'

(30) *Hanako*$_i$ *wa haha-oya o zibun*$_i$ *no hutyuui de ryuukan ni*
mother self's carelessness flu
kakar-ase-te simat-ta.
catch-cause-completive-past
'To her$_i$ regret, Hanako$_i$ had her mother catch flu through her$_i$ carelessness.'

It should be pointed out that in their complement sentences, (29′) and (30′), *zibun* is interpreted as coreferential with *tuma* and *haha-oya*, respectively. This means that no semantic oddity is involved in the coreferential reading of *zibun* with either *tuma* or *haha-oya*:

(29′) *Taroo no tuma*$_j$ *wa zibun*$_j$ *ga kat-ta kusuri de sin-de simat-ta.*
'Taro's wife died because of the medicine she bought.'

[22]Some speakers who are not very restrictive in the use of reflexives allow ambiguous readings to examples (27) and (28), but they prefer the readings indicated here by the same indexes over the other possible readings.

[23]Martin has suggested that the unique interpretation may be due to the fact that *zibun* appears in the NP denoting Instrument, because of the close relation between Agent and Instrument. However, the situation does not change in the cases in which *zibun* appears in other types of noun phrases. The following is one example:

(i) *Taroo*$_i$ *wa tuma o zibun*$_i$ *ga kat-ta bed no ue de sin-ase-te simat-ta.*
wife self buy-past on die-cause completive-past
'To his regret, Taro$_i$ had his wife die on the bed he$_i$ bought.'

(30′) *Hanako no haha-oya$_j$ wa zibun$_j$ no hutyuui de ryuukan ni kakat-te simat-ta.*
'Hanako's mother$_j$ caught flu through her$_j$ carelessness.'

Zibun in (31) and (32) does not always carry ambiguity, either, although the same prediction is made for such affective passives:[24]

(31) *Hanako$_i$ wa Taroo ni zibun$_i$ no kuruma ni nor-are-ta.*
self's car ride-passive-past
'?Taro rode in Hanako's car on her.'

(32) *Hanako$_i$ wa Taroo ni zibun$_i$ no nooto o nakus-are-ta.*
self's notebook lose-passive-past
'?Taro lost Hanako's notebook on her.'

Thus, examples (27)–(32) cannot be treated by the hypothesis of cyclic reflexivization.

The last argument in this connection is based on an observation concerning affective passives with causative complements. J. McCawley (1972b) argues, 'Indeed, affective passives of causatives appear to be ungrammatical even in cases where the meaning to be expressed would seem to demand such a combination [p. 71].' McCawley gives (33) as an example of such ungrammatical sentences:

(33) **Boku wa kanai ni Yamada-sensei o iti-zikan mo*
I wife by Prof. one hour even
mat-ase-rare-ta.
wait-cause-passive-past
'I was subjected to my wife making Prof. Yamada wait an hour.'

Example (33) is not entirely unacceptable, in the first place. The sentence would be acceptable in a context in which the wife was going to pick up Professor Yamada, the speaker at a meeting for which the subject (*boku*) was responsible. This is shown by the fact that (33) can be followed by a sentence like *Sore de kai o zikan ni hazime-rare-nakat-ta* 'Because of this (I) could not start the meeting on time.'

Second, we cannot say that affective passives of causatives are nonexistent on the basis of the questionable status of (33), because slight changes, as in (34), will make the sentence grammatical:

[24]In this work they are treated as affective passives, because the subjects of these sentences are not the objects of their active counterparts. Sentences like the following are also good affective passives:

Hanako wa Taroo ni Ziroo no nooto o nakus-are-ta.
'Taro lost Jiro's notebook to Hanako's disadvantage.'

(34) *Boku wa Yamada-sensei ni (zibun no) kanai o iti-zikan mo mat-ase-rare-ta.*
'I was subjected to Prof. Yamada making my wife wait an hour.'

In the case of (33), it is rather hard to imagine a situation in which the interests of the subject (*boku*) and *Yamada-sensei* coincide and both of them are affected by the conduct of one as closely related to the subject as his wife. In (34), *kanai* (wife) and *Yamada-sensei* are switched, thus making it possible to reconstruct a natural close relation of *boku* to *kanai*. Note, also, that *zibun* can optionally precede *kanai*. The underlying causative complement is (35), in which *boku* appears followed by the possessive particle *no*:

(35) *Yamada-sensei wa boku no kanai o iti-zikan mo*
Prof. my wife one hour even
mat-ase-ta.
wait-cause-past
'Prof. Yamada kept my wife waiting for an hour.'

Semantically, (34) is an affective passive sentence, with the subject identical with the possessor noun phrase in the complement sentence. This is also syntactically an affective passive if the criterion stated in footnote 24 is adopted. Similar examples follow:

(36) *Taroo$_i$ wa Hanako ni(zibun$_i$ no)kodomo o hatarak-ase-*
self's child work-cause-
rare-ta.
passive-past
'Taro was subjected to Hanako making his own child work.'

(37) *Hanako$_i$ wa Taroo ni(zibun$_i$ no)otooto o rakudai-s-ase-*
self's brother flunk cause-
rare-ta.
passive-past
'Hanako was subjected to Taro making her brother flunk the exam.'

The following is a tentative and informal discussion showing how these facts are semantically explained in terms of the case features Agent and Experiencer.

Because of limited space, we cannot go into a discussion of the justification of establishing Experiencer as a case feature carried by some verbs as one of their inherent semantic features.[25] In the following discussion, Experiencer is taken to be a case feature carried by verbs expressing sensation,

[25]Inoue (1974a) treats specific problems related to Experiencer.

perception, and psychological states. This case feature is copied to either the subject or the nonsubject noun phrase, and the choice between these two possibilities is made by each verb.[26] The nonsubject noun phrase, with Experiencer copied onto it, will get the case particle *ni* attached to it.

Besides these verbs, there are three types of sentences whose subjects are supposed to take the Experiencer case feature. One is the subject of an affective passive sentence, which is interpreted as the 'affectee' of the event. We can assume that the affective passive formative *rare* carries the Experiencer case feature.[27] The second is a special type of transitive sentence, the subject of which denotes the possessor of the object noun phrase undergoing the change expressed by the verb, as in:

(38) *Taroo ga yubi o kit-ta*
finger cut-past
'Taro cut his finger.'

(39) *Hanako ga ha o ot-ta*
tooth break-past
'Hanako broke her tooth.'

Although the verbs in (38) and (39), *kir-u* 'cut' and *or-u* 'break', are regular action verbs that usually require Agents for their subjects, the subjects of these sentences are not normally interpreted as Agents. They are, rather, the affectees of the events. These sentences are somehow related to (38′) and (39′), with *Taroo* and *Hanako* as possessor noun phrases.[28]

(38′) *Taroo no yubi ga kire-ta.*
'Taro's finger was cut.'

(39′) *Hanako no ha ga ore-ta.*
'Hanako's tooth broke.'

A similar situation obtains with causative sentences such as (29) and (30). The causative formative *sase* (*ase*) usually requires an Agent for its subject, but in these sentences the subjects are again affectees of the events. As was stated before, their matrix subjects are the same as the possessor noun

[26]Semantic case features carried by the verbs are copied to noun phrases (Inoue, 1972a). Perception verbs, such as *mie-ru* 'see' *kikoe-ru* 'hear', take the Experiencer followed by *ni*, while psychological verbs, such as *kizuk-u* 'notice', *sator-u* 'realize', take Experiencers as their subjects. Unless we treat morphologically complex verbs like *mie-ru*, *kikoe-ru*, and so on, as involving complementation (as in Inoue, 1973a), and derive experiencer-*ni* from an underlying experiencer-subject, we have to treat this distinction as a lexical idiosyncracy and mark the verbs as such.

[27]See Inoue (1974a) for arguments on this point.

[28]Syntactic peculiarities of sentences like (38) and (39) are discussed in Inoue (1974a). This does not necessarily mean that (38) and (39) are transformationally related to (38′) and (39′).

phrases in the complements. On the basis of this observation, we assume that the Experiencer case feature is added to the subjects on top of the original Agent case. With the newly added Experiencer reading, the Agentive reading is certainly reduced to the subject's inactive involvement in the event. Still, there is a clear semantic difference between the Agent–Experiencer and the simple Experiencer reading, as is attested by the contrast between the following examples:

(40) *Taroo ga* *tuma o ryuukan de sin-ase-ta.*
Agent-Experiencer wife flu of die-cause-past
'Taro's wife died of flu on him (but he could not prevent it).'

(41) *Taroo ga tuma ni ryuukan de sin-are-ta.*
Experiencer wife by flu of die-passive-past
'Taro's wife died of flu on him.'

With this much understood, let us try to explain the peculiarity of the coreferential relations in (27)–(37).

In (27) and (28), *zibun* is predominantly interpreted as coreferential with the complement subject *Ziroo*, with the Experiencer case feature assigned by psychological verbs, *sator-u* 'realize' and *tanosim-u* 'enjoy'. *Taroo* may be the Agent or the Cause of the event. In (29) to (32), on the other hand, the matrix subject is an Experiencer, while the complement subjects of (29), (30), and (32) are nonagentive, and that of (31) is agentive. This means that *zibun* is predominantly interpreted as coreferential to the Experiencer noun phrase, regardless of the cases of the other subjects.

The subjects of (36) and (37), *Taroo* and *Hanako*, are Experiencer noun phrases, according to our assumption. *Zibun* in these examples is, again, interpreted as coreferential to Experiencer noun phrases.[29]

When complement and matrix subjects of causatives of this kind are either Experiencers or Causes of events, ambiguity seems to remain, as in (42) and (43):

(42) *Taroo$_i$ wa Ziroo$_j$ ni ukkari zibun$_{ij}$ no kako o sator-ase-te*
unwittingly self's past realize-cause-
simat-ta.
completive-past
'Taro$_i$ unwittingly caused Jiro$_j$ to find out about his$_{ij}$ past.'

(43) *Taroo$_i$ wa Ziroo$_j$ ni zibun$_{ij}$ e no kitai o usinaw-ase-ta.*
self to hope lose-cause-past
'Taro$_i$ caused Jiro$_j$ to lose hope for him$_{ij}$.'

[29]This problem is taken up again in Section 4.

In a sentence without an Experiencer, an Agent noun phrase is so interpreted. The following examples are from Kuno (1972); they have Agents for both matrix and complement subjects:

(44) [Kuno's (85a)]
John$_i$ *wa zibun*$_i$ *ga kaita tegami o yaburi suteta*
self write-past letter tear throw away-past
'John tore and threw away the letter he wrote.'

(45) [Kuno's n16(i)]
George$_i$ *wa zibun*$_i$ *ga si-tai toki ni sigoto o suru.*
self do want time at work do-non-past
'George works only when he wants to work.'

Although it is impossible at this stage to state the roles of various other cases in semantic interpretation of reflexives, there is another rather clear situation in which the semantic case feature Object plays a negative role in the reflexive interpretation. Examples (46)–(50) are given by Kuno (1972) as not permitting the interpretation of *zibun* as coreferential with the matrix subjects:

(46) **John*$_i$ *wa, Mary ga zibun*$_i$ *ni ai ni kita toki*
self with meet to come-past when
moo sinde imasita.
already dead be-past
'John, when Mary came to see him, was already dead.'

(47) **John*$_i$ *wa Mary ga zibun*$_i$ *o miru toki wa itu mo*
self see when always
kaoiro ga warui soo da.
complexion bad I hear
'I hear that John looks pale whenever Mary sees him.'

(48) **John*$_i$ *wa zibun*$_i$ *ga sinda toki, issen mo motte*
self died when a penny have
imasen desita yo.
not did
'John didn't have a penny when he died.'

(49) **John*$_i$ *wa zibun*$_i$ *ga yopparatta toki dake, watasi ni*
self drunk-is when only I to
yasasiku narimasu.
kindly become
'John becomes tender to me only when he gets drunk.'

(50) *$John_i$ wa $zibun_i$ ga sissinsita toki, boku no oyazi no*
self fainted when I 's father's
byooin ni katugi-komaremasita.
hospital to was taken
'John was taken to my father's hospital when he fainted.'

In all of these sentences, both matrix and constituent subjects are semantically Objects, and the constituent sentences are adverbial clauses. One might suppose that the change of the constituent subjects to Agent noun phrases would rescue these sentences. This is not the case, however. Observe the following ungrammatical coreferential readings in sentences with the Agent constituent subject and the Object matrix subject:

(51) *$John_i$ wa $zibun_i$ ga sigoto ni ik-u toki wa, itu mo*
self work to go-non-past time always
kaoiro ga warui soo da.
look pale reportative non-past
'Whenever $self_i$ goes to work, $John_i$ looks pale.'

(52) *$John_i$ wa $zibun_i$ ga syoku o kae-ta toki,*
self job change-past time,
issen mo mot-te-i-masen desita yo.
a penny even have-polite-past
'When John changed his job, he did not even have a penny.'

(53) *$John_i$ wa $zibun_i$ ga ryokoo ni iku toki dake,*
self trip on go-non-past time only
watakusi ni yasasiku nari-masu.
I to
'John becomes tender to me only when he goes on a trip.'

It appears from these examples that in sentences with matrix subjects with the Object case feature, *zibun* in adverbial clauses cannot be coreferential with the matrix subject, regardless of the case assumed by the constituent subject.

It seems to be possible to set up a thematic hierarchy, with Experiencer and Agent on the top, Object at the bottom, and the other cases in the middle. Then this hierarchy will function as a mechanism for making the final adjustment of coreferential readings.[30]

The preceding is an attempt to show that some semantic factor other than

[30]See Jackendoff (1972) for a thematic hierarchy. The Source case feature seems to be rather high in this hierarchy, somewhere below the Agent. A detailed study is needed before anything definite could be proposed in this connection.

those already proposed is at work in the interpretation of the coreferential relation of reflexives with their antecedents.

Thus, there seems to be enough justification to have the reflexives, *zibun*, *ziko*, *zisin*, etc., already in the underlying structure. They are special lexical items with their own lexical specifications and [+Refl] feature, which indicates that their coreferentiality is to be determined by interpretive rules. Lexical items with [+ Refl] would be selected when the Experiencer or Agent case feature appears as a feature carried by the verb or there is some element in the sentence that requires Agent or Experiencer as the case of its subject. Stylistic distinctions, such as formal versus informal, polite versus plain, masculine versus feminine, reportive versus nonreportive, etc., seem to have to be specified in some way in the underlying structure, because they influence the choice of vocabulary.[31] These specifications also function as selectional restrictions on reflexives. Another possibility is to throw out reflexives violating selectional restrictions as semantically anomalous by interpretation rules. If such rules are worked out, they apply before the interpretation rules proposed in this chapter.

Cyclicity Questioned

In the preceding discussion, I gave three types of counterexamples to the assumption of transformational derivation of reflexives, and suggested that reflexives may be generated in the underlying structures and that their coreferentiality may be determined by interpretation rules. In order to present syntactic arguments for noncyclic interpretation rules, I have to argue against the other possible theories of reflexivization:

CT: cyclic transformation
PT: postcyclic transformation
DI: deep structure interpretation
CI: cyclic interpretation
PI: postcyclic interpretation[32]

Since Theory PI is proposed in this chapter, the first four theories will be discussed here. For this discussion, evidence is drawn from seven types of data: (a) relative clauses, (b) passives, (c) causatives, (d) causative-passives, (e) *te moraw-u* ‘ask a favor of’ sentences, (f) sentences with multiple center

[31]In Section 4 some further argument is given in connection to this problem.

[32]I have omitted the consideration of both precyclic and last-cyclic possibilities because no cases have been reported that might call for them. Deep structure transformation is not treated separately because arguments supporting the cyclic transformational approach refute the deep structure hypothesis. Comments by Bell, Haraguchi, and Martin, who read the first, sketchy version of this study, made me realize the necessity of a detailed discussion of these possibilities.

embedding,[33] and (g) complex noun phrases. Since (d), (f), and (g) have each two subclasses, we are going to examine ten types of sentences in this section.

RELATIVE CLAUSES

Cyclic Transformation and Cyclic Interpretation.

(54) *Taroo*$_i$ *ga zibun*$_{ij}$ *no kodomo o sinsatu-si-ta isya*$_j$ *o*
self's child examine-past doctor
sonkei-si-ta.
respect-past
'Taro$_i$ respected the doctor$_j$ who examined self's$_{ij}$ child.'

In (54), *zibun* is ambiguous between two readings, as coreferential with either Taro or the doctor. Assuming that the antecedent of a reflexive is the subject and commands the reflexive, let us follow the cyclic transformational derivation with the help of (54′), a schematic representation of the underlying structure of (54):

(54′)

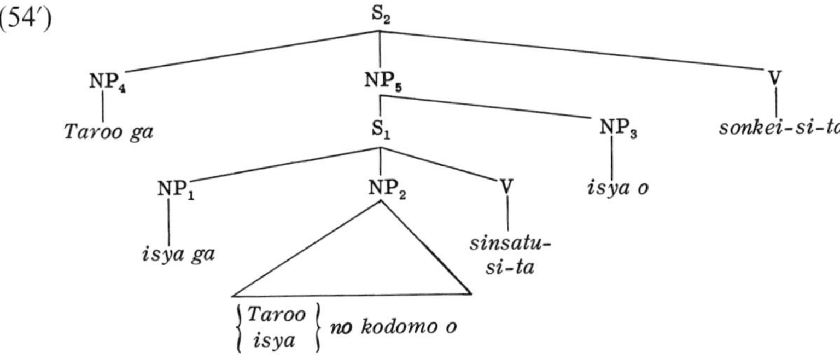

If *Taroo* appears under S_1, nothing happens on the S_1 cycle, but it gets reflexivized on the S_2 cycle. If, on the other hand, *isya* appears under S_1, it is reflexivized on the S_1 cycle. Hence the ambiguity. This type of sentence was used as evidence for the cyclic nature of reflexivization. Even though no one has yet proposed cyclic interpretive rules (Theory CI) for Japanese reflexives, it is obvious that this will be used as crucial evidence for their cyclicity. The argument will go as follows: Because *isya* under NP_3, which is the head NP of the relative clause S_1, is not the subject, it cannot be the antecedent for *isya* under NP_2 after NP_1 is deleted by relativization. With the assumption of cyclicity, reflexivization will take place on the S_1 cycle, at the stage when *isya* under NP_1, the subject of S_1, is still present.

[33]The term CENTER EMBEDDING is from Kuno (1974a).

Postcyclic Transformation. This theory fails to account for the ambiguity involved in active sentences such as (54). The derived structure of (54) when the cycles are over will look like the following:

(55)

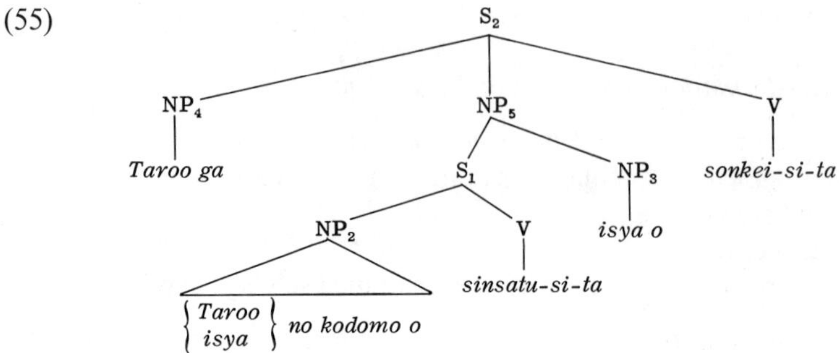

Taroo under NP_2 will be reflexivized because of the presence of *Taroo* (under NP_4) as the subject of S_2. If *isya* appears under NP_2, reflexivization is inapplicable, since the identical noun phrase is under the nonsubject noun phrase (NP_3). Thus, Theory PT is not capable of accounting for the ambiguity of (54).[34]

Deep Structure Interpretation. Theory DI establishes coreferential relations on the basis of the deep structure in (54′), so it successfully accounts for the ambiguity of (54).

PASSIVES

Cyclic Transformation and Cyclic Interpretation. Now, observe (56), which is the passive counterpart of (54):

(56) *Zibun$_j$ no kodomo o sinsatu-si-ta isya$_j$ ga Taroo ni sonkei-s-are-ta.*
'The doctor$_j$ who examined self's$_j$ child was respected by Taro.'

In (56), *zibun* is uniquely interpreted as coreferential with *isya*. Example (57) is a similar active–passive pair:

(57) a. *Taroo$_i$ ga zibun$_{ij}$ no heya ni i-ta gakusei$_j$ ni soto e*
self's room in be-past student to out to
de-ru yoo ni it-ta.
go-non-past to tell-past

[34]Theory PT is the only one among the four theories that is incapable of accounting for sentences like (54), i.e., active sentences with relative clauses.

'Taro$_i$ told the students$_j$ who were in self's$_{ij}$ room to go out.'

b. *Zibun*$_j$ *no heya ni i-ta gakusei*$_j$ *ga Taroo ni soto e de-ru yoo ni iw-are-ta.*
tell-passive-past
'The students$_j$ who were in self's$_j$ room were told to go out by Taro.'

Now, these are apparent counterexamples to theories of cyclicity, both transformational and interpretive. However, these theories can be saved by hypothesizing simple passive transformation, which switches the subject and the object, and by ordering passivization before reflexivization. According to this hypothesis, reflexivization takes place on the S_1 cycle, changing *isya* to *zibun* if *isya* appears under NP_2 of (54′). On the second cycle, passivization brings NP_5 to the subject position and NP_4 to the position vacated by NP_5. If *Taroo* appears under NP_2, the structure at this stage looks like the following:

(54″)

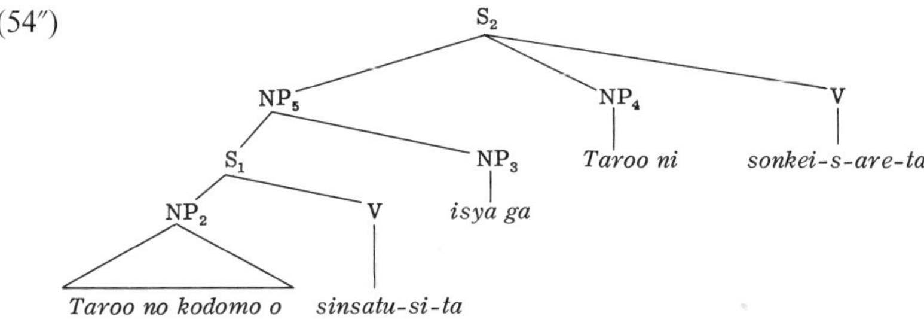

Since reflexivization is ordered after passivization, *Taroo* under NP_4 no longer qualifies as the antecedent of *zibun*. Consequently, there is only one possible interpretation for (56), namely, that *zibun* is coreferential only with *isya*. This is consistent with the facts about (56). Thus, such passive sentences do not provide evidence against Theories CT and CI.

Postcyclic Transformation. Let us assume that (54″) is the structure after all cyclic transformations are applied. Postcyclic reflexivization is then supposed to apply to this structure. Strictly speaking, NP_3 in (54″) is not the subject of S_2 by itself. However, let us assume the subjecthood of the head (NP_3 in this case) of the subject noun phrase (NP_5). Then, reflexivization applies if *isya* appears under NP_2, because NP_3 is the subject. If, on the other hand, *Taroo* appears under NP_2, as in (54″), it cannot be reflexivized, because *Taroo* is no longer the subject. Thus, Theory PT accounts for the unique interpretation of (56).

Deep Structure Interpretation. In this case, reflexivization applies to deep structure (54′), with *zibun* under NP_2. And this reflexive will be interpreted as coreferential with either *Taroo* or *isya*, because both of them appear as the subjects in the deep structure. Since the deep structure interpretation theory is blind to all subsequent syntactic changes, it fails to account for the unique interpretation of the reflexive in (56), the passive counterpart of (54).

CAUSATIVES

Regular Causatives: Cyclic Transformation and Cyclic Interpretation. Regular causatives provide strong evidence for the theory of cyclicity, both transformational and interpretive. Discussion is omitted here, since a detailed argument for this theory was given in Section 1.

Regular Causatives: Postcyclic Transformation. This theory fails to account for ambiguity involved in causative sentences such as (9):

(9) *Taroo*$_i$ *wa kodomo*$_j$ *o zibun*$_{ij}$ *no heya de benkyoo-s-ase-ta.*
child self's room in study-cause-past
'Taro$_i$ made (or let) his child$_j$ study in his$_{ij}$ room.'

The underlying structure in (10) is changed to (10′) at the time reflexivization applies, according to this theory:

(10)

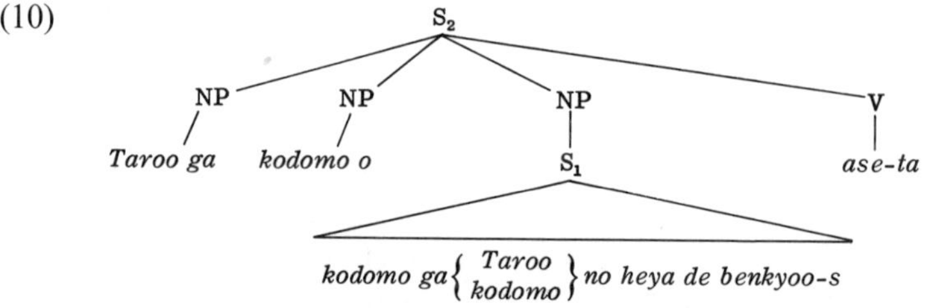

(10′)

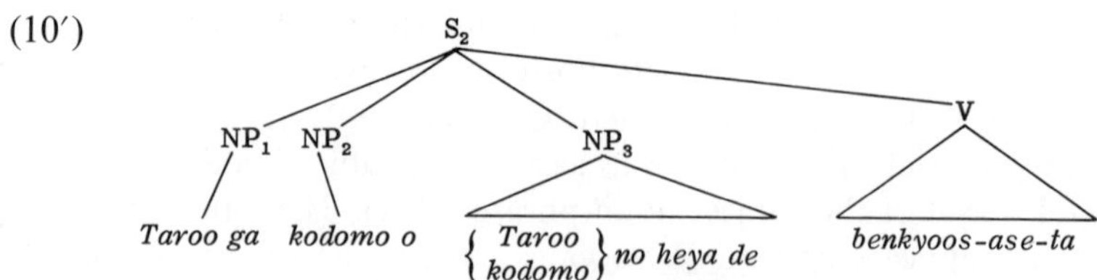

Now, *Taroo* under NP_3 can be reflexivized, but *kodomo* cannot, because *kodomo* as the object noun phrase (NP_2) is not qualified to be its antecedent. Thus, Theory PT fails to explain the ambiguity of coreferentiality in (9).

Regular Causatives: Deep Structure Interpretation. With a deep structure such as (10), Theory DI successfully interprets *zibun no* under S_1 to be coreferential with either *Taroo* or *kodomo.*

Causatives with Psychological Verbs: Cyclic Transformation. There have been interesting arguments about the derivation of causatives that crucially involve psychological verbs. The fact was first noted by Akatsuka (now N. McCawley) and extensively discussed in her chapter in this volume. Example (58) is from Akatsuka (1972):

(58) *Arisu wa zibun ga otokonoko ni moteru koto o yorokonda.*
she boys with popular that pleased, happy
'Alice was pleased (happy) that she was popular with boys.'

The causative version of (58) is (59):

(59) *Zibun ga otokonoko ni moteru koto ga Arisu o yorokobaseta.*
'That she was popular with boys pleased Alice.'

Let us assume that sentences like (58) and (59) are related, setting aside the problem of how to relate them. First, observe that the sentences in the following pair are equivalent in terms of the coreferentiality readings of *zibun*:

(60) a. *Hanako*$_i$ *wa Taroo*$_j$ *ga zibun*$_{ij}$ *no kuruma de dekake-ta*
self's car in go out-past
koto o sinpai-si-ta.
that worry-past.
'Hanako$_i$ was worried that Taroo$_j$ went out in self's$_{ij}$ car.'
b. *Taroo*$_i$ *ga zibun*$_{ij}$ *no kuruma de dekake-ta koto ga Hanako*$_j$ *o sinpai-sase-ta.*
worry-cause-past
'That Taro$_i$ went out in self's$_{ij}$ car worried Hanako$_j$.'

In both cases, *zibun* is ambiguous between the readings of *Taroo* and *Hanako.* However, the same situation does not obtain in (61):

(61) a. *Hanako*$_i$ *wa zibun*$_{ij}$ *no kuruma de dekake-ta tomodati*$_j$
self's car in go out-past friend
(no koto)[35] *o sinpai-si-ta*
worry-past
'Hanako$_i$ worried about the friend$_j$ who went out in self's$_{ij}$ car.'

[35]Kuno (in this volume) discusses the optional appearances of *koto* after human nouns. It appears mostly with the object human noun phrases of verbs of feeling, thinking, and saying.

b. *Zibun*$_j$ *no kuruma de dekake-ta tomodati*$_j$ *ga Hanako o sinpai-sase-ta.*
worry-cause-past
'The friend$_j$ who went out in self's$_j$ car worried Hanako.'

According to Theory CT, the underlying structure of (61) is supposed to be like (61′):

(61′)

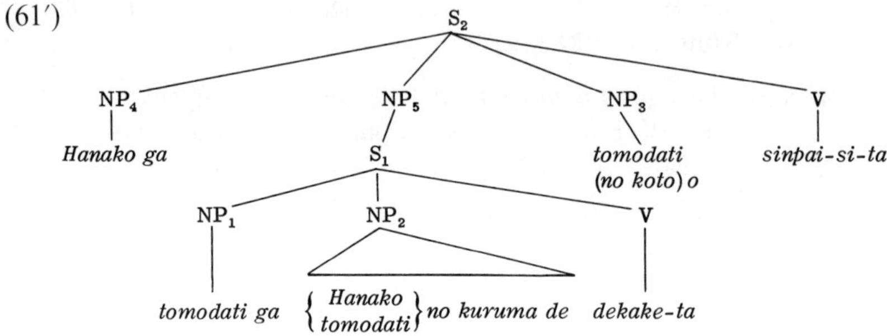

If *tomodati* is chosen under NP_2, it will be reflexivized in the first cycle, because the subject of the relative clause is also *tomodati*. If *Hanako* appears instead under NP_2, it will be reflexivized in the second cycle, because of its identity with the subject of S_2, *Hanako*.

Even though N. McCawley does not deal with sentences with relative clauses, we might propose the following underlying structure for both (61a) and (61b) on the basis of her general line of argument. Let us call this Theory CT-1:

(61″)

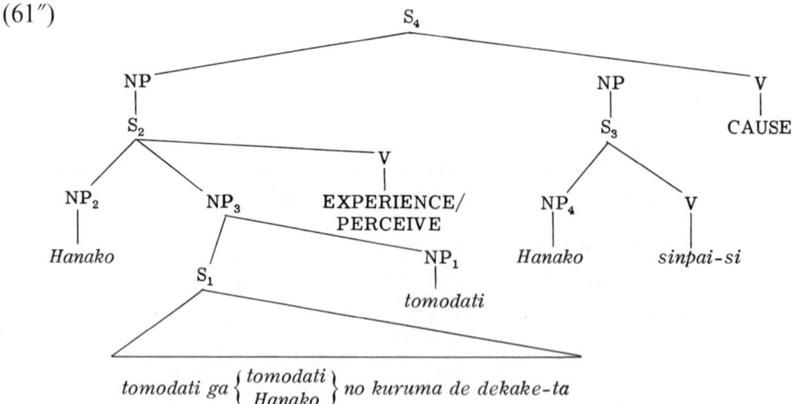

In this theory the ambiguity of (61a) is accounted for in the following way:

Tomodati and *Hanako* under S_1 are reflexivized on the S_1 and S_2 cycles, respectively. After deletion of *tomodati*, the subject of S_1, by relativization, *Hanako* (NP_2), the subject, and PERCEIVE/EXPERIENCE, the verb, of S_2 get deleted. At this stage causal object formation applies, bringing NP_3 after NP_4. Then verb raising and pruning of S_2 and S_3 will derive (61a).

Example (61b), the causative version of (61a), poses a serious problem, because it requires that reflexivization on the S_2 cycle, which reflexivizes *Hanako* under S_1 owing to its identity with the S_2 subject, be suspended until after this subject, *Hanako* (NP_2), is deleted. Otherwise, both *Hanako* and *tomodati* in (61b) would have the coreferential relation with the reflexive. It is now obvious that the derivations of (61a) and (61b) are in direct conflict with each other. To account for (61a), reflexivization must take place before the deletion of NP_2, the subject of S_2. And this is what N. McCawley assumes for all cases of backward reflexivization.[36] Now, to account for (61b), the deletion of this subject must be carried out before reflexivization. Thus, Theory CT-1 fails to account for certain causatives with psychological verbs.

If (62) is assumed to be the underlying structure of (61b), with (61′) as its complement (S_2), Theory CT cannot block the derivation of *zibun* on the basis of the identity of two *Hanako*'s on the S_2 cycle. Let us call this Theory CT-2:

(62)

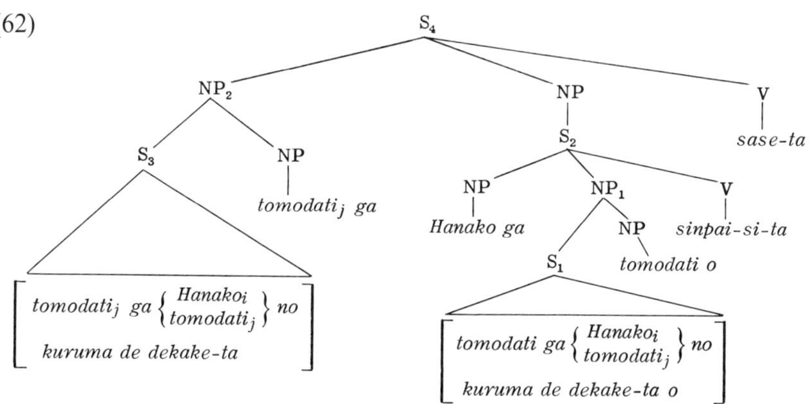

At the end of the S_2 cycle, either *Hanako* (*no*) or *tomodati* (*no*) under S_1 is reflexivized, followed by relativization, which deletes the subject (*tomodati*) of S_1. Next, on the S_3 cycle reflexivization applies, changing *tomodati* (*no*) to *zibun* (*no*). Then, on the S_4 cycle, relativization deletes the subject of S_3,

[36]Forward reflexivization has the antecedent precede the reflexive, backward reflexivization the reverse.

tomodati. At this stage, *zibun* appears under S_1 with either *tomodati* or *Hanako* as its antecedent, and *zibun* under S_3 is derived with *tomodati* as its only possible antecedent. Now, the structure at this stage is something like (62′):

(62′)

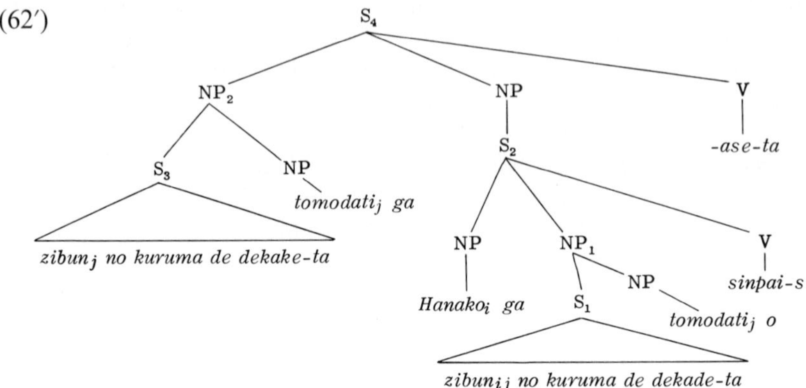

Now, NP_2 and NP_1 look exactly the same, except the indexes attached to *zibun*. For equi-NP deletion to apply to derive (61b), *zibun*$_j$ under S_1 is chosen, but *zibun*$_i$ must be thrown out, since *zibun* under NP_2 can never be coreferential with *Hanako*.[37]

Assuming this underlying structure, Theory CT-2 successfully accounts for the difference between the (a) and (b) sentences of (61) in reflexivization possibilities. However, (62), as the underlying structure for causatives in general, is at best problematic, since causatives with the same noun phrases for the matrix subject and complement object are ungrammatical. Example (63a) is a causative sentence with (63b) as its complement:

(63) a. **Otooto*$_i$ *ga Taroo ni zibun*$_i$ *o kyooiku-s-ase-ta.*
brother self educate-cause-past
'His brother made Taro educate him.'

b. *Taroo ga otooto o kyooiku-si-ta.*
'Taro educated his brother.'

To solve this problem, we can posit an underlying structure like (64) for causative sentences with psychological verbs, deriving sentences like (61b) by copying NP_1 in the position occupied by a dummy symbol under NP_2. Let us call this Theory CT-3:

[37]Thus, S_1, dominating *zibun*$_i$ is never deleted under identity with S_3. Since an obligatory transformation, equi-NP deletion, cannot apply, this string is thrown out as an ill-formed underlying structure.

(64)

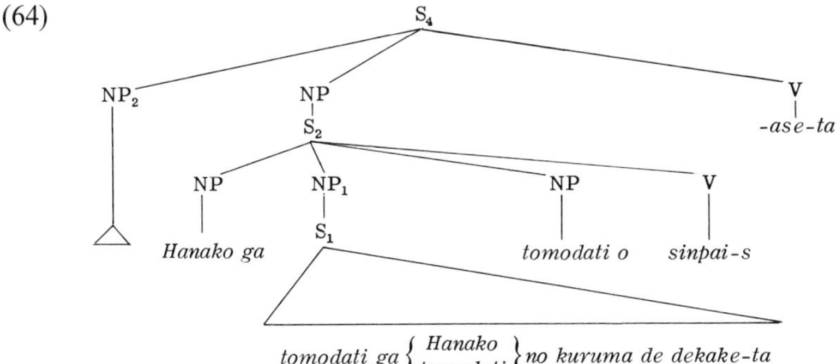

Now, the ambiguous reading of *zibun* assigned on the S_1 cycle will be carried over to NP_2, so that the unique interpretation of (61b) cannot be accounted for by this theory. Thus, causative sentences with psychological verbs work as counterexamples to all three versions of Theory CT.

Causatives with Psychological Verbs: Postcyclic Transformation. Regardless of which deep structure is chosen, the derived structure to which postcyclic reflexivization applies would be like (65):

(65) a. [for (61a)]

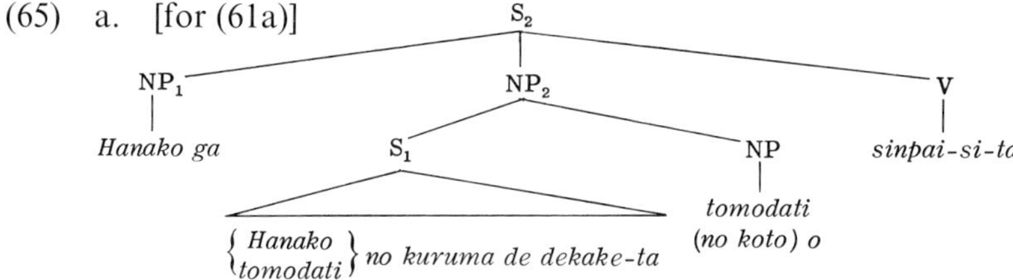

b. [for (61b)]

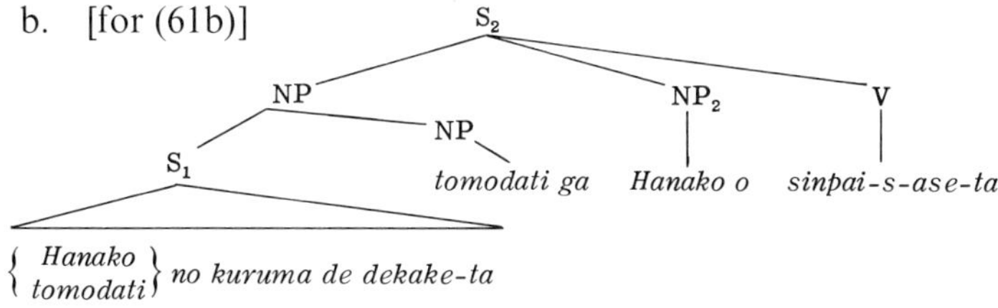

In (65a), *Hanako* under S_1 can be turned into *zibun* because of the identity with NP_1, but there is no way of deriving *zibun* from *tomodati* under S_1. Thus, Theory PT fails to account for the ambiguity of (61a). The unique coreferentiality in (61b), on the other hand, is successfully accounted for by Theory PT, because in (65b), NP_1 (*tomodati*), being the subject of S_2, triggers reflexivization of *tomodati* under S_1, while NP_2 (*Hanako*) does not. However, Theory PT cannot account for causatives with psychological verbs such as (60b), because in the derived structure *Hanako* is no longer the subject.

Causative with Psychological Verbs: Deep Structure Interpretation. Theory DI, with a deep structure similar to (61′), explains the ambiguous reading of (61a) but not the unique interpretation of (61b). With a deep structure similar to (61″), it again takes care of (61a) but not (61b). And lastly, the deep structure assumed by Theory CT-2 or CT-3 [(62) or (64)] will make Theory DI suffer from the same difficulty as that encountered by CT-2 and CT-3.

Causatives with Psychological Verbs: Cyclic Interpretation. Theory CI shares the strengths and weaknesses of Theory CT.

CAUSATIVE PASSIVES

Cyclic Transformation and Cyclic Interpretation. Examples (66) and (67) are causatives, which, as predicted by Theory CT, permit an ambiguous coreferential reading of *zibun*:

(66) *Gakubutyoo*$_i$ *wa Tanaka-san*$_j$ *ni zibun*$_{ij}$ *no kuruma de*
Mr. self's car in
Nakazima-kyoozyu o mukae-ni ik-ase-ta.
Prof. go and get-cause-past
'The dean$_i$ made Mr. Tanaka$_j$ go and get Prof. Nakajima in self's$_{ij}$ car.'

(67) *Tanaka-san*$_i$ *wa gakusei*$_j$ *ni zibun*$_{ij}$ *no peepaa o taipu-s-ase-ta.*
student self's paper type-cause-past
'Mr. Tanaka$_i$ made a student$_j$ type self's$_{ij}$ paper.'

From this we would expect that (68) and (69) involve the same ambiguity, since (66) and (67) appear as their complements:

(68) *Tanaka-san*$_i$ *wa gakubutyoo ni zibun*$_i$ *no kuruma de Nakazima-kyoozyu o mukae-ni ik-ase-rare-ta.*
cause-passive-past
'Mr. Tanaka$_i$ was made to go and get Prof. Nakajima in self's$_i$ car by the dean.'

(69) *Gakusei*$_i$ *wa Tanaka-san*$_j$ *ni zibun*$_{i(j)}$ *no peepaa o taipu-s-ase-rare-ta.*
'A student$_i$ was made to type self's$_{i(j)}$ paper by Mr. Tanaka.'[38]

Contrary to our expectation, *zibun* does not carry ambiguity in (68): It is uniquely interpreted as coreferential with *Tanaka-san*. Now, let us follow Theory CT in its derivation of *zibun*. The following is a schematic representation of its underlying structure:

(70)

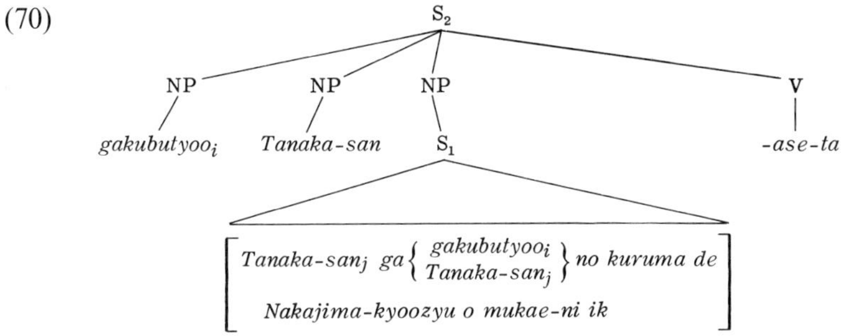

In (70), with *gakubutyoo* under S_1, nothing happens on the S_1 cycle. If *Tanaka-san* appears under S_1, reflexivization applies to it, changing it to *zibun*. *Gakubutyoo* under S_1, on the other hand, will be reflexivized on the S_2 cycle, because it is coreferential with the subject of S_2. Thus, at the end of the S_2 cycle *zibun* is derived from two sources. This is the structure to which the simple passive transformation applies.[39] Now, by ordering this transformation before reflexivization, as stated before, that is, by passivizing (70) before changing *gakubutyoo* under S_1 into *zibun* on the S_2 cycle, Theory CT can account for the unique interpretation of (68), because by the time reflexivization applies *gakubutyoo* has lost its subjecthood.

However, in the case of (69) some native speakers allow two readings. The difference of such native intuition may be crucially dependent on syntactic information such as the object of a sentence,[40] since in (69) *zibun* appears in the object noun phrase, while in (68) it appears in an adverbial phrase.

Some more examples similar to both kinds follow. Let us call (68) and (69) Type A and Type B, respectively, and group similar examples under these headings. In the following, the (a) sentences are causatives and the (b) sentences causative passives.

[38]Parentheses indicate the possibility of ambiguous readings.

[39]There may be a question as to whether (68) is a simple passive or an affective passive. However, let us assume that it is a simple passive, since the passive subject *Tanaka-san* is the indirect object of the causative complement.

[40]This point is developed in Section 3.

Type A.

(71) a. *Katyoo$_i$ wa Tanaka-san$_j$ o zibun$_{ij}$ no hiyoo de*
section chief self's expense at
syuttyoo sase-ta.
go on official trip cause-past
'The chief of the section made Mr. Tanaka go on an official trip at his expense.'

b. *Tanaka-san$_j$ wa katyoo ni zibun$_j$ no hiyoo de syuttyoo sase-rare-ta.*
'Mr. Tanaka$_j$ was made to go on an official trip at his$_j$ own expense by the chief of the section.'

(72) a. *Satoo$_i$ wa Tanaka$_j$ ni zibun$_{ij}$ no ie de paatii o s-ase-ta.*
house at cause-past
'Sato$_i$ made Tanaka$_j$ have a party at self's$_{ij}$ house.'

b. *Tanaka$_j$ wa Sato ni zibun$_j$ no ie de paatii o s-ase-rare-ta.*
'Tanaka$_j$ was made to have a party at his$_j$ house.'

Type B.

(73) a. *Oyazi$_i$ wa boku$_j$ ni zibun$_{ij}$ no kuruma o araw-ase-ta.*
Dad I self's car wash-cause-past
'Dad$_i$ made me$_j$ wash self's$_{ij}$ car.'

b. *Boku$_j$ wa oyazi$_i$ ni zibun$_{j(i)}$ no kuruma o araw-ase-rare-ta.*
'I$_j$ was made to wash self's$_{j(i)}$ car by Dad$_i$.'

(74) a. *Haha$_i$ wa Taroo$_j$ ni zibun$_{ij}$ no ryokoo-keikaku o*
self's tour plans
tate-sase-ta.
make-cause-past
'Mother$_i$ made Taro$_j$ work out self's$_{ij}$ tour plans.'

b. *Taroo$_j$ wa haha$_i$ ni zibun$_{j(i)}$ no ryokoo-keikaku o tate-sase-rare-ta.*
'Taro$_j$ was made to work out self's$_{j(i)}$ tour plans by his mother.'

If this intuition about Type B sentences is correct, they cannot be accounted for by ordering reflexivization after simple passivization. The distinction between Theory CT-1 and CT-2 and CT-3 is eliminated by this type of data, because there is no reason why Theory CT-1 should set up a deep structure of causatives different from that underlying (66) or (67).

Postcyclic Transformation. Theory PT will be capable of deriving reflexives in (68) correctly, with *Tanaka-san* as the only possible antecedent, because by the time it applies *gakubutyoo* has already lost its subjecthood by the previous application of passivization. This, in turn, makes Theory PT incapable of deriving *zibun* in (66) from two sources, since at the time of reflexivization *Tanaka-san* is no longer the subject [(66) is an example of regular causatives].

Deep Structure Interpretation. To Theory DI, only the deep structure represented as (70) is available for the interpretation of (66) and (68), so that it successfully assigns an ambiguous reading to (66) but fails to account for the unique reading of (68).

SENTENCES WITH *te moraw-u*

With Causative Complements. Next we will observe the case in which both Type A and Type B are counterexamples to the cyclicity hypothesis, both transformational (Theory CT) and interpretive (Theory CI):

Type A.

(68′) *Tanaka-san*$_j$ *wa gakubutyoo ni zibun*$_j$ *no kuruma de Nakazima-kyoozyu o mukae-ni ik-ase-te morat-ta.*
ask a favor of-past
'Mr. Tanaka$_j$ asked the favor of the dean to let him go and get Prof. Nakajima in his$_j$ car.'

(71′) *Tanaka-san*$_j$ *wa katyoo ni zibun*$_j$ *no hiyoo de syuttyoo-s-ase-te morat-ta.*
'Mr. Tanaka$_j$ had the chief permit him to go on an official trip on his$_j$ own expense.'

(72′) *Tanaka*$_j$ *wa Satoo ni zibun*$_j$ *no ie de paatii o s-ase-te morat-ta.*
'Tanaka$_j$ had Sato let him have a party at his$_j$ own house.'

Type B.

(69′) *Gakusei*$_j$ *wa Tanaka-san ni zibun*$_j$ *no peepaa o taipu-s-ase-te morat-ta.*
'The student$_j$ had Mr. Tanaka permit him to type his$_j$ paper.'

(74′) *Taroo*$_j$ *wa haha ni zibun*$_j$ *no ryokoo-keikaku o tate-sase-te morat-ta.*
'Taro$_j$ had his mother permit him to make his$_j$ tour plans.'

All of these examples show that one of the ambiguous coreferential relations, once established on the lower cycle, has to be canceled on the cycle above. Take, for example, (68), which permits *zibun* to be coreferential with either *gakubutyoo* or *Tanaka-san* at the end of the second cycle. If this is embedded in the *te moraw-u* sentence,[41] as in (69), the reading of *gakubutyoo* as the antecedent of *zibun* is not permitted. This means that the hypothesis of cyclicity of reflexivization can hardly be maintained. Here the distinction among Theories CT-1, CT-2, and CT-3 is eliminated.

As in the case of causative passives, Theory PT is capable, and Theory DI incapable, of giving nonambiguous readings to *te moraw-u* sentences.

Other Types of Complements. The same situation obtains with *te moraw-u* sentences with other types of complements. Observe the following:

(75) a. *Gakubutyoo*$_i$ *ga gakusei*$_j$ *ni zibun*$_{ij}$ *no heya de syorui o*
dean student self's room in documents
seiri-su-ru koto o yurusi-ta.
put in order-non-past that permit-past
'The dean$_i$ permitted the students$_j$ to put the documents in order in self's$_{ij}$ room.'

b. *Tanaka-san*$_k$ *wa gakubutyoo*$_i$ *ni gakusei*$_j$ *ga zibun*$_{kj}$ *no heya de syorui o seiri-su-ru koto o yurusi-te morat-ta.*
'Mr. Tanaka$_k$ asked a favor of the dean$_i$ to permit the students$_j$ to put the documents in order in self's$_{kj}$ room.'

(76) a. *Hanako*$_i$ *ga kodomo-tati*$_j$ *ni zibun*$_{ij}$ *no kaban o mot-te-*
children self's bag bring
ku-ru yoo ni it-ta.
come-non-past to tell-past
'Hanako$_i$ told the children$_j$ to bring self's$_{ij}$ bag.'

b. *Taroo wa*$_k$ *Hanako*$_i$ *ni (kara) kodomo-tati*$_j$ *ga zibun*$_{kj}$ *no kaban o mot-te-ku-ru yoo ni it-te morat-ta.*
'Taro$_k$ asked a favor of Hanako$_i$ to tell the children$_j$ to bring self's$_{kj}$ bag.'

In both (75) and (76), the (a) sentences permit the noun phrases with the indexes *i* and *j*, but in the (b) sentences, with the (a) sentences as complements, the noun phrases with the index *i*, *gakubutyoo* and *Hanako*, do not work as the antecedents of *zibun*. To see that such data are also counterexamples to the hypothesis of cyclicity, let us trace the derivation of (75) from the underlying structure in (77):

[41] We assume here that *te moraw-u* involves complementation. If we are to derive it by movement transformations and addition of *te-moraw-u*, it is hard to account for its specific semantic value and selectional restrictions between the subject, the indirect object, and *te moraw-u*.

(77)

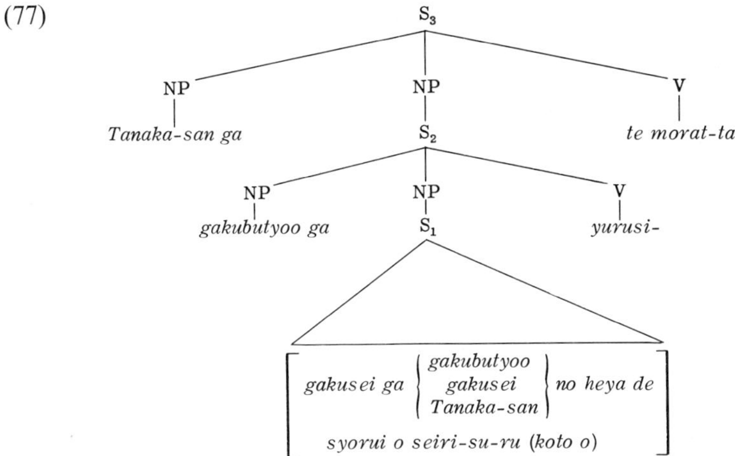

According to Theory CT, *gakusei no* under S_1 is reflexivized on the S_1 cycle, while *gakubutyoo no* will be turned to *zibun no* on the S_2 cycle. Hence the ambiguity of (75a). Next, on the S_3 cycle, *Tanaka-san* qualifies as the antecedent of the reflexive. This means that we would expect, on the basis of Theory CT, that (75b) involves three-way ambiguity, i.e., *Tanaka-san*, *gakubutyoo*, or *gakusei* as the antecedent of the reflexive. As pointed out before, this expectation is not supported by the data, in which only two noun phrases are interpreted as the antecedents. Since there is no way of blocking the noun phrases with the index *i* from working as the antecedents in the (b) sentences of (75) and (76), Theories CT and CI face a serious difficulty.

Theory PT, on the other hand, successfully accounts for two-way ambiguity involved in the (b) sentences of (75) and (76), since the structure to which reflexivization applies will be something like (78):

(78)

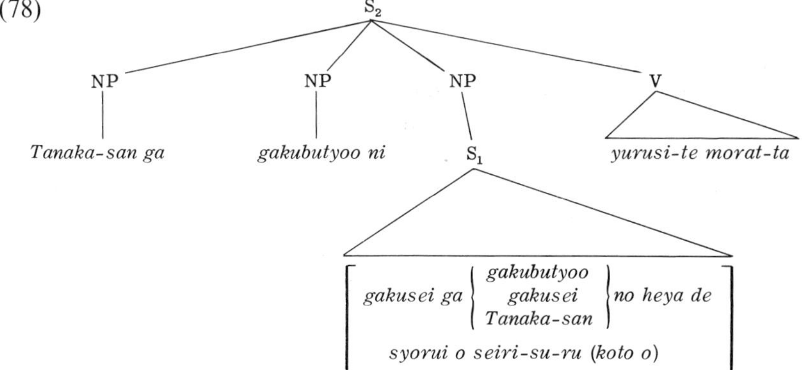

In (78), only *Tanaka-san* and *gakusei*, the subjects of the matrix and complement sentences, are qualified to be the antecedents of the reflexive, since *gakubutyoo* has already lost its subjecthood at this stage. Hence, the only possibility is two-way ambiguity.

Theory DI, with a deep structure like (77), will interpret *zibun* under S_1 as three ways ambiguous, since at this stage the three noun phrases are still qualified to be the antecedents. Thus, it is clear that this theory makes a false prediction.

SENTENCES WITH MULTIPLE CENTER EMBEDDING

Observe the following sentences of very low acceptability:

(79) ?**Taroo*$_i$ *wa watasi*$_j$ *ga Hanako*$_k$ *ga Ziroo ni zibun*$_{ijk}$ *no*
kuruma o kasi-ta to omot-ta to it-ta.
car lend-past that think-past that say-past
'Taro$_i$ said that I$_j$ thought that Hanako$_k$ let Jiro have self's$_{ijk}$ car.'

Unlike the English sentence, the Japanese version of (79) has an underlying structure with three center embeddings, as shown schematically by (80):

(80)

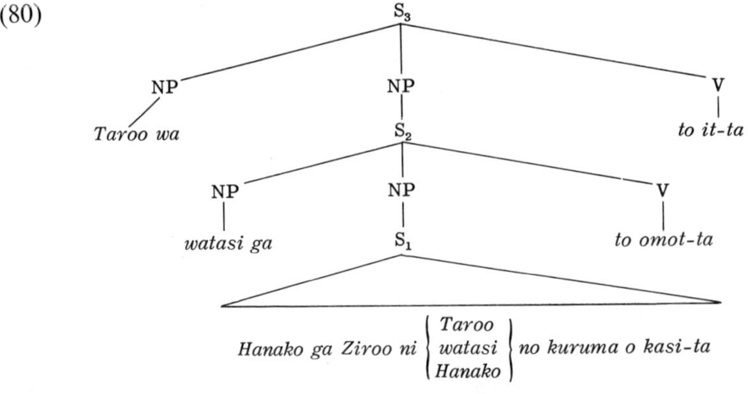

Since the center embedding reduces the acceptability radically, the sentence may be rejected regardless of whether the coreferentiality of *zibun* is decidable or not. Let us call this the center-embedding constraint. However, the crucial point here is that native speakers try to interpret sentences like (79) by placing a long pause after *Taroo wa.* This means that a long pause gives him a chance to reanalyze the sentence, so that he can start his interpretation with *watasi* as the first qualified element of the newly analyzed sentence. This suggests that the interpretation of reflexives is not a cyclic process, nor given to the deep structure, but heavily dependent on the structure very close to the surface.

Our next and more important argument in this connection is based on the comparison of sentences like (79) with causatives:

(81) *Taroo*$_i$ *wa Ziroo*$_j$ *ga Hanako*$_k$ *ni zibun*$_{ijk}$ *no kutu o*
shoes
migak-ase- te i- ru to omot-ta.
polish-cause-progressive-non-past that think-past
'Taro$_i$ thought that Jiro$_j$ was making Hanako$_k$ polish self's$_{ijk}$ shoes.'

(82)

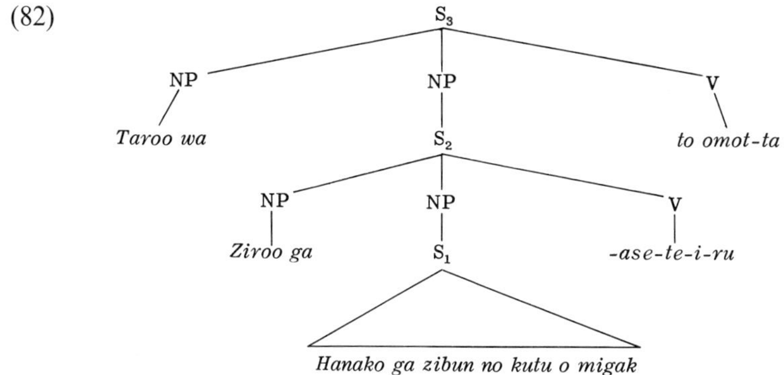

As shown by (82), (81) involves three center embeddings, but this sentence is far better, and in it *zibun* is far more easily interpreted as three ways ambiguous than in (79), with the same number of center embeddings. The center-embedding constraint does not explain this difference. What seems to be operative here is the number of S nodes in the structure close to the surface. In (79), the three underlying S nodes are retained in the derived structure, which is indicated by the appearance of the three noun phrases with the subject particle *ga* and the three finite verbs.[42] In (81), on the other hand, S_1 is pruned after the verb *migak* (polish) is raised to S_2, so that only two S nodes, i.e., S_2 and S_3, appear in the structure close to the surface, as shown in (83):

(83)

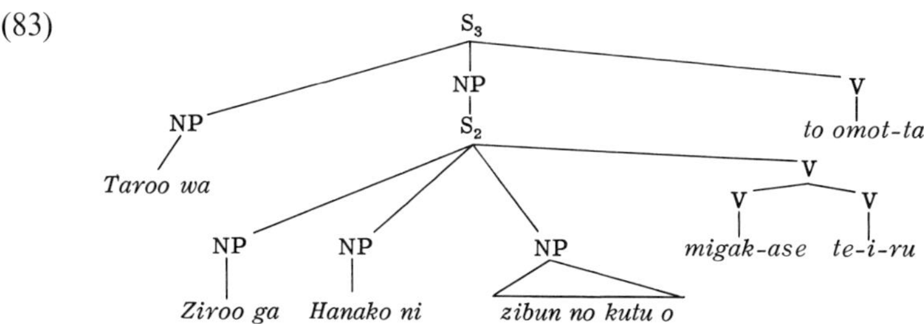

This strongly suggests that the interpretation of coreferentiality is not dependent on the underlying structure. This is a strong argument against Theory DI. And since the cyclic principle makes crucial use of underlying

[42]By a 'finite verb' I mean a verb affixed with tense.

S nodes, this is also an argument against Theories CT and CI. Postcyclic theories, PT and PI (our theory), do well in this respect.

COMPLEX NOUN PHRASES[43]

Relative Clauses of a Special Type. In certain contexts, Japanese relative clauses have reflexives and pronominals coreferential with their head noun phrases. Here we are not concerned with this phenomenon in general, but are concerned specifically with the reflexives within relative clauses that can be handled by none of the four theories under discussion. First, observe (84):

(84) *Yamada-sensei wa zibun*$_i$ *no ie ga yake-ta*
self 's house be burned down-past
gakusei$_i$ *o atume-ta.*
students gather-past
'Prof. Yamada gathered the students whose houses were burned down.'

Furthermore, in Japanese, relativization out of a relative clause is possible under certain conditions.[44] Thus, (85) is a grammatical sentence:

(85) *Katoo-si wa zibun*$_i$ *ga osie-te i-ta* *gakusei ga*
self teach-progressive-past student
zisatu-si-ta *sensei*$_i$ *ni ai-ni it-ta.*
suicide commit-past teacher meet to go-past
'Mr. Kato went to see the teacher$_i$ who the student self$_i$ was teaching committed suicide.'

In either of these cases, the antecedent, *gakusei* 'students' in (84), *sensei* 'teacher' in (85), is not the subject in the deep structure, nor is it the subject at any level of derivation. To see this, let us take a look at their deep structure representations, (84′) and (85′):

(84′)

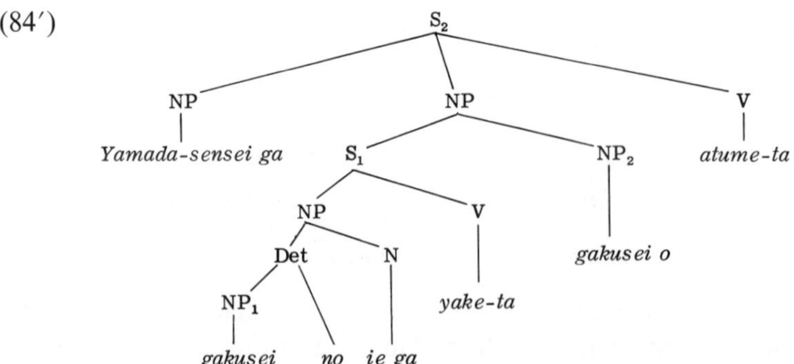

[43]Relative clauses and appositive clauses are complex noun phrases, according to Ross.
[44]See Inoue (1974b) for the reflexives and pronominal traces in Japanese relative clauses.

(85′)

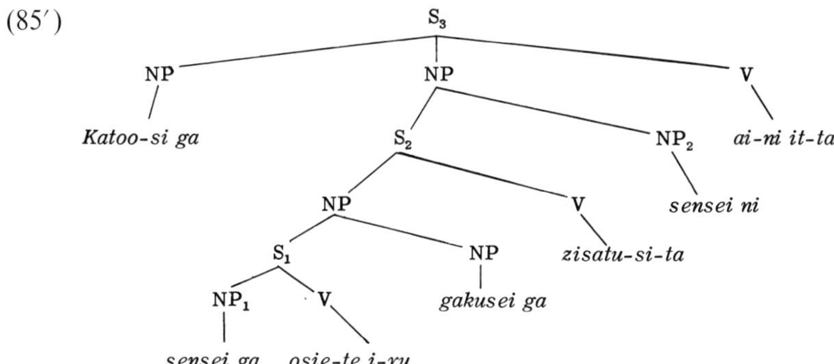

In both cases, NP_2 (*gakusei* or *sensei*) is not the subject in these deep structures. For the theory of deep structure interpretation, *zibun* appears under NP_1 in both (84′) and (85′), but it cannot be identified as coreferential with NP_2, since in each case NP_2 is not the subject. The situation does not improve for any one of the remaining three theories, because NP_2 can never be the subject at any point of derivation. There are many examples of this kind; (86) is one:

(86) *Watasi wa zibun*$_i$ *no kai-ta hon o syuppan-si-ta hon-ya ga*
I self write-past book publish-past publisher
hasan-si-ta gakusya o sit-te i-ru.
broke go-past scholar know-non-past
*'I know the scholar who the publisher that published the book that he wrote went broke.'

(86′)

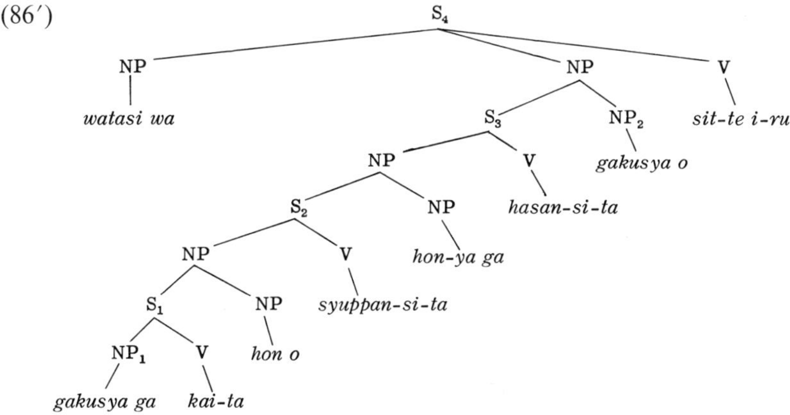

Appositive Clauses. A similar situation obtains with appositive clauses. The following is an example:

(87) *Zibun*$_i$ *ga kai-ta hon o syuppan-si-ta hon-ya ga*
self write-past book publish-past publisher
hasan-si-ta (to iu) zizitu ga Katoo-si ni tutawat-ta.
broke-go-past that fact to be given-past
'The fact that the publisher which published the book self$_i$ wrote went broke was reported to Mr. Kato.'

(87′)

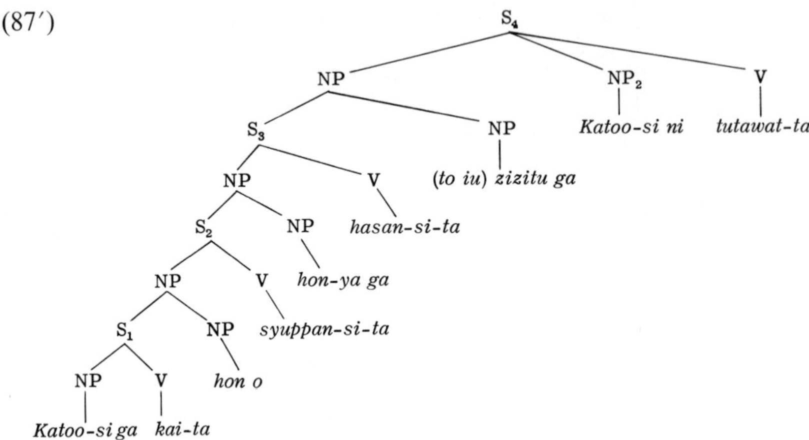

Again, in (87′), the deep structure representation of (87), NP_2 is not the subject, and can never be one at any point of derivation. This is another type of data that the four theories fail to account for.

There might be an argument that in all these cases topicalization applies first and then reflexivization, using topic phrases as antecedents. Take (84′), for example. It might be argued that instead of S_1 of (84′), i.e., *gakusei no ie ga yake-ta* 'The students' houses were burned down', the relative clause can be taken to be a topicalized sentence, *gakusei wa* ***gakusei*** *no ie ga yake-ta* 'As for the students, the students' houses were burned down', and reflexivization changes the second ***gakusei*** into *zibun*, using the topic NP *gakusei wa* as the antecedent. Finally, relativization deletes this topic NP. However, this argument is untenable, because ordering topicalization before reflexivization results in all sorts of ungrammatical sentences. The object, indirect object, and all other topicalizable noun phrases would become antecedents. The following is an example, in which topicalized object is used incorrectly as the antecedent:

(88) a. *Taroo*$_i$ *ga Ziroo o zibun*$_i$ *no ie de tatai-ta.*
self 's house in hit-past
'Taro$_i$ hit Jiro in his$_i$ house.'

b. **Ziroo*$_j$ *wa Taroo ga zibun*$_j$ *no ie de tatai-ta.*
'As for Jiro$_j$, Taro hit (him) in self's$_j$ house.'

SUMMARY

As a summary of the foregoing arguments about the four theories under discussion, in connection with reflexives, two charts are presented. In (89a), the sentence types taken up in this section are given on the top horizontal line. The circle in the chart indicates that the particular sentence type is correctly explained by each of the theories listed along the leftmost vertical line. An *X* means that the particular sentence type is a counterexample. The question marks indicate that the underlying structures posited to get the theory to work are problematic. In case a certain theory does not cover the entire range of data of a particular type, (O) is used. Abbreviations read as follows:

Rel = relative clauses	Te-M = *te moraw-u*
Pass = passives	W-Ca = with causatives
Caus = causatives	W-Oth = with other complements
Reg = regular	C-Em = center embedding
W-Psy = with psych verbs	Cx-NP = complex noun phrases
C-Pass = causative passives	App = appositive noun phrases

(89) a.

<table>
<tr><th rowspan="2" colspan="2"></th><th rowspan="2">Rel</th><th rowspan="2">Pass</th><th colspan="2">Caus</th><th rowspan="2">C-Pass</th><th colspan="2">Te-M</th><th rowspan="2">C-Em</th><th colspan="2">Cx-NP</th></tr>
<tr><th>Reg</th><th>W-Psy</th><th>W-Ca</th><th>W-Oth</th><th>Rel</th><th>App</th></tr>
<tr><td rowspan="3">CT</td><td>1</td><td rowspan="3">O</td><td rowspan="3">O</td><td rowspan="3">O</td><td>X</td><td rowspan="3">(O)</td><td rowspan="3">X</td><td rowspan="3">X</td><td rowspan="3">X</td><td rowspan="3">X</td><td rowspan="3">X</td></tr>
<tr><td>2</td><td>?</td></tr>
<tr><td>3</td><td>X</td></tr>
<tr><td colspan="2">PT</td><td>X</td><td>O</td><td>X</td><td>X</td><td>(O)</td><td>O</td><td>O</td><td>O</td><td>X</td><td>X</td></tr>
<tr><td colspan="2">DI</td><td>O</td><td>X</td><td>O</td><td>X</td><td>X</td><td>X</td><td>X</td><td>X</td><td>X</td><td>X</td></tr>
<tr><td colspan="2">CI</td><td>O</td><td>O</td><td>O</td><td>?</td><td>(O)</td><td>X</td><td>X</td><td>X</td><td>X</td><td>X</td></tr>
</table>

b.

	O	X and others
CT	4	6
PT	5	5
DI	2	8
CI	4	6

These charts indicate that even PT, apparently the best theory, among the four, accounts for only half of the data. It must also be pointed out that the cyclic transformational theory was proposed on the basis of passives and causatives, the data that work favorably for the theory, at the cost of disregarding all the other unfavorable types of data.

Interpretation Rules of Reflexives

Given so much evidence against cyclic and transformational treatment of reflexives, a possible alternative is to assume that coreferentiality of reflexives is determined in terms of the structures close to the surface. Let us assume that the point at which the interpretation of coreferentiality is decided is before the following reordering rules: topicalization, left and right dislocation, and scrambling.

To justify this assumption we have to show the noncyclicity of these reordering rules.

The first three transformations are supposed to be root transformations in the sense of Emonds (1970). This assumption is supported by such ungrammatical sentences as (90)–(92), which are produced by the application of these transformations in the embedded sentences. Examples (90′) and (91′) are underlying sentences for (90)–(92).[45]

(90) **Taroo ga hon wa Hanako kara Ziroo ni watas-ase-ru*
book from to give-cause-non-past
koto ni si-ta.
that decide-past
'*Taro decided as for the book to have Hanako give Jiro.'

(91) **Ano dendoo no taipuraitaa, sore ga ofisu ni miatar-*
that electric that be found
ana-i koto ga mina ni sire-ta.
negative-non-past that everybody to be known-past
'*That that electric typewriter, that is not found in the office became known to everybody.'

(92) **Ofisu ni miatar-ana-i, ano dendoo no taipuraitaa (ga) koto ga mina ni sire-ta.*
'*That is not found in the office, that electric typewriter became known to everybody.'

(90′) *Taroo ga Hanako kara Ziroo ni hon o watas-ase-ru koto ni si-ta.*
'Taro decided to have Hanako give the book to Jiro.'

[45]Haraguchi (1973) has an extensive discussion of the status of dislocation in Japanese. Deletion of subject and object noun phrases is frequent in Japanese when they are understood from context. This deletion seems to take place after the four reordering rules discussed here.

(91′) *Ano dendoo no taipuraitaa ga ofisu ni miatar-ana-i koto ga mina ni sire-ta.*
'That that electric typewriter is not found in the office became known to everybody.'

Scrambling[46] cannot be cyclic, either, since equi-NP deletion, which deletes the complement subject, has to have the complement word order intact. Observe the following:

(93) *Haha ga imooto o kawai-gat-ta.*
mother sister love-past
'My mother loved my sister.'

(94)

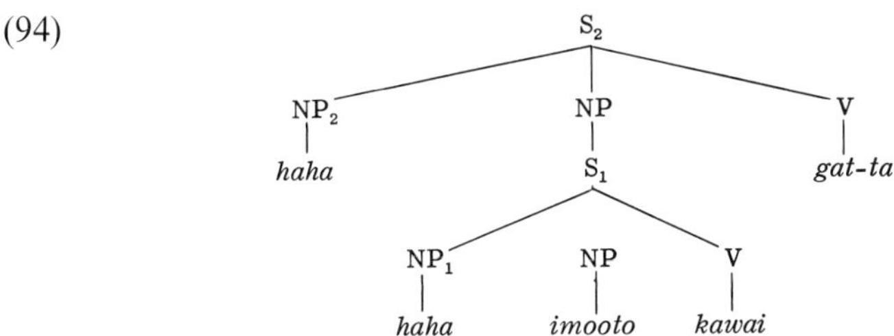

On the S_2 cycle of (94) Equi-NP deletion applies, deleting NP_1, which is identical to the matrix subject, NP_2. If NP_1 is scrambled on the S_1 cycle, NP_1 cannot be identified as the subject of S_1, so that it loses the chance of being deleted on the S_2 cycle. One argument to defend the cyclicity in this connection is to say that cyclic Scrambling applies at the end of each cycle, after case particles are assigned to mark the subject and object noun phrases. However, this argument does not hold. In (94), both *haha* and *imooto* will receive *ga*, the former being the subject and the latter the object of the stative verb *kawai*,[47] so that (95) is a good sentence:

(95) *Haha ga imooto ga kawai-i no da.*
'Mother loves my sister.'

Thus, even after the case marking has operated on the S_1 cycle, the crucial information 'subject of' is lost by scrambling. Hence the implausibility of cyclicity of scrambling.

[46]Scrambling is assumed to be a transformation in Japanese that permutes clausemate noun phrases. The question of whether this is a transformation or not does not have a direct bearing on our discussion.

[47]The object of stative verbs receive the case particle *ga*. This particle used to be called 'accusative *ga*' by traditional grammarians.

Finally, let us see that the coreferential relations before and after the four reordering rules are the same, as in (96b–e), which are derived from (96a) by the application of these rules:

(96) a. *Katoo-si*$_i$ *ga heya ni i-ta gakusei*$_j$ *ni zibun*$_{ij}$ *no*
room in be-past student self 's
tukue o huk-ase-ta.
desk clean-cause-past
'Mr. Kato$_i$ made the student$_j$ who was in the room clean self's$_{ij}$ desk.'

b. *Heya ni i-ta gakusei*$_j$ *ni wa Katoo-si*$_i$ *ga zibun*$_{ij}$ *no tukue o huk-ase-ta.* (topicalization)
'As for the student$_j$ who was in the room, Mr. Kato$_i$ made (him) clean self's$_{ij}$ desk.'

c. *Heya ni i-ta gakusei*$_j$, *Katoo-si*$_i$ *ga kare*$_j$ *ni zibun*$_{ij}$ *no tukue o huk-ase-ta.* (left dislocation)
'The student$_j$ who was in the room, Mr. Kato$_i$ made him clean the desk.'

d. *Katoo-si*$_i$ *ga zibun*$_{ij}$ *no tukue o huk-ase-ta, heya ni i-ta gakusei*$_j$ *ni.* (right dislocation)
'Mr. Kato$_i$ made (him) clean self's$_{ij}$ desk, the student$_j$ who was in the room.'

e. *Zibun*$_{ij}$ *no tukue o heya ni i-ta gakusei*$_j$ *ni Katoo-si*$_i$ *ga huk-ase-ta.*
Heya ni i-ta gakusei$_j$ *ni zibun*$_{ij}$ *no tukue o Katoo-si*$_i$ *ga huk-ase-ta.*
Zibun$_{ij}$ *no tukue o Katoo-si*$_i$ *ga heya ni i-ta gakusei*$_j$ *ni huk-ase-ta.*
Heya ni i-ta gakusei$_j$ *ni Katoo-si*$_i$ *ga zibun*$_{ij}$ *no tukue o huk-ase-ta.*
Katoo-si$_i$ *ga zibun*$_{ij}$ *no tukue o heya ni i-ta gakusei*$_j$ *ni huk-ase-ta.* (scrambling)

3. INTERPRETATION RULES OF JAPANESE REFLEXIVES[48]

The following is my proposal for post-cyclic interpretation rules of Japanese reflexives.

[48]Akmajian, Haraguchi, Kuroda, Martin, and Murray have made valuable comments that have contributed to the simplification of the rules, although they do not necessarily agree with this formulation. Haraguchi first suggested the formulation of the rules roughly in this form, which is different from my first version. He also pointed out the appearance of *zibun* in the second conjunct of coordinate structure, several examples of which were given to me by Ogawa.

(97) SD:

$$\left\{\begin{matrix}\#\\ //\end{matrix}\right\} X \left(\begin{bmatrix}+\text{H}\\ \text{NP}\end{bmatrix}\right) X \left(\begin{bmatrix}+\text{H}\\ \text{NP}\end{bmatrix}\right) X \begin{bmatrix}+\text{Refl}\\ \text{NP}\end{bmatrix} X\ V \left\{\begin{matrix}\#\\ //\end{matrix}\right\} X \left(\begin{bmatrix}+\text{H}\\ \text{NP}\end{bmatrix}\right) X\ \#$$

1 2 3 4 5 6 7 8 9 10 11 12 13 14

Conditions: (i) $\begin{bmatrix}+\text{H}\\ \text{NP}\end{bmatrix}$ commands $\begin{bmatrix}+\text{Refl}\\ \text{NP}\end{bmatrix}$.

(ii) 3 = Subj, 5 ≠ Subj.

(iii) 2, 4, and 11 do not contain $\begin{bmatrix}+\text{H}\\ \text{NP}\end{bmatrix}$.

Interpret (optional):

7 = {

3. (a)

5. Condition: 9 has [−Like Subj]. (b)

12. Conditions: 11 = ∅, $\begin{bmatrix}+\text{Refl}\\ \text{NP}\end{bmatrix}$ ≠ Subj unless bounded by more than one pair of //'s, 3 = ∅ unless 5 = ∅ and 9 = [−Like Subj]. (c)

12. Condition: If 11 contains Subj-conj, 11 contains no NP. (d)

3. Conditions: (i) does not hold, and 6 = Y $\left\{\begin{matrix}\#\ \text{Co-conj}\ \#\\ //\ \text{Co-conj}\end{matrix}\right\}$ Z, $\left(\text{where Z} \neq \begin{bmatrix}+\text{H}\\ \text{NP}\end{bmatrix}\right)$. (e)

}

This proposal makes crucial use of the sentence boundary # and the internal sentence boundary //. The topmost sentence is flanked by # from the time it first appears as the initial symbol of the base rules. Furthermore, both the topmost and internal sentence boundaries are indicated either by tree configurations or by square brackets as long as the S node stays in the structure. Therefore, the use of these boundary symbols does not mean that an undefined new notion is introduced just for this purpose. I use //, a conventional symbol representing an already existing well defined notion, in order to facilitate the explanation by eliminating the necessity of using troublesome names such as 'internal sentence boundary on the left or right'.

As stated before, noun phrases denoting higher animals such as *inu* 'dog', *neko* 'cat', and even *tori* 'bird' can sometimes be the antecedents of reflexives. Thus, $\begin{bmatrix}+\text{H}\\ \text{NP}\end{bmatrix}$ in (97) stands for not only a human noun phrase but also a noun phrase denoting such a higher animal.

General Conditions on (97)

Condition (i) stipulates that the antecedent command a reflexive.

Condition (iii) is a generalization of possible candidates for antecedents of reflexives. This condition actually makes the following statement. In a sentence flanked by a pair of # without any internal sentence boundaries, the maximum number of candidates is two, the first and second human noun phrases, i.e., terms 3 and 5. For 5 to be a candidate, 9 has to have a feature [−Like Subj], as stated as a condition on (b). (The explanation of [−Like Subj] is given later.) In a sentence that involves a pair of //, the maximum number of candidates are three, terms 3, 5, and 12. It means that for backward reflexive interpretation only one candidate exists, which is the first human noun phrase after //. To ensure that 3, 5, and 12 are the first or second human noun phrases in the contexts stated earlier, variables 2, 4, and 11 must not contain human noun phrases. The other variables, 6, 8, and 13, are irrelevant to reflexive interpretation, so that they may contain human noun phrases. Just one example is given here to show one of the typical structural analyses:

(98) # ∅ *Taroo*$_i$ *wa* ∅ *otooto*$_j$ *ni* ∅ *zibun*$_{ij}$ *no kuruma de Hanako o*
1 2 3 4 5 6 7 8
okur-ase-ta. #
[−Like Subj]
9
'Taro$_i$ had his brother$_j$ take Hanako home in self's$_{ij}$ car.'

In (98), either term 3 or term 5 can be the antecedent, so that the reflexive is ambiguously interpreted. Term 8 has a human noun phrase, *Hanako*, but it does not qualify to be a possible antecedent. Further details will be given as we go through rules (a) through (e).

A human noun phrase dominated by a determiner does not act as the antecedent. Following Chomsky (1970:200), I assume that a noun phrase followed by the possessive particle *no* is dominated by the node Det. Take, for example, sentences like (99):

(99) **Ziroo*$_i$ *no hon ga zibun*$_i$ *no tukue no ue ni ar-u.*
Jiro 's book self 's desk on be-non-past
'Jiro's$_i$ book is on self's$_i$ desk.'

The following is the structure to which (97) applies:

(100)

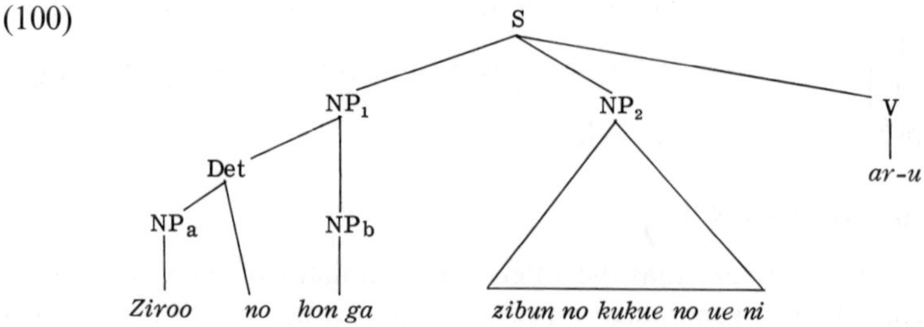

Since *Ziroo* in (100) is dominated by Det, this sentence is ungrammatical if *Ziroo* is interpreted as the antecedent. This is an automatic consequence of Condition (i) if we take NP to constitute a cycle. That is, NP , dominated by Det in (100), does not command NP_2 if NP_1 is a cycle node. Unless we follow this convention, we will need another condition: (iv) $\begin{bmatrix}+H\\NP\end{bmatrix}$ is not dominated by Det.[49]

Rules (a) and (b)

Together with Condition (i), (a) states that both matrix and constituent subjects can be the antecedents of following reflexives, thus accounting for the grammaticality of (101)–(103) and the ungrammaticality of (104). Here, 'ungrammaticality' means that reflexives do not get their coreferentiality decided:

(101) *Taroo*$_i$ *ga zibun*$_i$ *no heya o soozi-si-ta.*
room clean-past
'Taro cleaned his room.'

(102) *Taroo*$_i$ *ga katyoo ni zibun*$_i$ *ga kai-ta*
chief of the section to self write-past
hookoku-syo o mada mise-te i-na-i.
report yet show negative-non-past
'Taro has not yet shown his chief the report that he wrote.'

(103) *Taroo*$_i$ *ga Hanako ni zibun*$_i$ *ga Amerika e it-ta koto o*
to to go-past that
hanas-anakat-ta.
tell negative-past
'Taro did not tell Hanako that he had been to the States.'

(104) **Zibun*$_i$ *ga Taroo*$_i$ *no sigoto o hayaku katazuke-ta.*
work quickly finish-past
'*Himself finished Taro's work quickly.'

(105) **Taroo*$_i$ *ga kai-ta hon ga zibun*$_i$ *o yorokob-ase-ta.*
write-past book pleased-cause-past
'*The book Taro wrote pleased himself.'

[49] This kind of restriction was brought to my attention by Haraguchi. The possibility of eliminating Condition (iv) was suggested to me by Akmajian. The following is another example similar to (99):

(i) **Taroo*$_i$ *no hon ga zibun*$_i$ *ni yaku dat-ta.*
book self helpful be-past
'*Taro's$_i$ book was helpful to himself$_i$.'

In (101)–(103), *Taroo* appears as the subject and commands *zibun*, so that it is identified as the antecedent, whereas in (104) *Taroo* is not the subject, thus failing to meet Condition (ii). In (105). *Taroo* does not command *zibun*, since it is the subject of the relative clause. Hence the violation of Condition (i).

Note that in (102) *zibun* is the subject of a relative clause, while in (103) it is the subject of a complement sentence. As stated before, the subjects of embedded sentences can be reflexives because in Japanese the antecedent and the reflexive do not have to be clausemates. Now, let us see how Rule (a) works in (102) and (103). The following are their structural analyses:

(102′) # *Taroo*$_i$ *ga katyoo ni* // *zibun*$_i$ *ga kai-ta* // *hookoku-syo o*
1 3 5 7 8
mada mise-te i-na-i. #
9 10

(103′) # *Taroo*$_i$ *ga Hanako ni* // *zibun*$_i$ *ga Amerika e it-ta* //
1 3 5 7 8 9 10
koto o hanas-anakat-ta. #
11 13 14

Since *Taroo* in both sentences is the subject, it meets Condition (ii), and the coreferential relation between *Taroo* and the reflexive is decided by Rule (a).

Next, (a) and (b) of (97) account for the ambiguous reading of causatives, sentences with *yoo ni iituke* 'tell', and so on, which have the [−Like Subj] constraint:

(106) *Taroo*$_i$ *ga Ziroo*$_j$ *ni zibun*$_{ij}$ *no heya de benkyoo-s-ase-ta.*
room in study do-cause-past
'Taro$_i$ made Jiro$_j$ study in self's$_{ij}$ room.'

If (a) applies, *zibun* is interpreted as coreferential with *Taroo*. Otherwise, it is identified as coreferential with *Ziroo* in case the verb before # or // [term 9 in (97)] has the feature [−Like Subj]. Since the causative formative *sase* carries this feature, *zibun* receives the interpretation that it is coreferential with *Ziroo*. The feature [Like Subj] is not first introduced in this rule for this particular purpose. As is well known, this feature is independently motivated to account for complementation in many languages.[50] The following is an example similar to (106):

[50]It is not certain whether or not like and unlike subject constraints should be posited as deep structure constraints. However, one point is clear; that is, these constraints are determined by certain semantic properties of matrix verbs. [+Like Subj] represents the semantic property that requires identical matrix and complement subjects, [−Like Subj] the semantic property re-

(107) # *$Taroo_i$ wa $Ziroo_j$ ni // $zibun_{ij}$ no heya o soozi-su-ru //*
1 3 5 7 8
room clean-non-past

yoo ni iituke-ta. #
[− Like Subj]
9 10

'$Taro_i$ told $Jiro_j$ to clean self's$_{ij}$ room.'

Example (106) receives an analysis similar to that of (98), which is without any internal sentence boundaries.

Rules (a) and (b) take care of the straightforward cases that used to be handled by cyclic transformation with the subject-antecedent and antecedent-command conditions. The affective passive formative *rare* is also presumed to carry the feature [− Like Subj]; this is supported by the following data (the (a) sentences of (108)–(110) are underlying sentences):

(108) a. *Akanboo ga nai-ta.*
baby cry-past
'The baby cried.'

b. *Taroo ga akanboo ni nak-are-ta.*
cry-passive-past
'Taro was subjected to the baby's crying.'

(109) a. *Tanaka-san ga Russia o hoomon-si-ta.*
visit-do-past
'Mr. Tanaka visited Russia.'

b. *Satoo-san wa Tanaka-san ni Russia o hoomon-s-are-ta.*
visit-do-passive-past
'Mr. Tanaka visited Russia, to Mr. Sato's disadvantage.'

---

quiring nonidentical matrix and complement subjects. In the framework of this study, this feature works not only in the interpretation of reflexives but also as a semantic well-formedness condition, filtering out as semantically anomalous sentences that violate conditions placed by this feature.

Verbs that can take either like subjects or unlike subjects do not count as either [+ Like Subj] or [− Like Subj] verbs, e.g., *kitai-su-ru* 'hope', *yoki-su-ru* 'expect'. This point was brought to my attention by Shibatani. Consider:

(i) *Yamada-$sensei_i$ ga gakusei ni $zibun_i$ no ronbun no kansei o kitai-si-ta.*
student paper completion hope-past
'Professor $Yamada_i$ hoped that his student would complete self's$_i$ paper.'

In (i), for example, the reflexive is not coreferential with *gakusei*. If, however, both *Yamada-sensei* and *gakusei* appear as subjects, ambiguity arises, as in (ii):

(ii) *Yamada-$sensei_i$ ga $gakusei_j$ ga $zibun_{ij}$ no ronbun o kansei-su-ru koto o kitai-si-ta.*
'Professor $Yamada_i$ hoped that his $student_j$ would complete self's$_{ij}$ paper.'

(110) a. *Kinoo densya ga kosyoo-si-ta.*
yesterday train break down-past
'Yesterday the train broke down.'
b. *Kinoo boku wa densya ni kosyoo-s-are-ta.*
yesterday I train by break down-passive-past
'Yesterday the train broke down, to my disadvantage.'

It is clear that the (a) sentences of (108)–(110) do not contain noun phrases identical to the subjects of the (b) sentences. Therefore, we cannot explain the (b) sentences unless we posit a complement structure. Furthermore, the ungrammaticality of the following sentence gives another support for the assumption that the affective *rare* has the feature [−Like Subj]:

(111) **Taroo wa zibun ni tetuya de benkyoo-s-are-ta.*
through the night study-do-passive-past
'Taro was subjected to himself studying all through the night.'

Compare this sentence with (112), in which the [−Like Subj] condition is met:

(112) *Hanako wa Taroo ni tetuya de benkyoo-s-are-ta.*
'Hanako was subjected to Taro's studying all through the night.'

Simple passives, on the other hand, cannot be marked with regard to this feature if they are assumed to be derived from their active counterparts by movement transformations, rather than complementation, since [±Like Subj] is a feature carried by the verb that requires complementation.

Next, observe the following.

(113) *Hanako ni zibun$_i$ no syasin o okut-ta otoko$_i$ ga kono zimusyo de*
to self's picture send-past man this office in
hatarai-te i- ru.
work-progressive-non-past
'The man$_i$ who sent self's$_i$ picture to Hanako is working in this office.'

Hanako in (113) does not qualify as the antecedent because it is not the subject, nor does its verb have the feature [−Like Subj]. The interpretation of *otoko* 'man' as the antecedent is made by Rule (c).

Rule (c)

Rule (c) of (97) states that the human noun phrase immediately following // may be the antecedent of the preceding reflexive, provided that term 3 is $\emptyset$, or term 5 is $\emptyset$ and term 9 has the specification [−Like Subj]. When term 11 is ∅, as the condition states, the following human noun phrase is always the head of a relative clause. Rule (c) has a further condition that term 7 (reflexive) must not be the subject of a relative clause unless it is bounded by more than one pair of //'s. This means that if a reflexive appears in a relative clause embedded in another relative clause, i.e., bounded by more than one pair of //'s, as in (85), this condition does not hold. (For details, see the section on complex noun phrase, pp. 186–187.)

(114) is an example which meets these conditions on (c).

(114) # // *Zibun*$_i$ *no syukudai o oe-ta* // *gakusei*$_i$ *ga Taroo o*
homework finish-past student
tazune-te ki-ta #
visit-come-past
'The students who finished their homework came to visit Taro.'

Next observe the following.

(115) **Taroo ga zibun*$_j$ *no bokoo de at-ta gakusei*$_j$ *ga*
alma mater at meet-past student
tazune-te ki-ta.
visit-come-past
*'The students$_j$ who Taro met at self's$_j$ alma matar came to visit him.'

As is specified by (c), (115) is not accepted if *zibun* is interpreted as coreferential with *gakusei* 'students', because its relative clause has the subject *Taroo* and the verb is not marked with [−Like Subj]. In the only possible reading of this sentence, *zibun* is coreferential with *Taroo*, the interpretation given by (a).

Example (115′), on the other hand, has the subject of the relative clause (*Taroo*) and the verb marked with [−Like Subj] (*sase*), while term 5 is ∅. Hence the grammaticality of (115′), in which either term 3 or term 12 is interpreted as the antecedent.

(115′) *Taroo*$_i$ *ga zibun*$_{ij}$ *no heya o soozi-s-ase-ta*
room clean-do-cause-past
gakusei$_j$ *ga Taroo o tazune-te ki-ta.*
student visit-come-past [(a) and (c)]
'The student$_j$ Taro$_i$ made clean self's$_{ij}$ room came to visit Taro.'

Rule (c) also permits an ambiguous reading of a reflexive in a relative clause, if term 3 is ∅ and the condition of [−Like Subj] is met. Example (116) shows that this is actually the case.

(116) *Gakusei*$_i$ *ni zibun*$_{ij}$ *no heya o soozi-s-ase-ta* *sensei*$_j$ *ga*
student room clean-do-cause-past teacher
syakan *kara monku o iw-are-ta.* [(b) and (c)]
dormitory advisor from rebuke -passive-past
'The teacher$_i$ who had the students$_j$ clean self's$_{ij}$ room was rebuked by the dormitory advisor.'

In (116), the relative clause (*gakusei*$_i$ *ni zibun*$_{ij}$ *no heya o soozi-s-ase-ta sensei* 'the teacher$_j$ who had the students$_i$ clean self's room') does not have the subject, so Rule (c) can apply, marking coreferentiality of *zibun* with *sensei*. Furthermore, since the verb in the relative clause, i.e., *ase* (causative), is a [−Like Subj] verb, Rule (b) is applicable to establish the coreferentiality relation between *gakusei* 'students' and *zibun*. This is the reason for the ambiguity.

To (117), with both terms 3 and 5 present, Rule (c) does not apply. Therefore, the ambiguous readings given to (117) are due to (a) and (b).

(117) *Taroo*$_i$ *ga Hanako*$_j$ *ni zibun*$_{ij}$ *no hon o okur-ase-ta*
book sent-cause-past
tomodati$_k$ *ga yat-te ki-ta.* [(a) and (b)]
friend come-past
'The friend to whom Taro$_i$ made Hanako$_j$ send self's$_{ij}$ book came.'

Rule (d)

Rule (d) states that a reflexive can be coreferential with the following human noun phrase that is not immediately preceded by //. And Condition (iii) stipulates that term 11 not contain a human noun phrase. These statements are made to account for such sentences as (118)–(120), and for the ungrammaticality of sentences like (121), which have a human noun phrase for term 11:

(118) *Zibun*$_i$ *no uti ga kanemoti da to yuu koto ga Taroo*$_i$ *o*
family rich be-non-past that
omoiagar-ase-te i-ru.
conceited-cause-non-past
'That his$_i$ family is rich has made Taro$_i$ conceited.'

(119) *Zibun*$_i$ *ga zigyoo ni sippai-si-ta to yuu zizitu ga itumo Taroo*$_i$ *o*
business in fail-past fact always
nayam-ase-te i-ru.
worry-cause-non-past
'That he$_i$ failed in business always worries Taro$_i$.'

(120) *Hanako*$_i$ *ga zibun*$_{ij}$ *no heya ni i-ru* *hi* *ni* *Taroo*$_j$ *ga*
room in stay-non-past day on
sowasowa si-te i-ru
restless be-non-past
'On days when Hanako$_i$ stays in self's$_{ij}$ room, Taro$_j$ is restless.'

(121) *Otooto*$_i$ *ga zibun*$_{ij}$ *no ronbun o type si-te i-ta*
paper do-progressive-past
node Taroo$_j$ *ga asobi-ni ik-u* *no o yame-ta.*
play to go-non-past that give up-past
'As his brother$_i$ was typing self's$_{ij}$ paper, Taro$_j$ gave up the idea of going out to play.'

(122) **Itumo zibun*$_i$ *no heya ni tozikomot-te i-ru tomodati ga*
room in stay-non-past friend
Hanako$_i$ *o sinpai-s-ase-ta.*
worry-cause-past
'The friend who is always staying in self's$_i$ room worried Hanako$_i$.'

The complementizers, *koto* and *no* [as in (118)], abstract noun phrases such as *zizitu* 'fact', *hookoku* 'report' [as in (119)], and *hi* 'day' [in (120)] appear as term 11. Otherwise, subordinate conjunctions (Sub-conj) appear in this position. In this case, no noun phrase is permitted to appear in term 11. This condition blocks the establishment of coreferential relations such as that indicated in the following sentence.

(123)[51] **Zibun*$_i$ *ga tegami o dasi-ta node henzi ga Hanako*$_i$ *ni ki-ta.*
Sub-conj NP
11 12 13
letter send-past as answer to come-past
'*As self$_i$ sent a letter, an answer came to Hanako$_i$.

In (122), term 11 is filled with *tomodati* 'friend', so that term 12, *Hanako*, cannot be coreferential with term 7 (reflexive). Therefore, the sentence is ungrammatical if *zibun* and *Hanako* are taken to be coreferential.[52] The

[51]The ungrammaticality of this coreferential reading was pointed out to me by Harada (personal communication).

[52]Some speakers may give ambiguous readings to this sentence. Compare (122) with the following.

(i) *itumo zibun*$_i$ *no heya ni i-ru tomodati*$_i$ *ga Hanako o sinpai-s-ase-ta*
room in stay-non-past friend worry cause-past
'The friend$_i$ who always stays in self's$_i$ room worried Hanako.'

interpretation of *zibun* as coreferential with *tomodati* will make the sentence grammatical as is specified by (c). Notice that (124) without a human noun phrase as term 11 permits an ambiguous reading of *zibun*.

(124) # // *Taroo*$_i$ *ga zibun*$_{ij}$ *no kuruma de dekake-ta* // *koto ga*
1 2 3 7 ——— 9 10 11
8
Hanako$_j$ *o sinpai-s-ase-ta* #
12 13 14
'That Taro$_i$ went out in self's$_{ij}$ car worried Hanako$_j$.'

As discussed earlier, causatives with psychological verbs pose problems to transformational theory in one way or another. Setting aside all these problems, let us assume the correctness of the transformational derivation of *zibun* in these sentences for the time being. A sentence like (59) is supposed to underlie a sentence like (58):

(58) *Arisu wa zibun ga otokonoko ni moteru koto o yorokonda.*
'Alice was pleased that she was popular with boys.'

(59) *Zibun ga otokonoko ni moteru koto ga Arisu o yorokobaseta.*
'That she was popular with boys pleased Alice.'

In order to account for the coreferentiality relation in sentences like (15), we have to resort to the decomposition of lexical items such as *osie-ru* 'teach', *zetuboo e oiyar-u* 'drive to desperation', and so on into abstract verb complexes with CAUSE, as N. McCawley (1972) does.

(15) *Zibun*$_i$ *ga gan de aru to iuu sindan ga Mitiko*$_i$ *o zetuboo e*
self cancer is that diagnosis desperation to
oiyat-ta.
drive away-past
'The diagnosis that self$_i$ had a cancer drove Mitiko$_i$ to desperation.'

(ii) *itumo zibun*$_j$ *no heya ni ku-ru tomodati ga Hanako*$_j$ *o sinpai-s-ase-ta*
come-non-past worry-cause-past
'The friend who always comes to self's$_j$ room worried Hanako$_j$.'

To those speakers the same ambiguity exists in (i). However, (ii) is uniquely interpreted by most people with a coreferential relation between the reflexive and *Hanako*. The complement verb in (ii) is a directional verb which excludes the reading of *tomodati* as the antecedent, so that the Experiencer *Hanako* gets interpreted as the antecedent. To those who give ambiguous readings to (122) and (i) in the above, Experiencer is such a strong candidate for the antecedent that Condition (iii) that 11 does not contain $\begin{bmatrix}+\text{H}\\ \text{NP}\end{bmatrix}$ does not hold for them. (See Section 4 for details.)

Example (125) is another such sentence that calls for a similar decomposition:

(125) [Kuno, 1972a, (113a)]
Zibun$_i$ *ga Mary ni karakaware ta koto ga John*$_i$ *o*
by was-made-fun-of that
zetuboo e oiyatta.
desperation to drove
'That self (= he) was made fun of by Mary drove John to desperation.'

However, there are many sentences for which such lexical decomposition is impossible:

(126) *Zibun*$_i$ *no gakusei ga taiho-s-are-ta no de*
student arrest-passive-past as
Tanaka-sensei$_i$ *ga koogi o yasun-da.*
lecture be absent-past
'As self's$_i$ student was arrested, Prof. Tanaka$_i$ did not give the lecture.'

(127) *Zibun*$_i$ *no tate-ta keikaku ga Katoo-si*$_i$ *o kyuuti ni oikon-da.*
make-past plan corner drive-past
'The plan that self$_i$ made drove Mr. Kato$_i$ into a corner.'

(128)[53] *Zibun*$_i$ *no hatumeisi-ta omotya ga kyoozyu*$_i$ *ni bakudai na*
invent-past toy professor to big
zaisan o motarasi-ta.
fortune bring-past
'The toy that self$_i$ invented brought about an unexpected fortune to the professor$_i$.'

The coreferentiality of *zibun* in these sentences is decided by Rule (d) without any ad hoc manoeuvre.

Next, let us turn to (129), which is superficially a counterexample to our theory, since it does not involve the expected ambiguity.

(129) [Kuno, 1972: (113a)]
Mary ga zibun$_i$ *o hinansita koto ga John*$_i$ *o utinomesita*
self accused that floored
'That Mary accused self (= him) floored John.'

However, the somewhat dubious status of the sentence with *Mary* identified as the antecedent is supposed to be due to the semantic anomaly of the

[53]Examples (127) and (128) are from Oyakawa, with slight modification.

expression 'to accuse oneself'. The point will become clear if the verb in (129) is replaced by other, less limited ones:

(130) *Mary*$_i$ *ga zibun*$_{ij}$ *no koto o kamaw-ana-i*
take care of-negative-non-past
koto ga John$_j$ *o utinomesita.*
that
'That Mary does not take care of self (= him, her) floored John.'

Example (130) carries ambiguity, as predicted. It must be noted, however, that the preferred reading in (130) is, indeed, the coreferentiality of *zibun* with *John*. This is one of the cases where the semantic case feature Experiencer plays a role and picks out *John*, the Experiencer, as the preferable antecedent.

Next, let us examine more closely reflexives in adverbial clauses of time, place, reason, condition, and concession, which will be interpreted by Rule (d), as well as (a) and (b).[54] The following five pairs of sentences[55] contain such adverbial clauses:

(131) a. *Hanako*$_i$ *ga zibun*$_{ij}$ *no heya ni i-ru hi ni*
room in stay-non-past day on
Taroo$_j$ *ga sowasowa-si-te i-ru.* [(a), (d)]
restless-be-non-past
'On the days Hanako$_i$ stays in self's$_{ij}$ room, Taro$_j$ is restless.'

b. *Taroo*$_j$ *wa, Hanako*$_i$ *ga zibun*$_{ij}$ *no heya ni i-ru hi (ni) wa, sowasowa-si-te i-ru.*
'As for Taro$_j$, on the days when Hanako$_i$ stays in self's$_{ij}$ room, he is restless.'

(132) a. *Hanako*$_i$ *ga Ziroo*$_j$ *ni zibun*$_{ijk}$ *no heya o soozi-s-ase-te*
room clean-do-cause-
i-ru soba de Taroo$_k$ *ga terebi o*
progressive-non-past side at television
mi-te i-ta. [(a), (b), (d)]
watch-progressive-past
'Hanako$_i$ was making Jiro$_j$ clean self's$_{ijk}$ room, and by her side Taro$_k$ was watching television.'

b. *Taroo*$_k$ *wa Hanako*$_i$ *ga Ziroo*$_j$ *ni zibun*$_{ijk}$ *no heya o soozi-s-ase-te i-ru soba de terebi o mi-te i-ta.*

[54]Since Rules (c) and (d) are mutually exclusive, they never apply to the same string.
[55]The rules employed are indicated in parentheses.

'As for Taro$_i$. he was watching television where Hanako$_i$ was making Jiro$_j$ clean self's$_{ijk}$ room.'

(133) a. *Otooto$_i$ ga zibun$_{ij}$ no ronbun o taipu-si-te i-ta node,*
paper type-progressive-past
Taroo$_j$ ga asobi-ni ik-u no o yame-ta. [(a), (d)]
play to go-non-past that give up-past
'As his brother$_i$ was typing self's$_{ij}$ paper, Taro$_j$ gave up the idea of going out to play.'

b. *Taroo$_j$ wa otooto$_i$ ga zibun$_{ij}$ no ronbun o taipu-si-te i-ta node, asobi-ni ik-u no o yame-ta.*
'As for Taro$_j$, as his brother was typing self's$_{ij}$ paper, he gave up the idea of going out to play.'

(134) a. *Mitiko$_i$ ga zibun$_{ij}$ no koto o hito ni ii-hazime-tara*
others to say-begin if
Hanako$_j$ ga damat-te i- rare- na- i
also silent keep-potential-negative-non-past
daroo. [(a), (d)]
presumptive
'If Michiko$_i$ starts talking to others about self$_{ij}$, Hanako$_j$ will not be able to keep silent.'

b. *Hanako$_j$ wa, Mitiko$_i$ ga zibun$_{ij}$ no koto o hito ni ii-hazime-tara, damat-te i-rare-na-i daroo.*
'As for Hanako$_j$, if Michiko$_i$ starts talking to others about self$_{ij}$, she will not be able to keep silent.'

(135) a. *Mitiko$_i$ ga zibun$_{ij}$ no kodomo o sewa-si-te i-*
take care of-progressive
ru noni, Taroo$_j$ ga sir-ana-i
non-past though know-negative-non-past
huri o si-te i-ta. [(a), (d)]
pretend-past
'Though Michiko$_i$ was taking care of self's$_{ij}$ child, Taro$_j$ pretended that he was not aware of it.'

b. *Taroo$_j$ wa, Mitiko$_i$ ga zibun$_{ij}$ no kodomo o sewa-si-te i-ru noni, sir-ana-i huri o si-te i-ta*
'As for Taro$_j$, even though Michiko$_i$ was taking care of self's$_{ij}$ child, he pretended that he was not aware of it.'

In these examples, (131) has time, (132) place, (133) reason, (134) condition, and (135) concession. In all of them, the (b) sentences are the results of topicalization, and our rules apply to the (a) sentences before the subject of the main sentence is moved to sentence-initial position. I presume that the structure to which Rule (d) applies is schematically like (136):

(136)

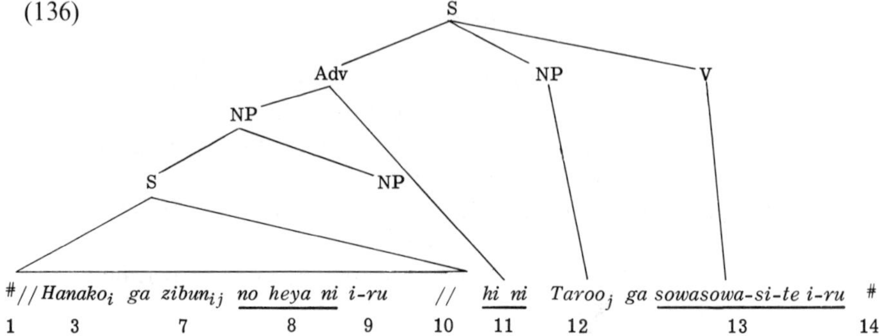

Now, Rule (a) could apply to (136), marking *zibun* as coreferential with *Hanako*. Otherwise, Rule (d) marks it as coreferential with *Taroo*. Hence the two-way ambiguity. Examples (134) and (135) are handled in exactly the same way.

Because of limited space, I cannot go into the independent justification of the underlying structure (136).[56] If this underlying structure proves to be wrong, or either (137a) or (137b) is independently motivated as the underlying structure of these sentences, our interpretive rules are defective, since in this structure the term 12 does not command the term 7 any more. This means that the term 12 cannot be identified as the antecedent, due to the antecedent-command condition. If this proves to be the case, then slight modification of Rule (d) will become necessary.

(137)a.

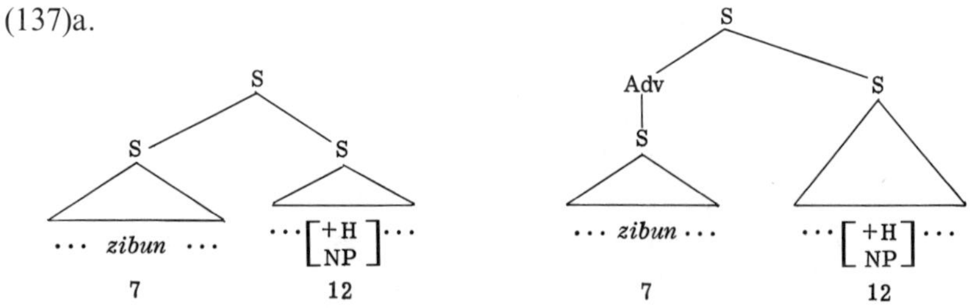

Now at this point let us recapitulate the conditions on (d). First, term 11 must not contain a human noun phrase, as is stipulated by Condition (iii). The ungrammaticality of (138a) is due to the violation of this condition.

[56]This is a justifiable assumption, because subordinate conjunctions preceded by a copula are used as sentence-initial connective particles; for example, *daga* 'but', *dakedo* 'but', *demo* 'even though'. The second plausible alternative is to assume that the subject precedes the subordinate clause. This assumption, however, does not falsify our assumption, because in that case Rule (a), instead of Rule (d), is applied.

Next, as the condition on (d) stipulates, term 11 must not contain any noun phrase, human or non-human, if it contains a subordinate conjunction. (138b) is an example of violation of this condition.

(138) a. *# // *Zibun*$_i$ *ga zaisan o nakusi-ta* // *koto ga Taroo ni*
1 2 7 8 9 10 $\begin{bmatrix}+H\\NP\end{bmatrix}$
fortune 11
Hanako$_i$ *o urayamasi-gar-ase-ta.* #
12 13 14
envy- cause-past
'*That self$_i$ lost fortune made Taro envy Hanako$_i$.'

b. [57] # // *Titi ga zibun*$_i$ *o yon-da* // *toki kozutumi ga Taroo*$_i$
1 2 3 7 9 10 Sub-conj NP 12
11
father call-past when parcel
ni ki-ta. #
13 14
'*When Father called self$_i$, a parcel came to Taro$_i$.'

It is to be noted in passing that most of the recent works on reflexives in Japanese have been concerned with the permissibility of *zibun* in adverbial clauses or in sentences containing sentential subjects, such as (118) and (119). In other words, the discussion has been concerned mostly with the issue of what contexts allow reflexives. Curiously enough, the question of ambiguous readings in those contexts has never attracted the attention of linguists.

Rule (e)

A reflexive in the first conjunct of a coordinate sentence can never be marked as coreferential with a human noun phrase in the second conjunct. Thus, we do not have sentences like the following.

(139) **Zibun*$_i$ *wa honya e yot-ta,* *sosite Taroo ga kudamono o*
bookstore drop in-past and fruit
kat-ta.
buy-past
'Self$_i$ dropped in at the bookstore, and Taro$_i$ bought fruit.'

[57] It is not the case that only the subject of a matrix sentence can be the antecedent of a reflexive in a clause followed by a subordinate conjunction. In (i) below, non-subject, Taro, is the antecedent.

(i) *titi ga zibun*$_i$ *o yon-da*// *toki Taroo*$_i$ *ni wa zizyoo ga zenzen wakar-anakat-ta*
11 12
father self call-past when state of affairs at all understand-not-past
'When father called self$_i$, the state of affairs was not clear to Taro$_i$ at all.'

Example (139) is ungrammatical if Rule (d) applies and identifies *zibun* as coreferential with *Taroo*. However, our antecedent-command condition blocks its application because, as (141) shows, *Taroo* does not command *zibun*.

A reflexive in the second conjunct, on the other hand, can be identified as coreferential with the subject of the first conjunct, as in (140):[58]

(140) *Taroo*$_i$ *wa inu o oi-kake-ta, sosite zibun*$_i$ *wa Ziroo ni*
dog chase-past and self by
oi-kake-rare-ta.
chase-passive-past
'Taro$_i$ chased the dog, and self$_i$ was chased by Jiro.'

As before, *Taroo* does not command *zibun*. However, Rule (e) says that a reflexive (term 7) is coreferential with the subject of the first conjunct (term 3), even if it does not command the reflexive, provided that term 6 has either two sentence boundaries connected by a coordinate conjunction (Co-conj) or an internal sentence boundary followed by a Co-conj. The following structure, which underlies (140), shows the first case:

(141)

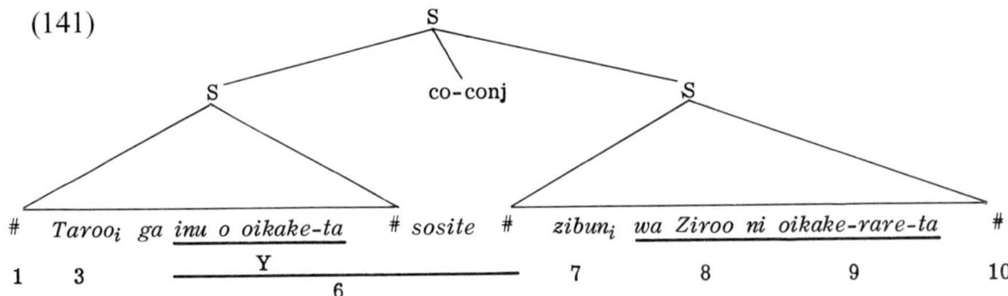

From (141), it is clear that *Taroo* qualifies as the antecedent under the specification of Rule (e). Next, let us turn to our second case:

(142)[59] # // *Taroo*$_i$ *ga utusi-ta*// *zibun*$_i$ *no syasin ga*
take-past self's picture
okur-are-te ki-ta.
send-passive come-past
'The picture of self$_i$ that Taro$_i$ took was sent to him.'

The pair of internal sentence boundaries (//) in (142) shows that *Taroo* in the embedded sentence, with *zibun* in the matrix, does not command the

[58] Reflexives in the second conjunct of coordinate sentences cannot be handled by a transformational approach. In some dialects, *zibun* in this context is interpreted to convey only the contrastive meaning, i.e., 'self, and not others'. If this is generally the case, this type of sentence must be taken care of by another semantic rule.

[59] This sentence is from Ogawa (personal communication).

reflexive. Then why is it legitimate to identify *Taroo* as the antecedent of *zibun* in this sentence? Let us figure out a plausible derived structure to which our interpretation rules apply. What is clear and unquestionable is that *Taroo ga utusi-ta* and *zibun no* form a coordinate structure jointly modifying the following noun, *syasin*. What should be the node dominating them is not a firmly settled question. However, the latter question does not have a direct bearing on the point at issue. Let us take one of the traditional analyses (e.g., Smith, 1964) of relative clauses[60] and set up (143) as the structure to which Rule (e) applies:

(143)

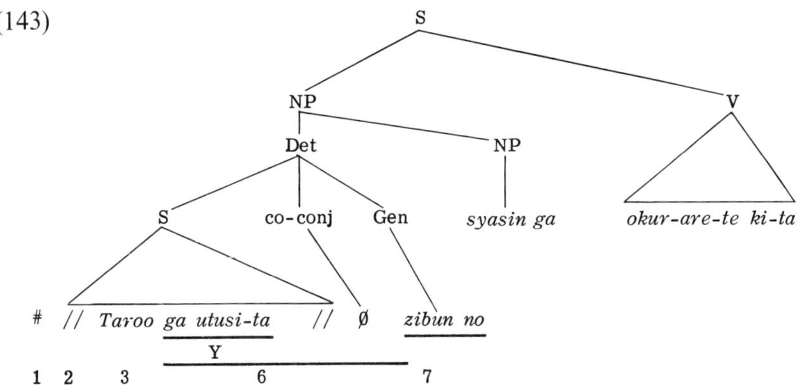

Again, in this case *Taroo* does not command *zibun*, but with term 6 analyzed as Y // Co-conj, it qualifies as the antecedent.

If, on the other hand, (144) is proposed as the structure relevant to reflexive interpretation, none of our rules can decide the coreferential relation in it:

(144)

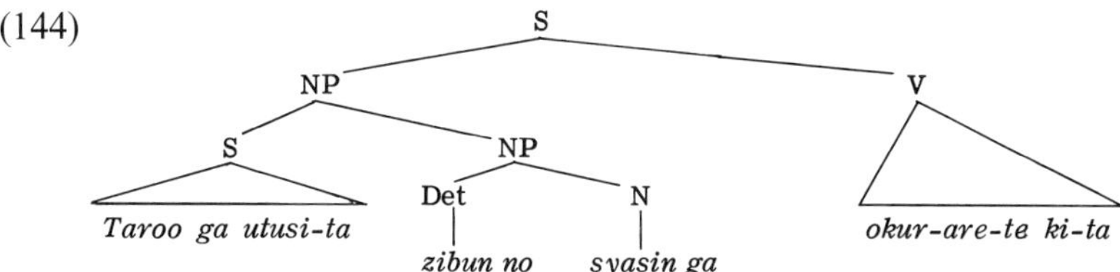

The position of Det in a structural analysis such as (144) has been questioned because relativization, which deletes a noun phrase identical to the head noun, does not require the identity of both articles (cf. Kajita, 1968a).

[60] *Zibun no* in (142) is ambiguous among such readings as 'possessive', 'picture of self', and 'picture that self took'. (The last meaning is excluded here due to the preceding sentence.) Regardless whether it is a possessive phrase dominated by Det or not, the position of *zibun no* in (144) is highly questionable.

Furthermore, the internal structures of both the determiner and the prenominal modifier string, including the status of the genitive, have not been studied. Therefore, the choice between (143) and (144) is still very much dependent on future study.

Generalizations Made by Rules (a), (b), (c), and (d)

First, our interpretation rules clarify possible candidates for antecedents of reflexives, as stated at the beginning of this section. Next, they specify possible combinations of candidates. For sentences without any internal sentence boundaries, the maximum number of possible antecedents is two [(145)]. For sentences in which a crucial use of one internal sentence boundary is made,[61] they permit nine possible combinations of antecedents. It is possible, furthermore, to add one more candidate between # and // at the initial position, as indicated by the (NP) in (146):

(145)

	# 1	3	5	7	# 10
(i)		*NP*		refl	
(ii)		*NP*	*NP*	refl	

(146)

	# 1		// 2	3	5	7	// 10	11	12	# 14
(iii)		(*NP*)		*NP*	*NP*	refl		∅	NP	
(iv)		(*NP*)		*NP*		refl		∅	NP	
(v)		(*NP*)		*NP*		refl		∅	*NP*	
(vi)		(*NP*)			*NP*	refl		∅	*NP*	
(vii)		(*NP*)				refl		∅	*NP*	
(viii)		*		*NP*	*NP*	refl		X	*NP*	
(ix)		(*NP*)			*NP*	refl		X	*NP*	
(x)		(*NP*)				refl		X	*NP*	
(xi)		(*NP*)				refl		X	*NP*	

In (145) and (146), all the italicized NPs are possible antecedents. Strings (iii)–(vii) have ∅ for their term 11, which means that they have relative clauses. The X in (viii)–(xi) means that term 11 is filled with some form other than a human noun phrase. String (viii) does not have a parenthesized NP, which means that the fourth candidate is not permitted. Thus, possible combinations total 19. Although all the possibilities are realized as actually occurring sentences, only 11 combinations are illustrated in (147), since the addition of (NP)s is nothing more than a repetition of the application of Rule (a).

Furthermore, (145) and (146) show that the maximum number of ante-

[61]Rule (a) makes crucial use of initial # or //, while Rules (c) and (d) use the internal //.

cedents for forward reflexive interpretation is three, as in (iii), including (NP), and the maximum number of antecedents for backward interpretation is only one. Interaction of forward and backward interpretation is attested only in the case of the relative clause with its own subject; namely, if its subject stays in the clause, the head of the relative clause cannot be the antecedent unless the verb in it is [−Like Subj] verb:

(147) (i) *NP* *NP* refl
\# *gakubutyoo*$_i$ *ga Tanaka-san*$_j$ *ni zibun*$_{ij}$ *no kuruma de*
car in
Nakazima-kyoozyu o mukae-ni ik-ase-ta. # [(a), (b)]
go and get-cause-past
'The dean made Mr. Tanaka go and get Prof. Nakazima.'

(ii) *NP* refl
\# *Taroo*$_i$ *ga zibun*$_i$ *no heya de sigoto o si-ta.* # [(a)]
'Taro worked in his room.'

(iii) *NP* *NP* refl
\# // *Taroo*$_i$ *ga Hanako*$_j$ *ni zibun*$_{ij}$ *no hon o*
book
NP
okur-ase-ta// *otoko ga Taroo o tazune-te ki-ta.* #
send-cause-past visit-come-past
[(a), (b); (c) is inapplicable]
'The man to whom Taro$_i$ had Hanako$_j$ send self's$_{ij}$ book came to visit Taro.'

(iv) *NP* refl
\# // *Hanako*$_i$ *ga zibun*$_i$ *no hon o kasi-ta//*
book lend-past
NP
otoko ga Hanako o suisen-si-ta. # [(a)]
recommend-past
'The man to whom Hanako lent her book recommended her.'

(v) *NP* refl
\# // *Hanako*$_i$ *ga zibun*$_{ij}$ *no heya o soozi-s-ase-ta//*
room clean-cause-past
NP
gakusei$_j$ *ga ryoo o de-ta.* # [(a), (c)]
student dormitory
'The student$_j$ who Hanako$_i$ made clean self's$_{ij}$ room got out of the dormitory.'

(vi) *NP* refl
\# // *Hanako*$_i$ *ni zibun*$_{ij}$ *no heya de benkyoo-su-ru yoo ni*
room study to
NP
iituke-ta// sensei$_j$ *ga watasi no tannin*
tell-past teacher I 's homeroom teacher
des-u. # [(b), (c)]
is-polite
'The teacher who told Hanako to study in self's$_{ij}$ room is my homeroom teacher.'

(vii) refl *NP*
\# // *Zibun*$_i$ *no ronbun o taipu-si-te i-ta// Taroo*$_i$ *ga kyuu*
paper progressive-past
ni heya no soto e tobidasi-ta. # [(c)]
'Taro, who was typing his paper, ran out of the room suddenly.'

(viii) *NP* *NP* refl
\# // *Taroo*$_i$ *ga Ziroo*$_j$ *ni zibun*$_{ijk}$ *no heya de*
room in
NP
type-s-ase-ta// koto ga Hanako$_k$ *o okor-*
cause-past that get angry-
ase-ta. # [(a), (b), (d)]
cause-past
'That Taro$_i$ had Ziro$_j$ type in self's$_{ijk}$ room made Hanako$_k$ angry.'

(ix) *NP* refl
\# // *Ziroo*$_i$ *ni zibun*$_{ij}$ *no heya de taipu-s-ase-ta// koto ga*
room in cause-past that
NP
Hanako$_j$ *ni ansin-kan o atae-ta.* # [(b), (d)]
relief sense give-past
'That Hanako made Jiro$_i$ type in self's$_{ij}$ room gave Hanako$_j$ a sense of relief.'

(x) refl *NP*
\# // *Zibun*$_i$ *ga baka de ar-u // koto ga Mitiko*$_i$ *o*
fool be-non-past that
kanasim-ase-ta. # [(d)]
be sorry cause-past
'That she was a fool grieved Michiko.'

(xi) *NP* refl *NP*
\# // *Noboru*$_i$ *ga zibun*$_{ij}$ *no heya ni i-ta* // *koto ga Hirosi*$_j$
room in stay-past that
ni iyana kanzi o atae-ta. # [(a), (d)]
to bad feeling give-past
'That Noboru$_i$ was in self's$_{ij}$ room gave Hiroshi$_j$ a bad feeling.'

Interpretation of the Five Cases Discussed in Section 2

Now, let us turn to the interpretation of the five cases discussed in Section 2, for which the other four theories do not always provide satisfactory explanations.

PASSIVES

First, the interpretation of active sentences such as (54) is straightforward within our theory:

(54) # *Taroo*$_i$ *ga* // *zibun*$_{ij}$ *no kodomo o sinsatu-si-ta*// *isya*$_j$ *o sonkei-si-ta.* #
'Taro$_i$ respected the doctor$_j$ who examined self's$_{ij}$ child.'

In (54), Rule (a) can apply and interpret *zibun* as coreferential with *Taroo*. If this option is not chosen, then Rule (c) establishes *zibun*'s coreferentiality with *isya*. The result is consistent with the data.

Next, our theory also gives a unique interpretation to the passive counterpart of (54), i.e., (56), by Rule (c):

(56) # // *Zibun*$_j$ *no kodomo o sinsatu-si-ta*// *isya*$_j$ *ga Taroo ni sonkei-s-are-ta.* #
'The doctor$_j$ who examined self's$_j$ child was respected by Taro.'

CAUSATIVES

Since quite a few examples have already been given for the interpretation of regular causatives, let us take up causatives with psychological verbs, using (61) as an example:

(61) a. # *Hanako*$_i$ *wa* // *zibun*$_{ij}$ *no kuruma de dekake-ta* // *tomodati*$_j$ *no koto o sinpai-si-ta.* #
'Hanako$_i$ worried about the friend$_j$ who went out in self's$_{ij}$ car.'

Now, Rule (a) may identify *Hanako* as the antecedent of *zibun*. If this possibility is not chosen, Rule (c) identifies *tomodati* as its antecedent. Thus, two readings are assignable. Next, let us turn to the causative counterpart:

(61) b. # // *Zibun*$_j$ *no kuruma de dekake-ta*// *tomodati*$_j$ *ga Hanako o sinpai-s-ase-ta.* #
'The friend$_j$ who went out in self's$_j$ car worried Hanako.'

Here, Rule (c) interprets *zibun* as coreferential with *tomodati*. *Hanako* can never be so interpreted, since it is the second human noun phrase after //.

AFFECTIVE PASSIVES WITH CAUSATIVES AND *te moraw-u* SENTENCES

The affective passive formatives *rare* and *te moraw-u* are [−Like Subj] verbs. Thus, they permit ambiguous readings, as in:

(148) # *Taroo*$_i$ *wa tomodati*$_j$ *ni zibun*$_{ij}$ *no heya de*
friend by room in
sin-are-ta. #
die-affective-passive-past
'Taro's friend died in self's$_{ij}$ room on Taro$_i$.'

(149) # *Taroo*$_i$ *wa tomodati*$_j$ *ni zibun*$_{ij}$ *no heya ni i-te*
friend room in stay-
morat-ta. #
ask a favor of-past
'Taro$_i$ asked a favor of his friend$_j$ to stay in self's$_{ij}$ room.'

Earlier, I argued that some passive sentences whose subjects do not appear in their active counterparts must be taken to involve complementation, and the passive *rare* in this case must be marked with [−Like Subj], since in these sentences matrix and complement subjects must not be identical. These are called 'affective passives' [(148) is one of them].

In the case of simple passives, the object noun phrase appears as the subject of its passive counterpart. In the following sentences, which appeared in Section 2, the passive subjects are not the active objects. This is indicated by (34′), (36′), and (37′), which are their active counterparts. Because of this characteristic, it does not seem quite adequate to treat these sentences as simple passives. This is a syntactic reason to classify them, with passives like (148), as affective passives:

(34) # *Boku*$_i$ *wa Yamada-sensei ni zibun*$_i$ *no kanai o iti-zikan mo mat-ase-rare-ta.* #
'I was subjected to Prof. Yamada making my wife wait an hour.'

(34′) *Yamada-sensei*$_j$ *wa* $\begin{Bmatrix} zibun_j \\ boku \end{Bmatrix}$ *no kanai o iti-zikan mo mat-ase-ta.*[62]

[62]In causative sentences, the subject is the antecedent of *zibun*. This reading does not remain in the causative passive version.

'Prof. Yamada_j made his_j (my) wife wait for an hour.'

(36) # *Taroo_i wa Hanako ni zibun_i no kodomo o hatarak-ase-rare-ta.* #
'Taro_i was subjected to Hanako making his_i child work.'

(36′) *Hanako_j wa* $\left\{\begin{matrix} \textit{zibun}_j \\ \textit{Taroo} \end{matrix}\right\}$ *no kodomo o hatarak-ase-ta.*
'Hanako made her (Taro's) child work.'

(37) # *Hanako_i wa Taroo ni zibun_i no otooto o rakudai-s-ase-rare-ta.* #
'Hanako_i was subjected to Taro making her brother flunk the exam.'

(37′) *Taroo_j wa* $\left\{\begin{matrix} \textit{zibun}_j \\ \textit{Hanako} \end{matrix}\right\}$ *no otooto o rakudai-s-ase-ta.*
'Taro made his (Hanako's) brother flunk the exam.'

Note that *zibun* in each of these sentences is unambiguous.

We saw in Section 2 that *te moraw-u* sentences, with causative and other types of complements, do not permit ambiguous readings, either:

(69′) # *Gakusei_j wa Tanaka-san ni zibun_j no peepaa o taipu-s-ase-te morat-ta.* #
'The student_j had Mr. Tanaka permit him to type his_j paper.'

(75b) # *Tanaka-san_k wa gakubutyoo ni // gakusei_j ga zibun_{kj} no heya de syorui o seiri-su-ru // koto o yurusi-te morat-ta.* #
'Mr. Tanaka_k asked a favor of the dean to permit the student_j to put the documents in order in self's_{kj} room.'

Observe that in both affective passives and *te moraw-u* sentences the feature [−Like Subj] appears twice consecutively, i.e., first on *sase* or *yurus* and next on *rare* or *te moraw*. Thus, we would predict four-way ambiguity if there are as many qualified antecedents. However, this prediction is not borne out in our data. They do not even permit two-way ambiguity. There are two possible explanations of this situation. One is to decide that sentences like (34), (36), and (37) are simple passives, and work out some way to account for *te moraw-u* sentences. J. McCawley does this. He argues that affective passives with causative complements do not exist, even when they are semantically called for. The reason for this is that, according to him, nonambiguous readings are given to all the cases of causative passives. The argument is circular, because he supports cyclic reflexivization on the basis of the ambiguity and nonambiguity involved in affective and simple passives, respectively. Then, he assumes sentences with nonambiguous interpretation of reflexives to be simple passives, regardless of their syntactic peculiarity. Furthermore, this argument is considerably weakened, since, as we have seen, *te moraw-u* (with [−Like Subj]) also loses this characteristic when it has a [−Like Subj] verb in the complement. If we derived *te moraw-u* sentences by simple movement transformations similar to simple passivization, we would not be able to explain the ambiguity in *te moraw-u* sentences like (149). Moreover, *moraw-u* has a distinct semantic value that selects an appropriate noun phrase for its subject, and can hardly be treated as an element automatically inserted as a result of transformation.

Taking sentences like (34), (36), and (37) as affective passives, the second explanation goes as follows: Since four-way ambiguity is utterly impossible, the feature specification seems to be nullified when two [−Like Subj] verbs appear consecutively, and these verbs are simply left without any specification as to [±Like Subj].

I adopt the second explanation because it covers all my data and explains syntactic and semantic peculiarities of affective passives. It also seems natural, within my framework, to regard nullification of complex semantic features as an interpretation process.

Finally, a comment about the difference in native intuition concerning Type A and Type B causative passives might be in order. We have assumed, so far, that both Type A and Type B causative passives are simple passives, because the subjects of the example sentences are the indirect objects of their active causative counterparts. In Japanese the indirect objects of causative sentences are obligatorily human noun phrases, so that (150a), with a nonhuman indirect object is ungrammatical, while (150b), with a nonhuman direct object, is grammatical:

(150) a. **Ware-ware wa ame **ni** hur-ase-ta.*
rain fall-cause-past
'We made it rain.'
b. *Ware-ware wa ame **o** hur-ase-ta.*
'We made it rain.'

Because of this factor, causative passives always have human subjects, which are originally the indirect objects of the embedded causatives.

When human noun phrases are the subjects of passive sentences, they are usually interpreted as affectees of the events. This is why simple passive sentences like (13) are often given ambiguous readings (see footnote 14). Thus, both Type A and Type B sentences are taken to be affective passives by many native speakers. The unique interpretation of Type A sentences seems to be the result of nullification, rather than the consequence of interpreting the sentences as simple passives. In this view, those who give ambiguous readings to Type B sentences are supposed to retain the affective passive reading. This is a plausible interpretation, because *zibun* in the object noun phrases of Type B sentences is more strongly connected with the affective passive reading than *zibun* in adverbial phrases of Type A sentences.

Inadequate though this particular semantic reasoning might be, data like this strongly suggest that the coreferential relation between the reflexive and the antecedent is a matter of semantic interpretation.

Center Embedding

First, take the case of two center embeddings:

(151) # *Watasi*$_i$ *wa* // *Hanako*$_j$ *ga Ziroo ni zibun*$_{ij}$ *no zisyo o*
dictionary
kasi-ta // *to omot-ta.* #
lend-past that think-past
'I thought that Hanako lent self's (her, my) dictionary to Jiro.'

This is the case of two possibilities of application of Rule (a), with *watasi* or *Hanako* identified as term 3 after # or //.

A few people who accept three coreferential readings of *zibun* in sentences with three center embeddings, such as (152), analyze them in the following way:

(152) # *Taroo*$_i$ *wa* # *watasi*$_j$ *ga* // *Hanako*$_k$ *ga Ziroo ni zibun*$_{ijk}$ *no kuruma o kasi-ta* // *to omot-ta* # *to it-ta.* #
'Taro$_i$ said that I$_j$ thought that Hanako$_k$ let Jiro have self's$_{ijk}$ car.'

Compare this with a sentence like (153), which involves three deep structure center embeddings, but is considerably higher in acceptability and receives three coreferential readings more easily than the preceding sentence:

(153) # *Taroo*$_i$ *wa* // *Ziroo*$_j$ *ga Hanako*$_k$ *ni zibun*$_{ijk}$ *no kutu o migak-ase-te i-ru* // *to omot-ta.* #
'Taro$_i$ thought Jiro$_j$ was making Hanako$_k$ polish self's$_{ijk}$ shoes.'

In the structure of (153), to which our rules apply, there are only two pairs of sentence boundaries. This explains the higher acceptability of this sentence with *zibun* interpreted in three ways. First, Rule (a) has two chances of application, identifying either *Taroo* or *Ziroo* as the antecedent. If neither one of them is chosen, then Rule (b) applies to establish *Hanako* as its antecedent, since it has a [−Like Subj] verb. The result is three-way ambiguity.

Complex Noun Phrases

It is obvious that the cyclic transformational theory misses the generalization about backward reflexivization. This is clearly shown by two facts:

1. It fails to account for reflexives in sentences with psychological verbs, regardless of what kinds of deep structures are posited (see Section 2).
2. It fails to account for reflexives in complex noun phrases of the type discussed in Section 2.

It is especially noteworthy that in the case of complex noun phrases certain conditions on reflexivization are inadequate.

Generalizations to be captured here are:

1. The subject-antecedent condition should not be placed on backward reflexivization.
2. For all cases of backward reflexivization, the relevant conditions are the antecedent-command condition and the condition that the first human noun after the internal sentence boundary (//) be the antecedent.

The differences between relative clauses and the other nominal clauses appear as conditions on Rule (c) of (97).

In my theory, the reflexives in complex noun phrases under discussion are not exceptions at all. They are interpreted in exactly the same way as those in other relative and nominal clauses are. Let us see how this is done by our rules (again, with examples from Section 2):

(84) # *Yamada-sensei wa* // *zibun*$_i$ *no ie ga yake-ta* //
1 3 4 7 8 9 10
∅ *gakusei*$_i$ *o atume-ta.* #
11 12 13 14
'Prof. Yamada gathered the students whose houses were burnt down.'

(85) # *Katoo-si wa* // // *zibun*$_i$ *ga osie-te i-ta* // *gakusei ga*
1 3 4 7 8
zisatu-si-ta // ∅ *sensei ni ai-ni it-ta.* #
9 10 11 12 13 14
'*Mr. Kato went to see the teacher$_i$ who the student self$_i$ was teaching committed suicide.'

(86) # *Watasi wa* // // *zibun*$_i$ *ga kai-ta hon o syuppan-si-ta* //
1 3 4 7 8
honya ga hasan-si-ta // ∅ *gakusya o sit-te i-ru.* #
8 9 10 11 12 13 14
'*I know the scholar who the publisher which published the book which he wrote went broke.'

In (84), 11 is ∅, so that Rule (c) applies, establishing a coreferential relation between 7 and 12 in a straightforward manner. In (85) and (86), *zibun* is the subject of relative clauses. However, the reflexive is bounded by two pairs of //'s in each case, so that the second condition on Rule (c), $\begin{bmatrix} +\text{Refl} \\ \text{NP} \end{bmatrix} \neq \text{Subj}$, does not hold. This is why the coreferentiality is established between the reflexive and *gakusei* and *gakusya* in (85) and (86). Appositive clauses are handled in the same way.

It should be noted that the matrix subject (term 3 in these examples) cannot be identified as the antecedent in any of these cases, though the four theories discussed in Section 2, as well as our theory, predict that there is a coreferential relation between them. This is a problem to be studied in the future, especially in relation to the study of relative clauses in general.[63]

There are sentences which yield two alternative analyses for the application of Rule (c). (154) is an example of this kind, which is given ambiguous readings by two possible applications of Rule (c).

(154) a. # *Katoo-si wa // // zibun*$_i$ *no sigoto o issyookenmei si-te i-ta*
1 3 4 7 8 9
// ∅ gakusei$_i$ *ga zisatu-si-ta // ∅ sensei ni ai-ni it-ta.* #
10 11 12 13 14
'*Mr. Kato went to see the teacher who the student$_i$ who was doing his$_i$ work in earnest committed suicide.'

b. # *Katoo-si wa // // zibun*$_j$ *no sigoto o issyookenmei*
1 3 4 7
si-te i-ta // ∅ gakusei ga zisatu-si-ta // ∅ sensei$_j$ *ni . . .*
8 9 10 11 12 13
'*Mr. Kato went to see the teacher$_j$ who the student who was doing his$_j$ work in earnest committed suicide.'

Further Clarification and Additional Facts

Clarification of Condition (iii) of (97). In the following examples, the second human noun phrases after // are interpreted as the antecedents.

(155) # // *Zibun*$_i$ *no daigaku ga zaisei-nan ni*
university financial difficulty in
oti-it-ta// koto ga watasi$_k$ *no syuzin*$_i$ *o itumo nayam-ase-*
get into-past that my husband always worry-cause
te i-masi-ta. #
state-polite-past
'That his$_i$ university had gotten into financial difficulty always worried my husband$_i$.'

[63]As a matter of fact, some speakers admit coreferential relation between the reflexive and the matrix subject, *Katoo-si* in both (85) and (154). The whole situation should be further clarified.

(156) # // *Zibun*$_i$ *no uti ga binboo na*// *noni* // *Yamada-san ga*
family poor be though
osie-te i-ru // *gakusei*$_i$ *wa*
teach-progressive-non-past student
mudazukai bakari si-te i-ru.
spend wastefully only do-progressive-non-past
'Though self's$_i$ family is poor, the student$_i$ Mr. Yamada is teaching is always wasteful.'

Watasi in (155) is not qualified as the antecedent, because it is dominated by Det and within the NP cycle. *Yamada-san* in (156) does not qualify to be the antecedent, either, owing to Condition (i), because it does not command the reflexive, as is clear in (157), the structure of (156) to which our rules apply:

(157)

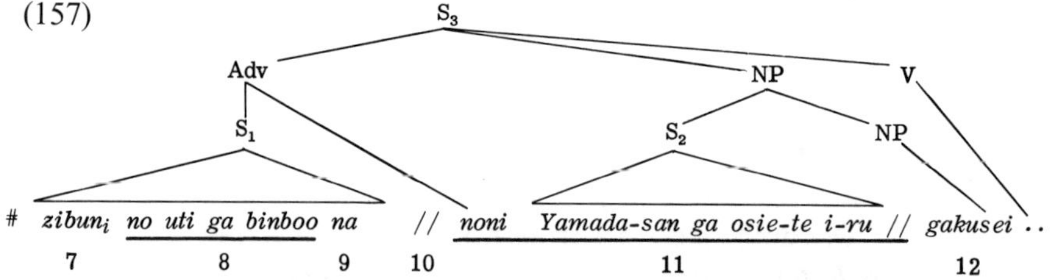

Because of the presence of S_2 over *Yamada-san*, *Yamada-san* does not command *zibun*$_i$. Therefore, *gakusei* is the only qualified antecedent, even though it is the second human noun phrase after //.[64]

The situation is the same in the case of forward reflexive interpretation, as is shown by (158):

(158) # *Katoo-san*$_i$ *wa* // *Mitiko ga osie-te i-ru* //
teach-progressive-non-past
gakusei$_j$ *o zibun*$_{ij}$ *no heya de benkyoo-s-ase-ta.* #
student self's room in study-do-cause-past
'Mr. Kato$_i$ made (let) the student$_j$ who Michiko is teaching study in self's$_{ij}$ room.'

(159)

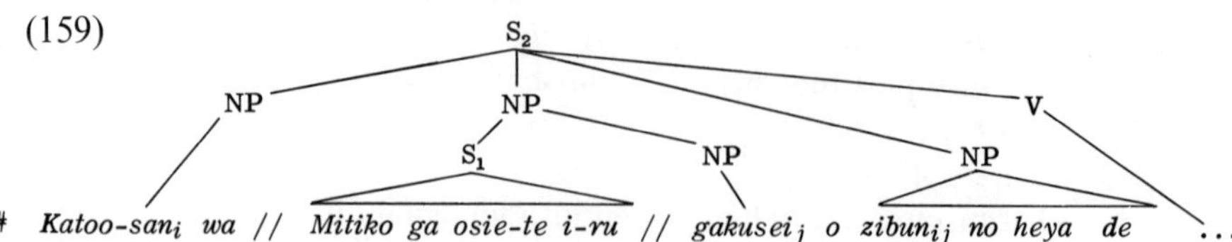

[64]It may not be adequate to take NP to constitute a cycle, because it makes it impossible to say that *gakusei* [term 12 in (157)] commands the reflexive. Then Condition (iv), $\begin{bmatrix}+\text{H}\\ \text{NP}\end{bmatrix}$ is not dominated by Det, is necessary.

As is clear in (159), *Mitiko* does not qualify as the antecedent owing to the presence of S_1 over it.

These examples show that Condition (iii) must be modified to read as follows:

CONDITION (iii): *Terms 2, 4, 11 do not contain an* $\begin{bmatrix} +H \\ NP \end{bmatrix}$ *that meets Condition (i).*

There is one case that must be accounted for by the A-over-A principle.[65] Observe the following:

(160) **Midori-san*$_i$ *to Kaoru-san*$_j$ *ga zibun*$_i$ *no syasin o*
and picture at
mi-te i-ru.
look-progressive-non-past
'*Midori$_i$ and Kaoru are looking at her$_i$ picture.'

In (160), the subject is a coordinate noun phrasc, so that one conjunct, *Midori-san*, cannot be picked out and interpreted as the antecedent, even though it is identified as term 3 of (97). This is the case where the coordinate structure constraint[66] works. However, a better explanation might be to say that the A-over-A principle is at work, because it explains not only why *Midori-san* alone cannot be the antecedent but also why the two conjuncts together can be the antecedent of the plural *zibun-tati* in (161):

(161) # *Midori-san to Kaoru-san* *ga* *zibun-tati* *no syasin o*
3 7 8
mi-te i-ru. #
9 10

MORE THAN ONE REFLEXIVE IN A SENTENCE

More than one reflexive may appear in a sentence,[67] as in (162):

[65]The principle states that transformations apply to the topmost category if it dominates the same category. The subject of (160) has the following structure:

(160)

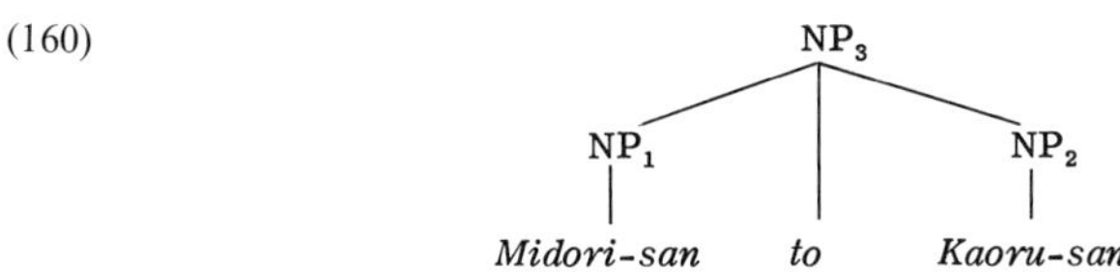

Since NP_3 is the topmost NP in this case, this rule must apply to NP_3.

[66]This constraint states that one of the conjuncts of a coordinate structure cannot be extracted from it by a movement rule. This constraint works in the identification of coreferentiality, too.

[67]The second, and possibly the third, reflexive appear as term 8.

(162) *Taroo$_i$ ga Hanako ni zibun$_i$ ga kari-ta zibun$_i$ no kyoori no*
borrow-past hometown
rekisi o kai-ta hon o mise-ta.
history write-past book show-past
'Taro$_i$ showed Hanako the book that he$_i$ borrowed that tells the history of his$_i$ hometown.'

The antecedent of both reflexives in (162) is *Taroo*. However, we cannot tell from this example alone whether reflexives in a sentence always share the same antecedent, because *Taroo* is the only qualified noun phrase in (162). Let us turn to a sentence with two qualified noun phrases:

(163)[68] # *Taroo$_i$ wa Hanako ni$_{(j)}$ zibun$_{i(j)}$ o tot-ta zibun$_{i(j)}$ no*
take-past
syasin o yaki-masi-sase-ta. #
picture get extra printing cause-past
'Taro$_i$ had Hanako$_j$ get extra prints of the picture of self$_{ij}$ which self$_{ij}$ took.'

Suppose that each reflexive in (163) is identified as coreferential with either one of the qualified noun phrases. Then we might expect that the sentence would be four ways ambiguous among the four possible combinations of coreferential relations:

	zibun	*zibun*
(a)	*i*	*i*
(b)	*i*	*j*
(c)	*j*	*j*
(d)	*j*	*i*

The fact is, however, that only (a) and (c), which permit pairs of identical coreferential relations, are accepted, as indicated by parentheses in (163). From this, it is clear that there must be a device to copy the coreferential reading from the first reflexive onto the following ones.[69]

A RESIDUAL PROBLEM

Perlmutter (1973) gives the following sentence as one piece of evidence for cyclic reflexivization. His point is that reflexivization should take place in (164) before the underlying subject *Mitiko* is raised in order to get the reading indicated by the indexes:

[68]I owe this sentence to Ogawa.

[69]Some speakers permit four way ambiguity in this case. To those speakers, the reflexives that appear as term 8 are independently assigned coreferential readings by (97). Then the rules should read that $\begin{bmatrix} +\text{Refl} \\ \text{NP} \end{bmatrix}$ in term 7 and 8 = 3, etc. Cf. Howard and Niyekawa-Howard (in this volume) for a discussion of multiple reflexives and a transformational treatment of the phenomenon.

(164) [Perlmutter, 1973:(19)]

Watasi wa Mitiko$_i$ *o zibun*$_i$ *ni tyuuzitu da to omotte iru.*
'I think Michiko to be faithful to herself.'

Some native speakers, including myself, are doubtful whether *Mitiko* can be the antecedent of the reflexive in this sentence, the interpretation of *watasi* as the antecedent being so predominant. However, we have to admit that our rules cannot explain the intuition of those who accept the coreferential relation between *Mitiko* and the reflexive.

4. ASSIGNMENT OF PREFERRED READINGS

The rules in (97) establish coreferential relations between reflexives and antecedents on the basis of syntactic information. Then final adjustments are made to the already-given readings by another set of semantic interpretation rules. In this section I shall point out some factors that play important roles in such semantic interpretation rules.

The role of underlying cases in deciding preferred readings has already been discussed in Section 2. I list here some of the sentences given there to show that our rules assign ambiguous readings to them:

(27)[70] *Taroo*$_{(i)}$ *wa Ziroo*$_j$ *ni zibun*$_{(i)j}$ *no sippai o sator-ase-ta.*
'Taro$_{(i)}$ made Jiro$_j$ realize his$_{(i)j}$ failure.'

(29) *Taroo*$_i$ *wa tuma*$_{(j)}$ *o zibun*$_{i(j)}$ *ga kat-ta kusuri de sin-ase-te simat-ta.*
'Taro$_i$ had his wife$_{(j)}$ die because of the medicine self$_{i(j)}$ bought.'

(31) *Hanako*$_i$ *wa Taroo*$_{(j)}$ *ni zibun*$_{i(j)}$ *no kuruma ni nor-are-ta.*
'Taro$_{(j)}$ rode in self's$_{i(j)}$ car on Hanako$_i$.'

The antecedents in these sentences are decided either by Rule (a) or Rule (b), because the verbs are marked with [−Like Subj]. However, in each case the preferred, or usual, reading is the coreferential relation between the underlying Experiencer and the reflexive.

Next, in case there is no noun phrase qualified as the antecedent, the Experiencer is interpreted as such:

(165) [Kuno, 1972: (117a)]

Sono keiken wa Mary$_i$ *ni zibun*$_i$ *ga baka de aru koto o osieta*
the experience to self fool is that taught.
'That experience taught Mary that she was a fool.'

[70]Parentheses indicate nonpredominant readings assigned by our rules.

(166) [Ibid., (117b)]
John no zisatu wa Mary$_i$ ni-totte zibun$_i$ ga kare ni
's suicide to self he by
uragir-are-ta koto o imisita.
betray-passive-ed *that* meant
'John's suicide meant to Mary that she had been betrayed by him.'

(167) [Ibid., (117c)]
Kono zizitu wa Mary$_i$ ni dare mo zibun$_i$ o aisite-inai
this fact to any one self love-not
koto o sisasita.
that suggested
'This fact suggested to Mary that no one loved her.'

Though *Mary* does not qualify as the antecedent in each case, there is no other qualified noun phrase, so that *Mary*, as an Experiencer, is so understood. If, for example, sono *keiken* in (165) is replaced by *John*, *Mary* cannot be taken as the antecedent:

(168) *John$_j$ wa Mary ni zibun$_j$ ga baka de aru koto o osieta.*
'John taught Mary that he was a fool.'

The same is true with the rest of the preceding examples.

A negative role played by the underlying Object was also discussed in Section 2. All the examples given in this connection are ungrammatical, because the underlying Object is supposed to be the antecedent of the reflexive in each case. Example (46) is among these:

(46) **John$_i$ wa Mary ga zibun$_i$ ni ai ni kita toki moo sinde-imasita*
'John, when Mary came to see him, was already dead.'

Rule (d), however, interprets *John* as the antecedent. At present, I do not know whether we should stipulate that the antecedent of the reflexive must be either an Agent or an Experiencer, or that it must not be the underlying Object. However, it is reasonable to try to account for this phenomenon by positing a thematic hierarchy with Experiencer and Agent on the top and Object at the bottom. With a more detailed study, it would become possible to specify the positions of the other cases in the hierarchy. Then this will work as a mechanism for final adjustment in the semantic component.[71]

[71]Example (i) below is an example to which Rule (d) does not apply. (The reflexive is the subject of the relative clause and bounded by only one pair of //'s.)

(i) ?# // *Zibun$_i$ ga rikon-si-ta* // ∅ *tuma ga kyoozyu$_i$ ni*
7 9 10 11 12 13
divorce-past wife professor to

The second factor in deciding preferred readings is the directional meaning of the verb. Observe the following:

(169) [Oyakawa, 1973: (15a)]
Yamada-si$_i$ *wa musuko*$_{(j)}$ *ga zibun*$_{i(j)}$ *no zimusyo ni*
son self's office to
ku-ru no o iyagat-ta.
come-non-past that dislike-past
'Mr. Yamada$_i$ did not like that his son$_{(j)}$ comes to self's$_{i(j)}$ office.'

In case *Yamada-si* is supposed to be in his office, which is the most common interpretation, *zibun* is interpreted as coreferential with *Yamada-si* because, roughly speaking, *ku-ru* (come) means[72] a motion of someone other than the speaker and/or the matrix subject (when *ku-ru* occurs in an embedded sentence) toward the location of the speaker and/or the matrix subject. Another, less preferable, reading is given in which *Yamada-si* is in his son's office and his son comes to his own office. If we change *o* after *ku-ru no* into *mo*, this reading is easily given:

(170) *Yamada-si wa musuko*$_j$ *ga zibun*$_j$ *no zimusyo ni ku-ru no mo kirat-ta.*
'Mr. Yamada did not like even his son's$_j$ coming to his$_j$ own office.'

Because of this directional sense, (171) below is grammatical, while (172) is not:

(171) [Kuroda, 1973b: (12)]
John wa zyuunen mae ni Mary ga zibun o tazunete kita
ten years ago self visit-come-past
ie de ima wa koohuku-ni kurasite-imasu.
house in now happily live-polite-non-past

---

bakudai na zaisan o motarasi-ta. #
13 14
big fortune bring-past
'The wife self$_i$ divorced brought a big fortune to the professor$_i$.'

(I owe this sentence to Harada.)
Some speakers interpret *Kyoozyu* in the above as the antecedent, but others do not. *Kyoozyu* is not an Experiencer in this case, which may be the reason for the difference in native reactions. Condition on Rule (c) of (97) block the coreferential interpretation between the reflexive and *tuma*, because the reflexive is the subject and it is not bounded by more than one pair of //'s.

[72] This is, necessarily, a very much simplified interpretation of deictic forms, which should be treated with more attention to the intricate relation between the speaker and the subject. Deixis is also sensitive to the reportive–nonreportive distinction.

'John now lives happily in the house where Mary came to visit him ten years ago.'

(172) [Ibid., (14)]
**John wa zyuunen mae ni Mary ga zibun o tazunete-itta ie de ima wa koohuku-ni kurasite-imasu.*
'John now lives happily in the house where Mary went to visit him ten years ago.'

Example (172) is ungrammatical because *ik-u* 'go' means the motion away from the speaker and/or the matrix subject. In this sentence the subject is now in the house, so that anyone who visited him came toward his present location.

The third factor is the case in which the verb does not permit the subject and the object to be identical. Let us call this the nonidentical subject object constraint. Consider the following examples [(129) was discussed in Section 3]:

(129) a. *Mary ga zibun$_i$ o hinansita koto ga John$_i$ o utinomesita*
'That Mary accused self (= him) floored John.'
b. **Mary$_j$ ga zibun$_j$ o hinansita*
'Mary accused herself.'

(173) [Oyakawa 1973: (13a)]
a. *Syoonen$_i$ wa roozin ni zibun$_i$ no iken o kii-te*
boy old man self's opinion listen
morat-ta.
to ask a favor of-past
'The boy$_i$ asked the old man a favor of listening to self's$_i$ opinion.'
b. **Roozin$_j$ ga zibun$_j$ no iken o kii-ta.*
'*The old man$_j$ listened to self's$_j$ opinion.'

(174) a. *Oedipus$_i$ wa Jocasta ga zibun$_i$ o unda ie de ima wa*
bore house in now
kodomotati to koohuku-soo-ni kurasite imasu.
children with happily living-is
'Oedipus now lives happily with his children in the house where Jocasta bore him.'
b. **Jocasta$_j$ ga zibun$_j$ o unda.*
'*Jocasta bore herself.'

The (b) sentences indicate that their verbs are subject to the nonidentical subject object constraint. That only the matrix subjects can be the antecedents in the (a) sentences is a natural consequence of this constraint.

The fourth factor is the distinction between the reportive and nonreportive styles discussed by Kuroda. If the information about this distinction is made available in some form in the base component, it will be possible to make insertion of reflexives sensitive to a selectional restriction of this type. As discussed before, style distinctions in general function as selectional restrictions on honorifics; special vocabulary used by men, women, children; and jargons of various kinds. Honorifics are especially relevant to this question because they are attached to discontinuous formatives in systematic agreement.[73]

Such being the general situation with style distinctions, there is no reason why the reportive–nonreportive distinction cannot be treated as part of it. Then the choice of *zibun* in the reportive style will be limited only to the case in which the clausemate subject appears as the antecedent and *zibun* as the object. In the reportive style, (175) receives only one coreferential reading between the clausemate subject *Hanako* and the reflexive:

(175) *Hirosi wa Hanako*$_i$ *ga zibun*$_i$ *o damasi-te i-ru*
fool-progressive-non-past
to omot-ta.
that think-past
'Hiroshi thought that Hanako was fooling herself.'

If *Hirosi* is the object, *kare* instead of *zibun* is used in this style, as in (176):

(176) *Hirosi*$_j$ *wa Hanako ga kare*$_j$ *o damasi-te-i-ru to omot-ta.*
'Hiroshi thought that Hanako was fooling him.'

(177) **Hirosi wa Hanako*$_i$ *ga kanozyo*$_i$ *o damasi-te-i-ru to omot-ta.*

Since *kanozyo* is the object and supposed to be coreferential with the clausemate subject *Hanako*, (177) is ungrammatical.[74]

The situation is complex when nonobject *zibun* appears. Observe the following contrast:

(178) a. *Gakusei wa zibun-tati no heya ni tate-komot-ta.*
students selves room in close up-past
'The students closed themselves up in their rooms.'
b. *Gakusei wa kare-ra no heya ni tate-komot-ta.*
'The students closed themselves up in their rooms.'

Because of the use of *zibun* in nonobject position, (178a) is interpreted as in

[73]This does not mean that actual honorific forms are decided in the deep structure. We should say that if certain information about stylistic distinctions is included in deep structures, this will trigger the attachment of honorifics to appropriate elements by low-level transformations.

[74]If the reflexive form *kanozyo-zisin* is used in place of *kanozyo*, the sentence will become grammatical.

the nonreportive style, while (178b), with *kare-ra* 'they', is taken to be in the reportive style. Even though the distinction is subtle in many cases, this principle seems to hold in general. Examples (179) and (180) are a similar contrastive pair:

(179) *Hirosi*$_i$ *wa Hanako*$_j$ *ga zibun*$_{ij}$ *no heya ni i-ru*
room in be-non-past
to omot-ta.
that think-past
'Hiroshi$_i$ thought Hanako$_j$ was in self's$_{ij}$ room.'

(180) a. *Hirosi*$_i$ *wa Hanako ga kare*$_i$ *no heya ni i-ru to omot-ta.*
'Hiroshi thought that Hanako was in his room.'
b. *Hirosi wa Hanako*$_j$ *ga kanozyo*$_j$ *no heya ni i-ru to omot-ta.*
'Hiroshi thought that Hanako was in her room.'

Example (179) is in the nonreportive style, while the sentences in (180) are in the reportive style.

As a matter of fact, native speakers who are restrictive in the use of *zibun* have the same limitation as the reportive style, namely, limiting the use of *zibun* to the object position, and only as coreferential with the clausemate subject, i.e., the subject within a simplex sentence. Those speakers use, in place of reflexives, *kare* 'he' *kanozyo* 'she', and other pronominal forms like *ano hito* 'that man', *sono onna* 'the woman', *aitu* 'that guy', etc., which consist of demonstratives and pronominals of various kinds.

The fifth factor is Kuno's proposal of direct discourse analysis, which seems to be effective in explaining properties of Kuroda's nonreportive (subject-oriented) speech style. At least, the awareness of the subject in Kuno's sense plays an important role in the selection of lexical items of various kinds. Selection of tense is also sensitive to this aspect (cf. Inoue, 1973b).

Finally, I have to point out a difficulty involved in the interpretation of reflexives in copular sentences and the so-called 'pseudo-cleft' sentences. The following are examples from Oyakawa (1974) that cannot be handled by our theory, nor by the other theories discussed in Section 2. First, observe the following:

(181) a. *Oosama*$_i$ *no ziman wa zibun*$_i$ *no yuuhukusa da.*
king's pride self's wealth be-non-past
'The king's$_i$ pride is self's wealth.'
b. **Zibun*$_i$ *no ziman wa oosama*$_i$ *no yuuhukusa da.*
'Self's$_i$ pride is the king's$_i$ wealth.'
c. **Oosama*$_i$ *no yuuhukusa wa zibun*$_i$ *no ziman da.*
'The king's$_i$ wealth is self's$_i$ pride.'

d. *Zibun*$_i$ *no yuuhukusa wa oosama*$_i$ *no ziman da.*
'Self's$_i$ wealth is the king's$_i$ pride.'

(182) a. *Sono risoosyugisya*$_i$ *no risoo wa zibun*$_i$ *ga risoo o*
the idealist's ideal self ideal
mot-ana-i koto dat-ta.
have-not-non-past that be-past
'The ideal of that idealist$_i$ was that self$_i$ would not have any ideal.'

b. **Zibun*$_i$ *no risoo wa sono risoosyugisya*$_i$ *ga risoo o mot-ana-i koto dat-ta.*
'Self's$_i$ ideal was that the idealist$_i$ would not have any ideal.'

c. **Sono risoosyugisya*$_i$ *ga risoo o mot-ana-i koto wa zibun*$_i$ *no risoo dat-ta.*
'That the idealist$_i$ would not have any ideal was self's$_i$ ideal.'

d. *Zibun*$_i$ *ga risoo o mot-ana-i koto wa sono risoosyugisya*$_i$ *no risoo dat-ta.*
'That self$_i$ would not have any ideal was the ideal of that idealist$_i$.'

It is clear that in these examples neither the subject-antecedent condition nor the antecedent-command condition holds. Let us set up the antecedent-precede condition exclusively to account for reflexives in copular sentences,[75] and assume that topicalization applies after reflexivization or reflexive interpretation. Then we can explain the grammaticality of the (d) sentences. As for the ungrammaticality of the (c) sentences, the four theories (that is, all except deep structure interpretation) are capable of accounting for them. The (c) sentences are ungrammatical because after topicalization is applied, the second identical noun phrases are reflexivized. However, there is no reason why we should not expect the (c) sentences also to be non-topicalized sentences, with reflexives derived by the antecedent-precede condition. The question is how we could decide that the (a) sentences are not topicalized, while the (c) sentences are. This problem cannot be explained unless we set up a semantic rule that decides the proper relation of the subject and the predicate noun phrase in a copular sentence.

Next, let us turn to pseudo-cleft sentences, again from Oyakawa (1974):

[75]The antecedent-command condition is to be given up in the interpretation of reflexives in copular sentences, as well as in coordinate sentences. There may be some other minor exceptions. However, this condition is necessary for the majority of cases. Without it, we cannot explain the grammaticality of sentences like (5) and many others that are handled by Rules (c) and (d).

(183) a. *Tyanpion*$_i$ *ga zimansi-ta koto wa zibun*$_i$ *no tuyosa da.*
champion be proud-past that self's strength
'What the champion$_i$ was proud of is self's$_i$ strength.'
b. **Zibun*$_i$ *ga zimansi-ta koto wa tyanpion*$_i$ *no tuyosa da.*
'*What self$_i$ was proud of is the champion's$_i$ strength.'
c. **Tyanpion*$_i$ *no tuyosa wa zibun*$_i$ *ga zimansi-ta koto da.*
'*The champion's$_i$ strength is what self$_i$ was proud of.'
d. ?*Zibun*$_i$ *no tuyosa wa tyanpion ga zimansi-ta koto da.*
'Self's$_i$ strength is what the champion$_i$ was proud of.'
e. *Tyanpion*$_i$ *ga zibun*$_i$ *no tuyosa o zimansi-ta.*
'The champion$_i$ was proud of self's$_i$ strength.'

Let us assume that we have pseudo-cleft transformation for Japanese, and take (183) as the input to this transformation. *Zibun* in (183) is accounted for in a straightforward manner by the five theories using the antecedent-precede condition. By ordering reflexivization or reflexive interpretation before pseudo-clefting, the five theories are all capable of accounting for the grammaticality of the (a) and (d) sentences and the ungrammaticality of the (b) and (c) sentences in (183). However, there is a set of sentences that follow exactly the same pattern as (183) and still are underivable by pseudo-clefting:

(184) a. *Keizi-butyoo*$_i$ *ga soosakaigi de teiansi-ta*
chief detective meeting for investigation propose-past
keikaku wa zibun$_i$ *ga otori ni nar-u koto*
plan self decoy become-non-past that
dat-ta.
be-past
'The plan that the chief detective$_i$ proposed at the staff meeting for investigation was that self$_i$ set himself up as a decoy.'
b. **Zibun*$_i$ *ga soosakaigi de teiansi-ta keikaku wa keizi-butyoo*$_i$ *ga otori ni nar-u koto dat-ta.*
'*The plan that self$_i$ proposed at the staff meeting for investigation was that the chief detective$_i$ set himself up as a decoy.'
c. **Keizi-butyoo*$_i$ *ga otori ni nar-u koto wa zibun*$_i$ *ga soosakaigi de teiansi-ta keikaku dat-ta.*
'*That the chief detective$_i$ set himself up as a decoy was the plan that self$_i$ proposed at the staff meeting for investigation.'
d. ??*Zibun*$_i$ *ga otori ni nar-u koto wa keizi-butyoo*$_i$ *ga soosakaigi de teiansi-ta keikaku dat-ta.*

'That self$_i$ set himself up as a decoy was the plan that the chief detective$_i$ proposed at the staff meeting for investigation.'

e. *Keizi-butyoo$_i$ ga soosakaigi de zibun$_i$ ga otori ni nar-u keikaku o teiansi-ta.*
'The chief detective$_i$ proposed at the staff meeting for investigation the plan that self$_i$ set himself up for decoy.'

f. *Keizi-butyoo$_i$ ga soosakaigi de teiansi-ta koto wa zibun$_i$ ga otori ni nar-u keikaku dat-ta.*
'What the chief$_i$ detective proposed at the staff meeting for investigation was the plan that self$_i$ set himself up for decoy.'

g. *Keizi-butyoo$_i$ ga zibun$_i$ ga otori ni nar-u keikaku o teiansi-ta no wa soosakaigi (de) dat-ta.*
'The time when the chief detective$_i$ proposed the plan that self$_i$ set himself up for decoy was at the staff meeting for investigation.'

If we take (184e) as the input sentence, then (184f) and (184g) are the only sentences derivable from this by pseudo-clefting, while none of the others in (184) are. Because of the head noun phrase (*keikaku* 'plan'), pseudo-clefting is very much limited. The adequacy of pseudo-clefting in English is seriously questioned by Higgins from syntactic and semantic points of view. Among various reasons he gives, the difficulty of specifying the relation between the subject and the predicate noun phrase in a copular sentence, and the nonexistence of underlying sentences for some pseudo-cleft sentences, are important ones. The situation in Japanese also strongly suggests the inadequacy of this transformation, together with the transformational derivation of reflexives.

Thus, it seems reasonable to keep our conditions on (97) and leave the interpretation of reflexives in copular sentences (including pseudo-cleft sentences) to another type of semantic interpretation rule, which is needed anyway to decide the grammaticality of copular sentences on the basis of whether or not subjects and predicate noun phrases hold semantically proper relations.

Needless to say, a sentence is not well-formed if it has a reflexive that is still without the specification of coreferential relation with its antecedent at the exit of the semantic component.

ACKNOWLEDGMENTS

This work was done while I was at Massachusetts Institute of Technology as a visiting scientist, partly supported by a grant from the Japan Private School Research Foundation. Portions of this work were presented at the Linguistic Colloquium at the University of California, San Diego; Stanford–Berkeley Center for East Asian Studies at the University of California, Berkeley; and the University of Massachusetts, Amherst. Comments by professors and students who attended those sessions contributed to the improvements of this chapter. I am indebted to A. Akmajian, S. Y. Kuroda, P. Murray, K. Ogawa, and M. Shibatani for their comments on specific points. I am particularly grateful to S. Bell, S. Martin, and S. Haraguchi, who read the preliminary versions of this chapter and gave me detailed comments.

PASSIVIZATION

IRWIN HOWARD AND AGNES M. NIYEKAWA-HOWARD

INTRODUCTION

The syntactic and semantic properties of the Japanese passive construction have attracted attention for many years. Only within the past decade, however, have we progressed beyond a superficial characterization and attempted to explore its properties in greater detail. The results of these investigations have been extremely rewarding, since it has been shown that the passive interacts with other phenomena in very interesting ways.

A work like this one seems almost redundant today, following so soon after the comprehensive overview of the controversy on the passive by Shibatani (1972b) and the compelling evidence introduced by N. McCawley (1972a, b)[1] for a particular view of the passive. However, our own research raises some questions that, we feel, call for a reappraisal of views that are currently widely accepted.

The focus of the following discussion is on arguments for the SYNTACTIC structure of the Japanese passive. It is inevitable, given the nature of this construction, that the relationship between its syntactic and semantic properties should form part of the argument, but many interesting and controversial aspects of the semantics of the passive that are peripheral to the

[1] N. McCawley (1972b) is a revised version of the third chapter of her dissertation, (1972a). Since the former is not only modified but also more accessible, we will refer to it exclusively when the two works overlap.

primary concerns here will be left for another study (Howard and Niyekawa-Howard, forthcoming (a)).

This chapter is divided into four major sections. Section 1 provides a general background to the two major positions on the syntactic structure of the passive. Section 2 presents the evidence that has been advanced in support of the view we shall refer to as the 'nonuniform'[2] theory and some counterarguments to that evidence. Section 3 presents an alternative explanation of the crucial interrelationship between reflexivization and passives. Finally, Section 4 is a brief summary and conclusion.

1. BACKGROUND

Direct and Indirect Passives

Many Japanese passive sentences are directly parallel to English passives in structure:

(1) a. *Taroo wa sensei ni sikarareta.*
teacher scold-passive
'Taro was scolded by the teacher.'
b. *Sensei wa Taroo o sikatta.*
scold
'The teacher scolded Taro.'

In both the Japanese and English sentences in (1), the object of the active sentence (1b) appears as the subject of the corresponding passive sentence (1a).

The most striking property of the Japanese passive is the fact that it often contains one more noun phrase than appears in its closest active counterpart. This noun phrase represents the individual indirectly affected by the action or event expressed in the remainder of the sentence:[3]

(2) a. *Tanaka-san wa sensei ni kodomo o sikarareta.*
child scold-passive
'Tanaka had his child scolded by the teacher.'
b. *Taroo wa ame ni hurareta.*
rain fall-passive
'Taro was rained on.'

[2]This term has been adopted from N. McCawley (1972b).

[3]No attempt will be made here to provide consistent glosses for passive sentences. The semantic content of the Japanese passive is at least as much in controversy as its syntactic structure (cf. Niyekawa, 1968a; Howard, 1969; Alfonso, 1971; Makiuchi, 1972; N. McCawley, 1972b; Shibatani, 1972b).

Example sentences taken from other works will be glossed as in the original, except for minor modifications of format and romanization.

There is no active sentence directly corresponding to either of these sentences. Sentence (2b) also demonstrates that even intransitive verbs may be 'passivized' in Japanese.

For the purposes of this exposition, we shall refer to passive sentences like (1a) as 'direct' passives and those with an extra noun phrase like the examples in (2) as 'indirect' passives. This terminological distinction is based on a single syntactic criterion and is not intended to make any claim about other syntactic or semantic properties of these constructions. It is strictly an empirical question as to whether this distinction or some other best captures the relevant facts about the passive.

Alternative Views of the Passive

Two major positions have been taken on the structure of the Japanese passive. These positions are in essential agreement about the nature of the indirect passive construction, both assuming that indirect passives are derived from a deep structure involving two sentences. The extra noun phrase (always the subject of the passive) is assumed to be the subject of the matrix sentence, and the passive morpheme *-rare*, or some abstract equivalent,[4] is the matrix verb. An active sentence expressing the action or event is embedded in this structure as a complement. Thus, the assumed underlying structure for sentence (2a) is as follows:[5]

(3)

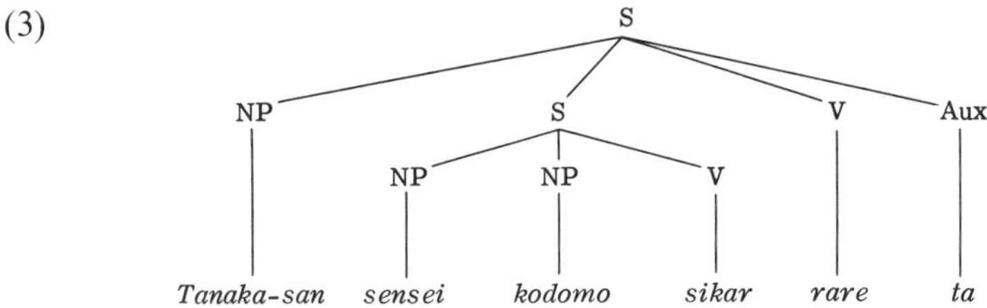

To convert this structure to the desired output string, it is necessary to assign the case markers by a set of rules such as those given in Kuno (1973) and to raise and adjoin the embedded verb to the matrix verb. Since verb raising leaves the embedded sentence without a verb, the S node dominating that sentence will be pruned by the universal convention proposed by Ross (1969).

[4]N. McCawley (1972b) assumes that *-rare* is added transformationally and that its place in the proposed deep structure in (3) is occupied, instead, by an abstract verb AFFECT. Makino (1973) proposes an abstract verb RECEIVE.

[5]This structure is presented solely to clarify the exposition and is not intended to make a claim with regard to the existence or nonexistence of a verb phrase node in Japanese. For an interesting discussion of this topic, see Hinds (1973b). The lack of an auxiliary in the embedded sentence may be due either to a rule of auxiliary deletion or to a deep structural restriction, as in the theory proposed by Kajita (1968b).

Although identical in their treatments of indirect passives, the two positions differ in their treatments of direct passives. In his pioneering study, Kuroda (1965b) proposes that both types of passives are derived from two-sentence sources like (3). With direct passive sentences, however, one of the arguments of the embedded sentence is identical with the subject of the matrix sentence. Thus, the deep structure of (1a) is assumed to be (4):

(4)

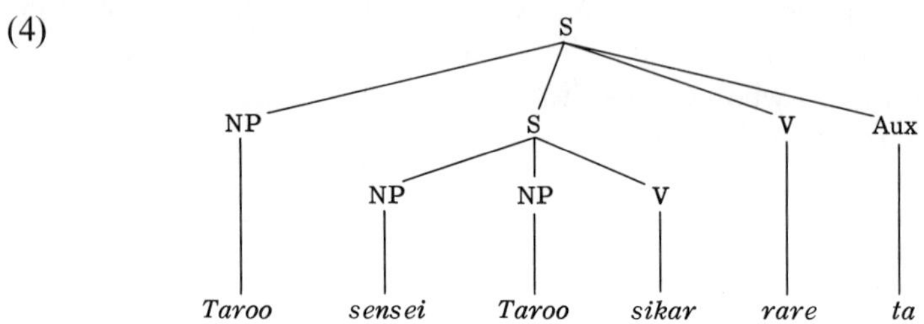

According to this view, direct passives are derived by deleting the embedded noun phrase under identity with the matrix subject, together with case marking and verb raising, as with indirect passives.

The second position is that indirect and direct passives are derived from different types of deep structures. This view has been most convincingly advocated by N. McCawley (1972b) and by Kuno (1973), and has gained widespread acceptance.[6] According to this view, indirect passive sentences are derived from a deep structure source containing two sentences, but direct passives are the result of a permutation transformation, which we shall refer to (following Kuno, 1973) as PURE PASSIVE FORMATION, applying to active sentences. The sentence underlying the direct passive sentence (1a) is, thus, held to be (1b).

We adopt here the terminology proposed by N. McCawley (1972b) to distinguish these two positions. The theory that holds that both types of passive sentences derive from a single type of deep structure will be referred to as the 'uniform' theory of the passive, while the theory that maintains that they have distinct deep structures will be called the 'nonuniform' theory.

One caution must be made with regard to this terminology, however. It expresses a dichotomy that is more severe than the range of theoretical positions actually taken in the literature. For example, Howard (1968, 1969) and Niyekawa-Howard (1968a) argue that passives with inanimate subjects and other 'translation-style' passives are derived by means of pure passive formation, as in the nonuniform theory, but that the remainder of the direct passive sentences are derived from a complex source, as in the uniform

[6]See, for example, J. McCawley (1972b), Harada (1973), Perlmutter (1973). However, Hasegawa (1964, 1968), Makino (1972, 1973), and others have been strong advocates of the uniform position.

theory. In the discussion that follows, the term NONUNIFORM will refer exclusively to the view that ALL direct passives are derived by pure passive formation, as in the McCawley–Kuno analysis.

2. EVIDENCE FOR AND AGAINST THE NONUNIFORM THEORY

The purpose of this section is to review and evaluate the various arguments that have been offered in favor of the nonuniform theory over the uniform theory. In each case, we will attempt to show that the evidence does not in fact support the nonuniform theory and, in one case, is actually in serious conflict with it. The first argument presented—that relating to the interaction between reflexives and passives—is discussed in this section only because it is a cornerstone on which the nonuniform theory is built and is, thus, crucial to the evaluation of the other arguments. In Section 3, we will deal with this argument in greater detail and show that the uniform theory is not only capable of handling the same facts but also correctly predicts some new facts that the nonuniform theory cannot account for.

The Reflexive Pronoun *Zibun*

The most interesting and most important single contribution to the controversy over the syntactic structure of the passive was the discovery that the reflexive pronoun *zibun* behaves peculiarly in passive constructions. This discovery and the conclusions as to its implications for the structure of the passive were apparently made independently by N. McCawley and by Kuno. To see this argument in proper perspective, it is first necessary to digress and discuss the behavior of the reflexive pronoun in other constructions.

One significant property of *zibun* is that its antecedent must be the subject of a sentence.[7] In (5), the antecedent of *himself* in the English translation is ambiguous, while *zibun* refers unambiguously to the subject of the sentence, *Taroo*:[8]

[7]Some authors (e.g., Oyakawa, 1973) argue for 'backward' as well as 'forward' reflexivization. Forward reflexivization is governed by the subject-antecedent condition, while in backward reflexivization the antecedent is never a subject. There is some controversy over whether backward reflexivization is attributable to an underlying subject that is subsequently removed from the subject position by a rule like psych movement (cf. especially Oyakawa, 1973; N. McCawley 1972a, 1971 under her maiden name, Akatsuka). For further details of Japanese reflexivization, cf. the chapters by N. McCawley and Inoue in this volume.

[8]In presenting sentences with reflexives, we will follow the practice of Kuno (1973) and N. McCawley (1972a) in sometimes using the word *self* in English translations to avoid the problems created by person, gender, and number distinctions with the English reflexive, as well as the problem of *X's own* in genitive constructions. Possible antecedents of the reflexive pronoun will be indicated by boldface type.

(5) a. ***Taroo*** *wa Ziroo ni* ***zibun*** *no syasin o miseta.*
self picture show
'Taro showed Jiro a picture of himself.'

A second property of *zibun* is that it does not have to be a clausemate (Postal, 1970a) of its antecedent.[9] In the following sentences (from Kuno, 1972:179), *zibun* is coreferential with the matrix subject *John*:

(6) a. ***John*** *wa [****zibun*** *ga kaita] tegami o yaburi suteta.*
write letter tearing-throw
'John tore to pieces and threw away the letter that {he / *himself} wrote.'

b. ***John*** *wa [Mary ga* ***zibun*** *o damasita] koto o urande iru.*
deceive that vengeful be
'John is vengeful of the fact that Mary deceived {him / *himself}.'

English reflexives, by contrast, must be clausemates of their antecedents, which accounts for the ungrammaticality of these sentences with *himself.*

A third property of *zibun* is that it must be commanded (Langacker, 1969) by its antecedent. In (7a), *zibun* is commanded by the noun phrase *Taroo*

[9]Actually, the normal case in Japanese is that the reflexive MAY NOT be a clausemate of its antecedent. Thus, of the following sentences (i) and (ii) are ungrammatical, since *zibun* is a clausemate of its antecedent, but (i′), (ii′), and (ii″) are not:

(i) **Mary wa zibun o damasita.*
deceive
'Mary deceived herself.'

(ii) [N. McCawley, 1972a:29]
**Tanaka wa zibun o tantoo de sasita.*
knife stab
'Tanaka stabbed himself with a knife.'

(i′) *Mary wa zibun zisin o damasita.*
'Mary deceived herself.'

(ii′) [Ibid.]
Tanaka wa Satoo o tantoo de sasita.
'Tanaka stabbed Sato with a knife.'

(ii″) *Tanaka wa zibun no sensei o tantoo de sasita.*
'Tanaka stabbed his teacher with a knife.'

N. McCawley (1972a) proposes the like-NP constraint to deal with these cases. While this principle will not be dealt with here, it is useful to point out that the ungrammaticality of (1) just given accounts for the fact that *zibun* in (6b) cannot be coreferential with *Mary*.

and is coreferential with it. In (7b), the sentence is ungrammatical in the intended meaning because the command condition is not met:[10]

(7) a. [***zibun*** *no hon o yonde iru*] *hito ni* ***Taroo*** *wa yuki atta.*
book reading be person chance to meet
'Taro chanced to meet someone who was reading self's book.'

b. *[***Taroo*** *no hon o yonde iru*] *hito ni* ***zibun*** *wa yuki atta.*
'Self chanced to meet someone who was reading Taro's book.'

The fact that the antecedent of *zibun* must be the subject of a sentence means that in any simplex sentence the antecedent of *zibun* is nonambiguous. However, since reflexivization may extend beyond clause boundaries, it is possible for *zibun* to be ambiguous in a complex sentence with two or more subjects. In (8), *zibun* may thus refer to either *Taroo* or *Hanako*, both of which are subjects of their clauses, but not to *Ziroo*:

(8) ***Taroo*** *wa* ***Hanako*** *ga* ***zibun*** *no syasin o Ziroo ni miseru no o mita.*
picture show see
'Taro saw Hanako show self's picture to Jiro.'

The important observation about reflexives and passives made independently by N. McCawley and by Kuno is that *zibun* tends to be ambiguous in indirect passives and unambiguous in direct passive sentences. Consider the following indirect passive sentences (from Kuno, 1973:303–304):

(9) a. ***John*** *wa* ***Mary*** *ni* ***zibun*** *no kazoku no hanasi bakari sareta.*
family talk only do-passive
'John was affected by Mary's talking only about self's family.'

b. ***John*** *wa* ***Mary*** *ni* ***zibun*** *no koto o ziman sareta.*
matter boast do-passive
'John suffered from Mary's bragging about self's matter.'

The ambiguity of *zibun* with indirect passive sentences is consistent, of course, with the view that these are derived from a complex deep structure containing two sentences. The subject of each of these sentences is a potential antecedent of *zibun*.

[10] Note that (7a) is three ways ambiguous. When *zibun* is coreferential with *hito*, this is due to the fact that the deleted subject of the relative clause is *hito* and not to the influence of the head of the clause. The remaining interpretation, in which *zibun* is coreferential with the speaker, is possible in many, if not all, of the sentences to be considered. No further mention of this possible interpretation will be made.

The following examples, also from Kuno (ibid., p. 307), illustrate the fact that direct passive sentences generally provide a single antecedent for *zibun*:

(10) a. ***Mary*** *wa John ni* ***zibun*** *no uti de korosareta.*
house kill-passive
'Mary was killed by John in self's house.'
b. ***Mary*** *wa John ni* ***zibun*** *no uti de hon o yomaserareta.*
house book read-causative-passive
'Mary was made by John to read the book in self's house.'

According to the uniform theory, in which both direct and indirect passives are derived from two-sentence sources, there is no obvious reason for the nonambiguity of *zibun* in these sentences (although a reason will be offered in Section 3). According to the nonuniform theory, however, in which direct passive sentences are derived by a transformation from the active sentence, this nonambiguity follows as a direct consequence of having a single subject noun phrase.

The nonuniform theory assumes that in the deep structure of (10a) *John* is the subject and *Mary* the object:

(11) *John (ga) Mary (o) Mary no uti de korosita*

Pure passive formation applies to this structure, inverting the subject and object, adding the postposition *ni* after *John*, and adding the morpheme *-rare* to the verb (see Kuno, 1973:327–350 for details). This yields the derived structure:

(12) *Mary (ga) John ni Mary no uti de korosareta*

Reflexivization, applying after pure passive formation, converts the second instance of *Mary* to *zibun*.

Notice that the crucial ordering of pure passive formation before reflexivization is responsible, in this view, for the nonambiguity of direct passives. Suppose that in the deep structure the house belonged to John rather than to Mary:

(13) *John (ga) Mary (o) John no uti de korosita*

Pure passive formation applying to this structure will yield:

(14) *Mary (ga) John ni John no uti de korosareta*

In this case, reflexivization will not be applicable, since the subject-antecedent constraint is not satisfied. The second instance of *John* may subsequently be pronominalized to *kare* or remain as *John*, but in this view it is impossible to derive (10a) with the incorrect reading in which *zibun* and *John* are coreferential.

By contrast, the uniform theory assumes that the deep structure of (10a) is the following:

(15) [*Mary* [*John Mary Mary no uti de koros-*]*-rareta*]

Reflexivization cannot apply on the first cycle, since *Mary* is not the subject of the sentence, but it will apply on the second, along with the deletion of the embedded object, to yield (10a). However, if the underlying string referred to *John's* house, the uniform theory is presented with a problem:

(16) [*Mary* [*John Mary John no uti de koros-*]*-rareta*]

The structural description of reflexivization is met on the first cycle, converting the second instance of *John* to *zibun*. On the second cycle, the embedded instance of *Mary* is deleted, yielding (10a). This incorrectly claims that (10a) is ambiguous between the semantic interpretations of (15) and (16).

The significance of these facts is twofold. First, the ambiguity of indirect passives and the nonambiguity of direct passives in relation to reflexives is PREDICTED by the nonuniform theory on the basis of the number of underlying sentences involved. Second, no proposal has yet been made as to how these facts can be handled within the uniform theory. As a result, these facts seem to lend strong support to the nonuniform theory and place the burden of proof on proponents of the uniform theory to show that some coherent explanation is available within that theory. We will return to this issue in Section 3.

Semantic–Syntactic Uniformity

It has commonly been argued that the Japanese passive differs markedly from the English passive not only in its syntactic behavior but in its semantic character as well. For example, Kuroda (1965b) states that 'the Japanese passive sentence is, in principle, not neutral as it is in English, but carries an implication of disadvantage for the subject [p. 160].' Other linguists working within widely divergent theoretical frameworks have distinguished between two classes of passive sentences, those that have a strong emotional implication for the subject and those that do not.[11] The former type has been called 'adversative passive' (Howard, 1968, 1969; Niyekawa (-Howard), 1968a, b), 'adversity passive' (Kuno, 1973), or 'affective passive' (N. McCawley, 1972b), while the latter type has often been called 'pure passive' or 'simple passive'.

Both the uniform and nonuniform theories assume that the emotional

[11]See, for example, Bloch (1946:310), Jorden (1963:306), Martin (1962:400), Elisseeff, Reischauer, and Yoshihashi (1944:39), Dunn and Yanada (1958:151), Taylor (1971:233). In fact, most authors writing on Japanese syntax appear to distinguish between two semantic classes of passives and attempt to define them along syntactic lines. Alfonso (1966, 1971) seems to be alone in ignoring the syntactic correlates of these meanings.

content of Japanese passives is a property of the higher verb *rare* (or its abstract counterpart). Within the uniform theory, in which both direct and indirect passives derive from an underlying structure containing *rare*, we would thus expect both types of passives to manifest this emotional implication. Within the nonuniform theory, on the other hand, in which all direct passive sentences are derived by pure passive formation and *rare* is not in the underlying structure, the claim is that NO direct passive sentences have this emotional content in common with indirect passives.

Proponents of the nonuniform theory have observed this difference in claims between the two theories and have used it as an argument in favor of their position. Thus, Kuno (1973) states that 'the connotation of suffering or inadvertant effect on the part of the main subject is completely lacking in pure passive sentences', arising 'only when there is an extra noun phrase ... that cannot be accounted for by the simplex deep structure of the active version [pp. 302–303].' He concludes from this semantic evidence that pure passive sentences—that is, all DIRECT passives—are derived from their corresponding active sentences, and brings in the behavior of *zibun* as independent corroborating evidence.

In the remainder of this section and in sections to follow, numerous examples will be given that clearly demonstrate that this claim of the nonuniform theory is false. Direct passive sentences may have the same emotional connotation found in indirect passives. The consequences of this fact for the nonuniform theory will be discussed more fully at the end of the section.

Consider the (b) sentences in examples (17)–(22). These direct passive sentences are not neutral statements of fact like the corresponding active (a) sentences but, rather, carry a definite, though subtle, emotional implication in relation to the subject of the sentence:

(17) a. *Oya wa kodomo o Nihon ni nokosita.*
parent child Japan leave
'The parent left his child in Japan.'
b. *Kodomo wa oya ni Nihon ni nokosareta.*
leave-passive
'The child was left in Japan by his parent.'

In this case, the passive sentence clearly implies that the child was rejected or otherwise suffered an adverse effect. This implication is absent from the active sentence.

(18) a. *Suzuki-san wa Ozawa-san o nizikan mo matta.*
two hours wait
'Suzuki waited as long as two hours for Ozawa.'
b. *Ozawa-san wa Suzuki-san ni nizikan mo matareta.*
wait-passive
'Ozawa was waited for by Suzuki for as long as two hours.'

Sentence (18b) implies that Ozawa was trying to avoid meeting Suzuki, but the latter unfortunately had the persistence to wait for him.

(19) a. *Butyoo wa Satoo o zinzika ni mawasita.*
director personnel transfer
'The director transfered Sato to the personnel section.'
b. *Satoo wa butyoo ni zinzika ni mawasareta.*
transfer-passive
'Sato was transfered by the director to the personnel section.'

While sentence (19a) could be used in any kind of transfer, (19b) implies that the transfer was a demotion or against Sato's wishes.

(20) a. *Katoo-san wa azukatte iru Mitiko o kuni ni kaesita.*
entrusted be home send
'Kato sent Michiko, who was entrusted to him/her, back home.'
b. *Mitiko wa Katoo-san ni kuni ni kaesareta.*
send-passive
'Michiko was sent back home by Kato.'

The implication of (20b) is that Michiko was sent back home against her will.

(21) a. *Satoo-sensei wa Hawai daigaku o yameta.*
Hawaii university quit
'Professor Sato quit the University of Hawaii.'
b. *Hawai daigaku wa Satoo-sensei ni yamerareta.*
quit-passive
'The University of Hawaii had Professor Sato quit.'

The implication of (21b) is that the institution suffered, either because the professor was a valued asset or because the manner in which he left was such as to bring discredit to the institution.

The existence of direct passive sentences with the same emotional content as indirect passives poses a serious problem for the nonuniform theory. Since the theory, as stated, attributes this content to the higher verb *rare* underlying indirect passive sentences only, it fails to provide any source for this content in direct passives. The significance of this fact for the nonuniform theory can be appreciated only when the major alternative ways of attempting to modify the theory are considered.

One possibility that might be explored is to find some different source for the emotional content of direct passives. No such alternative has yet been proposed, and it is difficult to imagine what one would be. A second possibility would be to abandon the idea that the higher verb is the source of the emotional content in indirect passives and to propose some other general principle to account for all passives. This would have the advantage over the first alternative of treating both in the same way and thereby not losing a generalization, but again, it is difficult to imagine what such a source would be.

The remaining possibility, that some direct passives are derived from the same type of deep structure as indirect passives, runs into conflict with the analysis of *zibun* discussed in the preceding section. The nonuniform theory would then be claiming that *zibun* in direct passive sentences that have the emotional content in question will be ambiguous. The sentences in (22) demonstrate that this is not the case:

(22) a. ***Taroo*** *wa Hanako o* ***zibun*** *no oya no moto ni nokosita.*
parent care leave
'Taro left Hanako in self's parent's care.'
b. ***Hanako*** *wa Taroo ni* ***zibun*** *no oya no moto ni nokosareta.*
leave-passive
'Hanako was left by Taro in self's parent's care.'

The facts presented in this section lead us to conclude that the behavior of *zibun* in passive sentences and the semantic content of passives do not constitute mutually supportive evidence, as has been claimed. Rather, they must be regarded as CONFLICTING evidence that calls the nonuniform theory into serious question. The burden of proof now falls upon the proponent of the nonuniform theory to show how this conflict may be resolved.[12]

Verbs That Allegedly Cannot Occur in Direct Passives

Another type of evidence that has been offered in support of the nonuniform theory involves certain verbs that supposedly do not appear as direct passives, even though they occur in indirect passive constructions.

[12]We do not intend to imply that the burden of proof is ever entirely on the advocate of one theory or the other. In actuality, each theory has its unresolved problems, and the choice between theories rests on how serious these problems are for each. When proponents of the nonuniform theory argued that the evidence from *zibun* strongly favors their view and placed the burden of proof on proponents of the uniform theory, they were correct in doing so. We feel that this challenge is more than adequately met in Section 3. Similarly, the fact that the evidence presented in this section conflicts with the analysis of *zibun* within the nonuniform theory poses a special challenge that must be met if the nonuniform theory is to be considered a viable alternative.

It must also be pointed out that the uniform theory is incorrect in predicting that all direct passives manifest this emotional content. When the direct passive sentence has an inanimate subject, this problem can be resolved by assuming a more limited version of pure passive formation (however, see Howard and Niyekawa-Howard (forthcoming, b) for some arguments relevant to this issue). Sentences in which the subject is animate but the emotional content is apparently lacking are much more problematic, however. Some suggestions as to how this might be explained were made in our earlier works, and further evidence will be presented in Howard and Niyekawa-Howard (forthcoming, a).

In each of the following examples (from N. McCawley, 1972b:264–265), the (b) sentence is ungrammatical when interpreted as a direct passive, while the (c) sentence shows clearly that these verbs can be used grammatically as indirect passives:

(23) a. *Satoo-san wa Tanaka-san ni kuruma o utta.*
car sell
'Sato sold a car to Tanaka.'
b. **Tanaka-san wa Satoo-san ni kuruma o urareta.*
c. *Tanaka-san wa Satoo-san ni sono kuruma o*
that car
tanin ni urarete simatta.
someone else sell-passive end up
'Tanaka was subjected to Sato's selling that car to someone else.'

(24) a. *Tanaka-san wa Satoo-san kara kuruma o katta.*
buy
'Tanaka bought a car from Sato.'
b. **Satoo-san wa Tanaka-san ni kuruma o kawareta.*[13]
c. *Tanaka-san wa dareka ni sono kuruma o saki ni*
someone ahead
kawarete zannengatte iru.
buy-passive sorry be
'Someone bought that car ahead of Tanaka and he is sorry.'

(25) a. *Satoo-san wa Tanaka-san ni omiyage o ageta.*
souvenir give
'Sato gave Tanaka a souvenir.'
b. **Tanaka-san wa Satoo-san ni omiyage o agerareta.*
c. *Daizi na sinamono o anna hito ni agerarete wa*
precious things such person give-passive
komaru
trouble
'I'll be in trouble if you give such precious things to such a person.'

(26) a. *Tanaka-san wa Satoo-san ni/kara omiyage o moratta.*
souvenir receive
'Tanaka got a souvenir from Sato.

[13] We do not agree that this sentence is ungrammatical as a direct passive. It is entirely appropriate when Tanaka, through repeated badgering, got Sato to part with his car. The sentence implies that Sato was really unwilling to sell.

b. **Satoo-san wa Tanaka-san ni omiyage o morawareta.*
c. *Okurete itta node, saki ni kita hitotati ni minna*
going late ahead come people all
ii sina o morawarete simatta.
good thing receive-passive end up
'As I was late, other people who arrived earlier got good things (to my disadvantage).'

N. McCawley argues that it is possible to account for these facts within the nonuniform theory by marking the verbs in question as exceptions to pure passive formation, yet allowing them to occur in the deep structure of indirect passive sentences. She also claims that no such straightforward solution is available within the uniform theory, which would have to explain why certain verbs can be combined with the higher verb *rare* only if the structural description of equi-object deletion is not met.

It is important to examine carefully how this solution would work within the nonuniform theory. The fundamental assumption of this position is that direct and indirect passive sentences are MUTUALLY EXCLUSIVE, at least to the extent that there are no direct passive sentences that are derived from a two-sentence deep structure like indirect passives. The reason for this, of course, is that *zibun* in such direct passive sentences would be potentially ambiguous, owing to the existence of two subjects. To ensure that no direct passive sentences are derived with an ambiguous reflexive pronoun, N. McCawley proposes a deep structure nonidentity constraint that prohibits an identity between the subject of the matrix verb in the indirect passive structure and any main noun phrase in the embedded sentence. This constraint also functions to account for the ungrammaticality of the following sentences, in which the object of the action is interpreted as coreferential with the subject of the sentence:

(27) a. **Ziroo wa Taroo ni zibun o sikarareta.*
scold-passive
'Jiro was scolded by Taro.'
b. **Ziroo wa Taroo ni Ziroo o sikarareta.*
c. **Ziroo wa Taroo ni kare o sikarareta.*

The nonidentity constraint plays a major role in the proposed solution to the ungrammaticality of the (b) sentences in (23)–(26) as well. It is not enough to mark the verb as unable to undergo pure passive formation if the (b) sentences were derivable from some other source.

It is our purpose in this section to demonstrate that the seemingly straightforward solution proposed by N. McCawley will not work and that the problem is more complicated than has been thought. While we do not have a convincing solution either, it can be concluded that these verbs do not constitute evidence for the nonuniform theory over the uniform theory.

The crucial fact negating N. McCawley's solution is that these verbs do, indeed, allow direct passives. In all of the examples in (23)–(26), the subjects of the ungrammatical (b) sentences correspond to the indirect object marked with *ni* in the active sentences. A different picture emerges, however, when we consider direct passives in which the subject corresponds to the direct object marked with *o*. One such example is given in (28):

(28) *Makaha no goruhu koosu wa Chinn Ho ni yotte Nihon no*
golf course Japan
kaisya ni urareta.
company sell-passive
'The golf course at Makaha was sold by Chinn Ho to a Japanese company.'

Since inanimate nouns are not normally appropriate subjects of passive sentences, this direct passive sounds 'translation style'.[14] However, by making the direct object animate, clearly natural direct passive sentences result. Thus, from the active sentences represented by (29) the direct passives in (30) can be formed:

(29) a. *Yamada-san wa otonari ni syepaado o utta.*
neighbor German shepherd sell
'Yamada sold his German shepherd to the neighbor.'

b. *Otonari wa Yamada-san kara syepaado o katta.*
'The neighbor bought the German shepherd from Yamada.'

c. *Yamada-san wa otonari ni syepaado o ageta.*
'Yamada gave his German shepherd to the neighbor.'

d. *Otonari wa Yamada-san kara syepaado o moratta.*
'The neighbor received the German shepherd from Yamada.'

(30) a. *Ano syepaado wa (Yamada-san kara) otonari ni urareta.*
'That German shepherd was sold by Yamada to the neighbor.'

b. *Ano syepaado wa otonari ni (Yamada-san kara) kawareta.*
'That German shepherd was bought by the neighbor from Yamada.'

[14]Cf. Niyekawa(-Howard) (1968a:15–16) for a brief discussion of translation style.

c. **Ano syepaado wa (Yamada-san kara) otonari ni agerareta.*[15]
'That German shepherd was given by Yamada to the neighbor.'

d. *Ano syepaado wa otonari ni (Yamada-san kara) morawareta.*
'That German shepherd was received by the neighbor from Yamada.'

The significance of these examples should be clear. If they are to be derived as direct passive sentences, then we cannot, after all, mark the verbs as exceptions to pure passive formation. Within the nonuniform theory, moreover, it is not possible to regard them as indirect passives, since the subject of the matrix sentence would be identical to an argument of the embedded sentence, violating the independently needed (for the nonuniform theory) nonidentity constraint.

Since the nonidentity constraint is crucial to the nonuniform theory and is thus 'nonnegotiable', it would be necessary to find a way to allow the derivation of sentences like those in (30) via pure passive formation without allowing the derivation of the (b) sentences in (23)–(26). One obvious approach is to constrain the pure passive formation transformation in general so that it can apply only to direct object phrases marked with *o* and not to *ni* or *kara* phrases. However, as is well known, such a general constraint is not possible.

Indirect object phrases marked with *ni*, for example, are often passivizable,[16] as the following sentences illustrate:

(31) a. *Okaasan wa kodomo o obaasan ni azuketa.*
mother child grandmother leave in care of
'The mother left the child in care of the grandmother.'

b. *Obaasan wa okaasan ni kodomo o azukerareta.*
'The grandmother had the child left in her care by the mother.'

[15]The ungrammaticality of (30c) is very peculiar but does not seem to be due to inability to passivize per se. Rather, for a reason we do not clearly understand, it seems to be inappropriate to use *agerareta* when the object given is an animal. The active sentence with *ageta* (29c) is not quite as bad, but *yarareta* seems to be preferable:

Ano syepaado wa (Yamada-san kara) otonari ni yarareta.

[16]The term PASSIVIZABLE or PASSIVIZED will be used henceforth in this work in a sense that is neutral between theories. A noun phrase in an active sentence will be said to be passivizable if there is a corresponding passive sentence, however derived, in which it appears as the subject.

c. *Kodomo wa (okaasan kara) obaasan ni azukerareta.*
'The child was left by the mother in care of the grandmother.'

(32) a. *Katoo-san wa sensei ni hondai o haratta.*
teacher book-price pay
'Kato paid the teacher for the book.'
b. *Sensei wa Katoo-san ni hondai o harawareta.*
'The teacher had Kato pay for the book.'

(33) a. *Hanako wa Taroo ni eigo o osieta.*
English teach
'Hanako taught Taro English.'
b. *Taroo wa Hanako ni eigo o osierareta.*
'Taro had Hanako teach him English.'

(34) a. *Hanako wa sensei ni/kara hon o karita.*
teacher book borrow
'Hanako borrowed the book from the teacher.'
b. *Sensei wa Hanako ni hon o karirareta.*
'The teacher had Hanako borrow the book.'

These examples confirm the fact that indirect object phrases with *ni* can be passivized. On the other hand, verbs like *uru*, *ageru*, and *morau* show that this is not always the case. It thus appears to be necessary to have some way of indicating which indirect object phrases with *ni* can be passivized and which cannot.

The facts here are similar to those encountered with the NP-*ga* NP-*ni* V construction, in which the verb takes what might be called a 'dative object'. N. McCawley (1972b:263) presents an example of this type:

(35) a. *Mitiko wa kossori koibito ni atta.*
secretly boyfriend meet
'Michiko met her boyfriend secretly.'
b. **Koibito wa Mitiko ni kossori awareta.*
c. *Oya no watasi ni mudan de daizi na musume ni*
parent I treasured daughter
awarete wa komaru.
meet-passive trouble
'I don't like the idea that you meet my dear daughter without my permission.'

Kuno (1973:346) points out that certain verbs that take objects of this type can undergo pure passive formation while others cannot, an observation he attributes to N. McCawley. The existence of this dichotomy further emphasizes the fact that pure passive formation cannot be constrained to apply only to direct objects marked with *o*.

Before returning to the question of how the two theories would handle these cases, we would like to present one of the most interesting examples given in N. McCawley's article (1972b:263):

(36) a. *Hirosi wa sakana o takusan totta.*
fish many catch
'Hiroshi caught a lot of fish.'
b. **Sakana wa takusan Hirosi ni torareta.*
c. *Tonari no wanpakuboozu ni ike no sakana o takusan*
neighbor naughty boy pond fish many
torareta.
catch-passive
'I was subjected to a little bastard who lives next door catching a lot of fish in our pond.'

Unlike the case considered earlier, here it is the DIRECT OBJECT that is not passivizable. However, the following sentences show that *toru* cannot be marked as exceptional to pure passive formation:

(37) a. *Taroo wa Hanako kara neko o totta.*
cat grab away
'Taro grabbed the cat away from Hanako.'
b. **Neko wa Taroo ni Hanako kara torareta.*
'The cat was grabbed away from Hanako by Taro.'
c. *Hanako wa Taroo ni neko o torareta.*
'Hanako had the cat grabbed away from her by Taro.'

(38) a. ?*Mitiko wa Taroo o Taroo no hahaoya kara totta.*
mother take away
'Michiko took Taro away from his mother.'
b. **Taroo wa Mitiko ni hahaoya kara torareta.*
'Taro was taken away from his mother by Michiko.'
c. *Hahaoya wa Mitiko ni Taroo o torareta.*
'(Taro's) mother had Taro taken away by Michiko.'

The various related meanings of *toru* share certain properties. All of them seem to prohibit the direct object from becoming the subject of the passive. At the same time, all of them seem to permit a passive in which the subject is the person from whom the active object is being separated. Although there are unexplained problems with sentences like (38a), it nevertheless seems that there is an underlying SOURCE noun phrase that is being passivized.[17]

All of the facts discussed in this section seem to point in one general direction: The limitations on passives are more complex than has been recognized. It is not possible to account for this variety of facts by making verbs exceptions to pure passive formation, nor is it possible to confine the application of such a transformation to 'the first unmarked NP in the verb phrase,' as proposed by Harada (1973:122).

For the nonuniform theory, this means that it will be necessary to state for a given verb which NPs it will allow to passivize and which it will not. For the uniform theory, these same facts will have to be dealt with by idiosyncratic nonidentity constraints (governed by the lower verb) rather than by constraints on a rule. However, the statements required by the two theories are entirely parallel, and neither has a significant advantage over the other.

It seems likely to us that deeper investigation will show that these constraints are based on case relations and other semantic considerations and not really on idiosyncratic properties of individual verbs. Should this be the case, both theories would profit by an increased generality of statement of the required constraints.

It is far from clear, then, that the nonuniform theory has any special advantage over the uniform theory in accounting for the constraints on direct passives that we have discussed. However, once again it is possible to show that the nonuniform theory fails to accord with the semantic facts of the passive, since the direct passive sentences presented throughout this section are not semantically neutral. Thus, all of the sentences in (30) show a kind of empathy with the German shepherd that is absent from those in (29). In (31b), the grandmother was displeased or inconvenienced by the child's being left in her care, unlike the case in the active sentence. In (32b), in the reading in which the money was paid to the teacher, the latter was insulted. A sentence like (33b) with *osierareta* (rather than *osowatta*) frequently is used when something bad is taught (e.g., where in English one would say with emphasis, '*Who taught you **that**?*'). Similarly with the remaining direct passive sentences in this section.

[17]Other examples of source NPs passivizing may be seen in (34b) and in the following sentence:

(i) *Taroo wa suri ni saihu o nusumareta.*
thief wallet steal-passive
'Taro had his wallet stolen by a thief.'

(ii) *Suri wa Taroo kara saihu o nusunda.*
'The thief stole the wallet from Taro.'

Adverbial Scope

Makino (1972) discusses the problem of scope in relation to certain attitudinal adverbials, such as *iyaiya* 'reluctantly, unwillingly' and *wazato* 'intentionally'. He claims that in active sentences the adverb unambiguously refers to the subject of the sentence, as in (39a), while in passive sentences such as (39b) it can refer to either the surface subject or the agent:

(39) a. *Taroo wa Hanako o iyaiya syootai sita.*
unwillingly invite do
'Taro unwillingly invited Hanako.'
b. *Hanako wa Taroo ni iyaiya syootai sareta.*
unwillingly invite do-passive
'Hanako was unwillingly invited by Taro.'

On the basis of sentences like these, Makino argues that the Japanese passive is derived from a complex structure with two underlying sentences. That is, he adopts the 'uniform' theory of the passive. Under this assumption, the adverbial may be attached in deep structure to either sentence, thus accounting for the ambiguity. His proposed deep structures for the two readings of (39b) are shown in (40) and (41):

(40)

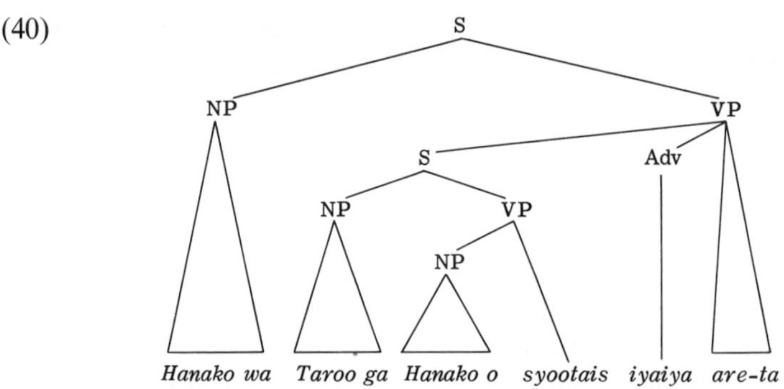

(41)

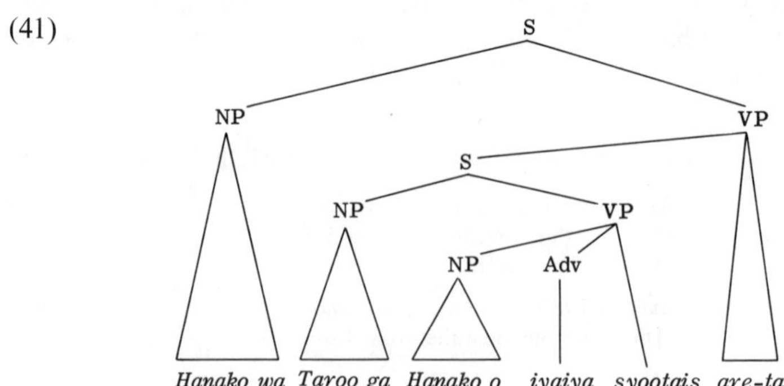

The passive sentence under consideration is a DIRECT passive sentence. N. McCawley (1972b:265–266) points out that no such ambiguity exists with indirect passives:

(42) a. *Taroo wa* ***Ziroo*** *ni koibito no Hanako o*
girlfriend
iyaiya syootai sareta.
reluctantly invite do-passive
'Taro had his girlfriend Hanako invited by Jiro reluctantly (on him).'

b. ****Tanaka-san*** *wa* ***zibun*** *kara susunde musuko o*
of his own accord son
keisatu ni tukamaerareta.
police arrest-passive
'Tanaka had his son arrested by the police of his own accord (on him).'

Since direct and indirect passives behave differently with regard to the problem of adverbial scope, this might be taken as an argument in favor of the nonuniform analysis of the passive. Such a conclusion would be unwarranted, however, since it leaves totally unexplained why the DIRECT passive is ambiguous in relation to adverbial scope, since only the indirect passive comes from two underlying sentences. Moreover, if Makino's general line of analysis is correct, neither theory accounts for the nonambiguity of indirect passives. We must conclude, therefore, that no satisfactory argument as to the deep structure of the passive has yet been given on the basis of adverbial scope.[18]

Passive-Causatives and the Syntactic Cycle

A further argument in favor of the nonuniform analysis has been presented by J. McCawley (1972b).[19] It involves determining the order of application of the rules of pure passive formation and reflexivization and utilizing this order to predict the behavior of passive-causatives.

[18]Shibatani (1972b:161–163) points out that the issue is much more complex than presented in any of these works. There are different classes of adverbs that behave differently from the attitudinal adverbs that Makino considered, and a theory of adverbial scope will have to encompass all of these. Moreover, adverbial scope depends to a considerable degree on where the adverb occurs in the surface string.

We would like to add that we find Makino's example (39b) totally unacceptable (in Japanese or in English) in the sense in which *Hanako* is the unwilling one. Consider the semantic interpretation of such a sentence. It is very vague, but, if anything, it indicates an unwillingness to ACCEPT the invitation, to GO to where she is invited, etc. What does it mean to be unwilling to BE INVITED?

[19]This evidence is also discussed in N. McCawley (1972b:268–269) and in Kuno (1973:305–306).

From the fact that direct passive sentences allow only a single interpretation of *zibun*, it can be concluded that in the nonuniform analysis pure passive formation must precede reflexivization. If we applied these rules in the opposite order, they would incorrectly yield direct passive sentences in which *zibun* is not coreferential with the surface subject. It is also clear that in indirect passive sentences reflexivization on the lower cycle must precede verb raising on the higher cycle. The reason for this is that the application of verb raising results in the embedded sentence node's being pruned, thereby making the underlying subject of the embedded sentence a constituent of the matrix sentence. That is, it no longer meets the structural description of reflexivization, since it is no longer structurally the subject of a sentence.

Consider a passive-causative sentence like (43):

(43) *Boku wa Tanaka-san ni iti-zikan mo mataserareta.*
I one hour wait-causative-passive
'I was made to wait an hour by Tanaka.'

J. McCawley points out that passive-causative sentences always involve the meaning of an *o* causative in the sense of Kuroda (1965a), in which a person is FORCED to do something, rather than the meaning of a *ni* causative, in which he is PERMITTED to do something. He then proposes that the deep structure of the causative sentence (44), as well as the passive-causative sentence in (43), is (45):

(44) *Tanaka-san wa boku o iti-zikan mo mataseta.*
'Tanaka made me wait an hour.'

(45)

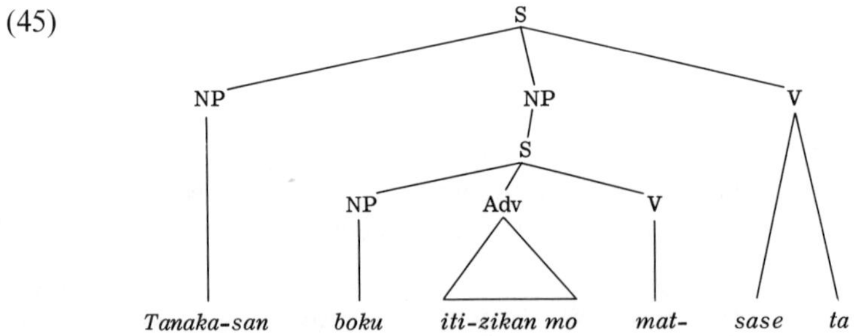

According to this analysis, the passive-causative sentence would be derived as follows. On the lower cycle, nothing of interest to us will happen. On the higher cycle, verb raising will apply, attaching the embedded verb to the matrix verb and making the other embedded phrases constituents of the matrix sentence. Then pure passive formation will apply, interchanging *boku* and *Tanaka-san*, etc. Notice that verb raising must precede pure passive formation, since *boku* must be a constituent of the matrix sentence before it can be passivized.

Combining this ordering observation with the earlier ones yields the following sequence of potential applications:

(46) a. *Reflexivization on the lower cycle precedes verb raising on the higher cycle.*
b. *Verb raising on the higher cycle precedes pure passive formation on the higher cycle.*
c. *Pure passive formation on the higher cycle precedes reflexivization on the higher cycle.*

This ordering not only justifies having the three rules in the cycle in the sequence (a) verb raising, (b) pure passive formation, and (c) reflexivization but also makes a prediction with regard to passive-causatives. It predicts that in sentence (47), *zibun* is unambiguously coreferential with *Yamada*:

(47) *Yamada-san wa Tanaka-san ni iti-zikan mo zibun no ie de*
one hour self house
mataserareta.
wait-causative-passive
'Yamada was made by Tanaka to wait an hour in his house.'

Note that if it were *Tanaka*'s house, reflexivization could never apply, because *Yamada* is the embedded subject and pure passive formation on the higher cycle will remove *Tanaka* from the subject position before reflexivization could apply on that cycle. The fact that *zibun* is unambiguous in this sentence and the prediction is thereby supported is taken as evidence in favor of the nonuniform theory, as well as for a syntactic cycle in Japanese. (For further discussion of the cyclic principle and reflexivization, cf. the chapter by Inoue in this volume.)

This argument, though straightforward and superficially convincing, suffers from two serious difficulties. One of these is that the deep structure proposed for *o* causatives in this analysis cannot be accepted without question, since it is at variance with that justified in other treatments.[20] For example, Kuno (1973:295–298), Shibatani (1973a:335–336), and Harada (1973:127–136) all argue convincingly that the *o* causative differs from the *ni* causative in having a noun phrase in the matrix sentence that is coreferential with the embedded subject. Thus, the deep structure for (44) may not be (45) but, rather, (48):

[20]Although it is consistent with proposals made by Inoue (1971) and Nakau (1973). See Harada (1973:129–131) for a criticism of this position, however.

(48)

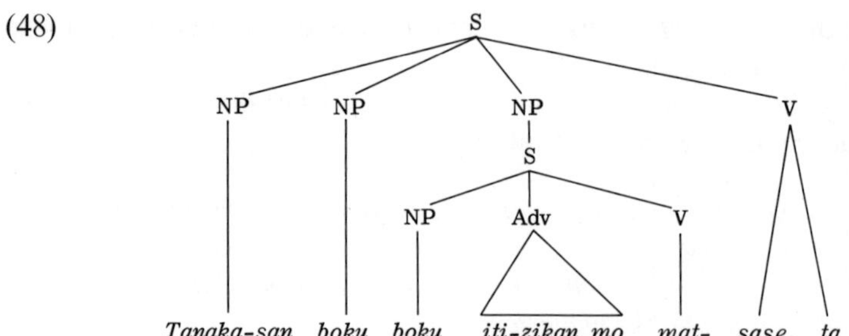

J. McCawley's argument for the cycle depends crucially on accepting the deep structure in (45) without an object in the matrix sentence, for it hinges on the need to raise the embedded subject into the matrix sentence before pure passive formation. That is, verb raising must intervene between two possible applications of pure passive formation and reflexivization. However, if the structure in (48) is valid, it is conceivable that pure passive formation and reflexivization apply to both sentences before verb raising.[21]

The second difficulty with this argument rests in the claim that the passive-causative is a 'simple passive, not an affective passive' (J. McCawley, 1972b:71; cf. also Kuno, 1973:306). The fact that passive-causatives do not normally tolerate the extra noun phrase is offered as support for this claim:

(49) **Boku wa kanai ni Yamada-sensei o iti-zikan mo*
wife one hour
matasareta.
wait-causative-passive
'I was subjected to my wife making Professor Yamada wait an hour.'

While it would be correct to say that passive causatives are direct passive sentences, it is misleading to say that they are not AFFECTIVE passives. The latter term has semantic implications as well as syntactic ones, and it is clear that passive-causatives differ from simple causatives by having an additional connotation of suffering with regard to the subject of the sentence. Consider the following pairs of sentences:

(50) a. *Taroo wa Hanaka no otooto o eiga ni ikaseta.*
younger brother movie go-causative
'Taro {made / let} Hanako's younger brother go to the movies.'

[21]To say that this particular argument does not justify a syntactic cycle in Japanese does not necessarily mean that no justification for the cycle exists. Perlmutter (1973) presents considerably more evidence for the cycle.

b. *Hanako no otooto wa Taroo ni eiga ni ikaserareta.*
'Hanako's younger brother was forced by Taro to go to the movies.'

(51) a. *Katyoo wa Suzuki ni rusutyuu dairi to site tegami o*
section chief during absence agent as do letter
kakaseta.
write-causative
'The section chief made Suzuki write letters in his place during his absence.'

b. *Suzuki wa katyoo ni rusutyuu dairi to site tegami o kakas(er)areta.*
'Suzuki was forced by the section chief to write letters in his place during his absence.'

(52) a. *Hahaoya wa Hanako ni itutu no toki kara piano o*
mother five time
narawaseta.
learn-causative
'(Hanako's) mother made Hanako learn piano from the age of five.'

b. *Hanako wa hahaoya ni itutu no toki kara piano o narawaserareta.*
'Hanako was forced by her mother to learn piano from the age of five.'

There are two major differences between the active (a) sentences and the passive (b) sentences. It is commonly known that the former have both a causative and a permissive sense, while the latter are strictly causative. There is also a more subtle but consistent meaning difference beyond this, however. In a sentence like (51a), the *katyoo* is in a position of authority to require that Suzuki perform a particular task. In (51b), there is the additional implication that Suzuki was made to do it against his will, or that the task was unpleasant for him.[22] Each of the (b) sentences (and passive-causative sentences in general) involves a similar implication for the subject that is not found in the active.

It may be concluded, then, that the passive-causative manifests yet another instance of the conflict between syntactic form and the interpretation of *zibun*, on the one hand, and semantic properties on the other, which the nonuniform theory is at a loss to explain. For the uniform theory, too,

[22]Passive-causatives may also be used to express humility. When a person is being praised or admired for an accomplishment, he may use the passive-causative to say that it was not really his own doing at all. Such cases are extended usages of the construction.

the passive-causative is a problem owing to the ungrammaticality of sentences like (49). The resolution of this problem appears to be related to what we have already seen with verbs like *uru* and *ageru*. In those cases it was necessary to constrain the passive deep structure so that the subject of the matrix verb *rare* may not be coreferential with particular noun phrases in the embedded sentence. With the passive-causative, there must be a different type of constraint: that the matrix subject must be coreferential with the embedded object of *sase*. This constraint, thus, holds between the two circled noun phrases in (53):

(53)

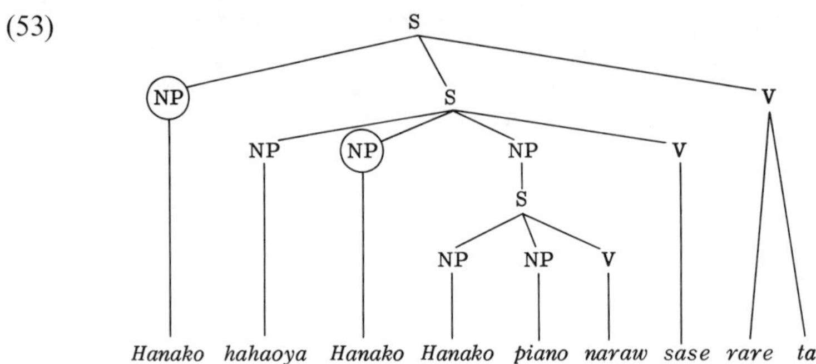

The fact that *zibun* in passive-causative sentences is unambiguous is open to the same explanation as that required for other direct passives, to be discussed in Section 3.

Summary

In the preceding discussion we have presented the main arguments that have been offered in support of the nonuniform theory of the Japanese passive.[23] On the basis of our evaluation of these arguments, the following

[23]There are two less significant arguments relevant to these issues that might be mentioned here. The first was given in Kuno (1973:346), where he points out that *ni yotte* may replace *ni* in direct passives but not in indirect passives. This is taken as support for the view that the two types of passives have different derivational histories. In order to account for this fact, Kuno introduces *yotte* optionally, along with the postposition *ni*, as part of his pure passive formation transformation. If the relevant distinction is simply between direct and indirect passive sentences, however, there is no compelling reason to conclude that the two types of passives have different DEEP structures or to introduce *yotte* directly as a part of pure passive formation. Moreover, the behavior of *ni yotte* is far too complex (cf. Inoue, 1972b:199–203, 216) and too little studied to draw significant conclusions from it.

The second argument is also due to Kuno. On the basis of data concerning the interpretation of quantifiers, he concludes (1971) that the Japanese passive 'is derived from a complex deep structure in which *rare*, the passive morpheme, appears in the matrix sentence [p. 362].' The

conclusions can be drawn. First, the claim that the indirect/direct passive distinction correlates with the affective or nonaffective semantic content of the passive completely falls apart. Since the nonuniform theory attributes the affective meaning to the verb *rare* (or the abstract verb AFFECT) in indirect passive constructions, it can offer no explanation for the affective content of direct passive sentences. This must be taken as strong evidence AGAINST the nonuniform theory as it has been presented. Second, the problems of verbs with 'defective' passives, of adverbial scope, and of passive-causatives provide no evidence for the nonuniform theory. Finally, the only facts that appear to lend support to the nonuniform theory are those involving the interpretation of *zibun* in passive sentences.

The crucial questions that remain are (a) whether it is possible to account for the behavior of *zibun* within the uniform theory and (b) whether there is any further evidence supporting either of these theories. An attempt to provide answers to these questions will be made in the next section.

3. AN ALTERNATIVE ANALYSIS OF *ZIBUN*

Let us briefly recapitulate the problem that reflexivization poses for the uniform theory. There is no difficulty at all in deriving a direct passive sentence containing a reflexive pronoun that is coreferential with the subject. Assume the following deep structure for sentence (10):

(54)

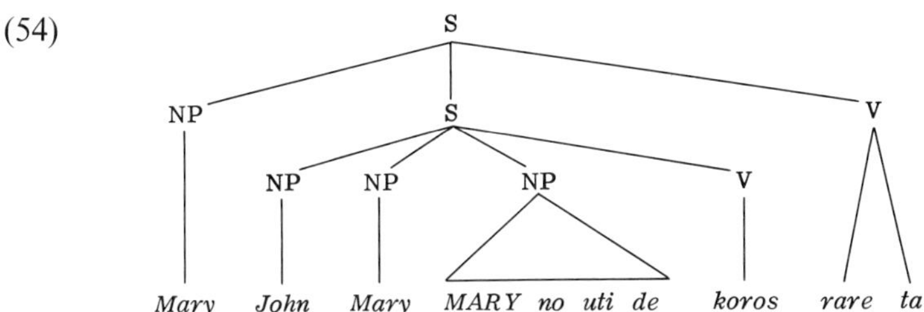

No reflexivization can take place on the first cycle, since *Mary* is not the subject of the embedded sentence. On the second cycle, however, reflexivization applies. The embedded object will then be deleted under identity with the matrix subject, yielding:

(55) ***Mary*** *wa John ni* ***zibun*** *no uti de korosareta.*

relevant example was a DIRECT passive sentence, which he now claims is derived by pure passive formation. The argument must, thus, be construed as supporting the uniform theory rather than the nonuniform theory. However, this argument was apparently either weak or ill-founded, since it was omitted when the text was republished as Chapter 28 of Kuno (1973).

The problem arises when the house belongs to John instead of Mary:

(56)

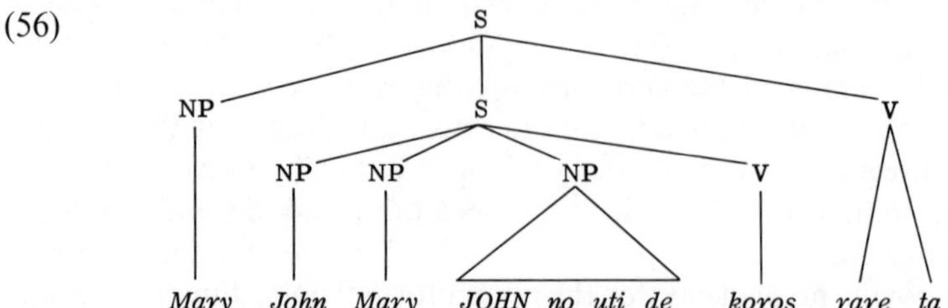

Here, reflexivization may apply on the first cycle, creating a *zibun* that is coreferential with *John*. After deletion of the embedded object on the second cycle, we are left with the following ungrammatical sentence:

(57) **Mary wa* ***John*** *ni* ***zibun*** *no uti de korosareta.*

The problem that confronts us, then, is how to prevent the derivation of such sentences in which *zibun* in a direct passive is coreferential with the embedded subject. It is clearly not possible to solve this problem by ordering arguments alone, since reflexivization must be applicable on the first cycle if its structural description is met.

The solution to this problem that we are proposing is based on the assumption that reflexivization is applied on the first cycle to *John* and on the second cycle to *Mary*. Thus, the output of the first cycle is as follows:

(58)

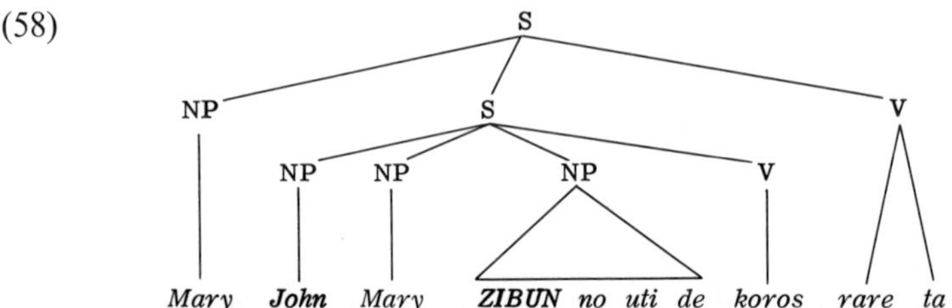

On the second cycle, the structural description of reflexivization is again met, this time between the matrix subject and the embedded object. Application of reflexivization will yield the following structure:

(59)

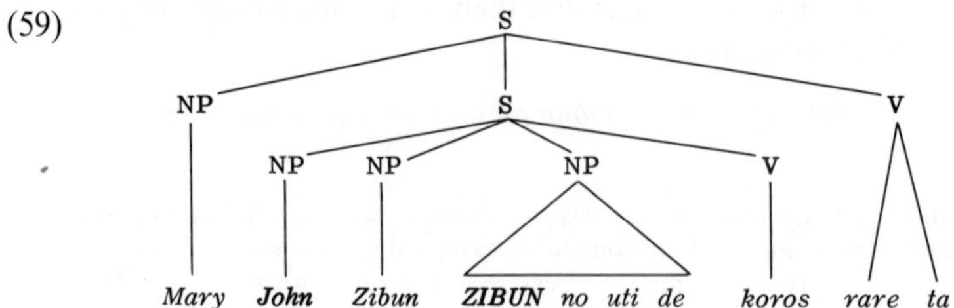

This structure now contains two instances of the reflexive pronoun that are not coreferential. Despite the fact that the embedded object will subsequently be deleted, there is good reason to assume that the noncoreferentiality of these two reflexives is responsible for sentence (57)'s being ungrammatical.

What we are assuming, to be more precise, is that before the embedded noun phrase is deleted it undergoes reflexivization. If the resultant structure involves two instances of *zibun* with different referents, the sentence is discarded via a constraint that we shall refer to as the REFLEXIVE COREFERENCE CONSTRAINT (RCC). The RCC may be stated roughly as follows:

(60) *Two instances of the reflexive pronoun* ***zibun*** *commanded by the same pair of possible antecedents must be coreferential. If they are not, the sentence is marked as ungrammatical.*

The RCC must follow the application of reflexivization and precede embedded object deletion if it is to account for the nonambiguity of *zibun* in direct passive sentences.[24]

In the next section we will attempt to justify the RCC by demonstrating that it is independently required to account for the behavior of *zibun* in nonpassive sentences as well, and not just an ad hoc invention to make our analysis work.

Some Evidence for the RCC

It was shown earlier that if a given instance of *zibun* is commanded by two noun phrases, each of which is the subject of an underlying sentence,

[24]It may also be shown that the RCC is a CYCLIC constraint, like N. McCawley's like-NP constraint (see footnote 9). Consider the following sentence:

(i) *Taroo wa Ziroo ga zibun ni sikarareru koto o syooti site iru to omotta.*
scold-passive understand do be think
'Taro thought that Jiro understood that he would be scolded by him.'

The deep structure for this sentence is assumed to be roughly the following:

(ii) [*T* [*Z* [*Z* [*T Z sikar-*] *rareru*] *koto syooti site iru*] *to omotta*]

The first opportunity for reflexivization to apply is on the second cycle, in which the object of *sikar-* is reflexivized owing to the influence of the subject of *rareru*. On the fourth cycle, reflexivization is once more applicable, this time between the subject of the matrix verb *omotta* and the subject of *sikar-*. Although two instances of *zibun* are created in the course of the derivation, each having a different antecedent, the sentence is grammatical. This can be explained by requiring embedded object deletion to apply in the cycle in which its structural description is met—hence, on the second cycle. At the point in the derivation at which reflexivization applies for the second time, the first instance of *zibun* will already have been deleted and therefore no violation of the RCC occurs. In unembedded direct passive sentences we have shown that the RCC must PRECEDE embedded object deletion, while in the sentence just given the RCC must FOLLOW embedded object deletion. This may be accounted for easily by the assumption that the RCC is a cyclically applied constraint.

then *zibun* is potentially ambiguous. By the same token, if there are two instances of *zibun*, they should both be ambiguous. The RCC makes a particular claim about the interpretation of reflexive pronouns in these circumstances that has not yet (to our knowledge) been advanced in studies of Japanese syntax: The ambiguity will normally be only a two-way ambiguity rather than a four-way ambiguity. To illustrate this point, consider the following sentence.[25]

(61) *Taroo wa Hanako ga zibun no heya de zibun no sigoto o site*
room work do
ita to itta.
be say
'Taro said that Hanako was doing self's work in self's room.'

This sentence may be interpreted such that it is either Taro's room or Hanako's room, either Taro's work or Hanako's work; but the two must go together:

(62) a. *Taro said that Hanako was doing his work in his room.*
b. *Taro said that Hanako was doing her work in her room.*
c. **Taro said that Hanako was doing his work in her room.*
d. **Taro said that Hanako was doing her work in his room.*

Notice what happens when we introduce another *zibun* whose reference is semantically nonambiguous:

(63) a. *Taroo wa Hanako ga zibun no kawari ni zibun no heya de zibun no sigoto o site ita to itta.*
'Taro said that Hanako was doing self's work in self's room in self's place.'
b. *Taroo wa Hanako ga zibun hitori de zibun no heya de zibun no sigoto o site ita to itta.*
'Taro said that Hanako was doing self's work by self in self's room.'

The phrase *zibun no kawari ni* in (63a) can refer only to *Taroo*. As a result, the other two instances of *zibun* must also refer to *Taroo*:

(64) a. *Taro said that Hanako was doing his work in his room in his place.*
b. **Taro said that Hanako was doing her work in his room in his place.*
(*etc.*)

On the other hand, *zibun hitori de* in (63b) can refer only to *Hanako*. There-

[25]We are indebted to Shigeo Tonoike for the beautiful examples in (61) and (63).

fore, the only available interpretation of the other reflexives is that they are coreferential with *Hanako* also:

(65) a. *Taro said that Hanako was doing her work by herself in her room.*
b. **Taro said that Hanako was doing her work by herself in his room.*
(*etc.*)

The RCC constitutes a claim that multiple instances of the reflexive pronoun within a given domain must share the same antecedent. It is easy to see why such a constraint might be imposed on a grammar, in that *zibun* usually serves a contrastive function, much like *his own* in English. If there are several instances of *zibun* and they are multiply ambiguous, the contrastive function will be largely defeated.

Consider now the following additional examples of the RCC:

(66) a. *Kazuko wa Hanako ga zibun no tanzyoobi ni wa zibun ga*
birthday
tukutta yoohuku o kiru koto o kitaisita.
make dress wear expect
'Kazuko expected Hanako to wear the dress that self made on self's birthday.'
b. *Kazuko wa Hanako ni zibun ga sakkyoku sita ongaku o*
compose do music
zibun no piano de hiite moratta.
play receive
'Kazuko had Hanako play the music that self composed on self's piano.'

To us, both of these sentences can be interpreted only with the two instances of *zibun* being coreferential.

The RCC is thus an independently motivated principle of Japanese grammar, which interacts with other principles to explain the peculiar behavior of reflexives in passive sentences. To make the case for the RCC and the uniform theory fully convincing, however, it is desirable to show (a) that the other principles required are independently motivated as well and (b) that there are additional data predicted by the uniform theory as proposed here which the nonuniform theory cannot handle. In the next section, we will attempt to provide both types of support for this analysis.

Justification and Further Evidence

It is interesting to note that the foundation for this position was laid down in Kuroda's impressive treatment of Japanese syntax written ten years ago.

Although he did not anticipate the difficulties that the interpretation of *zibun* would create for his analysis of passives, he nevertheless provided nearly all of the mechanisms necessary for their resolution. It is therefore appropriate to review his conclusions here.

In contrasting reflexivization and (zero) pronominalization, Kuroda argued that there are certain contexts in which reflexivization applies obligatorily and others in which it applies optionally. One context in which reflexivization is optional is when an identity exists between the matrix subject and the constituent subject. Consider the following sentences:

(67) a. *George wa George ga sitai toki ni sigoto o suru.*
do-want time work do
'George does his work when George feels like doing it.'
b. *George wa zibun ga sitai toki ni sigoto o suru.*
c. *George wa sitai toki ni sigoto o suru.*

Both (67b), in which the embedded subject is the reflexive pronoun *zibun*, and (67c), in which the embedded subject is deleted, are paraphrases of (67a).

Similarly, both (68a) and (68b) are interpreted with *John* as the embedded subject:

(68) a. *John wa zibun ga sono ie ni kakumatta Bill o uragitta.*
that house shelter betray
'John betrayed Bill, whom he sheltered in that house.'
b. *John wa sono ie ni kakumatta Bill o uragitta.*

By contrast, when there is identity between the matrix subject and the embedded object and the latter is in the object or complement of the matrix verb, reflexivization is obligatory. Consider the following sentences:

(69) a. *John wa sono ie ni zibun o kakumatta Bill o uragitta.*
that house shelter betray
'John betrayed Bill, who sheltered him in that house.'
b. *John wa Bill ga zibun o miru no o tometa.*
see prohibit
'John prohibited Bill from seeing him.'

In these cases, if *zibun* is replaced by zero the meaning of the sentence changes. That is, (69a) does not have the same meaning as the sentences in (68).

A parallel example is the causative verb. If there is identity between the subject of *sase* and the embedded object, reflexivization is obligatory and pronominalization changes the meaning:

(70) a. *John wa Bill ni zibun o misaseta.*
see-causative
'John made Bill see him.'
b. *John wa Bill ni misaseta.*
'John made Bill see (something).'

Sentence (70b) is not normally construed as containing the meaning of (70a).

After presenting this analysis of reflexivization, Kuroda discusses the passive construction in particular. He points out that it presents what appears to be a counterexample to his analysis in that it presumably has the same type of underlying structure as the causative but has deletion of the pronoun rather than reflexivization. Thus, if the deep structure of (71a) is (71b), as assumed in the uniform theory, we have an apparent violation of Kuroda's analysis of reflexivization:

(71) a. *John wa Bill ni mirareta.*
see-passive
'John was seen by Bill.'
b. [*John* [*Bill John mi-*] *rareta*]

The position taken by Kuroda is that the behavior of passives is not an isolated exception but, rather, a property shared with the *-te morau* construction. In both of these constructions, an embedded object is deleted if it is identical with the subject of the matrix verb. Kuroda provides the following sentences to illustrate the difference between the causative verb *sase*, which does not undergo embedded object deletion, and *-te morau*:

(72) a. *John ga Bill ni suisen saseta.*
'John made Bill recommend (someone).'
b. *John ga Bill ni suisen site moratta.*
'John got Bill to recommend him.'

(73) a. *John ga Bill ni syootai saseta.*
'John made Bill invite (someone).'
b. *John ga Bill ni syootai site moratta.*
'John got Bill to invite him.'

(74) a. *John ga Bill ni yurusaseta.*
'John made Bill forgive (someone).'
b. *John ga Bill ni yurusite moratta.*
'John got Bill to forgive him.'

The fact that embedded object deletion is applicable to *-te morau* thus provides independent support for the rule.[26]

Kuroda's analysis of reflexives and passives is relevant to our current proposal in several ways. Two of these were shown earlier: (a) It confirms that reflexivization applies OBLIGATORILY to noun phrases in the same structural configuration as the one that will be deleted in the passive construction—a crucial assumption of our analysis; (b) it provides independent justification for the embedded object deletion rule, which might otherwise appear ad hoc.

In addition, there are two less direct ways in which Kuroda's analysis can be shown to be supportive of our position. One of these has to do with contexts in which reflexivization is optional rather than obligatory. Although Kuroda did not deal specifically with possessive constructions, it can be shown that reflexivization in these contexts is optional:[27]

(75) a. *Tanaka-san wa zibun no senkyoku de enzetu sita.*
district give a speech
'Tanaka gave a speech in his prefectural electoral district.'
b. *Tanaka-san wa kare no senkyoku de enzetu sita.*
c. *Tanaka-san wa Tanaka-san no senkyoku de enzetu sita.*

(76) a. *Tanaka-san wa Miki-san ni zibun no senkyoku de enzetu saseta.*
'Tanaka made Miki give a speech in his prefectural electoral district.'
b. *Tanaka-san wa Miki-san ni kare no senkyoku de enzetu saseta.*
c. *Tanaka-san wa Miki-san ni Tanaka-san no senkyoku de enzetu saseta.*

All six sentences share the meaning that the prefectural electoral district

[26]It is interesting that Kuroda (1965b:158) offers a semantically based explanation for the fact that the embedded object of *-te morau* is deletable while it is not deletable with most other verbs:

> The difference shown between the *sase* form and the *-te moraw* form is due to the fact that the latter has the semantic implication that the action of the constituent sentence is done in favor of, or for the benefit of the matrix subject. This implication makes it possible for the deleted object of the constituent verb to be understood as referring to the matrix subject.

Kuroda then points out that the negative implication of the Japanese passive construction makes it similarly possible to interpret the deleted object of *rare* as coreferential with the matrix subject. These two verbs, thus, share an important property that explains their special treatment with regard to embedded object deletion.

[27]We are grateful to Shigeo Tonoike for the sentences in (75), (76), and (80).

involved is that belonging to the subject of the sentence, *Tanaka*. The (c) sentences are somewhat less natural in that they require stress and are contrastive, but these sentences represent a range of options that is not available in contexts in which reflexivization is obligatory.

While obligatory reflexivization of the noun phrase to be deleted is necessary to prevent ambiguous reflexive pronouns in direct passive sentences, optional reflexivization is necessary if sentences like the following are to be derived:

(77) *Mary wa John ni John no uti de korosareta.*
'Mary was killed by John in John's house.'

It is thus an important fact that there is independent evidence outside of the passive construction that shows that reflexivization is obligatory where we need it to be obligatory and optional where we need it to be optional.

The remaining implication of Kuroda's analysis for our explanation of the interaction of passives and reflexives is based on the fact that the *-te morau* construction also undergoes embedded object deletion. If our claim is correct that the embedded object in passives is obligatorily reflexivized and that the resultant structure is subject to the RCC before the embedded object is deleted, then we should find exactly the same behavior with the *-te morau* construction. That is, our proposal predicts that in *-te morau* constructions in which there is an embedded noun phrase identical with the matrix subject, *zibun* can refer only to the subject of the sentence, just as in direct passives.

Consider the following sentences:

(78) a. *Taroo wa Hanako ni zibun no iinazuke no mae de*
fiancé(e) front
homete moratta.
praise receive
'Taro had Hanako praise him in front of self's fiancé(e).'

b. *Yamada-sensei wa Tanaka-sensei ni zibun no byooin de*
hospital
syuzyutu site moratta.
operation do receive
'Doctor Yamada had Doctor Tanaka operate on him in self's hospital.'

c. *Yamada-san wa Tanaka-san ni zibun no uti made okutte*
house send
moratta.
receive
'Yamada had Tanaka send him to self's house.'

In each case, when we interpret the sentence so that the object of the embedded sentence is coreferential with the matrix subject (as indicated in the translations), *zibun* refers only to the subject of the sentence, despite the fact that the situation in which it would refer to the embedded subject is semantically plausible.[28]

These observations provide strong support for the theory we have proposed. Although these sentences behave exactly like direct passives, it is clearly not possible to invoke a permutation transformation to explain their lack of ambiguity. The nonuniform theory is, thus, incapable of accounting for these facts, or at least of doing so in a general way. The uniform theory as presented here, however, offers an explanation that is independent of the number of sentences in the underlying structure and correctly predicts nonambiguity in both the direct passive and parallel examples of the *-te morau* construction.

4. SUMMARY AND CONCLUSIONS

In this work, we have endeavored to present and evaluate two alternative views of the Japanese passive construction. A number of arguments in support of the nonuniform theory have been presented in the literature, and each of these was examined in some detail. It was shown that these arguments either failed to differentiate between the two theories or were invalidated by empirical evidence. In particular, the two major arguments that form the foundation of the nonuniform position were shown to be seriously inadequate or invalid. First, the claim that direct passive sentences do not (i.e., CANNOT) have the emotional connotation of indirect passives is clearly false, and numerous examples were presented to demonstrate that fact. Second, the explanation of the nonambiguity of *zibun* based on a pure passive for-

[28]It is interesting that not all *-te morau* sentences in which the matrix subject corresponds to an argument of the embedding are nonambiguous. The first such test sentence we tried with *zibun* seemed to refute our hypothesis:

(i) ***Taroo*** *wa* ***Hanako*** *ni* ***zibun*** *no syasin o misete moratta.*
picture show receive
'Taro had Hanako show him self's picture.'

It was subsequently discovered, however, that a passive version of the same sentence is also ambiguous:

(ii) ***Taroo*** *wa* ***Hanako*** *ni* ***zibun*** *no syasin o miserareta.*
'Taro was subjected to Hanako's showing him self's picture.'

This peculiarity is due to the fact that a 'picture noun' is involved (cf. Howard and Niyekawa-Howard, in press).

mation transformation not only conflicts with the semantic facts but fails to account for the nonambiguity of *zibun* in the *-te morau* construction.

The new proposal offered in Section 3, which makes crucial use of an independently motivated constraint on *zibun*, is consistent with and derives further support from the uniform theory of the passive. It not only permits an analysis that is more in conformity with the semantic facts of the passive but also correctly PREDICTS the nonambiguity of *zibun* in an entirely new class of cases.

While we feel that the RCC plays a major role in explaining the peculiar behavior of *zibun* in passive sentences, we do not wish to overstate our case, nor to minimize the difficulties involved in providing a comprehensive and explicit solution to the problem.[29] Rather, we hope that the direction of analysis presented in this chapter will stimulate further research in this fascinating area of Japanese grammar.

ACKNOWLEDGMENTS

We are pleased to acknowledge here the many individuals who have contributed to this work. A special debt of gratitude is owed to Shigeo Tonoike, who provided constant stimulation and is, directly or indirectly, responsible for many of the arguments and examples contained herein. Roderick Jacobs and the members of his syntax class, Gregory Lee, Lewis Josephs, and numerous others have served as sounding boards for our ideas and offered invaluable criticisms. Still others have shared with us their linguistic intuitions and grammaticality judgments of Japanese sentences. While we would be happy to spread the blame as widely as possible, we must take full responsibility for any mistakes, erroneous opinions, or unintended distortions of alternative positions that this work may contain.

[29]For example, several different idiolects exist with regard to how *zibun* is interpreted. To some individuals *zibun*, even in direct passives, is ambiguous, while to others there is great difficulty in interpreting *zibun* as anything other than the matrix subject, even in indirect passives. Another difficulty is in providing a precise definition of the domain in which the RCC is applicable. The so-called 'picture nouns' (cf. Howard and Niyekawa-Howard, in press) appear to fall outside of this domain, for example. Finally, we should mention the likelihood that reflexivization is not a transformation converting some NP to *zibun* but, rather, that *zibun* is an independent lexical item. If so, it must be subject to various cyclically applied constraints governing both its interpretation and its possibility of occurrence.

CAUSATIVIZATION

MASAYOSHI SHIBATANI

INTRODUCTION

Defining the causative construction is not an easy matter. In fact, a successful definition of the causative construction would approximate a thorough grammatical analysis of the construction. Nevertheless, it seems highly appropriate, or even necessary, to give a rough characterization of the causative construction before details of the Japanese causative construction are dealt with. Since a syntactic structure that conveys a causative expression varies from one language to another, a universally valid definition must be given in semantic terms.

The easiest way to define the causative construction is, perhaps, by characterizing the situation, which may be called the 'causative situation', that the construction expresses. Two events can be said to constitute a causative situation if the following two conditions hold:

(1) a. *The relation between the two events is such that the speaker believes that the occurrence of one event, the 'caused event', has been realized at t_2, which is after t_1, the time of the 'causing event.'*

b. *The relation between the causing and the caused event is such that the speaker believes that the occurrence of the caused event is wholly dependent on the occurrence of the causing event; the dependency of the two events must be to the extent that it allows the speaker to entertain a counterfactual in-*

ference that the caused event would not have taken place at that particular time if the causing event had not taken place, provided that all else had remained same.

According to this characterization of the causative situation, English sentences such as *I told John to go* and *I regret that John went* are not causative sentences. The sentence *I told John to go* does not commit the speaker to the belief that the event of John's going occurred after his telling him to do so. Thus, there is no contradiction involved in the sentence *I told John to go, but I don't think he did.* The sentence *I regret that John went* does commit the speaker to the belief that the event of John's going took place, yet the sentence is not a causative sentence.[1] This is because the occurrence of the second event, John's going, is in no way dependent on the event of the speaker's regretting.

On the other hand, sentences like *I caused John to go* and *I made John go*, as well as *I opened the door* and *I sent John to the market*, are causative sentences. All of these sentences commit the speaker to the belief that the caused event has taken place. Thus, sentences such as *I caused John to go, but I don't think he went* and *I opened the door, but it didn't open* involve contradiction. It is also the case that all of these sentences express situations in which the realization of the caused events is wholly dependent on the occurrence of the causing events. That is, these causative sentences would not be appropriate if the situations were such that John went or the door opened in any event, regardless of the speaker's having told John to go or of the speaker's having done something to the door.

In traditional grammar, verbs like *melt* and *kick* are classified as transitive verbs, but the terms CAUSATIVE VERBS and TRANSITIVE VERBS do not coincide. The verb *kick*, for example, is not a causative verb by itself, since a sentence such as *John kicked the ice* does not necessarily convey that there was any caused event following John's kicking the ice. One can, thus, say the sentence *John kicked the ice, but nothing happened to the ice* without involving any contradiction. However, the causative verb *melt* creates contradiction, as shown in the sentence *John melted the ice, but nothing happened to the ice.*

1. MORPHOLOGY

As we have seen, English has two types of causative sentences, one with auxiliary causative verbs such as *cause*, *make*, etc., and the other with morphologically irregular causative verbs, e.g., *open*, *melt*. Japanese causative forms may be also classified into two types on the basis of morphological

[1]The notion involved in this sentence is not that of causation but that of factivity (cf. Kiparsky and Kiparsky, 1971).

regularity. The regular type involves the suffix *sase*, which has a phonological variant form *ase*, as illustrated in (2):

(2)

	Noncausative	Causative
'work'	*hatarak-u*	*hatarak-ase-ru*
'look'	*mi-ru*	*mi-sase-ru*
'walk'	*aruk-u*	*aruk-ase-ru*

a. *Taroo ga hatarak-u.*
'Taro works.'

a′. *Hanako ga Taroo o hatarak-ase-ru.*
'Hanako makes Taro work.'

b. *Taroo ga e o mi-ru.*
'Taro looks at the picture.'

b′. *Hanako ga Taroo ni e o mi-sase-ru.*
'Hanako makes Taro look at the picture.'

c. *Taroo ga aruk-u.*
'Taro walks.'

c′. *Hanako ga Taroo o aruk-ase-ru.*
'Hanako makes Taro walk.'

The other type, illustrated in (3), includes the forms that are related to the noncausative forms in an irregular fashion:

(3)

	Noncausative	Causative
'open'	*hirak-u*	*hirak-u*
'die'	*sin-u*	*koros-u*
'withdraw'	*hikkom-u*	*hikkom-e-ru*
'cry'	*nak-u*	*nak-as-u*

a. *Mado ga hirak-u.*
'The window opens.'

a′. *Taroo ga mado o hirak-u.*
'Taro opens the window.'

b. *Kaeru ga sin-da.*
'The frog died.'

b′. *Taroo ga kaeru o koros-i-ta.*
'Taro killed the frog.'

c. *Musuko ga hikkon-da.*
'The son withdrew.'

c′. *Taroo ga musuko o hikkom-e-ta.*
'Taro withdrew the son.'

d. *Hanako ga nak-u.*
'Hanako cries.'

d′. *Taroo ga Hanako o nak-as-u.*
'Taro makes Hanako cry.'

The forms illustrated in (3) are irregularly related to the noncausative forms; some of the forms that belong to this irregular type have the same shape for both causative and noncausative forms, some causative–noncausative pairs show no morphological relation, and some others involve suffixation of one kind or another. The nonproductive nature of the forms in (3) can be known from the fact that even the suffixed forms cannot interchange the suffixes, while the suffix *sase* involved in (2) can be affixed productively, as shown in (4):

(4)

		Noncausative	Causative
a.	'withdraw'	*hikkom-u*	**hikkom-as-u*[2]
			hikkom-ase-ru
b.	'cry'	*nak-u*	**nak-e-ru*
			nak-ase-ru
c.	'die'	*sin-u*	*sin-ase-ru*

What the preceding observation shows is that, while the regular, productive causative forms in (2) need not be present in the lexicon, the irregular forms in (3) require either that they be present in the lexicon or that the noncausative forms be lexically marked as to the surface forms their causative counterparts take in case some kind of lexical derivational rule is involved. For ease of exposition, the regular causative forms and irregular forms are henceforth referred to as the 'productive causatives' and the 'lexical causatives', respectively.

2. SYNTAX

Syntactic Structures and Processes

It has been proposed in Shibatani (1973a) that the underlying syntactic structure for the productive causative sentence should have the basic form of (5) and that of the lexical causative sentence the basic form of (6):

(5)

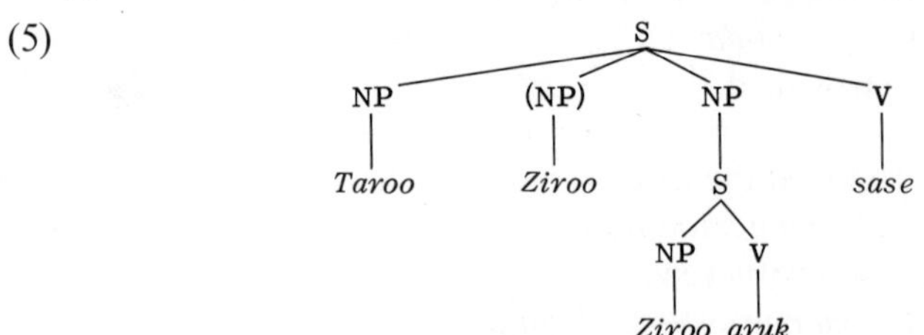

E.g., *Taroo ga Ziroo o/ni aruk-ase-ta.*
'Taro made/had Jiro walk.'

[2]There is a certain confusion among many speakers of Japanese who abbreviate *sase* as *sas*. For those speakers the *hikkom-as-u* form is well-formed as the abbreviated form of *hikkom-ase-ru*, but not as a variant of *hikkom-e-ru*.

(6)

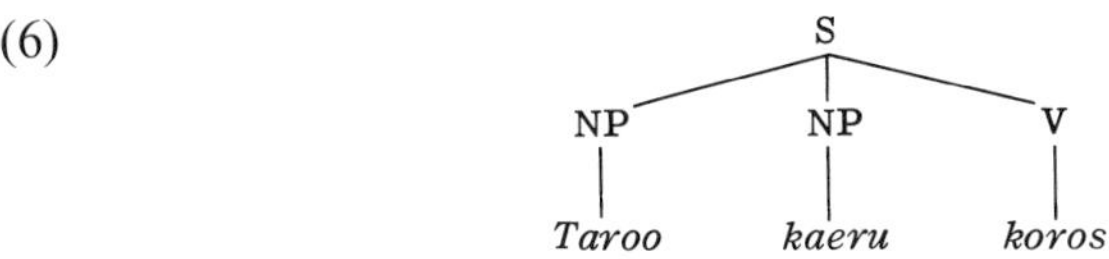

E.g., *Taroo ga kaeru o koros-i-ta.*
'Taro killed the frog.'

The presence or absence of an extra noun phrase in the matrix sentence in (5) is correlated with the fact that an English sentence such as (7a) translates into two Japanese sentences, (7b) and (7c):

(7)
a. *John caused Bill to walk.*
b. *Zyon ga Biru* **o** *aruk-ase-ta.*
c. *Zyon ga Biru* **ni** *aruk-ase-ta.*

The sentence with the *o*-marked 'causee' expresses coercive causation, and it corresponds more closely to an English sentence with *make*, while the sentence with the *ni*-marked causee expresses noncoercive causation like an English sentence with *have*.[3] It is for the purpose of reflecting this semantic difference that an extra noun phrase has been posited in the matrix sentence that underlies the coercive sentence.

In the case of the coercive sentence, the main syntactic processes involved are (a) equi-NP deletion, which deletes the subject of the embedded sentence, (b) verb raising, which raises the verb of the embedded sentence and adjoins it to the verb of the matrix sentence,[4] and (c) case-marking rules, which assign *ga* to the surface subject and *o* to the noun phrase that occurs as the second noun phrase in the matrix sentence. The structure underlying the noncoercive sentence, on the other hand, calls for (a) verb raising and (b) case-marking rules, one of which assigns *ni* to the subject of the embedded sentence that has been raised to the matrix sentence following verb raising and tree pruning.

In addition to these processes, there are two additional rules that are purely syntactic. One has to do with the surface neutralization of the coercive and noncoercive causative forms. As observed in (7), if the causative structure involves an intransitive sentence as the embedded sentence, there arise two causative forms, one with the *o*-marked causee and the other with the *ni*-marked causee, reflecting an underlying semantic difference. If, on the other hand, the embedded sentence is transitive, the surface particle for the causee invariably becomes *ni*. For example, a sentence like (8a) is ambiguous as to the coerciveness involved, and the corresponding sentence, (8b), with the *o*-marked causee, is ungrammatical:

[3]These sentences are subsequently referred to as the '*o* causative' and the '*ni* causative'.

[4]The terms VERB RAISING and PREDICATE RAISING are used interchangeably.

(8) a. *Taroo ga Ziroo* ***ni*** *hon o kaw-ase-ta.*
'Taro made/had Jiro buy a book.'
b. **Taroo ga Ziroo* ***o*** *hon o kaw-ase-ta.*

This phenomenon seems to be correlated with a surface structure constraint in Japanese that prohibits two occurrences of N-*o* in a sentence that has only one verb (provided that the sentence is not derived via conjunction reduction or gapping). It appears that the fact that the underlying verb *sase* becomes a suffix rather than remaining an independent verb at the surface level makes the productive causative sentence subject to this constraint. The phenomenon observed in (8) can be accounted for by positing a rule that turns an N-*o* phrase followed by another N-*o* phrase into N-*ni* under the condition that only one verb exists in the sentence. What this account amounts to is to say that there are two underlying structures for sentence (8a) corresponding to the two readings of the sentence, and that the noncoercive structure directly gives rise to (8a) while the coercive structure first becomes (8b), and then the above-mentioned rule turns (8b) into the surface structure identical with the noncoercive form.

The other rule has to do with double causatives. Japanese allows double causatives, but in the surface often only one causative morpheme appears. Observe:

(9) a. *Taroo ga Ziroo ni Itiroo o aruk-**ase-sase**-ta.*
'Taro made/had Jiro make Ichiro walk.'
b. *Taroo ga Ziroo ni Itiroo o aruk-**ase**-ta.*

Both convey the same double causative meaning, and the native speaker prefers the second sentence. Since (9b) also expresses double causation, it must be derived from the same structure that underlies (9a). The most reasonable account for (9b), then, is to posit a rule that says that the double causatives are preferably reduced to the single causative at the surface level; i.e., a *sase-sase* sequence is reduced to just *sase*.

The claims made in the analysis just outlined are the following: (a) While the productive causative involves an embedding structure, the lexical causative does not, and (b) despite the morphological difference, the productive causatives in English and Japanese essentially involve the same type of underlying structure.

When one compares only the pairs of noncausative and causative expressions (2a)–(2a′) and (3c)–(3c′), it is hard to see that the causative forms in these pairs are as different as the preceding analysis claims them to be. From a purely morphological point of view, the causative sentences in the pairs both involve suffixed verbs. However, the classification of the causative forms was made on the basis of productivity, and the fact that this classificatory basis indeed provides a meaningful classification can be shown by examining the syntactic patterns that the two types of causative forms display. I turn now to several syntactic phenomena in which causative forms classified as lexical causatives show syntactic behavior different from those classified as productive causatives. The phenomena to be presented will also render support to the claim that while the productive causative involves an embedding structure like the one involved in the English productive causative, the lexical causative involves a simplex structure, as illustrated in (5) and (6).

Adverbial Modification

In this section I consider how adverbial modification is correlated with lexical and productive causatives. With productive causative sentences, adverbs can be interpreted as being associated with either the causing event or the caused event. That is, in one interpretation the adverb is a constituent of the clause whose main verbs is *sase*, and in the other it is a constituent of the clause of a caused event. Sentence (10a), for example, may mean either that Taro was silent when he made Hanako come into the room or that Taro instructed Hanako in such a way that she came into the room silently:

(10) a. *Taroo wa Hanako o heya ni damatte hair-ase-ta.*
'Taro made Hanako come into the room silently.'
b. *Taroo wa Hanako o kyuuni tomar-ase-ta.*
'Taro made Hanako stop suddenly.'

Other adverbials behave similarly, as shown in (11):

(11) a. *Taroo wa Ziroo o te de ki ni agar-ase-ta.*
'Taro made Jiro go up the tree with the hands.'
b. *Taroo wa Ziroo o rokuzi ni oki-sase-ta.*
'Taro made Jiro get up at six o'clock.'
c. *Taroo wa Ziroo ni huku o heya de ki-sase-ta.*
'Taro made Jiro put on the clothes in the room.'
d. *Taroo wa Ziroo o heya ni sankai hair-ase-ta.*
'Taro made Jiro come into the room three times.'

One will notice that there is a slight difference in the patterns of modification between time and place adverbials and other adverbials, e.g., manner adverbs. The manner adverb may modify only the manner of the causing agent, as observed in (10). That is, in one interpretation of (10a), it can be the case that only Taro was silent. Time and place adverbials, however, cannot be interpreted as modifying just the causing event. One interpretation of (11b) is similar to one of the interpretations (10a) gives, and it says that only Jiro's getting up took place at six o'clock (with the understanding that Taro's instruction to Jiro occurred before six o'clock). The other interpretation, however, says that both Taro's instructing Jiro and Jiro's getting up took place at six o'clock, and the sentence does not allow the interpretation that only Taro's instructing Jiro took place at six o'clock (with the understanding that Jiro's getting up took place sometime after six o'clock).

The behavior of the time and place adverbial, as we have seen, is in fact a characteristic of the causative sentence. A noncausative sentence like (12) does not show the same pattern:

(12) *Taroo was Ziroo ni rokuzi ni okiru yoo it-ta.*
'Taro told Jiro to get up at six o'clock.'

Although (12) involves an embedding structure similar to (5), the adverb modifies the sentence differently from what we have seen. In (12), it is possible to have the interpretation that only Taro's telling Jiro took place at six o'clock (with the understanding that Jiro got up sometime after six o'clock, or even with the understanding that Jiro did not get up at all).

Returning now to the causative sentence, one will notice that the same observation holds in the English productive causative sentence; the translations of the preceding examples all have two interpretations with respect to the scope of adverbial modification. In the case of lexical causatives, however, only one interpretation of the adverbial scope is possible:

(13) a. *Taroo wa Hanako o heya ni damatte ire-ta.*
'Taro put Hanako into the room silently.'
b. *Taroo wa Hanako o kyuuni tome-ta.*
'Taro stopped Hanako suddenly.'
c. *Taroo wa Ziroo o te de ki ni age-ta.*
'Taro lifted Jiro up the tree with the hands.'
d. *Taroo wa Ziroo o rokuzi ni okos-i-ta.*
'Taro got Jiro up at six o'clock.'
e. *Taroo wa Ziroo ni huku o heya de kise-ta.*
'Taro put the clothes on Jiro in the room.'
f. *Taroo wa Ziroo o heya ni sankai ire-ta.*
'Taro put Jiro into the room three times.'

Sentence (13a), for example, does not allow two interpretations similar to those observed in (10a), and here the adverb modifies only Taro's activity. The time and place adverbial modifies whole causative events, and cannot be interpreted as modifying just the caused events (with the understanding that the causing events took place prior to the time specified or in places other than the place specified). For example, (13d), unlike (11b), gives only one interpretation, that both Taro's getting Jiro up and Jiro's getting up took place at six o'clock, and there is no reading that says only Jiro's getting up took place at six o'clock (with the understanding that Taro's causing activity took place before six o'clock).

If one compares the lexical causative *kise-ru* 'put (the clothes) on (someone)' and the productive form *ki-sase-ru* 'cause (someone) to put on (the clothes)' with the noncausative form *ki-ru* 'put on (the clothes)', it appears that the lexical form *kise-ru* also contains the suffix *-se* added to the stem *ki-*. Thus, from a purely morphological point of view, there does not seem to be much difference between *kise-ru* and *ki-sase-ru*. However, comparison of (11c) and (13e) reveals that they display a very different syntactic pattern; the lexical causative *kise-ru* patterns together with other irregular, hence, lexical causative verbs such as *ire-ru* 'put in', *tome-ru* 'stop', etc. Thus, the criterion based on the productivity of the form yields a significant classification of causative verbs. More instances that support this classification follow.

Reflexivization

Just as the scope of adverbial modification can be interpreted in two ways in the productive causative sentence, the reflexive pronoun can be interpreted ambiguously in such a sentence, while no such ambiguity arises in the lexical causative sentence. As extensively discussed by N. McCawley and by Inoue (in this volume), the Japanese reflexive pronoun *zibun* 'self' takes a subject noun as its antecedent as a general rule; consequently, when a sentence contains just one subject the reflexive pronoun refers uniquely to that subject. A sentence like the following, therefore, has no ambiguity as to which noun the reflexive pronoun refers to; it uniquely refers to the subject, Taro:

(14) *Taroo wa Hanako o zibun no heya de ket-ta.*
'Taro kicked Hanako in his room.'
(Lit.) 'Taro$_i$ kicked Hanako$_j$ in self's$_i$/*self's$_j$ room.'

Unlike English, Japanese reflexivization takes place across clause boundaries. Accordingly, if a sentence is derived from a complex structure with two or more subjects, an ambiguity arises as to which subject the reflexive pronoun refers to.[5] Sentence (15), for example, is assumed to derive from an underlying structure with two subjects, Taro and Hanako, and it so turns out that the sentence is ambiguous:

(15) *Taroo wa Hanako ni kagami ni ututta* ***zibun*** *o miru yoo ni it-ta.*
(Lit.) 'Taro$_i$ told Hanako$_j$ to look at self$_i$/self$_j$ reflected in the mirror.'

In one reading, the pronoun *zibun* refers to Taro, and in the other Hanako, since both Taro and Hanako are subjects underlyingly.

[5]See the chapter by Howard and Niyekawa-Howard in this volume for a constraint on this possibility.

Like the phenomenon of adverbial modification considered earlier, the phenomenon of Japanese reflexivization leads us to suspect that the underlying syntactic structure of a productive causative sentence is complex. This follows from the fact that the reflexive pronoun in a productive causative sentence is ambiguously interpreted; it may refer to the agent of the causing event or that of the caused event. Sentence (16a), for example, is ambiguous; in one reading *zibun* 'self' refers to Taro, and in the other to Hanako:

(16) a. *Taroo wa Hanako ni kagami ni ututta* ***zibun*** *o mi-sase-ta.*
(Lit.) 'Taro$_i$ made Hanako$_j$ look at self$_i$/self$_j$ reflected in the mirror.'
b. *Taro wa Ziroo ni* ***zibun*** *no huku o ki-sase-ta.*
(Lit.) 'Taro$_i$ made Jiro$_j$ put on self's$_i$/self's$_j$ clothes.'

A lexical causative sentence, on the other hand, displays characteristics found in simplex sentences, since the reflexive pronoun in it cannot be interpreted ambiguously. Unlike (16a), (17a), for example, does not allow the interpretation of the reflexive pronoun as referring to the causee, Hanako:

(17) a. *Taroo wa Hanako ni kagami ni ututta* ***zibun*** *o mise-ta.*
(Lit.) 'Taro$_i$ showed Hanako$_j$ self/*self$_j$ reflected in the mirror.'
b. *Taroo wa Ziroo ni* ***zibun*** *no huku o kise-ta.*
(Lit.) 'Taro$_i$ put self's$_i$/*self's$_j$ clothes on Jiro$_j$.'

Comparison of the sentences in (16) and (17) with those in (15) and (14) makes it clear that the productive causative sentence patterns together with the sentence arising from a complex structure, while the lexical causative sentence patterns together with a simplex sentence.

Soo Suru Replacement

The proverbal form *soo su-* replaces the verb and some other parts of a sentence under certain identity conditions.[6] Sentence (18a), for example, comes from the structure that underlies (18b) via the *soo-suru* rule:

(18) a. *Taroo ga uinkusu-ru to Hanako mo* ***soo si-ta.***
'When Taro winked, Hanako did so, too.'
b. *Taroo ga uinkusu-ru to Hanako mo uinkusi-ta.*
'When Taro winked, Hanako winked, too.'

We have already noted that the Japanese productive causative form appears to have just one verb in the surface, since the causative morpheme

[6] The conditions involved here are not yet precisely known. Cf. Hinds (1973a) for a relevant discussion.

turns into a suffix. The fact that the productive suffix *sase* really functions as an independent verb at a deeper level can be seen when a rule like the *soo suru* rule applies; the *soo suru* rule applies either to the verb of the caused event, i.e., the embedded structure, or to the whole causative verbal complex, i.e., *V-sase*, yielding ambiguous phrases:

(19) *Taroo ga otooto o tomar-ase-ru to, Ziroo mo* ***soo si-ta.***
'When Taro made his brother stop, Jiro did so, too.'

This sentence is ambiguous; in one reading the phrase *Ziroo mo soo si-ta* 'Jiro did so, too' means that Jiro made his brother stop, too, and in the other it means that Jiro (himself) stopped. This ambiguity can be attributed to the following two possible sources for (19):

(20) a. *Taroo ga otooto o tomar-ase-ru to, Ziroo mo otooto o tomar-ase-ta.*
'When Taro made his brother stop, Jiro made his brother stop, too.'
b. *Taroo ga otooto o tomar-ase-ru to, Ziroo mo tomat-ta.*
'When Taro made his brother stop, Jiro stopped, too.

The fact that the *soo suru* phrase in (19) allows the reading corresponding to (20b) presents evidence that the productive causative form *tomar-ase-* 'cause to stop' comes from a structure that contains the main verb, i.e., *tomar-* 'stop', as an independent verb. In other words, a sentence like *Taroo ga otooto o tomar-ase-ru* 'Taro makes his brother stop' comes from a structure like the one given in (5), in which there is an independent clause, *otooto ga tomar-u* 'the brother stops', beneath the structure that has the causative verb *sase* separately.

The lexical causative sentence behaves quite differently from its corresponding productive causative sentence with respect to the *soo suru* rule. Unlike the productive causative sentence, the *soo suru* phrase is in no way ambiguous when it occurs in the lexical causative sentence, as observed in (21):

(21) *Taroo ga otooto o tome-ru to Ziroo mo* ***soo si-ta.***
'When Taro stopped his brother Jiro did so, too.'

The *soo suru* phrase in (21) unambiguously says that Jiro stopped his brother, too, and one cannot get the reading from it that Jiro also stopped. In other words, (22) is not a possible source for (21), which means that the underlying structure of a sentence such as *Taroo ga otooto o tome-ru* 'Taro stops his brother' does not contain the clause *otooto ga tomar-u*, which is contained in the productive counterpart:

(22) *Taroo ga otooto o tome-ru to Ziroo mo tomat-ta.*
'When Taro stopped his brother, Jiro stopped, too.'

Here again, the lexical and productive causatives show different syntactic behavior.

Sentence Pronominalization

As in English, Japanese allows a sentence to undergo pronominalization. Sentence pronominalization may apply to the entire sentence or just to the embedded sentence of a complex sentence structure. For example, in (23b), the pronoun *sore* 'it' can be interpreted as referring to the entire sentence of (23a), while in (23c), *sore* has replaced only what is identical with the embedded sentence *Taroo ga atarasii setu o hakken si-ta* 'Taro discovered a new theory':

(23) a. *Taroo wa atarasii setu o hakken si-ta to syutyoo si-ta ga*
'Taro claimed that he had discovered a new theory, but'
b. *daremo* ***sore*** *o kini kakenakat-ta.*
'no one paid any attention to it.'
c. *Dare mo* ***sore*** *o sinzinakat-ta.*
'no one believed it.'

This fact indicates that when the pronoun refers back to a complex sentence structure, it is potentially ambiguous as to whether it refers to the entire sentence or just to an embedded sentence. In fact, such ambiguity is observed in the productive causative sentence, as in (24):

(24) a. *Zensin huzui no Taroo ga tiisana otooto ni huku o hitori de ki-sase-ta to syutyoo si-ta ga*
'Totally paralyzed Taro claimed that he made his small brother put on the clothes alone, but'
b. *minna wa* ***sore*** *wa hukanoo da to omot-ta.*
'everyone thought that it was impossible.'

Here, the pronoun *sore* in (24b) is ambiguous in that it may be referring to the whole causative sentence in (24a) or just to the embedded sentence *tiisana otooto ga huku o hitori de kiru* 'the small brother puts the clothes on alone.' The phenomenon of sentence pronominalization, thus, argues again for the presence of the independent embedded sentence in the productive causative structure.

A sentence with a lexical causative, on the other hand, does not present any ambiguity when the pronoun refers to it. For example, the lexical causative sentence (25a), corresponding to the productive causative sentence (24a), does not present any ambiguity for the pronoun *sore* in (25b); the pronoun has a unique antecedent, namely, the whole causative sentence in (25a):

(25) a. *Zensin huzui no Taroo ga tiisana otooto ni huku o hitori de kise-ta to syutyoo si-ta ga*
'Totally paralyzed Taro claimed that he put the clothes on his small brother alone, but'
b. *minna wa* **sore** *wa hukanoo da to omot-ta.*
'everyone thought it was impossible.'

The four phenomena just examined should suffice to show that there is a considerable amount of evidence to support the claims made in the analysis presented earlier. I turn now to semantic properties of the Japanese causative expression.

3. SEMANTICS

We have so far studied morphological and syntactic properties of causative forms. In this section we will be dealing with semantic properties of causative expressions.

Coercive versus Noncoercive Causation

In a situation in which both causer and causee are human, there is a wide range of activity that the causer can perform in effecting the caused event: He may force the causee, he may persuade the causee, or he may gently suggest that the causee perform an act that constitutes the caused event. Causative verbs, particularly productive forms, tend to be abstract in not specifying what the causer did to get something done. English sentence (26), for example, may be describing a situation in which the speaker just suggested that John go and he went, etc.:

(26) *I caused John to go.*

The range of activity the causer performs in a causative situation can be qualified or delimited by a phrase that describes the causer's activity, as in (27):

(27) a. *I caused John to go by suggesting that he do so.*
b. *I caused John to go by forcing him to do so.*
etc.

A similar observation appears to obtain in Japanese, since (28) can describe a wide range of situations as far as the activity on the part of the causer is concerned:

(28) *Taroo wa Hanako ni hon o yom-ase-ta.*
'Taro caused Hanako to read the book.'

Though both the English causative verb *cause* and the Japanese verb *sase* are quite abstract as to what kind of causation act the causer performs, both languages have a way to indicate at least the extent of coerciveness involved in the causation act. Thus, English sentence (26) may be translated as either (29a) or (29b), depending on whether coercion is involved or not:

(29) a. *Boku wa Zyon* ***ni*** *ik-ase-ta.*
b. *Boku wa Zyon* ***o*** *ik-ase-ta.*

The situation expressed by (27a) can be more appropriately expressed by (29a) than by (29b), while the situation expressed by (27b) corresponds to what (29b) expresses. This correlation can be observed by the naturalness and unnaturalness of the following sentences:

(30) a. *Boku wa yasasiku iikikasete Zyon* ***ni*** *ik-ase-ta.*
'I caused John to go by gently persuading him.'
b. ?*Boku wa tikarazuku de Zyon* ***ni*** *ik-ase-ta.*
'I caused John to go forcibly.'
c. *Boku wa tikarazuku de Zyon* ***o*** *ik-ase-ta.*
'I caused John to go forcibly.'
d. ?*Boku wa yasasiku iikikase te Zyon* ***o*** *ik-ase-ta.*
'I caused John to go by gently suggesting him.'

The adverbial phrase that expresses noncoercive manner goes naturally with the *ni* causative form only, while the phrase expressing coercive manner goes well only with the *o* causative form. Thus, in Japanese, noncoercive causation is expressed by the *ni* causative and the coercive causation by the *o* causative. Since these different particles on the causee are assigned on the basis of the difference in underlying structure (see Section 2), Japanese expresses the coercive–noncoercive distinction by syntactic means. We have already discussed that in a sentence like (28), which contains a transitive structure expressing the caused event, the structural difference distinguishing the coercive–noncoercive distinction is lost at the surface level.

While Japanese expresses the coercive–noncoercive distinction by syntactic means, some languages express such a distinction by lexical means. English, for example, has *make*, which can be used to express coercive causation. Forms like *have* and *get*, on the other hand, typically express noncoercive causation. Sentence (31a), being noncoercive, is quite natural in an ordinary situation, while (31b) is appropriate only in describing a situation in which John resorted to coercive action, e.g., twisting the doctor's arm:

(31) a. *John had the doctor come.*

b. *John made the doctor come.*

As in (30), the factor being considered here is apparently relevant to the selection of adverbial phrases; adverbial phrases that convey coercive meaning go well only with the coercive causative forms.

(32) a. *I forcibly made the doctor come.*
b. *I made the doctor come by twisting his arm.*
c. **I forcibly had the doctor come.*
d. **I had the doctor come by twisting his arm.*

Although the discussion so far has been concerned with the causative situation from the causer's perspective, the notion of coercive–noncoercive causation can be studied from the causee's perspective, as well. In particular, there is a close correlation between the extent of coerciveness involved in the causing event and the amount of resistance associated with the caused event. Coercive causation is applied when the causer encounters a strong resistance in effecting the caused event, while if the caused event can be effected without encountering resistance, coercive causation need not be applied. It is, thus, the resistance that the causer must overcome that calls for coercive causation.

The above-mentioned correlation between the coercion and the resistance seems to be reflected in the following pairs of sentences:

(33) a. *Taroo* ***o*** *tukai ni ik-ase-ru noni zyuppun kakat-ta.*
'It took (me) ten minutes to make Taro go on an errand.'
b. *Taroo* ***ni*** *tukai ni ik-ase-ru noni zyuppun kakat-ta.*
'It took (me) ten minutes to send Taro on an errand.'

As for my intuition, which is shared by a number of native speakers, it is the case that in (33a) ten minutes were spent in overcoming Taro's resistance to go on an errand; i.e., ten minutes were spent in persuading or threatening reluctant Taro. In (33b), on the other hand, ten minutes were likely to have been spent in giving directions, dressing Taro, etc., rather than in overcoming Taro's resistance.

To sum up, the notion of coercion in the causative situation can be viewed from two different points of view. From the causer's perspective, it relates to the amount of coerciveness involved in the causation act; from the causee's perspective, it relates to the extent of the causee's concurrence. The nature of human interaction is such that the extent of coerciveness in the causation act is most often correlated with the extent of the concurrence on the part of the causee: If the causer assumes that the causee would concur with his intention, no coercive causation act is exercised; if, on the other hand, the causer expects resistance, he resorts to a coercive causation act.

Permissive Causation

Japanese is one of those languages that allow the use of the causative morpheme to express 'permissive causation'. There appear to be, altogether, four types of permissive causation. The two most prevalent types are (a) a situation in which the causer forbears (or omits) prevention (or intervention), as a result of which the caused event takes place successfully, and (b) a situation in which the causer actively gives permission to the causee to do something. This second type can be understood as a type of forbearance, too; namely, the causer forbears withholding permission. The two less prevalent types are (c) a case in which the causer attempts but fails to prevent something from happening and (d) a situation in which the causer gives up and does not intervene with the caused event, knowing that his intervention would not succeed anyway.

Types (a), (c), and (d) are closely related in that prevention has not taken place, and as a result, the caused event has been realized; however, some aspects of presuppositions involved in each type may be different. All of these types involve the assertion that nonoccurrence of prevention (or forbearance of intervention), $\sim E_1$, which constitutes the causing event, has led to (or permitted) the occurrence of the caused event, E_2.

In the case of type (b), the causing event, E_1, is identified with withholding permission, and this type asserts that not withholding or giving permission $\sim E_1$, has led to the realization of the caused event, E_2. Thus, in all four types of permissive causation, the assertion takes the form '$\sim E_1$ leads to E_2.'

As far as the presuppositions are concerned, the prevalent types, (a) and (b) as well as (c), share the presupposition that if E_1 (prevention or withholding of permission) had been successful, E_2 would not have happened. That is, E_1 leads to $\sim E_2$. In the case of type (c), there should be some additional presupposition expressing that the causer attempts to prevent the caused event from occurring. Type (d), on the other hand, does not seem to share the presupposition that E_1 leads to $\sim E_2$. But what appears to be involved is the notion that, even if the causer attempted to prevent the caused event, he would not have been successful, and it would have occurred anyway.

Leaving aside for now the discussion of the formal properties of permissive causation, I turn now to the Japanese forms that express permissive causation. Since permissive causation holds only in the situation in which the caused event has a propensity to occur, the *ni* causative form, which typically expresses noncoercive causation, is the prevalent permissive causative form. Thus, of the following pair, (34a) can be much more readily interpreted in the permissive sense than (34b):

(34) a. *Taroo* ***ni*** *eiga e ik-ase-ta.*
'(I) had/let Taro go to the movies.'

b. *Taroo **o** eiga e ik-ase-ta.*
'(I) made Taro go to the movies.'

However, there are *o* causative sentences that express permissive causation, as observed in the following sentences from Kitagawa (1974):

(35) a. *Kawaisoo datta ga, yaru miruku mo nakatta no de sono mama akanboo o nak-ase-ta.*
'I felt bad, but since I did not have even milk to give it, I just let the baby cry.'

b. *Moo uma o turete kaeru zikan datta ga, amari yukaisoo ni kakoi no naka o hasitte iru no de Taroo wa sono mama moo sibaraku uma o hasir-ase-ta.*
'The time had come for Taro to take the horse back, but, because the horse was running so joyously in the corral, Taro let the horse run for a little while more.'

In addition to the sentences in (35), the causee takes the particle *o* if it is a nonvolitional entity, regardless of whether the situation involves permissive causation or ordinary causation:

(36) a. *Reizooko ni irezu ni hotte oite, yasai o/*ni kusar-ase-ta.*
'(I) let the vegetable rot without putting it in the refrigerator.'

b. *Omoiyari no aru isya wa konsuizyootai ni ari tasukaru mikomi no nai byoonin o/*ni sin-ase-ta.*
'The sympathetic doctor let the patient, who was in a coma and had no hope of survival, die.'

Sentences of this type give a certain clue as to the difference between the permissive causative forms expressed by the *o* causative and those expressed by the *ni* causative. In the case of the situations expressed by the *o* causative, it appears that the causer either fails to prevent the caused event from happening or does not actively give permission to the causee, but merely forbears his interfering act so that the ongoing event will persist or the imminent event will occur. In other words, the *o* causative forms express permissive causation of types (a), (c), and (d). In contrast, the situations expressed by the *ni* causative form involve the causer as an active participant; in particular, he would be actively giving (often oral) permission to the causee. That is, the *ni* causative expresses the type (b) permissive situation. The contrast can be observed in the following sentences:

(37) a. *Iede o siyoo to site iru musume o/?ni me o tubutte ik-ase-ta.*
'Pretending not to see, (I) let the daughter go who was trying to run away from home.'

b. *Tatoe tomete mo mudananode hotte oite masuko o/?ni ik-ase-ta.*

'Since stopping is no use, (I) let the son go without doing anything.'

c. *'Aa iiyo' to itte kodomo ni/?o motto asob-ase-ta.*
'(I) let the children play more by saying "Oh, OK."'

d. *'Ittemo iiyo' to kyoka o ataete musuko ni/?o ik-ase-ta.*
'(I) let the son go by giving a permission "OK, you can go."'

Undoubtedly, the fact that only *o* causative forms can express permissive causation if the causee is a nonvolitional entity is due to the situational difference discussed earlier. The essential difference between the permissive causative situation expressed by the *ni* causative form and the one expressed by the *o* causative form is that, in the former situation, the causer actively concurs with or enhances the causee's volition while, in the latter situation, there is no such active concurrence or enhancement given to the causee's volition. Thus, only a volitional entity can be the causee of the former situation, while there is no such restriction in the latter situation.

It is interesting to note here that in the case of the nonvolitional causee, if the causer actively participates or attempts to enhance the process, the situation cannot be interpreted as permissive causation; such a situation can be interpreted only as an ordinary causative situation. For example, in contrast to the sentences in (36), the following can be understood only as ordinary causative sentences:

(38) a. *Reizooko kara toridasite yasai o kusar-ase-ta.*
'(I) made the vegetable rot by taking it out from the refrigerator.'

b. *Omiyarino aru isya wa karyoo no kusuri o ataete konsuizyootai ni ari tasukaru mikomi no nai byoonin o sin-ase-ta.*
'By giving an overdose of medicine, the sympathetic doctor caused the patient to die who was in a coma and had no hope of survival.'

One other point to be noted here is that in the permissive causative situation expressed by the *o* causative form and involving the nonvolitional entity as the causee, the process must be such that it must have either inherent or programed potentiality to take place. The following sentences are, thus, not normally acceptable as permissive causative sentences:

(39) a. **Taroo wa yasai o nie-sase-ta.*
'Taro let the vegetable cook.'

b. **Taroo wa isu o taore-sase-ta.*
'Taro let the chair fall down.'

Sentence (39b), however, can be correctly interpreted in the situation in which someone knocked over the chair and it was slowly falling down, but

Taro, who could have prevented the chair from falling down, just let it fall down. Notice, however, that this type of permissive causation holds only in a situation in which the causer has a capacity to prevent the occurrence of the caused event. Thus, if Taro could have prevented the chair from falling down but did not, one can accuse Taro by saying (39b), but if Taro was in one corner of the room and therefore could not help when someone knocked over the chair in another corner of the room, no one can describe the situation or accuse Taro by saying (39b).

While the most permissive causative cases are expressed by the use of the productive causative form, there are certain cases in which lexical causative forms may be used for permissive causation. Typical cases involve natural forces such as gravity that add propensity to the caused event. For example, (40a) may be interpreted as ordinary causation if Taro intentionally dropped the books, but in the situation in which Taro was pulling a certain book from a high shelf, and, though he attempted to prevent it, he dropped a few neighboring books, the sentence may be interpreted as expressing permissive causation:

(40) a. *Taroo wa hon o otos-i-(te-simat-)ta.*
'Taro dropped the books.'
b. *Taroo wa mokei no hune o sizume-(te-simat-)ta.*
'Taro sank the model ship.'

When one carefully compares the situations appropriate for these sentences with those appropriate for the following productive forms, one will notice that an essential difference is involved:

(41) a. *Taroo wa hon o oti-sase-ta.*
'Taro let the books drop/fall.'
b. *Taroo wa mokei no hune o sizum-ase-ta.*
'Taro let the model ship sink.'

Sentences (41a) and (41b) are appropriate for situations in which Taro was an onlooker and could prevent the books from falling from the shelf or the ship from sinking, but he did not do anything and let the happenings take place. These situations, however, cannot be described by (40a) and (40b). On the other hand, (41a) and (41b) are inappropriate for situations in which Taro was directly involved in the events, e.g., he touched the books or he broke the model ship, and could not prevent the occurrence of the caused events. These situations are most appropriately expressed by (40a) and (40b). In other words, lexical causative forms are appropriate for situations in which the causer manipulates (or directly acts on) the causee, while productive forms are used for situations in which no manipulation of the causee is involved. This notion of manipulation is an important one, for it is inherent in the meaning of lexical causative forms, to be discussed.

The Relation between Ordinary and Permissive Causation

We have seen that Japanese is one of those languages that allow the use of the causative morpheme to express permissive causation. The fact that so many languages, e.g., French (*faire*), German (*lassen*), Korean (*ha-ta*), Turkish (e.g., *-dur-*), and Quechua (*-či-*), share this property indicates that there must be some deep-seated semantic relation between ordinary and permissive causation. In fact, a detailed semantic analysis of the two types of causation reveals that ordinary causation and permissive causation involve the same set of presuppositions, assertions, and negative conditions, but with different functions.

As is clear from the informal, expository characterization of the causative situation given in the introduction, the ordinary causative sentence asserts that the realization of the causing event, E_1, has led to the realization of the caused event, E_2. Let us formally express this relation as 'E_1 Lt E_2', where *Lt* stands for 'leads to'. The presupposition associated with the ordinary causative sentence is that if E_1 had not taken place, then E_2 would not have taken place. Using our notation, this presupposition would be expressed as '$\sim E_1$ Lt $\sim E_2$'. From this assertion and presupposition we can derive negative conditions under which an ordinary causative situation does not hold. They are '$\sim E_1$ Lt E_2' and 'E_1 Lt $\sim E_2$'. That is, no causal relation holds between E_1 and E_2 when the nonoccurrence of E_1 has led to the occurrence of E_2, or when the occurrence of E_1 has led to the nonoccurrence of E_2.

As discussed earlier, in the case of a permissive causative situation, prevention constitutes E_1, and what is asserted is that the nonoccurrence (or forbearance) of prevention, i.e., $\sim E_1$, has led to the realization of the caused event, E_2, i.e., $\sim E_1$ Lt E_2. The presupposition involved in the prevalent types of permissive causation is that if E_1 (prevention) had occurred, then E_2 would not have occurred, i.e., E_1 Lt $\sim E_2$. This presupposition holds crucially in permissive causation, since a permissive causative situation does not hold when (a) E_2 occurs even if the forbearance of prevention is **not** exercised, and when (b) E_2 does not occur even though the forbearance of prevention occurs. In other words, the assertion and the presupposition associated with permissive causation express the following negative conditions for a permissive causative situation: E_1 Lt E_2 and $\sim E_1$ Lt $\sim E_2$.

A careful reader may have noticed the systematic relation that exists between ordinary causation and permissive causation. The negative conditions for ordinary causation function as the presupposition and the assertion for permissive causation, and the presupposition and the assertion of ordinary causation correspond to the negative causations for permissive causation, and vice versa. Schematically, the situation can be summarized as follows:

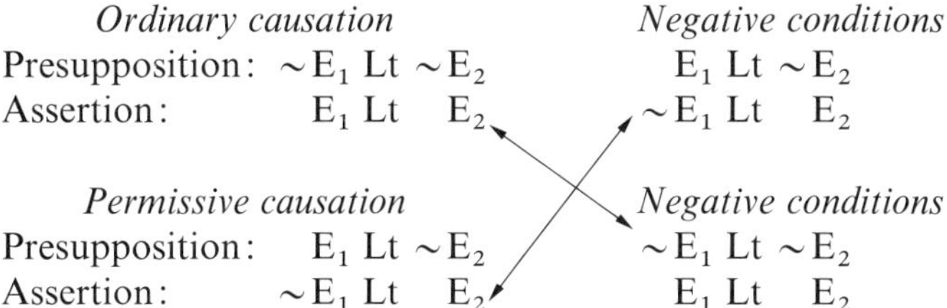

Since the set of negative conditions and the presupposition and the assertion of one type of causation function in completely reverse roles in the other type, the situational difference between ordinary causation and permissive causation is maximal. Thus, even if the same morpheme were to be used for the two situations, there should not arise any confusion. That is, when one uses the morpheme *x* in the ordinary causative sense, he is both presupposing and asserting what constitutes the negative conditions for the other permissive sense; hence, as long as the hearer understands the assertion and shares the presupposition correctly, there is no way he can misunderstand *x* as being used for the permissive sense. Exactly the reverse holds when *x* is used for the permissive sense.

Directive versus Manipulative Causation

The caused event can be effected in a number of different ways. Depending on whether the causee functions as a volitional entity or not, there arise two modes of causation. In a situation in which the causee functions as a volitional entity, giving a direction to the causee is the basic action associated with the causer. On the other hand, in a situation in which the volition of the causee is absent, the causer must physically manipulate the causee in effecting the caused event. The former case is henceforth referred to as 'directive causation', the latter 'manipulative causation'.

The fact that the nonvolitional entity does not very often function as the causee in the productive causative sentence shows that the productive form typically expresses a directive causative situation. Observe:

(42)
a. **Boku wa isu o/ni heya ni hair-ase-ta.*
'I *made/*had the chair enter the room.'
b. **Boku wa hon o/ni tat-ase-ta.*
'I made/*had the book stand up.'
c. *Boku wa Taroo ni/o heya ni hair-ase-ta.*
'I made/had Taro enter the room.'

d. *Boku wa Hanako o/ni taore-sase-ta.*
'I made/had Hanako fall down.'

The lexical causative form, on the other hand, allows both a volitional and a nonvolitional entity to occur as the causee:

(43) a. *Boku wa isu o heya ni ire-ta.*
'I put the chair in the room.'
b. *Boku wa hon o tate-ta.*
'I stood the book up.'
c. *Boku wa Taroo o heya ni ire-ta.*
'I put Taro in the room.'
d. *Boku wa Hanako o taos-i-ta.*
'I threw Hanako down.'

If one compares a situation expressed by a lexical causative sentence, e.g., (43d), and that expressed by a productive causative sentence, e.g., (42d), he will notice that there is a basic difference in the mode of causation involved in each case. In (42d), the situation involves the speaker's giving a directive in such a way that Hanako fell down. (One might imagine a situation involving the speaker as a movie director and Hanako as an actress.) It is also the case that if the situation were to involve any physical manipulation of the causee on the part of the causer, e.g., the speaker's physically throwing down Hanako, (42d) would not be appropriate. In contrast to the situation involved in (42d), the situation expressed by (43d) involves physical manipulation, and (43d) is appropriate for the second situation but not for the first. What is being discussed here is in line with the fact that the nonvolitional entity cannot be a causee of the productive causative form: One cannot give a direction to the nonvolitional entity; therefore, the latter cannot participate in directive causation, and since the productive form typically expresses a directive causative situation, the nonvolitional entity cannot occur as the causee in the productive causative sentence.

What is observed is the division of semantic function between the two types of causative forms: The productive causative primarily expresses the meaning of directive causation, and the lexical causative manipulative causation. Thus, one major semantic difference between the productive and lexical causatives lies in the dimension of the directive–manipulative distinction.

Productive Causatives Expressing Manipulative Causation

While what has been said in the preceding section about the directive–manipulative distinction generally holds true, there are certain cases in which productive forms express manipulative causation. Certain noncausative verbs may lack the corresponding lexical causatives, or even if they have the corresponding lexical causatives, the causative forms may impose a severe selectional restriction on the choice of the causee. The English verb *run* in the sense of 'to move rapidly by springing steps' illustrates the first case for not having the corresponding lexical causative form, and English *fall* illustrates the second case, since the lexical counterpart *fell* is restricted to situations involving a tree or a large animal as the causee.

To a large extent, each language has its own idiosyncracies with respect to this type of "lexical gap". Thus, Korean has the lexical causative form *talli-ta* for the noncausative verb *talli-ta* 'run' (both having the same phonological shape). In Japanese, the lexical causative form *taos-u* for the verb *taore-ru* 'fall down' is not confined to situations involving a tree or a large animal as the causee. On the other hand, unlike the English causative verb *stand up*, the corresponding Japanese verb *tate-ru* is confined to the situation involving an inanimate causee.

When the verbs lack their corresponding lexical forms or when the lexical causatives permit only a limited type of causee, languages in general allow the productive forms to be used to express the situation involving manipulative causation. Japanese shares this property. As noted earlier, the Japanese lexical causative verb *tate-ru* 'stand up' admits only an inanimate causee, while its noncausative counterpart *tat-u* 'stand (up)' admits both animate and inanimate subjects. Observe:

(44)
a. *Boo ga tat-te-i-ta.*
'There was a stick standing.'
b. *Kodomo ga tat-ta.*
'A child stood up.'
c. *Boku wa boo o tate-ta.*
'I stood the stick up.'
d. **Boku wa kodomo o tate-ta.*
'I stood the child up.'

The only well-formed sentence that can be used in place of (44d) is the following, with the productive causative form *tat-ase-ru*:

(45) *Boku wa kodomo o tat-ase-ta.*
'I made the child stand up./I stood the child up.'

As the English translation indicates, the sentence is ambiguous; the sentence may be used for a situation in which the speaker directed the child to stand up or one in which the speaker physically stood the child up. The point being made here becomes clearer if (45) is contrasted with a sentence with the productive form that has the corresponding lexical causative form. Unlike (45), (46a), for example, does not allow the manipulative causative reading, as this reading is expressed by the corresponding lexical causative sentence in (46b):

(46) a. *Boku wa kodomo o taore-sase-ta.*
'I made the child fall down.'
b. *Boku wa kodomo o taos-i-ta.*
'I threw down the child.'

One other point to note here is that it is only the *o* causative form that allows the manipulative reading. In contrast to (45), the following *ni* causative sentence gives only the directive reading:

(47) *Boku wa kodomo ni tat-ase-ta.*
'I had the child stand up.' ≠ 'I stood the child up.'

This situation has to do with the fact that the particle *ni* marks only the volitional causee, while the particle *o* may mark both volitional and nonvolitional causees. As discussed previously, in the manipulative situation the causee functions as an inanimate entity; hence, only the *o* causative form allows the manipulative reading. Also compare the following:

(48) a. *Boku wa sissin site iru kodomo o tat-ase-ta.*
'I stood the fainted child up.'
b. **Boku wa sissin site iru kodomo ni tat-ase-ta.*

Sentence (48b) is ungrammatical because while the sentence structure calls for a directive causative situation, the causee involved is nonvolitional. Furthermore, (48a) has only the manipulative reading, in spite of the fact that structurally comparable (45) gives both manipulative and directive readings. Further discussion on the relation of the volitional causee and the particles is given in a subsequent discussion.

To summarize here, the productive causative form may express the manipulative situation in case there is no corresponding lexical causative form, or in case the causee is something not permitted by the lexical form. This fact is significant because it indicates that the entire range of meaning of the productive causative form is not predictable by just looking at the form alone; one has to find out whether or not the language has the corresponding lexical form and whether or not the existing lexical form permits the entity in question as a causee. If there are both productive and lexical forms, and if the latter permits the causee in question, then the productive form expresses the directive meaning, and the lexical form the manipulative meaning. If, on the other hand, only the productive form is available, it expresses both directive and manipulative meanings.

Lexical Causatives Expressing Directive Causation

As there are certain cases in which productive causative forms express situations involving manipulative causation, there are certain lexical causative forms that are used in expressing directive causation. The verb *ire-ru* 'put in' in the following sentence is one such example:

(49) *Boku wa Taroo o heya ni ire-ta.*
'I put Taro in the room./I had Taro enter the room.'

Sentence (49) is ambiguous. In one reading the verb *ire-ru* has its literal meaning of 'put in', involving manipulative causation, but the sentence also allows the reading of the speaker's telling Taro to go into the room. Some other verbs that allow such ambiguous readings are seen in the following:

(50) a. *Boku wa tuukoonin o tome-ta.*
'I stopped a passer-by.'
b. *Hahaoya wa kodomo o nikai e age-ta.*
'The mother sent the child upstairs.'
c. *Hahaoya wa kodomo o gakkoo no mae de oros-i-ta.*
'The mother dropped off the child in front of the school.'

Some lexical causatives, however, never allow the directive reading, as seen in (51):

(51) a. *Hahaoya wa Taroo ni huku o kise-ta.*
'The mother put the clothes on Taro.'
≠'The mother had Taro put on the clothes.'
b. *Boku wa Taroo o ugokas-i-ta.*
'I moved Taro.'
≠'I had Taro move (over).'
c. *Hahaoya wa kodomo o nekas-i-ta.*
'The mother put the child to sleep.'
≠'The mother had the child go to sleep.'

The questions taken up here are: (a) What kind of semantic difference is there between the directive use of lexical causative forms and the corresponding productive causatives used in (52)?; and (b) Why do some verbs allow and some verbs, such as those in (51), not allow the directive reading? The questions raised here are closely related, and the answer to the first gives a clue to the answer for the second:

(52) a. *Boku wa tuukoonin o tomar-ase-ta.*
'I had a passer-by stop.'
b. *Hahaoya wa kodomo o nikai e agar-ase-ta.*
'The mother had the child go upstairs.'
c. *Hahaoya wa kodomo o gakkoo no mae de ori-sase-ta.*
'The mother had the child get out of (the car) in front of the school.'

The basic difference between (50) and (52) has to do with the purpose the causer has in mind in bringing about the caused event. In (50), the causer's purposes are not simply to see that a passer-by stops, the child goes upstairs, or the child gets out of the car. On the other hand, in (52), the causer's interest lies in the caused events themselves. In other words, when lexical causatives are used in the directive sense, they convey that the causer's interest lies in the ultimate purposes associated with the causative situations rather than the causative situations themselves, while there is no such implication in the case of the productive forms.

In sentence (50a), for example, the speaker's stopping a passer-by is an accidental event rather than the ultimate purpose of his action, the ultimate purpose being to ask for a light or for directions. In (52a), on the other hand, to see that a passer-by stops is the speaker's central concern. This difference is reflected in the unnaturalness of (53b):

(53) a. *Miti o kiku no ni tuukoonin o tome-ta.*
'In order to ask for directions, I stopped a passer-by.'
b. ?*Miti o kiku no ni tuukoonin o tomar-ase-ta.*
'In order to ask for directions, I had a passer-by stop.'

One other dimension of meaning that contributes to the oddness of (53b) is that while all productive causative forms express the causer's authority over the causee, lexical causative forms, including those used in (50), do not express such authority.

The fact that the productive form is called for in case the causer's interest lies in the caused event itself can be seen in the following pair:

(54) a. *Moo kaidan ga noboreru ka miyoo to akanboo o nikai e agar-ase-te mi-ta.*
'In order to see if he could climb the stairs, (I) made the baby go upstairs.'
b. **Moo kaidan ga noboreru ka miyoo to akanboo o nikai e age-te mi-ta.*

When one compares these sentences with the following, it becomes clear that the association of the purpose and the causative situation alone is not a sufficient condition for the directive use of the lexical causative form:

(55) a. *Hahaoya wa kodomo o tukue ni age-ta.*
'The mother lifted the child up onto the desk.'
b. *Boku wa Taroo o hako ni ire-ta.*
'I put Taro into the box.'

The sentences in (55), though the same lexical causatives are used in them as in (50), do not allow the directive reading. What makes the sentences in (50) different from those in (55) appears to be correlated with whether or not the purpose associated with the causative situation is conventionalized or well-defined. While sending a child upstairs and letting someone into the room have conventionalized purposes associated with them, e.g., sending a child to sleep and meeting with a person, respectively, getting a child onto the desk and putting someone into a box do not have any conventionalized purpose associated with them. That is, while in the cases of the sentences in (50), one can infer or narrow down sufficiently the range of purposes associated with the situations, this is not the case with the sentences in (55).

Now, in the light of the preceding distinction, compare (50c) and (52c). Sentence (50c), when read with the directive sense, definitely brings forth the conventionalized purpose associated with the sentence, namely, that the mother took the child to school, where he attended class. In contrast to (50c), (52c) does not readily bring forth the conveyed meaning. The sentence even gives the impression that it was a sheer accident that the mother made the son get out of the car in front of the school; e.g., it was because of a flat tire.

These observations point out that whether a particular lexical causative can be interpreted in the directive sense or not depends not only on the lexical item itself but also on whether or not the sentence as a whole expresses a situation that has a conventionalized purpose associated with it. This point suggests an answer to our second question, namely, that the reason that some lexical forms, e.g., *kise-ru* 'dress', *ugokas-u* 'move', never allow the directive interpretation is that these verbs do not occur in environments associated with conventionalized purposes.

There is an interesting phenomenon related to the present discussion. A lexical causative, which by itself has only the basic, literal sense, takes on additional meaning when it occurs in an environment associated with a conventionalized purpose. The Japanese lexical causative verb *ire-ru* by itself means 'put something/someone into something'. The productive counterpart *hair-ase-ru* means 'make/have someone enter into something'. However, when the former occurs in an appropriate environment, it takes on a unique meaning derived from the conventionalized purpose associated with the sentence. Thus, when *ire-ru* 'put in' occurs in the environment of a movie house, as in *eigakan ni ire-ru* (literally, 'put into a movie house'), it means 'to admit'; when it occurs in the environment of a school, as in *daigaku ni ire-ru* (literally, 'put into a university'), it means 'to enroll'; when it occurs in the environment of a mental institution, it means 'to commit'; and when it occurs in the environment of a prison, it means 'to imprison'. But the productive form in the same environments does not necessarily have the same meaning. Thus, if I actually want to see the movie, and if I happen to know the ticket puncher, I would say *Ire-te kudasai* 'Please admit me to the movie' rather than *Hair-ase-te kudasai* 'Please let me in'. But if I just want to buy cigarettes or use the rest room, I would use the latter rather than the former. In other words, *ire-ru* (a lexical form) in the environment of a movie house means 'to let someone in and let him see the movie', while the productive form *hair-ase-ru* in the same environment maintains the literal meaning of 'let someone in' without any implication of letting him see the movie. Similarly, *rooya ni ire-ru* (literally, 'put into the jail') means 'to imprison', and the corresponding productive form *rooya ni hair-ase-ru* means 'make/let someone go into the prison'. Thus, if I have committed a crime and want myself to be imprisoned, I must say *Rooya ni ire-te kudasai* 'Please imprison me'. But if I just want to see someone who is an inmate, I cannot use that expression; in this case I must say *Rooya ni hair-ase-te kudasai* 'Please let me go into the prison'.

To summarize, then, the lexical causative may be used to express a situation involving directive causation if the association of a well-defined purpose with the causative event is conventionalized, and when the causer's concern is centered on this well-defined purpose rather than on the actual causative event itself. The lexical causative, moreover, manifests a dimension of meaning derived from this well-defined purpose, while supressing its literal meaning. In the case of a productive causative, however, the literal meaning is retained strongly even in the same environment in which the preceding phenomenon occurs.

Before we move on let us take up the question of whether the directive meaning derivable from the lexical causative sentence under the condition studied earlier has any syntactic reflections. As studied in Section 2, the productive causative forms show syntactic behavior different from that of the lexical causative sentences. One may naturally ask whether the lexical causative forms that express the directive meaning, which is typically expressed by the productive forms, share syntactic patterns with the productive forms. Examinations of the manner of adverbial modification, *soo suru* replacement, and reflexivization reveal that the directive use of the lexical causative form does not permit the sentence to behave similarly to the productive form, and that it retains the properties of the regular lexical causative sentence. Thus, in the following examples the productive causative (a) sentences show ambiguity, while the lexical causative (b) sentences that permit the directive reading do not share the ambiguity that the corresponding (a) sentences show:

(56) a. *Taroo wa Hanako o yeha ni sankai hair-ase-ta.*
(i) 'For three times, Taro made Hanako enter the room.'
(ii) 'Taro instructed Hanako in such a way that she entered the room three times.'
b. *Taroo wa Hanako o heya ni sankai ire-ta.*
(Only the first reading, (i), is possible.)

(57) a. *Hahaoya ga Taroo o nikai e agar-ase-ru to, titioya mo soo si-ta.*

(i) 'When the mother made Taro go upstairs, the father also made him go upstairs.'
(ii) 'When the mother made Taro go upstairs, the father also went upstairs.'

b. *Hahaoya ga Taroo o nikai e age-ru to, titioya mo soo si-ta.*
(Only the first reading is possible.)

(58) a. *Taroo wa Hanako o zibun no kuruma kara ori-sase-ta.*
(i) 'Taro$_i$ made Hanako$_j$ get out of self's$_i$ car.'
(ii) 'Taro$_i$ made Hanako$_j$ get out of self's$_j$ car.'

b. *Taroo wa Hanako o zibun no kuruma kara oros-i-ta.*
(Only the first reading is possible.)

Direct versus Indirect Causation

In both directive and manipulative causation, the causer acts directly on the causee, whether it is done orally or physically. There are causative situations in which the causer's directly acting on the causee is either impossible or simply has not taken place. For example, normally one cannot manipulate someone else's psychological state. What the causer can do in bringing about a change in someone's psychological state is to do something indirect as a result of which a change is brought about. For example, in making someone happy, the causer can neither tell the causee to be happy nor physically manipulate the causee's mentality. But the causer can do something indirect, e.g., buy the causee an ice-cream cone, which brings about a change in the causee's psychological state. This manner of causation, thus, differs from both directive and manipulative causation. I will henceforth refer to the former as 'indirect causation', as opposed to the latter two types, which can be collectively termed 'direct causation'.

Since lexical causatives are typically correlated with manipulative, i.e., direct, causation, one seldom finds lexical causatives that express indirect causation.[7] Thus, Japanese does not have lexical forms for *kanasim-u* 'feel sad', *yorokob-u* 'be happy', *sabisigar-u* 'feel lonesome', etc. In other words, indirect causation is normally expressed by the productive form, as in (59):

(59) a. *Taroo wa Hanako o kanasim-ase-ta.*
'Taro made Hanako sad.'

b. *Taroo wa Hanako o yorokob-ase-ta.*
'Taro made Hanako happy.'

[7]One notable exception to this generalization is the metaphorical use of certain lexical causative forms, such as *oiyar-u* 'drive away', as in:

(1) *Sono ziken wa Taroo o kyuuti ni oiyat-ta.*
'That event drove Taro away into a difficult position.'

Cf. the chapter by Noriko McCawley in this volume on the properties of this type of expression.

Also, a sentence of the following type, which contains a sentence or inanimate object as its subject, typically express indirect causation:

(60) a. *Taroo ga okurimono o kaiwasure-ta koto ga Hanako o kanasim-ase-ta.*
'Taro's forgetting to buy a present made Hanako sad.'
b. *Taroo no syusse ga Hanako o yorokob-ase-ta.*
'Taro's success made Hanako happy.'

An indirect causative situation involving an active event as the caused event is also expressed by this type of construction, as seen in (61):

(61) a. *Taroo ga kyuuni kaettekita koto ga Hanako o isoide kaimono ni ik-ase-ta.*
'Taro's returning suddenly made Hanako go shopping in a hurry.'
b. *Teppoo no oto ga kodomotati o issei ni hasir-ase-ta.*
'The sound of the gun made the children run all at once.'
c. *Sono inu no sonzai ga kodomotati ni mawari-miti o s-ase-ta.*
'The presence of the dog made the children take a detour.'

In English, an inanimate object may occur as the causee of indirect causation. For example, the following sentences possibly can be used in describing a situation in which the causer indirectly moved the chair, e.g., by pulling a string attached to the chair, or indirectly opened the door, e.g., by banging against the wall:

(62) a. *John made the chair move.*
b. *John made the door open.*

In Japanese, however, an inanimate object is not usually permitted as the causee of an indirect causative sentence. The following sentences, for example, are not quite so grammatical as the English sentences in (62), even if the same situations are imagined:

(63) a. **Zyon wa isu o ugok-ase-ta.*
b. **Zyon wa doa o hirak-ase-ta.*

The only conceivable situations in which (63) may be used are those in which John, by using magic, could communicate with the chair and the door and could give them a direction, i.e., directive causative situations. Similarly, although sentences with sentential subjects and inanimate causees are possible in English, the corresponding Japanese sentences are not:

(64) a. *John's pulling the string made the chair move.*
b. *John's banging against the wall made the door open.*

(65) a. **Zyon ga himo o hipparu koto ga isu o ugok-ase-ta.*
b. **Zyon ga kabe ni butukaru koto ga doa o hirak-ase-ta.*

It thus appears that indirect causative sentences are possible only when the corresponding sentential subject forms are possible.

One notable exception to the generalization that an inanimate object cannot function as the causee in an indirect causative sentence that has been brought to my attention is the following sentence from J. McCawley (1972a):

(66) *Taroo ga enzin o tomar-ase-ta.*
'Taro made the engine stop.'

The lexical causative form *tome-ru* 'stop' must be used if Taro had stopped the engine by using a key in a normal manner, and this sentence is not appropriate for such a normal situation. Sentence (66), however, is not ungrammatical like those in (63), and it is appropriate in describing a situation like the one in which Taro's stopping the engine involves an unusual means such as putting sand and rocks in the engine or hammering the engine so that it jams up and comes to a halt. The fact that an engine is a piece of machinery conceivable as having its own force seems to differentiate it from other purely inanimate objects such as a chair and a wall. If what is involved is an automatic door, one can think up a situation appropriate for even a sentence like (63b).

Volition of the Causee and the Case Marking

In Shibatani (1973a), it was argued that 'case marking cannot be successfully done unless the rules take semantic considerations into account [p. 341]', and the following rules were proposed:

(67)
a. *x*
N——→N *ga*/ # #——
where *x* = any argument type

b. agent
N——→N *ni*/*X*——
where *X* ≠ # #

c. patient
N——→N *o*/*X*——
where *X* ≠ # #

Rule (67a) assigns *ga* to the sentence-initial noun regardless of its argument type. Rules (67b) and (67c) assign *ni* to the agentive noun and *o* to the patient noun, respectively, when they occur sentence internally.

The rules assign correct case particles to both coercive and noncoercive causative structures whose underlying structures are as follows:

(68) a. Noncoercive causative structure
(Taroo (Hanako aruk-) sase-ta)
Taroo ga Hanako ni aruk-ase-ta.
'Taro had Hanako walk.'

b. Coercive causative structure
(Taroo Hanako (Hanako aruk-) sase-ta)
Taroo ga Hanako o aruk-ase-ta.
'Taro made Hanako walk.'

In (68a), the agentive noun *Hanako* moves into the matrix sentence following verb raising and tree pruning, and it receives *ni* by Rule (67b). In (68b), on the other hand, the agentive noun *Hanako* of the embedded sentence is deleted by equi-NP deletion; what is left is the patient noun *Hanako* that originates in the matrix sentence, and it receives *o* by Rule (67c).

The preceding analysis accounts for the particle *o* and the nonoccurrence of *ni* in a permissive causative sentence like (36b):

(36b) *Omoiyari no aru isya ga konsuizyootai ni ari tasukaru mikomi no nai byoonin o/*ni sin-ase-ta.*

Since in this case there is no semantic motivation to posit the patient noun *byoonin* 'patient' in the matrix sentence, the underlying structure takes a form similar to the noncoercive structure (cf. 68a)—namely, the following:

(69) *(isya (byoonin sin-) sase-ta)*

The case marking rules in (67) most naturally account for the difference in case particles that the causees in (68a) and (69) receive: In the case of (68a), the causee *Hanako* functions as an agent, while in (69) the causee *byoonin* functions as a patient.

Now, it appears that, in the case of sentences (68a) and (36b), the argument types 'agent' and 'patient' correspond well to the presence and absence of the volition on the part of the causee. In (68a), Taro appeals to Hanako's volition, and Hanako VOLITIONALLY instigates an event of walking. In (39b), on the other hand, the doctor does not appeal to the patient, nor does the patient instigate any event; the latter simply undergoes (nonvolitionally) a process of dying. There are, however, certain cases in which the correspondence of the argument types and the presence and absence of the causee's volition does not hold completely. Consider the following sentences:

(70) a. *Taroo ga Hanako* ***ni*** *waraw-ase-ta.*
'Taro had Hanako laugh.'
b. *Taroo ga Hanako* ***o*** *waraw-ase-ta.*
'Taro made Hanako laugh.'

Sentence (70a) is a clear case of Hanako's laughing volitionally. (Again, imagine a situation in which Taro is a movie director and Hanako an actress.) Sentence (70b) has the same reading as (70a), the only difference being the extent of coerciveness. Sentence (70b), however, has another reading in which Hanako laughed nonvolitionally. This second reading usually involves some kind of indirect causation; a typical situation involves Taro's telling or doing something that induces laughter. The crucial difference between (70a) and the first reading of (70b), on the one hand, and the second reading of (70b), on the other, is that, in the former situations, Hanako, being instructed by Taro, laughs at her own volition while, in the latter case, Hanako's laughing is not accompanied by her volition. In other words, in the two former cases, Hanako plays a role as a volitional entity while, in the latter, she functions as a nonvolitional entity.

The problem here is that in both these situations Hanako appears to be functioning as an agent, since she instigates an event of laughing. If both volitional Hanako and nonvolitional Hanako in (70a) and (70b) function as agents, the case-marking rules in (67) cannot assign the correct particle *o* to the causee in the case of (70b), namely, when it expresses an indirect causative situation. Since, in the case of indirect causative sentences, there does not seem to be any evidence suggesting the presence of the causee in the matrix sentence, (70a) and the indirect causative case of (70b) have the same underlying structure. Furthermore, since in both cases Hanako functions as an agent, there is no way to account for the presence of *o* in the indirect causative case of (70b).

There are two ways to deal with this situation. One is to modify Rules (67b) and (67c) in such a way that they say 'attach *ni* to the volitional noun' and 'attach *o* to the nonvolitional noun', respectively, under the condition that the nouns in question do not occur sentence initially. The other way is to redefine the argument types 'agent' and 'patient'. My feeling at the moment leans toward the second solution. First, it appears that the definition of 'agent' as 'the instigator of the event' (Fillmore, 1971a:376) is too loose. In fact, when one laughs impulsively, it is not entirely clear that the one is really an instigator of laughing. Perhaps the term AGENT should be redefined as an entity that VOLITIONALLY instigates or engages in an event. Also, the term PATIENT should take in an entity that is engaged in an event nonvolitionally. In fact, this redefinition of the term AGENT seems in order, since the entities that appear to be playing the same agentive role in the earlier definition involve different semantic notions and different syntactic consequences, as observed earlier in Japanese.

Ballistic Causation

There is one class of verbs that behave differently from other causative expressions. This class includes the verb *okur-u* 'send' and a host of verb compounds that contain *okur-* as the first member, e.g., *okur-i-das-u* 'send out'. The verbs belonging to this class are causative verbs, since they assert that some kind of caused event follows after the realization of the causing event. Observe the contradiction involved in the following sentences:

(71) a. **Taroo wa hon o okut-ta ga, sono hon wa mada Taroo no moto ni atta.*
'Taro sent the book, but the book was still with him.'

b. **Hahaoya wa Taroo o gakkoo e okuridas-i-ta ga, Taroo wa mada ie ni ir-u.*
'The mother sent Taro out to school, but Taro is still at home.'

One general characteristic of causative expressions is that when the place or time adverb occurs sentence initially, the adverb designates the place or the time of both causing and caused event. Thus, (72a–b) assert that both Taro's giving a direction or doing something, i.e., the causing event, and Hanako's going into the room or Hanako's dying, i.e., the caused event, took place at the designated time or place. This is further confirmed by the contradictory nature of (72c–d):

(72) a. *Sanzi ni Taroo wa Hanako o heya ni hair-ase-ta.*
'At three o'clock, Taro made Hanako enter the room.'

b. *Sono heya de Taroo wa Hanako o koros-i-ta.*
'In that room, Taro killed Hanako.'

c. **Sanzi ni Taroo wa Hanako o heya ni hair-ase-ta ga, Hanako wa yozi made heya ni hair-anakat-ta.*
'*At three o'clock, Taro made Hanako enter the room, but Hanako did not enter the room until four o'clock.'

d. **Sono heya de Taroo wa Hanako o koros-i-ta ga, Hanako wa tonari no heya de sin-da.*
'*In that room, Taro killed Hanako, but Hanako died in the next room.'

The verb *okur-u* 'send', however, does not share this property, since the following sentences, unlike (72c–d), do not involve any contradiction:

(73) a. *Hatigatu-tuitati ni Taroo wa genkoo o syuppansya ni okut-ta ga, genkoo wa hatigatu tooka made tukanakat-ta.*
'On August 1, Taro sent the manuscript to the publisher, but the manuscript did not arrive at the publisher until August 10.'

b. *Rosanzerusu de Taroo wa nihon ni iru Hanako ni tegami o okut-ta.*
'In Los Angeles, Taro sent a letter to Hanako, who is in Japan.'

The verb *okur-u*, thus, appears to be asserting only that the caused event has begun to take place, rather than the completion of the caused event that other causative verbs assert. Observe the contrast:

(74) a. **Taroo wa Hanako o heya ni ire-ta ga Hanako wa heya ni hairanakat-ta.*
'Taro made Hanako enter the room, but Hanako didn't enter the room.'
b. **Taroo wa Hanako o koros-i-ta ga Hanako wa sinanakat-ta.*
'Taro killed Hanako, but Hanako didn't die.'
c. *Taroo wa genkoo o syuppansya ni okut-ta ga, genkoo wa syuppansya ni tukanakat-ta.*
'Taro sent the manuscript to the publisher, but it didn't reach the publisher.'
d. *Hahaoya wa Taroo o gakkoo e okuridas-i-ta ga, Taroo wa gakkoo ni ikazu ni eiga o mini it-ta.*
'The mother sent Taro out to school, but Taro went to see the movies instead of going to school.'

The type of causation expressed by the verb *okur-u* 'send' may be termed 'ballistic causation'. The preceding discussion of ballistic causation concludes our investigation of the semantic properties of various types of causative expressions.

4. INTEGRATION OF SYNTAX AND SEMANTICS

Several approaches toward integrating syntax and semantics have been developed in the past decade. The most notable ones are Fillmore's case grammar; interpretive semantics, developed primarily by Chomsky and Jackendoff; and generative semantics, developed primarily by G. Lakoff, J. McCawley, and Postal.[8] Because of the lack of space and also owing to the fact that the most comprehensive analysis of the causative construction has been done in the framework of generative semantics, the following discussion will focus on the generative semantic approach.

Generative Semantics and the Causative Construction

It is by no means an exaggeration to say that the theory of generative semantics has developed along with or in the process of the analysis of the causative construction. The causative construction, in other words, has provided the generative semanticist with the most rewarding field of investigation. The original treatment of causative sentences in an early phase of the development of generative semantics appeared in G. Lakoff's 1965 dissertation, subsequently published as G. Lakoff (1970a). A more generalized but still an earlier version of the generative semantic treatment of the subject was

[8]Cf., for example, Fillmore (1968), Chomsky (1971), Jackendoff (1972), G. Lakoff (1970b), J. McCawley (1973), and Postal (1970b).

proposed in J. McCawley (1968b). For all the sentences in (75), McCawley proposed the underlying (or semantic) representation given in (76a):

(75) a. *John killed Harry.*
b. *John caused Harry to die.*
c. *John caused Harry to become dead.*
d. *John caused Harry to become not alive.*

The predicates in the structure in (76a) are thought to be semantic 'primitives', and they do not necessarily coincide with real morphemes such as *cause*, *become*, etc., although undoubtedly these morphemes contain as part of their meaning the semantic components expressed by those primitives:

(76)

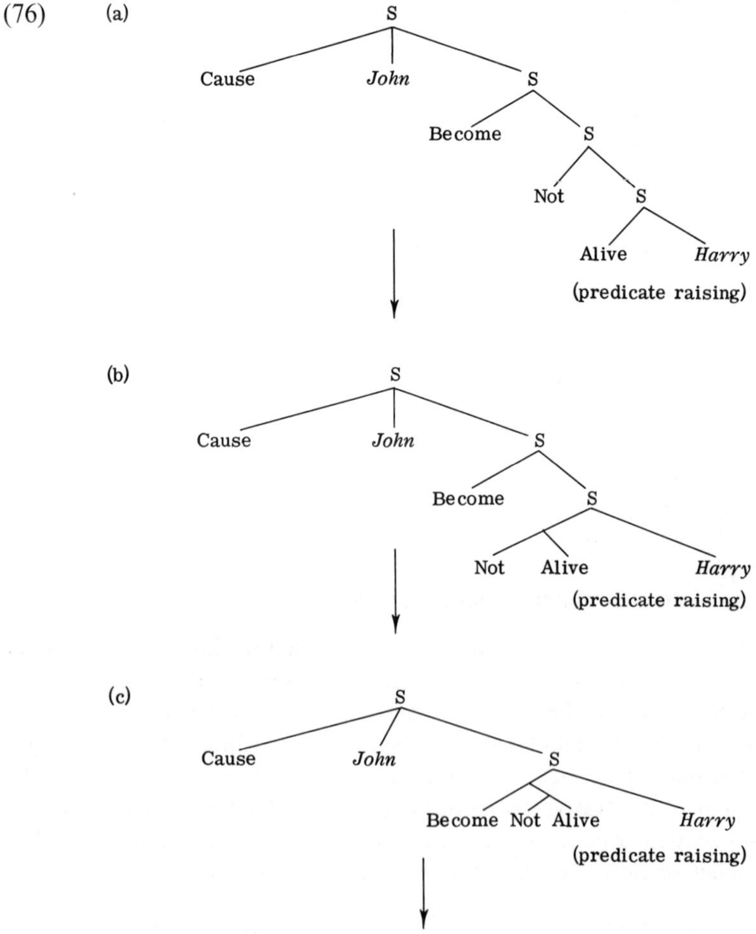

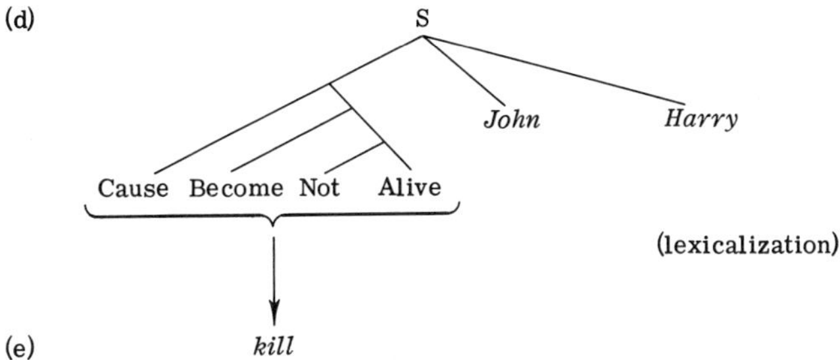

Within McCawley's model, (75a) was derived in the manner shown in (76b–e). The last structure, (76e), further undergoes the rule of subject formation that brings the subject to sentence-initial position in the case of English. The other sentences in (75) were considered mere surface variants of (75a) and were accounted for in terms of the optional rule of predicate raising. That is, lexical insertion may take place at any of the intermediate stages of the derivation, since there exist lexical entries matching the various constituents that appear during the derivation.

In a more recent publication, J. McCawley (1973) revised the structure of a causative sentence as in (77):

(77)

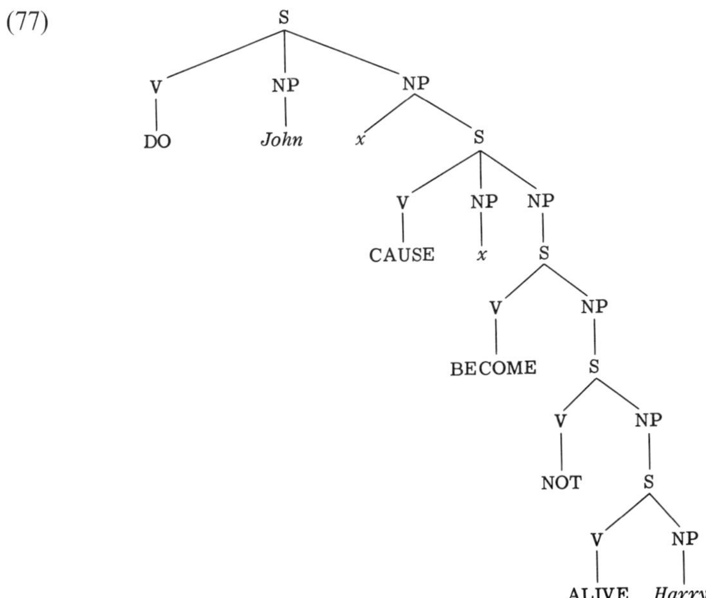

The most prominent characteristic of the generative semantic treatment is that both lexical and productive causative sentences are derived from the identical underlying representation. Before turning to the motivations behind such an analysis, let me note at this point that the generative semantic approach just outlined has been espoused for the analysis of the causative constructions in a number of languages, including Hindi (Kachru, 1966), Korean (Yang, 1972), and Japanese (Soga, 1970).[9]

Motivations for the Generative Semantic Treatment

The most fundamental motivation for the generative semantic treatment comes from the desire to account for the synonymy or paraphrase relations observed in (75). The sentences in (75) all appear to share the same truth value. There also exist entailment relations among the sentences in (75). Sentence (75c) entails (75d), (75b), (75c), and (75a) entails (75b). The relations here are transitive; therefore, (75a) entails (75c–d) as well, as does (75b). Again, these entailment relations are easily derivable within the generative semantic model. When viewed historically, the generative semantic approach to the causative construction follows most closely the tradition of transformational grammar: Sentences that are in a paraphrase relation are given the same underlying representation, the surface variations being accounted for in terms of transformations.

The fact that both lexical and productive causatives share the same semantic properties is another semantic motivation for the generative semantic approach. If both lexical and productive sentences are thought to involve the predicate CAUSE that relates the causing and the caused events, one need only give a semantic characterization for the construction S_1 CAUSE S_2 in accounting for the fact that lexical and productive causatives involve the same assertion and presupposition. For example, the fact that (78a) and (78b) are anomalous while (79a) and (79b) are not can be accounted for by first setting off the former sentences from the latter in terms of the presence and absence of the predicate CAUSE (the former contain it and the latter do not) and then defining the structure S_1 CAUSE S_2 common to (78a) and (78b), as in (80) (see the Introduction and Section 3 for discussion of the presupposition and assertion associated with the causative expression):

(78) a. **John opened the door, but it did not open.*
b. **John caused the door to open, but it did not open.*

(79) a. *John pushed the door, but it did not open.*
b. *John banged against the door to open it, but it did not open.*

(80) $$S_1 \text{ CAUSE } S_2: \begin{bmatrix} \text{Presupposition:} & \sim S_1 \text{ Lt} \sim S_2 \\ \text{Assertion:} & S_1 \text{ Lt } S_2 \end{bmatrix}$$

[9] Cf. Kachru (1975) and Shibatani (1973c) for further developments on Hindi causatives and Korean causatives, respectively.

In addition to the purely semantic motivations just given, there has been some syntax-oriented evidence for the generative semantic approach. One type of evidence has to do with a certain type of adverbial modification. In (81), the adverbs *for ten minutes* and *again* may modify a constituent that is not part of the surface structure:

(81) a. *I closed the door for ten minutes.*
b. *The door opened, and then I closed it again.*

That is, as discussed by J. McCawley (1971a), in addition to the reading in which the adverbs are interpreted as modifying the whole structure of *I closed the door*, the sentences in (81) give the reading in which the adverbs are interpreted as modifying the constituent *the door is closed*, which does not surface. If the sentence *I closed the door* is analyzed in the generative semantic fashion, i.e., as in (82), the second reading can be accounted for by attributing the adverbs to the bottom-most S:

(82)

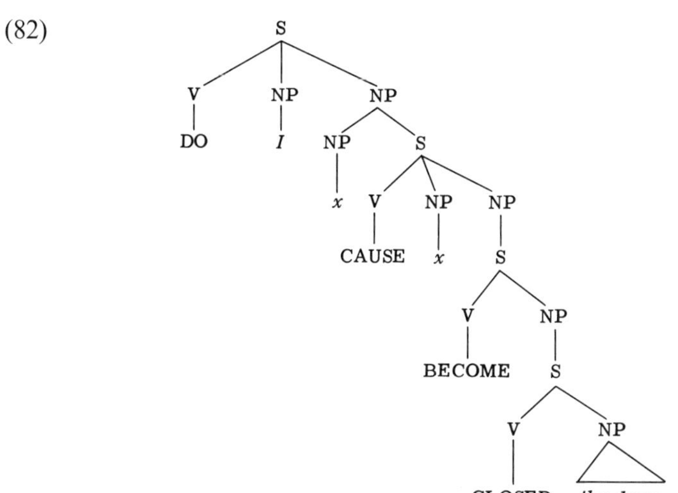

A similar observation holds in Japanese. Thus, the sentences in (83) are ambiguous in the same way as those in (81):

(83) a. *Boku wa doa o zyuppun-kan sime-ta.*
'I closed the door for ten minutes.'
b. *Doa ga aita node, mata sime-ta.*
'Since the door opened, I closed it again.'

Sentence (83a) may be interpreted as saying that for ten minutes the speaker repeatedly closed the door or that the speaker closed the door in such a way that the door remained closed for ten minutes. Similarly, in (83b), the adverb *mata* 'again' may be understood to modify the activity of the closing of the door or just to modify the state of the door's being closed.

Another type of evidence brought up in support of the generative semantic approach has to do with the sentence like the following, discovered by Lakoff:

(84) *The physicist finally hardened the metal, but it took him six months to bring* ***it*** *about.*

It is claimed that the second *it* refers to 'the metal's becoming hard', and that it indicates the presence of the constituent (BECOME (HARD *the metal*)) beneath CAUSE in the underlying representation.

One final argument in favor of the generative semantic approach taken up here has to do with the notion of 'possible lexical item'. As extensively discussed in phonology, a native speaker possesses an intuition as to whether a given nonsense word is a phonologically possible or impossible word in his language. It has been said that a native speaker of English feels that the actually nonoccurring 'word' *blik* is possible but that *ftik* is not. J. McCawley (1973c) notes that, in the generative semantic approach, it is possible to make this distinction of semantically possible-but-non-occurring words versus impossible words. He says that although it is conceivable that there may exist a verb that expresses the meaning 'cause to cease to be left-handed', it is inconceivable that we would ever admit in the English dictionary the verb **thork* meaning 'give to one's uncle and' or the verb **blirf* meaning 'to kiss a girl who is allergic to' as in (85):

(85) a. **John thorked Harry 5000 yen.* (paraphrasable as 'John gave his uncle and Harry 5000 yen')
b. **John blirfed eggs.* (paraphrasable as 'John kissed a girl who was allergic to eggs')

McCawley argues that in his approach one can explain why such a distinction holds. Specifically, he points out that in the case of the verb meaning 'cause to cease to be left-handed' the process of amalgamating semantic elements for the purpose of lexical insertion involves no violation of known constraints on transformations, while in the case of the verbs **thork* and **blirf* Ross' coordinate structure constraint and complex NP constraint would be violated (cf. Ross, 1967).

Syntactically oriented evidence like the one discussed above has been often used to underscore the generative semanticist's hypothesis that 'syntactic structure and semantic structure are the same general type', e.g., both involve a labeled tree (McCawley, 1973c:261), that what have been called syntactic transformations apply directly to the semantic structure, i.e., prelexically, and therefore, that one cannot maintain the syntax/semantics and transformation/semantic interpretation rule dichotomies. Thus, research into the causative construction has provided the linguist with a considerable amount of evidence for the tenets of generative semantics.

Problems with the Generative Semantic Approach

While the generative semantic approach to the causative construction has been hailed by many researchers and has been adopted in the analysis of a number of languages, as noted earlier, it is not free of problems. Some of the problems demand a certain amount of modification in the semantic structure originally proposed, some point up the need for closer semantic specifications, and others present devastating evidence against the generative semantic approach and challenge the tenets of generative semantics. I will first discuss syntactically oriented problems and then take up problems centering on semantics.

Syntactically based arguments against the generative semantic analysis of lexical causatives in English have been presented by Fodor (1970). Fodor gives three types of evidence that militate against the generative analysis. The first evidence is based on the *do-so* transformation (corresponding to the Japanese *soo suru* replacement discussed in Section 2) that replaces the verb phrase under certain identity conditions. By first showing that the productive causative form of the type given in (86a) produces two 'do so' phrases, (86b) and (86c), Fodor argues that if the corresponding lexical causative sentence in (87a) were to derive from the same structure as that underlying (86a), we would expect to find the two grammatical 'do so' phrases:

(86) a. *John caused Mary to die.*
b. *John caused Mary to die and it surprised me that he did so.*
c. *John caused Mary to die and it surprised me that she did so.*

(87) a. *John killed Mary.*
b. *John killed Mary and it surprised me that he did so.*
c. **John killed Mary and it surprised me that she did so.*

As seen in (87c), the lexical causative sentence fails to produce the two expected 'do so' phrases; hence, the derivation of such a sentence from the structure that underlies the productive form poses a problem.

Fodor's second argument is based on the fact that the productive causative sentence allows an adverbial phrase containing a time adverb that is different from the one that modifies the caused event. Thus, the underlying structure (88a) gives rise to a well-formed surface sentence, (88b):

(88) a. *(Floyd (caused (the glass to melt on Sunday)) (by (heating it on Saturday)))*
b. *Floyd caused the glass to melt on Sunday by heating it on Saturday.*

However, the lexical counterpart does not admit the same type of adverbial phrase, as observed in (89):

(89) **Floyd melted the glass on Sunday by heating it on Saturday.*

The same observation holds for other lexical-productive pairs such as *kill/cause to die*:

(90) a. *John caused Bill to die on Sunday by stabbing him on Saturday.*
b. **John killed Bill on Sunday by stabbing him on Saturday.*

The last argument offered by Fodor is concerned with the case that an instrumental adverb shares deep structure subjects. First, observe that while (91a), which contains only one subject, involves no ambiguity as to who uses the telephone, (91b) does involve ambiguity. This is because (91b), having two deep subjects, allows both (92a) and (92b), while (91a), with only one deep subject, allows only one version:

(91) a. *John contacted Mary by using the telephone.*
b. *Mary intimidated John into cutting the meat by using a knife.*

(92) a. *(Mary intimidate John (John cut the meat) (by (Mary use a knife)))*
b. *(Mary intimidate John ((John cut the meat) (by (John use a knife))))*

(92′) a. *(John contact Mary by (John use the telephone))*
b. **(John contact Mary by (Mary use the telephone))*

Now, in the case of productive causative sentences, ambiguity arises paralleling sentence (91b), for they clearly involve two deep subjects. Observe:

(93) *John caused Bill to die by swallowing his tongue.*
(i) *John swallowed Bill's tongue.*
(ii) *Bill swallowed his own tongue.*

Fodor argues that if *kill* comes from the structure underlying *cause to die* that contains the clause *(Bill) die*, then the same observation should hold. However, since this is not the case [as seen in (94)], Fodor concludes that this is evidence against the generative semantic analysis of the lexical causative form:

(94) *John killed Bill by swallowing his tongue.*
(i) *John swallowed Bill's tongue.*
(ii) **Bill swallowed his own tongue.*

I turn now to a discussion of the Japanese case. However, before I take up arguments against the generative semantic approach it is necessary to clarify the position taken up by the advocate of the generative treatment of Japanese causative forms. As mentioned earlier, Soga (1970) approaches the Japanese causative construction in the framework of generative semantics. Soga suggests that:

> We may be able to say that transitive [lexical causative] forms such as *hikkome* 'to draw (something) in', *ire* 'to put (something) in', and others, which are formally different from causative forms [productive causatives], are simply morphophonemic variants of the causative forms of their intransitive counterparts, and this consideration seems justifiable from the semantic point of view, too [p. 273].

and then goes on to conclude that:

> Thus, on the basis of semantic and grammatical evidence, we may now be able to say that many transitive verbs in Japanese become transitive [lexical causative] verbs by way of causativization, and this characteristic is the same as that of English [i.e. the transitive verb *harden* in *John hardened the metal* is also said to be derived from the underlying structure *(John cause (it (for the metal to harden)))*] [ibid., pp. 273–274].

According to Soga, then, sentences like (95a) and (95b) will be given a single semantic structure like (96), and the surface difference is to be accounted for in terms of what he calls a morphophonemic rule and what J. McCawley calls a lexicalization rule:

(95) a. *Taroo ga Ziroo o tomar-ase-ta.*
'Tato made Jiro stop.'
b. *Taroo ga Ziroo o tome-ta.*
'Taro stopped Jiro.'

(96) a.

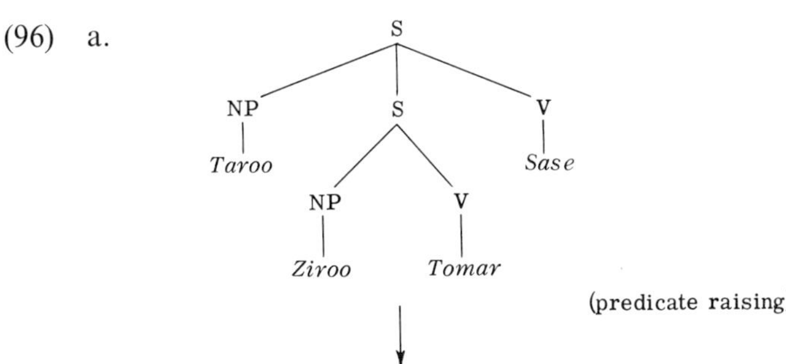

b.

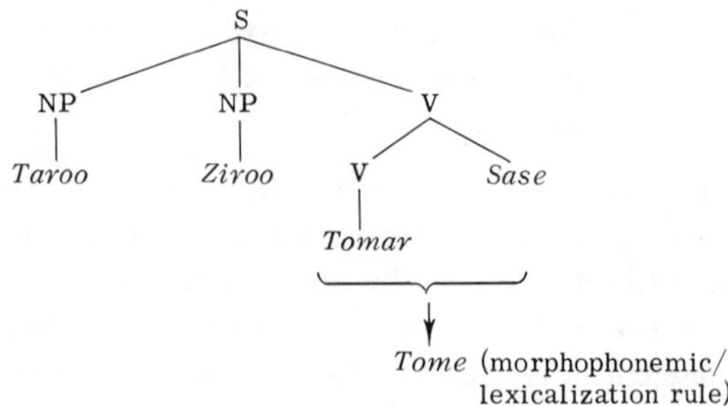

For the reader of this chapter, it is not necessary for me to repeat the kinds of argument against this analysis presented in Shibatani (1972a) and (1973a). It is only necessary to refer to the various syntactic differences between the lexical causatives and the productive counterparts discussed in Section 2. All of the evidence presented in that section argues against the putative embedding structure, e.g., (96a), posited for lexical causative forms. Nevertheless, it seems in order to briefly note that a theoretical device such as rule ordering does not help resolve the conflicts between the analysis presented in (96) and the phenomena discussed in Section 2. One might, for example, argue that the rules of reflexivization, *soo suru* replacement, and sentence pronominalization apply after the lexicalization (or Soga's morphophonemic) rule, and that since the structure resulting from lexicalization no longer contains an embedded clause, all of the rules referring to the embedded clause do not apply. The differences observed in Section 2 are, thus, due to at what point lexicalization applies; in the case of lexical causatives, lexicalization applies prior to the above-mentioned rules, and in the case of productive causatives, no lexicalization applies.

After a moment of reflection it is clear that an argument of this type does not hold water. One must realize that predicate raising must apply before lexicalization. Within the conception of generative semantics, semantic elements must be amalgamated by rules such as predicate raising before lexicalization inserts a lexical item. That is, the lexical item *tome-* 'stop' cannot be inserted in (96a) directly; predicate raising must bring the two predicates together under a single node, as in (96b), before lexicalization may take place.

Furthermore, the rules of reflexivization, *soo suru* replacement, and sentence pronominalization must apply before predicate raising. This is because predicate raising must apply in both lexical and productive form before it destroys the embedded structure. As briefly discussed in Section 2, predicatc raising brings the lower verb to the position immediately before the higher verb so that the surface configuration of *V-sase* would result as one verb. This process, together with the tree pruning that follows it, wipes out the embedded structure. Since reflexivization, *soo suru* replacement, and sentence pronominalization must, respectively, refer to the subject of the embedded sentence, the verb of the embedded sentence, and the embedded sentence itself, they must apply before the predicate raising that destroys the embedded sentence. The required order of application calls for the rules of reflexivization, *soo suru* replacement, and sentence pronominalization prior to predicate raising. Otherwise, one cannot account for the ambiguities involved in the productive causative forms. Now, if the rules of reflexivization, *soo suru* replacement, and sentence pronominalization must apply prior to predicate raising, and if predicate raising must apply before lexicalization, then it cannot be the case that lexicalization applies before reflexivization, *soo suru* replacement, and sentence pronominalization.

I turn now to the semantically oriented arguments against the generative semantic treatment. As pointed out earlier, and as is obvious in the quotations from Soga, the basic motivation for the generative semantic analysis was the synonymy or paraphrase relation found, for example, between (75a) and (75b), repeated here for convenience:

(75) a. *John killed Harry.*
b. *John caused Harry to die.*

Naturally, the discussion has centered on the validity of the observation that sentences of this type are synonymous. Many people who are against the generative semantic treatment seem to have concentrated on finding an environment in which either the lexical or the productive form can be used, but not both. On the other hand, very little has actually been done in explicating precise semantic differences that may exist between the lexical and the productive form. Jackendoff (1972:28), for example, points out that the lexical–productive pair does not involve true synonymy, for, as seen in the pair of sentences in (97), there are situations in which one is grammatical while the other is not:

(97) a. **Floyd dropped the glass to the floor by tickling Sally, who was holding it.*
b. *Floyd caused the glass to drop to the floor by tickling Sally, who was holding it.*

Jackendoff, however, merely notes that while the verb *drop* requires a situation involving direct causation, the *cause* form does not, without offering any definition of the term DIRECT CAUSATION, which has been used very vaguely by many. As far as I know, Shibatani (1973d) is the only work that has seriously attempted to explicate more systematically the differences involved in the pair like (97). It has been shown that in English, while lexical causatives and the productive forms with *make*, *have*, and *get* are associated with specific semantic notions such as manipulative, directive, coercive causation, and others discussed in Section 3, the verb *cause* is noncommital to these specifications. That is, the productive form with *cause* is semantically the most general causative expression in English. Thus, while on the one hand the *cause* form can be used for various causative situations, the actual use of the form, on the other hand, is fairly limited owing to lack of specifics. Thus, the sentences in (97) show a case in which the lexical form is ruled out because of the conflict in semantic specification. That is, the lexical causative form *drop* is associated with manipulative causation (see Section 3), but since the *by* clause in (97a) specifies that the situation did not involve manipulative causation, the two specifications come into conflict. The productive form with *cause*, on the other hand, does not specifically call for a manipulative situation, hence the acceptability of (97b).

Since the relation between the causative sentence with *cause* and the lexical causative is as we have discussed, the more general expression with *cause* can be used to express the specific situation expressible by the lexical causative form, but not vice versa.[10] One can, thus, use (98b) in describing the situation expressed by (98a), but (98a) cannot be used to express all the possible situations that (98b) can express:

(98) a. *I dressed the child.*
b. *I caused the child to be dressed.*

The relation, in other words, is that of inclusion; the more general *cause* form includes the more specific lexical form. Schematically represented, the relation looks like the following:

(99) Inclusion relation.

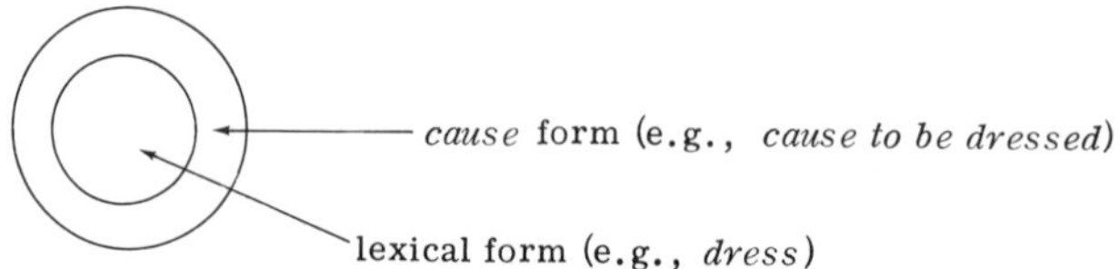

Thus, while (98a) implies (98b), (98b) does not imply (98a), since the expression with specifics implies the more general expression, but the reverse does not hold.[11]

The asymmetrical relation between the *cause* form and the lexical form is manifested in the following pairs of sentences:

(100) a. *I didn't dress the child, but I merely caused him to be dressed.*
b. **I didn't cause the child to be dressed, but I merely dressed the child.*

[10]Of course, if the general *cause* form were used, the specificity would be lost.

[11]For example, *I drove to school* implies *I went to school*, but not vice versa.

(101) a. *You shouldn't dress the child, but you may cause him to be dressed.*
b. **You shouldn't cause the child to be dressed, but you may dress him.*

Once one negates a more general statement [the larger circle in (97)] that includes a more specific statement [the smaller circle in (97)], he cannot assert the specific statement, whereas negating the specific statement does not prohibit assertion of the general statement.[12] Referring back to (99), one can see the relation more clearly: Negating the larger circle automatically leads to negating what is included in it, but negating the smaller circle does not lead to negating the larger circle, for the larger circle still has some area not covered by the smaller circle. Thus, both (100b) and (101b) involve contradiction, while (100a) and (101a) do not.

The same inclusion relation holds between the *cause* form and other productive forms with *make*, *have*, etc.; the following sentences parallel (100) and (101):

(102) a. *I didn't have the child stand up, but I caused the child to stand up.*
b. **I didn't cause the child to stand up, but I had the child stand up.*

(103) a. *You shouldn't have the child stand up, but you may cause the child to stand up.*
b. **You shouldn't cause the child to stand up, but you may have the child stand up.*

However, the relation between the *have* form and the lexical form is not that of inclusion; rather, they involve the intersecting relation. The intersecting relation can be schematically represented as follows:

(104) Intersecting relation.

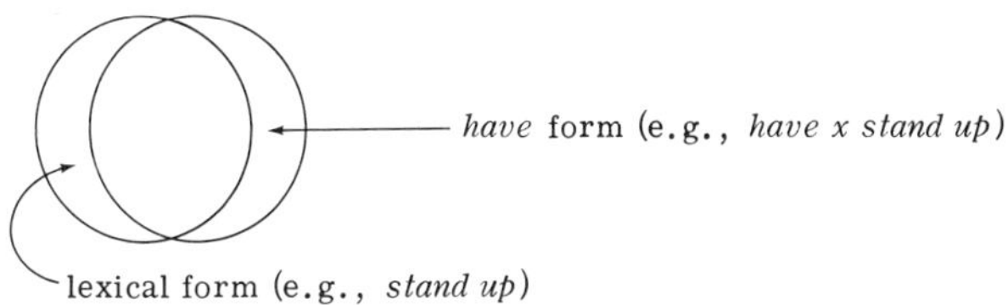

[12]Also compare:

(i) a. *I didn't drive to school, but I went to school today.*
b. **I didn't go to school, but I drove to school today.*

(ii) a. *You shouldn't drive to school, but you may go to school today.*
b. **You shouldn't go to school, but you may drive to school today.*

In the case of the intersecting relation, neither form implies the other, and negating one does not entail the negation of the other. In other words, the symmetrical pattern would be exhibited. Thus, unlike the cases in (100)–(101) and (102)–(103), the sentences in the following pairs are all well-formed:

(105) a. *I didn't stand the child up, but I had him stand up.*
b. *I didn't have the child stand up, but I stood him up.*

(106) a. *You shouldn't stand up the child, but you may have him stand up.*
b. *You shouldn't have the child stand up, but you may stand him up.*

Turning now to the question of the synonymy in the Japanese lexical and productive causative pair, one discovers that in Japanese only the intersecting relation holds. As discussed in Section 3, members of the Japanese lexical and productive causative pair involve fairly distinct semantic properties. The most salient feature that holds between the lexical form and the productive form is the manipulative–directive distinction (see Section 3). Since Japanese lacks a causative form as abstract as the English verb *cause*, there is no case involving the inclusion relation [see (99)]. The prevailing relation is the intersecting relation, and we find the same kind of situation that is observed in the pair of the English lexical causative and the *have* form [see (105) and (106)]. Observe the following:

(107) a. *Sono kodomo ni huku o kise-ta no de wa naku, ki-sase-ta no da.*
'It is not the case that I dressed the child, but it is the case that I had him get dressed.'
b. *Sono kodomo ni huku o ki-sase-ta no de wa naku, kise-ta no da.*
'It is not the case that I had the child get dressed, but it is the case that I dressed him.'

(108) a. *Sono kodomo ni wa huku o kise-nai de ki-sase-te kudasai.*
'As for that child, please don't dress him, but have him get dressed.'
b. *Sono kodomo ni wa huku o ki-sase-nai de kise-te kudasai.*
'As for that child, please don't have him get dressed, but dress him.'

(109) a. *Sono kodomo o tukue no ue ni age-ta no de wa naku, agar-ase-ta no da.*
'It is not the case that I lifted the child up onto the desk, but I had him get up there.'

b. *Sono kodomo o tukue no ue ni agar-ase-ta no de wa naku, age-ta no da.*
'It is not the case that I had the child get up onto the desk, but I lifted him up there.'

(110) a. *Sono kodomo wa tukue no ue ni age-nai de, agar-ase-te kudasai.*
'As for that child, please don't lift him up onto the desk, but have him get up there.'

b. *Sono kodomo wa tukue no ue ni agar-ase-nai de, age-te kudasai.*
'As for that child, please don't have him get up onto the desk, but lift him up there.'

Even though the relation between coercive and noncoercive causation is intersecting, the nonintersecting part is so small that the distinction does not show up as clearly as the case involving the manipulative–directive distinction. It is not entirely clear, therefore, whether the following are indeed well-formed:

(111) a. ?*Sono kodomo* ***o*** *hasir-ase-ta no de wa naku, sono kodomo* ***ni*** *hasir-ase-ta no da.*
'It is not the case I made the child$_i$ run, but I had him$_i$ run.'

b. ?*Sono kodomo* ***ni*** *hasir-ase-ta no de wa naku, sono kodomo* ***o*** *hasir-ase-ta no da.*
'It is not the case that I had the child$_i$ run, but I made him$_i$ run.'

This difference can be schematically shown as follows:

(112)

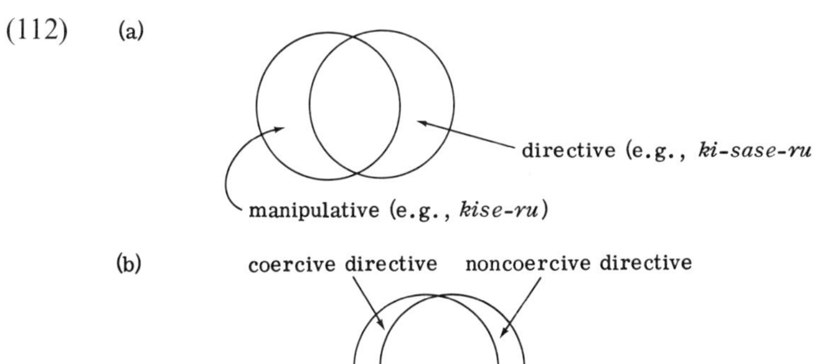

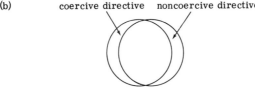

Thus, although some pairs of causative expressions may be close to true synonymy, the pair involving the lexical and productive forms has a fairly distinct meaning difference. In the case of Japanese, which does not have an abstract form comparable to English *cause*, it is particularly hard to maintain, in the light of well-formed expressions like (107)–(110), that the lexical causative form and the corresponding productive form are synonymous. What the generative semantic analysis has captured is the intersection of the semantic fields that is shared by the two types of causative expressions [see (112a)]. It has, however, left the semantic aspects unique to each type unaccounted for. In other words, deriving a sentence pair like (95) from the identical underlying structure captures what is common, but it entirely ignores what is not common between the sentences of the pair.[13]

How to Deal with the Problems

I have discussed both motivations for and problems associated with the generative semantic treatment of causative forms. The discussion has centered on the validity of the proposed uniform treatment of the lexical and productive causative forms. I will now discuss how some of these problems have been and can possibly be resolved within the framework of generative semantics.

In his reply to Shibatani (1972a), J. McCawley (1972a) has offered the following solution. He first notes that the analysis that attempts to derive a lexical causative form from the corresponding intransitive form by way of a causativization rule is wrong. That is, an analysis of the sort suggested by Soga (1970) that posits the intransitive embedded sentence to derive the corresponding lexical causative [see (95) and (96)] is wrong, since 'clauses containing *nokos-* ["leave behind"], *ire-* ["put in"], and *oros-* ["bring down"] [are derived] from structures containing "*x* be in *y*" or "*x* not be in *y*" ... [p. 144].' In this proposal the lexical expression *x ga y o z ni nokos-u* '*x* leaves *y* behind at *z*' does not come from the structure (*x* (*y ga z ni nokor-*) CAUSE) where the intransitive expression '*y* remains at *z*' is included, but rather, the expression originates from a structure like (*x* ((*y ga z ni* BE) BECOME)CAUSE), where only one agent is involved. On the other hand, the productive form *x ga y o z ni nokor-ase-ru* '*x* makes *y* remain at *z*' comes from a structure that contains two agents, the causer and the causee, which are subjects of the verbs *sase* and *nokor-*, respectively. McCawley goes on to say that the reason the *soo suru* replacement does not bring about ambiguity in the lexical causative expression (see Section 2) is that the phrase *soo suru* replaces only action verbs: Since the lexical causative contains only one action verb, namely, CAUSE (or perhaps DO), there is a unique antecedent for *soo suru*. In the productive expression, however, there may be two

[13]For a much more comprehensive overview of the controversy over the causative construction, see Shibatani (1975a).

action verbs, one that gives rise to *sase* and one that turns into an intransitive verb, hence two possible antecedents for the *soo suru* phrase.

McCawley's observation that the causee in the lexical causative expression does not function as an agent seems to be correct. The mere fact that the causee of a lexical causative never surfaces with the particle *ni* gives a clue to this, and the fact that the situations expressible by lexical causative sentences involve the causee as a nonvolitional participant (except in the conventionalized usage discussed in Section 3) corroborates the observation. McCawley's revision also accounts for the problems brought up by Fodor (see pages 279–281). The asymmetry observed in (113) can be explained by saying that *kill* is analyzed as (CAUSE(BECOME(NOT ALIVE))) involving only one agent, and that the *do so* phrase replaces only action verbs:[14]

(113) a. *John caused Mary to die, and it surprised me that he did so.*
b. *John caused Mary to die, and it surprised me that she did so.*
c. *John killed Mary, and it surprised me that he did so.*
d. **John killed Mary, and it surprised me that she did so.*

Also, the fact that the instrumental phrase does not bring about ambiguity in the lexical causative expression (e.g., 114b) can be accounted for similarly:

(114) a. *John caused Bill to die by swallowing his tongue.*
b. *John killed Bill by swallowing his tongue.*

Only an agent can be associated with an instrumental clause. Since the lexical causative expression contains only one agent, there is a unique agent that can be associated with an instrumental phrase.

While McCawley's revised model for the lexical causative structure accounts for a few problems brought up against the original conception of the generative semantic treatment, it involves the serious problem of underspecification of semantic contents involved in lexical causative forms. For example, McCawley says, as quoted previously, that lexical causatives such as *nokos-u* 'leave behind', *ire-ru* 'put in', and *oros-u* 'bring down' are derived from structures containing '*x* be in *y*' or '*x* not be in *y*'. The structures expressing these ideas are presumably embedded beneath the predicates BECOME and CAUSE, as well as DO. The obvious problem here is that the amalgamation of '*x* be in *y*', BECOME, CAUSE, and DO, or that of '*x* not be in *y*', BECOME, CAUSE, and DO, does not represent what the real verbs *nokos-u*, *ire-ru*, and *oros-u* mean. For example, if a chicken produces

[14]This leads us to the conclusion that the English verb *die* functions both as an action verb and as a process verb.

an egg in the room, thereby 'causing it to become that an egg is in the room', one should be able to say either *Niwatori ga tamago o heya ni nokos-u* 'A chicken leaves an egg behind in the room' or *Niwatori ga tamago o heya ni ire-ru* 'A chicken puts an egg into the room.' Similarly, if one smokes cigarettes in the car, thereby 'causing them not to be in the car', one should be able to say *Kare ga tabako o oros-i-ta* 'He took the cigarettes out (of the car).' But apparently these expressions do not express correctly what is really taking place.

What should be specified in place of '*x* be in *y*' or '*x* not be in *y*' is, perhaps, something representing the idea of *x ga nokotte-iru* '*x* is in the state of remaining' in the case of *nokos-u* 'leave behind', and *x ga orite-iru* '*x* is in the state of having gotton off' in the case of *oros-u* 'bring down'. Both *nokotte-iru* and *orite-iru* are noncommittal as to whether the events that entailed these states have involved *nokor-u* 'remain' or *nokos-u* 'leave behind' or *ori-ru* 'get down' or *oros-u* 'bring down'. But the real question is whether one can represent the meaning of *nokotte-iru* without making reference to either *nokor-u* or *nokos-u*. If one had to refer to either of them, then such an analysis would involve circularity and would be unable to analyze these verbs; one cannot say, in analyzing the verbs *nokor-u* or *nokos-u*, that the verb comes from the structure containing *nokotte-iru*, which expresses the resultative state of either *nokor-u* or *nokos-u*. McCawley's attempt to analyze the lexical causative does not refer to the form being analyzed, but his analysis, as shown earlier, patently fails to represent what the item really means.

In addition to this problem, McCawley's revision still leaves phenomena of reflexivization, sentence pronominalization, and adverbial modification involving time and place adverbs unaccounted for (cf. Section 2).

First, we have noted that, in English, the phenomenon of sentence pronominalization was used in support of the generative semantic arguments. However, even in English it is not entirely clear whether the phenomenon really supports the generative treatment. For example, it is the case that the second *it* in (115) cannot be correctly understood as referring to 'Mary's dying', contrary to the alleged possible interpretation of *it* involved in (84), which is repeated here for convenience:

(115) **John killed Mary, but it took him one hour to bring* ***it*** *about.*

(84) *The physicist finally hardened the metal, but it took him six months to bring* ***it*** *about.*

Lakoff and Ross (1972) have attempted to give possible reasons for these phenomena, but I have argued in Shibatani (1972c) that their reasons do not hold well even in English, and that the evidence drawn from (84) is highly questionable. In the case of Japanese, it is clear, as seen in Section 2, that the pronoun *sore* 'it' cannot refer to anything but the whole sentence when it refers back to the lexical causative sentence. Thus, one of the original motivations for the generative treatment is in fact in conflict with it.

The case of reflexivization also argues against the generative treatment, in which even the causee of a lexical causative sentence functions as the subject of one of the embedded sentences. Reflexivization is different from the *soo suru* or *do so* case in that it is not restricted to the case involving action verbs. That is, both agentive and patient subject can function as an antecedent in reflexivization. For example, the subjects in the following sentences are not agents, but they still function as an antecedent of the reflexive pronoun:

(116) a. *Taroo wa zibun no ani yori se ga takai.*
'Taro is taller than his own brother.'
b. *Taroo wa zibun o tuyoku aisite iru.*
'Taro loves himself strongly.'
c. *Taroo wa zibun no kuruma kara orite iru.*
'Taro is in the state of having gotten out of his own car.'

Thus, even if one adopts J. McCawley's revision, discussed earlier, the phenomena of reflexivization and sentence pronominalization cannot be adequately accounted for.

The phenomena of reflexivization and sentence pronominalization in Japanese, thus, strongly challenge the generative semantic treatment of the lexical causative form.[15] One way to deal with the problem within the framework of generative semantics is to say that the rules of reflexivization and sentence pronominalization apply only to the structure that contains real morphemes, and that they do not apply to the semantic structure that contains semantic elements directly. A solution of this type, however, is diametrically opposed to the very tenets of generative semantics—namely, that there is no separation of syntax and semantics and that syntactic rules apply prelexically, i.e., directly to the semantic structure, as well.

The adverbial modification of time and place adverbs must be treated in conjunction with the notion of 'event'. The fact that time or place adverbs must be interpreted as modifying the whole causative event in the case of a lexical form indicates that the causative situation is conceived as one cohesive event. In the case of the productive form, however, the causative

[15]This fact is ironical when viewed in light of Noriko McCawley's analysis of reflexivization (in this volume), in which reflexivization is used to support what appears to be an extreme practice of the generative semantic doctrine. Incidentally, N. McCawley has not offered any solution to the phenomenon discussed here.

situation is conceived of as comprising two distinct events that can be separately modified by a time or place adverb. In the generative semantic treatment that breaks up even a lexical causative expression into several distinct events in the semantic representation, it is not clear how a distinction of the sort discussed here can be made.

Finally, I turn to the problem of representing semantic properties such as the notions of directive causation, manipulative causation, coercive causation, and the others discussed in Section 3. Within the framework of generative semantics, it appears possible to divide semantic properties into two groups, one including pragmatic constraints and the other the 'basic' semantic elements, representable in terms of finite, universal semantic 'primitives' such as CAUSE and BECOME (cf. Lakoff, 1974). If this is really possible, then one can assume that while the 'core' causative meaning is represented directly in the semantic representation, those properties discussed in Section 3 are treated as pragmatic constraints.[16] Furthermore, if the separation of the 'core' meaning and pragmatic constraints is possible, one can account for the difference between the productive form and the lexical form in terms of the applicability of predicate raising. That is, by assuming that the applicability of predicate raising depends on pragmatic constraints, one can say, for example, that the insertion of *raise* takes place only when predicate raising brings semantic elements together under one node. But since predicate raising is made sensitive to the pragmatic constraints, it applies only when all the necessary constraints hold. If the pragmatic constraints do not hold, then no predicate raising applies, and as a result, lexical insertion inserts lexical items into each independent node, yielding the productive form *cause to rise*. The idea of making predicate raising sensitive to pragmatic constraints is obviously an extension of the idea discussed in Postal (1974), in which it is shown that presuppositions are affected depending on whether raising applies or not. By turning things around, Postal suggests that such a case is to be handled by making the applicability of raising sensitive to presuppositions. That is, if a certain presupposition holds, then raising applies; otherwise, it does not.

Now, this treatment does not call for the complication of the semantic structure of causative constructions itself, and the similarity between the lexical causative and the productive form can be maximally represented; but there is a problem, particularly in Japanese. In addition to the difficulty associated with differentiating the 'core' meaning from the so-called pragmatic constraints, the treatment suggested turns out to be in conflict with

[16]It is not entirely clear what this 'core' meaning would be. It is presumably something that is shared by all types of causative expressions.

the tenets of generative semantics. One will recall that, in Japanese, even the productive form involves predicate raising. Since the productive causative form and the lexical causative form involve a different set of pragmatic constraints, some provision must be made in order to avoid the confusion. One can allow either two types of predicate raising or require two separate types of pragmatic constraints. The first choice seems not very felicitous, since it essentially involves the recognition of 'semantic predicate raising' that raises semantic elements and 'syntactic predicate raising' that raises real morphemes. (The former is to apply in the lexical causative case, and the latter in the productive case.) The second solution, however, is no better than the first. It must say that one type of pragmatic constraints applies to predicate raising when what is raised are semantic elements, and the other type to raising when what is raised are real morphemes. This, in effect, is saying that a process dealing with semantic elements is sensitive to certain constraints that are different from those involved in a process dealing with morphemes. This is tantamount to saying that semantic processes and syntactic processes (or prelexical and postlexical processes) are different in nature, which is contradictory to the tenet of generative semantics that the syntax/semantics dichotomy does not hold.

This problem and the one associated with reflexivization and sentence pronominalization prompted me (Shibatani, 1973d) to explore a new model of semantic representation that allows one to include much more semantic information than is permitted in the generative semantic model. Also, the possibility of not involving predicate raising of semantic elements is explored. If one allows insertion of lexical items directly into the semantic structure, also allowing replacement of semantic elements that are not under one node by one lexical item, one cannot use McCawley's explanation of 'possible lexical items' (see page 278). However, it is still not entirely clear that one cannot discover a more general and self-explanatory condition on lexical insertion. One will notice that McCawley's, and for that matter Ross', accounts do not explain why constraints such as the coordinate structure constraint and the complex NP constraint hold in language.

5. CONCLUDING REMARKS

We have studied at length Japanese causative constructions from three dimensions—morphological, syntactic, and semantic. The study of causative constructions has proved to be worthwhile, since it relates not only to a number of other syntactic phenomena but also, in a very significant way, to grammatical theory. We have looked in detail at how the theory of generative semantics, one of the most promising current grammatical theories, can handle many intricate syntactic and semantic properties that causative constructions display. Though a complete formal analysis has not been achieved, the facts and problems have been fully explicated. Research on causative constructions in Japanese, English, and other languages continues, and the relevance of such research to the development of grammatical theory has been amply demonstrated in this chapter. Some of the recent achievements in this area are presented in Shibatani (1975b).

RELATIVIZATION[1]

JAMES D. McCAWLEY

INTRODUCTION

Within the past couple of years, so much really first-rate work on Japanese relative clauses has been produced that there is little left for me to do here beyond summarizing the observations of Kuno (1970, 1973), Teramura (1971a), and Muraki (1970) and commenting on the conclusions of those works.

In Japanese, a relative clause, whether restrictive or nonrestrictive, consists of a truncated sentence (specifically, a sentence that lacks the NP that is relativized over and any case markers that go with that NP). The relative clause precedes the NP that it modifies. For example:

(1) a. *Yamada-san ga sáru o*
Mr. NOMINATIVE monkey ACCUSATIVE
kát-te i-ru
keep-PARTICIPLE be-PRESENT
'Mr. Yamada keeps a monkey.'

b. [*Yamada-san ga kátte iru*] *sáru*
'the monkey which Mr. Yamada keeps'

c. [*Sáru o kátte iru*] *Yamada-san*
'Mr. Yamada, who keeps a monkey'
or
'the Mr. Yamada who keeps a monkey'

[1]This chapter originally appeared in *The Chicago Which Hunt, Papers from the Relative Clause Festival*, Chicago Linguistic Society. It is reprinted here with the permission of the author and the Chicago Linguistic Society.

The only exceptions to this are that (a) under some circumstances a pronoun may appear in the position of the relativized NP:

(2) a. [*sono máe ni kuruma ga tomatte*
its front DATIVE car NOMINATIVE stop-PARTICIPLE
iru] *misé*
is shop
'the shop which there is a car parked in front of'

b. [***zibun*** *ga kawigátte ita inú ga*
self NOMINATIVE kept-as-pet was dog NOMINATIVE
sinde simatta] *kodomo*
die-PARTICIPLE went-and child
'a child whose pet dog died on him'

and (b) the copula in the present tense takes a special dependent form in relative clauses:

(3) [*kinben na*] *hito*
diligent is person
'a diligent person'

This is the only remnant in modern Japanese of the distinct dependent (*rentaikei*) and independent (*syuusikei*) verb and adjective forms of older Japanese, which have otherwise fallen together.

In addition to NPs such as (1b), (1c), and (2), which are clearly relative constructions, there are a number of other types of NP with the surface form $[\mathrm{S\ NP}]_{\mathrm{NP}}$; it is not completely clear whether they should be treated as relative clauses.[2] The following is an example:

(4) [*Káre ga Tookyoo e itta*] *yokunen ano dai-zísin ga átta.*
He went next-year that big-earthquake was
'The year after he went to Tokyo, there was that big earthquake.'

While *káre ga Tookyoo e itta* is not a 'truncated sentence', its occurrence in (4) should probably be analyzed as a reduced form of *káre ga Tookyoo e itta tosí /toki no* 'of the year/time when he went to Tokyo', and *NP no yokunen* should probably be analyzed as itself a relative clause construction ('the year which follows NP'). If these conjectures are correct, then (4) contains in its logical structure a relative clause within a relative clause, but *káre ga Tookyoo e itta*, which occurs in the surface position of a relative clause, is not itself a relative clause but merely a constituent of an underlying relative clause, the rest of which has been either deleted or incorporated into the noun *yokunen*. I conjecture that the reason why so many 'relational nouns' can occur in structures like (4) is that the syntactic rules involved in such nouns give rise to structures in which they are modified by a genitive NP,

[2]A comprehensive collection of such structures is presented in Teramura (1971a).

for example :

(5) *tunami no yokunen*
'the year after the tidal wave'

and that when the modifying NP of such a construction is a clause, deletion of the genitive marker *no* gives rise to a surface configuration that (thanks to the absence of relative pronouns in Japanese) exists in Japanese anyway.

Another class of NPs of the surface form S NP that may have to be analyzed as relative clause constructions, but in which the S is not the relative clause but merely a constituent of it, is illustrated by the following examples (Mikami, 1960:87; Teramura, 1971a:65):

(6) a. [*gásu ga moréru*] *niói*
'the smell of gas leaking'
b. [*sanma o yaite iru*] *niói*
'the smell of (someone) frying samma (a kind of fish)'
c. [*piano o hiku*] *otó*
'the sound of (someone) playing the piano'

1. CONDITIONS ON RELATIVIZATION

I turn now to the important question of the conditions under which an NP may be relativized. It appears that the rule responsible for the deletion of the relativized NP is subject to Ross' coordinate structure constraint, but to only a restricted version of the complex NP constraint:

(7) a. *Tároo to Zíroo ga otagai ni naguriátta.*
mutual hit-met.
'Taro and Jiro hit each other.'
*[*Zíroo ga otagai ni naguriátta*] *tinpira*
'The punk who and Jiro hit each other.'
b. *Tanaka-senséi ga kyoositu ni háitte,*
Prof. classroom DATIVE enter
zyúgyoo ga hazimatta.
instruction NOMINATIVE began
'Prof. Tanaka entered the classroom and the class began.'
*[*kyoositu ni háitte zyúgyoo ga hazimatta*] *kyóosi*
'the teacher who entered the classroom and the class began'

(8) a. *Tároo wa uísukii o nónde ita hito*
whiskey ACCUSATIVE drink was person
ni hanasi-káketa.
DATIVE speak-hung
'Taro spoke to a man who was drinking whiskey.'
*[*nónde ita hito ni Tároo ga hanasikáketa*] *nomímono*
'the beverage which Taro spoke to a man who was drinking'

b. *Mítiko wa [zibun ga Hírosi o korosita] yumé o mita.*
self killed dream saw
'Michiko dreamed that she had killed Hiroshi.'
[Mítiko ga [zibun ga korosita] yumé o míta] hito
'the person who Michiko dreamt that she had killed'

c. *Hitóbito wa [tikyuu ga sikakúi] to yuu uwasa o sínzite ita.*
people world square say rumor believe were
'People believed the rumor that the world was square.'
[sikakúi to yuu uwasa o sínzite ita] tikyuu wa marúkatta
'the world, which they believed the rumor that it was square, was really round'

d. *[Tanaka-san ga kite iru] yoohuku ga yogorete iru.*
put-on suit get-dirty
'The suit which Mr. Tanaka is wearing is dirty'
[[kite iru] yoohuku ga yogorete iru] sínsi
'a gentleman such that the suit that he is wearing is dirty'

e. *[Ano kodomo ga kawaigátte ita] inú ga sinde simatta.*
'The dog that that child kept as a pet died on him.'
[[Kawaigátte ita] inú ga sinde simatta] kodomo. [= (2b)]

The kinds of ostensibly conjoined structures in English from which items can be moved (Ross, 1967:168–170) have parallels in Japanese, which, indeed, appears to allow this phenomenon even more freely than English does:

(9) a. *Tároo wa Mitukósi e itte, harámaki o katte kitá.*
go haramaki buy came
'Taro went to the Mitsukoshi and bought a haramaki.'
[Tároo ga Mitukosi e itte katta kitá] harámaki
'the haramaki which Taro went to the Mitsukoshi and bought'

b. *Tároo wa daigaku e itte, boodoo o okósita.*
university go riot caused
'Taro went to the university and started a riot.'
[Tároo ga daigaku e itte okósita] boodoo
'the riot which Taro went to the university and started'

A large number of other constraints on the NP to be relativized have been discussed in Kuno (1970, 1973) in the context of an argument that all relative clauses have an embedded topic. Before discussing this argument, I must first say a little about the topic in Japanese. A topic NP ends with the particle *wa*. Some topics have a 'standard grammatical relation' to the rest of the clause:

(10) a. *Yamada-san wa sáru o kátte iru.*
'Mr. Yamada keeps a monkey.' (subject)

b. *Ano okási wa bóku ga moo tábete simatta.*
cake I already eat finished
'I have already eaten that cake.' (direct object)

c. *Tookyoo kará wa denpoo ga kitá.*
ABLATIVE telegram
'A telegram has come from Tokyo.' (ablative)

However, some do not:

(11) (Mikami, 1960)

a. *Sakana wa tái ga ii.*
fish snapper good
'As for fish, snapper is good/best.'

b. *Sinbun o yomi-ta-i hito wa, koko ni arimásu.*
newspaper read-want-PRESENT person here DATIVE exist
'As for people who want to read newspapers, there are some (papers) here.'

In the former class of cases, the nominative marker *ga* never occurs before *wa*, the accusative marker practically never does, and the other case markers can occur before *wa*, though sometimes they are absent. I will assume in this work that, at some stage of the derivation, the topic (without any case marker) appears as a sister to the sentence in question:

(12)

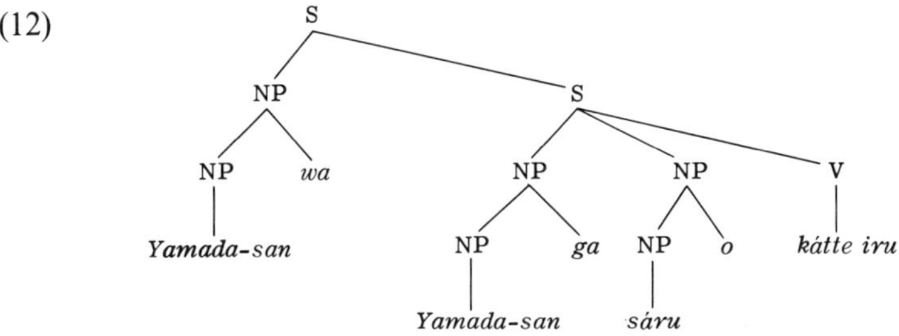

and that there is a rule that replaces the topic by the corresponding NP WITH CASE MARKER from the sister S:

(13)

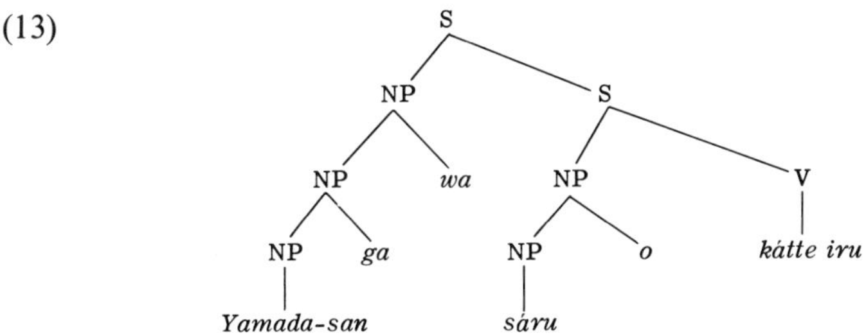

and later rules that delete various case markers before *wa*, sometimes optionally and sometimes obligatorily. This deletion is actually more general, applying also before *mo* 'also' and *sika* 'only' and before the copula in cleft sentences:

(14) a. *Yamada-san (*ga) mo sáru o kátte iru.*
'Even Mr. Yamada keeps a monkey.'
b. *Yamada-san (*ga) sika sáru o kátte inai.*
'Only Mr. Yamada keeps a monkey.'
c. [*Sáru o kátte iru*] *no wa Yamada-san (*ga) da.*
'It's Mr. Yamada who keeps a monkey.'
d. *Tookyoo kará mo denpoo ga kitá.*
'A telegram came also from Tokyo.'
e. *Tookyoo kará sika denpoo ga kónakatta.*
'A telegram came only from Tokyo.'
f. [*Denpoo ga kitá*] *no wa Tookyoo kará da.*
'It's from Tokyo that a telegram came.'

Kuno argues that a relative clause is possible if and only if (he actually weakens this somewhat) there is a corresponding sentence in which the counterpart of the relativized NP is a topic WITHOUT CASE MARKER. For example, Kuno notes that the comitative case marker *to* is generally not deletable but becomes deletable when such an expression as *issyo ni* 'together' is present:

(15) a. *Hánako to/*∅ wa Tároo ga benkyoo sita.*
'Taro studied with Hanako.'
b. *Hánako to/∅ wa Tároo ga issyo ni benkyoo sita.*

The possibility of forming a relative clause here parallels the possibility of deleting *to*:[3]

(16) *[*Tároo ga benkyoo-sita*] *gakusei.*
'The student with whom Taro studied.'
[*Tároo ga issyo ni benkyoo-sita*] *gakusei.*

Kuno's explanation of the parallelism between (15) and (16) is in terms of

[3]For reasons that I do not understand, the deletion of *to* observed here is not possible before the copula of a cleft sentence or before *mo* or *sika*:

(i) a. [*Tároo ga issyo ni benkyoo-sita*] *no wa Hánako to/*∅ da.*
'It was Hanako that Taro studied with.'
b. *Tároo wa Hánako to/*∅ mo issyo ni benkyoo-sita.*
'Taro studied even with Hanako.'
c. *Tároo wa Hánako to/*∅ sika issyo ni benkyoo-sinákatta.*
'Taro studied only with Hanako.'

an underlying structure such as (17):[4]

(17)

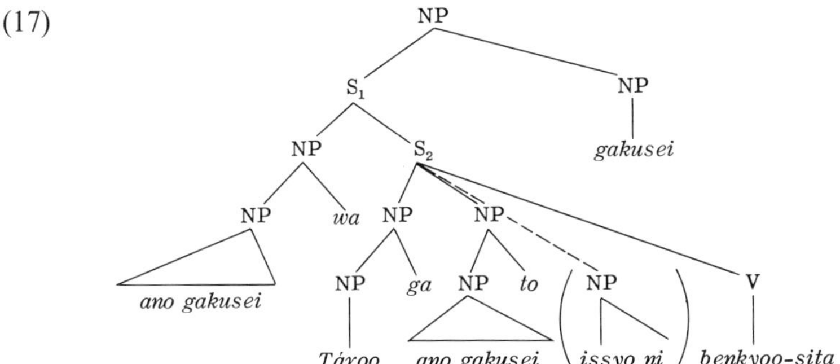

In the case of either (16a) or (16b), *ano gakusei to* replaces the topic *ano gakusei* in S_1. Deletion of *to* is possible if *issyo ni* is present [as in (16b)] but not otherwise [as in (16a)]. If the case marker has been deleted, the topic may also be, and a good relative clause results. Otherwise, no output results.

The facts about deletion of case markers that Kuno gives do not, in my opinion, constitute much evidence for his analysis. Regardless of the underlying structure of relative clauses, their derivation must involve the deletion of the case marker on the relativized NP, and it may well be that the parallelism of (15) and (16), and similar pairs, merely reflects some constraint on deletability of case markers that has nothing directly to do with *wa* or the other morphemes mentioned earlier. By the same token, I do not regard as particularly damaging one class of counterexamples to Kuno's claims, adduced in Muraki (1970). Specifically, the particle *de* and the dative (as opposed to locative) occurrences of *ni* cannot be deleted before *wa*; nevertheless, corresponding relative clauses are possible:

(18) a. *Ano hootyoo dé/*∅ wa Tanaka-san ga níku o kizanda.*
That cleaver INSTRUMENTAL meat chopped
'Tanaka chopped the meat with the cleaver.'
b. [*Tanaka-san ga níku o kizanda*] *hootyoo*
'the cleaver with which Tanaka chopped the meat'

(19) a. *Ano basyo dé/*∅ wa Yamada-san ga sinda.*
place died
'Mr. Yamada died at that place.'

[4]Since Kuno does not make clear how topicalization is to be represented in deep structure, I have arbitrarily imposed on his analysis the treatment sketched earlier. Kuno also does not make completely clear whether the relativized NP in a restrictive clause is identical to the 'head' NP or is, e.g., a 'definite' analog to it, as in (17). The structure in (17) is not a deep structure but an intermediate stage to which rules inserting predictable case markers have already applied.

b. [*Yamada-san ga sinda*] *basyo*
'the place where Mr. Yamada died'

(20) a. *Yamada-senséi ni/*∅ wa syatyoo ga butyoo o syookai-sita.*
'The (company) president introduced the manager to Prof. Yamada.'
b. [*syatyoo ga butyoo o syookai-sita*] *gakusya*
'the scholar to whom the president introduced the manager'

It would not be fatal to Kuno's analysis to have to allow the conditions for deletion of particles before *wa* and for deletion of particles in a relativized NP to differ to the extent that *de* and dative *ni* could be deleted in the latter case but not in the former. A real counterexample to Kuno's claim would be a case where a NP could be relativized but could not be topicalized, with or without deletion of the particle. Muraki gives a couple of cases in which the topicalization is a bit odd, but none that provides a clear counterexample of this type:

(21) a. ??*Sono riyuu dé wa Tároo ga kesseki sita.*
'For that reason, Taro was absent.'
b. [*Tároo ga kesseki sita*] *riyuu*
'the reason why Taro was absent'

I will return later to the other class of counterexamples presented by Muraki: cases in which, allegedly, topicalization is possible but not relativization.

Among the parallelisms between relativization and topicalization that Kuno cites, the most noteworthy are the following:

1. The possibility of a 'resumptive' pronoun under restricted circumstances:

(22) a. *Ano kodomo wa* ***zibun*** *no gakkoo no senséi ga*
that child self GENITIVE school teacher
kootuu-zíko de sinda.
traffic-accident INSTRUMENTAL died
'A teacher at that child's school died in an auto accident.'
b. [***zibun*** *no gakkoo no senséi ga kootuu-zíko de sinda*] *kodomo*
'a child, a teacher at whose school died in an auto accident'

(23) a. *Ano doobutu wa (****sono****) mawari ni kodomo ga atumátte ita.*
animal its surrounding gathered
'There were children gathered around that animal.'
b. [*(****sono****) mawari ni kodomo ga atumátte ita*] *doobutu*
'an animal around which there were children gathered'

This is an especially compelling case for an embedded topic, since otherwise there is no available antecedent for *zibun*, which must follow its antecedent except under conditions that are not met here (see N. McCawley (in this volume) for details).

2. Cases in which the NP is in various adverbial clauses:

(24) a. *Sono hito wa, sindá node, minná ga kanasínda.*
person died because all sorrowed
'Everyone was sad because that man died.'
b. [*sindá no de minná ga kanasínda*] *hito*
'a person who everyone was sad because (he) died'

(25) a. *Sono sínsi wa kite iru yoohuku ga yogorete iru.*
'The suit that that gentleman has on is dirty.'
b. [*kite iru yoohuku ga yogorete iru*] *sínsi*
'a gentlemen such that the suit that he has on is dirty'

3. The difference between genitive *no* and appositive *no*:

(26) a. *Syatyoo no okusan ga nakunátta.*
president GENITIVE wife died
'The president's wife died.'
b. [*okusan ga nakunátta*] *syatyoo*
'the (company) president whose wife died'

(27) a. *Syatyoo no Yamada-san ga nakunátta.*
'Mr. Yamada, the president, died.'
b. *[*Yamada-san ga nakunátta*] *syatyoo*

2. 'RANGE TOPIC' AND 'INSTANCE TOPIC'

I turn now to Muraki's other class of counterexamples to Kuno's proposals. The following are a sample:

(28) a. *Amerika wa Kariforúnia e itta.*
'As for America, I went to California.'
b. *[*Kariforúnia e itta*] *Amerika*

(29) a. *Nékutai wa aói no o katta.*
necktie blue one ACCUSATIVE bought
'As for neckties, I bought a blue one.'
b. **aoi no o katta nekutai*

(30) a. *Bukka wa Nyuu-yóoku ga tákakatta.*
'As for prices, New York was high.'
b. *[*Nyuu-yóoku ga tákakatta*] *bukka*

(31) a. *Ásawa ítumo usugurai úti ni ókita.*
morning always semi-dark inside got-up
'In the mornings, I always got up while it was twilight.'
b. *[*ítumo usugurai úti ni ókita*] *ása*

Kuno has pointed out that many of Muraki's supposedly bad relative clauses are good in appropriate contexts, for example:

(32) *Kariforúnia e itta Amerika, Efferu-táwaa ni nobotta Huransu, zóo ni notta Índo no koto ga wasure-rare-na-i.*
'I can't forget America, where I went to California; France, where I climbed the Eiffel Tower; and India, where I rode an elephant.'

An interesting point emerges if the topics in this group of Muraki's counterexamples are compared with the other topics that have appeared in earlier examples. In this group of examples, the topic indicates the range of a variable. For example, in (30a), the topic restricts the range of the variable x in 'x was high' to price levels in various places, and says that of the things in that range, it is (the member corresponding to) New York for which 'x was high' is true. In (31), there is an overt quantifier (*ítumo*), whose range is given by the topic. The sentence means 'For every morning x, I got up on x while it was still twilight.'[5] In the earlier examples, the topic provided not the range of a variable but an instance of a variable. For example, in (10a), Mr. Yamada is being said to have the property 'x keeps a monkey'; the meaning of (10a) does not involve a variable that ranges over (parts of?) Mr. Yamada. The contrast between the two kinds of topics, which I hereby

[5]Compare (31a) with the following, slightly different example:

(i) a. *Ano gakki wa ítumo/máiasa usugurai úti ni ókita.*
'That school term, {I always got up / got up every morning} while it was still twilight.'
b. [*ítumo/máiasa usugurai úti ni ókita*] *gakki*
'the term when I {always got up / got up every morning} while it was still twilight'

The difference between (31a) and (i) is that in (31a) the topic is 'bound' by the quantifier, whereas in (i) it is not. The topic in (i) is an instance topic: That school term is being said to be an x such that 'on every morning of x, I got up while it was still twilight'. It is also possible to alter (31) slightly so as to get a topic that denotes a specific set of mornings (and, thus, is not bound by the quantifier) rather than denoting just 'morning' in general:

(ii) [*Ítumo usugurai úti ni ókita*] *Kumamoto no ása ga natukasii.*
'I miss the mornings (back) in Kumamoto when I always got up while it was still twilight.'

baptise 'range topic' and 'instance topic'[6], is brought out by the following pair of sentences:

(33) a. *Nihón wa Tookyoo ga sumi-yó-i.* (range topic)
live-good-PRESENT
'As for Japan, Tokyo is a good place to live.'
Among the x such that [x is (a place) in Japan],
Tokyo is an x such that [x is a good place to live].

b. *Nihón wa syúto ga sumiyói.* (instance topic)
'As for Japan, its capital is a good place to live.'
= Japan is an x such that [the capital of x is a good place to live].

The difference between range topics and instance topics has syntactic consequences. Note the different possibilities for comparatives:

(34) a. **Nihón wa Huransu yóri Tookyoo ga sumiyói.*
France than
b. *Nihón wa Huransu yóri syúto ga sumiyói.*
'Thc capital of Japan is a better place to live than that of France.'

and, most important, the different possibilities for RESTRICTIVE relative clauses:

(35) a. *[*Tookyoo ga sumiyói*] *kuni*
'a country whose Tokyo is a good place to live'
b. [*syúto ga sumiyói*] *kuni*
'a country whose capital is a good place to live'

Note that the relative clauses in (32) are nonrestrictive. There seems to be no difference in the possibility of forming nonrestrictive clauses corresponding to the two kinds of topics, save only for the fact that those corresponding to range topics seem most normal when in a context like (32), in which the nonrestrictive clause gives a reason why the thing in question is mentioned. It thus appears as if Kuno's correlation between topicalization and relativization has to be modified so as to accomodate the distinctions between instance and range topics and between restrictive and nonrestrictive clauses: Restrictive clauses can be formed only by relativization over an NP that corresponds to an instance topic, whereas nonrestrictive clauses can be formed by relativization over an NP that corresponds to either kind of topic.

I wish, finally, to consider briefly the most basic question that Kuno's proposal raises: Why should there be any connection between topicalization

[6]The distinction between these two kinds of topics has been arrived at independently by Householder and Cheng (1971).

and relative clauses? I do not have a real answer to that question, but can at least offer as a ground for the plausibility of Kuno's claim the fact that *such that* turns up quite naturally in renditions of both instance topics and restrictive clauses into quasi-mathematical English. For example:

(36) a. *Yamada-san wa sáru o kátte iru.*
b. [*sáru o kátte iru*] *hito*

could be rendered as 'Mr. Yamada is an x such that [x keeps a monkey]' and 'a man x such that [x keeps a monkey]'. The clause that follows *such that* denotes a propositional function, and the material that it is combined with provides an instance of that propositional function. This observation gives some plausibility to the claim that the relation of an instance topic to its 'comment' is the same as that of the relativized NP in a restrictive clause to that clause. However, this leaves me without a clue as to why there should be any relationship between nonrestrictive clauses and both instance and range topics. I will probably lack such a clue until someone provides an answer to the important but neglected question, When a person uses a nonrestrictive clause, why does he do so rather than just expressing the material in question in a separate sentence?

COMPLEMENTATION

LEWIS S. JOSEPHS

1. BACKGROUND AND SCOPE OF THIS CHAPTER

In the recent literature on Japanese syntax, there has been considerable discussion about the form and meaning of Japanese complement constructions. The studies that have appeared thus far, however, present us with a rather fragmented picture of Japanese complementation, since some of them focus on certain SYNTACTIC properties of complement sentences while others attempt to clarify problems relating to the SEMANTIC interpretation of complement sentences and nominalizers. The main purpose of this chapter is to bring together the major observations about the syntax and semantics of Japanese complementation that have accumulated over the past several years, and to offer new observations and generalizations where possible.

Alfonso's (1966) monumental textbook contains a wealth of data on Japanese complement types, supplemented by syntactic explanations that are intended to be practical, rather than theoretical, in nature (see especially pp. 614–645, 994–1006, 1036–1041, 1153–1168). Semantic explanations for complementation phenomena are given rarely, but nevertheless insightfully: Thus, as we will see in Section 5, Alfonso attempts to relate the deletability of the noun complementizer *to yuu* to the semantic features of the following head noun (pp. 1155–1158).

Makino (1970) and Watanabe (1972) are mainly syntactic in their orientation. Makino's overriding interest in the syntactic properties of Japanese complements is typified by his concern for differentiating relative clauses ('relativizing nominalizations') from complement sentences ('nonrelativizing nominalizations'), while much of Watanabe's analysis is an attempt to establish transformational relationships between the various complement types and formulate rules for deleting the noun complementizer *to yuu* on the basis of certain syntactic features (see Section 5).

Nakau (1973) is the most comprehensive study available on the syntax of Japanese complementation. Following the tradition of Rosenbaum (1967), Nakau establishes a basic distinction between noun and predicate complementation in Japanese (cf. Rosenbaum's noun phrase versus verb phrase complementation) and draws convincingly upon a wide range of syntactic phenomena to justify this distinction. He also argues plausibly that the noun complementizer *to yuu*, the predicate complementizers *to* and *yoo ni*, and the abstract sentential nominalizers *koto*, *no*, and *tokoro* are deep structural rather than transformationally introduced elements. Though Nakau's study is of considerable value because it presents a clear picture of the syntactic structures involved in Japanese complementation, it conspicuously fails to consider the possibility that there might be a correlation between the INHERENT MEANINGS of a complementizer like *to yuu* or nominalizers like *koto*, *no*, and *tokoro* and their actual distribution. This semantically based position is the one I shall pursue. In all fairness, however, I should note that Nakau does not disregard semantic features altogether: Thus, he makes significant use of the notion of factivity [see Kiparsky and Kiparsky (1971)] in distinguishing *koto* complements from *to* complements with certain verbs (pp. 121–124), though such an analysis is undoubtedly borrowed from Kuno (1970) (to be discussed).

Harada (1973) attempts to prove that the grammar of Japanese contains a rule that operates in a way that is counter to the normal operation of the equi-NP deletion rule: In other words, Japanese has a rule that, roughly stated, 'delete[s] an NP in the MATRIX SENTENCE if it is identical to the subject of the COMPLEMENT SENTENCE [p. 114; emphasis added].' In support of his analysis, Harada examines the salient syntactic features of circumstantial *tokoro* complements and concludes that they are essentially adverbial (as opposed to nominal) in nature. Thus, Harada's study makes a valuable contribution to our knowledge of the syntax of complement sentences by demonstrating the unique grammatical properties of *tokoro* complements.

The first really insightful attempt at a preliminary classification of Japanese complement types along semantic lines appears in Kuno (1973: Chapter 18, '*Koto*, *No*, and *To*'). In this chapter (which appeared as Section V of Kuno, 1970), Kuno points out that the factive versus nonfactive distinction discovered by the Kiparskys is applicable in Japanese, where it is realized by *koto*/*no* complements and *to* complements, respectively. Kuno's greatest contribution, however, is his attempt to account for the distribution of the nominalizers *koto* and *no* in terms of the general semantic properties of the propositions they nominalize: Thus, *koto* is used to nominalize a proposition that the context allows (or forces) us to construe as an ABSTRACT

CONCEPT, while *no* nominalizes a proposition that can (or must) be understood as a CONCRETE EVENT (1973:221). Accordingly, there are significant correlations between semantic classes of matrix verbs (e.g., verbs of perception, verbs of mental activity) and the type of cooccurring complement (S *koto* versus S *no*).

Directly developing from the above-mentioned work of Kuno, Josephs (1972a:Chapter 2, '*Koto* and *No*') draws heavily on cooccurrence restrictions between *koto*/*no* and various sets of matrix verbs in order to determine the inherent semantic features of these nominalizers. In that study, it becomes clear that *koto* and *no* are semantically distinct from each other in a very basic way and that the cooccurrence restrictions observed between *koto*/*no* and matrix verbs are not idiosyncratic but are due to a principle of semantic compatibility. Furthermore, the fact that 'direct' *no* and 'indirect' *koto* have presuppositional as well as nonpresuppositional readings is illuminated. Because this material has not been previously published, considerable space will be devoted to it here.

Although Nakau's (1973) discussion of complement sentences covers a wide range of structures from S *koto*/*no*/*tokoro* and S *to*/*yoo ni* to embedded sentences associated with higher verbs (or predicates) such as *-rare-* (passive), *-sase-* (causative), *-ta-i* (desiderative), etc., the focus of interest in the following sections will be on the former types. Detailed analyses of higher verbs such as *-rare-* and *-sase-* can be found in the works of Howard and Shibatani, respectively, in this volume.

2. NOUN VERSUS PREDICATE COMPLEMENTATION

By far the major contribution of Nakau's (1973) study of Japanese complementation is its painstaking effort to establish the difference between noun and predicate complementation. These contrasting types of complementation are represented by the following different phrase marker fragments:

(1)

(2)

The configurations in (1) and (2) exhibit the obvious difference that in noun complementation the embedded sentence S′ (called a noun complement) precedes N (the head noun) and is dominated by NP, while in predicate complementation the embedded sentence (called a predicate complement) precedes Pred (the predicate—usually a verb) and is dominated by Pred Phr. Furthermore, the Comp (i.e., noun complementizer) of (1) will be realized as *to yuu*,[1] while the Comp (i.e., predicate complementizer) of (2) will be either *to* or *yoo ni*. Since noun complementation structures like (1) can occur as sentence subject or object, they strictly subcategorize cooccurring predicates in various ways: Thus, Nakau says (p. 4) that predicates are subcategorized by the type of head noun (e.g., abstract sentential nominalizers such as *koto*, *no*, and *tokoro* or lexical head nouns such as *hanasi* 'story', *uwasa* 'rumor', etc.) and, in some cases, by the internal structure of the complement sentence. In predicate complementation structures like (2), predicates are subcategorized by the type of cooccurring complementizer (*to* versus *yoo ni*) and, occasionally, by elements within the complement sentence.

What is common to the noun and predicate complementation structures in (1) and (2) is the presence of an embedded sentence—S′—which is expanded into S-Comp. This expansion reflects Nakau's assumption (p. 128ff) that the noun complementizer *to yuu* and the predicate complementizers *to* and *yoo ni* are deep structure elements. As we will see in Section 5, the correctness of this assumption is partly supported by the fact that the noun complementizer *to yuu* has meaning and can contrast with ∅ in the pre-head noun position. The presence of a head noun N in the noun complementation structure of (1) reflects Nakau's further assumption that abstract sentential nominalizers such as *koto*, *no*, and *tokoro* are deep structure elements, just as lexical head nouns like *hanasi* 'story' and *uwasa* 'rumor' are (pp. 104–109). This assumption is strongly supported by the discussions in Section 3 and 4, in which *koto*, *no*, and *tokoro* are shown to be contrasting lexical items with quite distinct meanings.

The node S′ is justified in the configurations in (1) and (2) because there are various transformations that move or affect the sentential complement TOGETHER WITH the complementizer. Thus, Nakau points out (pp.139–140) that when a noun sentential complement is preposed within the domain of an NP, the noun complementizer *to yuu* must be preposed along with it. This phenomenon is illustrated in the following example taken from Nakau:

[1]This statement, which implies that there is only one noun complementizer, namely, *to yuu*, is deliberately oversimplified. Nakau (pp. 156–158) argues quite insightfully that 'syntactically frozen' clause-final elements such as *to ka yuu*, *to itta*, and *to ka itta* should also be regarded as noun complementizers. A further possibility, namely, that there may be a ∅ noun complementizer, arises out of a major difficulty in Nakau's phrase structure rules (see Section 5).

(3) a. [*Taroo no* [*yuurei ga dete kita*]$_S$ *to yuu kotoba*]$_{NP}$
ghost came out words
'Taro's statement that a ghost appeared'
b. [[*Yuurei ga dete kita*]$_S$ *to yuu, Taroo no kotoba*]$_{NP}$
c. *[[*Yuurei ga dete kita*]$_S$ *Taroo no to yuu kotoba*]$_{NP}$

Similarly, Nakau observes (pp. 148–149) that when the process of *soo* sentential pro-formation applies to a predicate sentential complement, the pro-form *soo* substitutes for the WHOLE sequence of sentential complement plus complementizer. Thus, in the following example (also Nakau's), only *soo*, but not *soo to*, is possible in the second conjunct:

(4) *Boku wa*, [*baka wa sinanakya naoranai*]$_S$ *to omotta;*
I fool unless he dies won't improve thought
*hoka no hitotati mo soo (*to) omotta.*
other people so thought
'I thought that a fool could not be cured until he had died, and other people thought so, too.'

As partial evidence that the grammar of Japanese must contain the contrasting configurations in (1) and (2), Nakau demonstrates that transformations that move or affect simple NPs can also apply to structures like (1), but not to structures like (2). In other words, the fact that a sequence of the form S-Comp-N of (1) functions as a single unit under topicalization, cleft formation, NP deletion, and the like indicates that it is an NP and that the S-Comp portion of it is a 'noun complement' embedded before a head noun. By contrast, the fact that no part of (2) can be moved or deleted by the very same syntactic tests shows that no NP is involved anywhere in this structure and that the S-Comp portion of it is a 'predicate complement' embedded before a predicate.

To illustrate one of these syntactic tests, observe the effects of applying the rule of cleft formation to sentences containing the configurations in (1) and (2):

(5) Noun complementation:
a. *Watakusi wa* ***Tanaka-san ga zisyoku sita to yuu uwasa*** *o kiita.*
I Mr. Tanaka resigned rumor heard
'I heard the rumor that Mr. Tanaka resigned.'
b. *Watakusi ga kiita no wa* ***Tanaka-san ga zisyoku sita to yuu uwasa*** *da.*
'What I heard was the rumor that Mr. Tanaka resigned.'

(6) Predicate complementation:

a. *Watakusi wa* ***Tanaka-san ga zisyoku sita to*** *omotta.*
I Mr. Tanaka resigned thought
'I thought that Mr. Tanaka resigned.'

b. **Watakusi ga omotta no wa* ***Tanaka-san ga zisyoku sita to*** *da.*
'What I thought was that Mr. Tanaka resigned.'

If we assume that cleft sentences are derived from a deep structure of the following form:

(7)

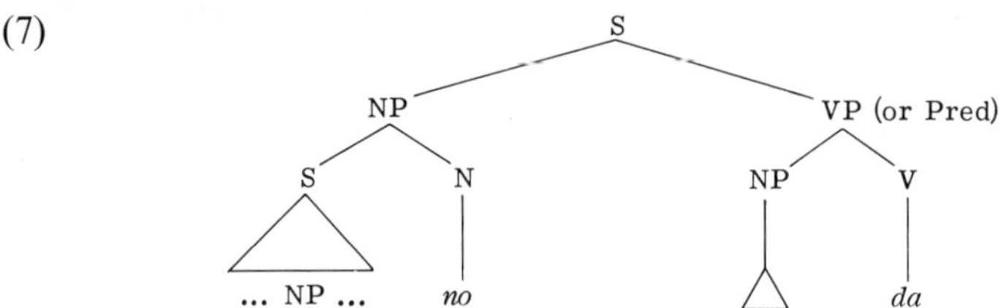

by removing an NP from the embedded sentence and placing it in the precopular position of focus (where it substitutes for the dummy),[2] we can see that the cleft sentences of (5b) and (6b) would be derived from a structure like (7) in which the (noncleft) sentences of (5a) and (6a) are embedded before the nominalizer *no*. But the cleft sentence of (5b) is grammatical, while that of (6b) is not. We therefore conclude that the boldface sequence *Tanaka-san ga zisyoku sita to yuu uwasa* (i.e., S-Comp-N) of (5a) is an NP because it can be 'isolated' by the cleft construction of (5b), while the boldface sequence *Tanaka-san ga zisyoku sita to* (i.e., S-Comp) of (6a) is not an NP because its occurrence in the precopular (NP) position of (6b) is precluded.[3] Similar conclusions can be reached by observing the effects of

[2]This is one of the alternative analyses of cleft formation suggested in Harada (1973:117–118), where the configuration in (7) is also given. For further discussion of Japanese cleft formation, see Nakau (1973:60–69) and Muraki (1970).

[3]Nakau remarks (pp. 112–113) that a grammatical cleft sentence like the following [cf. (6b)]:

(i) *Watakusi ga omotta no wa Tanaka-san ga zisyoku sita to yuu koto da.*
I thought Mr. Tanaka resigned fact
'What I thought of was the fact that Mr. Tanaka resigned.'

cannot be derived from a structure like (7), in which (6a) appears as the embedded sentence before *no*. The main objection to such an analysis would be that the cleft formation transformation does not preserve meaning: Thus, while S *to* in (6a) is a complement of the nonfactive verb *omou* 'think' and therefore involves no presupposition, clefted S *to yuu koto* in (i) above does presuppose the truth of the embedded proposition. The actual derivation of (i) poses a real problem because its apparent source is ungrammatical:

(ii) **Watakusi wa Tanaka-san ga zisyoku sita to yuu koto o omotta.*
'I thought of the fact that Mr. Tanaka resigned.'

applying such transformations as topicalization, NP deletion, *sore* pronominalization, subject–object inversion (e.g., passivization), and *soo* sentential pro-formation. Since Nakau discusses these transformations in detail and illustrates their effects with copious examples (pp. 93–103, 109–116), no further discussion is necessary here.[4]

3. THE NOMINALIZERS *KOTO* AND *NO*

The most challenging semantic and syntactic problems presented by the phenomena of Japanese sentential complementation are found within the noun complementation system. Of particular difficulty is the question of accounting for the distribution of the noun complementizer *to yuu* and of the abstract sentential nominalizers *koto*, *no*, and *tokoro*. As we will see in this and the following sections, an analysis that assigns specific meanings to these elements and tries to explain their distribution in terms of semantic compatibility with cooccurring predicates appears to be the only way of making sense out of what would otherwise be totally chaotic and idiosyncratic phenomena. In an attempt to clarify the major problems of the Japanese noun complementation system, we will divide our discussion into three separate topics. In this and the immediately following subsections, we will examine the nominalizers *koto* and *no* and demonstrate that they have contrasting semantic features; in Section 4, we will discuss the semantic contrast between *no* and *tokoro* after presenting arguments about the syntactic status of clauses headed by these nominalizers; and in Section 5, we will clarify the meaning and use of the noun complementizer *to yuu*, pointing to a serious flaw in Nakau's analysis. Compared with the problem areas just enumerated, the Japanese predicate complementation system is relatively straightforward and unchallenging; for this reason, only a quick survey of certain phenomena related to predicate complementation will be given in Section 6.

Among native Japanese grammarians, nominalizers like *koto* and *no* have traditionally been regarded as semantically empty formatives. Thus, as early as 1930, Matsushita referred to words of this kind as *keisiki meisi*

[4]There are, of course, simpler arguments than those proposed by Nakau for supporting the basic syntactic difference between S-Comp-N (noun complementation) of (5a) and S-Comp (predicate complementation) of (6a). Thus, Makino (1970:77) cites the almost trivially obvious fact that S-Comp-N of (5a) can be followed by a case-marking particle like *o* because it is an NP, while such a particle is prevented after S-Comp of (6a) because this sequence is not an NP. This type of observation, Makino notes, was made by Hashimoto (1948:86–87). Here, Hashimoto says that a sequence of the form verb + nominalizer (e.g., *iku no*) constitutes a unit that, like any ordinary noun (e.g., *hana* 'flower'), can be followed by particles such as *ga*, *o*, *wa*, etc.

'formal nouns'—i.e., nouns that have '. . . only formal (empty) meaning without having any substantial meaning.'[5] Expanding somewhat on Matsushita's definition, Kieda asserted that the Japanese *keisiki meisi* '. . . does not have a certain substantial concept corresponding to a name [It] has no more than a general form. Therefore, it is necessary to add some limiting (or defining) words in front of it.'[6]

Some of the more recent transformational studies of Japanese nominalization have, implicitly or explicitly, perpetuated the notion that nominalizers like *koto* and *no* are devoid of meaning. For example, though Makino (1970:45) recognizes that 'nonrelativizing nominalizations' like S *koto* and S *no* involve the conversion of a whole sentence into a kind of abstract noun phrase whose distributional features are similar to those of a simple (i.e., single-word) noun phrase, he goes no further on the issue of the semantic interpretation of the nominalizers *koto* and *no* than to quote the opinions of Matsushita, Kieda, and others. In addition, Makino presents many examples (see especially pp. 81–91) that imply that *koto* and *no* can be used interchangeably without any apparent effect on the meaning. This interchangeability, of course, would be compatible with an analysis that assigns no substantial (or contrasting) meaning to these nominalizers.

Nakau (1973:100) says that *koto* and *no* (as well as *tokoro*) are abstract sentential nominalizers which are obligatorily preceded by an embedded sentence and, in some cases, by the noun complementizer *to yuu*. These abstract sentential nominalizers, Nakau argues (p. 104ff), should be analyzed as deep structural rather than transformationally introduced elements because their syntactic behavior resembles that of such independently occurring head nouns as *hanasi* 'story', *zizitu* 'fact', and *tamesi* 'attempt', whose presence in the deep structure cannot be denied. The most important syntactic characteristic that the abstract sentential nominalizers *koto*, *no*, and *tokoro* share with the independently occurring head nouns just mentioned is that they subcategorize predicates. Thus, Nakau observes (pp. 106–108) that some predicates require S *no*, others require S *koto*, still others allow both S *koto* and S *no*, and so on. These unusual and potentially interesting distributional restrictions, however, are simply viewed as idiosyncratic and unpredictable phenomena, as the following summary of Nakau's position indicates:

> . . . there is no syntactic basis for distinguishing among the three sentential nominalizers with respect to their cooccurrence relations with Predicates, because all nominalizers

[5]See Matsushita (1930:24–25). This reference, as well as the translation of Matsushita's definition, is due to Makino (1970).

[6]See Kieda (1937:75). This reference and the translation from Kieda are also due to Makino (1970).

> can occur as the head Nouns of the Noun sentential complements in both subject and pre-Predicate position. ... Nor is there any semantic basis for distinguishing among the three nominalizers, because no semantic restrictions can be found which are common to the Predicates which require a particular nominalizer [pp. 108–109].

In the following discussion we will see that the second part of Nakau's statement cannot be maintained: In other words, we will discover that there is, indeed, a semantic basis for distinguishing among the nominalizers and, consequently, for explaining the restrictions on their distribution.

Kuno [(1973:213–222) (= Kuno, 1970:V)] is a landmark study which attempts to account for the distribution of the predicate complementizer *to* and the abstract sentential nominalizers *koto* and *no* in terms of the semantic features of cooccurring predicates. Of major consequence are the following two observations: first, that predicate complements marked with *to* are used with nonfactive predicates while noun complements nominalized with *koto* or *no* occur with factive predicates, and, second, that *koto* nominalizes propositions designating abstract concepts while *no* nominalizes propositions denoting concrete events. The latter discovery gave impetus to the analysis in Josephs (1972a:43–134), in which it is claimed that *koto* and *no* have inherent meanings that are distinct—indeed, opposite—from each other and that the distribution of these nominalizers can be explained in terms of semantic compatibility with cooccurring predicates. Taken together, Kuno (1973) and Josephs (1972a) represent a striking departure from the earlier view that the nominalizers *koto* and *no* are semantically empty elements.

Presupposition in Japanese

Using the concepts of presupposition and factivity, as discussed by Kiparsky and Kiparsky (1971), Kuno (1973) calls attention to the basic distinction between factive *koto/no*, on the one hand, and nonfactive *to*, on the other. Thus, just like English, Japanese has predicates that are uniquely factive or nonfactive, as in the following examples (modeled after Kuno's):

(8) *Ziroo wa Taroo ga tunbo de aru* { *koto/no o* / **to* } *omoidasita.*
deaf is recalled
'Jiro recalled that Taro was deaf.'

(9) *Hanako wa Hirosi ga sinda* { *to* / **koto/*no o* } *gokai sita.*
died misunderstood
'Hanako formed the mistaken notion that Hiroshi had died.'

As these examples show, a factive predicate like *omoidasu* 'recall, remember' requires a noun complement nominalized with *koto* or *no*, while a nonfactive predicate like *gokai suru* 'misunderstand, misapprehend' must be preceded by a predicate complement marked with *to*. The S *koto/no* 'complement' accompanying factive *omoidasu* in (8) represents a proposition that the speaker presupposes to be a true fact; by contrast, the S *to* complement co-occurring with *gokai suru* in (9) does not involve the speaker's presupposition but merely describes a belief that some third party (Hanako) is asserted to have held.

There are a number of Japanese predicates that participate indifferently in both factive and nonfactive paradigms. As expected, predicates of this kind occur with either *koto/no* (factive) or *to* (nonfactive), resulting in a subtle, yet significant, difference in meaning. Observe, therefore, the following pairs of sentences (also modeled after Kuno's):

(10) a. *Taroo wa Mitiko ga baka na koto o nageita.*
stupid is lamented
'Taro lamented the fact that Michiko was stupid, which she was.'
b. *Taroo wa Mitiko ga baka da to nageita.*
'Taro lamented that Michiko was stupid—she might or might not have been stupid.'

(11) a. *Ziroo wa Satiko ga sinda koto o sinzinakatta.*
died didn't believe
'Jiro didn't believe that Sachiko was dead, which she was.'
b. *Ziroo wa Satiko ga sinda to sinzinakatta.*
'Jiro didn't believe that Sachiko was dead—she might or might not have been dead.'

The expanded English translations for (10) and (11) are designed to show that in the factive (a) sentences the speaker presupposes the embedded proposition to be a true fact, while in the nonfactive (b) sentences no such presupposition by the speaker is involved.[7]

Nonpresuppositional Uses of *Koto* and *No*

The semantic properties of the nominalizers *koto* and *no* are considerably more complex than the preceding discussion would lead us to believe. Thus, Kuno notes (p. 219ff) that there are several groups of Japanese predicates

[7]According to Kuno (1973:215–217), the following predicates are also indifferently factive or nonfactive: *utagau* 'doubt', *suitei suru* 'infer', *zihaku suru* 'confess', and *kiku* 'hear'. Nakau (1973:121–124, 144, 146) supplements this list with the following examples: *setumei suru* 'explain', *uttaeru* 'complain', *tutaeru* 'tell, convey', and *hookoku suru* 'report'.

that take *koto/no* but cannot be classified as factive because they do not seem to involve any presupposition. One such group of predicates is illustrated in the following examples:

(12) a. *Ziroo wa tyuugokugo o hanasu koto ga dekiru.*
Chinese speak is able
'Jiro is able to speak Chinese.'

b. *Kanozyo wa kaimono ni iku* {*koto* / *no*} *ga kirai da.*
she shopping go dislike
'She dislikes going shopping.'

c. *Gitaa o hiku* {*koto* / *no*} *wa yasasii.*
play easy
'It is easy to play the guitar.'

d. *Sensei o sonna ni hayaku hoomon suru* {*koto* / *no*} *wa yorosiku nai.*
teacher so quickly call on isn't good
'It isn't advisable to call on one's teacher so soon.'

The examples of (12) are all general statements in which the action or activity of the embedded sentence is construed as a habit or skill rather than as a specific, actually realized event. Thus, the predicates *dekiru* 'be able', *kirai* 'dislike', etc., of (12) do not involve the speaker's presupposition that the embedded proposition is a true fact; instead, they impose on the embedded proposition the interpretation that the designated action or activity is being viewed as a general habit or skill. In uttering (12a), for example, the speaker is not necessarily presupposing that Jiro is speaking Chinese at the present moment, nor is he even presupposing that Jiro speaks or has spoken Chinese on numerous occasions. All that the predicate *dekiru* 'be able' does is to signal (or imply) that the activity of the embedded proposition (i.e., *tyuugokugo o hanasu* 'speak Chinese') is being looked upon as a habit or skill.

Because the predicate *dekiru* 'be able' involves the aforementioned implication, the following sentences are ungrammatical:

(13) a. **Ziroo wa tyuugokugo o hanasite iru koto ga dekiru.*
Chinese is speaking is able
'*Jiro is able to be speaking Chinese.'

b. **Ziroo wa tyuugokugo o hanasita koto ga dekiru.*
spoke
'*Jiro is able to have spoken Chinese.'

The ungrammaticality of (13a) and (13b) is due to the fact that the embedded propositions no longer involve activities that could be construed as habits or skills: Thus, both progressive *hanasite iru* 'is speaking' and past *hanasita* 'spoke' can refer only to some SINGLE EVENT of speaking which is in progress or completed. Semantic anomaly, therefore, results when the embedded predicates of (13), which designate discrete events, are forced to cooccur with the higher predicate *dekiru*, which implies a habit or skill.

The examples in (13) point out an important syntactic difference between the nonpresuppositional predicates of (12) and the presuppositional (factive) predicates found in sentences like (8), (10a), and (11a). Whereas factive predicates do not place any restrictions whatsoever on the tense (or aspect) of the accompanying embedded sentence, nonpresuppositional predicates characteristically require the embedded sentence to contain the present tense. If the nonpresuppositional predicate involves the implication of a habit or skill, as in (12a–d), the present tense marker (*-u* or *-ru*) found in the embedded sentence has no particular time reference and is, indeed, nothing more than a semantically empty element. In other cases, however, the present tense marker which is required in the embedded sentence specifically refers to simultaneous time or to future time, as we will see.[8]

Another group of predicates that take complements nominalized with *koto/no* but do not involve presupposition is exemplified in the following sentences:

(14) a. *Watakusi wa Ziroo ga okane o toru no o mita.*
I money take saw
'I saw Jiro take the money.'

b. *Watakusitati wa sono mati o tooru no o saketa.*
we that town pass through avoided
'We avoided passing through that town.'

c. *Watakusi wa kare ga seikoo suru* {*koto* / *no*} *o kitai site ita.*
I he succeed was expecting
'I was expecting him to succeed.'

In these examples, too, the predicates taking S *koto/no* involve phenomena of implication rather than presupposition; in particular, the types of implication found here closely resemble those discussed in Karttunen (1970b). Thus, when used in the affirmative, the predicate *miru* 'see' of (14a) implies the truth of the embedded proposition (provided, of course, that the speaker is neither lying nor suffering from hallucinations): In other words, by as-

[8]For some clarification of the use of tense markers in Japanese complement sentences, see Nakau (1973:224–227).

serting that he SAW Jiro take the money, the speaker automatically implies that the proposition 'Jiro took the money' is true. In contrast with *miru* 'see' of (14a), the predicate *sakeru* 'avoid' of (14b) implies the falsity of the accompanying proposition: Thus, the speaker who says *We avoided passing through that town* implies that the embedded proposition 'We passed through that town' is false. Finally, whereas the predicates of (14a) and (14b) unequivocally imply the truth or falsity, respectively, of the nominalized propositions, the predicate *kitai suru* 'expect' of (14c) does not allow us to infer whether the accompanying proposition is true or false. In other words, the mere expectation of an event does not necessarily guarantee its actual realization.

The nonpresuppositional predicates of (14), like those of (12), place restrictions on the tense of the embedded sentence. Thus, *miru* 'see' and *sakeru* 'avoid' of (14a) and (14b) require that the embedded sentence contain the present tense marker and, furthermore, that this marker refer to SIMULTANEOUS time. This means that the time point of the embedded sentence proposition is implied (or understood) to be cooccurrent with that of the nonpresuppositional predicate. In (14a), for example, the event designated by the embedded proposition *Ziroo ga okane o toru* (lit.) 'Jiro takes the money' is understood to have occurred in the past, at the same moment in time as the event of the higher predicate *mita* 'saw': This interpretation holds in spite of the fact that the predicate of the embedded sentence (i.e., *toru* 'take') has the present tense marker. The predicate *kitai suru* 'expect' of (14c) also requires that the accompanying embedded sentence have the present tense marker, but in such cases this marker must refer to FUTURE time. The occurrence of the present tense marker to designate future time in embedded sentences accompanying *kitai suru* 'expect' is confirmed by the fact that such embedded sentences can contain future tense adverbials,[9] as in the following:

(15) *Watakusi wa tomodati ga asita kuru* $\left\{\begin{matrix} \textit{koto} \\ \textit{no} \end{matrix}\right\}$ *o kitai site iru.*
I friend tomorrow come am expecting
'I'm expecting that my friend will arrive tomorrow.'

Since a predicate like *kitai suru* implies the possible future occurrence of the embedded sentence action or event, we shall call it a 'futuritive' predicate. Futuritive predicates will be examined further in a later discussion.

In embedded sentences accompanying nonpresuppositional predicates such as those of (14), occurrence of the past tense marker is precluded. Thus, if a complement sentence nominalized with *koto/no* contains the past tense

[9]For a very insightful discussion of the distinction between 'tense' adverbials and 'time' adverbials, see Kajita (1968b:47–49).

marker, the cooccurring predicate must be factive.[10] Note, therefore, the contrasting interpretations of the following two sentences modeled after Nakau (1973:230–231):

(16) a. *Ziroo wa tegami o dasita* {*koto* / *no*} *o wasurete ita.*
letter mailed forgot
'Jiro forgot that he (= Jiro) had mailed the letter.'

b. *Ziroo wa tegami o dasu* {*koto* / *no*} *o wasurete ita.*
mail
'Jiro forgot to mail the letter.'

In (16a), in which the complement sentence contains the past tense form *dasita* 'mailed', the speaker first presupposes that the embedded proposition *tegami o dasita* 'he (= Jiro) mailed the letter' is a fact and then goes on to assert that Jiro himself forgot this fact. In (16b), however, in which the complement sentence contains the present tense form *dasu* 'mail', no such presupposition is involved; instead, it is merely implied that the embedded proposition is false (i.e., Jiro did not mail the letter). Thus, we can see that the higher predicate *wasureru* 'forget' can be used indifferently as a factive predicate, as in (16a), or as a nonpresuppositional predicate, as in (16b). In the latter usage, the implicational features of *wasureru* are the same as those of *sakeru* 'avoid' [cf. (14b)] and *kotowaru* 'refuse'.[11]

[10]The only exception to this claim is found in existential sentences like the following, in which the embedded sentence accompanying nonpresuppositional *aru* 'exist' contains the past tense marker to indicate PAST EXPERIENCE:

Hanako (ni) wa Taiwan ni itta koto ga aru.
to went exists
'Hanako has had the experience of going to Taiwan.'

A brief study of Japanese existential sentences containing S *koto* appears in Nakau (1973: 227–230).

[11]Nakau (1973:231–233) notes the following additional differences between factive and nonpresuppositional *wasureru* 'forget'. First of all, factive *wasureru* places no restriction on the type of complement sentence predicate, which can be either active, as in (16a), or stative, as in the following:

Masaru wa Hanako ga kyoosansyugisya de aru {*koto* / *no*} *o wasurete ita.*
communist is forgot
'Masaru forgot that Hanako is a communist.'

By contrast, nonpresuppositional *wasureru* allows active, but not stative, predicates in the complement sentence, as in (16b). Second, the nominalizer *koto* cooccurring with factive *wasureru* can be replaced by the lexical item *zizitu* 'fact', while the *koto* accompanying nonpresuppositional *wasureru* cannot.

Factive and nonpresuppositional predicates taking S *koto/no* in object position can be partially differentiated from each other in terms of whether or not they impose the identity condition on the subject of the accompanying complement sentence. Thus, with one or two exceptions, factive predicates never require that the complement subject be identical in deep structure to some noun phrase (the subject or indirect object) of the matrix sentence[12]—hence, the grammaticality of (8), (10a), and (11a), in which the subject of the factive complement and that of the matrix sentence are not the same. If, however, the subject of a factive complement happens to be identical to a noun phrase of the matrix sentence, it can be either deleted, as in (16a), or replaced by the reflexive pronoun *zibun* 'self'.

In contrast with factive predicates, some (but by no means all) nonpresuppositional predicates taking S *koto/no* in object position require the complement subject to be identical to the subject or indirect object of the matrix sentence. In the surface structure the embedded sentence (identical) subject is missing because the rule of complement subject deletion has obligatorily applied.[13] Thus, in examples (12a), (12b), (14b), and (16b) we have nonpresuppositional predicates that require deep structure identity between the complement subject and the matrix subject. Other predicates in this category include *kokoromiru* 'try', *hazimeru* 'begin', *tuzukeru* 'continue,' *yameru* 'stop, cease', and *yakusoku suru* 'promise'. And in the following examples we find nonpresuppositional predicates (primarily verbs of ordering, request, and advice) that require deep structure identity between the complement subject and the matrix indirect object:

(17) a. *Bosu wa Yamada-san ni yoku hataraku koto o meizita.*
boss Mr. Yamada well work ordered
'The boss ordered Mr. Yamada to work diligently.'

[12]Two exceptional factive predicates that require the complement subject to be identical to the matrix subject are *kookai suru* 'regret' and *kuiru* 'regret'. Note the following examples:

(i) a. *Watakusi wa hooritu o manabanakatta* {*koto* / *no*} *o kookai site iru.*
I law didn't learn am regretting
'I regret the fact that I didn't study law.'

b. *Taroo wa sensei no kanzyoo o gaisita* {*koto* / *no*} *o kuita.*
teacher feeling hurt regretted
'Taro regretted that he hurt the teacher's feelings.'

English factive verbs such as *repent for* and *be sorry for* involve the same requirement.

[13]See Nakau (1973:211–224) for elaborate proof that particular predicates require the identity condition and subsequent application of complement subject deletion.

b. *Watakusi wa bosu ni zisyoku suru koto o tanonda.*
I boss resign asked
'I asked the boss to resign.'

c. *Ziroo wa Taroo ni narubeku hayaku zisyoku suru koto o*
as soon as possible resign
kankoku sita.
advised
'Jiro advised Taro to resign as soon as possible.'

Further predicates of this type will be examined later.

Examples (14a) and (14c) contain nonpresuppositional predicates that do not impose the identity condition on the subject of the complement sentence. This feature characterizes many classes of nonpresuppositional predicates, including verbs of sense perception, helping, prevention, prediction, and others. Since these classes of predicates will be discussed in detail later, no further elaboration is necessary here.

The Meaning Contrast between *Koto* and *No*

As we have seen, the abstract sentential nominalizers *koto* and *no* can cooccur with both factive and nonpresuppositional predicates. Regardless of the type of predicate that accompanies them, these two nominalizers maintain a clear-cut contrast in meaning. This inherent difference in meaning comes into focus when we examine the distribution of S *koto* and S *no* and attempt to find semantic properties common to predicates which uniquely take the one or the other. We also find that the semantic content of the embedded proposition seems to affect the appropriateness of *koto* versus *no* (to be discussed). In general, we discover that the cooccurrence restrictions observed between S *koto* and S *no* and matrix predicates are not idiosyncratic but are due to a principle of semantic compatibility that relates the inherent semantic features of the nominalizers with those of the cooccurring predicates (and, occasionally, with those of the embedded proposition as a whole).

Kuno's analysis provides us with an essential clue to discovering the difference in meaning between *koto* and *no* by focusing on the overall semantic interpretation of the nominalized proposition and relating this to the meaning of the cooccurring predicate. Thus, Kuno (1973) observes that:

> ... *koto* is used for nominalizing a proposition and forming an abstract concept out of the proposition, while *no* is used for representing a concrete event. From this point of view, it is natural that only *no* can be used for marking the [sentential] object of perceptive verbs. ... One can see or hear a concrete event, but not an abstract concept. There are verbs that can take only a concrete event as their object, such as those of perception,

> and there are verbs that can take only an abstract concept, such as *kangaeru* 'to think' ... There are also some verbs that can take both an abstract concept and a concrete event as their object: *wasureru* 'to forget', *omoidasu* 'to recall', *nageku* 'to deplore', *sinziru* 'to believe', etc. [p. 221] ...

To summarize Kuno's position, *no* occurs as nominalizer only if the embedded proposition names a concrete action or event, while *koto* is less restricted in its distribution because it can follow both 'event' and 'nonevent' propositions, the latter including, for example, propositions that designate abstract concepts or constitute generic (or habitual) statements. Thus, we can account for the contrasting acceptability of these nominalizers in sentences like the following (borrowed from or modeled after Kuno):

(18) a. *Watakusi no kodomo wa sensei ga Mitiko o butte iru*
I child teacher is hitting
{*no* / **koto*} *o mita.*
saw
'My child saw the teacher hitting Michiko.'

b. *Ningen ga hane no nai nihon asi no doobutu de aru* {*koto* / *?*no*}
man featherless two-legged animal is
wa syuuti no zizitu desu.
well-known fact is
'It is a well-known fact that man is a featherless biped.'

c. *Watakusi wa Koronbusu ga Amerika o hakken sita* {*koto* / *no*} *o*
I Columbus discovered
siranakatta.
didn't know
'I did not know (the fact) that Columbus discovered America.'

Because the embedded proposition *sensei ga Mitiko o butte iru* (lit.) 'the teacher is hitting Michiko' in (18a) cooccurs with the verb of perception *miru* 'see', it can designate only a concrete event (i.e., an event perceivable by one of the five senses). Therefore, 'concrete' *no* is acceptable in this sentence, while 'abstract' *koto* is totally ungrammatical. By contrast, the embedded proposition *ningen ga hane no nai nihon asi no doobutu de aru* 'man is a featherless biped' in (18b) is a generic statement or abstract idea; for this reason, *koto* is appropriate, while *no* is ungrammatical (or, at best, very awkward). Finally, the embedded proposition *Koronbusu ga Amerika o hakken sita*

'Columbus discovered America' in (18c) can be construed as either an abstract concept or a concrete event because of the meaning of the cooccurring verb *siru* 'get to know'—that is, one can acquire knowledge of abstract concepts as well as concrete events. Therefore, both *koto* and *no* are grammatical in (18c).

Since the polarization in meaning between *koto* and *no* manifests itself most clearly with certain groups of nonpresuppositional predicates taking S *koto/no* as object, we will first focus our attention on these. We will discover that *no* is used as nominalizer when the matrix predicate imposes connotations of directness, simultaneity, immediacy, or urgency on the event of the embedded proposition. Thus, S *no* is required with verbs of sense perception such as *miru* 'see', *kiku* 'hear', and *kanziru* 'feel', and verbs of discovery such as *mitukeru* 'find' and *tukamaeru* 'catch', all of which have inherent semantic features that impose upon the embedded proposition the interpretation of a directly perceived, simultaneously occurring event. Similarly, S *no* must be used with verbs of helping, such as *tasukeru* 'help' and *tetudau* 'help', which do not involve sense perception but, nevertheless, imply a simultaneously occurring event (or state), and with verbs of stopping, such as *tomeru* 'stop', *seisi suru* 'stop, check', and *hurikiru* 'shake off', which describe immediate, undelayed reaction to a simultaneously occurring or imminent event. Occurrence of S *no* is also possible with verbs of prevention, such as *boosi suru* 'prevent', *husegu* 'prevent', and *zyama suru* 'hinder', but only when these verbs connote a sense of urgency or a relatively strong conviction on the part of the speaker that the event of the embedded proposition will be realized. As we will see, verbs of prevention can also take S *koto*, resulting in a significant difference in meaning.

The nominalizer *koto*, by contrast, cannot cooccur with predicates connoting directness, simultaneity, immediacy, or urgency. Instead, *koto* is used when the matrix predicate imposes connotations of indirectness, abstractness, nonsimultaneity, or nonrealization on the embedded proposition. Thus, with certain types of futuritive predicates—e.g., verbs of ordering or request, such as *meiziru* 'order' and *tanomu* 'ask' and verbs of proposal or advice, such as *teian suru* 'propose' and *susumeru* 'advise'—only S *koto* can occur. This is apparently due to the fact that any proposition constituting an order, request, proposal, or piece of advice is still unrealized (and, therefore, not directly or immediately perceivable) at the moment when the order is given, the request made, etc. In addition, factive predicates designating particular types of mental activity—e.g., verbs of deduction and thinking, such as *suitei suru* 'infer' and *kangaeru* 'think about', and verbs of learning, such as *narau* 'learn' and *manabu* 'learn'—require S *koto* because they invariably impose upon the embedded proposition the connotation of 'abstract concept'. In other words, abstract concepts, but not concrete events, can be grasped or manipulated by such mental processes as deduction, thinking, and learning.[14]

Some classes of Japanese predicates allow both S *no* and S *koto*. Thus, as remarked previously, verbs of prevention take S *no* when the need to forestall the event of the embedded proposition is felt to be urgent or immediate—i.e., when the speaker has a relatively strong conviction that the event is about to take place. Verbs of prevention also cooccur with S *koto*, but, as expected, the connotation of urgency or immediacy is lost: Instead, the speaker looks upon the event of the embedded proposition as some relatively distant future happening against which certain precautions might be taken. In other words, with S *koto* the speaker has a weaker conviction that the event of the embedded proposition will be realized. A similar contrast in meaning between S *no* and S *koto* is observed among other groups of futuritive predicates, including verbs of expectation, such as *kitai suru* 'expect' and *tanosimi ni site iru* 'look forward to', and verbs of prediction, such as *yogen suru* 'predict'. Interesting contrasts in meaning also result from using S *no* versus S *koto* with factive verbs of emotional response such as *heikoo suru* 'be annoyed', and with verbs designating the mental activities of understanding and realization, such as *wakaru* 'understand' and *siru* 'come to know' (further details will be given later).

On the basis of the preceding discussion, we propose that the nominalizers *no* and *koto* are independent lexical items with opposing meanings: *No* means something like 'directly perceived, simultaneously occurring, or imminent action, event, etc.', while *koto* means 'nonsimultaneous, nonrealized, or abstractly perceived action, event, state, etc.' We can summarize this inherent meaning difference by characterizing *no* with a semantic feature like ⟨direct⟩ and *koto* with a semantic feature like ⟨indirect⟩. Each of these features is merely a cover term for the wide range of meanings that the nominalizers *no* and *koto* individually subsume. The distribution of the two nominalizers can be plausibly explained in terms of semantic compatibility with cooccurring predicates (and, sometimes, with the whole embedded proposition). For example, since verbs of sense perception, discovery, helping, and stopping have an inherent semantic feature such as ⟨direct⟩, they occur compatibly with ⟨direct⟩ *no*, but not with ⟨indirect⟩ *koto*. Conversely, verbs of ordering,

[14]Reference to Weinberg's distinction between 'signal reactions' and 'symbol reactions' (1959:34ff, and 48ff) may be helpful in clarifying the dichotomy introduced here. Of the two differing types of reaction to external phenomena, signal reactions are direct and undelayed, such as yelling when touching a hot stove, while symbol reactions require some kind of mental activity (deliberation, inference, etc.) and, therefore, involve delay, as when one says *That certainly hurt*! or *I should have been more careful* at some time following the initial (signal) reaction to the stimulus. A symbol reaction is a response to an entire situation or experience, while a signal reaction represents the initial perception of it. In Japanese, use of S *no* is the analog of a signal reaction, while use of S *koto* is the analog of a symbol reaction.

request, proposal, and advice contain the feature ⟨indirect⟩ and cooccur harmoniously with ⟨indirect⟩ *koto*, but not with ⟨direct⟩ *no*. By contrast, certain groups of predicates—e.g., verbs of prevention or expectation—can be either ⟨direct⟩ or ⟨indirect⟩; for this reason, they allow both of the nominalizers.

In order to justify the above-mentioned conclusions, we are now compelled to examine the various sets of data on which they are based. Therefore, in the following sections we will look at the distribution of S *no* versus S *koto* with respect to three major groups of predicates. Then, further observations on the semantic features of the two nominalizers will be given by way of final summary.[15]

Verbs of Sense Perception, Discovery, Helping, and Stopping

In this section, we will deal with four groups of nonpresuppositional predicates—verbs of sense perception, discovery, helping, and stopping—which cooccur with S *no* almost exclusively[16] and allow S *koto* only in a few special cases. The verbs in these four groups all share the semantic feature ⟨direct⟩—that is, they involve actions in which the subject directly perceives or directly responds to a simultaneously occurring or imminent event (or, occasionally, state). Characteristic of nonpresuppositional predicates in general, these groups of verbs place restrictions on the tense of the embedded proposition. Thus, the embedded sentence cannot be in the past tense but must always contain the present tense marker in the meaning of simultaneous time. In addition, the embedded sentence can contain the progressive aspect *-te iru*, as we will see.

In the following examples various verbs of sense perception are used in

[15]A few precautionary remarks may be necessary before examining the relevant data. First of all, it goes without saying that the judgments of informants about the grammaticality, acceptability, or semantic interpretation of sentences are often at variance with each other, no matter how straightforward the material to be examined apparently is. In a study of this kind, however, the problem of conflicting or unclear responses is particularly heightened, since we are attempting to clarify a fairly subtle semantic distinction between two lexical items. Therefore, the claims made will not hold in every single case for every single speaker—rather, they represent the general trends and more preferred usages.

Second, in the course of elicitation, it was sometimes difficult to decide whether the sentence under consideration was 'normal colloquial' Japanese or whether it was somewhat literary or formal in style. Thus, with certain pairs of sentences differing only in the presence of *koto* versus *no*, informants often responded that there was no discernible difference in semantic content but that while sentences with *koto* were reserved for formal or 'official' speech situations, sentences with *no* were more informal and 'intimate'. Responses of this kind might be due in part to the fact that *koto* is frequently used in literary or 'translation' style and is associated with the Chinese character 事, while *no* is always written with the native syllabary symbol の.

[16]This statement is made with specific reference to the contrast between S *no* and S *koto*. As we will see in Section 4, some of the verbs in these groups also cooccur with S *tokoro*.

the matrix sentence. The cooccurring embedded sentence must be nominalized with *no*, but not *koto*:

(19) a. *Watakusi wa Hanako ga* {*oyoide iru* / *oyogu*} *no o mita.*[17]
I {is swimming / swims} saw
'I saw Hanako {swimming / swim}.'

b. *Kodomotati ga asonde iru no ga tooku kara mieta.*
children are playing afar from could see
'From a distance one could see the children playing.'

c. *Boku wa kiteki ga tooku de natte iru no o kiita.*[18]
I whistle far away is sounding heard
'I heard a whistle sounding a long way off.'

d. *Tori ga naite iru no ga kikoeta.*
bird is singing could hear
'One could hear birds singing.'

e. *Watakusi wa sesuzi ga samuku naru no o kanzita.*[19]
I spine get cold felt
'I felt a chill run down my spine.'

[17]In the following example, *miru* 'see' is used figuratively in the sense of 'experience/enjoy the fruits of one's labor'. In spite of this fact, only S *no* is grammatical:

Kare wa sono doryoku ga mukuwareru no o mizu ni sinda.
he his efforts be rewarded not seeing died
'He died without seeing his efforts rewarded.'

[18]In this example (borrowed from Nakau, 1973:106), the matrix verb *kiku* 'hear' refers to direct auditory perception of a simultaneously occurring event. This verb, however, can also be used in the sense of 'be informed/find out (that ...)', in which case it does not imply direct sense perception at all. In this latter usage, *kiku* cooccurs with both factive and nonfactive paradigms (as discussed earlier). Since factive and nonfactive verbs do not place any restrictions on the tense of the embedded sentence, the past tense marker in particular can appear in the embedded proposition, as the following examples show:

(i) Factive.

Watakusi wa Matusita-san ga zisyoku sita koto o kiita.
I resigned heard
'I've heard about the fact that Mr. Matsushita resigned.'

(ii) Nonfactive.

Watakusi wa Matusita-san ga zisyoku sita to kiita.
'I've heard that Mr. Matsushita resigned (but is it true?)'

[19]According to Kuno (1973:220), from whom this example is taken, *kanziru* 'feel' can also occur with S *koto*. In such a case, *kanziru* would be more or less equivalent to English 'think': In other words, it would express a mental activity rather than actual sense perception.

f. *Kanozyo ga sono uta o utatte iru no ni kikiitta.*[20]
she that song is singing listened to
'I listened enraptured to her singing of the song.'

g. *Watakusi wa kodomotati ga asonde iru no o nagamete ita.*
I children are playing was watching
'I was watching the children playing.'

h. *Kare wa runpen ga kooen o sanpo site iru no o*
he hobo park is taking a walk
mikaketa.
caught sight of
'He caught sight of a hobo walking through the park.'

i. *Kanozyo wa takeyabu ga zawazawa suru no ni*
she bamboo thicket rustle
obieta.[21]
became frightened
'She became frightened at the sound of rustling in the bamboo thicket.'

In most of these examples the embedded sentence contains an action verb in the (present) progressive *-te iru* form. Therefore, it is understood that the event of the embedded proposition was perceived just as it was taking place—i.e., while it was in progress. For example, (19a) with progressive *oyoide iru* (lit.) 'is swimming' expresses rather vividly that the speaker-subject saw a particular part of the ongoing action of Hanako's swimming. By contrast, (19a) with nonprogressive *oyogu* (lit.) 'swim' lacks this vivid focus and implies, instead, that the speaker-subject saw the total event from start to finish.

Verbs of discovery, such as *mitukeru* 'discover, find, catch' and *tukamaeru* 'catch', involve direct visual perception of a simultaneously occurring event. These verbs impose upon the embedded proposition a connotation of 'action in progress' or 'imminent action' and, therefore, require that the embedded predicate be in the *-te iru* (progressive) form or the *-(y)oo to suru* (imminent) form, respectively. Interestingly enough, embedded predicates in the simple present tense form are ungrammatical or awkward when verbs of discovery

[20]The verb *kikiiru* 'listen intently to' takes S *no ni* rather than S *no o*. Here, the particle *ni* perhaps designates the GOAL of the action (see Kuno, 1973:96–100). Another verb with similar characteristics is *miiru* 'look intently at', as in the following:

Watakusi wa kanozyo ga odotte iru no ni miitta.
I she is dancing gazed at
'I gazed intently at her as she danced.'

[21]The verb *obieru*, which takes S *no ni*, is included with the verbs of sense perception because it describes a feeling of fright that develops while the stimulus itself is still being perceived. Thus, an appropriate English equivalent might be 'get frightened at the perception of'.

occur in the matrix sentence. Observe the following examples, in which *no*, but not *koto*, is grammatical:

(20) a. *Heya ni hairu to watakusi wa kodomo ga tabako o*
room enter I child cigarette
{*nonde iru* / *nomoo to suru* / ?**nomu*} *no o mituketa.*
{is smoking / about to smoke / (smoke)} discovered
'When I entered the room, I caught the child {smoking / about to smoke}.'

b. *Keisatu wa doroboo ga Hanako no saihu o*
police thief purse
{*totte iru* / *toroo to suru* / ?**toru*} *no o tukamaeta.*
{is stealing / about to steal / (steal)} caught
'The police caught a thief {just as he was stealing / as he was about to steal} Hanako's purse.'

With *-te iru* in the embedded sentence, the examples in (20) involve the discovery of some event just as it was taking place. However, with *-(y)oo to suru*, these very same examples indicate the discovery of an imminent event—i.e., one that was just about to take place and whose preliminary or preparatory stages were observed.[22]

[22]The verb *mitukeru* 'discover, find, catch' can also be used with S *koto*, but only in a factive interpretation. In such a case, *mitukeru* does not refer to direct visual perception but, instead, involves some kind of mental activity (usually inference). As expected, the embedded sentence does not necessarily have to indicate simultaneous time, nor are there any restrictions on the tense of its predicate. Note the following sentence:

Watakusi wa kodomo ga tabako o {*nomu* / *nonde ita*} *koto o mituketa.*
I child cigarette {smokes / was smoking} discovered
'I discovered (the fact) that the child {smokes / had been smoking} cigarettes.'

In this example, the speaker-subject is mentioning a fact that he discovered or inferred on the

Verbs of helping, such as *tetudau* 'help' and *tasukeru* 'help', involve a direct, immediate response to a simultaneously occurring event or state. In other words, the inherent semantic nature of these verbs is such that the time of helping must necessarily be cooccurrent with the time of the action or situation that requires the help. Predictably, S *no* is grammatical, while S *koto* is not:

(21) a. *Boku wa haha ga* {*sara o arau* / *tegami o taipu suru*} *no o tetudatte ageta.*
I Mother {wash the dishes / type the letter} helped
'I helped Mother {wash the dishes / type the letter}.'

b. *Boku wa kanozyo ga* {*komatte iru* / *booto ni noru*} *no o tasukete ageta.*
I she {is in trouble / get in the boat} helped
'I helped her {when she was in trouble / get in the boat}.'

Semantically, *tetudau* and *tasukeru* differ in the following significant way: While *tetudau* means helping by doing the same action as expressed in the embedded proposition, *tasukeru* means helping by doing some action other than that expressed in the embedded proposition. Thus, *tetudau* is appropriate in (21a) because *sara o arau* 'wash the dishes' and *tegami o taipu suru* 'type the letter' are activities in which both the matrix and embedded subjects can participate equally. By contrast, *tasukeru* is required in (21b) because *komatte iru* 'be in trouble' and *booto ni noru* 'get in the boat' do not allow equal participation: that is, one does not help someone in trouble by getting in trouble oneself, nor does one normally help someone get into a boat by getting into a boat oneself.[23]

---

basis of certain perceived evidence. It is entirely possible that he did not actually catch the child at a moment when the child was smoking; i.e., the time of the embedded proposition need not be simultaneous with that of the matrix predicate *mituketa.* Rather, he may have formed his conclusion on the basis of secondary evidence such as seeing cigarette butts in the wastebasket, smelling the smoke, and so forth.

[23]The above-mentioned observation about the semantic difference between *tetudau* and *tasukeru* is due to Kuno (personal communication). Kuno also notes the following syntactic difference between these two verbs. While *tasukeru* can also take S *tokoro o* [(a 'circumstantial' *tokoro* complement—Harada, 1973:114ff)], *tetudau* cannot. This suggests the possibility that complements cooccurring with *tasukeru* are adverbial in nature, while those accompanying *tetudau* are not. Further discussion of this problem will be given in Section 4.

Verbs of stopping describe a direct, immediate reaction to a simultaneously occurring or imminent event. The action designated by the verb of stopping invariably serves to cut off the forward progress or potential realization of the action expressed by the embedded proposition. Because verbs of stopping are instantaneous (i.e., the actions that they designate are momentary rather than durational), they normally occur only with embedded propositions that express a single, discrete event. The most frequently used member of this group is *tomeru* 'stop', which is illustrated in the following examples:

(22) a. *Sensei wa kodomo ga tabako o* {*sutte iru* / *suoo to suru*} *no o tometa.*
teacher child cigarette {is smoking / try to smoke} stopped
'The teacher stopped the child from {smoking / trying to smoke} the cigarette.'

b. *Keisatu wa gakusei ga demo ni sanka suru no o tometa.*
police student participate stopped
'The police stopped the students from participating in the demonstration.'

c. *Settoku site Hanako ga kaeru no o tometa.*
persuade-and return stopped
'I dissuaded Hanako from returning (home).'

Whether the action of stopping involves physical force, as is most likely in (22a) and (22b), or nonphysical force (e.g., persuasion), as in (22c), it cannot take place unless the stimulus is immediate and easily perceivable. For this reason, S *no*, but not S *koto*, is acceptable in the preceding examples.[24] Though the past tense marker is prevented in the embedded sentence, progressive *-te iru* and imminent *-(y)oo to suru* are compatible with the semantic features of *tomeru*, as the grammaticality of (22a) indicates.

Now, observe the following sentences, in which *tomeru* is used in the 'potential' form *tomerareru* 'can stop':

(23) a. *Gasutanku ga bakuhatu suru* {*no* / *(koto)*} *o tomerarenakatta.*
explode couldn't stop
'They couldn't stop the gas tanks from exploding.'

[24]Matsuo Soga reports (personal communication) that *koto* is acceptable to him in sentences like (22b–c). The reason for this may be that any action that is stopped or interrupted is not completely realized and, therefore, not directly perceivable—hence the possibility of *koto*. Compare the later discussion of verbs of ordering.

b. *Sono byooki ga hirogaru* {*no* / *(koto)*} *o tomerarenakatta.*
that disease spread couldn't stop
'They couldn't stop that disease from spreading.'

While most speakers use S *no* in (23a) and (23b), certain speakers also find S *koto* acceptable. This acceptability is undoubtedly due to the presence of the potential suffix *-rare-*, which changes the instantaneous action verb *tomeru* 'stop' into a (durative) state verb *tomerareru* 'can stop'. Because *tomerareru* lacks the strong implication of simultaneity and directness that *tomeru* itself has, ⟨indirect⟩ *koto* becomes possible as nominalizer, and the embedded sentence can designate either a repeated action, as in (23a), or an action of considerable duration, as in (23b). Needless to say, if the action of the embedded sentence is not repeatable, then *koto* is impossible, as the following pair of sentences shows:

(24) a. *Keisatu wa Taroo ga Ziroo o korosu no o tomerarenakatta.*
police kill couldn't stop
'The police couldn't stop Taro from killing Jiro.'

b. **Keisatu wa Taroo ga Ziroo o korosu koto o tomerarenakatta.*
'*The police couldn't stop Taro from (repeatedly) killing Jiro.'

The ungrammaticality of (24b) illustrates particularly clearly that the nature of the embedded proposition as a whole has a bearing on the acceptability of *koto* versus *no* as nominalizer. In other words, since the cooccurrence of S *koto* with *tomerareru* is not necessarily incompatible, as the sentences in (23) with *koto* prove, the inability of S *koto* to occur with *tomerareru* in (24b) can be due only to the content of the embedded proposition.[25]

Japanese has many verbs of stopping whose syntactic properties resemble those of *tomeru*. Thus, verbs such as the following require S *no* almost exclusively: *hurikiru* 'shake off, free oneself from (by force), pass off', *kuitomeru* 'check, hold, resist', *seisi suru* 'stop, check, control, hold back (a crowd), push back (with the hands)', *ukenagasu* 'ward off, elude (a question)', *saegiru* 'interrupt, stop', and *uketomeru* 'stop/catch (a blow) (restricted to fencing)'.

FUTURITIVE PREDICATES

As already noted, Japanese has a class of nonpresuppositional predicates whose object complements obligatorily contain the present tense marker in

[25]Kuno (1973) also presents some interesting examples that show 'that the relation between *koto* and *no* is controlled not only by verbs, adjectives, and nominal adjectives of the main sentences but also secondarily by the semantic content of the subordinate clause [p. 222].'

the meaning of future time and optionally include future tense adverbials [cf. (15)]. Such 'futuritive' predicates can be divided into two groups, depending on the type of cooccurring nominalizer. As we will see, there are no futuritive predicates that cooccur exclusively with S *no*; rather, there are some that require S *koto* only, and others that allow both S *no* and S *koto*, resulting in a predictable difference in meaning.

In (17a) and (17b), we have already seen examples of verbs of ordering (*meiziru* 'order') and verbs of request (*tanomu* 'ask'). Some further examples containing verbs from these classes follow:

(25) a. *Kare wa kanozyo ni zisyoku suru koto o yookyuu sita.*
he she resign demanded/requested
'He {demanded of / requested} her to resign.'

b. *Watakusi wa kare ni hoken ni hairu koto o kan'yuu sita.*
I he insurance enter encouraged
'I encouraged him to subscribe to insurance.'

c. *Boku wa Taroo ni konai to inoti wa nai zo to*
I if you don't come life not be
odokasite asita kuru koto o kyoosei sita. [26]
threaten-and tomorrow come forced
'Threatening Taro with his life if he didn't come, I gave him unconditional orders (*lit.* forced him) to come tomorrow.'

With verbs of ordering and request, such as those just given, S *koto* is required, while S *no* is totally ungrammatical. A plausible explanation for this phenomenon is offered by Kuno (1973), who says that the inability to use S *no* with verbs of ordering (and, presumably, verbs of request) 'might be due to the fact that actions ordered cannot yet be perceived by any of the five senses [p. 220].' In other words, at the time when an order is given or a request is made, the desired future event (i.e., that of the embedded

[26] While Japanese *kyoosei suru* allows future tense adverbials in the accompanying embedded sentence (as in this example), English *force* does not. Therefore, the following sentence is ungrammatical:

(i) **Yesterday I forced Mary to come tomorrow.*

Also, the Japanese and English sentences in the following are not exactly equivalent because of differences in implication:

(ii) *Taroo wa Ziroo ni kuru koto o kyoosei sita.*
'Taro forced Jiro to come.'

Kuno reports (personal communication) that while Japanese *kyoosei suru* in (ii) does not necessarily imply the truth of the embedded proposition, English *force* does.

proposition) is as yet unrealized. Since an unrealized event is neither simultaneous nor directly perceivable, occurrence of ⟨direct⟩ *no* is completely ruled out, while ⟨indirect⟩ *koto* is acceptable.[27]

Sentences with verbs of ordering and request may or may not have an indirect object NP *ni* phrase in the surface structure, as the following examples indicate:

(26) a. *Watakusi wa Ziroo ga yoku hataraku koto o meizita.*
I well work ordered
'I ordered that Jiro work diligently.'

b. *Watakusi wa Ziroo ni yoku hataraku koto o meizita.*
'I ordered Jiro to work diligently.'

Although a sentence like (26a), which lacks NP *ni*, describes an order about what Jiro should do, it is not necessarily an order directly given to Jiro; i.e., it is entirely possible that the influence or agency of some unspecified intermediate party is being solicited. By contrast, a sentence like (26b), which contains NP *ni*, describes an order directly received by Jiro (most likely verbally). As the English equivalents show, the English verb *order* participates in identical paradigm types.

Verbs of proposal and advice are similar to verbs of ordering and request in that S *koto*, but not S *no*, is grammatical. Here, too, S *no* is apparently prevented because a proposed or suggested action is as yet unrealized, and therefore not directly perceivable, at the time when the proposal is made, the advice given, etc. Some verbs of proposal and advice [other than *kankoku suru* 'advise'; see (17c)] are used in the following sentences:

(27) a. *Sihainin wa raisyuu no nitiyoobi ni kooba o heisa suru*
manager next week Sunday factory close
koto o {*teian* / *sisa*} *sita.*
proposed
'The manager proposed to close the factory next Sunday.'

b. *Watakusi wa kare ni sono kurabu ni hairu koto o susumeta.*
I he that club enter advised
'I advised him to join that club.'

Whereas the futuritive verbs discussed so far allow only S *koto*, verbs of prevention occur with both S *no* and S *koto*, resulting in a subtle, but not unexpected, difference in meaning. Although the verbs in this group invari-

[27]It should be noted that verbs of ordering and request can also occur with predicate complements of the form S *yoo ni*, with no apparent difference in meaning. Some verbs of advice (e.g., *susumeru* 'advise') likewise take both S *koto o* and S *yoo ni*. As expected, the embedded sentence preceding *yoo ni* must contain the present tense marker in the meaning of future time. Further discussion of *yoo ni* will be given in Section 6.

ably impose upon the embedded proposition the connotation of 'future event', they are 'noncommittal' with respect to such factors as the likelihood of the event or its exact point in time. For this reason, they are compatible with either S *no* or S *koto*, with the following meaning difference. When a verb of prevention cooccurs with ⟨direct⟩ *no*, the need to prevent the action or event of the embedded proposition is considered to be urgent or immediate—in other words, the speaker has a strong conviction or belief that the event is likely to occur in the very near future. With ⟨indirect⟩ *koto*, however, the sense of urgency or immediacy is absent, and instead, the speaker has a weaker conviction about the likelihood of the future event, which is viewed as a relatively distant occurrence against which precautions might be considered.

As a typical example of this contrast, observe the following sentence with *boosi suru* 'prevent':

(28) *Hanzai ga syoorai okoru* {*no* / *koto*} *o boosi sinakereba narimasen.*
crime future arise must prevent
'We've got to prevent crime from occurring in the future.'

Though undistinguished in the English translation, (28) with S *no* versus S *koto* involves the following difference in connotation: With S *no* the speaker feels that the situation is urgent and that crime is likely to occur, but with S *koto* there is less urgency and time still remains for taking precautions.

In a sentence like the following, *no* is grammatical while *koto* is not:

(29) *Daigaku ni tuku to keisatu wa gakusei ga sono tatemono ni*
university arrive police student that building
hairoo to suru no o boosi site imasita.
about to enter were preventing
'When I arrived at the university, the police were preventing the students from entering the building.'

Here, the semantic content of the embedded proposition influences the choice of nominalizer. Thus, the imminent quality of the embedded predicate *hairoo to suru* 'about to enter' is compatible with ⟨direct⟩ *no* but not with ⟨indirect⟩ *koto*.[28] In a similar way, an embedded proposition

[28]An embedded predicate in -(*y*)*oo to suru* can cooccur with *koto*, however, if it is part of a general statement. In such cases, *koto* is required because general statements necessarily involve abstract concepts:

Egetu nai hoohoo de hito o dasinukoo to suru koto wa yoku nai.
low-handed method person try to outdo isn't good
'It's not right to try to get the better of people by using under-handed methods.'

expressing a violent, abrupt action allows only ⟨direct⟩ *no* as nominalizer, presumably because any accompanying act of prevention would have to be immediate and undelayed. Observe, therefore, the following examples with *husegu* 'prevent, ward off':

(30) a. *Mitiko wa doroboo ga osotte kuru no o huseida.*
robber accost warded off
'Michiko warded off the robber's attack.'
b. *Kumiko wa te kara handobakku o hittakuru no o huseida.*
hand from snatch warded off
'Kumiko warded off an attempt to snatch her handbag.'

Many other verbs of prevention allow both S *no* and S *koto* in object position, with the above-mentioned difference in meaning. Thus, similar phenomena can be observed for *zyama suru* 'hinder', *boogai suru* 'disturb, interrupt, interfere', *sosi suru* 'hinder, prevent, retard', and *samatageru* 'disturb, preclude'.

The now-familiar distinction between S *no* and S *koto* is also observed with another group of futuritive predicates—namely, verbs of expectation. Thus, with respect to an example like (31):

(31) *Watakusi wa Ziroo ga kuru* $\left\{\begin{array}{l}\textit{koto}\\ \textit{no}\end{array}\right\}$ *o kitai site ita.*
I come was expecting
'I was expecting Jiro to come.'

Kuno (1973) comments as follows:

> ... [Given (31) with *koto* versus *no*.] it seems to be the case that the latter represents a stronger conviction on the part of the [speaker-] subject that [Jiro] would come. This might be due, again, to the fact that *no* represents a concrete action, state, or event directly perceived by any of five (or six) senses, while *koto* represents a more abstract concept [p. 221].

In an example like the following, the semantic content of the embedded sentence seems to influence the choice of nominalizer:

(32) *Watakusi wa kanozyo ga syoorai erai gakusya ni naru* $\left\{\begin{array}{l}\textit{?no}\\ \textit{koto}\end{array}\right\}$ *o*
I she future great scholar become
kitai site imasu.
am expecting
'I expect that she'll become a great scholar in the future.'

Here, *koto* is preferred by most speakers because the embedded sentence designates a relatively abstract process—*erai gakusya ni naru* 'become a great scholar'—which requires a long period of time for completion. In other words, ⟨indirect⟩ *koto* is more suitable than ⟨direct⟩ *no* in this example because the 'event' of the embedded proposition is rather remote and not directly perceivable by the senses.[29]

Verbs of expectation, like those of ordering and request, may or may not occur with an indirect object NP *ni* phrase in the surface structure. Thus, contrast the following with (32):

(33) *Watakusi wa kanozyo ni syoorai erai gakusya ni naru* {*koto* / **no*} *o*
kitai site imasu.
'I have faith in her to become a great scholar in the future.'

While (32) simply describes, in a fairly neutral way, the expectation that some situation will obtain, (33) has a special connotation. In (33), the person designated by the indirect object noun phrase (i.e., *kanozyo* 'she') is being especially relied upon or depended upon to achieve the action of the embedded proposition. Interestingly enough, use of *no* is totally unacceptable in (33). That this phenomenon is related to the presence of NP *ni* is confirmed by a further example [cf. (31)]:

(34) *Watakusi wa Ziroo ni kuru* {*koto* / **no*} *o kitai site ita.*
I come was expecting
'I was relying on Jiro to come.'

The ungrammaticality of ⟨direct⟩ *no* in (33–34) might possibly be due to the fact that the action or process of the embedded sentence is being regarded

[29]Compare the following examples, in which *koto* is required as nominalizer because the embedded proposition is an abstract concept rather than a concrete event:

(i) *Nihon ga minsyusyugi no daidoo o ayumu* {*koto* / **no*} *o kitai site imasu.*
Japan democracy great road follow are expecting.
'We are expecting/hoping that Japan will follow the great path of democracy.'

(ii) *Wareware wa syoorai Nihon ga daiittookoku ni naru* {*koto* / **no*} *o kitai*
we future Japan first-class country become are
site iru no de arimasu.
expecting
'We are hoping that in the future Japan will become a first-class nation.'

as a kind of obligation which the indirect object NP must fulfil; as such, this action or process would be viewed abstractly and would, therefore, be incapable of any immediate or direct perception.

Since other verbs of expectation (e.g., *tanosimi ni site iru* 'look forward to', *matu* 'wait', and *inoru* 'pray, hope') can take either S *no* or S *koto* with the same contrast in meaning, no further examples will be given here. A few verbs of expectation (e.g., *kokorozasu* 'plan', *osoreru* 'fear', and *yume miru* 'fancy') tend to be used more frequently with ⟨indirect⟩ *koto* than with ⟨direct⟩ *no*, apparently because they impose upon the accompanying proposition connotations such as 'hard-to-attain goal', 'imagined event', and so on.

Verbs of prediction can occur with either S *no* or S *koto*, but there is considerable variation among speakers as to the consequences of using one nominalizer or the other. For some speakers, the expected difference in meaning arising from the contrast between ⟨direct⟩ *no* and ⟨indirect⟩ *koto* is observed, but for others it is absent. For speakers in the latter category, the use of *no* versus *koto* seems to reflect nothing more than a difference of style: Thus, *no* is used in rather informal conversation, while *koto* is appropriate to formal speech or writing. Some typical examples of verbs of prediction are *yogen suru* 'predict', *yoti suru* 'predict, foretell', *yoki suru* 'forecast, contemplate', and *yokoku suru* 'give advance notice'.[30]

Factive Predicates

We have seen in Section 3 that the distribution of *no* and *koto* depends on compatibility between the semantic features of these nominalizers and the semantic features of cooccurring nonpresuppositional predicates. Occasionally, too, the semantic features of the embedded sentence as a whole influence the choice of nominalizer. Here, we will examine various groups of 'factive' predicates and discover that they support the hypothesis that *no* and *koto* are distinguished by the inherent semantic features ⟨direct⟩ and ⟨indirect⟩, respectively. As with the futuritive predicates treated earlier, factive predicates can be divided into two groups according to the type of cooccurring nominalizer. Thus, we will see that some factive predicates take S *koto* exclusively, while others allow either S *no* or S *koto*, with a predictable difference in meaning.

Factive verbs designating certain types of mental activity, such as deduction, thinking, and learning, require S *koto* exclusively. The obligatory

[30]Some sample sentences containing these verbs of prediction are given in Josephs (1972a: 86–88).

occurrence of ⟨indirect⟩ *koto* is undoubtedly due to the fact that these verbs impose upon the embedded proposition the connotation of 'abstract concept'. In other words, the processes of deduction, thinking, and learning involve the formulation of abstract ideas, which can be manipulated in the mind but not directly perceived by the senses.

A typical verb of deduction—*suitei suru* 'infer, deduce'—is illustrated in the following example:

(35) *Taroo wa Ziroo ga sensei o korosita koto o tadasiku suitei sita.*
teacher killed correctly inferred
'Taro inferred, correctly, that Jiro killed the teacher.'

Because *suitei suru* is used here as a factive verb,[31] the speaker presupposes that the embedded proposition is a fact and then goes on to assert that the subject of the sentence (*Taroo*) correctly inferred this fact. The embedded sentence can contain the past tense marker because factive verbs place no restrictions on the tense of the accompanying proposition. Some additional verbs of deduction that take S *koto* object complements are *suiri suru* 'infer, deduce', *suiron suru* 'infer, deduce (in a formal way—e.g., using syllogisms, arguments, etc.)', *suisatu suru* 'guess', and *suisoku suru* 'guess'.

Since a verb of thinking like *kangaeru* 'think about, consider' always imposes on the accompanying proposition the connotation of 'abstract concept',[32] it is natural that only *koto* occurs as nominalizer:

[31]This verb (and other verbs of deduction as well) can also occur in a nonfactive paradigm with S *to*. For many speakers, this nonfactive use is more common than the factive one. Thus, with (35) compare the following:

Taroo wa Ziroo ga sensei o korosita to suitei sita.
'Taro inferred that Jiro killed the teacher (but his inference may have been wrong).'

[32]Even when the object of *kangaeru* 'think about, consider' is not sentential, it must be abstract, as the ungrammaticality of (ii) indicates:

(i) {*Kanozyo no koto* / *Sono koto*} *o kangaeta.*
{things about her / that fact} thought about
'I thought about {her / that (fact)}.'

(ii) *{*Kanozyo* / *Sore*} *o kangaeta*
{she / that} thought about

(36) *Otukisan ni roketto ga tuita koto o kangaete (mo) goran.*
moon landed just try to imagine
'Just think about the fact that a rocket has landed on the moon!'

Although the embedded proposition of (36)—*otukisan ni roketto ga tuita* 'a rocket landed on the moon'—could be construed as a concrete event in other contexts (e.g., when spoken in isolation), it must be understood as an abstract concept in (36) because of the presence of *kangaeru.*

In a similar way, verbs of learning, such as *narau* 'learn' and *manabu* 'learn', take S *koto* exclusively. This is because the accompanying proposition expresses an abstract concept which comes to be known rather indirectly—e.g., through experience, through understanding what someone has said, etc. Observe, therefore, the following examples:

(37) a. *Kodomotati wa Koronbusu ga Amerikatairiku o*
children American continent
hakken sita koto o naratta.
discovered learned
'The children learned that Columbus discovered America.'

b. *Watakusi wa Nihongo ga muzukasii koto o mananda.*
I Japanese difficult learned
'I learned that Japanese is a difficult language.'

Whereas verbs of deduction, thinking, and learning require S *koto* exclusively, as observed earlier, certain other factive verbs of mental activity—namely, verbs of understanding and realization—allow both S *no* and S *koto*. The resulting difference in meaning is consistent with the inherent semantic distinction between ⟨direct⟩ *no* and ⟨indirect⟩ *koto*. Verbs of understanding and realization are compatible with either of the two nominalizers because the types of mental activity they designate can themselves be direct or indirect. Thus, one's understanding or realization of something is 'indirect' if it is achieved through deliberation, inference, or any type of mental process that takes place over a period of time. By contrast, understanding or realization is 'direct' if it comes to one immediately upon exposure to the stimulus; deliberation, thinking, and so on are not necessary, and instead, understanding is achieved through intuition (a kind of sixth sense).

In the following examples we observe object complements accompanying three common verbs of understanding and realization—*wakaru* 'understand, come to know', *siru* 'come to know',[33] and *satoru* 'understand':

[33]The verb *siru* 'come to know' can be used with S *to* in certain contexts. See Kuno (1973: 217–218) for some comments on this problematical matter.

(38) a. *Kanozyo wa sono kutiburi kara keikaku ga umaku itte inai*
she that way of speaking from plan isn't going well
$\left\{\begin{matrix} \textit{koto} \\ \textit{no} \end{matrix}\right\} \left\{\begin{matrix} \textit{ga wakatta} \\ \textit{o sitta} \end{matrix}\right\}.$
$\left\{\begin{matrix} \text{understood} \\ \text{came to know} \end{matrix}\right\}$
'From the way he spoke, she understood that the plan wasn't going well.'

b. *Tanaka-san to hanasite miru to kare wa kuni ga maketa*
when he spoke he country lost
$\left\{\begin{matrix} \textit{koto} \\ \textit{no} \end{matrix}\right\}$ *o satotta.*
understood
'When he talked with Mr. Tanaka, he perceived, correctly, that the country had been defeated.'

In (38a) and (38b) with *koto*, the subject of the sentence came to know the information of the embedded proposition INDIRECTLY—i.e., as a result of analyzing and thinking about the actual content of the interlocutor's words. In the very same sentences with *no*, however, the subject came to know the information more DIRECTLY and with less thinking—e.g., by feeling or sensing, on the basis of some observable signs (the interlocutor's tone of voice, mannerisms, etc.), that something was wrong.

In sentences containing verbs of understanding and realization, certain contextual elements can determine the appropriateness of one or the other nominalizer. Consider the following example:

(39) *Yoku kangaeru to zibun ga matigaeta* $\left\{\begin{matrix} \textit{koto} \\ \textit{?no} \end{matrix}\right\}$ *ga wakatta.*
well think myself erred understood
'When I thought about it carefully, I realized that I had made a mistake.'

The awkwardness of ⟨direct⟩ *no* in (39) appears to be caused by the presence of the introductory clause *yoku kangaeru to* 'when I thought about it carefully', which makes it clear that the understanding involved is 'indirect'—i.e., the result of some type of mental deliberation.

Factive verbs designating various types of emotional response (e.g., surprise, shock, fright, annoyance, embarrassment) to an event or state are compatible with both S *no* and S *koto*. Observe, for example, the following sentences with *heikoo suru* 'be annoyed/bored/embarrassed/nonplused by', which takes S$\left\{\begin{matrix} \textit{no} \\ \textit{koto} \end{matrix}\right\}$ *ni (wa)*:

(40) a. *Kanozyo ga watto nakidasita* {*no* / **koto*} *ni wa heikoo sita.*
she burst out crying was embarrassed
'I was embarrassed that she burst into tears.'

b. *Kare ga anmari teinei ni hanasita* {*no* / **koto*} *ni wa heikoo sita.*
he too politely spoke was at a loss
'I was at a loss because he spoke so politely.'

(41) a. *Kanozyo ga watto nakidasita* {*koto* / *no*} *ni wa heikoo site iru.*
am annoyed
'I'm annoyed that she burst into tears.'

b. *Kare ga anmari teinei ni hanasita* {*koto* / *no*} *ni wa heikoo site iru.*
'I'm (still) annoyed that he spoke so politely.'

When *heikoo suru* is used in the past tense, as in (40a) and (40b), it portrays a quick, relatively instantaneous response to a directly experienced event: Therefore, only ⟨direct⟩ *no* can serve as nominalizer. However, when *heikoo suru* is used in the present progressive form, as in (41a) and (41b), it designates a delayed response—i.e., a continuing emotional state that is not instantaneous and is separated from the stimulus event by a considerable duration of time. For this reason, ⟨indirect⟩ *koto* becomes acceptable, if not even preferred, in these sentences.[34]

In the following sentences we observe further factive verbs of emotional response. If the verb is in the past tense, it represents an instantaneous reaction to a directly experienced event; therefore, the accompanying embedded sentence must be nominalized with *no* [cf. (40a) and (40b)]. If, however, the verb is in the present tense, it represents a durative state that

[34]Note also the following example, in which the embedded predicate is in the present tense form:

Koogi ga anmari nagai {*koto* / *no*} *ni wa minna heikoo site iru.*
lecture too long everyone is annoyed
'Everyone's annoyed that the {lectures are / lecture is} so long.'

With *koto*, the embedded proposition is construed as a habitually occurring event, but with *no* the speaker is focusing vividly on a single event that everyone is in the throes of experiencing.

is separated from the stimulus event, and, therefore, the cooccurring embedded sentence can also be nominalized with *koto* [cf. (41a) and (41b)]:

(42) a. *Kare ga biiru o zyuppon mo nonda* {*no* / **koto*} *ni wa*
he beer ten bottles drank
{*odoroita* / *akireta*}.
{was shocked / was taken aback}
'I was {shocked / taken aback} by his having drunk all of ten bottles of beer.'

b. *Sensei wa kare ga kirei na Oosakaben de* {*hanasita* / *hanaseru*} {*no* / **koto*}
teacher he pretty Osaka dialect {spoke / can speak}
ni wa bikkuri sita.
was surprised
'The teacher was amazed that he {spoke / could speak} a good Osaka dialect.'

c. *Kanozyo ni kekkon site kure to iwareta* {*no* / **koto*} *ni wa*
she 'marry me!' was told
{*maitta* / *yowatta*} *nee.*
was nonplused
'It was quite a thing, wasn't it, to have her say to me, "Marry me!"'

d. *Ano okusan ga akanboo o nakasete ita* {*koto* / *no*} *ni wa gaman*
that wife baby was letting cry can't
dekimasen.
stand
'I can't stand it how that woman just let her child keep crying.'

e. *Hanako-san ga okurete kuru* {*koto* / *?no*} *wa gaman dekimasen.*
come late can't stand
'I can't stand Hanako's (always) coming late.'

Summary: The Lexical Items *Koto* and *No*

The complexities of distribution exhibited by the nominalizers *no* and *koto* cannot be plausibly accounted for unless we assume, as we have in the preceding sections, that we are dealing with two independent lexical items with very distinct meanings. For this reason, ⟨direct⟩ *no* and ⟨indirect⟩ *koto* cannot be related to each other transformationally, nor can transformations be used to introduce them into sentences. As Nakau proposed (1973:104–109), they must be analyzed as deep structure elements—i.e., as lexical items that can occupy the position of head noun in various noun complement structures.

The nominalizers *no* and *koto* are characterized, respectively, by the inherent semantic features ⟨direct⟩ and ⟨indirect⟩. The very same semantic features are inherent to predicates as well. Thus, verbs of sense perception (*miru* 'see'), helping (*tetudau* 'help'), and so on are marked in the lexicon with the feature ⟨direct⟩; verbs of ordering (*meiziru* 'order'), thinking (*kangaeru* 'think about'), and the like contain the feature ⟨indirect⟩; and verbs of prevention (*boosi suru* 'prevent'), expectation (*kitai suru* 'expect'), etc., can be either ⟨direct⟩ or ⟨indirect⟩.[35] Embedded sentences as a whole can also be assigned either of these two features, depending on the type of proposition they contain. The distribution of the nominalizers *no* and *koto* is determined by a principle of semantic compatibility which states that cooccurring nominalizers, predicates, and embedded sentences must have matching features—i.e., they must all be either ⟨direct⟩ or ⟨indirect⟩.

Because the features ⟨direct⟩ and ⟨indirect⟩ are inherent and basic to the nominalizers *no* and *koto*, respectively, they effectuate the same contrast in meaning regardless of whether the cooccurring predicate is factive or nonpresuppositional. In other words, the contrast between 'directly perceived, simultaneously occurring event' and 'nonsimultaneous, nonrealized, or abstractly perceived event, state, etc.' is maintained with both ⟨factive⟩ and ⟨nonpresuppositional⟩ predicates. Whereas predicates will be marked in the

[35] If we follow Weinreich (1963) and the arguments offered in favor of Weinreich's position in McCawley (1968a), we would define a 'lexical item' as:

> ... the combination of a single semantic reading with a single underlying phonological shape, a single syntactic category, and a single set of specifications of exceptional behavior with respect to rules. Under this conception of "lexical item", ... there would simply be four lexical items pronounced *bachelor* rather than a single four-ways ambiguous lexical item [McCawley, 1968a:125ff].

Accepting this definition, we would have to view a verb like *boosi suru* 'prevent' as two lexical items, one containing the feature ⟨direct⟩ and cooccurring with *no*, and the other containing the feature ⟨indirect⟩ and cooccurring with *koto*.

lexicon for inherent presuppositional and implicational features (i.e., for semantic features such as ⟨factive⟩ and ⟨nonpresuppositional⟩), the nominalizers *no* and *koto* will not. In some sense, however, *no* and *koto* seem to acquire such features from the cooccurring predicate. Thus, when the feature ⟨factive⟩ is 'read onto' either *no* or *koto*, these lexical items take on the specific meaning 'fact'—i.e., we have:

(43)	*no* ⟨direct⟩, ⟨factive⟩	'directly perceived fact'
	koto ⟨indirect⟩, ⟨factive⟩	'abstractly perceived fact'

On the other hand, when the feature ⟨nonpresuppositional⟩ is imposed upon either *no* or *koto*, these nominalizers function like the (semantically empty) English complementizers (*for* ...) *to* or *-ing*—i.e., we have:

(44)	*no* ⟨direct⟩, ⟨nonpresuppositional⟩	'directly perceived, simultaneously occurring event, etc.'
	koto ⟨indirect⟩, ⟨nonpresuppositional⟩	'abstractly perceived, nonsimultaneous event, etc.'

The semantic complexities exhibited by the nominalizers *no* and *koto* are not exhausted by the rough approximations given in (43) and (44). Thus, as we will see in Section 5, both *no* and *koto* can be preceded by S *to yuu* (i.e., an embedded sentence and the noun complementizer), in which case they take on a connotation that resembles that of the nonfactive paradigm.[36]

4. THE SYNTACTIC STATUS OF *TOKORO* COMPLEMENTS

At first glance, it would appear that embedded propositions nominalized with *tokoro* 'place, point in time' are to be analyzed as the direct objects of the sentences in which they occur. Such *tokoro* complements, which are

[36]Since my purpose has been to bring out the basic difference between *no* and *koto* in the clearest possible manner, I have concentrated on a relatively small number of the grammatical constructions in which these nominalizers are actually observed to occur. A complete analysis of all such constructions, though necessary for testing the ultimate validity of my hypothesis about *no* versus *koto*, would go far beyond the scope of this study; therefore, no additional data will be given here. For a summary of constructions with *no* and *koto* that require further study, see Josephs (1972a:106–115).

invariably followed by the object-marking postposition *o*, would presumably function just like *no* or *koto* complements in object position. Thus, in analyzing sentences like the following:

(45) *Keikan ga Taroo ga Ziroo to kenka site iru tokoro o tukamaeta.*
policeman is quarreling caught
'A policeman caught Taro quarreling with Jiro.'

Nakau (1973) specifically rules out the possibility that they 'may be derived from underlying forms which have as higher object a Noun Phrase identical to the complement subject [p. 70, n. 10].' In other words, Nakau does not accept the following deep structure for (45):

(46) *Keikan ga Taroo*$_i$ *o* [*Taroo*$_i$ *ga Ziroo to kenka site iru*]$_S$ *tokoro o tukamaeta.*

and presumably S *tokoro o* is the deep structure object of the (transitive) predicate *tukamaeru* 'catch'.

Harada (1973) shows that there is considerable evidence for rejecting Nakau's (implicit) 'no extra NP analysis' in favor of an analysis that, indeed, posits deep structures like (46) for sentences containing *tokoro* complements. Acceptance of deep structures like (46) involves the claim that the real direct object of *tukamaeru* 'catch' is the human NP *Taroo o* and that S *tokoro o* is not a (deep structure) direct object at all but, rather, a type of adverbial. Very convincing evidence for the adverbial nature of S *tokoro o* is found in the fact that such complements occur in intransitive sentences, in which case they could not possibly be analyzed as direct objects. This phenomenon is observed in examples like the following:

(47) a. *Taroo wa kanningu o site iru tokoro o sensei ni mitukatta.*[37]
is cheating teacher was found
'Taro was caught cheating by the teacher.'

b. *Oisogasii tokoro o wazawaza okosikudasaimasite arigatoo gozaimasita.*
busy on purpose come-and thank you
'Thank you very much for making an effort to come at a time when you are busy.'

c. *Benkyoo siyoo to suru tokoro o okyakusan ni korareta.*
about to study guest had...arrive
'I had the misfortune of having guests arrive just as I was about to study.'

[37]This example is borrowed from Harada (1973:122).

As Harada claims (1973:122–123), the no extra NP analysis is unable to account for the examples of (47) in a principled way because of its implicit assumption that S *tokoro o* must be a direct object. The fact that S *tokoro o* appears to be a direct object in the surface structure, Harada concludes, does not necessarily imply that it is a direct object in the deep structure: Indeed, S *tokoro o* is a deep structure adverbial, and the postposition *o* that follows it is not the *o* of object marking but a homonymous *o* of different origin.[38]

In a structure like (46) the direct object of the matrix sentence must be identical to the subject of the embedded sentence preceding *tokoro o*. Because of this identity condition, which depends, of course, on the presence of the extra NP, Harada's (but not Nakau's) analysis can account for the ungrammaticality of a sentence like the following (borrowed from Harada):

(48) **Keisatu wa ame ga hutte iru tokoro o tukamaeta.*
police rain is falling caught
'*The police caught the rain (while it was) falling.'

In Harada's analysis, (48) would have to be derived from the deep structure in (49), namely:

(49) **Keisatu wa* ame_i *o* $[ame_i$ *ga hutte iru*$]_S$ *tokoro o tukamaeta.*

by applying the rule of 'counter equi-NP deletion' (to be discussed) to delete the NP *ame (o)* of the matrix sentence. But the deep structure in (49) would itself be ill-formed because a selectional restriction is violated: The transitive predicate *tukamaeru* 'catch' requires a human direct object, whereas the co-occurring direct object of (49) is inanimate *ame* 'rain'. Therefore, in Harada's analysis, the ungrammatical sentence (48) could never be generated simply because its source—i.e., (49)—could not be generated either, owing to the violation of a selectional restriction that holds between the matrix predicate and its object. For Nakau's no extra NP analysis, however, accounting for the ungrammaticality of (48) would necessitate a problematical modification of the theory of selectional restriction, since the absence of a matrix direct object would require that the selectional restriction in question be stated as

[38]See Harada (1973: 142–143, n. 14) for additional discussion on the possible origin of the *o* of S *tokoro o*. The very same *o* is probably found in S *saityuu o* 'in the midst of', which occurs in the following intransitive sentence [from Makino (1970:114)]:

Ame ga hagesiku huru saityuu {*o* / *ni*} *Taroo wa kaetta.*
rain violently fall midst returned
'Taro returned in the midst of the violent rainstorm.'

a relationship between the matrix predicate (*tukamaeru* 'catch') and the embedded sentence *subject* (*ame* 'rain'). The difficulty here is that:

> While there are cases in which a matrix ... verb imposes a selectional restriction on the complement ... *verb* (e.g., *force* requires its complement ... verb to be a self-controllable verb), there is no known case of a matrix ... verb imposing a restriction on an NP in its complement [Harada, 1973:125].

In accepting (46) as the correct deep structure of (45), Harada finds it necessary to posit a transformational rule of equi-NP deletion which operates in a manner opposite from that of 'traditional' equi-NP rules—that is, we need a 'counter equi-NP deletion' rule that deletes a MATRIX SENTENCE NP under identity with the subject NP of the COMPLEMENT SENTENCE.[39] As we have seen, some of the crucial evidence for proposing such a rule comes from sentences containing *tokoro* complements.[40]

THE MEANING CONTRAST BETWEEN *Tokoro* AND *No*

The nominalizer *tokoro* requires special attention because it contrasts (at least in the surface structure) with the nominalizer *no*. Thus, as we will see, S *tokoro o* cooccurs with many of those same predicates which were described in Section 3 as taking S *no o* but not S *koto o*. Specifically, S *tokoro o* appears regularly in sentences containing nonpresuppositional, nonfuturitive predicates, i.e., verbs of sense perception, discovery, helping, and stopping. It is difficult to ascertain whether any or all of the instances of S *no o* examined in Section 3 are to be analyzed like S *tokoro o*, that is, as deep structure adverbials. Although a preliminary investigation indicates that some of Harada's arguments for proving that S *tokoro o* is an underlying adverbial seem to apply to sentences containing S *no o* as well, much additional research will be necessary before this question can be adequately answered.

Leaving aside the question of whether object complements of the form S *no o* are actually deep structure adverbials like S *tokoro o*, we will now concentrate our attention on the meaning difference that the two nominalizers *tokoro* and *no* effectuate in the surface structure. Harada (1973) is essentially correct in identifying *tokoro* complements as 'circumstantial', that is, as referring to 'a physically perceptible state of affairs which indicates the situation in which the event referred to by the matrix sentence takes place [pp. 114–115].' Thus, *tokoro* complements describe the circumstances that serve as the situational backdrop or context for another event. This function is clearly seen in the following sentences, in which the *tokoro* complement

[39]For a discussion of the conditions of applicability of this rule, see Harada (1973:136–140).

[40]Further evidence to support the existence of such a rule—namely, the phenomena of clefting and passivization in sentences containing *tokoro* complements—is given in Harada (1973:117–122).

denotes a completed event that provides the background for the matrix sentence event:[41]

(50) a. *Doroboo wa Hanako ga yudan sita tokoro o osotta.*
thief relaxed attention attacked
'The thief attacked Hanako the instant she relaxed her attention.'

b. *Taroo wa Hanako ga tyoodo gaisyutu sita tokoro o*
just went out
kanozyo no ofisu o tazuneta.
she visited
'Taro visited Hanako's office at the very moment when she had gone out.'

In addition to supplying the situational backdrop for the accompanying matrix sentence event, the *tokoro* complements of (50) place special emphasis on the circumstantial cooccurrence or juxtaposition of the two events. Thus, in (50a), the event of the matrix sentence (the thief's attacking Hanako) took place as an immediate consequence of the embedded sentence event (Hanako's relaxing her attention), i.e., at the very moment after the embedded sentence event was completed. And, in (50b), the matrix sentence event (Taro's coming to Hanako's office) just happened to occur at the same moment as the embedded sentence event (Hanako's leaving the office). From these examples, then, it is clear that the nominalizer *tokoro* means something like 'moment' or 'instant'. This word also functions as an independently occurring noun meaning 'place' or 'location'. Evidently, the more basic function of *tokoro*—namely, to refer to a location in physical space—has been extended to cover the concept of '(precise) location in time'.

Because *tokoro* means 'moment' or 'instant', it can nominalize propositions denoting simultaneously occurring or imminent events. In this respect, it is similar to the nominalizer *no*, which was observed in Section 3 to occur with propositions of the same type. As a result of this overlap in function, S *tokoro o* can be found in some of the same environments as S *no o*—in particular, in sentences whose predicates are characterized by the semantic features ⟨direct⟩ and ⟨nonpresuppositional⟩ (i.e., verbs of sense perception, discovery, helping, and stopping).[42] Although *tokoro* and *no* would appear

[41]These examples are adapted from Harada (1973).

[42]S *tokoro o* cannot occur with most of the classes of futuritive predicates (see Section 3). This is evidently due to the fact that *tokoro* complements, which designate a situational backdrop in terms of a past, present, or imminent event or state, are semantically incompatible with futuritive predicates, which impose upon the cooccurring complement a connotation of 'unrealized, unperceivable future event'. In addition, S *tokoro o* is prevented with all factive predicates of mental activity and emotional response (see Section 3).

to be interchangeable in many cases, careful examination of the data shows that they indeed result in a subtle difference in meaning.

In the following examples both *tokoro* and *no* cooccur with the verb of sense perception *miru* 'see':

(51) a. *Satiko ga mukoogisi kara kotira made oyogu tokoro o*
opposite side from here up to swim
mita.
saw
'I saw Sachiko just as she was {swimming / about to swim} from the other side to here.'

b. *Satiko ga mukoogisi kara kotira made oyogu no o mita.*
'I saw Sachiko swim from the other side to here.'

As we might expect, *tokoro* 'moment, instant' in (51a) puts vivid focus on the (unusual or interesting) coincidence of the matrix sentence and embedded sentence events; i.e., the subject happened to perceive the embedded sentence event just as it was in progress or about to begin. By contrast, *no* in (51b) does not emphasize the coincidental nature of the two events, nor does it pinpoint an instant in time when the embedded sentence event was in progress or imminent. For this reason, (51b) merely states, in a rather neutral way, that the subject observed the TOTAL EVENT of the embedded proposition.

A rather similar contrast in meaning is found in the following pair, in which the nominalizers *tokoro* and *no* cooccur with the verb of discovery *tukamaeru* 'catch':

(52) a. *Keisatu wa doroboo ga Hanako no saihu o nukitoroo to suru*
police thief purse about to take
tokoro o tukamaeta.
caught
'The police caught the thief at the very instant he was taking Hanako's purse.'

b. *Keisatu wa doroboo ga Hanako no saihu o nukitoroo to suru no o tukamaeta.*
'The police caught the thief when he was trying to take Hanako's purse.'

While (52a) with S *tokoro o* implies that the police happened to discover and catch the thief at the exact moment when he was putting his hands on Hanako's purse, (52b) with S *no o* does not involve such a precise coincidence of events. Thus, (52b) simply states that the police caught the thief at some point during his attempt to steal Hanako's purse: It is entirely possible that they arrested him before he actually touched the purse (e.g., while he was making suspicious movements, etc.).

Because sentences with S *tokoro o* focus on a single instant or moment when two events coincide, the matrix sentence predicate must designate an action that is either instantaneous or of relatively short duration. Thus, compare the following examples, which contain the verb of helping *tasukeru* 'help':

(53) a. *Boku wa kanozyo ga komatte iru tokoro o tasukete ageta.*
I she is in trouble helped
'I helped her at the very moment she was in trouble.'
b. ??*Boku wa kanozyo ga komatte iru tokoro o sannenkan* for three years *tasukete ageta.*
'*I helped her over a period of three years at the very moment she was in trouble.'

The strangeness of (53b) is clearly due to the semantic incompatibility between S *tokoro o* and the matrix predicate, which can no longer be instantaneous because of the addition of the durational time adverbial *sannenkan* 'for three years'. Interestingly enough, S *no o* can occur in either of the environments (53) because the direct perception of, or response to, a simultaneously occurring event does not necessarily have to be instantaneous but can take place over a period of time:

(54) a. *Boku wa kanozyo ga komatte iru no o tasukete ageta.*
'I helped her when she was in trouble.'
b. *Boku wa kanozyo ga komatte iru no o sannenkan tasukete ageta.*
'I helped her for a period of three years while she was in trouble.'

Thus, in (54b) the action of helping is described as having continued over a period of three years as a direct response to the persisting situation mentioned in the embedded proposition. In contrast with (53a), which focuses on the very moment when the embedded sentence event reached its peak or crisis point, (54a) tends to view the embedded sentence event in its entirety. For this reason, the predicate *tasukete ageta* of (54a) does not have the strong connotation of instantaneousness that is associated with its counterpart in (53a).[43]

[43]In footnote 23 I remarked that the verb of helping *tasukeru* can cooccur with S *tokoro o* while *tetudau* cannot. This phenomenon can be plausibly related to the difference in meaning between these verbs. Because *tasukeru* means helping by doing some action other than that expressed in the embedded proposition, the two actions involved would be sufficiently different from each other that it would be of interest to speak of their coincidental occurrence—hence the possibility of S *tokoro o*. On the other hand, since *tetudau* means helping by doing the very same action as that expressed in the embedded proposition, the two actions would be very similar, and their cooccurrence would be of relatively trivial interest.

With certain verbs of stopping, *tokoro* complements occur compatibly, as in the following examples:

(55) a. *Utikonde kuru tokoro o katate de uketometa.*
approach with a blow with one hand caught
'I stopped the oncoming blow with one hand.'

b. *Keisatu wa gakusei ga daigaku no tatemono ni hairoo to suru tokoro o seisi sita.*
police student university building about to enter checked
'The police stopped the students just as they were about to enter the university buildings.'

In an example like the following, however, S *tokoro o* is ungrammatical:

(56) **Sono byooki ga hirogaru tokoro o tomerarenakatta.*
that disease spread couldn't stop
?'They couldn't stop that disease just as it was spreading.'

Here, too, the unacceptability of S *tokoro o* seems to be due to the fact that the matrix predicate is not instantaneous: Thus, as we saw in (23), addition of the potential suffix *-rare-* changes the normally instantaneous action verb *tomeru* 'stop' into a (durative) state verb *tomerareru* 'can stop'.

When we examine the cooccurrence restrictions between S *tokoro o* and verbs of sense perception more carefully, we find sentences like the following:

(57) a. ?*Boku wa kodomotati ga asobu tokoro o (itizikan) nagamete ita.*
I children play one hour was watching
'?(For one hour) I was watching the children just as they were playing.'

b. **Watakusi wa sesuzi ga samuku naru tokoro o kanzita.*
I spine become cold felt
'?I felt a chill just as it was running down my spine.'

c. **Boku wa kiteki ga tooku de natte iru tokoro o kiita.*
I whistle far away is sounding heard
'?I heard a whistle just as it was sounding a long way off.'

Whereas the awkwardness of (57a) is expected because the matrix predicate (*nagamete ita* 'was watching') is not instantaneous, the ungrammaticality of (57b) and (57c) cannot be explained in the same terms. It is possible that Harada's definition of circumstantial *tokoro* complements as referring to a 'physically perceptible state of affairs' is somewhat too broad and that S *tokoro o* is appropriate only if a cooccurring sense perception verb refers to visual perception. This restriction would then explain the ungrammaticality of (57b) and (57c), in which tactile and auditory perception are involved. The nominalizer *no*, of course, can appear in these sentences without any difficulty.

Although the preceding discussion has clarified the basic meaning of *tokoro* and illustrated how it contrasts with *no* in certain environments, there remain many relevant phenomena worthy of study. Thus, it will be necessary, for example, to determine the relationship between S *tokoro o* and S *tokoro ni/e/de*. The latter constructions are observed in sentences like the following:

(58) a. *Watakusi wa Ziroo ga isoide hasitte iku tokoro ni*
I in a rush run off
butukatta.
bumped into
'I bumped into Jiro as he was quickly running off.'

b. *Binboo de komatte iru tokoro e byooki ni kakatte simatta.*
poor and is in trouble sick fell prey to
'He was already troubled by poverty, and on top of that he fell prey to sickness.'[44]

c. *Kusuri o nonda tokoro de kirei ni naranai desyoo.*
medicine drank pretty probably won't become
'Even if she takes medicines for it she's not going to improve her looks.'

5. PREVIOUS ANALYSES OF *TO YUU*

Except for a lengthy analysis by Nakau, to be discussed in detail, the noun complementizer *to yuu* has received relatively little attention from scholars of Japanese. As a result, we have at best only a partial picture of the grammatical and semantic characteristics of this problematical construction. Even some of the most recent studies—e.g., Watanabe (1972)—leave the true nature of *to yuu* shrouded in mystery. Although I will not give a complete description of Watanabe's analysis here, the following fragment of it is typical. In discussing constructions of the form S *to yuu koto* + particle, Watanabe proposes the following deep structure (1972:98):

(59)

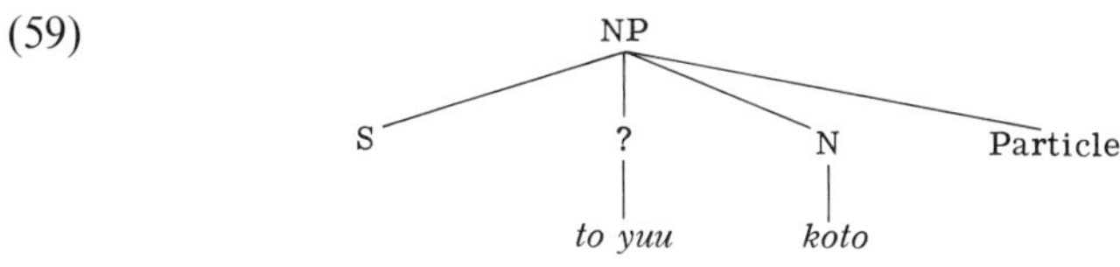

[44]This and the following example are borrowed from Alfonso (1966:1002). Further examples, as well as grammatical explanations, are presented on pp. 1003–1004.

Based on this deep structure, she proposes optional deletion rules such as the following:

(60) a. *Delete* ***yuu koto*** *if (i) Particle is* ***o*** *and (ii) main S verb is of correct class of verb.*
 b. *Delete* ***to yuu*** *if (i) Particle is* ***ga, o, wa*** *and (ii) clause ends in tense.*
 c. *Delete* ***to yuu koto*** *if (i) Particle is* ***ga, o, wa*** *and (ii) clause ends in* ***ka***.

The rules of (60) are ad hoc and unmotivated because their sole purpose is to generate *to yuu koto*, *to*, or *koto* in the positions where they are observed to occur. Only vague recognition is given to the possibility that the distribution of *to yuu* might be predicted in some principled way—e.g., in terms of semantic compatibility between the inherent meaning of *to yuu* and the meaning of cooccurring head nouns or predicates. All that Watanabe says on the subject is the following, which is meant as a comment on the use of the undefined expression CORRECT CLASS OF VERB in (60a):

> We would hope that the verbs relevant here are not merely an arbitrary list ... but a coherent class definable independently on the basis of other (perhaps semantic) characteristics [1972:133, n.8] ...

Another difficulty with Watanabe's rules is that they arbitrarily derive elements of different meaning and function one from the other. Thus, Rules (60a) and (60b) imply that the independently motivated complementizer *to* and the independently motivated nominalizer *koto* both come from the same source, namely, *to yuu koto*, and therefore mean the same thing. Since *to* and *koto* are indeed very different from each other in meaning and function, Watanabe's analysis leads to absurd consequences and requires no further consideration.

In a discussion of considerable insight, Alfonso (1966:1155–1158) attempts to relate the deletability of *to yuu* to the semantic features of the following head noun. In so doing, he comes to conclusions such as the following:

(61) a. *With head nouns of communication (e.g.,* ***hanasi*** *'story',* ***uwasa*** *'rumor',* ***tegami*** *'letter',* ***sirase*** *'information',* ***nyuusu*** *'news', etc.),* ***to yuu*** *is normally obligatory (i.e., cannot be deleted) when the embedded sentence preceding it represents the contents of communication.*
 b. *With head nouns expressing emotions, feelings, and mental states (e.g.,* ***osore*** *'fear',* ***kanzi*** *'feeling',* ***yokan*** *'presentiment',* ***kakusin*** *'conviction', etc.)* ***to yuu*** *is 'not absolutely needed but*

its use is extremely frequent'—i.e., in certain cases ***to yuu*** *can be optionally deleted.*

While the statements in (61) require further elaboration and qualification, they represent a valuable preliminary attempt at discovering the semantic nature of *to yuu*. They are, by and large, compatible with the hypothesis about *to yuu* to be presented later.

In his treatment of Japanese complementation, Nakau presents a lengthy discussion of the noun complementizer *to yuu* (1973:129ff). He claims that *to yuu* must be a deep structure element because it subcategorizes predicates and because its presence or absence has an effect on the semantic interpretation. Before examining this claim in detail, let us review the deep structure configuration that Nakau proposes for noun complementation (cf. the discussion at the beginning of Section 2), as well as the phrase structure rules on which it is based (1973:139):

(62) Noun complementation:

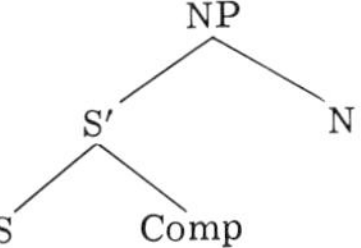

(63) Phrase structure rules:

(i) $\text{NP} \rightarrow \left(\begin{Bmatrix}\text{NP}' \\ \text{Det}\end{Bmatrix}\right) (\text{S}')\ \text{N}$

(ii) $\text{S}' \rightarrow \text{S Comp}$

Nakau's claim that *to yuu* must be in the deep structure is quite plausible. First of all, there are clear cases of predicates that either require or prevent the occurrence of *to yuu* before the accompanying head noun. Assuming that strict subcategorizational features can be expressed only in terms of deep structure constituents, the use of features such as +[S *to yuu* N—] or +[S N—] to subcategorize predicates in the lexicon would require that the complementizer *to yuu* be present in the deep structure as a possible expansion of the Comp node. In the following examples we observe predicates that cooccur with an embedded proposition nominalized with *koto*; in (64a), *to yuu* must obligatorily precede the nominalizer, while in (64b), *to yuu* is prevented:

(64) a. *Taroo ga Ziroo o uragitta* {*to yuu* / *∅} *koto wa* {*utagawasii* / *uso da*}.
betrayed {doubtful / lie is}

'It's {doubtful / not true} that Taro betrayed Jiro.'

b. *Sensei wa Rosiago o hanasu* {∅ / *to yuu} *koto ga dekiru.*
teacher Russian speak is able
'The teacher can speak Russian.'

Although Nakau is obviously aware of the cooccurrence restrictions exemplified in (64a) and (64b), he does not explain them adequately. He does recognize (1973:130) that if *to yuu* were omitted from (64a), this example would become unacceptable because of a logical contradiction between the predicates *utagawasii* 'doubtful' or *uso da* 'be false', which are nonfactive, and the S *koto* subjects, which could be interpreted only as factive. In other words, only S *to yuu koto*, which means something like 'the statement/claim that ...', is compatible with the nonfactive predicates of (64a). In spite of this observation, however, Nakau never comes to the natural conclusion that *to yuu* has what appears to be an inherent nonfactive meaning in sentences like (64a). This conclusion, which lends even more credibility to Nakau's claim that *to yuu* is a deep structure element, will be considered further later.

Whereas Nakau's discussion of (64a) at least approaches a significant generalization—namely, that there is a possible correlation between the inherent meaning of *to yuu* and its distribution—his treatment of (64b) is merely descriptive. In other words, he makes no attempt to explain why a nonpresuppositional predicate like *dekiru* 'be able' prevents the noun complementizer *to yuu* from intervening between the embedded sentence and the cooccurring head noun *koto*. This phenomenon will also be touched upon later.

Another type of evidence that Nakau cites in support of his position that *to yuu* is a deep structure element involves the fact that the presence versus absence of *to yuu* has an effect on the semantic interpretation. Here, too, Nakau appears to be approaching the claim that *to yuu* has an inherent meaning that might account for the observed differences in semantic interpretation, but unfortunately, he fails to make this point explicit. Because the relevant examples presented by Nakau (1973:134–139) are extremely complex, the following pair of sentences will suffice to illustrate the point under discussion:

(65) a. *Kinoo no sinbun de Tanaka-san ga rikon sita koto wa*
yesterday newspaper in got divorced
hookoku sareta.
was reported
'The fact that Mr. Tanaka got divorced was reported in yesterday's newspaper.'

b. *Kinoo no sinbun de Tanaka-san ga rikon sita to yuu koto wa hookoku sareta.*
'In yesterday's newspaper it was reported that Mr. Tanaka got divorced (but is it true?).'

As the English equivalents make clear, the distinction between (65a) and (65b) closely resembles that observed for factive versus nonfactive paradigms, respectively. In (65a), *hookoku sareru* 'be reported' is used as a 'true' factive predicate: In other words, the speaker presupposes that the embedded proposition is a fact and then asserts that this fact got reported in yesterday's newspaper. It is quite likely that the speaker considered the embedded proposition to be an established fact prior to, rather than as a result of, its being printed in the paper. In (65b), however, the true factive sense of *hookoku sareru* is lost because the speaker does not presuppose that the embedded proposition was a fact previous to its being reported, nor does he have complete confidence in its factual status even after it was reported. The presence of *to yuu* in (65b), therefore, connotes some degree of doubt on the part of the speaker that the embedded proposition is true, while leaving open the possibility that the speaker might accept the embedded proposition as a fact if he had proper confirmation or verification. This special connotation—namely, that the speaker considers the embedded proposition to be a possible or potential fact—is what differentiates 'nonfactive' *to yuu koto* of (65b) from true nonfactive constructions involving S *to* [e.g., (10b) and (11b)], since in the latter the speaker is totally neutral or noncommittal about the truth value of the embedded proposition.

In the discussion of noun complementation presented here, we have seen that the conditions of occurrence on the noun complementizer *to yuu* are of three different types:

1. The occurrence of *to yuu* is obligatory [e.g., with the head nouns of communication in (61a) and with *koto* and predicates like *utagawasii* 'doubtful' in (64a)].
2. The occurrence of *to yuu* is optional [e.g., with the head nouns expressing emotions, feelings, and mental states in (61b) and with *koto* and predicates like *hookoku sareru* 'be reported' in (65a) and (65b)].
3. The occurrence of *to yuu* is prevented [e.g., with *koto* and predicates like *dekiru* 'be able' in (64b)].

Although Nakau's examples and discussion show beyond a doubt that he recognizes the three distinct cases just listed (see, for example, 1973:132), his phrase structure rules conspicuously fail to account for cases (2) and (3), in which *to yuu* is either optionally or obligatorily absent in deep structure.

This failure results from the fact that his phrase structure rule (63ii) introduces Comp (the complementizer) as an OBLIGATORY, rather than optional, constituent.

Since Nakau ultimately rejects a transformational analysis for the placement of the noun complementizer (1973:132–134), he concludes that:

> ... the Phrase Structure Rules contain a node which can dominate the Noun Complementizer so that Predicates can be subcategorized for the obligatory occurrence or non-occurrence of this Complementizer under certain cooccurrence conditions. Under this hypothesis, there will be a transformational rule which deletes the Noun Complementizer from those instances of Noun sentential complementation where it occurs optionally without relevance to Predicates [ibid., p. 134].

Two major difficulties are found in Nakau's analysis. First, if the Comp node is to be obligatory, as the phrase structure rule (63ii) implies, then there will simply be no way of strictly subcategorizing predicates for the obligatory NONOCCURRENCE of *to yuu*, since *to yuu* would always be present in deep structure in the environment S__N. In order to save Nakau's claim that the complementizer *to yuu* is an obligatory deep structure element, and still account for those instances in which *to yuu* is prevented, we could introduce a transformational rule that would obligatorily delete *to yuu* in just the proper cases. Such an analysis, however, would require an idiosyncratic marking on predicates and would be totally ad hoc. Second, Nakau's statement that a transformational rule will optionally delete the noun complementizer in those instances in which it is observed to occur optionally without relevance to predicates needs further clarification; certainly, such an optional transformation would not be justified if it resulted in a change of meaning, as would be the case if (65a) were to be derived from (65b).

In seeking a solution to the dilemma that Nakau's phrase structure rule (63ii) creates, we come upon two possible solutions. The first alternative would be to keep (63ii) in its present form but expand Comp in the following way:

(66) $$\text{Comp} \rightarrow \left\{ \begin{matrix} \textit{to yuu} \\ \emptyset \end{matrix} \right\}$$

In this analysis, we would posit a ∅ noun complementizer that would subcategorize predicates and contrast with *to yuu*. Two disadvantages arise, however: First, 'phantom' ∅ elements are suspect unless very painstakingly motivated, and second, the assignment of a meaning to this ∅ complementizer would be extremely difficult. Furthermore, the meaning difference between (65a) and (65b) does not seem to result from a contrast between two distinct complementizers, *to yuu* and ∅, but, instead, from the fact that *to yuu* provides an ADDITIONAL element of meaning (namely, a connotation of speaker's doubt) in (65b).

The second alternative in improving Nakau's phrase structure rules would simply be to make the Comp node in (63ii) optional. In other words, this rule would then be formulated as:

(67) $S' \rightarrow S\ (\text{Comp})$

Under this analysis, the complementizer *to yuu* would be either present or absent in deep structure, and this factor would be used to subcategorize predicates. In addition, the presence of *to yuu* in a given phrase marker would contribute to the semantic interpretation, since this complementizer has an inherent meaning. This alternative appears to be relatively problem free and is therefore to be preferred.

The Meaning and Use of *To Yuu*

Many interesting facts about the distribution of *to yuu* can be plausibly accounted for if we assume that this complementizer has an inherent meaning that is essentially nonfactive. Because *to yuu* connotes varying degrees of doubt on the part of the speaker that the embedded proposition (i.e., the noun complement) is true, it is appropriate only to certain types of situations. Specifically, it can be used when the speaker does not presuppose the truth of the embedded proposition, or when the speaker cannot verify or guarantee the factual status of the embedded proposition.

In our discussion of (64a) we have already observed that *to yuu* is required when a subject complement nominalized with *koto* cooccurs with nonfactive predicates of DOUBT or DENIAL such as *utagawasii* 'doubtful', *uso da* 'be a lie, be false', *matigai da* 'be a mistake, be incorrect', and so on. Kuno implies (1973:218–219) that the S *to yuu koto* (and S *to yuu no*) subjects occurring in sentences like (64a) are nonfactive complements that substitute for the expected S *to*, which is prevented in such environments because the nonfactive predicate complementizer *to* idiosyncratically cannot form subject noun clauses. In other words, the following sentence [cf. (64a)] is ungrammatical:

(68) **Taroo ga Ziroo o uragitta to (wa) utagawasii.*
betrayed doubtful
'It's doubtful that Taro betrayed Jiro.'

The only way of rephrasing (68) would be to use a *koto* complement in subject position, but since S *koto* is normally interpreted as factive if the embedded sentence contains the past tense marker, a sentence like the following would be unacceptable because of semantic anomaly:

(69) **Taroo ga Ziroo o uragitta koto wa utagawasii.*
'The fact that Taro betrayed Jiro is doubtful.'

In order to obviate semantic anomaly between a factive S *koto* subject and a nonfactive predicate (*utagawasii* 'doubtful'), the noun complementizer *to yuu* must appear in the sentential subject, as in:

(70) *Taroo ga Ziroo o uragitta to yuu koto wa utagawasii.*
'It's doubtful that Taro betrayed Jiro.'

The grammaticality of (70) is clearly due to the presence of *to yuu*, which makes the subject complement nonfactive and, therefore, allows for total semantic compatibility with the accompanying nonfactive predicate.

As we have seen in (70), nonfactive predicates require the presence of *to yuu* in a subject complement nominalized with *koto* (or *no*). Kuno notes, however, that with factive predicates, the occurrence of *to yuu* is optional in the same kind of environment. Thus, Kuno presents examples like the following (adapted from Kuno 1973:218):

(71) *Ziroo ga kekkon tyokugo sinde simatta* {*koto/no* / *to yuu koto/no*} *wa*
marriage right after died
higeki da.
tragedy
'It is a tragedy that Jiro died right after he got married.'

The function of *to yuu* in (71) (not explained by Kuno) is by no means clear. Even though *higeki da* 'be a tragedy' is primarily a factive predicate and normally involves the speaker's firm presupposition that the embedded proposition is true, it can apparently cooccur with *to yuu* and undergo a slight weakening in the firmness of the presupposition. Thus, according to some informants, the versions of (71) with *to yuu* have a certain sense of surprise or wonder which might indicate a slight weakening of conviction on the part of the speaker that the embedded proposition is really true. For certain other informants, *to yuu* in (71) maintains some of the flavor of its literal meaning; i.e., it has the sense of 'say that ...' that derives from the sequence predicate complementizer *to* + nonfactive quotative verb *yuu* 'say'.[45] Since the information of the embedded proposition of (71) would therefore be hearsay, and not something the speaker has verified for himself, it is plausible that the firm presupposition normally associated with *higeki da* might undergo some weakening.[46]

[45]Nakau considers the noun complementizer *to yuu* to be a single 'syntactically frozen' element (cf. footnote 1) that is distinct from sequences involving the predicate complementizer *to* and the verb *yuu* 'say'. For arguments in favor of this distinction, and against the 'verb hypothesis' as the origin of *to yuu*, see Nakau (1973:155–163).

[46]Nakau's summary of Japanese complement types (1973:294ff) shows that there are quite a few predicates that work like *higeki da* 'be a tragedy' of (71). Thus, the following predicates have a basically factive meaning but allow *to yuu* to optionally occur in a subject complement nominalized with *koto* or *no*: *hanmei suru* 'become clear', *medatu* 'stand out', *akiraka da* 'be

In discussing the distribution of the noun complementizer *to yuu*, we have so far only treated examples in which the embedded sentence is nominalized with the abstract sentential nominalizers *koto* or *no*. When we examine the distribution of *to yuu* before various head nouns of more concrete meaning, we find a considerable amount of confirmation for our hypothesis that *to yuu* introduces a degree of doubt or a weakening of the speaker's conviction. As Alfonso noticed (1966: 1155–1158), most head nouns designating messages or forms of communication characteristically require the noun complementizer *to yuu*. This is undoubtedly due to the fact that the embedded proposition represents hearsay, reports, rumors, etc., which the speaker himself cannot fully vouch for. In other words, the degree of doubt that *to yuu* connotes is compatible with the speaker's inability to guarantee the truth value of the embedded proposition, which must remain tentative until verified. Some typical sentences containing head nouns of communication follow:

(72) a. *Sooridaizin ga zisatu sita to yuu hookoku o razio de kiita.*
prime minister committed suicide report heard
'On the radio I heard a report that the prime minister committed suicide.'

b. *Sora tobu enban ga tyakuriku sita to yuu uwasa ga tutawatte*
flying saucer landed rumor is
iru.
circulating
'There's a rumor circulating that a flying saucer landed.'

c. *Titi ga sinda to yuu sirase wa uso datta.*[47]
father died news lie was
'The news that my father died was erroneous.'

---

obvious', *husigi da* 'be strange', *toozen da* 'be natural', *hontoo da* 'be true', and *hen da* 'be odd'. A large number of factive predicates taking object complements headed by *koto* or *no* also allow the optional occurrence of *to yuu*. Typical examples are *siru* 'come to know', *wakaru* 'come to know, understand', *tutaeru* 'tell, report', and *setumei suru* 'explain'. For many speakers, the addition of *to yuu* to the subject or object complements of the above-mentioned predicates appears to have no effect whatsoever on the meaning. For others, however, there is a slight connotation of surprise, or a weakening of conviction, as in (71).

[47]In this example, the predicate *uso datta* 'was a lie' makes it clear that the information of the embedded proposition was not authentic—hence the compatibility of *to yuu*. However, if the predicate is neutral as to implication of authenticity, the appearance of *to yuu* before *sirase* 'news' is optional for some speakers. Observe the following example:

Titi ga sinda {*to yuu* / ∅} *sirase o kiita no wa sono toki datta.*
father died news heard that time was
'It was at that time that I got the information that my father had died.'

As expected, this sentence with *to yuu* implies that the speaker had some doubts as to whether the information that he heard was true.

d. *Kon'ya taihuu ga kuru daroo to yuu yohoo o kikimasita ka.*
tonight typhoon come forecast heard
'Did you hear the forecast which said that a typhoon would probably come tonight?'

e. *Hitobito wa tanuki ga kitune o bakasu to yuu densetu o iitutaeta.*[48]
people raccoon fox bewitch legend handed down
'People handed down the legend that a raccoon bewitched a fox.'

With head nouns expressing emotions, feelings, and mental states, the conditions of occurrence of the noun complementizer *to yuu* are particularly difficult to describe, and there is much disagreement among speakers. In certain cases, we observe a contrast between the presence and absence of *to yuu*, as in the following example:

(73) *Watakusi wa ano hito ga sensei o korosita* $\left\{\begin{matrix}\emptyset \\ \textit{to yuu}\end{matrix}\right\}$
I that man teacher killed
kanzi $\left\{\begin{matrix}\textit{ga sita} \\ \textit{o uketa}\end{matrix}\right\}$.
feeling $\left\{\begin{matrix}\text{had} \\ \text{got}\end{matrix}\right\}$
'I $\left\{\begin{matrix}\text{had} \\ \text{got}\end{matrix}\right\}$ the $\left\{\begin{matrix}\text{feeling} \\ \text{impression}\end{matrix}\right\}$ that that man killed the teacher.'

As expected, (73) without *to yuu* implies that the speaker had a rather direct, strong feeling that the embedded proposition was true. When *to yuu* is added, however, the speaker's feeling about the possible truth of the embedded proposition becomes perceptibly weaker, i.e., is reduced to a rather vague impression. A similar difference between strong and weak feeling is found in the following example:

(74) *Zibun ga sinu ka mo sirenai* $\left\{\begin{matrix}\emptyset \\ \textit{to yuu}\end{matrix}\right\}$ *yokan ga Hanako o*
self die may presentiment
nayamaseta.
troubled
'The $\left(\left\{\begin{matrix}\text{strong} \\ \text{vague}\end{matrix}\right\}\right)$ presentiment that she might die troubled Hanako.'

[48]This example is borrowed from Nakau (1973:98).

The semantic content of the proposition embedded before a given head noun can also influence the appropriateness of *to yuu*. Observe, for example, the following sentences containing S (*to yuu*) *ki ga suru* 'feel':

(75) a. *Boku wa Hanako ga wareware no himitu o sitte iru* $\left\{ \begin{array}{l} \textit{to yuu} \\ ?\emptyset \end{array} \right\}$
I we secret know
ki ga suru.
feel
'I get the feeling that Hanako knows some of our secrets.'

b. *Boku wa biiru o nomitai* $\left\{ \begin{array}{l} \emptyset \\ {}^{*}\textit{to yuu} \end{array} \right\}$ *ki ga suru.*
I want to drink feel
'I feel like drinking some beer.'

Because the embedded sentence *Hanako ga wareware no himitu o sitte iru* 'Hanako knows our secrets' of (75a) designates a state of mind of someone other than the speaker, it is not something the speaker can directly perceive. In other words, since the speaker can observe only certain external manifestations of Hanako's mental state (e.g., her behavior, her manner of speaking, etc.), he can never be totally sure that the embedded proposition is really true. For this reason, *to yuu* is required in (75a) because it introduces the necessary connotation of speaker's doubt or weaker conviction. By contrast, the embedded sentence *biiru o nomitai* 'I want to drink beer' of (75b) represents the speaker's own internal feeling, which he can obviously perceive in a direct way and can have no doubts about. Therefore, *to yuu* would be incompatible in (75b) because the possibility of speaker's doubt is excluded.

With certain head nouns indicating belief or conviction, the occurrence of the noun complementizer *to yuu* appears to be obligatory. Observe, for instance, the following sentences:[49]

(76) a. *Ziroo wa yatto sono hon ga iru to yuu kakusin ga tuita.*
finally that book need became convinced
'Jiro finally became convinced that he needed that book.'

b. *Taroo wa sono yotto ga kessite sizumanai to yuu sinnen o*
that yacht never not sink belief
motte iru.
hold
'Taro holds the belief that that yacht will never sink.'

[49]Example (76a) is borrowed from N. McCawley (1972a:74), and (76b) is adapted from Nakau (1973:59).

The obligatory nature of *to yuu* in (76a) and (76b) seems to be due to the fact that the speaker cannot vouch unequivocally for the truth, correctness, authenticity, etc., of someone else's belief, i.e., the belief of the sentence subject (Jiro or Taro). Therefore, *to yuu* is required to express the inevitable element of speaker's doubt or weaker conviction.

In Section 3, we observed that many groups of Japanese nonpresuppositional predicates take subject or object complements nominalized with *koto* and/or *no*. With nonpresuppositional complements of this type, the noun complementizer *to yuu* is strictly prevented. This phenomenon is illustrated in the following ungrammatical sentences:

(77) a. **Watakusi wa Ziroo ga okane o toru to yuu no o mita.*
I money take saw
'I saw Jiro take the money.'

b. **Watakusi wa kodomo ga tabako o nonde iru to yuu no o*
I child cigarette is smoking
mituketa.
found
'I found the child smoking.'

c. **Watakusitati wa sono mati o tooru to yuu no o saketa.*
we that town pass through avoided
'We avoided passing through that town.'

d. **Watakusi wa kare ga seikoo suru to yuu* {*koto* / *no*} *o kitai*
I he succeed was
site ita.
expecting
'I was expecting him to succeed.'

e. **Bosu wa Yamada-san ni yoku hataraku to yuu koto o meizita.*
well work ordered
'The boss ordered Mr. Yamada to work diligently.'

f. **Kanozyo wa kaimono ni iku to yuu* {*koto* / *no*} *ga kirai da.*
she shopping go dislike
'She dislikes going shopping.'

g. **Kanozyo wa mada papaya o tabeta to yuu koto wa nai.*
she yet ate isn't
'She hasn't ever eaten papaya.'

The nonoccurrence of *to yuu* in the noun complements of (77) can be plausibly explained as follows. Since all of the predicates of (77) are nonpresuppositional, they impose various types of implications on the proposition embedded before *koto* or *no*. In other words, the implicational features of a given nonpresuppositional predicate indicate unequivocally whether the embedded proposition is true or false [as in (77a–c)], or whether its truth value is impossible to determine [as in (77d–e)]. In addition, they provide other types of information about the embedded proposition, such as whether or not it is to be construed as a habit or experience [as in (77f–g)]. Whenever a speaker utters a sentence with a nonpresuppositional predicate, he is therefore always sure about the truth value (true, false, or indeterminate) or other aspects (e.g., the habitual nature) of the embedded proposition. For this reason, the use of *to yuu* would be inappropriate because it would imply, falsely, that the speaker had some doubts about these very features of the embedded proposition.[50]

In the preceding discussion, I have attempted to shed some light on the semantic and syntactic complexities of the noun complementizer *to yuu*. My conclusions, however, should be regarded as tentative because the data on which they are based are by no means shared by all speakers of Japanese. Furthermore, there are numerous sets of relevant data that require careful examination but are beyond the scope of the present study. At the least, the material presented here will serve to show that Nakau's view of the complementizer *to yuu* is far oversimplified. Thus, we have seen that many of the distributional characteristics of *to yuu* can be explained if this complementizer is assigned an inherent meaning (something Nakau neglected to do) and, furthermore, that it is a misrepresentation to say that 'in the greatest majority of instances of Noun complementation, the Noun Complementizer occurs optionally without relevance to Predicates [Nakau, 1973:129].'

6. SURVEY OF PREDICATE COMPLEMENTATION

In the preceding sections we have examined some of the major problems within the Japanese noun complementation system. The predicate complementation system, by comparison, poses fewer difficulties and, consequently, has found adequate treatment in the literature. For this reason, I will present only a broad survey of Japanese predicate complementation in this section, touching on the major observations of Kuno (1972, 1973) and Nakau (1973).

[50]In a few rare, but interesting, cases, noun complements accompanying nonpresuppositional predicates can contain the complementizer *to yuu*. In such environments, *to yuu* seems to provide a connotation of wonder or surprise, as in the following examples:

(i) *Taroo wa zyuppun mo mizu no naka ni mogutte iru to yuu koto ga dekiru.*
for all of ten minutes under water is diving be able
'Taro can dive (and stay) under water for ten whole minutes!'

(ii) *Bosu ga zisyoku suru to yuu koto wa kitai site inakatta.*
resign was not expecting
'I certainly wasn't expecting the boss to resign.'

As we saw in Section 2, Nakau proposes that Japanese predicate complementation involves the following structure:

(78) Predicate complementation:

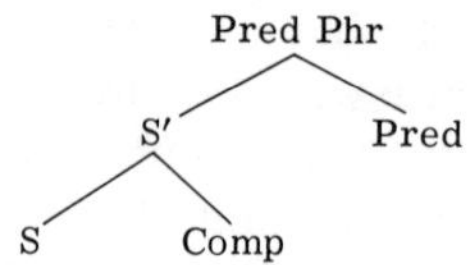

The Comp (i.e., predicate complementizer) is realized as *to* or *yoo ni*, and predicates are subcategorized in terms of the cooccurring complementizer.[51] There is considerable syntactic evidence (already discussed in Section 2) that predicate complementation is to be distinguished from noun complementation.

Kuno notes that the predicate complementizer *to* is used primarily with nonfactive predicates (cf. Section 3). Regarding this usage, he observes that:

> ... it is natural that *to*, which was originally a particle for reporting someone else's statement, be used for representing an action, state, or event about which the speaker has not made a presupposition [1973:215].

Certain predicates—e.g., *omou* 'think', *yuu* 'say', *hayagatten suru* 'come to a hasty conclusion', *kantigai suru* 'make the wrong guess', *gokai suru* 'misunderstand', *soozoo suru* 'imagine', etc.—are exclusively nonfactive and, therefore, cooccur only with S *to*. Other predicates, however, are indifferent as to factivity and allow either (nonfactive) S *to* or (factive) S *koto/no*; this group includes predicates such as *nageku* 'lament' [cf. (10)], *sinziru* 'believe' [cf. (11)], *kiku* 'hear', *zihaku suru* 'confess', and so on. In general, nonfactive

[51]Nakau (1973:164ff) proposes that predicates such as *tumori da* 'intend', *yotei da* 'plan', *rasii* 'likely', *yoo da* 'seem', etc., are preceded by (predicate) complements that lack the complementizer. In other words, the UNDERLINED parts of:

(i) *Taroo wa paatii e iku tumori datta.*
go intended
'Taro intended to go to the party.'

(ii) *Taroo wa okane o totta yoo da.*
money took seems
'Taro seems to have taken the money.'

are predicate complements that show that 'there are salient instances where no Complementizer is permitted [ibid., p. 4].' Because Nakau's phrase structure rule for expanding the S′ of predicate complementation (ibid., p. 147) is the same as that for expanding the S′ of noun complementation, namely, (63ii), his analysis of predicate complementation meets with difficulties identical to those observed at the end of Section 5. Thus, the obligatory nature of Comp in rule (63ii) makes it impossible to account for those instances of predicate complementation in which the complementizer is obligatorily absent, as in (i) and (ii) of this footnote.

predicates do not place any restrictions on the internal structure of the accompanying embedded sentence, which can, therefore, contain such elements as the past tense marker and the presumptive mood marker *daroo*;[52] furthermore, the condition of identity need not hold between matrix and embedded subject. In these respects, nonfactive verbs resemble factive verbs but differ markedly from nonpresuppositional verbs.[53]

Kuno (in this volume) maintains that a small number of Japanese nonfactive verbs of thinking (or internal feeling) permit the application of a subject-raising rule. This rule raises the embedded subject (NP *ga*) into the position of matrix object (NP *o*) and thus derives (79b) from (79a) without any change in meaning:

(79) a. *Taroo wa Ziroo ga baka da to omotte ita.*
crazy thought
'Taro thought Jiro was crazy.'
b. *Taroo wa Ziroo o baka da to omotte ita.*
'Taro thought Jiro to be crazy.'

Since Kuno provides cogent arguments in favor of a subject-raising rule and points out an interesting peculiarity of this rule, no further discussion is necessary here. The small group of verbs that allow subject raising includes *omou* 'think, believe', *sinziru* 'believe', *dantei suru* 'conclude', *suitei suru* 'guess', *omoikomu* 'believe erroneously', and *kantigai suru* 'make the wrong guess'.

As noted earlier, an S *to* complement usually identifies a cooccurring nonfactive predicate. In addition, S *to* complements are found to accompany a small group of nonpresuppositional predicates that designate efforts or

[52]A typical example of a predicate complement containing *daroo* is the following:

Kare wa kyoo yuki ga huru daroo to omotta.
he today snow fall thought
'He thought it would snow today.'

[53]As Nakau notes (1973:88–91), the complementizer *to* serves to embed both direct and indirect quotations. When direct quotation is involved, the internal structure of the predicate complement is totally unrestricted, since a direct quotation simply repeats, word for word, what someone said, thought, etc. For this reason, imperative sentences and sentences ending in various mood markers (e.g., assertive *yo* and *zo*) can even be embedded before *to* when direct quotation is intended. Note the following examples, borrowed from Nakau (1973:88–89) and N. McCawley (1972a:93), respectively:

(i) *Sono syookoo wa buka ni atumare to meizita.*
that officer men gather! ordered
'That officer ordered his men, "Fall in!"'

(ii) *Taroo wa kanarazu yaritogeru zo to zibun de zibun ni tikatta.*
by all means accomplish by himself to himself swore
'Taro swore to himself that he would accomplish it by all means.'

determination. In such cases, the verb of the embedded sentence must take the volitional mood marker -(*y*)*oo*. Thus, in the following sentences, we observe predicates that are subcategorized with the feature + [(. . .-*yoo*)s *to*]—:[54]

(80) a. *Ziroo wa atarasii keikaku o tateyoo to kessin sita.*
new plan build resolved
'Jiro resolved to formulate a new plan.'

b. *Sono gakusei wa sensei no hon o nusumoo to sita.*
that student teacher book steal tried
'That student tried to steal the teacher's book.'

c. *Yakuza wa keikan o korosoo to kuwadateta.*
gangster policeman kill undertook
'The gangster undertook to kill the policeman.'

In the deep structures of (80a–c), the embedded subject must be identical with the matrix subject; then, equi-NP deletion applies obligatorily to derive the correct surface structures.

Nonpresuppositional predicates designating orders, commands, requests, advice, and related concepts commonly take S *yoo ni*. In the surface structure, these classes of futuritive predicates (cf. Section 3) may or may not be accompanied by an indirect object NP *ni* phrase. Since the difference in meaning resulting from the presence versus absence of NP *ni* parallels that observed in (26a) and (26b), no further remarks are needed here. In all of the following examples, the futuritive predicate is accompanied by an NP *ni* phrase; N. McCawley (1972a) proposes that this NP is present in the deep structure as the matrix sentence indirect object and that the relevant predicates 'are subject to a deep structure constraint that their complement subject must be coreferential to their indirect object [p. 9].' Thus, the following sentences are derived by the obligatory application of equi-NP deletion:

(81) a. *Sensei wa Mitiko ni yoku hataraku yoo ni* {*meizita* / *itta* / *tanonda*}.
teacher well work {ordered / told / requested}
'The teacher {ordered / told / requested} Michiko to work diligently.'

b. *Bengosi wa sihainin ni zisyoku suru yoo ni susumeta.*
lawyer manager resign advised
'The lawyer advised the manager to resign.'

[54]Nakau (1973:297) uses a similar feature for identifying this verb class.

c. *Watakusi wa bosu ni sono tegami o sutenai yoo ni settoku sita.*
I that letter not throw away persuaded
'I persuaded my boss not to throw away the letter.'

d. *Ziroo wa Hanako ni sensei o okorasenai yoo ni tyuui sita.*
teacher not anger warned
'Jiro warned Hanako not to get the teacher angry.'

As Nakau notes (1973:297), a very small number of futuritive verbs that take S *yoo ni* require that the complement subject be identical to the subject, rather than indirect object, of the matrix sentence. In such cases, of course, there is no NP *ni* indirect object in the deep structure:

(82) a. *Sono gakusei wa yoku benkyoo suru yoo ni tutometa.*
that student well study endeavored
'That student endeavored to study hard.'

b. *Hayaku kaku yoo ni sinasai.*
fast write please try
'Please try to write it quickly.'

ACKNOWLEDGMENTS

I am especially indebted to Shigeo Tonoike, who generously provided much data for this paper and who stimulated my thinking with many insightful observations. I should also like to thank Irwin Howard, Masaru Kajita, Hiromi Nema, and Nobuo Sato, whose ideas and suggestions have been of considerable value.

NEGATION[1]

NAOMI HANAOKA McGLOIN

INTRODUCTION

There are two types of negative formation that appear in many languages. One of these is formed by verbal modifiers such as *not*, *never*, *hardly*, etc., in English and *na* in Japanese (sentence negation). The other type of negative makes use of negative prefixes, such as *in-*, *dis-*, *un-* in English and *hi-*, *hu-*, *mu-*, etc., in Japanese (affixal negation).

Affixal negation, although it renders the sentence negative in meaning, does not always manifest the same kind of syntactic properties as sentence negation. While 'negative words'[2] occur in the environment of sentence negation, as in (1), they do not occur in the environment of affixal negation, as in (2):

(1) *Watasi wa moo doko e mo ik-ana-i.*
I anymore nowhere go-negative-present
'I won't go anywhere anymore.'

(2) **Nani mo hu-kanoo-da.*
nothing im-possible-copula

[1]This is a shortened version of my Ph.D. dissertation entitled "Some Aspects of Negation in Japanese," University of Michigan, 1972.

[2]Negative words are words like *any*, *at all*, *drink a drop*, etc., in English, which usually appear only in the presence of the negative. Indefinites + *mo*, such as *nani-mo*, *dare-mo*, and *doko-e-mo*, are such words in Japanese. These words will be further investigated in Section 5.

It is an interesting question whether *na* and *hu-* are derived from the same underlying source or not. If, in fact, they are derived from the same underlying form, the lexically incorporated[3] negative forms an island[4] with respect to providing a favorable environment for negative words.

In this chapter, however, sentence negation is our main concern. Some syntactic–semantic properties of sentence negation in Japanese will be discussed, such as (a) *nakute* versus *naide*, (b) negative environments, and (c) scope of negation.

It has been argued by G. Lakoff and J. McCawley (1970) that NEGATIVE is an underlying intransitive verb that takes a sentential subject. I can only strengthen their claim by bringing in a Japanese example. Consider the following sentence:

(3) *Tieko wa kessite baka-de-wa-na-i noni, zibun de wa soo*
at all fool although self so
omot-te-i-ru.
think stative
'Chieko is not a fool by any means, but she thinks (she is).'

Sentence (3) argues for two things:

1. Notice that *soo* is a sentential pronoun. The fact that it is not an NP pronoun can be shown by the following sentence:

   (4) *Yoozoo wa mootakutoo-goroku o yon-de-i-ta.*
   read
   Yoozoo wa $\left\{\begin{matrix} \textit{sore} \\ \textit{*soo} \end{matrix}\right\}$ *o ani kara morat-ta no dat-ta.*
   elder brother get-past
   'Yozo was reading Mao's little red book. He got it from his elder brother.'

   Therefore, whatever *soo* refers to must be a sentential element.
2. In (3), *soo* refers to *Tieko ga baka da*, which is a positive counterpart of the preceding negative clause. Under the normal assumption that transformation operates on a single constituent, *Tieko ga baka da* has to be a single constituent at the time *soo* pronominalization applies.
3. Moreover, that NEGATIVE is a surface stative VERB is also supported in Japanese in that *na* is inflected exactly like an adjective. Since adjectives are verbs, it is not difficult to conclude that *na* is a verb.

[3]By 'lexical incorporation' I mean the process of substituting a word (i.e., *hukoo*) for a phrase (i.e., *koohuku-de-na-i*).

[4]The concept of 'island' was first developed by Ross in his thesis and subsequently employed by Paul Postal in the form of 'anaphoric' island.

Thus, *na* as in (1) will be derived from an underlying NEGATIVE, and we will assume the following underlying structure for sentence negation:

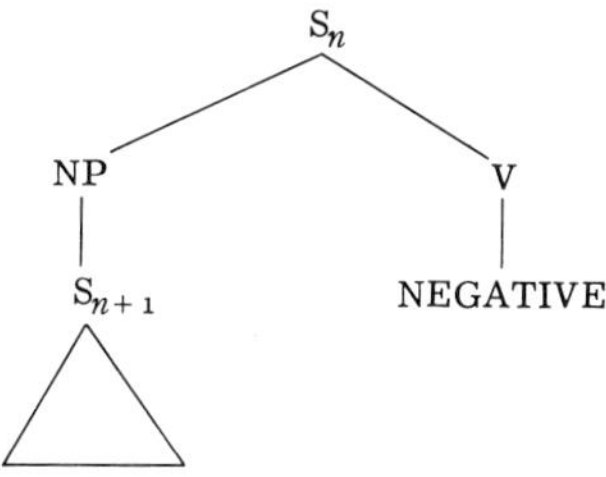

1. *NAIDE* VERSUS *NAKUTE*

Sentence negation in Japanese is characterized by the presence of the sentence-final *na* (or its variants *zu* or *n*). The negative formative *na* can be attached to verbs [as in (5)], adjectives [as in (6)], or nominal adjectives [as in (7)]:

(5) *Kyoo wa ik-ana-i.*
Today go-negative
'I am not going today.'

(6) *Hana wa akaku-na-i.*
flower red
'Flowers are not red.'

(7) *Hana wa kirei-de-wa-na-i.*
pretty
'Flowers are not pretty.'

There has been much controversy among traditional Japanese grammarians concerning the classification of *na* in (5)–(7). Many grammarians have claimed that there are, in fact, two *na(i)*'s—an adjective *na(i)* for those in sentences (6) and (7), and an auxiliary *na(i)* for sentence (5).

One of the main reasons for distinguishing two *na(i)*'s is the existence of two conjunctive (*-te*) forms—*nakute* and *naide*—for an auxiliary *na(i)* and the nonexistence of *naide* for an adjective *na(i)*. Observe the following sentences:

(8) *Hana wa akaku-* $\left\{\begin{matrix}\textit{nakute,} \\ \textit{*naide,}\end{matrix}\right\}$ *siroi.*
'Flowers are not red, but white.'

(9) *Hana wa kirei-de-* $\left\{\begin{matrix}\textit{nakute,} \\ \textit{*naide,}\end{matrix}\right\}$ *kitana-i.*
'Flowers are not pretty, but dirty.'

(10) *Kyoo wa ik-* { *anakute,* / *anaide,* } *i-i.*

'It is all right that you don't go for today.'

In this section I would like to show that the distribution of *nakute* and *naide* is not simply morphological but semantic, and that both of them can be derived from an underlying NEGATIVE.

1. Consider the following sentences:

(11) *Taroo wa tabe-* { *naide* / **nakute* } { *iru.* / *ageta.* / *kita.* / *itta.* / *kureta.* / *hosii.* / *moratta.* }

'Taro { hasn't eaten.' / didn't eat for *x*.' / came without eating.' / went without eating.' / didn't eat for us.' }

'I want Taroo not to eat.'

'Taroo asked someone not to eat.'

In the *te* complement constructions, as in (11), only *naide* occurs. Notice that adjectives and nominal adjectives do not occur in this environment:

(12) *Taroo wa kanasiku-nakute* { **iru* / **ageru* / **itta* / **kita* / **kureta* / **hosii* / **moratta* }.

2. If V_2 is a predicate like *ii* 'good', *sumu* 'be over', *komaru* 'be in trouble', *daizyoobu* 'all right', etc., *nakute* occurs as well as *naide*. Consider the following sentences:

(13) *Tegami wa kak-anakute i-i.*
letter write
'You don't have to write a letter.'

(14) *Kyoo wa kaimono ni ik-anakute sun-da.*
shopping
'I didn't have to go shopping today.'

(15) *Tomodati ga tittomo ko-nakute sabisi-i.*
friend at all come lonesome
'I feel lonesome since my friends do not visit me at all.'

(16) *Taroo wa kakitori ga deki-nakute komari-mas-u.*
spelling do well
'I feel troubled because Taro does not do well in spelling.'

(17) *Anata wa ko-nakute daizyoobu-des-u.*
'It is all right that you don't come.'

Sentences (13)–(17) really involve the speaker's judgment or emotional states generated as a result of S_1. For example, in (16), the person who feels *komaru* is the speaker, not Taro. Therefore, all of these sentences actually involve two different subjects for S_1 and S_2. The subject of S_2, however, must always be the SPEAKER.

Now, both adjectives and nominal adjectives also occur in this context. Consider sentences (18) and (19):

(18) *Kono okasi wa amari amaku-nakute, i-i.*
this cake too sweet

(19) *Uti no mawari wa sizuka-de-nakute, komari-mas-u.*
house around quiet-copula-negative
'It's too bad that it is not quiet around my house.'

Sentence (18) is interesting in that it is ambiguous between two readings, (a) and (b):

(a) 'This cake need not be so sweet.'
(b) 'This cake is good because it is not too sweet.'

In reading (a), the subject of S_1 has to be interpreted as 'generic'—'this kind of cake'.[5] If the sentence has a specific subject, therefore, the sentence can be interpreted only in reading (b), as in (20):

[5]Consider the following sentence:

(i) *Kono okasi wa, otoosan ni age-ru-n-da kara, amari amaku-nakute i-i.*
'Since this cake is for the father, it does not have to be sweet.'

Sentence (i) implies a specific cake. However, for a sentence like (i) with a specific subject to be interpreted in the sense of 'need', the speaker must presuppose that every cake for the father is supposed to be not too sweet. In this sense, then, some kind of genericness is still implied in (i).

(20) *Kono aka-i pen wa yawarakaku-nakute i-i.*
red pen soft
'This red pen is good, since it is not soft.'

The particles *wa* and *ga*, again, affect this interpretation:

(21) *Kono heya wa hon ga nakute i-i.*

(22) *Kono heya wa hon wa nakute i-i.*
room book negative

Sentence (21) has the (b) reading, while (22) has the (a) reading. Sentence (21) means that it is nice that there are no books in this room. Sentence (22) means that there need not be any books in this room. This is presumably related to the above-mentioned 'genericness' of the subject of S_1 in reading (a). Only *wa* introduces generic nouns.

Stative verbs[6] also have this ambiguity. Consider the following examples:

(23) *Eigo wa hanas-e-nakute i-i.*
English speak-can

(24) *Eigo ga hanas-e-nakute i-i.*

Sentence (23) means that you do not need to be able to speak English. Sentence (24) means that you are lucky that you cannot speak English. This, then, seems to be related to the causal reading of the *-te* form, which will be discussed later.

3. When S_1 and S_2 have different subjects, *nakute* also occurs:

(25) *Kyoo wa Taroo mo Hanako mo ko-* {*nakute,* / *naide,*} *sekkaku no*
special
gotisoo ga muda ni nat-ta.
dinner wasted become
'Today, neither Taro nor Hanako came and the dinner that I prepared with special care was wasted.'

[6]Concerning classifications of verbs in Japanese, the readers are referred to Kindaichi (1952), D. Smith (1970), and Kitagawa (1972). According to Akira Ota (1971:132–136), stative verbs in Japanese are subclassified into two groups:

(1) +stative, +durative	*aru* 'be', *iru* 'be', *dekiru* 'be capable', etc.
(2) +stative, −durative	*niru* 'resemble', *tomu* 'be rich', *arihureru* 'be common', etc.

Verbs of the first group are never used in resultative *-te iru* forms, while those of the second group are normally used in *-te iru* forms.

(26) *PTA ni wa okaasan ga ik-* {*anakute,* / *anaide,*} *otoosan ga it-ta.*
mother father
'My mother did not go to the PTA meeting and my father did.'

(27) *PTA ni wa okaasan ga ik-are-* {*nakute,* / *naide,*} *otoosan ga it-ta.*
'My mother could not go to the PTA meeting so my father did.'

(28) *Sigoto ga umaku ik-* {*anaide,* / *anakute,*} *rikon no ketui o si-ta.*
work well divorce decision do
'The work did not go well and I decided to get a divorce.'

4. The problem arises when both S_1 and S_2 have the same subject. Consider the following sentences:

(29) *Taroo wa mada gohan o tabe-* {*naide* / **nakute*} *mat-te i-ru.*
still dinner eat wait
'Taro is still waiting without eating the dinner.'

(30) *Ooku no hito-bito wa nan no mokuteki mo mot-* {*anaide* / **anakute*}
many people any purpose hold
ryuugaku-su-ru.
go abroad
'Many people go to study abroad without having any purpose.'

(31) *Gakkoo no ato, uti e kaer-* {*anaide* / **anakute*} *eiga o mi ni it-ta.*
school after house return movie see for
'After school, he went to see the movie without going home.'

(32) *Watasi wa kinoo wa sanpo si-* {**nakute* / *naide*} *hirune si-masi-ta.*
yesterday walk nap
'Instead of taking a walk I took a nap yesterday.'

Sentences (29)–(32) are ungrammatical if *nakute* is used. However, *nakute* is permitted in this environment if V_1 is a stative verb or adjective:

(33) *Taroo wa eigo ga deki-nakute sibu sibu eigo-zyuku e*
reluctantly class
kayot-ta.
attend
'Taro was not good at English and attended the English class against his will.'

(34) *Kooiti wa gihu to no koto de moo uti ni wa i-rare-nakute,*
stepfather fact stay-can
iede si-ta.
leave home
'Kooichi could not stay home anymore because of his stepfather, and left home.'

(35) *Kono eiga wa omosiroku-nakute kudar-ana-i.*
interesting worthless
'This movie is uninteresting and worthless.'

In (29)–(31), one usually expects S_1 to have occurred before S_2. However, contrary to one's expectation, S_1 does not happen. For example, in (31) the speaker expected him to go home before he went to the movie. Surprisingly, however, he did not go home first. I call this kind of relation between S_1 and S_2 'denial of expectation'. In (32) and (35), S_1 and S_2 are merely juxtaposed to each other. This kind of relation I call 'symmetrical'. In (33) and (34), S_1, being negated, is the cause for S_2. In (33), for example, the fact that he could not speak English caused him to go to the English classes against his will. I call this kind of relation 'causal'.

When V_1 is a nonstative verb, denial of expectation characteristically holds between S_1 and S_2. When V_1 is a stative verb, on the other hand, the causal relation most distinctly holds between S_1 and S_2.

To summarize these observations, the types of verbs in S_1 and whether S_1 and S_2 have like subjects or not are relevant to the kind of semantic relations that are observed between S_1 and S_2. The following chart will show this more clearly:

Subject	V_1	Relation between S_1 and S_2	*Nakute*	*Naide*
Different	stative	symmetrical/causal	yes	yes
	nonstative	denial/symmetrical/causal	yes	yes
Same	nonstative	symmetrical/denial[a]	no	yes
	stative	symmetrical/causal	yes	yes

[a]Denial = denial of expectation.

Notice that, when S_1 and S_2 have like subjects, the following triplets are characteristically associated with each other:

stative verb—*nakute*—causal
nonstative verb—**nakute*—*causal

This, then, suggests that there is a nonarbitrary relation between the occurrence of *nakute* and the 'causal' interpretation; namely, *nakute* is used when causal interpretation is possible.

There are cases, however, in which S_1 and S_2 have the like subject and a nonstative verb seems to be acceptable with *nakute*. Consider the following sentences:

(36) *Yamanaka-san wa peepaa o kak-* {*anaide* / *?anakute*} *kyuudai-si-ta.*
paper write pass
'Mr. Yamanaka passed the course without writing a paper.'

(37) *Ano hito wa yoboo-tyuusya o si-* {*naide* / *nakute*} *byooki ni nat-ta.*
that person preventive injection ill
'That man did not have a preventive injection, and he got sick.'

Sentence (36) with *naide* is interpreted as either denial of expectation or symmetrical. Everyone is expected to write a paper in order to pass a course, but Mr. Yamanaka passed the course without writing a paper. Sentence (36), with *nakute*, although it sounds a little awkward, forces a causal interpretation. In other words, (36) is acceptable with *nakute* only if there is a strong presupposition that Mr. Yamanaka's not writing a paper was a necessary and sufficient condition for his passing the course. This reading is difficult to obtain, presumably because one has to imagine a rather unusual situation in which the teacher has decided not to pass anybody who has written a paper. Compared with (36), (37) is more readily acceptable with *nakute*. This is due to the fact that it is easier for one to imagine a situation in which there is a cause–effect relation between not getting an injection and getting sick. In (37), too, when *nakute* is used the causal interpretation is generated.

Moreover, with *naide* [as in (36) and (37)] it is felt that negation is emphasized compared with *nakute*.[7] With *nakute*, the emphasis is more on the relationship between S_1 and S_2. The assertive power of *naide* exists in the very meaning of 'contrary to expectation': In (36), one expects that everyone had to write a paper, but Mr. Yamanaka did not. In other words, it is felt that the speaker makes an assertion by negating S_1 (which might be contained

[7] I am indebted to Chisato Kitagawa for pointing this out to me.

in an expectation) and then continues by asserting S_2. In (37), for example, it is equally emphasized that the man did not get an injection and that he became sick. With *nakute*, however, the speaker takes $(\sim S_1)$ as a unit and relates it to S_2. The relation holds between $(\sim S_1)$ and S_2.

On the basis of the preceding observations, the denial of expectation and causal relations between S_1 and S_2 are presented as follows. Both share the same basic $[S_1$ -te $S_2]$ structure. The differences, then, are mainly due to presuppositional differences. When denial of expectation holds, it is presupposed that one expects S_1 to precede S_2. The speaker then asserts $\sim S_1$. Of course, the notion 'precede' here does not necessarily correspond to the temporal sequence that exists in the real world. It can be a mental precedence; some event or state can have precedence over some other event or state in the speaker's mind.[8] Schematically, then, (29)–(31) will be presented as follows:

(38) Presupposition: EXPECT (a, (PRECEDE (S_1, S_2)))
Assertion: ASSERT (a, $\sim S_1$) & ASSERT (a, S_2)

On the other hand, when the causal interpretation holds, it is presupposed that S_1 CAUSE S_2. This will be presented as follows:

(39) Presupposition: CAUSE $(\sim S_1, S_2)$
Assertion: ASSERT (a, $(\sim S_1$ & $S_2)$)

Naide will be introduced in a structure like (38), and *nakute* will be introduced in a structure like (39). The symmetrical usages of *naide* and *nakute* are cases in which the presuppositions of (38) and (39) are reduced to null. In these cases, the difference between *nakute* and *naide* reflects the difference of the structures of their assertions.

In relation to the above-mentioned verb types, both stative and nonstative verbs can occur in S_1 of (39) if appropriate presuppositions hold. In (29)–(32), *nakute* was unacceptable, since appropriate presuppositions did not hold for these cases. If V_1 is a nonstative verb, the difference in the subjects of S_1 and S_2 more readily contributes to the appropriate presupposition of (39). Stative verbs can occur with *naide*, but only with the symmetrical reading. Only nonstative verbs can occur in S_1 of (38).

We may conclude that *nakute* reflects a structure like (39) and, hence,

[8]For example, in (32) 'taking a walk' does not necessarily actually precede 'taking a nap'. However, it is felt that the speaker usually takes a walk every day or has taken a walk at least once before, and therefore, in the speaker's mind, taking a walk has a precedence over taking a nap. Of course, in (32), if this kind of precedence is not presupposed, the sentence will be simply a juxtaposition of S_1 and S_2.

shows a more strongly causal implication. On the other hand, *naide* reflects a structure like (38) and shows a stronger negative assertion.

2. THE INHERENT NEGATIVE *MAI*

Mai,[9] somewhat archaic, also expresses negation in the following sentence:

(40) *Watasi wa moo nidoto sonna tokoro e wa ik-u mai.*
I twice such place

Sentence (40) is actually ambiguous between readings (a) and (b). Reading (a) will be paraphrased by (40a) and reading (b) by (40b):

(40a) *Watasi wa moo nidoto sonna tokoro e wa ik-ana-i tumori-da.*
'I intend not to go to such a place again.'

(40b) *Watasi wa moo nidoto sonna tokoro e wa ik-ana-i daroo.*
'It will probably be the case that I will never go to such a place again.'

In reading (a), (40) can be embedded in the following verbs:

(41) *Watasi wa moo nidoto sonna tokoro e wa ik-u mai to*

$$\left\{\begin{array}{ll} \textit{omot-te i-ru.} & \text{'think'} \\ \textit{kokoro ni tikat-te i-ru.} & \text{'swear in mind'} \\ \textit{kessin-si-te i-ru.} & \text{'have made up my mind'} \\ \textit{it-ta.} & \text{'said'} \end{array}\right\}$$

In reading (b), (40) can be embedded as a complement of a different class of verbs:

(42) *Watasi wa moo nidoto sonna tokoro e wa ik-u mai*

$$\textit{to} \left\{\begin{array}{l} \textit{omoi-mas-u} \\ {}^{*}\textit{kokoro ni tikat-te i-ru} \\ {}^{*}\textit{kessin-si-te i-ru} \end{array}\right\}.$$

Also, in reading (b) *mai* can be modified by adverbs like *osoraku* or *tabun*:

(43) *Watasi wa osoraku moo nidoto sonna tokoro e wa ik-u mai to*
probably
omoi-mas-u.

The difference seems to lie in that the (a) sense of (40) can be embedded as

[9]The *-i* in *mai* will probably be the marker of the non-past tense like *-i* in *nai*.

the complement of verbs that denote one's volition or resolution, while the (b) sense of (40) cannot.

Now, consider sentence (44):

(44) *Taroo wa ik-u mai.*

With the third person as a subject, (44) is not ambiguous and means 'It will probably be the case that Taro does not go.' Note, however, that (44) can be embedded as complement of certain verbs:

(45) $$\textit{Taroo wa }{}_{S}[\textit{ik-u mai}]_{S}\textit{ to}\begin{Bmatrix}\textit{omot-ta}\\ \textit{kessin-si-ta}\\ \textit{si-ta}\\ \textit{kokoro ni tikat-ta}\end{Bmatrix}.$$

When thus embedded, with the third person as a higher subject, (44) gives a volitional reading.

This seeming complexity of the volitional versus probability readings and the corresponding restrictions on the part of the subjects can be accounted for if we make the following assumptions:

1. In the underlying structures of these sentences, we posit a two-place predicate *mai* for the volitional sense and a one-place predicate *mai* for the probability sense.
2. Two-place predicate *mai* has a restriction on its subject NP in that this NP must be identical to the subject NP of a higher sentence.
3. An abstract performative verb underlies every declarative sentence, and its subject is in the first person.

Now, the next problem is concerned with whether *mai* is decomposable or not. As may be seen in (46), *mai* provides a favorable environment for INDETERMINATES + *mo*:

(46) *Dare mo ik-u mai.*
'Nobody will go.'

Accordingly, *mai* does contain an element NEGATIVE. Note that the ambiguity between (a) and (b) readings of (40) exists with the English *will*:

(47) *I won't be going to that class anymore.*

Sentence (47) is ambiguous between (47a) and (47b):

(47a) *I do not intend to go to that class anymore.*

(47b) *It will probably be the case that I do not go to the class anymore.*

I propose, then, the following underlying structures for (40a) and (40b):

(48)

(49)

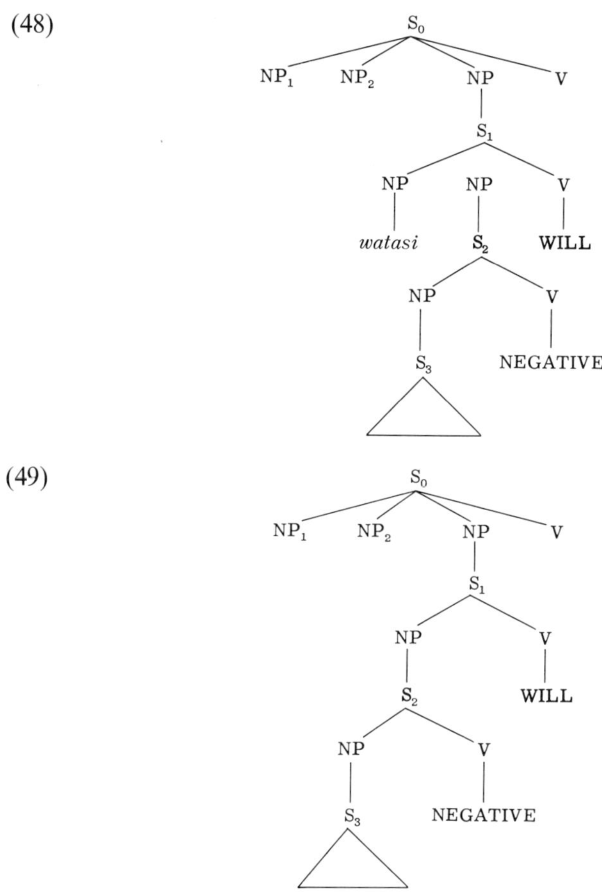

The abstract verb WILL is used here for lack of a better term. It will eventually be ascribed to something like [certain to almost 100 percent].

Now, WILL in (48), in Japanese, will be lexicalized as *tumori*, and WILL in (49) will be lexicalized as *daroo*. That a two-place abstract verb WILL is lexicalized as *tumori* accounts for two facts: (a) It has to undergo the rule of equi-NP deletion; (b) it is subject to the rule of negative transportation. Accordingly, NEGATIVE in (48) and (49) is optionally transported to a higher sentence. [WILL NEGATIVE] then will be lexicalized as *mai*. If the NEGATIVE is not raised, we will get (40a) and (40b), which are the paraphrases of two readings of (40).

One difficulty in deriving *mai* and *tumori* from the same underlying predicate is that *mai* is more restricted than *tumori*. For example, while *mai* requires the first person as its subject, *tumori* does not have this restriction. While *mai* will never occur in the past tense, *tumori* does occur in the past tense, as in (50):

(50) *Boku wa ano hito to kekkon-su-ru tumori-dat-ta.*
I marry
'I intended to marry that person.'

This led Kindaichi (1952) to say that *mai* is a subjective expression of the speaker, while *tumori* is an objective expression. He then says that *mai* can be treated in the same manner as interjections or interjectional particles. I think, however, that this difference will be accounted for by putting a restriction on the *mai* insertion rule. It will be necessary, then, to make the *mai* insertion rule a global rule.

Thus far we have shown that a NEGATIVE also underlies *mai.*

3. NEGATIVE RAISING

Consider the following two dialogs, in which the answers both seem to involve the negation of the main sentence:

(51) A: *Kono yoohuku doo kasira? Zidai okure kasira ne?*
this dress how question-feminine old-fashioned
'What do you think about this dress? Is it old-fashioned?'

B1: *Soonee, tittomo zidaiokure-da to omow-ana-i wa.*
well at all
'Well, I don't think it is old-fashioned at all.'

B2: # *Tittomo zidaiokure-zya-na-i to mo omow-ana-i kedo.*[10]
'Although I don't think it isn't old-fashioned at all either.'

(52) A: *Taroo-san wa kyoo no atumari ni ku-ru kasira?*
meeting
Kurut-te it-te-ta?
come quote say
'I wonder if Taro is coming to today's meeting. Did he say he was coming?'

B1: *Ku-ru to wa it-te-na-kat-ta yo.*
'He didn't say he was coming.'

B2: *Ko-na-i to mo it-te-na-kat-ta kedo ne.*
'Although he didn't say he wasn't coming either.'

[10]Of course, (B2) of (51) is grammatical by itself. The symbol # indicates that it is unacceptable in this particular context.

In (51), the addressee of A, by uttering (B1), seems to be expressing her opinion about the dress—whether it is old-fashioned or not—in this case, a negative opinion. Thus, modifying (B1) by (B2) sounds very awkward or almost nonsensical. In (52), on the other hand, the addressee is not really expressing his opinion about whether Taro is coming or not, but is reporting what Taroo said. Therefore, (B1) can be modified by the statement (B2). I would like to claim, then, that the negative in (B1) of (51) really modifies the embedded proposition.

For similar sentences in English, a rule of negative raising has been proposed. By this rule, negative originates in the embedded sentence in its logical structure and later is transported to the higher sentence. The arguments in favor of this rule involve very fine semantic judgments and are often inconclusive. However, I would argue here that such a rule must also exist in Japanese in order to account for sentences like (B1) of (51), and that it applies to a very small class of verbs.

The first argument involves negative words such as *tittomo* 'at all', *kessite* 'never', and *made* 'until', which require the presence of the negative in the same simplex sentence at some level of the derivation. Therefore:

(53) a. **Kono e wa tittomo okasi-i.*
picture at all funny
'This picture is at all funny.'
b. *Kono e wa tittomo okasiku-na-i.*
'This picture is not funny at all.'

(54) a. **Sono yoohuku wa kessite zidaiokure-da.*
'That dress is at all old-fashioned.'
b. *Sono yoohuku wa kessite zidaiokure-de-na-i.*
'That dress is not old-fashioned at all.'

(55) a. **Hunabin no kozutumi wa raigetu made tuk-u.*
sea mail package next month until arrive
'The sea mail package will arrive until next month.'
b. *Hunabin no kuzutumi wa raigetu made tuk-ana-i.*
'The sea mail package won't arrive until next month.'

These negative words also occur in an embedded sentence when the embedded sentence itself does not contain any negative morpheme. Consider the following sentences:

(56) a. *Watasi wa sono e wa tittomo okasiku-na-i to omo-u.*
'I think that picture is not funny at all.'
b. *Watasi wa sono e wa tittomo okasi-i to omow-ana-i.*
'I don't think that picture is funny at all.'

(57) a. *Hunabin no kozutumi wa raigetu made tuk-ana-i to omo-u.*
'I think the sea mail package won't arrive until next month.'
b. *Hunabin no kozutumi wa raigetu made tuk-u to omow-ana-i.*
'I don't think the sea mail package will arrive until next month.'

Compare (56) and (57) with the following sentences, in which the main verb is *yuu* 'say':

(58) a. *Watasi wa sono e wa tittomo okasiku-na-i to it-ta.*
'I said that picture is not funny at all.'
b. # *Watasi wa sono e wa tittomo okasi-i to iw-ana-kat-ta.*
'I didn't say that picture is funny at all.'

(59) a. *Hunabin no kozutumi wa raigetu made tuk-ana-i to it-ta.*
'I said that the sea mail package won't arrive until next month.'
b. **Hunabin no kozutumi wa raigetu made tuk-u to iw-ana-kat-ta.*
'I didn't say the sea mail package will arrive until next month.'

Note that the sentence pairs in (56) and (57) are both grammatical and semantically equivalent, while (58b) and (59b), in which the negative and negative words do not immediately command each other, are ungrammatical.

This phenomenon can be explained if we make the following assumptions and observations:

1. The negative words *tittomo*, *kessite*, and *made* require the presence of an overt negative morpheme in such a way that the negative word and the negative both immediately command each other at some level of the derivation. Hence the ungrammaticality of (53a), (54a), and (55a).
2. The negative originates in the embedded sentences in the underlying structures of (56b) and (57b) and is then optionally transported to the higher sentences.

The next argument depends on the quantifier-like particle *sika*, which requires the negative in the same simplex S at some level of the derivation. Sentence (60b) is ungrammatical because it lacks this negative in the simplex S:

(60) a. *Kaze ga huk-u to okeya sika mookar-ana-i no wa*
wind blow when cooper only gain that
omosiro-i.
interesting
'It is interesting that only a cooper gains when the wind blows.'

b. **Kaze ga huk-u to okeya sika mookar-u no wa omosi-roku-na-i.*

c. *Kaze ga huk-u to okeya ga mookar-u no sika omosi-roku-na-i.*
'Nothing is interesting except that a cooper gains when the wind blows.'

Now, consider the following sentences:

(61) a. *Watasi wa Taroo ni sika ki-te hosiku-na-i.*
want
'I want only Taro to come.'
b. **Watasi wa Taroo ni sika ko-naide hosi-i.*

Sentence (61a) means something like 'I want nobody but Taro to come.' It has a logical structure roughly represented as follows:

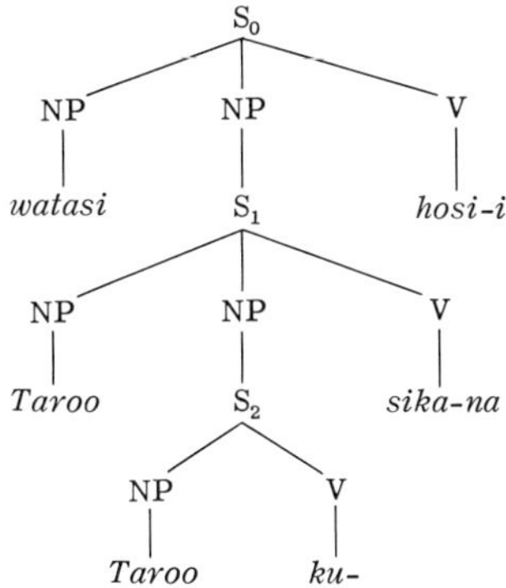

First, *sika-na* will be lowered into S_2:

Watasi [Taroo sika ku-na-i] hosi-i.

Second, the subject *ni* extraction applies:

Watasi Taroo ni sika [ku-na-i] hosi-i.

We have noted that *sika* requires NEGATIVE in the same simplex S. Since *sika* is now outside of the scope of NEGATIVE, NEGATIVE is raised in order to make this derivation grammatical:

Watasi Taroo ni sika [ku] hosi-na-i.

Thus, (61b), which disobeys the constraint that NEGATIVE must immediately command *sika*, is ungrammatical. With the application of *te* complementizer insertion and case marking, we get the correct surface form. In order to account for the grammaticality of (61a) and the ungrammaticality of (61b), we have to resort to the rule of negative raising.

Now, verbs or abstract nominalizers that allow the negative to be optionally moved out of the lower sentence consist of the following:

1. Verbs of thinking such as *omou* and *kangaeru*.[11]
2. A class of modals such as *hosii*, *sase*, *rare*, *tai*, *hazu*, and *tumori*.

Examine the following sentences:

(62) a. *Watasi wa daihyoodan wa asita no asa made tuk-u to*
contingent tomorrow morning
{*omow-ana-i.* / *kangae-na-i.*}
'I don't think the contingent will be arriving until tomorrow morning.'

b. *Watasi wa Taroo ni wa asita no asa made tui-te hosiku-na-i.*
'I don't want Taro to arrive until tomorrow morning.'

c. *Yoru no zyuu-ni-zi made benkyoo-s-ase-na-kat-ta.*
night midnight study-do-cause
'I made him not to study until midnight.'

d. *Boku wa gaarufurendo ni sin-are-na-kat-ta.*
girlfriend die-passive
'My girlfriend did not die on me.'

e. *Boku wa asita made iki-taku-na-i.*
'I don't want to go until tomorrow.'

f. *Taroo wa asita no asa made tuk-u hazu-de-wa-na-i.*
'There is a strong reason to believe (except) that Taro won't arrive until tomorrow morning.'

g. *Watasi wa asita made ik-u tumori-de-wa-na-i.*
'I don't intend to go until tomorrow.'

In all of these sentences, the *made* phrase modifies the embedded verb rather than the main verb. In other words, in these sentences, one is not denying the existence of thought, causation, desire, expectation, or intention. In (62b), then, it is not the case that 'I do not have any desire at all' but, rather, 'I

[11]English verbs of thinking like *believe*, *guess*, *suppose*, *expect*, *feel* are considered negative-raising verbs. The corresponding Japanese verbs *sinziru*, *kanziru*, *kitaisuru*, etc., which take *to* as a complementizer, however, do not seem to allow the negative to be optionally moved out of the lower sentence. This seems to make sense in light of the following fact. English verbs of thinking are usually translated by the Japanese verb *omou* or other modals. Consequently, when the above-mentioned verbs are used, they carry their own meanings more distinctively and cannot be used as a kind of modal, as the corresponding English verbs are. On the other hand, *omou*, as Uyeno (1971) points out, can be used as a kind of modal equivalent to *daroo* 'probably'.

have a desire for Taro not to come until tomorrow morning.' Sentence (62c) is actually ambiguous. In one reading, the speaker did something (e.g., talking) that prevented him from studying before midnight. In the other reading, the speaker did make him study, but it was not until midnight. In the first sense, then, the negative originates in the embedded sentence and is obligatorily raised to the main sentence. Sentence (62d) always implies the negation of the complement—'my girlfriend did not die'. It usually also implies that I did not suffer or was not adversely affected by the event. It CAN mean, however, that the subject—I—suffered in the sense that I expected my girlfriend to die but she did not.

4. THE PARTICLE *WA* AND THE SCOPE OF NEGATION

The Role of *Wa* in Negative Sentences

Observe the following sentences:

(63)
a. **Ame wa hut-te i-ru.*
rain fall
b. *Ame wa hut-te i-na-i.*
c. *Ah, ame ga hut-te i-ru.*
look
d. ?*Ah, ame ga hut-te i-na-i.*

As Kuroda (1965b) and Kuno (1970) discuss in detail, only generic or anaphoric NPs can become themes of the sentence. Sentence (63a), therefore, is ungrammatical with a thematic interpretation of *wa*, since *ame* is a non-generic, nonanaphoric NP. When the sentence is negated, however [as in (63b)], it is perfectly acceptable. In other words, in negative sentences, the speaker is making a certain judgment about a proposition that has been registered in the discourse or in the speaker's mind. *Ame* in (63b), then, is anaphoric in some sense, while *ame* in (63a) is not. While (63c) is acceptable as a description of the scene, (63d) can be interpreted only as a surprise, expressing a sharp contradiction between what one perceives and what one has expected—'it would be raining'. So, when we utter a negative sentence in which negation is the primary focus of the sentence, a certain object, event, or state is presupposed and the speaker negates the existence of such an object, event, or state.

Now, (63b) is ambiguous between two readings of *wa*:

(a) Thematic *wa*: 'As for rain, it is not raining.'
(b) Contrastive *wa*: 'It is not raining (but it's snowing).'

The two readings, in an actual conversation, will be disambiguated as follows. Consider a question like (64):

(64) *Ima ame ga hut-te i-ru?*
'Is it raining right now?'

Question (64) can be answered in two ways:

(64) a. *Iie, hut-te i-masen.*
'No, it is not.'

(64) b. *Iie, ame wa hut-te i-masen.*
'No, it is not raining.'

Normally, if the addressee answers with (64b), he intends to suggest that something else is falling or something else is happening—e.g., the wind is blowing. Of course, one could answer by saying *Iie, ame wa hut-te i-masen*, to mean (64a). In this case, *wa* in (64b) will be distinguished from *wa* in (64a) by the emphatic stress on *wa*. Similarly, for (65), the speaker can choose either (65a) or (65b) as an answer:

(65) *Kiyosi-san wa hanbaagaa o tabe-mas-u ka?*
'Does Kiyoshi eat hamburgers?'

(65) a. *Iie, tabe-masen.*

(65) b. *Iie, hanbaagaa wa tabe-masen.*
'No, he doesn't eat hamburgers.'

Sentence (65a) is a flat denial of the proposition, whereas (65b) implies that the answerer has a specific intention of conveying the idea that he eats something but, unfortunately, does not eat hamburgers. In other words, in (65b), the speaker is not denying Kiyoshi's eating but denies that what he eats is a hamburger. The particle *wa* that is attached to *hamburger*, accordingly, marks the scope of negation.

The particle *wa*, then, is attached to various constituents of the sentence and marks the scope of negation. Consider the following sentences:

(66) a. *Kiyosi wa Kurisumasu ni okaasan ni purezento o*
Christmas mother present
age-na-kat-ta.
give-negative-past
'Kiyoshi did not give a present to his mother for Christmas.'

b. *Kiyosi wa Kurisumasu ni* ***wa*** *okaasan ni purezento o age-na-kat-ta.*

c. *Kiyosi wa Kurisumasu ni okaasan ni* ***wa*** *purezento o age-na-kat-ta.*
d. *Kiyosi wa Kurisumasu ni okaasan ni purezento* ***wa*** *age-na-kat-ta.*
e. *Kiyosi wa Kurisumasu ni okaasan ni purezento o age* ***wa*** *si-na-kat-ta.*

Sentences (66a–e) may all be translated as 'Kiyoshi did not give a present to his mother for Christmas.' Sentences (66a–e), however, do not mean the same thing. Sentence (66b) means that Kiyoshi gave a present to his mother but it was not for Christmas. Sentence (66c) means that Kiyoshi gave somebody a present for Christmas, but it was not his mother. Sentence (66d) negates 'a present' and says that Kiyoshi gave something to his mother for Christmas, but it was not a present. Sentence (66e) means that Kiyoshi did something with his present to his mother for Christmas, but it was not giving. Sentence (66a) carries no presupposition, unless *wa* is stressed. With the stressed *wa*, the sentence means that someone gave a present to his mother but it was not Kiyoshi.

Presuppositional Analysis of the Scope of Negation

Basically, there seem to be two ways of approaching this problem. One is to allow the negative to be freely attached to any constituent of the sentence, whether NP or V (including adverbial phrases, etc.). NEGATIVE, then, will be transposed to the end of the sentence, leaving the particle *wa* behind. By this operation (67a) will be converted into (67b):

(67)
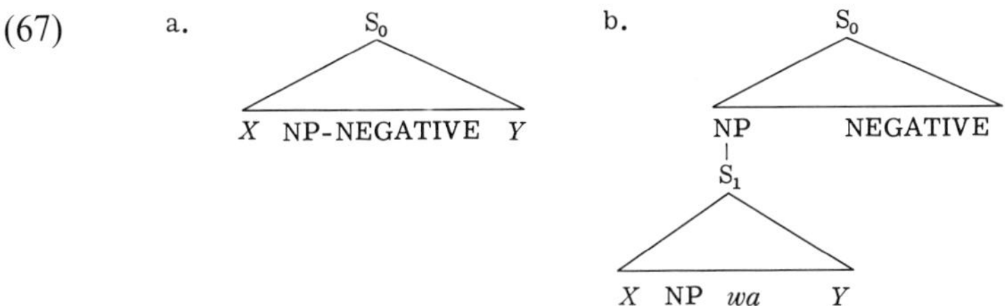

If we take this approach, however, it is necessary to distinguish sentence negation from NP or verb phrase negation.

Generative semantics has generally accounted for the scope differences in terms of higher predicates and the relative height of these predicates. For example, G. Lakoff's (1970) famous sentence *I don't beat my wife because I like her* is ambiguous between the following two readings. In the first reading, I do not beat my wife, and the reason is that I like her. In the second reading, on the other hand, I beat my wife, but the reason is something other than the fact that I like my wife. G. Lakoff (1970) accounts for these ambiguities by the relative height of two predicates—NEGATIVE and the reason adverbial. Namely, in the first reading, the reason adverbial is placed higher in the tree than the NEGATIVE, whereas, in the second reading, NEGATIVE is higher. Moreover, in the first reading, the speaker presupposes that he likes his wife, while in the second reading, it is presupposed that the speaker beats his wife. In terms of a higher predicate analysis, this distinction between presupposition and assertion, however, is not systematically handled.

Now, the use of this *wa* is not restricted to the negative sentences. Consider the following sentence:

(68) *Ano hito wa mainiti sake* **wa** *nomi-mas-u.*
that person every day wine drink

Sentence (68) implies that the man usually does not drink some unspecified thing every day, but he drinks wine every day.

The function of *wa*, then, is to exclude NP introduced by *wa* from the set of objects of a specified function. Kuroda notes (1969a) that the non-subjective use of *wa* is of the same character as *mo* 'also', *sae* 'even', and *demo* 'even', and that the meaning of *wa* will be formalized in a similar fashion, 'perhaps, in the scheme of some kind of modal logic [pp. 146–147].'

Formalization aside, I will introduce the contrastive *wa* from the interaction of presupposition and assertion. According to this analysis, only the sentence negation is required. Sentence (69), for example, is assumed to have the following underlying structure:

(69) *Ano hito wa sake* **wa** *nom-ana-i.*
'That person does not drink wine.'

(69′)

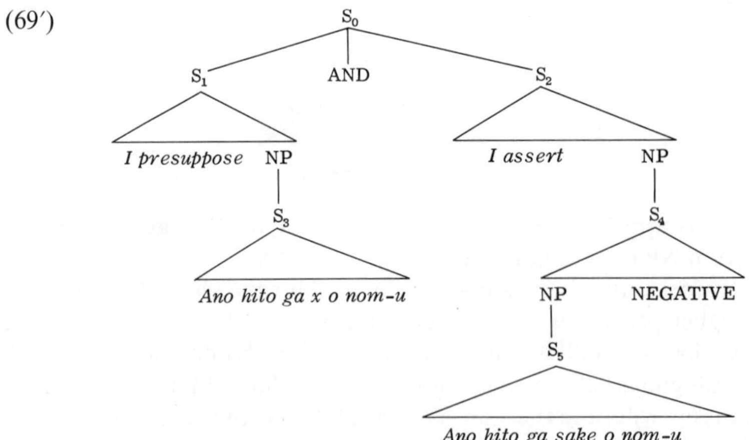

The rule of contrastive *wa* insertion, then, will insert *wa* immediately after a constituent in S_5 that is not identical to a constituent in S_3, if and only if $[_{\alpha}\text{NEG}]_{S_3}$ and $[-_{\alpha}\text{NEG}]_{S_4}$ hold.[12] S_1, then, will be deleted.[13]

Wa and the Quantifiers

The position of the particle *wa* seems to play a crucial role in determining the total versus partial negation readings of quantifiers. Observe the following sentences:

(70) *Misigan no gakusei ga minna demo ni it-ta soo-da yo.*
students all demonstration hear
'I hear that all the students at Michigan went to the demonstration.'

(71) *Sonna koto wa na-i yo.*
'Such a thing can't be.'
a. *Misigan no gakusei* ***wa*** *minna ik-ana-kat-ta yo.*
'None of the students at Michigan went.'
b. *Misigan no gakusei ga minna iki* ***wa*** *si-na-kat-ta yo.*
'Not all the students at Michigan went.'
c. %*Misigan no gakusei ga minna* ***wa*** *ik-ana-kat-ta yo.*
'Not all the students at Michigan went.'
d. *Minna ga iki* ***wa*** *si-na-kat-ta yo.*
'Not all went.'

[12] I do not have a good argument for introducing the presupposition in the logical structure here. Muraki (1970), in accounting for presuppositional differences associated with different stress patterns of sentences (e.g., *Jóhn gave Mary the book*, *John gave Máry the book*, etc.), incorporates presuppositions into the deep structures. He introduces a two-place predicate *presuppose*, whose first argument is the presupposition for the second argument. The presupposition is, then, subsequently deleted. However, it might turn out, as Karttunen (1970b:329) mentions, that implied proposition is derivable from the original sentence by certain rules of inference.

[13] Although he does not talk about presupposition and assertion, Soga (1966) also derives the contrastive *wa* from the interaction of positive and negative sentences. His *wa* insertion rule is formulated as follows:

$$\text{X} - \text{Y} - \text{Z} - \text{T} - ga_2 - \text{X}' - \text{Y}' - \text{Z}' - \text{T} \Longrightarrow$$
$$\text{X} - \text{Y} - wa - \text{Z} - \text{T} - ga_2 - \text{X}' - \text{Y}' - \text{wa} - \text{Z}' - \text{T}$$

Y $\neq$ Y′, but they share the same semantic features

$\text{Z} = \text{Z}' - \text{A} + na$ or $\text{Z}' = \text{Z} - \text{A} + na$

$$\text{Y, Y}' = \begin{Bmatrix} \text{Nom} \\ \text{I-}te \\ \text{Aj-}ku \\ \text{Av} \end{Bmatrix}$$

Then, an optional transformation deletes sentence$_2$:

$$\underbrace{\text{X} - \text{Y} - wa - \text{Z} - \text{T}}_{1} - \underbrace{ga_2 - \text{X}' - \text{Y}' - wa - \text{Z}' - \text{T}}_{2} \Longrightarrow 1$$

e. *Minna* ***wa*** *ik-ana-kat-ta yo.*
'Not all went.'

f. *Minna ik-ana-kat-ta yo.*
'Nobody went.'

Sentences (71a) and (71f) are unmarked cases and imply total negation. Sentences (71b–e) are cases of partial negation.

Now, compare (71b) and (71c) with (72):

(72) *Misigan no gakusei ga minna ik-ana-kat-ta yo.*

Sentence (72) is formed by deleting the particle *wa* from (71b) and (71c). Sentence (72), then, is a total negation, and means that none of the students at Michigan went. *Ga*, here, has the exhaustive listing interpretation. So, it is clear from these examples that the total versus partial negation readings depend crucially on the position of the particle *wa*. If *wa* follows the quantifier, the partial negation reading is rendered.

Compare the following two sentences:

(73) a. *Amerikazin* $\textbf{\textit{wa}}_1$ *minna syooziki-de-*$(wa)_2$ *na-i.*
Americans all honest
'None of the Americans are honest (but they are something else.)'

b. *Amerikazin ga minna syooziki-de-****wa*** *na-i.*
'Not all Americans are honest.'

Sentence (73a) has the total negation reading, while (73b) has the partial negation reading. Notice here that both (73a) and (73b) contain the particle *wa* following the quantifier. The difference here is that (73a) remains as a total negation even if the second *wa* is deleted, but (73b) will not remain a partial negation. In other words, wa_2 in (73a) is optional, whereas *wa* in (73b) is obligatory, to render the respective interpretations.

There is a dialect split on the acceptability of (71c), in which *wa* immediately follows the quantifier. Among six native speakers whom I asked about these sentences, about half of them accepted (71c). If, however, the subject NP—*Misigan no gakusei*—is deleted [as in (71e)], everybody accepts the sentence. Sentence (71e) implies the partial negation. Moreover, if the quantified NP is in the object position, as in (74):

(74) *Syukudai o zenbu* ***wa*** *yat-te ik-ana-kat-ta.*
homework all do
'I didn't go having finished all the homework.'

the sentence is unanimously accepted, with the partial negation reading. Even for those who accept sentence (71c), the following sentences are not acceptable:

(75) a. ***Nihonzin ga dare mo* **wa** *kanemoti-de na-i.*
Japanese rich

b. ***Basu to densya to dotira mo* **wa** *benri-de na-i.*
bus train both convenient

Therefore, there are quantifiers that cannot be immediately followed by *wa*, such as *dare mo*, *nani mo*, and *dotira mo*. Those that do take an immediately following *wa* are *minna* 'everybody', *subete* 'all', *zenbu* 'all', etc. This will be taken care of by an output condition on the surface structure that particles *mo* and *wa* are incompatible with each other.[14]

Sentences that contain quantifiers and *wa*, then, are also derived from the interaction of presupposition and assertion, as the earlier analysis of contrastive *wa* suggested. Sentence (71a), then, will be derived, if the contrastive stress is placed on *wa*, from a structure like the following:[15]

(71a) *Misigan no gakusei wa minna ik-ana-kat-ta yo.*
'None of the students at Michigan went.'

(76)

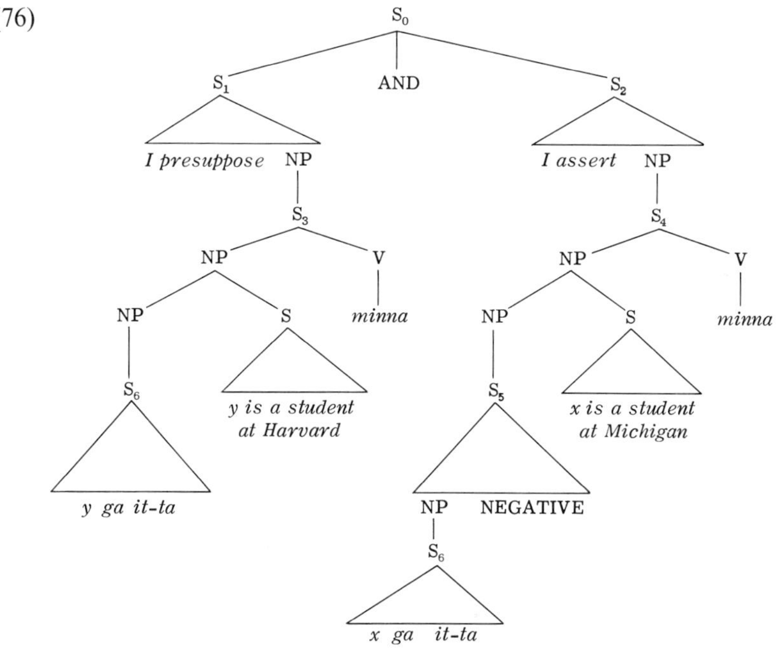

[14]The time quantifier *itumo* 'always', although it contains *mo*, can be followed by *wa*, as in (i):

(i) *Itumo wa koohii-zya na-i.*
'Usually I do not drink coffee, but today I take coffee.'

Thus, the output condition does not apply to *itumo*. *Itumo*, however, seems to behave a bit differently from other quantifiers, and needs further investigation.

[15]Concerning the deep structures of quantifiers, see J. McCawley (1973c).

Wa assignment will insert *wa* after x; then the quantifier will be lowered.

Sentences (71b) and (71c) are derived from the following underlying structure:

(71b) *Misigan no gakusei ga minna iki wa si-na-kat-ta yo.*
'Not all the students of Michigan went.'

(71c) *Misigan no gakusei ga minna wa ik-ana-kat-ta yo.*

(77)

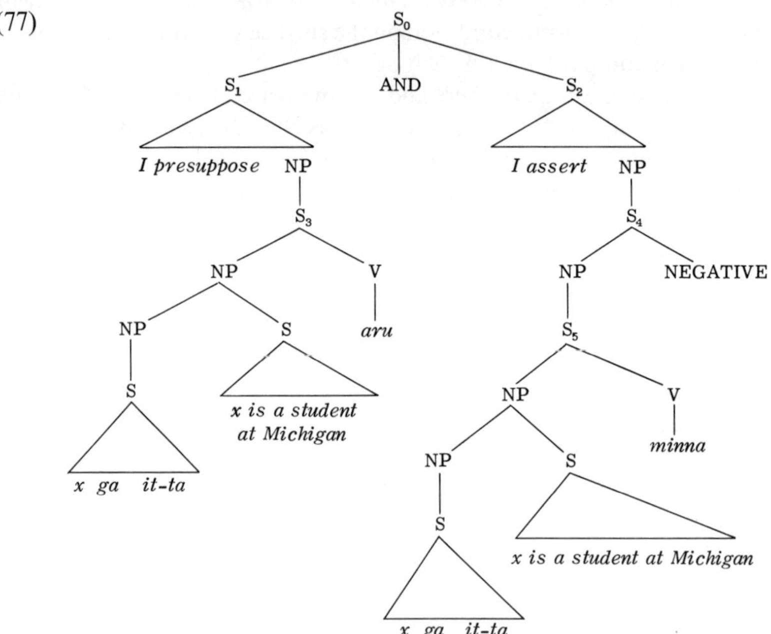

Wa assignment will insert *wa* after *minna*, and then, by quantifier lowering, *minna wa* will be lowered. With the deletions mentioned before, (71c) is rendered.

Now, there is a rule of *wa* shifting that will transpose any *wa* in a sentence to the end of that sentence.[16] In other words, (78), with proper intonation, can be interpreted as (78a) and (78b):

[16]Curiously, *wa* is not necessarily shifted to the end of the sentence. Observe the following sentences:

(i) *Watasi wa benkyoo-su-ru tame ni wa gakkoo e iki-masen.*
I study-do in order to school go

Sentence (i) presupposes that I go to school, and says that it is not for studying that I go. Compare (i) with (ii):

(ii) *Watasi wa benkyoo-su-ru tame ni gakkoo e wa iki-masen.*

Sentence (ii), in one reading, is synonymous with (i). That is to say, in cases like (ii), *wa* merely is shifted to the following constituent and still retains the same reading.

(78) *Taroo wa kinoo Masao ni ai wa si-na-kat-ta.*
yesterday meet
'Taro didn't meet Masao yesterday.'

(78a) *Taro didn't meet Masao* ***yesterday*** *(but some other day).*

(78b) *Taro didn't meet* ***Masao*** *yesterday (but some other person).*

Of course, (78) has the regular reading 'Taro didn't ***meet*** Masao yesterday (but did something else).' It is noted, also, that the contrastive *wa* that is attached to the subject of the sentence cannot be shifted.

Sentence (71b), therefore, results by shifting *wa* after Q (quantifier) to the end of the sentence.

In this section, we have observed the role of *wa* in negative sentences, particularly *wa* as defining the scope of negation. It was suggested that the presupposition of the sentence must somehow be represented in order to account for the scope differences of negative sentences.

5. NEGATIVE POLARITY ITEMS

Preliminary Look at Polarity Items

In English, items like *any*, *at all*, *drink a drop*, and many others are considered negative polarity items (i.e., require the presence of the negative in the sentence). It has been observed, however, that these items also occur in sentences without an overt negative if certain conditions are met: If a sentence is a question, *if* clause, or comparative, and if a sentence contains items like *odd*, *too*, *surprised*, *difficult*, etc. Moreover, as R. Lakoff (1969b) and Borkin (1971) point out, presuppositions of the speaker play a crucial role in determining the distribution of polarity items. Our task here, then, is to find out what are the negative polarity items in Japanese and what are the negative environments.

In Japanese, the items under the column NEGATIVE in Table 1 represent some of the negative polarity items.

Table 1

Positive	Positive-Negative	Negative
Indeterminate + *ka/mo*		
dare-ka 'somebody'		*dare-mo* 'nobody'[17]
nani-ka 'something'		*nani-mo* 'nothing'
doko-ka e 'somewhere'		*doko e mo* 'nowhere'

(Continued)

[17] *Dare-mo*, *nani-mo*, and *doko-e-mo* must be read as da|re-mo, na|ni-mo, and do|ko-e-mo.

Positive	Positive-Negative	Negative
itu-ka 'sometime'	*itu-mo* 'always, never'	
doka-ka 'somewhere'	*doko-mo* 'everywhere, nowhere'	
dore-ka 'some one of'	*dore-mo* 'every one of, none of'	
dotira-ka 'either one of'	*dotira-mo* 'both, neither'	
ikura-ka 'somewhat'	*ikura-mo* 'a lot, not a whole lot'	
Indeterminate + *demo*		
nan-demo 'everything, anything'		
⋮		
Negative adverbs		*kessite* 'never'
		yomoya 'surely not'
		masaka 'by no means'
		Sika 'only, nothing but'
Degree adverbs		
zuibun 'extremely'	*zenzen* 'at all'	*tittomo* 'not at all'
taihen 'very'	*mattaku* 'utterly'	*sukosi-mo* 'not a bit'
totemo 'very'	*sibaraku* 'a while'	*ikkoo ni* 'not a bit'
hizyooni 'considerably'	*zutto* 'all during'	*kaimoku* 'not at all'
sootoo 'fairly'		
hidoku 'extremely'		
kanari 'quite'		*anmari* 'not too'
naka naka 'quite'		*mettani* 'rarely'
issoo 'all the more'	*zyuubunni* 'enough'	*taisite* 'not so'
taitei 'nearly'	*takusan* 'much/many'	*rokuni* 'not much'
motto 'more'	*sukkari* 'completely'	*betuni* 'particularly'
	kanzenni 'completely'	
sukosi 'a bit'		*sonnani* 'not very'
ikubun 'to some extent'		
tasyoo 'somewhat'		
Idiomatic phrases:		
		sasitukae (nai) 'be all right'
		x ni oyob (anai) 'don't need to'
		manziri to mo si (nai) 'do not sleep a wink'
		me ga (nai) 'be crazy about'
		⋮
Numbers 1 and 2 + counter:		
	itido 'once'	*itido-mo* 'not once'
	nido-mo 'twice'	*nido-to* 'not even twice'

Some comments follow:

1. INDETERMINATES + *ka* are positive polarity items. The corresponding INDETERMINATES + *mo*, however, are divided into two groups: (a) *Dare-/nani-/doko e-mo* occur only in a negative environment and, hence, will

be referred to as type N; (b) others occur in both positive and negative sentences. When they occur in positive sentences, they mean 'every-' while, in the negative sentences, they mean 'none'. Among them, *doko-mo*, *dore-mo*, and *dotira-mo*, however, carry no accent when they are used under negation, a characteristic of negative indefinites. These items will be discussed later.

2. Some of the degree adverbs like *zuibun, taihen, totemo*, etc., are positive polarity items. Observe the following sentences:

(79) a. *Taroo wa* {*taihen* / *totemo* / *hizyooni*} *yorokonde* {*i-ta.* / **i-na-kat-ta.*}
very be glad

b. *Kinoo wa* {*kanari* / *sootoo* / *zuibun*} {*tukare-ra.* / **tukare-na-kat-ta.*} {'got tired' / 'wasn't tired'}

c. *Paatii de* {*sukosi* / *hidoku*} {*yot-ta.* / **yow-ana-kat-ta.*} {'got drunk' / 'didn't get drunk'}

Some of these words, however, do appear in sentences that contain the negative *na*. Observe the following sentences:

(80) *Ano hito wa* {*hidoku* / *taihen* / *totemo* / *kanari*} {*otituki ga na-i.* / *hin ga na-i.*} {'be restless' / 'be vulgar'}

However, these items also occur with negative prefixes that do not allow the occurrence of negative words in their environment:

(81) *Ano hito wa* {*hidoku* / *taihen* / *totemo* / *kanari*} *hu-koona hito-da.*
un-happy.

It seems necessary, then, to distinguish between absolute and relative positiveness. If we take two points—A meaning happiness and B meaning its opposite, unhappiness—we can approach A and B from point C.

A ⇠ X ⇢ B
(happiness) C (unhappiness)

As far as we approach A and B from the point of view of C, the direction of both is positive (toward the poles A and B), whether the absolute values of A and B are positive or not. In other words, in (80) and (81) we can take 'unhappiness' or 'restlessness' as a fixed quality of a person and describe the extent to which a person IS unhappy or restless. If we want to mark the extent to which a person is 'negatively marked' from the point of view of C (as in the direction of dotted lines in the preceding chart) concerning qualities A and B, positive polarity degree adverbs cannot be used, regardless of the absolute values of A and B. So:

(82) **Ano hito wa* {*hidoku* / *taihen* / *totemo* / *kanari*} *hu-koo-de-na-i.*

In this sense, then, I think we can still call items like *hidoku, taihen, totemo, kanari*, etc., 'positive polarity items'.

3. Numerals plus counters present an interesting pattern. In Japanese, when one counts things one has to use counters, depending on the nature or type of object in question. For example, *-hon* is a counter for objects that are long and cylindrical in shape; *-do* is used for counting frequency; etc. Numeral 1 + COUNTER + *mo* occurs only in negative sentences. Numeral (2 ... *n*) + COUNTER + *mo*, however, occurs in both positive and negative sentences. Numeral 2 + COUNTER + *to* occurs only in negative sentences. Consider the following sentences:

(83)

a. *Itido* {*ik-ana-kat-ta.* / *it-ta.*}
'I did not go once.'
'I went once.'

b. *Itido-mo* {*ik-ana-kat-ta.* / **it-ta.*}
'I did not go even once.'

c. {*Ni* / *San* / ⋮} *do-mo* {*it-ta.* / *ik-ana-kat-ta.*}
'I went (or didn't go) as many as ... times'

d. *Nido-to* {**it-ta.* / *ik-ana-kat-ta.*}

In (83c), with negative, the sentence is ambiguous between the 'less than' interpretation (I went once but not twice) and the 'exactly' interpretation (it was twice that I did not go). In the latter reading, the sentence also implies a disproof on the part of the speaker in the sense that not going twice is against the norm.

Mo Words and *Ka* Words

In the preceding subsection, a number of polarity-sensitive items in Japanese were listed. In the rest of this chapter, I would like to focus my attention on indeterminates + *ka/mo* and investigate what triggers the occurrence of these words. Henceforth, indeterminates + *ka* and indeterminates + *mo* will be referred to as '*KA* words' and '*MO* words', respectively. *MO* words require the presence of NEGATIVE in the sentence, while *KA* words do not occur in negative sentences, as shown in (84) and (85):

(84) a. *Dare-mo ko-na-kat-ta.*
b. **Dare-mo ki-ta.*

(85) a. *Dare-ka ki-ta.*
b. **Dare-ka ko-na-kat-ta.*

In connection with *MO* and *KA* words, I would like to note two observations. First, although Kuroda (1965b), in his analysis of *KA* and *MO*, derives *MO* from *DEMO*, I think there are slight meaning differences between *mo* and *demo* and, hence, that *MO* cannot be a surface reflection of *DEMO*. Kuroda correctly observes that *MO* words only occur in the negative sentence, while *DEMO* words are restricted to positive sentences. However, this is true only with *nanimo* and *daremo*, and there are other *MO* pronouns that occur not only in negative sentences but also in positive sentences. Consider the following sentences:

(86) a. *Ano hito wa nihongo mo eigo mo dotira mo hanas-e-na-i.*
'That man can speak neither Japanese nor English.'
b. *Ano hito wa nihongo mo eigo mo dotira mo hanas-e-ru.*
'That man can speak both Japanese and English.'

(87) a. *Eigakan wa doko mo man'in-da.*
movie theatre full
'The movie theatres are full everywhere.'
b. *Eigakan wa doko mo man'in-de-na-i.*
'The movie theatres are not full anywhere.'

Now, (86b) and (87a) contrast with (88a) and (88b), respectively, which contain the DEMO words:

(88) a. *Ano hito wa nihongo to eigo to dotira demo hanas-e-ru.*
b. *Eigakan wa doko demo man'in-da.*

So, if the indeterminates are *dotira*, *doko*, *dore*, and *itu*, *demo* and *mo* contrast in positive sentences. If we want to account for indefinites other than *nanimo* and *daremo*, then, we cannot simply consider *demo* the only source for *mo*.

Moreover, there seems to be a slight meaning difference between *MO* words and *DEMO* words when they both occur in positive sentences. Compare (86b) with (88a). Sentence (86b) simply states that this person can speak both languages. Sentence (88a) also asserts that this person can speak both languages, but here the assertion seems to apply to one at a time. It implies that he can speak either English or Japanese, whichever the situation demands. Sometimes the situation demands English, and sometimes Japanese. As a result, the assertion extends to the whole set, which includes, in this case, English and Japanese.

The difference becomes a bit clearer in the following examples:

(89) a. *Tikatetu to basu to dotira mo tukai-mas-u.*
subway and bus and both use
'I use both the subway and the bus.'
b. *Tikatetu to basu to dotira demo tukai-mas-u.*
'I use either the subway or the bus.'

Sentence (89a) can mean one of two things:

(90) a. '*I use both the subway and the bus to commute. I have to change from one to the other on the way.*'
b. '*I can go to my destination using only one means of transportation, but I sometimes use the subway and sometimes the bus.*'

Sentence (89b), on the other hand, cannot mean (90a). It means something like (90b). In addition, it says that I can use either the subway or the bus, whichever is more appropriate at the time, for example, whichever arrives first. Therefore, it seems that *demo* implies, basically, a choice of that which is more (or most) appropriate.

Schematically, then, *mo* 'also' and *demo* 'even' seem to have a basic structure like the following:

mo: $(\exists x)\,(\exists y)\ \mathrm{F}x$ and $\mathrm{F}y$
demo: $(\exists x)\,(\exists y)\ \mathrm{F}_{\mathrm{L}}$ whether $\mathrm{L} = x$ or $\mathrm{L} = y$

Sentence (86b) says that the man can speak x and y, where $x =$ Japanese and $y =$ English. Sentence (88a) says that the man can speak L whether $\mathrm{L} = x$ or $\mathrm{L} = y$, where $x =$ Japanese and $y =$ English. The assertion, then, is immediately directed to x and y in the case of *mo*, but not in the case of *demo*.

Demo and *mo* are attached not only to indeterminates but also to ordinary NPs. Consider the following sentences:

(91) *Tanaka-san* {*mo* / *demo*} *toohyoo-si-ni ik-u daroo.*
vote-do-purpose probably
'Tanaka will also be voting.'
'Even Tanaka will be voting.'

With *mo* in (91), the speaker knows that other people will vote and says that Tanaka-san will also vote, in addition to all the other voters. When *demo* is used in (91), however, the speaker's presupposition is quite different. Sentence (91) with *demo*, moreover, is ambiguous between the two readings:

(91) a. '*(We don't have to worry about voting.) Mr. Tanaka or somebody will vote.*'

(91) b. '*(This election is very important and everybody is urged to vote.) So, even Mr. Tanaka (who usually does not vote) will probably vote.*'

Sentence (91) with reading (a) gives a sense of 'irresponsibility' on the part of the speaker. The speaker makes an assumption about Mr. Tanaka—that he is a kind of person who would vote. However, Mr. Tanaka is given merely as an example, and anybody will do for that matter. In reading (b), the speaker is making a completely different assumption concerning Mr. Tanaka—that Mr. Tanaka does not usually participate in voting. Hence, the 'even' sense of *demo* is generated. Consider the negation of (91):

(92) *Tanaka-san demo toohyoo-si-ni ik-ana-i daroo.*
'Even Mr. Tanaka won't go to vote.'

Reading (a) is difficult to obtain here, since a very construed situation has to be established, e.g., 'it is necessary that somebody does not vote'. With the 'even' sense of *demo*, (92) presupposes the opposite of (91), namely, that Mr. Tanaka usually never misses voting. So it seems that the 'even' sense of *demo* is generated when presupposition and assertion do not share the same positive-negative value—when presupposition is negative and assertion is positive, and vice versa. In reading (b), *demo* is usually stressed and is more or less interchangeable with *sae*:

(93) *Tanaka-san sae toohyoo-si-ni ik-u daroo.*

In reading (a) of *demo*, the presupposition is that the thing that is talked about is a typical or normal example. Thus, when the item introduced by *demo* is not typical, as in (94), the statement bears a sarcastic tone:

(94) *Ano mazu-i koohii demo non-de kudasai.*
that bad coffee drink please
'Please drink that bad coffee or something.'

Bad coffee is not something that one would normally drink—therefore, is not something that one would normally invite other people to drink. In either reading of *demo*, then, it is clear that the speaker's subjective feelings toward the proposition are quite different between *demo* and *mo*. The function of *mo* is simply to add an item to other instances of the same function. *Demo*, on the other hand, introduces typical or extreme choices. *Demo*, then, leaves choices other than those introduced by *demo* itself.

Second, both *mo* and *ka* behave like conjunctions. *Mo* conjoins arguments, as in (95), and *ka* disjoins arguments, as in (96):

(95) *Taroo mo Ziroo mo hon o kat-ta.*
'Both Taro and Jiro bought a book.'

(96) *Taroo ka Ziroo ga hon o kat-ta.*
'Either Taro bought a book or Jiro bought a book.'

Now, recall (84a) and (85a):

(84) a. *Dare mo ko-na-kat-ta.*

(85) a. *Dare ka ki-ta.*

As Kuroda indicates, *mo* in (84a) and *ka* in (85a) are also conjunctions. When (84a) is uttered, for example, it is felt that a shadow sentence like (97) underlies (84a):

(97) *(Watasi no tomodati wa) (Taroo) mo ko-na-kat-ta, (Ziroo) mo ko-na-kat-ta, (Saburoo) mo ko-na-kat-ta, ... (n) mo ko-na-kat-ta.*

It is felt in (84a) that by negating each one of the members of a predetermined set, all of them are negated. Sentence (85a) will be paraphrased as follows:

(98) *(Watasi no tomodati wa) (Taroo) ga ki-ta ka, (Ziroo) ga ki-ta ka, (Saburoo) ga ki-ta ka, ... (n) ga ki-ta ka des-u.*
'(Among my friends), Taro came, or Jiro came, or Saburo came, ... somebody came.'

Sentence (85a) says that among the members of some predetermined set that includes Taro, Jiro, Saburo, etc., some member came.

Mo in (84a), then, functions like the universal quantifier ∀, and *ka* in (85a) functions like the existential quantifier ∃.[18] Sentences (97) and (98), then, can also be paraphrased as follows:

[18]This was first brought to my attention by J. McCawley in his course offered at the University of Michigan in winter 1970.

(97′) $\forall x\ (x \in \text{my friends})\ (x\ \textit{ga ko-na-kat-ta})$

(98′) $\exists\ x\ (x \in \text{my friends})\ (x\ \textit{ga ki-ta})$

Mo and *ka* after indeterminates will, henceforth, be derived from higher predicates of *MO* and *KA*, respectively, which are in fact quantifiers. Sentence (84a), then, will have the following logical structure:

(99)

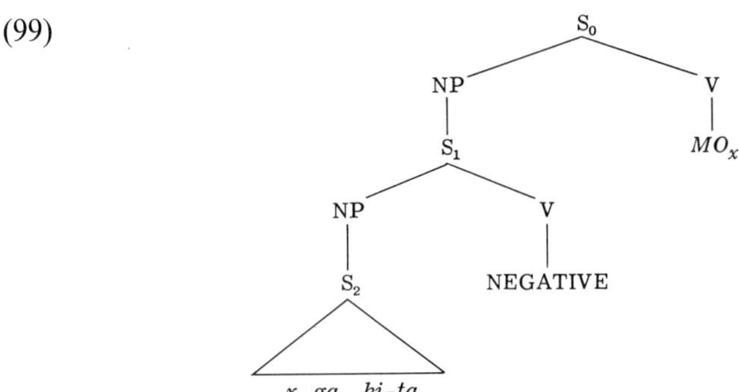

MO immediately commands NEGATIVE in the logical structure and is subsequently lowered into S_2.

Negative Environment in Japanese

Indefinites and Complement Sentences

MO words occur in the complement sentences of NEGATIVE transport verbs, as in (100)–(102), and non-NEGATIVE transport verbs, as in (103)–(105), while *KA* words do not occur in negative sentences. Examine the following sentences:

(100) a. *Dare-mo ku-ru hazu-de-wa na-i.*
'Nobody is supposed to come.'

b. **Dare-ka ku-ru hazu-de-wa na-i.*
'Somebody is not supposed to come.'

(101) a. *Watasi wa titi ni nani-mo kat-te hosiku-na-i.*
'I don't want my father to buy anything for me.'

b. **Watasi wa titi ni nani-ka kat-te hosiku-na-i.*[19]

(102) a. *Kyoo wa dare-mo ku-ru to omow-ana-i.*
'I don't think anybody is coming today.'

b. **Kyoo wa dare-ka ku-ru to omow-ana-i.*

[19]Sentence (101b) might be acceptable if *nani-ka* is interpreted as *nani-ka iroiro to* 'many things, this and that' or *nani ya ka ya.*

(103) a. *Ganzii wa nani-mo tabe-ru koto ga deki-na-kat-ta.*
'Gandhi could not eat anything.'
b. *Ganzii wa nani-mo tabe-na-i koto ga deki-ta.*
'Gandhi was capable of not eating anything.'
c. **Ganzii wa nani-ka tabe-ru koto ga deki-na-kat-ta.*

(104) a. *Watasi wa Zimu ni nani-mo kasi-te moraw-ana-kat-ta.*
'I didn't ask Jim to lend me anything.'
b. *Watasi wa Zimu ni nani-mo kas-ana-i-de morat-ta.*
'I asked Jim not to lend (him) anything.'
c. **Watasi wa Zimu ni nani-ka kasi-te moraw-ana-kat-ta.*

(105) a. *Watasi wa asa kara nani-mo tabe-te i-masen.*
'I haven't eaten anything since morning.'
b. *Watasi wa asa kara nani-mo tabe-na-i-de i-mas-u.*
'I haven't eaten anything since this morning.'
c. **Watasi wa asa kara nani-ka tabe-te i-masen.*

Now, in cases (103)–(105) the (a) and (b) sentences are not paraphrases of each other. For example, in (104a), *nani-mo* modifies [*moraw-ana-kat-ta*]. Sentence (104a) means that there is nothing I asked Jim to lend me. In (104b), on the other hand, *nani-mo* modifies [*kas-ana-i*]. Sentence (104b) means that I specifically asked Jim not to lend (him) anything. Take (105a), which simply means that I have not eaten anything since morning. Sentence (105b) means that I made a point of not eating since morning (because, e.g., I am on a hunger strike.) Sentences (104a) and (104b) will have the following logical structures:

(104a′)

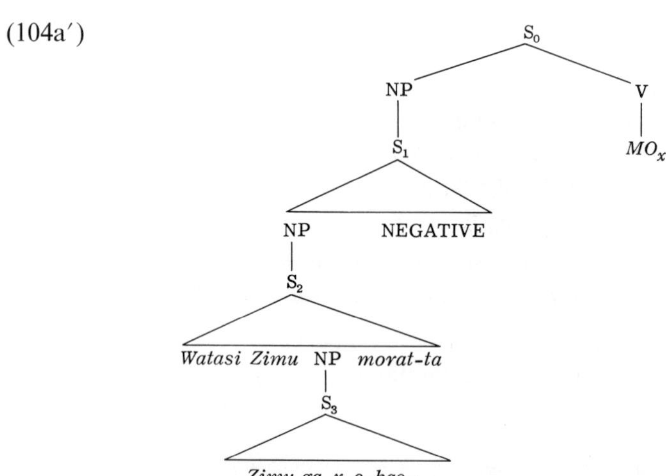

(104b′)

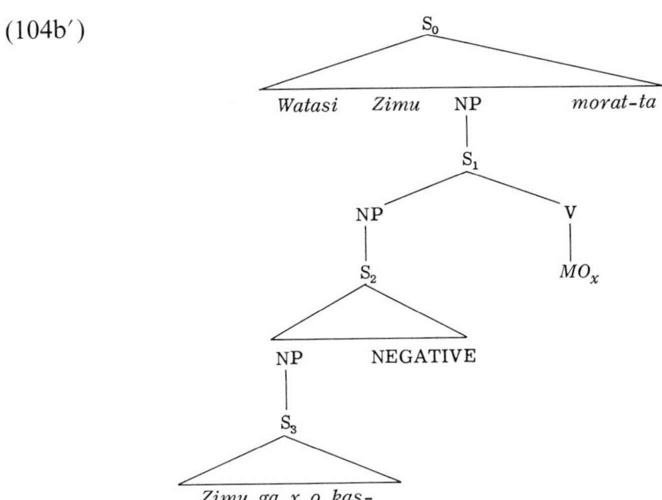

In both cases, *MO* immediately commands NEGATIVE in the logical structure, and is subsequently lowered into a sentence that is simply commanded by NEGATIVE.

Now, observe the following sentences:

(106) *Kyoo wa dare-mo ku-ru to wa iw-ana-kat-ta yo.*
'I didn't say that anybody will come today.'

(107) *Boku wa anata no tomodati wa dare-mo hannin-da to wa*
friend criminal
ii-masen-desi-ta yo.
'I didn't say that any of your friends were criminals.'

(108) a. *Boku wa boku no tomodati wa dare-mo uragirimono-da*
traitor
to wa sinzi-te i-na-i.
believe
'I don't believe that any of my friends are traitors.'

b. ?**Taroo wa dare-mo sin-da koto o sinzi-na-kat-ta.*
'Taro didn't believe the fact that anybody died.'

(109) a. *Watasi wa kondo no sensoo de wa dare-mo sin-da to*
this last war die
wa kii-te i-na-i.
hear
'I haven't heard that anybody died in the last war.'

b. ?**Watasi wa sensoo de dare-mo sin-da koto o kik-ana-kat-ta.*

(110) *Watasi wa Taroo wa ki-te-mo nani-mo yu-u to wa kitai-si-te i-na-i.*
'I don't expect Taro to say anything even if he comes.'

(111) **Watasi wa dare-mo mikata ni nat-te kure-ta koto o*
supporter become
wasure-na-kat-ta.
forget
'I didn't forget the fact that anybody became my supporter.'

As Kuno observes (1973, pp. 213–222), *koto* represents 'an action, state, or event which the speaker presupposes to be true', while with *to* there is no such presupposition. (Cf. the chapter on complementation in this volume.) *MO* words are acceptable in the complements with *to*, given a certain context. Sentence (107) is quite acceptable as a reply to the following statement—almost an accusation:

(112) *Anata wa watasi no tomodati no Tanaka-san ga hannin-da to it-ta soo-des-u ne.*
'I hear that you said that Tanaka-san, who is my friend, is a criminal, didn't you?'

The speaker is almost making an apology, emphasizing that he did not make such an assertion as (107)—there really is no one among the addressee's friends whom the speaker said is a criminal.

To recapitulate, then, (106), (107), (108a), and (109a) are acceptable given a certain context; namely, an assertion has reportedly been made and the speaker denies that such an assertion has been made. In other words, in these sentences, the scope of *mo* includes the main verb. As in (108b), (109b), and (111), *mo* words are not acceptable in *koto* factive complements.

There is, however, one exception, and that is a class of verbs that show one's emotion—*nageku* 'grieve', *yorokobu* 'be pleased', *kanasimu* 'be sad', etc. Consider the following sentences:

(113) a. *Taroo wa dare-mo ko-na-kat-ta to yorokon-da.*
'Taro was pleased that nobody came.'
b. **Taroo wa dare-mo ki-ta to wa yorokob-ana-kat-ta.*

(114) a. *Taroo wa doko-e-mo ik-e-na-i to kanasin-da.*
'Taro was sad that he could not go anywhere.'
b. **Taroo wa doko-e-mo ik-e-ru to wa kanasim-ana-kat-ta.*

Notice that, with emotive verbs, it is possible to replace *to* with *to itte*, without changing the meaning of the sentence. Consider the following sentence:

(115) *Taroo wa dare-mo ko-na-kat-ta* $\left\{\begin{array}{l}\textit{to} \\ \textit{to it-te}\end{array}\right\}$ *yorokon-da.*
'Taro was pleased saying that nobody came.'

This, then, is accounted for by formulating a constraint that *mo* is not lowered into the complement sentences of the verbs that hold the redundancy rule [*to* → *to itte*].

To summarize, *MO* immediately commands NEGATIVE in the logical structure, and is lowered into a sentence that is commanded by NEGATIVE. Like English *any*, *MO* is lowered into a nonfactive complement sentence, but not into a factive complement sentence. *KA* words do not occur if they are commanded by NEGATIVE, except when a direct quotation reading is possible.

Indefinites and Questions

Consider the following sentences:

(116) a. *Rusutyuu ni dare-ka ki-masi-ta ka?*
while absent somebody
'Did somebody come while I was gone?'
b. *Rusutyuu ni dare-ka ki-masen-desi-ta ka?*
'Didn't somebody come while I was gone?'
c. *Rusutyuu ni dare-mo ki-masen-desi-ta ka?*
'Didn't anybody come while I was gone?'
d. **Rusutyuu ni dare-mo ki-masi-ta ka?*

In ordinary questions, namely, questions ending with *ka*, *MO* words require the presence of an overt NEGATIVE. Hence, sentence (116d) is ungrammatical. *KA* words, however, seem to be a lot freer in this respect. *KA* words, in questions, can occur under an immediately commanding NEGATIVE, as in (116b). While (116a) is a question requesting the addressee to give him information as to whether someone came or not, (116b) will be uttered when the speaker has a much firmer basis for believing that someone came.

Consider the following sentences:

(117) a. *Nani-ka tabe-masen ka?*
'Aren't you going to eat something?'
b. *Nani-mo tabe-masen ka?*
'Are you not going to eat anything?'
c. *Asita wa doko-ka-e iki-masen ka?*
'Aren't we/you going somewhere tomorrow?'

d. *Asita wa doko-e-mo iki-masen ka?*
'Are you/we not going anywhere tomorrow?'

Sentences (117a) and (117c) are explicit invitations, while (117b) and (117d) are information-seeking questions.

Sentences (116c), (117b), and (117d) can also be uttered when the speaker already has some information that nobody came, he does not eat anything, or he is not going anywhere tomorrow. For example, (117b) can be uttered when the speaker notices that the addressee has not eaten anything or has shown signs of not eating, and the speaker wants to check with the addressee on whether it is his real intention not to eat. In these cases, in which the information is partly known to the speaker, (116c), (117b), and (117d) at the same time express various emotional attitudes of the speaker—e.g., disappointment, accusation, etc.

Although most negative polarity words do not occur in positive questions, there are some that do. NP + 'comparative marker' *hodo* is a negative polarity item, while *yori* is a positive polarity item:[20]

(118) a. *Inu wa kitune hodo* {*rikoo-de-na-i.* / **rikoo-da.*}
dog fox
'Dogs are not as smart as foxes.'

b. *Kitune wa inu yori* {*rikoo-da.* / **rikoo-de-na-i.*}
'Foxes are smarter than dogs.'

Now, observe the following sentences:

(119) *Inu wa kitune* {(a) *hodo* / (b) *yori*} *rikoo-des-u ka?*

(120) *Inu wa kitune* {(a) *hodo* / (b) *yori*} *rikoo-zya ari-masen ka?*

As I have predicted, *yori* occurs in a negative question, (120b). Here, (120b) is not an invitation per se, but the speaker believes that dogs are smarter than foxes and seeks the addressee's confirmation or agreement. Question

[20]Only the case of NP *hodo* is the negative polarity item. Sentence *hodo*, as in the following examples, does occur in positive sentences:

(i) *Asi ga itaku nar-u hodo hasit-ta.*
'I ran so much that my legs began to hurt.'

(ii) *Namida ga de-ru hodo warat-ta.*
'I laughed so much that the tears fell.'

(119b) is an ordinary information-seeking question. Unlike other negative polarity items, *hodo* occurs in a positive question, (119a), which expresses the speaker's suspicion about the truth of the proposition, or his surprise at the addressee's opinion that dogs are as smart as foxes. Question (120a), however, does not suggest such an attitude on the part of the speaker.

Now, there is another type of question—rhetorical—ending with *monoka*. In sentences ending with *monoka* (or *monka*), *MO* words occur but not *KA* words. Moreover, the sentence itself cannot contain an overt negative *na*. Yet *monoka* gives a strong 'negative assertion' to the sentence, not allowing any disagreement from the addressee. Observe the following sentences:

(121) a. *Dare ga ik-u monoka.*
'Who will go? (Nobody will)'
b. *Dare-mo ik-u monoka.*
'Nobody will go.'
c. **Dare-mo ik-ana-i monoka.*
d. **Dare-ka ik-u monoka.*

(122) a. *Doko-e-mo ik-u monoka.*
'I am not going anywhere.'
b. **Doko-ka-e ik-u monoka.*

(123) a. *Nani-mo kat-te yar-u monoka.*
'I am not going to buy anything for you.'
b. **Nani-ka kat-te yar-u monoka.*

Sentences with *monoka* do not begin the discourse, but are preceded by some statement or assumption to which the speaker strongly disagrees. For example, (124a) will be preceded by a statement like (124b):

(124) a. *Dare ga nan to it-ta-tte ik-u monoka.*
who what say-even if
'I am not going whatever people say.'
b. *Onegai-da kara, goryoosin ni ai ni it-te kudasai.*
parents see
'I beg you to go to see your parents.'

Monoka can be decomposed to a noun *mono*, which is traditionally called *keisiki-meisi* in Japanese grammar, or nonabstract nominalizer (by Makino, 1968), and the question marker *ka*. Strong negative assertiveness expressed by *monoka* seems to lie in the particle *ka* or, rather, in one usage of questions. In other words, as in the following sentences, a question is often used to deny its own content. Then, *ka* by itself without *mono* attains the same effect when accompanied by a falling intonation:

(125) *Sonna hutugoona koto ga ari-mas-u ka.*
such unreasonable thing exist
'There can't be such an unreasonable thing.'

(126) *Sonna kattena koto ga i-e-ru mibun des-u ka.*
such selfish thing say-can position
'You are in no position to say such selfish things.'

According to Makino, *no* and *koto* are abstract nominals, while *mono* is a nonabstract nominal. As nominalizers, they share the same syntactic property in that they have to be modified by a sentence:

(127) a. *Sumidagawa ni turi ni it-ta mono-da.*
Sumida River fishing
'We used to go fishing in the Sumida River.'
b. **Mono-da.*

(128) a. *Sumidagawa ni turi ni it-ta koto ga ar-u.*
'I have had the experience of fishing in the Sumida River.'
b. **Koto ga aru.*

(129) a. *Sumidagawa ni turi ni it-ta no-da.*
'I did go fishing in the Sumida River.'
b. **No-da.*

The semantic content of *mono* will become clear when the following sentences are observed:

(130) a. *Yoku Sumidagawa de turi o si-ta mono-da.*
'I used to fish in the Sumida River.'
b. *Sumidagawa de turi o si-ta mono-desyoo ka?*
'Do you think I should fish in the Sumida River?'
c. *Kodomo wa oya no meirei ni sitaga-u mono-da.*
children parents order follow
'Children are supposed to obey their parents' orders.'

Mono, in the past tense, expresses the past habitual action—'we used to'. In (130b), the speaker is asking whether it will be appropriate to fish or not. Sentence (130b) will be contrasted with (131):

(131) *Sumidagawa de turi o si-ta* $\left\{\begin{matrix} koto \\ no \end{matrix}\right\}$ *daroo ka?*

The complement of *koto* is factive, while *no* and *mono* do not suggest the factuality of the complement S. With *no*, the sentence implies that the speaker has perceived something that suggests that these people might have gone fishing. Sentence (130c) seems best to bring out the semantic content of *mono*. Compare (130c) with the following sentence:

(132) *Oya no meirei ni sitaga-u* $\left\{\begin{matrix} \textit{koto} \\ \textit{no} \end{matrix}\right\}$ *da.*

Sentence (132) with *koto* offers advice, namely, that it is best to obey one's parents. With *no*, (132) is almost an order or command, implying that 'you have to obey your parents whether you like it or not'. Kuno (1973) observes that *koto* represents an abstract concept while *no* represents a concrete event that can be perceived by the five senses. (For elaboration on this point, cf. the chapter on complementation in this volume.) This seems to explain the difference between *koto* and *no* in (132); namely, the speaker can assert more strongly a concrete event than an abstract one. *No* bears a strongly emphatic tone and, hence, implies an order. On the other hand, *koto* has a much milder tone and, hence, implies advice. Now, with *mono*, (130c) bears a scolding tone. It implies that 'it is a matter of course that children obey their parents, and what happened to you not to follow this natural law?' *Mono* implies that something is *yo no tune* (way of life) or *toozen-da* (matter of course). Hence the sense of being controlled by natural law.

We have observed the following points:

1. *Monoka* sentences do not begin the discourse.
2. Although *ka* is a question marker, the *monoka* sentence is not a question. It is a strong negative assertion. There is no question in the speaker's mind what the answer is (or should be).
3. *Monoka* can occur in a sentence disjunctively:

(133) *It-ta monoka iw-ana-i monoka mayot-te i-ru.*
say wonder
'I am wondering whether I should say it or not.'

On the basis of these observations, sentences with *monoka* are analyzed into the following meaning postulate:

(I TELL YOU (~(S or ~S)))

Sentence (121b), for example, will have the following semantic structure:

(121b) *Dare-mo ik-u monoka.*

(121b′)

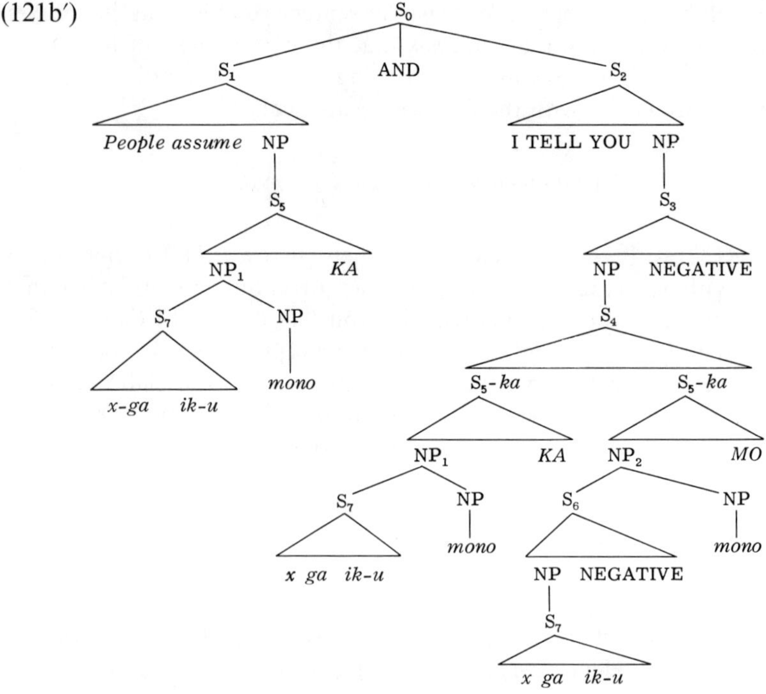

When the speaker utters a sentence like (121b), he believes that nobody will go. This negative assertion is implied in (121) in that what people think should be the case is positive, and this will be subsequently deleted.

To this, quantifier lowering applies first. Second, by forward pronominalization, the first occurrence of NP_1 is deleted under S_4. Third, by context deletion, S_1 is deleted. The performative deletion will subsequently apply, leaving the following structure:

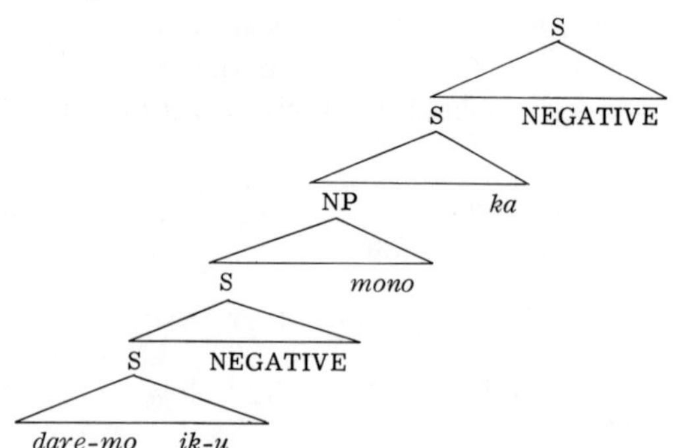

Here the two negatives cancel each other. The presence of the topmost

NEGATIVE will secure *ka* in sentence-final position; otherwise, it will be deleted.[21] This will yield (121b). This cancelation of negatives, however, is purely a syntactic phenomenon and does not change meaning. The meaning is defined by the logical structure.

This analysis will explain the following facts:

1. that *MO* words appear under *monoka*
2. that no NEGATIVE is overtly present, although in meaning it is negative
3. that *KA* words do not appear here. *KA* words do not appear here because, if negative NP_2 is deleted, the topmost NEGATIVE will not be canceled, thus leaving the sentence unacceptable. [KA-NEGATIVE] cannot be lexicalized in Japanese.

INDEFINITES AND CONDITIONALS

Conditional sentences are another negative environment in English. However, here too, we find that, in Japanese, *MO* words have to be commanded by an overt NEGATIVE, while *KA* words are less restricted. Observe the following sentences:

(134) a. *Nani-mo tabe-na-kat-tara, eiga e ture-te it-te.*
eat movie bring go
age-na-i yo.
give
'If you don't eat anything, I won't take you to the movie.'

b. **Nani-mo tabe-tara, eiga e ture-te it-te age-na-i.*

c. *Nani-ka tabe-tara, eiga e ture-te it-te age-ru.*
'If you eat something, I will take you to the movie.'

d. *Nani-ka tabe-tara, eiga e ture-te it-te age-na-i yo.*
'If you eat something, I won't take you to the movie.'

e. *Nani-ka tabe-na-kat-tara, eiga e ture-te it-te age-na-i yo.*
'Unless you eat something, I won't take you to the movie.'

[21] Kuroda (1965b) convincingly showed that in the ordinary declarative sentence, sentence-final *ka* is deleted, as in:

(i) *Taroo ga it-ta* ***ka*** *Ziroo ga it-ta.*

On the other hand, if *ka* is followed by elements like *da* or a question marker, since *ka* is not in the sentence-final position anymore, it is not deleted:

(ii) *Taroo ga it-ta ka Ziroo ga it-ta ka da.*

(iii) *Taroo ga it-ta ka?*

Since, in (134e), the speaker implies that the addressee should eat something, *nani-ka* is acceptable. Consider (135):

(135) $\left\{\begin{array}{l}\textit{Nani-mo}\\ \textit{*Nani-ka}\end{array}\right\}$ *tabe-na-kat-tara, eiga e ture-te it-te age-ru.*
'If you don't eat anything, I will take you to the movie.'

Sentence (135) is ungrammatical with *nani-ka* unless *nani-ka* is interpreted as some object that is actually known to both the speaker and the addressee, or as *nani-ya ka-ya*. Sentence (134e) differs from (135) in that the consequent contains a negative in (134e) while it does not in (135). Now, if, in (134e) and (135), [*x o tabe-ru*] is replaced by A and [*eiga e ture-te ik-u*] by B, those sentences will have the following logical structures:

(134e′) $\sim A \supset \sim B$

(135′) $\sim A \supset B$

In (134e), the speaker presupposes that the addressee wants to go to the movie (the use of *ageru* suggests this). The speaker, by uttering (134e), suggests that if the addressee does A, then B will be the consequence. What Geis and Zwicky (1971)[22] call 'invited inference' is involved here; namely, in ordinary conversation, by uttering (134e) the speaker is committed to the truth of both $\sim A \supset \sim B$ and $A \supset B$.[23] Sentence (134e) PROMISES (134e′) and invites an inference of the form $A \supset B$. The speaker, then, concludes A from $A \supset B$ and B, although this is not a logically valid argument. However, this conclusion A, in turn, affects the syntactic form of (134e) and permits the occurrence of *ka*.

In (135), the speaker presupposes that the addressee wants to go to the movie and, hence, infers that it is necessary for him to do A. Therefore, *ka* is not permitted in (135). However, if in (135) the speaker presupposes that the addressee does not want to go to the movie ($\sim B$), as in (136), then, the *KA* word occurs:

(136) *Nani-ka tabe-na-kat-tara, eiga e ture-te it-te sima-u yo.*
'If you don't eat anything, I will take you to the movie, which you don't want.'

Sentence (136) is a threat, but since the speaker knows that the addressee does not want B to happen, the speaker hopes for the addressee to eat something. Sentence (136) has the logical form $\sim A \supset B$. This invites an inference

[22] I am indebted to Masaaki Yamanashi for calling this reference to my attention.

[23] As Geis and Zwicky say, when $X \supset Y$ invites an inference of the form $\sim X \supset \sim Y$, this inference is not a logically valid one. Similarly, logically invalid arguments are (concluding X from $X \supset Y$ and Y) and (concluding $\sim Y$ from $X \supset Y$ and $\sim X$).

of the form A ⊃ ~B. The speaker, then, concludes A from A ⊃ ~B and ~B. Hence, *KA* words are permitted under this condition.

It was observed earlier that (134d) is a threat in that the speaker warns the addressee not to eat anything. Sentence (134d) has the logical form A ⊃ ~B. This, then, could invite an inference of the form ~A ⊃ B. Although this could be an environment in which *MO* words occur, *MO* words are not acceptable here, as is seen in (134b). My conjecture is that *MO* words are not sensitive to the negative inferred by an invited inference.

Similar sentences containing the conditional *to* follow:

(137) a. *Nani-{mo/ka} si-na-i to, uti e kaer-e-na-i yo.*
do home return-can-NEGATIVE
'Unless you do something, you can't go home.'

b. *Nani-{mo/*ka} si-na-i to, uti e kaer-e-ru yo.*
'If you don't do anything, you can go home.'

c. *Nani-{ka/mo} si-na-i to, uti e kaesi-te sima-u yo.*
'Unless you do something, I will send you back home.'

d. *Nani-{ka/*mo} su-ru to, uti e kaer-e-na-i yo.*
'If you do something, you cannot go home.'

It has been shown that *MO* words occur only in negative conditionals. *KA* words occur in both negative and positive conditionals. When *KA* words occur in negative conditionals, inferences that are made by the speaker play a crucial part in determining their occurrence. These inferences are not necessarily logically equivalent to the statement. Furthermore, the speaker's knowledge of whether or not the addressee wants to fulfill the consequence plays an important part in these inferences.

The Japanese fixed phrases *-te wa ikenai* and *-te mo ii* express prohibition and permission, respectively. So:

(138) a. *It-te wa ike-na-i.*
go not OK
'You should not go.'

b. *It-te mo ii.*
'You may go.'

c. *Ik-ana-kute wa ike-na-i.*
'You must go. (It's not all right if you don't go.)'

Literally, (138a) means 'It is not all right if you go.' Sentence (138b) means 'It is all right if you go.' Sentence (138c) means 'It is not all right if you do not go', thus meaning 'It is necessary to go.' *MO* and *KA* words interact with these phrases in an interesting way. Consider the following sentences:

(139) a. *Reizooko no naka no mono wa nani-mo tabe-te wa*
refrigerator inside thing
{*dame-des-u yo.* / *ike-masen yo.*}
'You may not eat anything in the refrigerator.'

b. *Reizooko no naka no mono o nani-ka tabe-te wa ike-masen yo.*
'You may not eat something in the refrigerator.'

c. *Rusutyuu ni* {*nani-ka* / **nani-mo*} *tabe-te mo i-i des-u.*
'You may eat something while I am gone.'

d. {*Nani-mo* / *Nani-ka*} *tabe-na-kute wa* {*ike-masen yo.* / *dame-des-u yo.*}
'You must eat something.'

The occurrence of the *KA* word in (139d) is predicted, since semantically (139d) is a positive sentence. The occurrence of the *MO* word here is due to the presence of the negative. However, when an expression that more strongly idiomatically implies 'have to' is used, as in (140), *MO* words do not occur:

(140) {**Nani-mo* / *Nani-ka*} *tabe-na-ker-eba narimasen.*
'We have to eat something.'

Although there are some dialectal variations, *MO* words are seen to occur in the positive conditionals, as in (139a), when they are followed by expressions like *ikemasen* or *dame desu*. This can be explained by saying that semantically (139a) is a prohibition, and there is a NEGATIVE commanding *nani* in the deeper structure. As in (140), even if *nani-mo* is commanded by NEGATIVE in the surface structure, *MO* words do not occur here. This is presumably because (140) is logically equivalent to the sentence without any NEGATIVE. It seems, then, that in these idiomatic expressions, the occurrence of *MO* words is sensitive to the logical equivalence relations of sentences.

On the basis of the preceding investigation of *MO* and *KA* words, we might conclude the following: Japanese is different from English with respect to what constitutes a negative environment. The investigation of *MO* words has shown that they are fairly strictly bound by the syntactic presence of the negative. *KA* words, on the other hand, are much more influenced by the presence or absence of a semantic negative, via inference. Even when

MO words are affected by a semantic negative, as in conditionals, *MO* words in Japanese are sensitive to the presence or absence of the negative deduced only by logical equivalence and not by the invited inferences or presuppositions. Whether this is a mere reflection of surface differences between English and Japanese or reflects deeper differences such as basic word order is not clear. It is hoped that similar problems in other languages like Japanese (i.e., SOV languages) will be investigated.

TENSE, ASPECT, AND MODALITY

MINORU NAKAU

INTRODUCTION

This chapter is concerned with explicating various temporal, aspectual, and modal phenomena involved in independent and dependent clauses in Japanese. It intends to provide a basic, but not an exhaustive, description of some limited interesting factual observations and the generalizations underlying them. It thus leaves problems of their theoretical relevance unexplored.

The outline of this chapter is as follows: Section 1 deals with the temporal and aspectual phenomena in independent clauses in an attempt to clarify the tense system and its temporal and aspectual relations. It is further hoped that the results of this section will provide a background for the study of the same phenomena in various types of dependent clauses in the sections that follow.

Section 2 discusses tense and aspect in subordinate clauses—in particular, those phenomena in temporal and conditional clauses. It focuses primarily on finding bases for determining a choice between the perfective and imperfective aspects of the aspectual tense.

Section 3 examines tense and aspect in three other major types of dependent clauses: spatial, relative, and predicate complement clauses. It also constitutes confirming evidence for the generalizations obtained in the preceding section. This section further examines the interchangeability of the three types of dependent clauses in question, coming to the conclusion that they are not interchangeable with each other.

The final section attempts to bring out clearly various types of modal phenomena in both independent and dependent clauses, centering its attention on the question of what type of psychological attitude of the speaker is expressed toward whom and about what. This section will, thus, serve as a first approximation to the grammar of speaker and hearer.

1. TENSE AND ASPECT IN INDEPENDENT CLAUSES

The term TENSE is used to represent a syntactic category because there is in Japanese a set of elements falling into this category that display the same syntactic behavior. On the other hand, the term ASPECT is used to represent a semantic notion because there is no set of elements to be subsumed under this name that exhibit distributional convergence. It will, thus, be shown that aspect is reflected in various syntactic forms, including, among others, tense and verbal forms. It will also be shown that tense refers semantically to either time or aspect in Japanese.

The first of the following subsections discusses tense and its temporal relations, and the second examines tense and its aspectual relations. These two subsections will serve the dual purpose of providing a basic, if not exhaustive, description of the temporal and aspectual phenomena in independent clauses and of providing a perspective from which to explicate the same phenomena in dependent clauses.

Tense and Its Temporal Relations

There are three different temporal notions that are syntactically relevant: past, present, and future time. They are syntactically reflected in different tense forms, but they cannot be determined only in terms of tense forms; rather, they are determined in terms of the action/state properties of predicates (i.e., verbs, adjectives, and nominal-adjectives, and the copula), and of whether a given sentence makes a generic or specific statement.

Most verbs designate action, as in (1a), and certain other verbs designate state, as in (1b); there are, further, other stative verbs that show syntactically and semantically different behavior, as in (1c):

(1) a. *tabe-(ru)* 'eat', *oyog-(u)* 'swim', *sin-(u)* 'die', *nige-(ru)* 'escape', *hanas-(u)* 'speak'
b. *deki-(ru)* 'be able', *i-(ru)* 'need', *i-(ru)* 'exist', *ar-(u)* 'exist'
c. *sir-(u)* 'know', *mot-(u)* 'have', *ni-(ru)* 'resemble', *sum-(u)* 'reside/live', *mie-(ru)* 'see', *kikoe-(ru)* 'hear', *wakar-(u)* 'understand', *hukum-(u)* 'contain', *sobie-(ru)* 'tower'

Adjectives, nominal-adjectives, and the copula *da* are all inherently stative.

Examples follow:

(2) a. *hazukasi-(i)* 'be ashamed of', *uresi-(i)* 'be glad of', *suzusi-(i)* 'be cool', *kasiko-(i)* 'be clever', *na-(i)* 'not exist'
b. *nigate-(da)* 'be poor at', *suki-(da)* 'be fond of', *oroka-(da)* 'be foolish', *mondai-(da)* 'be problematical'

First to be noted is the fact that the past tense forms of all types of predicates, regardless of whether they indicate action or state, represent past time, as exemplified in (3):

(3) a. *Boku wa, (kinoo) itaria-ryoori o tabe-**ta**.*
'(Yesterday) I had Italian dishes.'
b. *Kare wa, kodomo no koro, eigo ga deki-**ta**.*
'In his childhood, he was proficient in English.'
c. *(Mikka mae) kiteki ga kikoe-**ta**.*
'I heard a whistle (three days ago).'
d. *Kono heya wa, (kinoo) suzusi-kat-**ta**.*
'This room was cool (yesterday).'
e. *Kodomo no toki, oyogi ga heta-dat-**ta**.*
'In my childhood, I was poor at swimming.'
f. *Tanaka-san wa, sono toki gakusei dat-**ta**.*
'Mr. Tanaka was a student then.'

Nonpast time (i.e., present and future time), by contrast, is syntactically reflected in different predicate tense forms, depending on whether a given predicate designates action or state. The nonpast tense forms of stative predicates of all types refer to present time, as is illustrated in (4):

(4) a. *Kare wa, (ima) gakkoo ni i-**ru**.*
'He is (now) at school.'
b. *Boku wa, eigo ga wakar-**u**.*
'I understand English.'
c. *Kono heya wa, suzusi-**i**.*
'This room is cool.'
d. *Kippu wa, (ima) hatubai-tyuu-**da**.*
'The tickets are (now) on sale.'
e. *Tanaka-san wa, gakusei* ***da****.*
'Mr. Tanaka is a student.'

On the other hand, the nonpast tense forms of action verbs refer to present time only in their habitual, iterative, or generic use, as in (5):

(5) a. *Boku wa, mai asa roku zi ni oki-**ru**.*
'I get up at six every morning.'

b. *Taroo wa, sono si o nando mo ansyoo si-te-i-**ru**.*
'Taro is reciting the poem over and over.'
c. *Tikyuu wa, taiyoo no mawari o mawar-**u**.*
'The earth moves around the sun.'

The nonpast tense forms of action verbs otherwise refer to future time, as in (6):

(6) a. *(Asu) kitto ame ga hur-**u**.*
'It will surely rain (tomorrow).'
b. *Mamonaku Taroo ga yat-te-ku-**ru**.*
'Taro will come soon.'

An interesting phenomenon can be observed in certain idiomatic expressions for which the action/state distinction is determined not by the idiosyncratic properties of the predicates involved but, rather, by those of the predicate phrases or the whole sentences involved.

Thus, contrast the sentences in each of the following pairs:

(7) a. *Boku no tokoro ni wa, **denwa ga ar-u**.*
'We have a phone.'
b. *(Asu) Kare kara **denwa ga ar-u**.*
'I will have a call from him (tomorrow).'

(8) a. *Boku wa, kimi no it-ta koto ni **utagai ga ar-u**.*
'I have some doubt about what you said.'
b. *Boku wa, kimi ni tyotto **hanasi ga ar-u**.*
'I want (to have) a word with you.'

(9) a. *Kare no kangae wa, **rikutu ni a-u**.*
'His idea is reasonable.'
b. *Kare wa, (asu) **tomodati ni a-u**.*
'He will meet a friend (tomorrow).'

As is clearly shown in the English translations, the (a) sentence in each pair is interpreted as stative, while the (b) sentence is interpreted as nonstative. Thus, for instance, in (7b), the expression *denwa ga ar-u* serves to indicate action, contrary to the stativity of *ar-u*, but not in (7a). In (9a), the expression *rikutu ni a-u* 'stand to reason' indicates state, contrary to the activity of *a-u*, but in (9b), *tomodati ni a-u* 'will meet a friend' indicates action, according to the activity of *a-u*. A similar contrast holds for the sentences in (8).

The preceding observations, then, show that the action/state property of idioms is determined in terms of the action/state property not of the predicates within the idioms but, rather, of the whole phrases that constitute the idioms.

Another interesting observation can be made for the action/state property of the dependent predicates constituting part of complex predicates. As it will turn out, there are two types of dependent predicates. The first type includes those that are idiosyncratically specified for the action/state distinction. Examples that express action are illustrated in (10) and examples that express state in (11):

(10) *-sase-(ru)* (causative), *-hazime-(ru)* 'begin', *-tuzuke-(ru)* 'continue', *-oe-(ru)* 'end up', *-te-sima-(u)* 'finish', *-gar-(u)* 'show signs of/get interested in', *-nar-(u)* 'become (inchoative)', *-su-(ru)* (causative, as in *akaru-ku-su-ru* 'make something bright'), *-rare-(ru)* (passive), *-te-ok-(u)* (preparatory)

(11) a. *-te-i-(ru)* (progressive), *-te-ar-(u)* (preparatory), *-rare-/-re-(ru)* 'be able (potential)'
b. *-ta-(i)* (desiderative), *-te-hosi-(i)* (desiderative), *-tewaikena-(i)* 'must not', *-temoyo-(i)* 'may (permission)', *-nakerebanarana-(i)* 'must'
c. *-gati-(da)* 'tend', *-soo-(da)* 'look like'

Complex predicates that end in dependent predicates of the type under consideration, when combined with the nonpast tense, designate action or state, depending on the action or state property of the dependent predicates involved. Consider the following data:

(12) a. *Kare wa, yuuhan o* ***tabe-te-i-ru***.
'He is eating supper.'
b. *Mado ga* ***sime-te-ar-u***.
'The window remains shut.'
c. *Taroo wa,* ***oyog-e-ru***.
'Taro can swim.'
d. *Boku wa, ano eiga o* ***mi-ta-i***.
'I want to see the movie.'
e. *Kimi wa, motto benkyoo* ***si-nakerebanarana-i***.
'You must work harder.'
f. *Kare wa, gakkoo o* ***yasum-i-gati-da***.
'He tends to be absent from school.'
g. *Ame ga* ***hur-i-soo-da***.
'It looks like rain.'

The sentences in (12) show that the whole complex predicate is stative, despite the fact that the last but one component predicate (i.e., the predicate immediately preceding the dependent predicate involved) is nonstative; therefore, the dependent predicate in question is stative. Thus, for instance, in (12a) *-te-i-* is stative, because the last but one predicate, *tabe-*, is nonstative, yet the whole complex predicate, *tabe-te-i-*, is stative. Similar observations apply in the other sentences.

Analogously, observe the following data:

(13) a. *Asu Taroo o uti ni* ***i-sase-ru****.*
'I will have Taro stay at home tomorrow.'
b. *Kodomo-tati wa, kitto zoo o* ***mi-ta-gar-u****.*
'The children will surely get interested in seeing elephants.'
c. *Kare wa, mamonaku* ***genki-ni-nar-u****.*
'He will get well soon.'
d. *Asu kara heya o* ***suzusi-ku-su-ru****.*
'I will have the room cool from tomorrow on.'

The sentences in (13) show that the whole complex predicate is nonstative, despite the fact that the last but one component predicate is stative; therefore, it follows that the dependent predicate in question is nonstative. Thus, for instance, in (13a) *-sase-* is nonstative, because the last but one predicate, *i-* 'stay', is stative, yet the whole complex predicate, *i-sase-*, is nonstative. Similar observations apply in the other sentences.

Dependent predicates of the second type are those that cannot be described as inherently expressing action or state. In other words, they are neutral with respect to the action/state distinction. Included in this type are the following, among others:

(14) *-na-(i)* 'not (negative)', *-mas-(u)* (polite), *-masen* (polite negative)

Complex predicates that end in dependent predicates of the type under consideration, when combined with the nonpast tense, designate action or state, depending on the action or state property of the last but one component predicate rather than on that of the dependent predicate in question.

Compare the complex predicates in each of the following pairs:

(15) a. *Taroo wa, asu wa, yuuhan o* ***tabe-na-i****.*
'Taro will not eat supper tomorrow.'
b. *Taroo wa, yuuhan o* ***tabe-te-i-na-i****.*
'Taro is not eating supper/Taro has not eaten supper.'

(16) a. *Asu wa, gakkoo e* ***ik-i-mas-u****.*
'I will go to school tomorrow.'
b. *Ano ko wa, tenisu ga* ***deki-mas-u****.*
'That child/boy/girl is able to play tennis.'

(17) a. *Kono kusuri wa, konya wa,* ***nom-i-masen****.*
'I won't take this medicine tonight.'

b. *Sono sakana wa, **tabe-rare-masen**.*
'That fish is not edible.'

The contrast between the two complex predicates *tabe-na-i* and *tabe-te-i-na-i* in (15), which constitute a minimal pair, most clearly indicates that the activity of *tabe-na-i* is based on the activity of *tabe-*, while the stativity of *tabe-te-i-na-i* is based on the stativity of *(tabe)-te-i-*. It thus follows that *-na-(i)* is neutral with the action/state distinction and is not lexically specified for it. Similar observations may be made for the other pairs, and thus, *-mas-* and *-masen* are also lexically unspecified for the action/state distinction.

Tense and Aspect

In this subsection, we are concerned with investigating four types of aspectual phenomena: perfective, durative, progressive, and resultative aspect. These aspectual phenomena are reflected syntactically in certain specific elements, including, among others, the simple past and nonpast tense markers *-ta* and *-ru*, the progressive verbal forms *-te-i-ta/-ru*, and the preparatory verbal forms *-te-at-ta/te-ar-u* and *-te-oi-ta/-te-ok-u*. In particular, it will be shown, first, that the simple past and nonpast tense forms function as indicators of present perfect/imperfect aspect, as well as indicators of past/nonpast time, and second, that the progressive tense forms indicate different types of aspect, depending on what class of verbs immediately precede them.

Present perfect aspect can be represented by the simple past tense *-ta* form suffixed to action verbs. Thus, observe (18a), which is potentially ambiguous between temporal and aspectual interpretations, as is illustrated in the English translations (18b) and (18c):

(18) a. *Boku wa, ano hon o **yon-da**.*
b. 'I read that book (yesterday).'
c. 'I have (already) read that book.'

Evidence for this potential ambiguity is supplied by the following different contexts, in which the sentence in question is a proper response to two different types of questions:

(19) a. *Kimi wa, **kinoo** ano hon o **yon-da** ka?*
'Did you read that book yesterday?'
b. *Un, (boku wa, **kinoo** ano hon o) **yon-da**.*
'Yes, I did/I read that book yesterday.'
c. *Iya, (boku wa, **kinoo** ano hon o) **yom-a-na-kat-ta**.*
'No, I didn't (read that book yesterday).'

(20) a. *Kimi wa, **moo (sudeni)** ano hon o **yon-da** ka?*
'Have you read that book yet?'

b. *Un, (boku wa,* ***moo (sudeni)*** *ano hon o)* ***yon-da****.*
'Yes, I have (already read that book).'

c. *Iya, (boku wa,* ***mada*** *ano hon o)* ***yon-de-i-na-i****.*
'No, I have not (read that book) yet.'

On the one hand, a sentence like (18a) appears as an affirmative response like (19b) to a question like (19a), in which the simple past tense agrees with a past time adverb, *kinoo* 'yesterday'; on the other hand, the same sentence appears as an affirmative response like (20b) to a question like (20a), in which the simple past tense agrees with a perfectively oriented adverbial, *moo (sudeni)* 'already'. This clear-cut contrast, thus, provides supporting evidence for the potential ambiguity of a sentence like (18a) with an action verb in the simple past tense.

What is particularly noteworthy is the fact that reference to present time, not past time, is involved in the aspectual interpretation of (18a). Confirmation comes from the contrast between the two negative responses shown in (19c) and (20c); while *yom-a-na-kat-ta* in (19c) involves past time reference, as evidenced by the past tense marker *-ta* and its agreement with *kinoo* 'yesterday', *yon-de-i-na-i* in (20c) refers to present time, as evidenced by the nonpast tense marker *-i*. This sharp contrast constitutes the clearest piece of evidence for the potential ambiguity of (18a).

The preceding observations, therefore, indicate that the simple past tense *-ta* form of action verbs can represent present perfect aspect, designating an action that is perfected at the moment of speech, and that the *-te-i-na-i* form can represent present imperfect aspect, designating an action that is not perfected at the moment of speech.

No stative predicates of any type can be used to express perfect/imperfect aspect on their own; on the contrary, they can be used alone to express durative aspect:

(21) a. *Taroo wa, ikkagetu mae kara ie ni* ***i-ru****.*
'Taro has been at home since a month ago.'

b. *Sono ko wa, moo mono ga* ***i-e-ru****.*
'That baby has already become able to talk.'

c. *Kare wa, kodomo no koro kara eigo ga* ***deki-ru****.*
'He has been proficient in English since he was a child.'

d. *Nihon wa, mada* ***samu-ku-na-i****.*
'It is not cold yet in Japan.'

e. *Kare wa, moo ni-san-niti mae kara* ***genki-da****.*
'He has been well since a couple of days ago.'

In (21a), the *i-ru* form indicates a state that lasts for a certain span of time stretching from a certain point in the past up to the present moment. Similar observations apply in the other sentences. Present durative aspect can, thus, be reflected syntactically in the simple nonpast tense forms combined with state predicates of the type exemplified in (21), those of the type that cannot cooccur with the progressive *-te-i-(ru)*.

With stative verbs of the type that can cooccur with the progressive *-te-i-*, their *-te-i-ru* forms express present durative aspect rather than present progressive aspect, as in:

(22) a. *Sono uwasa wa, dare demo* ***sit-te-i-ru.***
'Everybody knows that rumor.'
b. *Haha-oya wa, Koobe ni* ***sun-de-i-ru.***
'Mother lives in Kobe.'
c. *Ano hito wa, buta ni* ***ni-te-i-ru.***
'That person resembles a pig.'
d. *Ano ozii-san wa, taikin o* ***mot-te-i-ru.***
'That old man has a large amount of money.'

Each of the *-te-i-ru* forms in (22) describes a state that exists at the present moment, possibly stretching into the future.

With some stative verbs of this type, both the simple and progressive tense forms are permissible and designate state, but they have different shades of meaning. Thus, compare the sentences in (23):

(23) a. *(Hare-ta hi ni wa,) koko kara Huzi san ga mie-ru.*
'(When it is a fine day,) you see Mt. Fuji from here.'
b. *(Ima) koko kara Huzi san ga* ***mie-te-i-ru.***
'From here, we see Mt. Fuji.'

The *mie-ru* form in (23a) may make a general statement in appropriate contexts or describe a permanent state that exists at the present moment, possibly extending into the future. By contrast, the *mie-te-i-ru* form in (23b) describes a temporary state that continues up to the present but might cease at any moment in the near future.

Contrast, further, the sentences in (24):

(24) a. *Boku ni wa, sore ga* ***wakar-u.***
'I understand it.'
b. *Kare ni wa, sore ga* ***wakar-u.***
'He will understand it.'
c. *{Boku / Kare} ni wa, sore ga* ***wakat-te-i-ru.***
'I have/He has understood it.'

Interestingly enough, *wakar-u* in (24a) expresses the present mental state of the speaker, but the same verbal form in (24b) expresses a future mental state of someone other than the speaker. This difference is due to the fact that the speaker cannot know the present mental state of someone else and, further, suggests that *wakar-(u)* is not strictly stative. Sentence (24c) lends confirmation to this view, because the *wakat-te-i-ru* form in (24c) designates a temporarily continuing state and, thus, enables the speaker to know someone else's present state of mind.

The *-te-i-ru* form, when attached to certain action verbs, represents present progressive aspect, indicating an action that is in progress at the present moment, as in (25):

(25) a. *Boku wa, (ima) tegami o* ***kai-te-i-ru****.*
'I am (now) writing a letter.'
b. *Taroo wa, Ziroo o* ***nagut-te-i-ru****.*
'Taro is beating Jiro.'
c. *Kare wa,* ***sin-i-kakat-te-i-ru****.*
'He is dying.'
d. *Kuruma ga supiido o* ***otos-i-te-i-ru****.*
'The car is slowing down.'

The sentences in (25) contain different subclasses of action verbs; thus, *kai-te-i-ru* 'be writing' refers to a specific single event, while *nagut-te-i-ru* 'be beating' refers to a series of repetitive actions and the *-te-i-ru* forms in (25c) and (25d) both refer to an event shifting from one state to another. Each of the verbal forms in (25), however, signals an action that is going on at the moment of speech.

The *-te-i-ru* form, when suffixed to certain other action verbs, represents present resultative aspect, thus designating a state that is resultant from the perfection of the action involved, as in (26):

(26) a. *Ano yama wa, (sudeni) yuki ga* ***tumot-te-i-ru****.*
'That mountain has (already) been covered with snow.'
b. *Taroo wa, (moo)* ***nemur-i-kon-de-i-ru****.*
'Taro has (already) fallen asleep.'
c. *Uti wa, (moo) yuuhan o* ***tabe-owat-te-i-mas-u****.*
'We are (now) finished with supper.'

In (26a), *tumot-te-i-ru* expresses a presently continuing state that has resulted from the event of snow falling, and in (26b), *nemur-i-kon-de-i-ru* expresses the present state of affairs that has followed naturally from the momentary action of going to sleep. In (26c), focus seems to be placed on a resulting state, rather than a perfected action, the latter being most clearly represented by *tabe-owat-ta.*

The following contrast reveals an interesting point:

(27) a. *Taroo wa, ima hasigo* ***ni*** *nobot-te-i-mas-u.*
'Taro has climbed up the ladder and is up on the ladder.'

b. *Taroo wa, ima hasigo **o** nobot-te-i-mas-u.*
'Taro is now climbing up the ladder.'

These two sentences differ only in the choice of the particle, and have different implications as exemplified in the English translations. Sentence (27a) normally implies a resulting state that necessarily follows from the action involved, because the particle *ni* signals a goal that the movement involved reaches, whereas (27b) implies an ongoing action that is not at all perfected at the present moment, because the particle *o* signals a path along which the movement involved takes place. In short, present resultative aspect is involved in the *-te-i-ru* form of (27a), while present progressive aspect is involved in the same form of (27b). The preceding observations, therefore, suggest that there are cases in which a whole predicate phrase, rather than a predicate alone, participates in determining a preference among different aspectual interpretations.

It has been shown that the simple nonpast tense form of stative adjectives and nominal-adjectives expresses present durative aspect, but in the following discussion, it will be shown that present perfective and resultative aspect are represented by the simple past tense *-ta* forms of the adjectives and nominal-adjectives verbalized by the inchoative *-nar-(u)* (e.g., *utukusi-ku-nat-ta* 'became beautiful') or by the progressive nonpast tense *-te-i-ru* forms of the same inchoativized adjectives and nominal-adjectives. Thus, observe (28):

(28) a. *Hanako wa, hatati ni nat-te, **utukusi-ku-nat-ta**.*
'Hanako, who has turned twenty, has become beautiful.'
b. *Obaa-san wa, **genki-ni-nat-te-i-mas-u**.*
'My grandmother has gotten well.'
c. *Kare no musuko wa, moo daigakusei ni **nat-te-i-ru**.*
'His son has already become a college student.'

The *-nat-te-i-ru/-mas-u* forms in (28b) and (28c) definitely denote a resulting state that necessarily comes about after the event mentioned has been perfected. By contrast, the *-nat-ta* form in (28a) normally, if not necessarily, denotes a resulting state rather than simply a perfected action.

An interesting syntactic form in which present resultative aspect is reflected is the *-te-ar-u* form suffixed to certain transitive action verbs, as in the following:

(29) a. *Tukue no ue ni hon ga takusan **tum-i-kasane-te-ar-u**.*
'There are many books piled up on the desk.'
b. *Boku no uti ni wa, denwa ga **hii-te-ar-u**.*
'We've gotten a phone.'

It is implied in (29a) that someone piled up many books on the desk at a certain point in the past and that the books still remain piled up there.

The understood agent is evidenced by the transitive verb *tumi-kasane-(ru)* 'pile up', but cannot be explicitly specified syntactically in (29a). A similar observation may be made for (29b).

The contrast between the three verbal forms in (30) illustrates the crucial differences at issue:

(30) a. *Denki ga* ***tuke-te-ar-u***.
'The lights have been switched on.'
b. *Denki ga* ***tui-te-i-ru***.
'The lights are on.'
c. *(Dareka ga) Denki o* ***tuke-te-i-ru***.
'Someone is switching on the lights.'

Resultative, durative, and progressive aspect are involved in (30a), (30b), and (30c), respectively. It is denoted in both (30a) and (30b) that the lights are on at the moment of speech, but it is implied only in (30a), not in (30b), that someone turned on the lights at a certain point in the past. This difference is due to the fact that (30a) contains a transitive verb, while (30b) contains its intransitive counterpart. An understood agent is involved in both (30a) and (30c), but it has a legitimate syntactic position in the *-te-i-ru* construction, as in (30c), and not in the *-te-ar-u* construction, as in (30a). Both (30b) and (30c) are *-te-i-ru* constructions, but (30b) describes a durative state while (30c) describes an ongoing action. The preceding observations, therefore, suggest that the *-te-ar-u* construction in (30a) is a syntactic and semantic amalgam of the transitive and intransitive *-te-i-ru* constructions in (30b) and (30c).

Another syntactic form of a similar sort that represents resultative aspect is the *-te-ok-(u)* form suffixed to certain transitive action verbs, as in (31):

(31) a. *Boku wa, denki o* ***tuke-te-ok-i-mas-u***.
'I will leave the lights switched on (by me).'
b. *Tukue no ue ni hon o takusan* ***tumi-kasane-te-oi-ta***.
'I left/have left many books piled up (by me) on the desk.'

First to be noted is the fact that *-te-ok-(u)* by nature designates action and, thus, refers to future time when it is in the simple nonpast tense form, while it involves reference to either past or present time when it is in the simple past tense form. Thus, in (31a) it is implied that I will turn on the lights at a certain point in the future and that I will leave the lights on afterwards. By contrast, in (31b), it is implied that I piled up many books at a certain point in the past and that I (have) left the books piled up afterwards. Contrast further (31b) with the following sentence with *-te-at-ta*, the past tense counterpart of (29a):

(32) *Tukue no ue ni hon ga takusan* ***tum-i-kasane-te-at-ta.***
'There were many books piled up on the desk.'

Unlike the *-te-oi-ta* form in (31b), the *-te-at-ta* form here involves only past time reference, because *-te-ar-* is inherently stative.

The preceding observations, then, show the following points: First, the *-te-ok-u* form expresses future resultative aspect, as contrasted with the *-te-ar-u* form, which expresses present resultative aspect, and second, the *-te-oi-ta* form expresses present or past resultative aspect, as contrasted with the *-te-at-ta* form, which expresses past resultative aspect.

As should be apparent from the preceding discussion, resultative aspect entails that the action involved was or will be perfected at a certain point in the past or the future, respectively. In short, it can be said that two facets are involved in resultative aspect, that is, the perfection of an action and the resulting state of the perfected action. There is one interesting example that I can think of in which these two facets of resultative aspect have independent syntactic correlatives; that is, the expression *-ta mama ni nat-te-i-(ru)*, in which *-ta* is the past tense marker of the dependent clause; *mama*, translatable literally as 'a state of affairs', serves as the head noun of the complement clause; and *nat-te-i-(ru)* is the verbal phrase of the main clause.

Thus, observe the sentences in (33):

(33) a. *Mada* [*denki ga* {*tuke-**ta*** / *tuke-rare-**ta*** / *tui-**ta***}] ***mama ni nat-te-i-ru.***
'The lights have still remained (switched) on.'

b. *Kinoo* [*tokei ga tomat-**ta***] ***mama ni nat-te-i-ta.***
'Yesterday I noticed that the clock had stopped.'

In (33a), the *-ta* form of the dependent clause indicates that the action of switching on the lights has been perfected at a certain point of time earlier than the point signaled by the main clause predicate, that is, the present time, and *mama ni nat-te-i-ru* indicates that the resulting state of the lights being on extends over a span of time lasting up to the present moment. On the other hand, in (33b), the *-ta* form of the dependent clause indicates that the event of the clock stopping had been perfected at a certain point of time in the past earlier than the time of the main clause, that is, before yesterday, and the *mama ni nat-te-i-ta* phrase indicates that the resulting state of the perfected action persisted up to a certain point in the past, that is, yesterday. These observations, thus, clearly show that the *-ta* form of the dependent clause signals perfective aspect and that the *mama ni nat-te-i-ru/-ta* form of the main clause signals (present/past) resultative aspect.

There are some other cases that require special comment. The first case is the *-te-i-ta* form of action verbs, which is potentially ambiguous between past progressive and perfective aspect, as in:

(34) a. *Boku wa, kinoo go zi ni yuuhan o* ***tabe-te-i-ta***.
'I was eating supper at 5 o'clock yesterday.'
b. *Boku wa, kinoo go zi made ni yuuhan o* ***tabe-te-i-ta***.
'I had eaten supper by 5 o'clock yesterday.'

The *tabe-te-i-ta* form in (34a) designates an action that was going on at a certain point in the past, that is, at 5 o'clock yesterday, and the same form in (34b) designates an action that had been perfected at a certain point in the past, that is, by 5 o'clock yesterday.

It should be noted here that this potential ambiguity can be observed also for the *-te-i-ru* form of action verbs, when it appears in future time contexts, as in:

(35) a. *Boku wa, asu no asa ronbun o* ***kai-te-i-ru*** *desyoo*.
'I will be writing a paper tomorrow morning.'
b. *Boku wa, asu no hiru made ni wa ronbun o* ***kai-te-i-ru*** *desyoo*.
'I will have finished writing a paper by noon tomorrow.'

The *-te-i-ru* form in (35a) indicates an action that will be going on at a certain point in the future, and the same form in (35b) indicates an action that will have been perfected at a certain point in the future. It is, thus, clear that the *-te-i-ru* form of action verbs in future contexts is potentially ambiguous between future progressive and perfective aspect. However, the same form, when it appears in present time contexts, indicates only present progressive aspect, as we have seen.

The *-te-i-ta* form of stative verbs is also potentially ambiguous—ambiguous between past durative and perfective aspect, as in:

(36) a. *Kare no kangae wa, ano toki (sudeni)* ***wakat-te-i-ta***.
'I had (already) known his idea then.'
b. *Kinoo, hare-ta toki, Huzi san ga* ***mie-te-i-ta***.
'Yesterday, Mt. Fuji was visible when it was fine.'
c. *Kinoo, o-hiru goro made, Huzi san ga* ***mie-te-i-ta***.
'Yesterday, Mt. Fuji had been visible until around noon.'

The *wakat-te-i-ta* form in (36a) tends to be interpreted as indicating past perfective aspect rather than past durative aspect. In (36b), the *mie-te-i-ta* form indicates a state that came about at a certain point in the past, and the same form in (36c) indicates a state that had been durative up to a certain point in the past.

Similar observations apply to stative predicates that cannot appear in the *-te-i-ta* form. Thus, the simple past tense form *-ta* of such predicates is potentially ambiguous between past durative and perfective aspect, as in (37):

(37) a. *Taroo wa, kinoo ie ni* ***i-ta***.
'Taro was at home yesterday.'
b. *Taroo wa, ni-san pun mae made ie ni* ***i-ta***.
'Taro had been at home until a couple of minutes ago.'
c. *Taroo wa, kinoo made Hanako ga* ***kirai-dat-ta***.
'Taro had disliked Hanako until yesterday.'
d. *Ano toki kare wa, sudeni gakusei* ***dat-ta***.
'He had already become a student at that time.'

The first two sentences constitute a minimal pair; the *i-ta* form in (37a) exhibits past durative aspect, and the same form in (37b) past perfective aspect. The *kirai-dat-ta* and *dat-ta* forms in the last two sentences exhibit only past perfective aspect, because they are associated with the perfectively oriented adverbs *kinoo made* 'until yesterday' and *ano toki sudeni* 'already at that time', respectively.

2. TENSE AND ASPECT IN SUBORDINATE CLAUSES

The purpose of this section is to provide a basic description of the temporal and aspectual phenomena involved in subordinate clauses—in particular, temporal and conditional clauses. The first subsection examines the temporal and aspectual functions of tense in order to clarify what determines a preference for one or the other function of tense in subordinate clauses, and the second subsection asks the question of what determines a preference for the perfective or imperfective aspect of the aspectual tense in subordinate clauses. Finally, the third subsection discusses the interpretation of simultaneous and sequential occurrence involved in perfective and imperfective aspect, and attempts to pinpoint in broader perspective what determines a preference for one or the other interpretation.

It will, thus, be shown, in particular, that the simple past/nonpast tense forms *-ta/-ru* of subordinate clause verbs function as indicators of present perfective/imperfective aspect or as indicators of past/nonpast time. The following contrast should then be noted here: Present perfective aspect, when associated with independent clauses, indicates an action that has been perfected at the moment of speech, namely, at the present moment, whereas, when associated with subordinate clauses, it indicates an action that has been perfected not at the moment of speech but, rather, at the moment represented by the main clause. The point here is that the 'present' of present perfective aspect in an independent clause is 'present as of the speech moment', while in a subordinate clause it is 'present as of the main clause time'.

The Temporal and Aspectual Functions of Tense

Whether the simple past and nonpast tense forms *-ta* and *-ru* in subordinate clauses undergo a temporal or an aspectual interpretation depends entirely on the idiosyncratic properties of the subordinate conjunctions involved. Examples subject to a temporal reading are enumerated in Class (a) of (38), and those subject to an aspectual reading in Class (b):

(38) Class a. *node* 'because', *kara* 'because', *nara* 'if', *ga* 'but', *keredomo* 'though', *noni* 'although', *to* 'if'
Class b. *mae (ni)* 'before', *ato (ni/de)* 'after', *made* 'until', *made ni* 'before/by', *uti ni* 'before/while', *to* 'when', *toki (ni)* 'when', *aida (ni)* 'while', *ya-ina-ya* 'as soon as', *totan (ni)* 'as soon as', *ta-ra* 'if/when', *kekka* 'as a result of'

What we must do here is provide grounds for this classification. Thus, consider, for example, the following minimally contrastive pair:

(39) a. *Sono seito wa, sensei ni sakubun o home-rare-ta* ***node****, taihen yorokon-da.*
'Since he was praised for his composition by his teacher, the pupil was very delighted.'
b. *Sono seito wa, sensei ni sakubun o home-rare-ta* ***toki****, taihen yorokon-da.*
'When he was praised for his composition by his teacher, the pupil was very delighted.'

My claim is that the *-ta* form of the *node* clause in (39a) refers to past time, while the same form of the *toki* clause in (39b) refers to present perfective aspect.

Quite analogously, compare the sentences in the following pair:

(40) a. *Kare wa, boku ga denwa o su-ru* ***node****, ie ni i-ru daroo.*
'He will be at home since I've arranged to call him up.'
b. *Kare wa, boku ga denwa o su-ru* ***toki****, ie ni i-ru daroo.*
'He will be at home when I call him up.'

My claim is that the *-ru* form of the *node* clause in (40a) refers to future time, while the same form of the *toki* clause in (40b) refers to present imperfective aspect.

Firstly, one could reasonably expect that if the tense form of a subordinate clause has a time referent of its own (i.e., past or nonpast), then it will allow the subordinate clause to contain a time adverbial independently of the main clause. This expectation seems well justified in Class (a) clauses, but not in Class (b) clauses, as shown in the following:

(41) a. *Kare wa, boku ga* ***ototoi*** *denwa o si-****ta*** *node,* ***kinoo*** *ai ni ki-ta.*
'He came to see me yesterday, because I called him up the day before yesterday.'
b. **Kare wa, boku ga* ***ototoi*** *denwa o si-****ta*** *toki,* ***kinoo*** *ai ni ki-ta.*
'(Lit.) He came to see me yesterday, when I called him up the day before yesterday.'

The contrast in grammaticality between (41a) and (41b) finds an exact parallel in the following pair of sentences with the *-ru* form instead of the *-ta* form in the subordinate clause:

(42) a. *Kare wa, boku ga* ***asu no asa*** *dekake-****ru*** *node,* ***konban-zyuu ni*** *denwa o si-te-ku-ru daroo.*
'He will call me up this evening, since I am going to leave tomorrow morning.'
b. **Kare wa, boku ga* ***asu no asa*** *dekake-****ru*** *toki,* ***konban-zyuu ni*** *denwa o si-te-ku-ru daroo.*
'(Lit.) He will call me up this evening, when I am going to leave tomorrow morning.'

It is shown in (41a) and (42a) that both the simple past and nonpast tense forms in *-ta* and *-ru* of the *node* clause have their own time referents, past time and nonpast time, respectively. However, it is shown in (41b) and (42b) that the same forms of the *toki* clause cannot have time referents of their own.

Secondly, the *-ta/-ru* forms of subordinate clause verbs have the function of perfective/imperfective aspect if the time of the subordinate clause event is under control of the tense of the main clause, another indication that the aspectual tenses in question do not have time referents of their own.

The best examples that confirm this claim are provided by sentences like those in (43), in which the main clause and subordinate clause predicates are in different tense forms:

(43) a. *Ame ga hut-****ta*** *noni, atu-****i****.*
'Although it rained, it is hot.'
b. *Ame ga hut-****ta*** *toki wa, atu-****i****.*
'It is hot when it has rained.'

The *-i* form of the main clause in (43a) describes the present state of affairs, while the same form in (43b) describes a general state that can be recurrent in the future without particular relevance to the present state of affairs. The important point here, however, is that the *-i* form of the main clause in either sentence has its own time referent, that is, reference to nonpast time. On the other hand, the *-ta* forms of the subordinate clauses in (43) contrast sharply with each other: In (43a), the *-ta* form indicates an event that occurred in the past, thus involving reference to past time independently of the tense of the main clause. By contrast, in (43b), the *-ta* form is interpreted as indicating an event that will occur in the future, and thus its reference to future time is not independent of, but under control of, the tense of the main clause.

Exactly the same observations may be made with respect to the sentences in the following pair, in which the main clause verb is in the past tense, while the subordinate clause verb is in the nonpast tense:

(44) a. *(Kyoo no gogo) ryokoo ni de-**ru** node, (sakuya wa) zyuubun suimin o tot-te-oi-**ta**.*
'Since I am going to set out on a journey (this afternoon), I had a good sleep (last night).'
b. *(Kinoo,) ryokoo ni de-**ru** toki, zyuubun suimin o tot-te-oi-**ta**.*
'(Yesterday) I had a good sleep when/before I set out on a journey.'

In (44a), since the *-ru* form of the *node* clause indicates an action that is going to take place in the near future, it has its own time referent independently of the main clause tense that refers to past time. In (44b), however, since the *-ru* form of the *toki* clause is interpreted as indicating an action that took place in the past, but not an action that will take place in the future, it follows that the *-ru* form of the *toki* clause cannot have its own time referent, and that the time of the *toki* clause action is under control of the main clause tense.

The preceding observations, thus, suggest that the *-ta/-ru* forms of the *toki* clause, unlike those of the *noni* and *node* clauses, are subject to present perfective/imperfective interpretations. The temporal scopes of the tenses of the main and subordinate clauses in (43) and (44) may be shown schematically as in (45) and (46), respectively:

(45) a. [*Ame ga hut*] ***-ta*** *noni*, [*atu*] ***-i***
b. [*Ame ga hut-**ta** toki wa, atu*] ***-i***

(46) a. [*Ryokoo ni de*] ***-ru*** *node*, [*zyuubun suimin o tot-te-oi*] ***-ta***
b. [*Ryokoo ni de-**ru** toki, zyuubun suimin o tot-te-oi*] ***-ta***

It is, thus, clear that whether the subordinate clause tense is aspectual or temporal here depends on whether it is under control of, i.e., within the scope of, the main clause tense with respect to time reference.

Another thing that might be clear from the schemata just shown is that when the *-ta/-ru* forms of the subordinate clause have the function of present perfective/imperfective aspect, they serve to represent certain sequential time relationships between the two events described by the main and subordinate clauses, and seem to demand that there be some point of convergence between the two events. Thus, in (45b), the *-ta* form is interpreted as signaling that the *toki* clause event precedes the main clause state in the order of occurrence, but in (46b), the *-ru* form is interpreted as signaling that the *toki* clause action is preceded by the main clause action. Furthermore, in either case, the two events are interpreted as occurring or having occurred together at least at one point in the future or in the past, respectively. We will come back to these questions of sequential occurrence and simultaneity. The preceding observations are generally true, except for the cases to be treated in the following discussions, of subordinate clauses with conjunctions of Class (b), but not Class (a).

It should be noted, however, that the simple nonpast tense form of a subordinate clause with a conjunction of Class (a) may have the function of present imperfective aspect if the two events described by the main and subordinate clauses are interpreted as converging at some point of time. Thus, observe the following sentences:

(47) a. *Kinoo kare wa, tenki ga i-**i** node, yamanobori o si-**ta**.*
'Yesterday he went mountaineering because it was fine.'
b. *Ame ga hur-**u** noni, kasa mo sas-a-na-kat-**ta**.*
'Although it rained, he did not put up his umbrella.'

It is implied in (47a) that he went mountaineering in fine weather, and in (47b) that he did not put up his umbrella in the rain. These implications, then, suggest the coming together of the two events represented by the main and subordinate clauses. Only in such cases as these can the nonpast tense form of the subordinate clause be replaced by its past counterpart without change of meaning. Thus, the sentences in (48) have the same meanings as those in (47), respectively:

(48) a. *Kinoo kare wa, tenki ga yo-kat-**ta** node, yamanobori o si-**ta**.*
'Yesterday he went mountaineering because it was fine.'
b. *Ame ga hut-**ta** noni, kasa mo sas-a-nak-kat-**ta**.*
'Although it rained, he did not put up his umbrella.'

On the other hand, if the interpretation of simultaneous occurrence is impossible, then the nonpast tense form of a subordinate clause with a conjunction of Class (a) cannot have the function of present imperfective aspect. Thus, observe the following sentences:

(49) a. *(Mamonaku) raikyaku ga ar-**u** node, isoide ie ni kae-te-ki-**ta**.*
'Since I am going to have company (soon), I came home in a hurry.'

b. *(Konban) yakoo de ryokoo ni de-**ru** noni, (yuube) zyuubun suimin o tor-e-nak-kat-**ta**.*

'Although I am going on a trip in a night train (this evening), I couldn't sleep too well (last night).'

(50) a. *Syakkin o kaes-a-nakerebanarana-**i** node, ginkoo de o-kane o oros-i-te-ki-**ta**.*

'Since I have to pay my debt, I have withdrawn money from the bank.'

b. *Boku wa yuk-u tumori-**da** keredomo, kare wa yuk-a-na-i yoosu-dat-**ta**.*

'While I intend to go, he seemed not to be going.'

c. *Ame ga hur-u kamosirena-**i** noni, Taroo wa kasa o mot-te-yuk-a-nak-kat-**ta**.*

'Although it may happen to rain, Taro didn't carry his umbrella.'

In each of these sentences it is observed that the two events or states represented by the main and subordinate clauses are not interpretable as converging at any point of time. Thus, for example, in (49a), since *raikyaku ga ar-u* 'will have company' refers to a future event and *kaet-te-ki-ta* 'came home' refers to an action completed in the past, there is definitely some time lag between the two events. Similarly in (49b). In (50a), the *-i* form of the *node* clause refers to a state existent in the present, while the *-ta* form of the main clause refers to an action perfected in the past, and therefore, there is some time lag between the state and the action. Similarly in the other sentences of (50). These observations, thus, show that the nonpast tense form in each of the preceding sentences has a temporal rather than an aspectual interpretation.

The replacement of the nonpast tense forms in question by the past tense forms makes the sentences different in meaning. Thus, contrast (49b) and (50c), for instance, with the following sentences:

(51) a. *Yakoo de ryokoo ni de-**ta** noni, zyuubun suimin o tor-e-nak-kat-**ta**.*

'Although I went on a trip in a night train, I couldn't sleep too well.'

b. *Ame ga hur-u kamosirena-kat-**ta** noni, Taroo wa kasa o mot-te-yuk-a-nak-kat-**ta**.*

'Although it might happen to rain, Taro didn't carry his umbrella.'

It is implied in (51a), but not in (49b), that it was in the night train in which I went on a trip that I could not sleep too well, and thus, given our common knowledge that a night train is not a comfortable place to sleep in, (51a) strikes us as a strange sentence. Of course, this does not hold of (49b). Furthermore, the contrast between (50c) and (51b) reveals their difference: In (50c), the *-i* form of the *noni* clause signals the speaker's present presumption of a future event, but in (51b), the *-ta* form of the *noni* clause signals the speaker's past presumption.

One might ask whether there is any syntactic or semantic clue to guide us in a choice for the convergence or nonconvergence of two events in such cases as those we have seen. Unfortunately, none exists. Thus, compare the sentences in (47), in which the nonpast tense of the subordinate clause has an aspectual interpretation, with the sentences in (49) and (50), in which the same form has a temporal interpretation. The action/state distinction, the most likely candidate, does not work at all, because in both groups of sentences the nonpast tense form of the subordinate clause is suffixed to both action and state predicates.

It has been shown that only the tense form of a subordinate clause that is subject to a temporal interpretation allows the subordinate clause to contain a time adverbial independently of the main clause. This holds true of subordinate conjunctions of Class (a). There is, however, only one subordinate conjunction of Class (b) of which this holds true, that is, the conditional *-ta ra* 'if', which requires the main clause to be in the nonpast tense (i.e., to refer to a nonpast action or state).

Thus, observe the following sentences:

(52) a. {***Asu*** / ***Kyoo***} *taamu peepaa o kai-te-simat-**ta** ra*, ***assate no asa*** *mot-te-ki-te-kudasai.*
'If you get done with your term paper tomorrow/today, then won't you please bring it along on the morning of the day after tomorrow?'

b. ****Kinoo*** *taamu peepaa o kai-te-simat-**ta** ra*, ***asu no asa*** *mot-te-ik-i-mas-u.*
'(Lit.) If I finished writing my term paper yesterday, I will bring it along tomorrow morning.'

The contrast in grammaticality between (52a) and (52b) shows that the *-ta* form of the conditional clause undergoes a perfective interpretation. The reason is that the *-ta* form in (52b) conflicts with a past time adverb, *kinoo* 'yesterday'; if the past tense form referred to past time, then (52b) would be grammatical. The grammaticality of (52a), then, suggests that the perfective *-ta* form is interpreted as signaling that the conditional clause action precedes the main clause action in the order of occurrence. What lends further support to this interpretation is the fact that the conditional clause action is associated with time adverbs that indicate points in the nearer future than that indicated by the time adverb with which the main clause action is associated. The point that is relevant to the present discussion, however, is that the conditional clause with the past tense as subject to a perfective interpretation can contain a time adverbial independently of the main clause, but that the time indicated by the time adverbial falls within the scope of future time required of the main clause.

The Perfect/Imperfect Contrast

The task with which we are faced now is to investigate when present perfective aspect is involved in subordinate clauses and when present imperfective aspect is involved. As will be shown, the choice between the perfective and imperfective tenses depends crucially on the idiosyncratic properties of the associated subordinate conjunctions. The following lists, thus, provide a classification of the subordinate conjunctions of Class (b):

(53) a. Subordinate conjunctions of the type that require the occurrence of the past tense and, hence, the involvement of present perfective aspect in the subordinate clause:
ato (de/ni) 'after', *ato kara* '(lit.) from after', *ato made* 'until after', *ageku* 'after', *kekka* 'as a result of', *totan (ni)* 'the moment'

b. Subordinate conjunctions of the type that require the occurrence of the nonpast tense and, hence, the involvement of present imperfective aspect in the subordinate clause:
mae (ni) 'before', *made* 'until', *made ni* 'by/before', *mae kara* '(lit.) from before', *mae made* 'until before', *uti ni* 'before/while', *ya-ina-ya* 'as soon as', *to* 'when', *magiwa ni* 'right before'

c. Subordinate conjunctions of the type that allow the occurrence of either the past or the nonpast tense and, hence, the involvement of either present perfective or imperfective aspect in the subordinate clause:
toki (ni) 'when/before/after', *aida (ni)* 'while'

Some representative examples will be examined in an attempt to demonstrate that their idiosyncratic properties determine the choice between the perfective and imperfective tenses and, further, to pinpoint exactly what semantic interpretations are involved in those aspectual tenses.

Firstly, as a typical example of present perfective aspect, observe the following sentences, in which the subordinate clause functions as the complement of the conjunction *ato de* 'after':

(54) a. *Kinoo Taroo wa, huro ni* {*hait-**ta*** / **hai-**ru***} *ato de, toko ni tui-**ta**.*
'Yesterday, Taro went to bed after he had taken a bath.'

b. *Konban Taroo wa, huro ni* {*hait-**ta*** / **hai-**ru***} *ato de, toko ni tuk-**u** daroo.*
'This evening, Taro will go to bed after he has taken a bath.'

It is observed in (54) that the temporal conjunction *ato de* requires the temporal clause verb to be in the past tense, regardless of whether the main clause verb is in the past or nonpast tense; furthermore, the *-ta* form in the temporal clause of (54b) is interpreted as referring not to past time but, rather, to nonpast time, under control of the main clause tense. These observations, thus, show that the past tense form of the *ato de* clause has the primary function of present perfective aspect rather than of past time.

It is further observed that in (54a), the *ato de* clause action took place at an earlier point in the past, namely, yesterday, than the main clause action, while in (54b), the *ato de* clause action will take place at an earlier point in the future, namely, this evening, than the main clause action. It is, thus, clear that such a sequential time relationship between two actions is definitely due to the inherent nature of the conjunction *ato de*, which is correlated with the perfective function of the past tense. This particular sequential relationship will be referred to as forward sequential occurrence.

Secondly, as a typical instance of present imperfective aspect, consider the following sentences with *mae ni* 'before' as subordinate conjunction:

(55) a. *Kinoo Taroo wa, toko ni* {*tuk-**u*** / **tui-**ta***} *mae ni, huro ni hait-**ta**.*
'Yesterday, Taro took a bath before he went to bed.'

b. *Asu Taroo wa, toko ni* {*tuk-**u*** / **tui-**ta***} *mae ni, huro ni hai-**ru** daroo.*
'Tomorrow, Taro will take a bath before he goes to bed.'

It is observed in (55) that the temporal conjunction *mae ni* requires the *mae ni* clause verb to be in the nonpast tense, regardless of whether the main clause verb is in the past or nonpast tense. Furthermore, the *-ru* form of the *mae ni* clause in (55a) is interpreted as referring not to nonpast time but, rather, to past time, under control of the tense of the main clause verb. These observations, thus, show that the nonpast tense form of the *mae ni* clause has the primary function of present imperfective aspect rather than of nonpast time.

It is further observed in (55a) that the temporal clause action took place at a later point in the past, namely, yesterday, than the main clause action, whereas in (55b), the temporal clause action will take place at a later point in the future, that is, tomorrow, than the main clause action. It is, thus, clear that such a sequential time relationship between two actions is definitely due to the inherent nature of the conjunction *mae ni*, which is correlative with the imperfective function of the nonpast tense. This particular sequential relationship will be referred to as backward sequential occurrence.

It should, incidentally, be noted that the time of the *mae ni* clause action is not necessarily under control of the tense of the main clause verb. Thus, compare the sentences in the following pair:

(56) a. *Kare wa, sin-**u** mae ni, isyo o kai-**ta**.*
'He drew up a will before he died.'
b. *Kare wa, isyo o kak-**u** mae ni, sin-**da**.*
'He died before he drew up a will.'

In (56a), it is implied under normal conditions that he has been dead, whereas in (56b), it can never be implied that he has drawn up a will, because he had been dead before he could draw up a will.

By contrast, consider the following pair of sentences with *ato de* 'after' as subordinate conjunction:

(57) a. **Kare wa, sin-**da** ato de, isyo o kai-**ta***
'(Lit.) He drew up a will after he had died.'
b. *Kare wa, isyo o kai-**ta** ato de, sin-**da***
'He died after he had drawn up a will.'

Sentence (57a) sounds anomalous, because nobody can draw up a will after he has died, and this anomaly stems from the idiosyncratic nature of the conjunction *ato de*, which requires the *ato de* clause action to be perfected earlier than the main clause action. In (57b), however, it is implied that he drew up a will.

Thirdly, as another typical example of present imperfective aspect, consider the following sentences, in which the subordinate clause functions as the complement of the conjunction *ya-ina-ya* 'as soon as':

(58) a. *Kare wa,* { *tat-i-agar-**u*** / **tat-i-agat-**ta*** } *ya-ina-ya, tob-i-kakat-te-ki-**ta**.*
'He threw himself upon me as soon as he stood up.'
b. *Kare wa, itumo toko ni* { *tuk-**u*** / **tui-**ta*** } *ya-ina-ya, neit-te-sima-**u**.*
'He always drops off to sleep as soon as he goes to bed.'

It is observed in (58) that the temporal *ya-ina-ya*, like *mae ni* 'before', requires the temporal clause verb to be in the nonpast tense, regardless of whether the main clause verb is in the past or nonpast tense. Furthermore, the *-ru* form of the *ya-ina-ya* clause of, say, (58a) is interpreted as referring not to nonpast time but, rather, to past time, and thus, this interpretation is made available under control of the main clause tense. These observations, thus, show that the nonpast tense form of the *ya-ina-ya* clause functions as an indicator of present imperfective aspect rather than of nonpast time.

What should be particularly noted here is the following: In (58a), the action of the *ya-ina-ya* clause is interpreted as having occurred at almost the same moment in the past as that when the action of the main clause occurred, and similarly, in (58b), the action of the *ya-ina-ya* clause is interpreted as always occurring at almost the same moment as that when the action of the main clause occurs. The point here, therefore, is that this momentarily simultaneous interpretation is psychological rather than logical, because, in the instance of, say, (58b), one normally cannot drop off to sleep at exactly the same moment that one goes to bed. This interpretation of psychological simultaneity is obviously attributable to the inherent nature of the conjunction *ya-ina-ya* 'as soon as'; moreover, this is another aspect of meaning involved in the imperfective function of the nonpast tense.

As another instance that exemplifies that the perfective/imperfective interpretation is psychological rather than logical, consider the following sentences, in which the temporal conjunction *totan-ni* 'the moment', as compared with *ya-ina-ya*, requires the subordinate clause verb to be in the past tense, regardless of whether the main clause verb is in the past or nonpast tense:

(59) a. *Taroo wa, Hanako o* {*mi-**ta*** / **mi-**ru***} *totan ni, kao-iro ga waru-ku-nat-**ta**.*

'The moment Taro saw Hanako, he turned pale.'

b. *Kare wa, itumo toko ni* {*tui-**ta*** / **tuk-**u***} *totan ni, neit-te-sima-**u**.*

'The instant he goes to bed, he always drops off to sleep.'

In (59a), the action of the *totan ni* clause is interpreted as having occurred in the past, and in (59b) as always occurring right before the main clause action. What is at issue here is that this forward sequential interpretation is psychological rather than logical. This will be made apparent, in particular, by the contrast between (58b) and (59b), because both sentences are understood as describing exactly the same actual situation.

In summary, it has so far been shown that there are three different types of interpretation involved in the present perfective and imperfective functions of the past and nonpast tenses contained in subordinate clauses with conjunctions of the type shown in (53). They may be summarized as follows:

1. Forward sequential occurrence, involved in the perfective function of the past tense verbal form of the subordinate clause;
2. backward sequential occurrence, involved in the imperfective function of the nonpast tense verbal form of the subordinate clause;
3. simultaneous occurrence, involved in the imperfective function of the nonpast tense verbal form of the subordinate clause.

It should be noted in particular that backward sequential occurrence and simultaneous occurrence are two aspects of meaning involved in the imperfective function of the nonpast tense. This is because present imperfective aspect specifies a sequential relation such that the subordinate clause action is NOT perfected at the time of the main clause action, as contrasted with present perfective aspect, which specifies a sequential relation such that the subordinate clause action is perfected at the time of the main clause action.

Finally, the following sentences, in which the subordinate clause functions as the complement of the temporal conjunction *toki ni* 'when', constitute a typical case that allows all three types of interpretation:

(60) a. *Genkan o de-**ta** toki ni, denwa ga nat-ta.*
'The telephone rang right after I had stepped out of the front door.'
b. *Genkan o de-**ru** toki ni, denwa ga nat-ta.*
(i) 'The telephone rang right before I stepped out of the front door.'
(ii) 'The telephone rang when I was about to step out of the front door.'

Here, it is observed that the temporal *toki ni* allows the occurrence of either the past or the nonpast tense verbal form in the subordinate clause. In (60a), the action of the *toki ni* clause is interpreted as having occurred in the past right before the time of the main clause event, but on the other hand, (60b) is ambiguously interpretable as having occurred in the past, either at the same moment as or immediately after the main clause event.

In particular, the ambiguity of (60b) provides confirming evidence for the involvement of the two aspects of meaning (2 and 3 in the list just given) in the imperfective function of the nonpast tense. As should be obvious, the availability of the three types of interpretation for the *toki ni* clauses is directly attributable to the semantic nature of the temporal conjunction *toki ni*, because it is inherently neutral between sequential and simultaneous occurrence.

Simultaneous versus Sequential Occurrence

In this subsection we will consider in broader perspective the conditions under which the interpretation of simultaneous or sequential occurrence is possible. The data to be examined will, thus, include examples with various subordinate conjunctions of the type given in (53).

The interpretation of simultaneous occurrence is possible insofar as the predicate form of the main or subordinate clause is interpretable as designating some degree of duration in actual situations. Thus, observe the sentences in (61), which are interpreted as involving partial simultaneity:

(61) a. *Sono hon wa, o-kane ga* ***ar-u*** *aida ni, kat-te-oi-ta.*
'I bought the book while I had money.'
b. *Terebi o* ***mi-te-i-ru*** *to, siri-ai ga de-te-ki-ta.*
'While I was watching television, an acquaintance came out on the screen.'
c. *Huro ni* ***hait-te-i-ta*** *ra, doaa no beru ga nat-ta.*
'When I was taking a bath, the door bell rang.'
d. *Ano ko wa, umare-ta toki, otoo-san ni* ***ni-te-i-ta.***
'That boy resembled his father when he was born.'

It is the verbal forms of the subordinate clauses in (61a–c) and the verbal form of the main clause in (61d) that designate states and, hence, certain degrees of duration. The point here is that partial simultaneity is involved in the interpretation of each of these sentences. Thus, for instance, in (61a), the action of my buying the book took place at a certain point of time in the past during the period when the state of my having money was existent. Similar observations may be made for the other sentences.

Consider next the sentences in (62), which are interpreted as involving total simultaneity:

(62) a. *Kanozyo wa, dokusin* ***dat-ta*** *koro,* ***utukusi-kat-ta.***
'When she was single, she was beautiful.'
b. *Boku ga denwa o* ***kake-te-i-ru*** *aida, minna* ***damat-te-i-ta.***
'Everybody kept silent while I was phoning.'
c. *Boku ga denwa o* ***kake-ru*** *aida, minna tinmoku o* ***tamot-ta.***
'Everybody kept silence while I was phoning.'

In (62a), the state of her being a beauty was existent in the past for the whole period during which the state of her being single was existent, and thus, the two states coincide entirely with each other. This interpretation of total simultaneity is made possible by the stativity of the two predicate forms of the main and subordinate clauses. A similar observation may be made for (62b).

The contrast between (62b) and (62c), however, reveals an interesting point. In (62b), both the main and subordinate clause verbal forms in *-te-i-(ru/ta)* designate state by definition, while both verbal forms in (62c) designate action. Nevertheless, both sentences describe exactly the same actual situation, and thus, both action verbal forms in (62c), exactly like the stative verbal forms in (62b), are interpreted as involving certain degrees of duration. The reason for the availability of this interpretation to (62c) is directly attributable to the semantic nature of the temporal conjunction *aida*, which means 'for the whole period during which' and, thus, requires total convergence of two actions or states. Sentence (62c) should be contrasted with (61a), in which the availability of partial simultaneity is evidenced by the presence of *aida ni* (instead of *aida*), which means 'at a certain point of time during the period when' and, thus, requires partial simultaneity.

Observe, further, the sentences in (63), which are interpretable as involving either partial or total simultaneity:

(63) a. *Kare wa,* ***waka-i*** *toki, yoku* ***ason-da***.
'When he was young, he used to live a fast life.'
b. *Ozii-san wa,* ***genki-na*** *ori wa, mago o* ***kawai-gat-ta***.
'The grandfather, when he was well, showed fondness for his grandchildren.'

In either sentence, the predicate form of the subordinate clause is stative and the verbal form of the main clause is nonstative. In fact, however, the main clause verbal form is preferably interpreted as referring to a series of recurrent actions over a single specific action, and thus, the totally simultaneous interpretation seems to be preferable, in which the series of actions represented by the main clause were recurrent at regular intervals for the whole span of time during which the state represented by the subordinate clause was existent.

One additional remark on the partially simultaneous interpretation of such sentences as those in (61) might be in order, namely, that the length of the span of simultaneous occurrence depends on how durative the action of the action verb involved is. Thus, in (61c), since the action represented by *beru ga nat-ta* 'the bell rang' is interpretable as having lasted fairly long rather than having occurred instantaneously, it follows that this action was concurrent for some duration of time with the progressive action represented by *huro ni hait-te-i-ta* 'was taking a bath'. Similar observations may be made for the other sentences in (61).

Consider, by contrast, the sentences in (58) and (60b), which are also subject to an interpretation of simultaneous occurrence. Since the verbal forms of the main and subordinate clauses in each of those sentences designate action, the two actions mentioned are interpretable only as being instantaneously simultaneous. It seems generally true that if instantaneously simultaneous occurrence is involved in the interpretation of a sentence, then the verbal forms designating action must appear in both the main and subordinate clauses of the sentence, but not vice versa (cf. (62c), with *aida* 'for the whole period during which' as temporal conjunction).

There exists only one type of instance that does not exhibit simultaneous occurrence even if a stative predicate form appears in either the main or the subordinate clause. This is the case in which the subordinate clause contains a stative predicate in its past tense form, whereas the main clause contains a stative or nonstative predicate in its nonpast tense form. Only in such a particular case as this does any point of convergence not occur. Thus, observe the following:

(64) a. **Huro ni hait-te-i-**ta** ra, nemuta-**i**.*
'(Lit.) While I was taking a bath, I am sleepy.'
b. **Samu-kat-**ta** toki, kaze o hik-**u**.*
'(Lit.) When one was cold, one catches cold.'
c. **Kanozyo wa, dokusin dat-**ta** koro, bizin **da**.*
'(Lit.) When she was single, she is a beauty.'

The ungrammaticality of each of these sentences is due to the fact that there exists no point of time when the state represented by the subordinate clause converges with the action or state represented by the main clause, in spite of the constraint of convergence imposed by the temporal conjunction involved. Thus, in (64b), for example, the temporal *toki* 'when' requires the stative predicate past tense form of the temporal clause to have the function of past rather than present perfective aspect, because present perfective aspect is possible only with the past tense form of action verbs, as shown in Section 1. Thus, we expect the main clause predicate to be in the past tense, but it actually is in the nonpast tense; hence, there is no point of convergence. Similar observations may be made for the other sentences in (64).

Forward or backward sequential occurrence, unlike simultaneous occurrence, can be represented only by simple past or nonpast tense forms suffixed to action verbs or a certain type of stative verb. Thus, observe the following sets of sentences:

(65) a. *Huro ni* {*hait-**ta*** / **hait-**te-i-ta***} *ato de, toko ni tui-ta.*
'I went to bed after I had taken a bath/(lit.) after I had been taking a bath.'
b. *Taroo wa, Hanako o* {*mi-**ta*** / **mi-**te-i-ta***} *totan ni, kao-iro ga waru-ku-nat-ta.*
'The moment Taro saw/(lit.) was looking at Hanako, he turned pale.'

(66) a. *Toko ni* {*tuk-**u*** / **tui-**te-i-ru***} *mae ni, huro ni hait-ta.*
'I took a bath before I went to bed/(lit.) before I was going to bed/(lit.) before I had gone to bed.'

b. *Singoo ga ao ni* {*kawar-**u*** / **kawat-**te-i-ru***} *made, mat-ta.*
'I waited until the traffic light turned green/(lit.) until the traffic light was turning green.'

c. *Kare wa,* {*tat-i-agar-**u*** / **tat-i-agat-**te-i-ru***} *ya-ina-ya, tob-i-kakat-te-ki-ta.*
'He threw himself upon me as soon as he stood up/(lit.) as soon as he was standing up.'

The sentences in (65) contain temporal conjunctions of the type that require forward sequential occurrence, and those in (66) contain temporal conjunctions of the type that require backward sequential occurrence. These sentences are all ungrammatical with the *-te-i-ta*/*-ru* forms, which are interpreted as designating state by definition, in the temporal clause.

Observe, next, the following sentences, which show that the temporal conjunctions under consideration require the temporal clause to contain a stative adjective or nominal-adjective in its inchoativized form, which is no longer stative:

(67) a. {***Sizuka-ni-nat-ta*** / ****Sizuka-dat-ta***} *ato de, benkyoo o hazime-ta.*
'I started studying after it had become quiet.'

b. {***Kura-ku-nar-u*** / ****Kura-i***} *made, mat-e.*
'Wait until dark.'

c. *Singoo ga* {*ao ni **nar-u*** / **ao de **ar-u***} *ya-ina-ya, tob-i-das-i-ta.*
'He rushed out as soon as the traffic light turned green.'

Consider, by contrast, the following sentences, in which the temporal clause contains an inherently stative verb in its simple past or nonpast tense form:

(68) a. *Kiteki ga **kikoe-ta** ato de, sanbasi ni it-ta.*
'I went to the pier after I had heard a whistle.'

b. *Subete no mondai ga **tok-e-ru** mae ni, zikan ga na-ku-nat-te-simat-ta.*
'Time ran out before I could solve all the problems.'

c. *Taroo wa, sono himitu ga* ***wakar-u*** *ya-ina-ya, hara o tate-ta.*
'Taro got angry as soon as he understood/knew that secret.'

It is observed that while the temporal clause verbal forms in (65)–(67) express point action, those in (68) express the initial or final stage of a state. Thus, in (68a), it is implied that the action of my going to the pier took place after the final stage of the state of my hearing a whistle. Similar implications are found in the other sentences in (68).

All the preceding observations, then, suggest the conclusion that only verbal forms that represent point action or the initial or final stage of a state are permissible in subordinate clauses with temporal conjunctions of the type that require sequential occurrence, forward or backward.

Finally, there are several temporal conjunctions that are potentially ambiguous between sequential and simultaneous occurrence. The existence of such conjunctions constitutes supporting evidence for the correctness of the conclusion suggested previously, because the choice between the two interpretations is determined on the basis of whether the predicate form of the temporal clause designates action or state.

Thus, observe the following sentences, in which the temporal *uti ni*, which is ambiguous between 'before' and 'while', appears as subordinate conjunction:

(69) a. ***Kura-ku-nar-a-na-i*** *uti ni, ie ni modot-ta.*
'I came home before it got dark.'
b. *Ame ga* ***hur-a-na-i*** *uti ni, tukai ni it-te-ki-ta.*
'I have been on an errand before it rains.'
c. *Kare wa, boku no* ***sir-a-na-i*** *uti ni, kaet-ta.*
'He left before I knew.'

(70) a. *Hon o* ***yon-de-i-ru*** *uti ni, nemu-ku-nat-ta.*
'I became sleepy while I was reading a book.'
b. ***Akaru-i*** *uti ni, tukai ni it-te-ki-ta.*
'I have been on an errand while it is light.'

The sentences in (69) are subject to a backward sequential interpretation, since *uti ni* here is interpreted as meaning 'before', while those in (70) are subject to a simultaneous interpretation, since *uti ni* here is interpreted as meaning 'while'. The basis for this distinction is that the temporal clause predicate forms in (69) express point action or the initial or final stage of a state, whereas the temporal clause predicate forms in (70) express state. Thus, for example, *hur-a-na-i* 'will not rain' in (69b) indicates action, because *hur-* indicates action but yet *na-(i)* is neutral with respect to the action/state distinction (cf. Section 1). Similarly in the other sentences in (69). On the other hand, *yon-de-i-ru* 'am reading' in (70a) indicates state, because *yon-* indicates action but yet *-de-i-(ru)* indicates state (cf. Section 1). Similarly in (70b).

This difference stands out most conspicuously in the minimally contrastive pair of sentences shown in (71):

(71) a. *Amari* ***atu-ku-nar-a-na-i*** *uti ni, benkyoosi-ta.*
'I studied before it became too hot.'
b. *Amari* ***atu-ku-na-i*** *uti ni, benkyoosi-ta.*
'I studied while it was not too hot.'

Atu-ku-nar-a-na-i 'will not become hot' in (71a) exhibits action, while *atu-ku-na-i* 'is not hot' in (71b) exhibits state. It is, thus, clear that this action/state distinction serves as the basis for distinguishing between the sequential interpretation of (71a) and the simultaneous interpretation of (71b).

3. TENSE AND ASPECT IN SPATIAL, RELATIVE, AND VERB COMPLEMENT CLAUSES

This section is centered primarily on an examination of the temporal and aspectual phenomena involved in two types of sentential complements. The first type I call 'spatial clauses', by which I mean subordinate clauses that function as the complements of nominal elements of the type that characterize a spatial relationship between the two actions or states represented by the main and subordinate clauses. The second type includes sentential complements of various predicates, including verbs, adjectives, and nominal-adjectives; but here I will restrict myself to sentential complements of verbs of perception. The temporal and aspectual phenomena involved in relative clauses will also be examined, but only in comparison with those in the above-mentioned two types of complement clauses.

The following points especially will be brought out in the coming discussion: Firstly, the verbal tense forms of spatial clauses and perception verb complements must undergo the interpretation of simultaneous occurrence. Secondly, this particular interpretation is due to the idiosyncratic properties of spatial elements and main clause verbs. Finally, neither spatial clauses nor perception verb complements are interchangeable with relative clauses.

Tense and Aspect in Spatial Clauses

Among spatial elements of the type under consideration are the following nominal elements, accompanied by one of the particles *de*, *ni*, and *o*, to be chosen under the influence of the idiosyncratic properties of the main clause predicate:

(72) *naka* 'in/inside', *soto* 'outside', *ue* 'above/over/on', *sita* 'under', *usiro* 'behind', *kage* 'behind', *tikaku* 'near/close to', *tooku* 'far away', *soba* 'by/beside', *mae* 'before/in front of', *yoko* 'at the side of', *migi(-te/-gawa)* 'on/to the right-hand side of', *hidari (-te/-gawa)* 'on/to the left-hand side of'

These nominal elements, when combined with any of the three particles just mentioned, can also function as postpositional expressions that specify a spatial relationship between two particular objects described in the associated sentence.

Before going into the main topic, therefore, observe the following simple sentences, in which some of the nominal elements exemplified in (72) function as characterizing certain spatial relations:

(73) a. *Boku wa, mori* ***no naka o*** *sanposi-ta.*
'I took a walk in the woods.'
b. *Gunsyuu* ***no ue o*** *sentooki ga tob-i-sat-ta.*
'A fighter flew away over the crowd of people.'
c. *Sono kazan* ***no soba de*** *syasin o tot-te-morat-ta.*
'I had a picture of myself taken beside the volcano.'
d. *Taroo wa, Ziroo to Hanako* ***no aida ni*** *warikon-da.*
'Taro squeezed himself between Jiro and Hanako.'
e. *Doroboo wa, kuruma* ***no kage ni*** *mi o kakus-i-te-i-ru.*
'The thief is hiding himself behind the car.'
f. *Yuubinkyoku* ***no migite ni*** *koohiiya ga ar-u.*
'There is a coffee shop on/to the right of the post office.'

In each of these sentences, it is observed that a spatial relation holds between two entities in which an action takes place or a state exists. In (73a), for instance, the postpositional phrase *no naka o* 'inside' specifies that there is a spatial relation between *boku* 'I' and *mori* 'the woods' viewed along the inside/outside dimension, and that in this spatial relation the act of taking a walk took place. In (73f), the postpositional phrase *no migite ni* 'on/to the right of' specifies that a spatial relation viewed along the right/left dimension obtains between *yuubinkyoku* 'post office' and *koohiiya* 'coffee shop', and that the two entities are located in this particular relation. Similar observations may be made for the other sentences in (73).

The relevant point here is that no spatial relation exists unless two entities actually exist on the same spatial dimension. It thus necessarily follows that the simultaneous occurrence of two entities is involved in the nature of a spatial postpositional phrase.

With the preceding observation as a preliminary, we can proceed to examine the temporal and aspectual phenomena of spatial clauses that function as the complements of spatial elements.

Observe, first, the following sentences, in which the spatial clause contains the simple nonpast tense verbal form in *-ru*:

(74) a. *Boku wa, [mori ga ussoo-to sige-**ru**] naka o hitori sanposi-ta.*
'I strolled alone in the forest when it grew thick.'

b. *[Gunsyuu ga nak-i-sakeb-**u**] ue o sentooki ga tob-i-sat-ta.*
'A fighter flew away over the crowd of people when they were screaming.'

c. *[Sono kazan ga hunkasu-**ru**] soba de syasin o tot-te-morat-ta.*
'I had a picture of myself taken beside the volcano when it was erupting.'

d. *Taro wa, [Ziroo to Hanako ga yoriso-**u**] aida ni warikon-da.*
'Taro squeezed himself between Jiro and Hanako when they nestled close to each other.'

e. *Doroboo wa, [nimotu ga takaku tum-i-kasanar-**u**] kage ni mi o kakus-i-te-i-ru.*
'The thief is hiding himself behind the pieces of baggage that have been piled up high.'

f. *[Yuubinkyoku ga hiro-i sikiti o sime-**ru**] migite ni tiisa-na koohiiya ga ar-u.*
'There is a small coffee shop on the right of the post office that occupies a spacious site.'

It is observed that the sentences in (74) differ from those in (73) only in that the former contain clauses where the latter contain noun phrases. It is, thus, clear in each of the preceding sentences that the contained clause functions as the complement of the spatial head noun. Notice, incidentally, that the English translations are far from corresponding in structure to the Japanese examples.

The point that is relevant to the present discussion is that the *-ru* verbal form of the spatial clause in each of the preceding sentences is interpreted as involving simultaneous occurrence. Thus, in (74c), for instance, it is implied that the volcano was erupting at the moment when the speaker had a picture of himself taken, and in (74d), that Jiro and Hanako were nestling close to each other at the moment when Taro squeezed himself between them. Similar observations hold for the other sentences in (74).

The availability of this simultaneous interpretation in (74) stems from the present imperfective function of the *-ru* verbal form of the spatial clause. Confirmation comes from the fact that in (74a–d), in which the main clause verb is in the past tense, the spatial clause refers to an event that took place in the past under the influence of the main clause verbal tense, and further, from the fact that the spatial clause cannot contain a time adverbial independently of the main clause, as shown in the sentences in (75), which correspond to (74a) and (74e):

(75) a. **Kinoo* *boku wa*, [*mori ga* ***ima*** *ussoo-to sige-**ru***] *naka o hitori sanposi-ta.*
'(Lit.) Yesterday I strolled alone in the forest when it has now grown thick.'

b. **Doroboo wa*, [*nimotu ga* ***asu*** *takaku tum-i-kasanar-**u***] *kage ni mi o kakus-i-te-i-ru.*
'(Lit.) The thief is hiding himself behind the pieces of baggage that will be piled up high tomorrow.'

It was shown in Section 2 that the nonpast tense verbal form of the temporal or conditional clause, when it has the function of present imperfective aspect, is interpretable as involving either simultaneous or backward sequential occurrence. It has turned out that the preceding observations about the simple nonpast tense verbal forms of the spatial clauses in (74) are quite compatible with this generalization. The interpretation of simultaneous occurrence in (74) is, thus, directly attributable to the idiosyncratic properties of the spatial nominals involved.

This simultaneous interpretation can also be represented by the *-te-i-ru* verbal form of the spatial clause. Thus, observe the following sentences:

(76) a. *Boku wa*, [*mori ga ussoo-to siget-**te-i-ru***] *naka o hitori sanposi-ta.*
'I strolled alone in the forest when it had grown thick.'

b. *Doroboo wa*, [*nimotu ga takaku tum-i-kasanat-**te-i-ru***] *kage ni mi o kakus-i-te-i-ru.*
'The thief is hiding himself behind the pieces of baggage that have been piled up high.'

c. [*Ano kazan ga hunkas-i-**te-i-ru***] *soba de syasin o tot-te-morat-ta.*
'I had a picture of myself taken beside that volcano when it was bursting into eruption.'

d. *Taroo wa*, [*Ziroo to Hanako ga yorisot-**te-i-ru***] *aida ni warikon-da.*
'Taro squeezed himself between Jiro and Hanako when they were nestling close to each other.'

The *-te-i-ru* forms of the spatial clauses in (76a) and (76b) designate resulting states, whereas the *-te-i-ru* forms of the spatial clauses in (76c) and (76d) designate progressive actions (cf. Section 1). What is at issue here is that all the *-te-i-ru* forms in question refer to states or actions that are in existence or process at a certain point of time identical to that of the main clause verbal form: hence the interpretation of simultaneous occurrence.

Particularly noteworthy is the fact that the simple past tense form in *-ta*, when suffixed to a spatial clause verb, allows a simultaneous interpretation if it is interpretable as having the function of present resultative aspect, as illustrated in (77):

(77) a. *Boku wa*, [*mori ga ussoo-to siget-**ta***] *naka o hitori sanposi-ta-i.*
'I want to stroll alone in the forest when it has grown thick.'
b. *Doroboo wa*, [*nimotu ga takaku tum-i-kasanat-**ta***] *kage ni mi o kakus-i-te-i-ru.*
'The thief is hiding himself behind the pieces of baggage that have been piled up high.'
c. [*Ano kazan ga hunkasi-**ta***] *soba de minna issyo-ni syasin o tor-oo.*
'Let's have a picture of us all taken beside that volcano when it has burst into eruption.'
d. *Taroo wa*, [*Ziroo to Hanako ga yorisot-**ta***] *aida ni warikom-i-ta-gat-te-i-ru.*
'Taro shows signs of wishing to squeeze himself between Jiro and Hanako when they have nestled close to each other.'

The *-ta* forms of the spatial clauses in (77a) and (77b) are definitely interpretable as expressing resultative states, but those in (77c) and (77d) are not. This difference finds an exact parallel in (76); namely, the *-ta* forms in (77a) and (77b) are interchangeable with the *-te-i-ru* forms in (76a) and (76b), but this relation does not hold between the *-ta* forms in (77c) and (77d) and the *-te-i-ru* forms in (76c) and (76d).

The following conclusions can, therefore, be drawn from the preceding observations: Sentences (77c) and (77d) are acceptable if and only if the spatial clause *-ta* verbal forms are interpretable as exhibiting present resultative aspect, that is, resulting states that are existent at certain points of time identical to those of the main clause verbal tense forms; hence the interpretation of simultaneous occurrence. In fact, however, these sentences sound to me somewhat unnatural, or at least less natural than (77a) and (77b), and this unnaturalness seems to stem from the fact that the *-ta* forms in the former, but not in the latter, tend to be interpreted as indicating present perfective aspect, thus referring to actions that are perfected at certain points of time earlier than those of the main clause verbal tense forms. Hence, there is no interpretation of simultaneous occurrence, a situation that is in conflict with the idiosyncratic properties of the spatial nominals involved.

In the preceding discussion, it has been shown that the simultaneous occurrence of two objects or events is obligatorily involved in the semantic interpretation of a sentence when the contained subordinate clause functions as the complement of spatial nominals like those in (72). It might, then, be hypothesized that spatial clauses like that in (78a) and relative clauses like that in (78b) would be interchangeable with each other because the former have the same semantic property, and the latter have the same syntactic structure, as that of postpositional phrases like that in (78c):

(78) a. *Boku wa,* [***mori*** *ga ussoo-to* {*sige-ru* / *siget-te-i-ru*}] *naka o hitori sanposi-ta.*
'I strolled alone in the forest when it grew dense.'

b. *Boku wa,* [*ussoo-to* {*sige-ru* / *siget-te-i-ru*}] ***mori*** *no naka o hitori sanposi-ta.*
'I strolled alone in the forest that grew dense.'

c. *Boku wa,* ***mori*** *no naka o hitori sanposi-ta.*
'I strolled alone in the forest.'

Sentence (78a) contains a complete sentence that functions as the sentential complement of the spatial nominal *naka* 'inside', but (78b) has a noun phrase *mori* 'forest', moved out of the sentential complement of (78a), functioning as the head of the relative clause. The whole complex noun phrase in (78b), thus, finds an exact parallel in structure in (78c).

Insofar as the preceding observations are concerned, spatial and relative clauses of the type under consideration appear to be interchangeable with each other, but in fact they are not. Particularly noteworthy is the fact that, regardless of whether the main clause predicate is in the past or nonpast tense, the nonpast tense form in either *-ru* or *-te-i-ru* of the spatial clause requires simultaneous occurrence, while the same form of the relative clause allows both simultaneous and nonsimultaneous occurrence. It might, thus, be conceivable that only in the interpretation of simultaneous occurrence would the spatial and relative clauses be interchangeable with each other.

Compare the sentences in each of the following pairs:

(79) a. *Taroo wa,* [***Ziroo to Hanako*** *ga* {*yoriso-u* / *yorisot-te-i-ru*}] *aida ni warikon-da.*
'Taro squeezed himself between Jiro and Hanako when they were nestling close to each other.'

b. *Taroo wa,* [{*yoriso-u* / *yorisot-te-i-ru*}] ***Ziroo to Hanako*** *no aida ni warikon-da.*
'Taro squeezed himself between Jiro and Hanako, who were nestling close to each other.'

(80) a. *Boku wa,* [**mori** *ga ussoo-to* {*sige-ru* / *siget-te-i-ru*}] *naka o hitori sanposi-ta-i.*
'I want to stroll alone in the forest when it grows dense.'

b. *Boku wa,* [*ussoo-to* {*sige-ru* / *siget-te-i-ru*}] ***mori*** *no naka o hitori sanposi-ta-i.*
'I want to stroll alone in the forest that grows dense.'

The *-ru* and *-te-i-ru* forms of the spatial clause in (79a) are uniquely interpretable as signifying an action that occurred and one that was occurring, respectively, at a certain point in the past identical to that of the main clause action. Similar observations apply in (80a). By contrast, the *-ru* and *-te-i-ru* forms of the relative clauses in (79b) and (80b) are both potentially ambiguous between this simultaneous interpretation and another interpretation, namely, a nonsimultaneous interpretation in which the forms in question have their own time referents independently of the verbal forms of the main clauses.

Evidence for the availability of this nonsimultaneous interpretation for sentences with relative clauses like (79b) and (80b) comes from the following sentences with different time adverbials in the main and relative clauses:

(81) a. ***Kinoo*** *Taroo wa,* [***itumo*** {*yoriso-**u*** / *yorisot-te-i-**ru***}] *Ziroo to Hanako no aida ni warikon-**da.***
'Yesterday Taro squeezed himself between Jiro and Hanako, who always nestle close to each other.'

b. ***Rainen*** *mo boku wa,* [***ima*** *ussoo-to* {*sige-**ru*** / *siget-te-i-**ru***}] *(kono) mori no naka o hitori sanposi-ta-**i**.*
'Next year also I want to stroll alone in this forest, which has now grown dense.'

As is apparent in the English translations, the relative clauses in (81) are interpreted as involving nonrestrictive use, thus providing extra information only for expository purposes. Thus, in (81a), the *-ru* and *-te-i-ru* forms express present habitual or recurrent actions, quite independently of the main clause verbal form, which expresses a past action. In (81b), the *-ru* and *-te-i-ru* forms indicate states that have been existent this year, quite independently of the main clause predicate form, which indicates the present mental attitude of the speaker-subject toward a future action.

It should be recalled here that this nonsimultaneous interpretation is not available for sentences with spatial clauses, as shown in (75). It should, further, be obvious that the interpretation of simultaneous occurrence involved in the spatial or relative clause is due to the aspectual function of their *-ru*/*-te-i-ru* verbal forms, while the interpretation of nonsimultaneous occurrence involved in the relative clause is due to the temporal function of the same verbal forms.

Tense and Aspect in Complements of Perception Verbs

There is a class of verbs in Japanese that require the occurrence of sentential complements with the abstract nominalizer *no* or *tokoro* (which has not entirely lost its original meaning 'place') as head noun. This class includes verbs of physical perception like those in (82a), and also what might be called verbs of physical contact and approach like those in (82b):

(82) a. *mi-(ru)* 'look at', *mie-(ru)* 'see', *kik-(u)* 'listen to', *kikoe-(ru)* 'hear', *mituke-(ru)* 'find', *mimamor-(u)* 'watch', *mokugekisu-(ru)* 'witness', *mitume-(ru)* 'stare at'
b. *torae-(ru)*, *tukamae-(ru)* 'catch/capture'; *oikake-(ru)*, *tuisekisu-(ru)* 'run after/chase'

In the discussion that follows, it will be shown that these verbs allow the occurrence of the complement verb only in the tense forms undergoing a simultaneous interpretation. It will also be shown that the same observation can be made about sentential complements of such set phrases as those in (83), which also indicate physical perception:

(83) *oto ga su-(ru)* 'hear the sound of', *nioi ga su-(ru)* 'smell of'

Firstly, observe sentences like those in (84), in which the complement verb appears in the simple nonpast tense form:

(84) a. *Boku wa, [kare ga kinko o kakus-**u**] no o mi-**ta**.*
'I saw him hide the safe.'
b. *Keikan wa, [doroboo ga nige-**ru**] tokoro o tukamae-**ta**.*
'The policeman captured the thief running away.'

The *-ru* form of the complement verb in each of these sentences is interpreted as indicating an action that took place at a certain point in the past identical to that of the main clause action; hence the simultaneous occurrence of the two actions involved. The availability of this particular interpretation shows that the *-ru* tense form has an aspectual rather than a temporal function, namely, the function of imperfect aspect. This aspectual function allows the *-ru* form to refer actually to past time under control of the main verb tense.

Clearer evidence comes from the fact that the *-ru* form does not allow the complement clause to contain a time adverb independently of the main clause, as is shown in the sentences in (85), contrasted with those in (84):

(85) a. **Kinoo* boku wa, [***asu*** *kare ga kinko o kakus-***u**] *no o mi-***ta**.
'(Lit.) Yesterday I saw him hide the safe tomorrow.'
b. **Kinoo* keikan wa, [***ima*** *doroboo ga nige-***ru**] *tokoro o tukamae-***ta**.
'(Lit.) Yesterday the policeman captured the thief running away right now.'

Secondly, consider sentences like those in (86), in which the complement verb appears in the progressive nonpast tense form:

(86) a. *Boku wa*, [*kare ga kinko o kakus-i-***te-i-ru**] *no o mokugekisi-ta*.
'I witnessed him hiding the safe.'
b. *Keikan wa*, [*doroboo ga nemur-i-kon-***de-i-ru**] *tokoro o torae-ta*.
'The policeman seized the thief while he was asleep.'

The *-te-i-ru* form of the complement verb in (86a) represents an action that was going on at a certain point in the past identical to that of the main verb action, while the *-de-i-ru* form of the complement verb in (86b) represents a resulting state that was existent at a certain point in the past identical to that of the main verb action. A simultaneous interpretation is, thus, involved in either of these sentences. What is shown by the availability of this interpretation is that the *-te/de-i-ru* form has an aspectual rather than a temporal function, namely, the function of progressive aspect in (86a) and that of resultative aspect in (86b). This aspectual function allows the *-te/de-i-ru* form actually to refer to past time under control of the main verb tense.

Finally, notice that even the simple past tense form is permissible with the complement verb insofar as it is interpretable as involving some degree of simultaneity, whether instantaneous or durative. Thus, observe the following sentences:

(87) a. [*Yama-yama ni yuki ga takaku tumot-***ta**] *no ga mie-ta*.
'I saw the snow being piled up high on the mountains.'
b. *Keikan wa*, [*hannin ga kuruma o tome-***ta**] *tokoro o taihosu-ru tumori-da*.
'The policeman intends to seize the criminal$_i$ when he$_i$ has stopped the car.'

The *-ta* form of the complement verb in (87a) is interpreted as referring to a state resulting from the event of snow falling, which was existent at a certain point in the past when the main verb action took place. On the other hand, the *-ta* form of the complement verb in (87) is interpreted as referring to an action that will be perfected at a certain point in the future when the main verb action will happen. Thus, the simultaneity involved in (87a) is fairly long, but that involved in (87b) is instantaneous.

It should also be noted that the *-ta* tense form has an aspectual rather than a temporal function, that is, the function of perfect aspect. Evidence is provided by the ungrammaticality of the following sentence, as compared with (87b):

(88) ****Asu*** *keikan wa*, [***kinoo*** *hannin ga kuruma o tome-****ta***] *tokoro o taihosu-****ru*** *tumori-da.*
'(Lit.) The policeman intends to seize the criminal$_i$ tomorrow when he$_i$ stopped his$_i$ car yesterday.'

Here, the past tense form in *-ta* does not allow the complement clause to contain a past time adverbial *kinoo* 'yesterday' independently of the main clause containing a future time adverbial *asu* 'tomorrow'.

A comparison of the following three sentences brings out clearly the differences in meaning among the three tense forms of the complement verb, namely, the *-ru*, *-te-i-ru*, and *-ta* forms:

(89) a. *Keikan wa*, [*aru otoko ga yane ni yozi-nobor-****u***] *tokoro o tukamae-ta.*
'The policeman caught a man$_i$ when he$_i$ was about to climb onto the roof.'

b. *Keikan wa*, [*aru otoko ga yane ni yozi-nobot-****te-i-ru***] *tokoro o tukamae-ta.*
'The policeman caught a man$_i$ while he$_i$ was climbing onto the roof.'

c. *Keikan wa*, [*aru otoko ga yane ni yozi-nobot-****ta***] *tokoro o tukamae-ta.*
'The policeman caught a man$_i$ when he$_i$ finished climbing onto the roof.'

All of these sentences are the same in that there is definitely at least one point of time involved at which the two actions coincide with each other, but they differ in the manner of convergence of the two actions, depending on what type of aspectual function is involved. Thus, in (89a) the *-ru* form, which indicates present imperfective aspect, implies an action that was not perfected when the main verb action took place; in (89b), the *-te-i-ru* form, which expresses present progressive aspect, implies an action that was in process when the main verb action took place; and in (89c), the *-ta* form, which shows present perfective aspect, implies an action that was perfected when the main verb action occurred. These differences may be clearly seen in the English counterparts.

Such clear-cut differences cannot be observed for all the verbs exemplified in (82). However, the underlying generalization has emerged that the verbs under consideration allow the occurrence of the complement verb only in the tense forms undergoing a simultaneous interpretation. Why is this the case? The reason seems to be simply that when one performs an act of physical perception or contact, there must necessarily exist a physical object that (at least one believes) one is actually perceiving or contacting at the very same moment. Thus, this semantic fact serves to impose a constraint on the tense of the complement verb in such a way that the two actions involved are interpreted as occurring simultaneously. There are, of course, verbs other than those of physical perception or contact for which similar observations apply; one example is *tetuda-(u)* 'help', as illustrated in (90):

(90) *Ware-ware wa,* [*kare ga kuruma o* {*ara-**u*** / ?*arat-**te-i-ru*** / **arat-**ta***}] *no o tetudat-ta.*
'We helped him wash his car.'

Now, turning our attention to set phrases such as those in (83), we observe that they also require the occurrence of the complement verb in the tense forms undergoing a simultaneous interpretation. Thus, contrast, first, the following sentences with *nioi ga su-(ru)* 'smell of':

(91) a. [*Sanma no* {*yake-**ru*** / *yake-**te-i-ru***}] *nioi ga si-ta.*
'I smelled of mackerel pike broiling.'
b. [*Sanma no koge-**ta***] *nioi ga su-ru.*
'I smell of mackerel pike being scorched.'

In (91a), with the complement verb in the *-ru* tense form, it is implied that the speaker smelled of mackerel pike when it broiled: on the other hand, in (91a), with the complement verb in the *-te-i-ru* form, it is implied that the speaker smelled of mackerel pike while it was broiling. However, in (91b), with the *-ta* tense form, it is implied that the speaker smells of mackerel pike when it has been scorched. It is, thus, clear that the interpretation of simultaneous occurrence is involved in each of these sentences, and that the *-ru*, *-te-i-ru*, and *-ta* tense forms of the complement verb have aspectual rather than temporal functions.

Next, compare (91) with the following sentences with *oto ga su-(ru)* 'hear the sound of':

(92) a. [*Ame ga hur-**u***] *oto ga si-ta.*
'I heard the sound of rain falling.'
b. *[*Ame ga hut-**ta***] *oto ga su-ru.*
'(Lit.) I hear the sound of rain having fallen.'

The *-ta* form in (91b) implies that there is a smell that comes out after fish has been scorched, and this implication is factually correct. By contrast, the same form in (92b) implies, contrary to fact, that there is a sound that is produced after it has rained, rather than one that is produced when it rains, as implied in (92a). This counterfactive implication makes (92b) unacceptable because it makes it impossible for the two actions involved to converge at any moment.

Analogously to such set phrases as these, it should be noticed, verbs of perception of the type shown in (82a) allow the occurrence of semantically significant lexical items like *oto* 'sound', *koe* 'voice', *sugata* 'figure', *arisama* 'scene', in place of the abstract nominalizers *no* and *tokoro*, as the head noun of the complement clause. Observe:

(93) a. [*Tonari de huuhu ga kenkasi-te-i-ru*] ***koe*** *ga kikoe-te-ki-ta.*
'I heard the voice of the couple next door quarreling with each other.'

b. *Boku wa*, [*aru otoko ga kinko o nusum-u*] ***usiro-sugata*** *o mokugekisi-ta.*
'I witnessed a man stealing the safe/(Lit.) I witnessed the back-figure of a man's stealing the safe.'

In these instances as well, the same restriction holds for the tense of the complement verb, namely, that there must be some point of time when the two actions converge.

It might, then, be speculated that complement clauses of this type would be interchangeable with relative clauses, but this speculation is factually incorrect. Some differences between the two types of clauses will, thus, present themselves. First to be noted is the fact that the relation of the complement clause to its head noun is quite different from that of the relative clause to its head noun: The head noun of the complement clause, unlike that of the relative clause, is not at all recoverable internally to the clause. In other words, the complement clause, as such, can occur as a complete sentence, whereas the relative clause is incomplete as an independent sentence unless the head noun is recovered within the clause.

Second, the *-te-i-ta* tense form is not allowed in the complement clause, but only in the relative clause, regardless of whether the main clause verb is in the past or nonpast tense. Thus, compare the following sentences:

(94) a. *[*Ame ga hut-**te-i-ta***] *oto ga kikoe-ta.*
'(Lit.) I heard the sound of rain having been falling.'

b. *[*Kodomo-tati ga oozei umi de oyoi-**de-i-ta***] *no ga mie-ru.*
'(Lit.) I see many children having been swimming in the sea.'

c. [*Umi de oyoi-**de-i-ta***] *kodomo-tati ga oozei mie-ru.*
'I see many children who were swimming in the sea (yesterday).'

The unacceptability of (94a) and (94b) is due to the fact that there is no point of convergence between the two actions involved; thus, (94a) has the self-contradictory implication that the speaker heard the sound of rain falling that had been produced and was gone before he could hear it, and (94b) that the speaker sees the action of many children's swimming in the sea that has been perfected before he can see it. By contrast, (94c), which contains a relative clause, is perfectly acceptable because nothing forces the two actions to converge at any moment, and it is, thus, interpreted as implying that many children whom the speaker sees at the moment of speech happen to be those who were swimming in the sea at a certain moment in the past.

Third, no tense form that represents what might be called a permanent state is allowed in the complement clause, but only in the relative clause. The only tense permissible is the simple nonpast tense suffixed to adjectives, nominal-adjectives, and nouns. Thus, compare the following sentences:

(95) a. *[*Onna-no-ko ga tenisu ga* ***uma-i***] *no o mituke-ta.*
'(Lit.) I found a girl being good at tennis.'
b. [*Tenisu ga* ***uma-i***] *onna-no-ko o mituke-ta.*
'I found a girl who was good at tennis.'

The contrast in grammaticality between (95a) and (95b) is due to the fact that one can find a physical object like *onna-no-ko* 'girl', but not a permanent state like that of a girl's being good at tennis. However, compare the following sentences:

(96) a. *[*Sora ga kura-i*] *no ga mie-ru.*
'(Lit.) I see the sky dark.'
b. [*Sora ga kura-ku-nar-u*] *no ga mie-ru.*
'I see the sky getting dark.'

The contrast between (96a) and (96b) shows that the sentence becomes acceptable if the stative form is actionalized (i.e., inchoativized). Thus, one can see an ongoing action or event as well as a physical object.

Finally, the difference in meaning between complement and relative clauses can be seen most clearly from the contrast between (97a), on the one hand, and (97b) and (97c), on the other:

(97) a. *Boku wa*, [*keikan ga hannin o torae-te-i-ru*] *no o mi-ta.*
'I saw the policeman capturing the criminal.'
b. *Boku wa*, [*hannin o torae-te-i-ru*] *keikan o mi-ta.*
'I saw the policeman who was capturing the criminal.'
c. *Boku wa*, [*keikan ga torae-te-i-ru*] *hannin o mi-ta.*
'I saw the criminal whom the policeman was capturing.'

The first sentence differs in meaning from the last two. While focus is placed on the head noun in the last two sentences, it is placed on the entire event represented by the complement clause in the first sentence. It could never reasonably be maintained that one complement clause, like that in (97a), would have two different semantic correlates expressible by relative clauses, like those in (97b) and (97c).

4. MODALITY IN INDEPENDENT AND DEPENDENT CLAUSES

Modality may be interpreted as a psychological attitude on the part of the speaker toward an event, an action, or a state. Various modal phenomena in Japanese are reflected syntactically in such elements as tense markers, modal particles, modal predicates, and certain dependent clauses like conditional clauses and sentential complements of nouns and predicates. The speaker may or may not be involved syntactically, though he must be semantically. There may or may not be a particular person involved toward whom the speaker directs his psychological attitude, and in cases in which a particular person is involved, regardless of whether he appears syntactically or not, he will be provoked to perform a particular action or to make an appropriate verbal reaction; otherwise, he will not do or say anything overtly. These matters may be determined by the idiosyntactic properties of such modal elements as those mentioned earlier. In this section, I will, thus, discuss some interesting modal phenomena in an attempt to clarify precisely what psychological attitude the speaker expresses toward whom and about what.

Modal Particles

The most salient examples that express various psychological attitudes on the part of the speaker are the sentence-final particles that may be called moods. The moods may be subdivided into two groups, one in which a particular person, namely, the hearer, toward whom modality is directed, is involved, and another in which such a particular person is not involved.

Firstly, some of the moods that belong to the first group provoke a particular action on the part of the hearer, that is, provoke the hearer to perform the action represented by the associated sentence. Some examples are shown in (98), and their syntactic behavior is exemplified in (99):

(98)
a. abrupt imperative *-ro/-e/-yo/-yare*
b. abrupt prohibitive *-na*
c. polite imperative *-nasai*
d. friendly request *-kure*
e. polite request *-kudasai*
f. hortative *-yoo/-oo*

(99) a. *Nige-**ro**.*
'Run away!'
b. *Motto hayaku hasir-**e**.*
'Run much faster!'
c. *Sore o kanketu-ni nobe-**yo**.*
'State it briefly!'
d. *Nagusame-te-**yare**.*
'Soothe her/him!'
e. *Nige-ru-**na**.*
'Don't run away!'
f. *Zisyo o sirabe-**nasai**.*
'Consult the dictionary!'
g. *Denki o tuke-na-i-de-**kure**.*
'Don't turn on the light (for me)!'
h. *Mado o ake-te-**kudasai**.*
'Open the window (for me)!'
i. *Sore de wa, hazime-mas-**yoo**.*
'Now, let's get started.'
j. *Aru-i-te-yuk-**oo**.*
'Let's walk (there).'

The moods here express different types of attitudes of command and request on the part of the speaker toward the hearer's future performance of the actions mentioned. Thus, they take on a strong performative flavor. In (99e), the speaker abruptly orders the hearer not to perform the action of running away, and in (99h), the speaker politely requests the hearer to perform the action of opening the window. In (99j), as in (99i), in which the mood is associated with a plural first-person subject, e.g., *ware-ware/watasi-tati/boku-ra (wa)*, the speaker plainly suggests to those present, including himself, that they perform the action of going there on foot. Similar observations may be made for the other sentences.

In the sentences in (99), the speaker's mental attitudes are expressed at the present moment, namely, at the moment of speech, whereas the events indicated by the sentences will invariably take place in the nonpast (i.e., present or future), as is sometimes evidenced by the obligatory occurrence of the nonpast tense marker, e.g., *-ru* in (99e) and *-i* in (99g). Those future events will be realized by the actions that the hearer is provoked to perform in the future.

Secondly, some moods provoke the hearer to make a verbal reaction to the sentence uttered by the speaker, rather than performing a particular action. Some examples of this subtype are shown in (100), and their syntactic performance is illustrated in (101):

(100) a. interrogative *ka*
b. confirmative *ne*
c. presumptive-interrogative *daroo-ka/desyoo-ka*

(101) a. *Kimi wa, konya dansu-paatii ni ik-i-mas-u* ***ka****?*
'Are you going to the dance tonight?'
b. *Kinoo wa, ame ga hur-i-mas-i-ta* ***ne****!?*
'It rained yesterday, didn't it?'
c. *Ano hito wa, densya ni maniat-ta daroo-ka?*
'Do you think that he has caught the train?'

The moods here express mental attitudes of the speaker that require an appropriate verbal reaction on the part of the hearer to the action or state mentioned. Thus, in (101b), for instance, the speaker makes a statement of request, for reassurance, that his belief that it rained yesterday is really correct. Without any proper verbal response, therefore, the sentence will sound incomplete. Natural responses of the hearer to the sentences in (101) would look something like the following, respectively:

(102) a. *Ee, ik-i-mas-u.*
'Yes, I will.'
b. *Iie, hur-i-mas-en des-i-ta.*
'No, it didn't.'
c. *Un, kitto maniat-ta daroo.*
'Yes, I'm sure he has been in time.'

In the sentences in (101), the event time, as contrasted with that of the sentences in (99), may be either in the past, as evidenced by the past tense marker *-ta* in (101b) and (101c), or in the nonpast, as evidenced by the nonpast tense marker *-(r)u* in (101a). The speaker's mental attitude is expressed at the present moment, and therefore, the hearer's verbal reaction will take place afterwards, namely, in the future.

Thirdly, there is a group of moods that provoke neither a particular action nor a verbal reaction on the part of the hearer, although the hearer is definitely involved. Some examples are presented in (103), and their syntactic behavior is illustrated in (104):

(103) a. assertive *yo*
b. plain presumptive *daroo*
c. polite presumptive *des-yoo*
d. polite presumptive *-mas-yoo*

(104) a. *Sonna koto o si-te-wa dame des-u* ***yo****!*
'You should not do that.'

b. *Tabun asu yuki ga hur-u* ***daroo****.*
'Perhaps it will snow tomorrow.'
c. *Ano ziko de wa, ooku no hito ga sin-da* ***des-yoo****.*
'I presume that many people were killed in that accident.'
d. *Asu gogo ni nat-te ame ga hur-i-das-i-****mas-yoo****.*
'Tomorrow it will presumably start to rain in the afternoon.'

It is hardly possible to find any clear evidence for the involvement of the hearer in the moods in question, but what is particularly noteworthy is the fact that it is due to the presence of the polite verbs *des-* and *-mas-* that a polite attitude of the speaker toward the hearer is expressed in (104c) and (104d). It can, thus, be inferred that the absence of the polite verbs in (104b) implies the absence of a polite attitude of the speaker toward the hearer.

Viewed along these lines, the volitional moods *-yoo/-oo*, when associated with a singular first-person subject, can be said to show the politeness or nonpoliteness of the speaker toward the hearer according to whether they are accompanied by the polite verbs or not. Thus, compare the following sentences:

(105) a. *Sore wa, boku ga hanas-****oo****.*
'I will talk about that.'
b. *Sore wa, watasi ga hanas-i-****mas-yoo****.*
'I will talk about that.'

It should be noted that the *yo*, *daroo*, and *des-yoo* modal forms may be associated with either a past or a nonpast event, as in (104a–c), whereas the presumptive and volitional *-mas-yoo* forms may be associated only with a nonpast event, as in (104d) and (105b).

There is, finally, another type of mood that does not imply the involvement of a particular person, e.g., the hearer, toward whom modality is directed. The following exemplify the moods of this subtype:

(106) a. exclamatory *naa*
b. negative-volitional *mai*
c. negative-presumptive *mai*

Consider the sentences in (107), which represent their syntactic behavior:

(107) a. *Kyoo wa, totemo samu-i* ***naa****!*
'How cold it is today!'
b. {*Watasi* / *Kimi* / *Kare*} *wa, syoosetu wa kak-e(-ru)* ***mai****.*
'Presumably, I/you/he will not be able to write novels.'

c. *Kimi* / *Kare* } *wa, syoosetu wa kak-u* ***mai***.
'Presumably, you/he will not write novels.'

d. *Watasi wa, syoosetu wa kak-u* ***mai***
(i) 'Presumably, I will not write novels.'
(ii) 'I won't write novels.'

Extremely interesting are the modal phenomena involved in the mood *mai*. Two factors participate in determining the idiosyncratic properties of this mood, one being what the subject is and the other being whether the predicate involved designates action or state. When the predicate is stative, without relevance to the choice of the subject, the mood *mai* expresses a presumptive attitude of the speaker, as exemplified in (107b). Here, the complex predicate *kak-e-* 'be able to write' indicates state under control of the most external component *-(ra)re-* 'be able'. On the other hand, when the predicate designates action, the situation is rather complicated. With a second- or third-person subject, as in (107c), the mood *mai* expresses the same presumptive attitude of the speaker, but, with a first-person subject, as in (107d), it is ambiguous between presumptive and strong volitional attitudes of the speaker, although the latter reading is preferred.

What must be particularly noted is the fact that the negative element of *mai* negates the proposition mentioned rather than the speaker's presumption or volition and, therefore, that the mood *mai* expresses a presumptive or volitional attitude of the speaker toward the negated proposition involved. It must, further, be noted that the negated proposition may be either a state, as in (107b), which neither exists at the present moment nor possibly extends into the future, or an action, as in (107c) and (107d), which will not occur in the future. Evidence that the time of the state or action is in the nonpast is provided by the obligatory or optional occurrence of only the nonpast tense marker *-ru*, as in (107b–d).

The Polite Verbs *-mas-*/*-masen*/*des-*

Another modal phenomenon in which a polite attitude on the part of the speaker is directed toward the hearer can be observed for the polite verbs. This particular property makes it necessary that the hearer be present at the moment when the speaker's attitude is expressed, and that the tense directly attached to the polite verbs, past or nonpast, indicate the time of the event mentioned. These points are illustrated in the following sentences:

(108) a. *Yamada wa, yoku okure-te-ki-**mas**-u.*
'Yamada often comes late.'

b. *Aitu wa, kinoo sin-i-**mas**-i-ta.*
'That fellow died yesterday.'

c. *Tanaka-san wa, mada mie-te-i-**masen** (**des**-i-ta).*
'Mr. Tanaka has not yet shown up (Mr. Tanaka had not yet shown up (then)).'

It is shown in (108a) and (108b) that the polite verb is associated with the hearer but not with the subject, because if the reverse were correct, then the bluntness of the title-less *Yamada* and the vulgar *aitu* 'fellow' would contradict the politeness of the verb *-mas-*; but this is not what happens. Thus, in (108a), for instance, the speaker politely informs the hearer of the event that Yamada often comes late, and similarly in (108b).

It is shown in (108c) that the negative element *-en* of *masen* negates the resultative state-indicating verbal *mie-te-i-* rather than the polite verb *-mas-* itself, so that the speaker can display a polite attitude toward the hearer when he tells him about the present state of affairs, namely, that Mr. Tanaka has not yet shown up. Note, incidentally, that the past counterpart of *-masen* is *-masen des-i-ta*, in which *des-* is another polite verb. This is shown in (108c). (For a formal treatment of the polite forms as well as other honorifics, cf. the chapter by Harada in this volume.)

The Simple Past/Nonpast Tense Markers *-ta/-ru*

One modal aspect reflected in the simple past tense *-ta* form of true verbs is the speaker's present awareness, with some degree of surprise, that his past desired or anticipated event has been realized. It is characteristically associated with interjective expressions such as *hora* 'look!', *nanda* 'what/why!', and *yappari/yahari*, translatable as 'as I expected/anticipated'.

Thus, observe the following sentences:

(109) a. *Hora, asoko ni itiban-bosi ga mie-**ta**!*
'Look! There's the first evening star over there!'
b. *Nanda, konna tokoro ni megane ga at-**ta**!*
'Look! I've found my glasses/Here are my glasses!'
c. *Yappari anna tokoro de oyoi-de-i-**ta** no-ka!*
'Just as I had anticipated, you were swimming over there.'

In (109a), the speaker becomes aware at the moment of speech that the event of his seeing the first evening star, which he has expected to take place over a period lasting up to the present moment, has actually come true. Similarly observations hold for the other sentences.

The point is that this connotation is explainable only by assuming that the simple past tense has a present perfective function rather than a past time function, because two mental states of the speaker are involved in the modal phenomenon under consideration, one being the speaker's past anticipation that the event mentioned will be realized and the other being the speaker's present awareness of its realization. This aspectual interpretation, however, is not so straightforward in sentences with the simple nonpast tense form corresponding to the sentences in (109), because the predicates involved are all stative.

However, the contrast between the simple past and nonpast tense forms of action verbs demonstrates the point, as in (110):

(110) a. *(Yatto) basu ga ki-**ta**!*
'The bus has come after all!'
b. *(*Yatto) basu ga ku-**ru**!*
'Here comes a bus (?after all)!'

It is implied in (110a), but not in (110b), that the speaker has hoped for a bus for a certain period stretching from the past into the present. This difference stems from whether the function of perfective aspect, rather than that of time, is involved in the tense forms in question, because the latter function forces, counterfactively, (110a) and (110b) to undergo the readings 'a bus came' and 'a bus will come', respectively, by general interpretive rules of tenses in independent clauses (cf. Section 1). In (110a), sharper focus is placed on the present perfection of an event desired in the past, but in (110b), on the present imperfection of an event not necessarily anticipated in the past, implying that a bus has just come in sight but has not yet actually arrived.

We have seen in Section 1 that the simple nonpast tense marker *-ru*, when combined with action verbs, refers to future time. In this particular case, different types of modality are involved, depending on whether the subject is in the first, second, or third person.

Thus, observe the following three sentences, which differ in the choice of the subject:

(111) a. *Boku ga yuk-**u**.*
'I will go.'
b. *Kimi ga sore o tantoo si-mas-**u**.*
'You will take charge of it.'
c. *Sore wa, Taroo ga mot-te-ku-**ru**.*
'Taro will (surely) bring it along.'

All these examples represent future actions, i.e., actions that will take place later than the moment of speech. In addition, they all imply an assertive attitude of the speaker toward an event, regardless of who the subject is, but this modal implication has subtle differences depending on who the subject is.

In (111a), in which the speaker is the subject, the speaker asserts his own certainty that he will go, and in (111c), with a third-person subject, the speaker makes clear his previous understanding or present belief that Taro will surely bring it along. In (111b), with a second-person subject, the speaker exhibits his own assertive or, sometimes, imperative attitude toward the hearer, depending on extralinguistic contexts, meaning that it is understood that 'you' will take charge of it, that 'I' command 'you' to take charge of it, and so forth. In particular, (111b), without the polite verb *-mas-*, will sound extremely abrupt and imperative, since the subject coincides with the hearer.

The Copulas in Their Past Tense Forms

There are several interesting copular expressions that indicate the speaker's present awareness that either (a) he had forgotten about something he once knew or (b) he does not know about something he believes he should have known. These are the existential simple past tense form in *at-ta* 'existed', the copular simple past tense form in *dat-ta* 'was/were', and its polite counterparts *des-i-ta* and *dat-ta no-des-u*.

A cursory glance at the following examples reveals this point:

(112) a. *Aa, asu go-zi ni kaigoo ga* ***at-ta****!*
'I now remember that we will hold a meeting at five tomorrow.'

b. *Siturei des-u ga, anata wa, Kyuusyuu no go-syussin* ***des-i-ta*** *ne?*
'Excuse me, but, if I remember rightly, you are from Kyushu, aren't you?'

c. *Gakkoo wa, rai-getu nan-niti kara* ***dat-ta (des-u ka)****?*
'Do you happen to know (and I hope you know) at what date next month school will start?'

d. *Nanika watasi ni* { (i) *go-yoo ga* ***ar-i-mas-i-ta*** *ka?* / (ii) *go-yoo* ***des-i-ta*** *ka?* }
'Is there something I can do for you?'

In (112a), the speaker recollects at the moment of speech what he knew previously but yet had forgotten until just now, that is, the event that a meeting will be held at five tomorrow. In (112c), at the moment of speech, when he is aware that he does not know when school will start although he should have known about it, he asks the question of the hearer. Similar observations apply for (112b) and (112d).

These observations suggest that the examples in (112) are paraphrasable as sentences with *no-dat-ta/no-des-i-ta* 'it was the case that' in final position, as in (113):

(113) a. *Asu go-zi ni kaigoo ga* ***ar-u n(o)-dat-ta***.
(Lit.) 'It was the case that we would hold a meeting at five tomorrow.'

b. ??*Siturei des-u ga, anata wa, Kyuusyuu no go-syussin* ***de-ar-u no-des-i-ta*** *ne?*
(Lit.) 'Excuse me, but it was the case that you were from Kyushu, wasn't it?'

c. *Gakoo wa, rai-getu nan-niti kara* {(i) ***hazimar-u no-des-i-ta*** / (ii) ??***de ar-u no-des-i-ta***} *ka?*
(Lit.) 'At what date next month was it the case that school would begin?'

d. *Nanika watasi ni* {(i) *go-yoo ga* ***ar-u no-des-i-ta*** / (ii) ??*go-yoo* ***de-ar-u no-des-i-ta***} *ka?*
(Lit.) 'Was it the case that there was something I could do for you?'

The sentences with question marks are low on the scale of acceptability, because different levels of style are confused and the copular phrase *de-ar-u no-des-i-ta* is redundant and clumsy; nevertheless, they must definitely be high on the scale of grammaticality. On the other hand, the sentences without question marks are perfectly acceptable.

It might, then, be concluded that the sentences in (112) are transformationally or interpretively related to those in (113); thus, a contraction rule would optionally delete the nonconstituents *-ru n(o) dat-* from (113a) and *-ru no-des-i-* from (i) of (113d); another rule would obligatorily delete the nonconstituent *de-ar-u no-* from the sentences with question marks. Still another contraction rule would optionally delete *hazimar-u no-* from (i) of (113c). Undoubtedly, all these rules, particularly the last one, are extremely ad hoc.

One advantage of this treatment, however, is that it would provide a natural explanation for disagreement between a tense and a time adverbial in sentences like those in (112). Thus, for example, the fact that the future time adverbial *asu go-zi ni* 'at five tomorrow' in (112a) is in conflict with the past time tense of *at-ta* 'existed' would, indeed, be a superficial phenomenon, because what the future time adverbial is associated with in the underlying source, (113a), would be the fragment *kaigi ga ar-u* 'will hold a meeting', which implies future time. The superficial time disagreement involved in (112a) could, thus, be a function of the rule of deletion involved. Exactly the same observations hold for (112c), in which a future time adverbial, *rai-getu nan-niti kara* 'at what date next month', is in apparent contradiction with the main predicate form *dat-ta (des-u)*.

Modal Adjectives and Nominal-Adjectives

There are many adjectives and nominal-adjectives that themselves express various mental states of the speaker relating to the events indicated by the sentential complements they require; but only under certain conditions do some of them take on counterfactive overtones. In the following discussions I will examine some of these predicates in an attempt to clarify different types of modality and counterfactive implication.

The nominal-adjective *mono-(da)*, which constitutes an isolated example, serves to indicate a series of past habitual actions. The peculiar property of this predicate is that it requires the complement verb to be in the past tense, indicating past time. Evidence for the past time indication comes from the fact that a past time adverbial occurs in the complement sentence even when the main predicate is in the nonpast tense. Thus, observe

(114) *Kodomo no koro, Taroo wa, [tomodati to kenkasi-te yoku nakas-are-ta/*-ru]* {(i) *mono-**da**.* / (ii) *mono-dat-**ta**.*}

'In his childhood, Taro used to be brought to the point of tears in quarrels with his friends.'

Furthermore, with either the past or the nonpast tense form of the main modal predicate *mono-*, the speaker has, at the moment of speech, a recollection of a series of past habitual or iterative events, and both forms imply that the speaker himself witnessed those events taking place in the past. As will be seen, this predicate sharply contrasts with the other modal predicates of the type in question.

There is a group of adjectives and nominal-adjectives that carry counterfactive overtones when they, as main predicates, are in the past tense while the associated complement predicates are in the nonpast tense. Typical examples are *hazu-(da)* 'it is expected that/ought to', *no-(da)* 'it is the case that', and *beki-(da)* 'should'.

First, observe the following sentence with *hazu-* as main predicate:

(115) *Taroo wa, kinoo [gakkoo o yasum-**u**] hazu-dat-**ta**.*

'Taro was expected to be absent from school yesterday (but in fact he was not absent).'

A counterfactive implication is involved in this sentence, and it stems from the fact that two factors conflict with each other; namely, the event that actually happened in the past was that Taro was not absent from school yesterday, but nevertheless, the speaker had the expectation, at a certain point in the past before the event happened, that Taro would be absent from school. Therefore, the speaker's past expectation conflicts with the past event.

In summary, two modal phenomena are observed in (115): One is the speaker's expectation or anticipation, indicated by the main predicate *hazu-*, and the other is the speaker's counterfactive implication, jointly effected by the nonpast tense of the complement verb and the past tense of the main predicate.

Similar modal phenomena are involved in sentences like those in (116) with *beki-(da)* and *no-(da)* as main predicate, but something different is going on:

(116) a. *Taroo wa, kinoo [kaigi ni de-**ru**] beki-dat-**ta**.*
'Taro should have attended the meeting yesterday (but in fact he did not).'

b. $\left.\begin{matrix}\textit{Boku}\\ {}^{*}\textit{Taroo}\end{matrix}\right\}$ *wa, kinoo [gakkoo o yasum-**u**] no-dat-**ta**.*
'I/Taro should have been absent from school yesterday (but in fact I/he was not).'

Counterfactive implications should be clear from the English translations. What is particularly interesting is the involvement of two additional restrictions in (116b). One restriction is that the subject be the speaker, and the other is that the complement contain an action verb in the simple nonpast tense *-ru* form.

Thus, contrast (116b) with the following sentences, which do not meet these conditions because the complement verb is in the simple past tense or in the progressive nonpast tense and because the subject may be a third person (e.g., Taro):

(117) $\left.\begin{matrix}\textit{Boku}\\ \textit{Taroo}\end{matrix}\right\}$ *wa, kinoo mo* $\left[\textit{gakkoo o}\left\{\begin{matrix}\textit{yasun-}\textbf{\textit{da}}\\ \textit{yasun-}\textbf{\textit{de-i-ru}}\end{matrix}\right\}\right]$ *no-dat-**ta**.*
'It was the case that I/Taro was absent from school yesterday as well.'

A counterfactive implication is involved in (116b), but not in (117). Moreover, the two occurrences of the modal predicate *no-* mean different things, obligation in (116b) and truth judgment in (117).

In summary, the modal predicate *no-* carries a counterfactive overtone only when the following conditions are met: that the predicate itself is in the past tense form, that the associated complement contains an action verb in the simple nonpast tense form, and that the speaker coincides with the subject.

It should be noted, by contrast, that there are some modal nominal-adjectives that never carry counterfactive overtones of the sort observed for the nominal-adjectives just discussed, even when they themselves appear in the past tense form and the associated complement predicates appear in the nonpast tense form. Some examples are *yoo-(da)* 'seem', *yoosu-(da)* 'seem/appear', *mitai-(da)* 'appear/look like'. Observe (118):

(118) a. *Hanako wa, ano toki [nai-te-i-**ru**] yoo-dat-**ta**.*
'Hanako seemed to be weeping at that time.'
b. *Taroo wa, kinoo [asu no kaigi ni de-**ru**] yoosu-dat-**ta**.*
'It appeared yesterday that Taro would attend the meeting tomorrow.'

The only modal phenomenon involved in each of these sentences is the likelihood or appearance of an event, indicated by the main modal predicate itself.

A different type of counterfactive implication can be observed for the nominal-adjective *tumori-(da)* 'intend' under certain conditions. This predicate, like other nominal-adjectives, including *keikaku-(da)* 'plan', *yotei-(da)* 'plan', *kakugo-(da)* 'be resolved', *ketui-(da)* 'be determined', and *netui-(da)* 'be enthusiastic', imposes a humanness constraint on the subject, and therefore, all these predicates express mental states of the subject but not of the speaker, as in the following sentences:

(119) a. *Kinoo Taroo wa, [kondo no doyoobi tetuya maazyan o su-ru] tumori-dat-ta.*
'Yesterday Taro intended to sit up all night next Saturday playing mahjong.'
b. *Ziroo wa, [rainen no natu Amerika ni yuk-u] keikaku-da.*
'Jiro is planning to go to America next summer.'
c. *Taroo wa, [nani o kik-are-te-mo damat-te-i-ru] kakugo-da.*
'Taro is determined to keep silence for any question he will be asked.'

What is expressed in these sentences is Taro's past intention to perform his future action, Jiro's present plan for his future action, and Taro's present determination for his future state. It is, thus, clear that the subject's mental state is indicated by the main predicate.

However, *tumori-* 'intend', unlike the other nominal-adjectives, designates a counterfactive assertion on the part of the speaker when the complement predicate is in the past tense, regardless of whether *tumori-* itself is in the past or the nonpast tense. Thus, observe the sentences in (120):

(120) a. *Taroo wa, arede [benkyoo si-**ta**] tumori-**da**.*
'Taro himself believes that he has studied enough by studying that much (but I don't believe that he has studied enough).'

b. *Kinoo Hanako wa, arede [monku o it-**ta**] tumori-dat-**ta**.*
'Yesterday Hanako herself believed that she complained enough by saying that much (but I don't believe that she complained enough).'

In either sentence, as should be clear from the English counterpart, the speaker makes a counterfactive assertion that is present in his mind at the moment of speech.

This particular predicate also designates a counterfactive assertion of the speaker when the complement predicate appears in any other tense form than those indicating a future action or state, as in:

(121) a. *Taroo wa, arede [kasiko-**i**] tumori-**da**.*
'Taro himself believes that he, as he is, is clever (but I don't believe that he is).'

b. *Ziroo wa, arede [me o samas-i-**te-i-ru**] tumori-dat-**ta**.*
'Jiro himself believed that he was awake as he was (but I don't believe that he was).'

c. *Ziroo wa, arede [me o samas-i-**te-i-ta**] tumori-**da**.*
'Jiro himself believes that he was awake as he was (but I don't believe that he was).'

The contrast between the sentences in (120) and (121), on the one hand, and (119a), on the other, reveals the point under consideration. What is involved in the first group of sentences is either a past action or a state (past or present), as evidenced by the tense forms of the complement predicates, whereas what is involved in (119a) is a future action, as evidenced by the simple nonpast tense form of the action verb in the complement sentence. The presence or absence of a counterfactive implication of the sort we have observed arises from this difference. Another difference to be noted here is that *arede*, variously translated in (120) and (121), is correlative only with the counterfactive *tumori-*.

It should, incidentally, be noted that the other nominal-adjectives mentioned earlier are not capable of expressing a counterfactive implication of the sort observed for *tumori-*, because they allow the complement predicate to take only a tense form indicating a future action or state, as in (119b) and (119c); a future action is involved in (119b), and a future state in (119c).

Verbs of Favor Doing and Favor Receiving

There is a class of verbs that are generally called verbs of favor doing and favor receiving. They express psychological attitudes that the speaker assumes toward a particular person, who may be either a second or a third person. The property peculiar to these verbs is the fact that both the speaker and the particular person involved occupy legitimate syntactic positions, their positions being lexically determined by the idiosyncratic properties of the verbs.

First, observe the following sentences, in which *-age-(ru)* and *-yar-(u)* appear as main predicate:

(122) a. {*Watasi* / *Boku*} *wa*, {*Tanaka-san* / *ano kata*} *ni eigo o osie-te-**age**-mas-u.*
'I will do Mr. Tanaka/that person the favor of teaching him English.'

b. *Ore wa*, {*Tanaka* / *aitu*} *ni kuruma o kas-i-te-**yar**-i-mas-u.*
'I will do Tanaka/that guy the favor of lending him my car.'

The *-age-(ru)* form is a polite counterpart of the nonpolite or abrupt *-yar-(u)*, both forms being roughly translatable as 'do a person the favor of'. As shown in (122), they require, roughly, that the speaker appear as subject and that the person toward whom the speaker's mental attitude is directed appear as indirect object with the recipient particle *ni*.

The *-age-* form, thus, expresses a polite attitude of the speaker toward the recipient, while the *-yar-* form expresses a nonpolite or abrupt attitude of the speaker toward the recipient. Evidence comes from the contrast between (122a) and (122b); only the polite forms *watasi* 'I', *Tanaka-san* 'Mr./Ms. Tanaka', and *ano kata* 'that person', along with the familiar form *boku* 'I (said only by a male person)', are compatible with the polite *-age-*, whereas only the vulgar forms *ore* 'I (said only by a male person)' and *aitu* 'that guy', and the title-less *Tanaka* are compatible with the nonpolite *-yar-*, and thus, they are not interchangeable.

Special mention should be made of the occurrence of the combined form of the abrupt *-yar-* and the polite *-mas-* in (122b). This combined form is not at all self-contradictory, because the abruptness of the speaker signaled by *-yar-* is directed toward the recipient, but the politeness of the speaker signaled by *-mas-* is directed toward the hearer, as discussed earlier in this section. Confirmation comes from the contrast between the following sentences, in which the recipient coincides with the hearer:

(123) a. *Ore wa, omae ni eigo o osie-te-**yar**-u.*
'I will do you the favor of teaching you English.'

b. **Ore wa, omae ni eigo o osie-te-**yar-i-mas**-u.*
'I will do you the favor of teaching you English.'

Omae is a vulgar form referring to a second person. The contrast between (122b) and (123b) shows that the vulgarity of the hearer-recipient *omae* 'you' conflicts with the property of *-mas-* that the speaker's politeness is directed toward the hearer. Supporting evidence is provided by the contrast between (123a) and (123b); (123a), with *-mas-* left out of the unacceptable (123b), is acceptable.

Consider, next, the following sentences, in which *-itadak-(u)* and *-mora-(u)* appear as main predicate:

(124) a. *Watasi wa,* {*sensei* / *anata*} *ni/kara kityoo-na zoosyo o kas-i-te-**itadai**-ta.*
'I received the favor of my teacher's/your lending me a precious book.'

b. *Boku wa,* {*tomodati* / *kimi*} *ni/kara eigo o osie-te-**morat**-ta.*
'I received the favor of my friend's/your teaching me English.'

c. *Ore wa,* {*aitu* / *omae*} *ni syasin o tot-te-**morat**-ta.*
'I received the favor of his/your taking a picture of me.'

As is shown in (124), both the *-itadak-* and *-mora-* forms, roughly translatable as 'receive the favor of', require that the speaker appear as subject and that the person toward whom the speaker's mental attitude is directed appear as a noun phrase with the agent/source particle *ni/kara*.

The *-itadak-* form exhibits a condescending attitude of the speaker toward the agent-source, while the *-mora-* form exhibits a noncondescending or plain attitude of the speaker toward the agent-source. Thus, for instance, (124a), with the condescending *-itadak-*, will be unacceptable if it contains as agent-source the familiar *kimi* 'you' or the vulgar *omae* 'you' instead of the polite *anata* 'you'.

Finally, observe the sentences in (125), in which *-kudasar-(u)* and *-kure-(ru)* appear as main predicate:

(125) a. *Sensei* / *Anata* } *ga watasi ni kityoo-na zoosyo o kas-i-te-**kudasat**-ta.*
'My teacher/You did me the favor of lending me a valuable book.'

b. *Tomodati* / *Kimi* } *wa, boku ni eigo o osie-te-**kure**-ta.*
'My friend/You did me the favor of teaching me English.'

c. *Tanaka* / *Omae* } *wa, ore ni syasin o tot-te-**kure**-ta.*
'Tanaka/You did me the favor of taking a picture of me.'

As is shown in (125), both the *-kudasar-* and *-kure-* forms, translatable as 'do me the favor of', require that the speaker appear as indirect object with the beneficiary particle *ni*, and that the person toward whom the speaker's mental attitude is directed appear as subject. This sharply contrasts with the requirement imposed by the verbs observed earlier.

The *-kudasar-* and *-kure-* forms designate honorific and nonhonorific (or plain) attitudes of the speaker toward the subject, respectively. Thus, in (125b) and (125c) the honorific *-kudasar-* cannot substitute for the nonhonorific *-kure-*, because the honorific form conflicts with the friendliness of *tomodati* 'friend', *kimi* 'you', and *boku* 'I' or with the abruptness of the title-less *Tanaka*, *omae* 'you', and *ore* 'I'. For a similar reason, the *-kure-* form cannot take the place of the *-kudasar-* form in (125a).

The Frozen Idiom *-rare-ta-i*

An extremely peculiar phenomenon of modality is observed for the verb-*rare-ta-i* form, in which *-rare-* (or *-are-* after consonant-final verbs) is an honorific verb and *-ta-* is a desiderative adjective. The *-rare-* form expresses an honorific attitude of the speaker toward a second or third person who invariably appears as subject, as in (126a), and the desiderative *-ta-*, when combined with the nonpast tense form *-i*, requires the subject to coincide with the speaker, thus exhibiting the speaker's desire, as in (126b):

(126) a. *Ano toki wa,* { *Yamada-san* / *anata* } *ga iken o nober-**are**-ta.*
'On that occasion, Mr. Yamada/you expressed his/your opinion.'

b. *Watasi* / **Taroo* / **Anata* } *wa, zibun no iken o nobe-**ta-i**.*
'I/*Taro/*You want to express my/his/your own opinion.'

The combined form *-rare-ta-i* should, then, be expected to be internally contradictory because the complement predicates impose different constraints on the subject, but in fact this is not the case.

Curiously enough, the combined form imposes a completely different constraint on the subject, namely, that the hearer, but not the speaker, occupy subject position, though he preferably does not appear overtly. Despite this syntactic difference, the modal phenomena involved independently in *-rare-* and *-ta-i* are carried over to the *-rare-ta-i* form; thus, this combined form represents the speaker's honorific attitude toward the hearer-subject, on the one hand, and on the other, the speaker's wish that the hearer-subject will perform the action mentioned.

These points are illustrated in the following sentences:

(127) a. *Sono ken wa, zensyos-**are-ta-i**.*
'I wish you to take a proper step toward that matter.'
b. *Tugi no ree o sansyoos-**are-ta-i**.*
'Compare the following examples.'
c. *Kari-ta hon wa, kigen made ni henkyakus-**are-ta-i**.*
'The borrowed books should be returned by the date when they are due.'
d. *Go-yoo no setu wa, go-ippoo kudas-**are-ta-ku**-omoi-mas-u.*
'If you have business with me, I hope you will let me know.'

These sentences typically appear as formal statements: (127a) in Diet speeches, (127b) in papers and theses, (127c) in library bulletins, and (127d) in formal letters. In (127a), the speaker honorifically wishes the hearer to perform the action of dealing with that matter properly, and similarly in the other sentences.

It should particularly be noticed that, in (127d), the understood subject of *omoi-mas-u* 'think', or rather, that of the combined form *-ta-ku-omoi-mas-u* 'hope', is the speaker. Evidence is provided by (128), which sounds clumsy compared to (127d) but has the speaker and the hearer legitimately recovered:

(128) *Watasi wa, anata ga go-ippoo kudas-are-ta-ku-omoi-mas-u.*
'I sincerely hope that you will let me know.'

Here, the speaker is associated with *-ta-ku-omoi-mas-u*, while the hearer is associated with *kudas-are-*. Verbs of cognition, when they appear in the simple nonpast tense form, as in *-ta-ku-omoi-mas-u*, express the present mental state of the speaker, even though the speaker does not appear overtly.

Confirmation comes from consideration of such sentences as those in (129):

(129) a. *Taroo wa, asu yuk-a-na-i to **omo-u**.*
'I don't think that Taro will go tomorrow.'

b. *Tanaka-san ga zen sekinin o tot-ta to* ***handans-i-mas-u***.
'I judge that Mr. Tanaka has taken full responsibility.'

c. *Sono sensei wa, ano toki hontoo-ni oroka-dat-ta to wa* ***omoi-masen***.
'I don't think that that teacher was really stupid then.'

In each of these sentences, the explicitly mentioned subject is hardly interpretable as the subject of the main verbal form. Thus, in (129a), *Taroo* is not interpretable as the subject of *omo-u* 'think', and (129a) cannot mean that Taro does not think that he will go tomorrow. Similar observations apply to the other sentences. The reason is that no one can tell the present internal state of anyone else. Thus, it is only the speaker who is responsible for the present mental states represented by such verbal forms as those that appear in bold type in (129).

ACKNOWLEDGMENTS

Special mention should be made here of two papers, Teramura (1971b) and Josephs (1972b), which, while I was working on this chapter, served as a constant source of information and speculation and provided me with a great deal of inspiration. I am also greatly indebted to Julie Lovins for many stylistic improvements of the English in the original version of this chapter. I have also benefited greatly from Yoshiko Otsubo, Yasuko Tajima, and Masaki Oka, who worked as patient informants of the data presented in this chapter. Whatever mistakes remain are, of course, my own.

NOMINAL COMPOUNDS

SEIICHI MAKINO

INTRODUCTION

The study of nominal compounds within generative transformational grammar started with R. Lees' (1960) classic monograph on English nominalizations. There, Lees attempted to derive all the productive nominal compounds by a set of both general and specific transformational rules. He argued that the English nominal compound *pronghorn*, for example, can be derived in the following way:

The sheep has a horn }
The horn is like a prong } ⟶ relativization
⟶ The sheep has a horn which is like a prong
⟶ *wh* and copula deletion ⟶
The sheep has a horn like a prong
⟶ The sheep with a horn like a prong
⟶ The sheep with a prong horn
⟶ a prônghòrn

However, some major difficulties of the Lees transformational approach to English compounds have been brought up by linguists and psycholinguists.

Summarized in my own terms, they are as follows:

1. Some compounds are lexemes or idioms learned as un unanalyzable lexical unit.[1]

[1]See Householder (1962:333–334) and Berko (1958:150–177).

2. How can we avoid violating the recoverability condition on a transformational rule, especially when we are dealing with a deletion rule that nullifies the verb?[2]
3. It does not seem to be the case that the often proposed underlying sentential structure for a compound represents the semantics of the compound. In other words, transformational rules for the compounding formation seem to violate a basic assumption that transformations should not alter meaning.[3]
4. The posited transformational rules for the compounding will end up generating a large number of possible but nonexistent compounds of low acceptability.[4]

Most of the generative transformational linguists who have shown skepticism toward the transformational approach to compounds also have admitted that some types of compounds are fairly easily relatable to sentential deep structures. Thus, for example, one cannot ignore the fact that *garden flower* and *flower garden* are somehow related to 'flower that grows in a garden' and 'garden where flowers grow', respectively.[5] In other words, in order to capture the grammatical relations observable between the two nominal elements (*flower* and *garden*), it appears reasonable to represent the relations in the deep structures, only once, at some level of representation, preferably at the deep sentential structure because the paraphrasability between a compound and a sentence seems to hold. Actually, this was Lees' major motivation for deriving nominal compounds from the underlying sentential structures.[6]

Perhaps the difficulties listed here have come about mainly owing to Lees' rigorous yet monolithic approach to compounds, or else to his indiscriminate application of powerful transformational apparatus to compounds.[7]

[2]See Gleitman and Gleitman (1970:94).

[3]See Gleitman and Gleitman (1970:96); Geer, Gleitman, and Gleitman (1972:348–355); L.Gleitman and Berheim (1967:16–17); and Marchand (1966:134–142).

[4]See Schacter (1962:145).

[5]See Geer, Gleitman, and Gleitman (1972:355).

[6]Lees (1960) writes this: '... English nominal compounds incorporate the grammatical forms of many different sentence types, and of many different internal grammatical relationships within sentences, such as subject-predicate, subject-verb, subject-object, verb-object, etc. Thus the variety of grammatical form in compounds must compare with that found within different sentences, and from this point of view the profusion would not seem to be too great [p. 119].'

[7]My statement here should not be taken to belittle Lees' contribution to the study of compounds; rather, it is Lees' considerable contribution that guides our thinking and enables us to come closer to a more plausible theory of compounds. Lees (1970) has shown that he became keenly aware of some difficulties—especially that of recoverability—and tried to solve the difficulty of defining the underlying, verb for a compound in terms of deep cases (of Fillmoreian case grammar). Yet he does not seem to have changed his mind as to the transformational derivations of compounds.

As I am going to show in what follows, Japanese compounds are not subject to such a black-and-white approach; rather, they could be more realistically viewed as a continuum that ranges from those that are more easily susceptible to transformational derivation to those that are most difficult to derive transformationally. However, none of the compounds can be derived transformationally as long as we adhere to the strict sense of the word TRANSFORMATION.

Bloomfield (1933) made an analysis of compounds, akin to Panini's, which is basically taxonomic typology because he classifies compounds according to 'the relation of the members'[8] and 'the relation of the compound as a whole to its members',[9] but he does imply that compounds occupy a murky position between phrases and words.

As far as I know, the basic approach taken by Japanese linguists has been very similar to Bloomfield's approach.[10] Makino (1968), which includes, among other things, an extensive study of nominal compounds, has adopted the transformational approach. My own approach is about as monolithic as Lees (1960). What I am doing here, then, is a reevaluation of my own past work on compounds in light of the major theoretical difficulties just discussed.

1. COMPOUND TYPES

Let me turn to a more specific discussion of Japanese compounds. To a transformation-minded linguistic observer, most of the Japanese compounds appear to be derivable either from an underlying relative clause or from a nominalized clause. The Japanese relative clause consists of the head noun modified by a sentential clause without any *wh* pronoun intervening between the head noun and the sentential clause. The nominalized clause is superficially similar to the relativized clause; the head noun is a quasi-noun, *koto* or *no*, plus the sentential clause preceding *koto* or *no*, again without any intervening *wh* pronoun. Thus, schematically, the relative clause and the nominalized clause are S + head noun and S + *koto*/*no*. Since both clauses have a nominal function, I call the relative clause and the nominalized clause RELATIVIZED NOMINALIZATION (= Rel Nom) and NONRELATIVIZED NOMINALIZATION (= Nonrel Nom), respectively.

I will not cover the Japanese nominal compounds in toto; instead, I will give just a set of typical compounds along with the surface morphemic characterization of the compounding elements. For each instance the morphemic boundary is indicated by the hyphen and a literally gloss is given in parenthesis.

[8]See Bloomfield (1933:233–234).

[9]See Bloomfield (1933:235).

[10]See, for example, Hashimoto (1948:16–17) or Izui (1967:12–20).

A. Noun-intransitive verb
   a. *gake-kuzure* (cliff-break) 'landslide'
   b. *mizu-asobi* (water-play) 'playing in water'
   c. *huna-yoi* (boat-get sick) 'seasickness'
   d. *natu-yasumi* (summer-rest) 'summer vacation'
   e. *gaikoku-iki* (foreign country-go) 'going abroad'
   f. *ie-de* (house-leave) 'leaving home'
   g. *inu-zini* (dog-die) 'to die like a dog'

B. Noun-transitive verb
   a. *hana-mi* (flower-see)
      'flower viewing' (especially cherry blossoms)
   b. *hito-gorosi* (man-kill) 'manslaughter' or 'killer'
   c. *tume-kiri* (nail-clip) 'nail clipper'
   d. *mae-barai* (before-pay) 'advance payment'
   e. *mado-kake* (window-hang) 'curtain'

C. Intransitive verb-noun
   a. *uki-bukuro* (float-bag) 'lifebuoy'
   b. *ne-basyo* (sleep-place) 'sleeping place'
   c. *hike-doki* (retire-time) 'time for retirement'
   d. *nori-mono* (get on-thing) 'vehicle'
   e. *de-guti* (leave-mouth) 'exit'
   f. *ne-zake* (sleep-*sake*) 'nightcap'

D. Transitive verb-noun
   a. *nomi-mizu* (drink-water) 'drinking water'
   b. *mamori-gami* (guardian-god) 'guardian deity'
   c. *sentaku-sekken* (wash-soap) 'washing soap'
   d. *otosi-ana* (drop-hole) 'pitfall'
   e. *nozoki-ana* (peep-hole) 'peeping hole'
   f. *tabe-kuzu* (eat-remains) 'scraps of food'

E. Adjective-noun[11]
   a. *huru-hon* (old-book) 'secondhand book'
   b. *aka-hige* (red beard)
      'redbeard' or 'a red-bearded person'
   c. *ao-byootan* (green-calabash)
      'green calabash' or 'a pale-faced person'
   d. *oo-ame* (heavy-rain) 'heavy rain'

F. Adjective verb-noun
   a. *anzen-titai* (safe-area) 'safety zone'

[11]The noun-adjective, e.g., *asi-baya* (leg-fast) 'swift-footedness', is productive but it is normally used not as a nominal compound but as a predicative adjective, as in *Ano hito wa* ***asi-baya*** *da* 'He is swift-footed.'

G. Noun-noun
  a. *kasi-zara* (cake-plate) 'cake plate'
  b. *asa-gohan* (morning-meal) 'breakfast'
  c. *yanagi-gosi* (willow-waist)
     'waist like a willow', 'a slender figure'
  d. *hoken-gaisya* (insurance-company)
     'insurance company'
  e. *kawa-zakana* (river-fish) 'fish in the river'
  f. *ago-hige* (chin-hair) 'beard'
  g. *mati-naka* (town-inside) 'inside of a city'
  h. *tizyoo-zikken* (above-ground-experiment)
     'above-ground experiment'
  i. *dansi-gakusei* (men-student) 'male student'
  j. *kami-bukuro* (paper-bag) 'paper bag'
  k. *zyooki-kikansya* (steam-locomotive) 'steam engine'

H. Verb-verb
  a. *kui-nige* (eat-run) 'to eat and run'
  b. *ni-bosi* (cook-dry) 'dried small sardine'
  c. *nomi-kui* (drink-eat) 'drinking and eating'

I. Adjective-verb
  a. *haya-wakari* (quick-understand) 'superficial understanding'

Now, generally, if the second element (or the last element if there are more than two elements) of the compound is a noun, the surface compound APPEARS to be relatable to a structure underlying a Rel Nom, and if it is a verb, the compound APPEARS to be relatable to a structure underlying a Nonrel Nom; thus, compound types C (intransitive verb-noun), D (transitive verb-noun), E (adjective-noun, with the exception of Ed), F (adjective verb-noun), and G (noun-noun, with the exception of Gf and Gg) seem reducible to Rel Nom clauses in the following way:

C′
  a′ *uku hukuro* 'bag that floats'
  b′ *neru basyo* 'place where you sleep'
  c′ *hikeru toki* 'time when you retire'
  d′ *noru mono* 'thing you get on'
  e′ *deru kuti* 'mouth through which you go out'
  f′ *neru mae ni nomu* ***sake*** '*sake* you drink before going to bed'
     neru mae ni ***sake*** *o nomu koto* 'to drink *sake* before going to bed'

D′
  a′ *nomu mizu* 'water you drink'
  b′ *mamoru kami* 'god who protects you'

c′ *sentaku o suru sekken* ‘soap with which you wash’
d′ *hito o otosu ana* ‘hole you make people fall into’
e′ *nozoku ana* ‘hole you peep through’
f′ *tabete dekiru kuzu* ‘remains you leave behind after eating’

E′

a′ *hurui hon* ‘old book’
b′ *akai hige (o sita hito)* ‘(person with) a red beard’
c′ *aoi hyootan (ni nita hito)* ‘(person resembling) a green calabash’
d′ **ooki*$_i$ *ame* ‘big rain’

F′

a′ *anzen na titai* ‘safe area’

G′

a′ *kasi o ireru sara* ‘plate you put cake on’
b′ *asa taberu gohan* ‘meal you have in the morning’
c′ *yanagi ni nita kosi* ‘waist resembling a willow tree’
d′ *hoken o atukau kaisya* ‘company dealing with insurance’
e′ *kawa de toreru sakana* ‘fish you can catch in a river’
(f′) *ago no hige* ‘hair of chin’
(g′) *mati no naka* ‘inside of the city’
h′ *tizyoo de suru zikken* ‘experiment you make above-ground’
i′ *dansi dearu gakusei* ‘student who is male’
j′ *kami de dekita hukuro* ‘bag made of paper’
k′ *zyooki de ugoku kikansya* ‘locomotive powered by steam’

The rest of the compound types, namely A (noun-intransitive verb, with the exception of Ad, where one version should be derived from the Rel Nom), B (noun-transitive verb, with the exception of the so-called exocentric version of Bb and Bc and Be), H (verb-verb, with the exception of Hb), and I (adjective-verb), seem to be derivable, as shown in the following examples, from a structure underlying the Nonrel Nom:

A′

a′ *gake ga kuzureru koto* ‘for land to slide’
b′ *mizu de asobu koto* ‘to play in water’
c′ *hune de/ni you koto* ‘to get seasickness’
d′ *natu ni yasumu koto* ‘to rest in summer’
e′ *gaikoku ni iku koto* ‘to go abroad’
f′ *inu no yoo ni sinu koto* ‘to die like a dog’

B′

a′ *hana o miru koto* ‘to view flowers’
b′ *hito o korosu koto* ‘to kill a person’
(c′) *tume o kiru mono/doogu* ‘thing with which you clip your nails’
d′ *mae ni kane o harau koto* ‘to pay in advance’
(e′) *mado ni kakeru mono* ‘thing you hang before the window’

H′

a′ *kutte nigeru koto* 'to escape right after eating'[12]

(b′) *nite hosita (tiisai) sakana* '(small) fish you cook and dry'

c′ *nondari kuttari suru koto* 'drinking and eating and the like'

I′

a. *hayaku wakaru koto* 'to understand quickly'

Next, I will discuss why those compounds should not be derived from these putative underlying structures. Throughout the following discussion, I will assume that the putative underlying representation includes no modifier (adverbial or otherwise) of any of the two elements of a compound, because if there is a modifier of some compounding element, the derivation just has to be blocked. To give a few examples:

(1) **Tumetai* ***mizu-asobi*** *o kinsi sareta.* ←——
Tumetai mizu de asobu koto o kinsi sareta.
'They were forbidden to play in cold water'
Ano hito wa takusan* ***sake-nomi* *da.* ←——
Ano hito wa takusan sake o nomu hito da.
'He is a man who drinks *sake* a lot'
Kore wa totemo* ***huru-hon* *da.* ←——
Kore wa totemo hurui hon da.
'This is a very old book'

One will notice that the following argument against the transformational approach to the compound is not dependent on the modification problems.

2. ARGUMENTS AGAINST TRANSFORMATIONAL ANALYSIS

Prior to the discussion of each type of compound, I have to present very general pieces of evidence against the transformational derivation: First, if the putative underlying structure is a Nonrel Nom, we cannot derive from it either the surface structure (a) compound-*no*-noun or the structure (b) compound-*o-suru* (if the compound represents some action), because the assumed underlying structure is ill-formed, as shown in the following examples:

(2) ***Gake-kuzure*** *no hoodoo ga haitta.* ←——
'The news of the landslide came in'
**Gake-ga kuzureru koto no hoodoo ga haitta.*

[12] There are quite a few examples that are so idiomatic that they just defy analysis: For type Ha we have *kawari-bae* 'successful service in another's place', *maki-zoe* 'involvement', etc., and for type Hb we have *huki-nagasi* 'streamer', *kiri-dasi* 'knife', etc.

Mizu-asobi *o suru.* ⟵
'They play in water'
**Mizu de asobu koto o suru.*

Second, regardless of the putative underlying structure, it is generally impossible to derive from it (a) an exclamatory sentence, or (b) a definition expression, simply because the underlying structure is ill-formed. Thus:

(3) Exclamatory sentence.
Gake-kuzure *da!* ⟵ **Gake ga kuzureru koto da!*
'Oh! Landslide!'
Asa-gohan *da!* ⟵ **Asa taberu gohan da!*
'Breakfast!'

(4) Definition expression.
Gake-kuzure *wa* ***gake-kuzure*** *da.* ⟵
'Landslide is landslide'
Gake-kuzure *wa gake ga kuzureru koto da.*
'By landslide is meant the sliding of land.'
Asa-gohan *wa* ***asa-gohan*** *da.* ⟵
'Breakfast is breakfast.'
Asa-gohan *wa asa taberu gohan no koto da.*
'Breakfast is a meal you have in the morning.'

I will not repeat these four cases against the transformational derivation in my more specific discussion of compounds. It should be, therefore, remembered that, even when no evidence against the transformational approach is given, there are automatically at least two or four pieces of evidence, depending on whether the particular compound is putatively derivable from a Rel Nom or a Nonrel Nom structure.

In what follows, I will present, whenever possible, at least one piece of evidence for each example that shows the impossibility of deriving the surface compound transformationally from its putative underlying representation:[13]

(For Aa): ***Gake-kuzure*** *ga okita* 'Landslide occurred' has to be derived from an ill-formed deep structure: **Gake ga kuzureru koto ga okita.*

(For Ab): *Kodomo ga* ***mizu-asobi*** *de kaze o hiita* 'The child caught cold because he played in the water' has to be derived from the underlying structure **Kodomo ga mizu de asobu koto de kaze o hiita.*

[13]As for the transformational rules that were assumed to be necessary to derive surface compounds, see Makino (1968:Chapter V).

(For Ac): ***Huna-yoi*** *ni kakatta* 'I got seasick' and *Huna-yoi de komatta* 'I had a hard time because of seasickness' have to be derived from the underlying structures **Hune ni you koto ni kakatta* and **Hune ni you koto de komatta*, respectively.

(For Ad): ***Natu-yasumi*** *wa arigatai* 'I like summer vacation' and *Natu-yasumi o yuukoo ni tukau* 'They make the most of summer vacation' have to be derived from **Natu ni yasumu koto wa arigatai* and **Natu ni yasumu koto o yuukoo ni tukau*, respectively.

(For Ae): None.

(For Af): ***Ie-de*** *ga ooi* 'Deserting one's home is frequent' is not semantically identical to *Ie o deru koto ga ooi* 'They often leave home'.

(For Ag): None.

(For Ba): ***Hana-mi*** *ni iku* 'They go to see the cherry blossoms' and ***Hana-mi*** *kara kaeru* 'They return after viewing the cherry blossoms' have to be derived from **Hana o miru koto ni iku* and **Hana o miru koto kara kaeru*, respectively.

(For Bb): ***Hito-gorosi*** *ni kita* 'He came to kill people' has to be derived from **Hito o korosu koto ni kita*. For the exocentric version of Bb, no evidence is available.

(For Bc): There is a recoverability problem as to whether the underlying *mono* 'tangible thing' or *doogu* 'instrument' or other, similar noun is to be deleted.

(For Bd): None.

(For Be): Nonrecoverability problem with the noun *mono*.

(For Ca): The grammaticality of *Uku hukuro wa kanarazusimo* ***uki-bukuro*** *de wa nai* 'A floating bag is not always a lifebuoy' shows the semantic discrepancy between the compound and its putative deep structure.

(For Cb): None.

(For Cc): None.

(For Cd): ***Nori-mono*** *ni noritai* 'I want to get on a vehicle', ***Nori-mono*** *ni you* 'I get sick in a vehicle', and ***Nori-mono*** *de iku* 'I go by a vehicle' have to be derived from **Noru mono ni noritai*, **Noru mono ni noru*, and **Noru mono de iku*, respectively.

(For Ce): ***De-guti*** *wa koko da* 'The exit is right here' and ***De-guti*** *kara dete kita* 'He came out of the exit' have to be derived from **Deru kuti wa koko da* and **Deru kuti kara dete kita*, respectively.

(For Cf): None.

(For Da): None.

(For Db): None.
(For Dc): None.
(For Dd): None.
(For De): None.
(For Df): There is a recoverability problem as to whether the underlying *dekiru* or some other alternative verb is to be deleted.
(For Ea): *Kyonen deta bakari no hon o* ***huru-hon*** *de katta* 'I bought second-hand the book that came out only last year' has to be derived from **Kyonen deta bakari no hon o hurui hon de katta.*
(For Eb): **Aka-hige o site iru* may be generated from *Akai hige o site iru* 'He wears red beard'. Note that ... *o site iru* expresses not an action but an inalienable possession. There is a recoverability problem in the exocentric version of Eb as to whether the underlying *sita* or some alternative verb should be deleted.
(For Ec): ??*Ao-byootan to ao-byootan ni nite inai hito* 'a person like green calabash and a person unlike green calabash' will be generated from *Aoi hyootan ni nite iru hito to aoi byootan ni nite inai hito*. There is a recoverability problem in the exocentric version of Ec as to whether the underlying verb *nite iru* or some alternative verb has to be deleted.
(For Ed): ***Oo-ame*** has to be generated from **ooi ame* 'large amount of rain'. A peculiar thing about *oo-ame* and other, similar compounds such as *oo-akinai* 'great business', *oo-ase* 'profuse perspiration', *oo-gane* 'big money', *oo-yuki* 'heavy snow', etc., is that *oo* is represented not by 多 (*oo*) but by 大 (*ooki*) and that **ooki-ame* is nonexistent.
(For F): *Anzen na titai* 'safe area', which is the putative underlying form for *anzen-titai*, is not necessarily *anzen-titai*, because the latter is a special median for safety in the street.
(For Ga): One cannot always use *kasi-zara* 'cake-plate' simply because cake happens to be on a plate, unless one uses the particular plate for cake habitually for some time. However, if we assume that the verb *ireru* 'put on' of *kasi o ireru sara* 'plate on which they put cake) is deletable only when it is specified as [+generic], we do not need to worry about the usage of *kasi-zara* at the utterance level.[14]
(For Gb): None.
(For Gc): There is a problem of recoverability of the deleted verb *nita* 'resemble'.

[14]See Zimmer (1972)

(For Gd): *Hoken-gaisya* 'insurance company' is not always identical to *hoken o atukau kaisya* 'a company dealing with insurance', because any company may deal with insurance at one time or another.
(For Ge): Nonrecoverability of the deleted verb *toreru*.
(For Gf): None.
(For Gg): None.
(For Gh): None.
(For Gi): None.
(For Gj): Nonrecoverability of the deleted verb *dekiru*.
(For Gk): Nonrecoverability of the deleted verb *ugoku*.
(For Ha): None.
(For Hb): None.
(For Hc): None.
(For I): *Haya-wakari* is not semantically identical to *hayaku wakaru koto*, because the compound version always has the implication of 'superficial understanding'.

The compounds for which I could not find any convincing evidence against transformational analysis (except the generally applicable pieces of evidence) are summarized in the following table:

The Putative Underlying Structure	
Rel Nom	Nonrel Nom
Cb, Cc, Cf	Ae, Ag
Da, Db, Dc, Dd, De	Bd
Gb, Gf, Gg, Gh, Gi	Ha, Hc
Hb	

Noteworthy is the fact that, apart from the fossilized, idiomatic compounds, roughly speaking, the compound having a Rel Nom putative underlying structure seems more amenable to transformational treatment than the one having a Nonrel Nom putative underlying structure, although amenability to transformational treatment can never be perfect. Closer observation reveals that among the compounds of Rel Nom origin, the transitive verb-noun is the most transformational, and the adjective-noun and the adjective verb-noun are the least transformational in character. Intransitive verb-noun, noun-noun, and verb-verb come between in order of more to less transformational. The relative order of the transformational nature of compounds seems to correlate with the semantic specificity of the particular compound and the recoverability of the underlyingly posited verb. Among the Rel Nom compounds, the noun-noun type is barely transformational in nature because of the enormous problems of recoverability, as shown previously. The least transformational nature of adjective-noun and adjective verb-noun seems to be due to the semantic specificity of each compound, a point also shown earlier.

I have shown that no compound is impeccably transformational, in spite of the fact that some compounds are relatively more so than others. If my observation holds and unless we alter the notion of transformation itself, especially by relaxing the recoverability constraint, it seems empirically wrong to derive any type of compound (discussed here) transformationally, although doing so is relatively more appropriate for some compounds than for others, as I have indicated.

3. SEMANTICS OF COMPOUNDS

The next problem we face is how the semantic structure of compounds should be described. As it is, the straightforward transformational mapping of the underlying sentential structure onto the surface compound seems impossible, but nonetheless, the compound is a so-called *mot motivé* (an analyzable word), unlike the so-called *mot simple* (an unanalyzable word); it is subject to semantic analysis. For example, the transitive verb-noun compound shows different deep case relations in the semantic structure. Thus:[15]

Da. *nomi-mizu* 'drinking water' (verb, direct, object ⟨agent⟩)
Db. *mamori-gami* 'guardian deity' (verb, agent, ⟨experiencer⟩)
Dc. *sentaku-sekken* 'soap' (verb, instrumental, ⟨agent⟩)
Dd. *otosi-ana* 'pitfall' (verb, direction, ⟨experiencer⟩)
De. *nozoki-ana* 'peeping hole' (verb, source, ⟨direct object⟩)
Df. *tabe-kuzu* 'remains of food' (verb, resultative, ⟨agent⟩, ⟨direct object⟩)

The case specification in the angle brackets will not show up on the surface. Formalization aside, it is certainly possible to classify the compounds in terms of their deep case relations within the lexicon as a part of the semantic analysis, but the exact mapping of the semantic representation onto the surface phonetic compound seems out of the question. If we did so, we would end up generating all sorts of nonoccurring compounds with varying degrees of acceptability. On both intuitive and empirical bases, the transformational sentence formation and the putatively transformational compound formation seem basically different in that the former will generate

[15] I am not assuming any specific order of elements in the semantic representation.

all sorts of novel but very acceptable outputs, but the latter, if assumed to be a generative mechanism at all, will generate novel yet usually unacceptable compounds. In a word, the compound formation is much less productive than the sentence formation. Sentences are NOT LISTABLE but compounds are usually claimed, correctly, to be LISTABLE by lexicographers. If the compound were functionally identical to a sentence, there would be no raison d'être for the compound. It is not by accident at all that the compound has, universally, a unifying accent just like a simplex word. The compound is bound to represent some specific meaning that a sentence with the same deep case relations and lexical items cannot represent. Therefore, there are lots of cases of unacceptable compounds due to the violation of the semantic specificity. Thus, for example, the following are all ungrammatical, despite the fact that each satisfies the deep case relations.

**kaki-tegami*	'write-letter'	(cf. Da)
**kiki-banasi*	'listen-talk'	(cf. Da)
**osie-sensei*	'teach-teacher'	(cf. Db)
**naosi-isya*	'cure-doctor'	(cf. Db)
**kai-gane*	'buy-money'	(cf. Dc)
**kaki-enpitu*	'write-pencil'	(cf. Dc)

Notice that the semantic banality—or absence of semantic specificity, if you like—of each of these compounds is due to the second element, which can predict fairly well whatever is represented by the first. It seems to be the case that whenever the second element can semantically predict the first in an asymmetrical way, that combination is too banal to form a compound. If one reverses the order of the elements in the preceding examples, the banality does not come about, simply because the second element cannot semantically predict the first any more. Thus, the following are generally acceptable:

tegami-kaki	(letter-write) 'letter writing'
??*hanasi-kiki*	(talk-listen) 'talk listening'
??*sensei-osie*	(teacher-teach) 'teaching teacher'
?*isya-naosi*	(doctor-cure) 'doctor curing'
??*kane-gai*	(money-buy) 'money buying'
(cf. *doru-gai*	(dollar-buy) 'dollar buying')

To prove my point with regard to what might be called the 'semantic specificity condition', more examples follow:

**tobi-tori*	(fly-bird) (cf. Ca)
**tabe-syokudoo*	(eat-dining room) (cf. Cb)
**siro-mesi*	(white-rice) (cf. Ea)
**yoru-ne*	(night-sleep) (cf. Ad)

Very importantly, the semantic banality in a compound is fatal, but not so in a sentence. Thus, the sentences that are putatively assumed to be in a paraphrase relation to the ungrammatical compounds are all grammatical in spite of the same semantic banality. Thus:

Tegami o kaku 'They write letters' (cf. **kaki-tegami*)
Hanasi o kiku 'They listen to a talk' (cf. **kiki-banasi*)
Sensei ga osieru 'Teachers teach' (cf. **osie-sensei*)
Isya ga naosu 'Doctors cure them' (cf. **naosi-isya*)
Kane de kau 'They buy things with money' (cf. **kai-gane*)
Enpitu de kaku 'They write with a pencil' (cf. **kaki-enpitu*)

If my argument about the semantic specificity condition is correct, it is another strong point against the transformational derivation of a compound from an underlying sentential structure. The condition in question involves such a fairly general semantic notion that it is unnecessary to specify it for each compound.

There are, however, cases in which one can exclude the ungrammatical compound by making a finer semantic representation for a compound. For example, ungrammatical compounds such as **naga-tegami* and **aka-enpitu*, exocentric compounds meaning 'a person who writes a long letter' and 'a person who has a red pencil', respectively, can be excluded if we specify the noun element as « bodily part or something you wear ». The following is another example of a similar type: **eki-basiri* 'station-run', **gake-oti* 'cliff-fall', and **kuruma-ori* 'car-get off' cannot mean 'running from the station', 'falling from a cliff', and 'getting off a car', respectively, simply because the verb of the second element has to represent « horizontal motion with a direction ».

There are also cases in which possible compounds simply do not exist, because if they did they would clash with the compounds of Chinese origin in the entire network or 'field' of the lexicon. Compounds such as **gakkoo-tatemono* 'school building', **atama-hage* 'head baldness', and **tukue-ue* 'table top' do not seem to have gained ground, owing to the prior existence of the borrowed Chinese compounds *koo-sya* (校舎), *toku-too* (禿頭), and *taku-zyoo* (卓上), respectively.

Zimmer (1972) has introduced the notion of 'Appropriately classificatory' (AC) to account for the grammaticality of noun-noun compounds. He explains it this way:

> A noun A has an AC relationship to a noun B if this relationship is regarded by a speaker as significant for his classification—rather than description—of B. (This is actually an abbreviated and somewhat misleading way of stating things: strictly speaking the AC relationship exists between components of a situation referred to by linguistic forms rather than between the linguistic forms themselves) [pp. 4–5].

Zimmer's AC principle can certainly explain why *kasi-zara* 'cake plate' is unacceptable in a situation in which someone has just put cake on a plate that is not usually used for that purpose. However, in cases of other types of compounds than the noun-noun compound, the AC principle does not seem to be working. For example, the unacceptable compounds given in connection with my discussion of the semantic specificity condition are totally immune to the AC principle; the fact that **kaki-tegami*, **kiki-banasi*, and **osie-sensei* are unacceptable cannot be accounted for by the notion of AC. Interesting is the fact that *kasi-zara* is listed in the dictionary as a well-established lexical item in spite of the fact that one may USE it in an unacceptable way by violating the AC principle. But in a case like **kaki-tegami* (intended to mean 'a letter one writes', it is unacceptable whether or not one violates the AC principle, and it is totally out of the question that it will be entered in the dictionary. Actually, there are metaphorical compounds in which emphasis is placed more on DESCRIPTION than on CLASSIFICATION: For example, *usagi-basiri* 'hare run' (cf. Ag, *inu-zini* 'to die like a dog'), *ao-hebi* 'green snake' (cf. Ec, *ao-byootan* 'green calabash'), *neko-otoko* 'cat man' (cf. Gc, *yanagi-gosi* 'waist like a willow tree') are possible compounds to DESCRIBE the way someone looks or behaves at a given moment; in other words, the compounds may be used to describe a phenomenon of the moment.

4. CONCLUSION

To sum up my discussion, I have argued that none of the Japanese compounds can be derived transformationally from the underlying sentential structure as long as we adhere to the 'recoverability' condition, although some compounds appear more susceptible to transformational treatment than others. If we do not adhere to the recoverability condition, the generative transformational approach in compounds will not work unless we dump the notion of 'generativity' of grammatical rules. I do not think that we have any decisive argument at this point for discarding the generativity of grammatical rules when it comes to explaining sentence formation.[16] Anyway, it is possible to analyze the semantic structure of each compound without any generative mechanism.

In view of my conclusion, one seems justified in asking the question: How can one decompose a SIMPLEX word into an underlying semantic representation in such a way that one can argue for prelexical transformation (à la J. McCawley, 1968b) when one can hardly use transformation even when

[16] See, however, J. McCawley (1973a: esp. p. 235).

the decomposition appears transparent and promising, as in the case of compounds?

At this point, compound analysis seems to exist somewhere between the sentence level and the lexical level but much closer to the latter, and its nature should be very close to whatever the lexical analysis is or will be. To be sure, this is a reactionary conclusion and sounds pretransformational, but the generative transformational grammar seems, after all, extremely powerless before lexical phenomena.

HONORIFICS

S. I. HARADA

INTRODUCTION

Every language has some means for making utterances sound polite and not offensive to the addressee. In English, for instance, we achieve this effect by adding the word *please* to a request [cf. (1b)], using the *will you* ...? interrogative instead of the imperative construction [cf. (1c)] or substituting a subjunctive form for an indicative form [cf. (1d)], and so on:

(1) a. *Show me the picture.*
b. *Show me the picture, please.*
c. *Will you show me the picture (please)?*
d. *Would you show me the picture (please)?*

Another well-known linguistic tool for polite speech concerns second-person categories, i.e., second-person pronouns and vocatives. In most Indo-European languages we find a special second-person singular pronoun used to refer to an addressee toward whom the speaker feels a need for showing some deference. The etymology of that special pronoun varies from language to language, but the essence is the same in each. A new form is transplanted from somewhere else to show the speaker's deference, with the original second-person singular pronoun now confined to reference to a person to whom the speaker does not need to show deference.[1] In the case of vocatives

[1]The special pronoun derives from the second-person plural pronoun in French (*vous*), from the third-person plural pronoun in German (*Sie*), and from a third-person noun in Spanish (*usted*). In languages like English, what was once such a translocated honorific pronoun (*you*, from the second person plural) has expelled the original second-person singular pronoun (*thou*) altogether and, thus, has become nonhonorific. See Brown and Gilman (1960) for an important discussion of the history of second-person pronouns in the Indo-European languages.

(or address forms), we observe that in most languages difference in the choice of address forms correlates to the degree of the speaker's deference toward the addressee. For instance, it is generally the case that a name preceded by a title (e.g., 'Mr. Smith', 'Dr. Smith', 'Prof. Smith') is a more polite address form than a mere name (e.g., 'Smith', 'John').[2] In a broad sense, such linguistic tools as *please*, the *will you* ...? construction, the subjunctive mood, the special second-person singular pronoun, and titled address forms can all be called 'honorific expressions' (or simply 'honorifics'). In this sense, honorifics prevail in every human language.

Honorifics in this broad sense do not appear to form a grammatical system, however. Most of the honorifics, in this sense, are not intended primarily for use in polite speech (e.g., the subjunctive mood), and those that are peculiar to polite speech (e.g., *please*) are isolated and quite unproductive. On the other hand, such languages as Japanese, Korean, Javanese, and Tibetan have developed a grammatical system of honorifics.[3] In these languages, honorific forms occur in a wider range of categories. Thus, in Japanese not only pronouns but also verbs, adjectives, nouns, and so on are put in the honorific form. What seems more important is the fact that the occurrence of an honorific form is, by and large, conditioned by grammatical factors. Thus, in Japanese, certain honorific forms occur only when the subject denotes a person to whom the speaker wants to show his deference, certain others only when the object denotes such a person, and so on. The question as to what properties are associated with a person who is referred to through honorifics is not a problem to which a grammatical description is addressed, though it is an interesting subject matter for sociolinguistic researches.[4] My purpose in the present chapter is to investigate the grammatical system of honorifics, which I shall refer to as 'honorification'. Sociolinguistic questions are not my immediate concern here.

Honorification is, as mentioned earlier, one of the salient features of the Japanese language that are absent in most other languages, in particular, the Indo-European languages. For this reason, nonnative speakers often find it hard to master. In fact, even native speakers need a considerable

[2]See Brown and Ford (1961) for some interesting observations.

[3]See Hayashi and Minami (1974b) for detailed descriptions of the honorific systems in languages other than Japanese.

Incidentally, it is an interesting question whether the honorific systems have developed independently in those languages, or their existence is due to some features common to them, e.g., genealogical relationships, similarity of the societies in which they have been spoken, etc. Current views lean toward the former conclusion. It is important to observe in this connection that, even in a language with an honorific system, some dialects lack it entirely. There remains a mystery, however, in that no Indo-European language has anything comparable to an honorific system, though the Indo-European family exhibits almost every typological possibility in other respects (cf. Greenberg, 1963).

[4]See Kokuritsu Kokugo Kenkyujo (1957, 1971) and Hayashi and Minami (1974a) for some attempts at sociolinguistic investigation of this matter.

amount of time for full acquisition of this system. The difficulty, however, does not lie in the grammatical system itself but, rather, in the formation of an appropriate conception of the interhuman relations that underlie the employment of honorifics. Once such a conception is shaped in the mind of the learner, the grammatical derivations are simple and straightforward.

Let us take the process of forming what we shall call 'subject honorifics' as an illustration. The key notion is that of 'social superiority'. Given an appropriate definition of this notion, we can see which NP refers to a person socially superior to the speaker (an SSS) and which NP does not. All that a grammatical description has to say is that a predicate is put in the subject honorific form if its subject denotes an SSS.

The notion of social superiority, on the other hand, does not seem definable in a simple, culture-independent way. For example, those who are accustomed to the American campus atmosphere would be surprised to know that in Japanese universities teachers are to be treated as socially superior to their former students even after the latter have become members of the faculty, as far as honorifics are concerned. Generally, in most Japanese institutions the members are hierarchically classified, and members of a lower rank are expected to use honorifics in talking to people of higher rank. The hierarchical organization also penetrates into noninstitutional societies. Thus, in a shopping situation, for instance, customers are treated as socially superior to the salesmen. Honorifics are used even within a family, especially in the upper or upper middle class, in which the wife may use honorifics in talking to the husband but not vice versa. I mentioned all this just in order to show that the notion of social superiority requires an extensive sociolinguistic research of Japanese. Since the purpose of my contribution to this volume is to present and discuss the grammatical system of honorifics, I will not go further into such questions here. For the sake of this chapter's intelligibility, however, I will sketch in Section 3 the most rudimentary facts about such matters that are presupposed in the example sentences quoted herein.

1. CLASSIFICATION OF THE HONORIFICS

Traditional grammars of Japanese all agree that Japanese honorifics are classifiable into three categories, exemplified in (2a–c):

(2) a. *Sasaki sensei*[5] *wa* *watasi ni*
topic marker I indirect object marker
koo ***o-hanasi ni nat-****ta*.
this way speak past
'Sasaki *sensei* told me this way.'

[5]For the meaning of this word, see Section 3 for some explanations. It is untranslatable into English, and I shall use it untranslated in the English translations of example sentences.

b. *Watasi wa Sasaki sensei ni koo* ***o-hanasi si****-ta.*
'I told Sasaki *sensei* this way.'
c. *Watasi wa sono hito ni koo hanasi-****masi****-ta.*
that man
'I told him this way.'

A number of names have been proposed for these categories, but the most widely accepted terminology refers to these as *sonkei-go* (respect words), *kenzyoo-go* (condescending words), and *teinei-go* (polite words), respectively.

In this chapter, however, I shall devise a new terminology in order to avoid the lengthy but fruitless discussion of interpretation that is often caused by the adoption of such semantically oriented terms as *sonkeigo.* I shall refer to the three categories, respectively, as 'subject honorifics', 'object honorifics', and 'performative honorifics', for reasons that will become clear in the course of presentation. Actually, the first two constitute a single category, which we call 'propositional honorifics', in opposition to the last. The classification of honorifics can be represented as in (3):

(3)

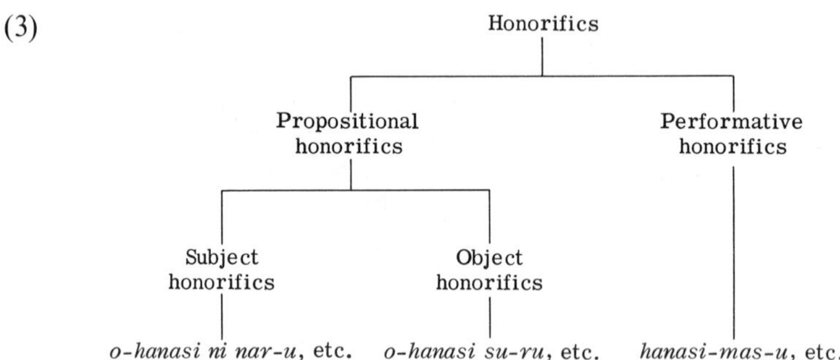

This hierarchical binary classification is motivated primarily by the location of the NP referring to an SSS. Performative honorifics differ from propositional honorifics in that they do not require the presence of an SSS in the propositional content of the sentence. Thus, corresponding to the sentence:

(4) *Ame ga hut-ta.*
rain subject marker fall
'It rained.'

we have a performative honorific sentence, (5a), but not propositional honorific ones like (5b) or (5c):

(5) a. *Ame ga huri-masi-ta.*
'It rained.' (polite speech)
b. **Ame ga o-huri ni nat-ta.*

c. **Ame ga o-huri si-ta.*

The ungrammaticality of the latter two is due precisely to the inadmissibility of human NPs (and hence of SSS's) in their propositional contents. Additional evidence is obtained from the observation that performative honorifics are not allowed to occur in nondirect discourse clausal complements, while propositional honorifics are fully permitted:

(6) a. *Boku wa [kyoo Yamada sensei ga* ***irassyar-u****] koto*
I today come complementizer
o sukkari wasure-te i-ta.
object marker entirely forget gerund marker be
'I completely forgot that Yamada *sensei* is coming today.'

b. **Boku wa [kyoo Yamada sensei ga* ***ki -mas-u/o-ide ni nari-***
come come
mas-u*] koto o sukkari wasure-te i-ta.*

(7) a. *Taroo ga [sensei no o-nimotu o* ***o-moti su-ru****] koto ni nat*
baggage bring it is decided
-te i-ru.
'We have arranged for Taro to carry the *sensei*'s baggage.'

b. **Taroo ga [sensei no o-nimotu o* ***moti-mas-u/o-moti si-mas-u****]*
koto ni nat-te i-ru.

where [] indicates the boundaries of a complement sentence, and the relevant honorifics are in bold type.

The distinction between the subject honorifics and the object honorifics is based on the difference in the grammatical relation of the NP referring to the SSS that conditions the occurrence of an honorific. As suggested by the terminology, subject honorifics are used when the subject refers to the SSS, and object honorifics are used when the indirect or direct object refers to the SSS. It is important to note, however, that there is a kind of asymmetry between subject and object honorifics: While the former can be found on almost any predicates (i.e., not only on verbs but also on adjectives), the latter is quite limited in distribution (for example, there is no object honorific form for adjectives). I shall discuss this problem in Section 6.

2. MORPHOLOGY

Regular Forms

Example (8) summarizes the most typical patterns of honorific forms. Some explanations are in order:

(8)

	Subject Honorifics	Object Honorifics	Performative Honorifics
Verbs	HP + INF *ni nar-*	HP + INF *su-*	INF + *mas-*
Adjectives	HP + ADJ	—	ADJ *des-*
Nouns	HP + N	HP + N	HP + N

where HP = the 'honorific prefix', i.e., *o-*/*go-*, and
INF = the infinitive form, or *ren'yoo-kei*, of a verb.

The most important characteristic of honorific forms is the recurrent use of the honorific prefix. It is used primarily in the formation of propositional honorifics, but the performative honorific form of a noun is also formed with this prefix.[6] The honorific prefix has two major variants, *o-* and *go-*. The choice depends on the lexical class of the following element. If the element is a Sino-Japanese morpheme (*kango*), the prefix takes the form *go-*; otherwise, it takes the form *o-*.[7]

(9) a. Sino-Japanese morphemes.
go-byooki 'disease'

[6]Typical examples of performative honorific nouns are the following:

o-biiru 'beer'
o-hana 'flower'
o-ikura 'how much'
o-ningyoo 'doll'
o-syooyu 'soy-sauce'
o-tenki 'weather'
o-tya 'tea'

Such honorifics are often used in contexts in which no SSS appears in the propositional content or in the environments irrelevant to the occurrence of the honorifics. Cf.:

(i) *Kyoo wa i-i o-tenki des-u ne.*
SENTENCE PARTICLE
'It's a fine weather, isn't it?'

(ii) *O-biiru ikaga?*
how
'Would you care for some beer?'

[7]There are, of course, exceptions. Except in such few cases as *go-yukkuri* 'please relax yourself', they are Sino-Japanese morphemes taking the *o-* form of the honorific prefix:

o-bentoo 'lunch'
o-denwa 'phone (call)'
o-genki (da) 'be fine'
o-ryoori 'cooking'
o-syasin 'picture, photo'
o-tenki 'weather'

go-kazoku	'family'
go-tyosyo	'work, publication'
go-kekkon	'marriage'
go-ryokoo	'travel'
go-seikoo	'success'

b. Native morphemes.

o-kao	'face'
o-tegami	'letter'
o-tosi	'age'
o-hanasi	'talk'
o-kangae	'thought'
o-sawagase	'trouble'
o-yorokobi	'pleasure'

When the honorific prefix is added to a verb, there is a further complexity. In the first place, the prefix is affixed not to a finite form but, rather, to the infinitive. The resulting combination will be referred to as the 'honorific infinitive'. In addition, such auxiliary verbs as *nar-* are employed to carry the inflectional endings, which the main verb, being an infinitive, cannot bear. In (8), I listed only one auxiliary for each category, but in fact there are several others. Example (10) is a list of such secondary auxiliaries:

(10) a. Subject honorifics.

HP + INF *da*[8]	(very common)
HP + INF *nasar-*	(obsolete in Standard Japanese; dialectal)
HP + INF *asobas-*	(hyperpolite)

[8]There is a fair possibility that the *da* honorific form is not a mere stylistic variant of the regular form. It seems that its occurrence is limited to places where, in the plain speech, an auxiliary of perfect or progressive (most often denoted by (*-te*) *i-ru*) would be expected. Consider the following examples:

(i) a. *Go-yoo wa moo o-sumi des-u ka?*
business already QUESTION MARKER
'Are you OK with the business?' (lit. 'Is your business already finished?')

b. *Kono hon, ima o-yomi des-yoo ka?*
this book now read SUBJUNCTIVE MARKER
'Are you reading this book right now?'

Sentence (ia) would be paraphrased in the plain speech by either (iia) or (iib), and (ib) by (iii):

(ii) a. *Yoo wa moo sun-da ka?*
b. *Yoo wa moo sun-de i-ru ka?*

(iii) *Kono hon (o) ima yon-de i-ru ka?*

Though the syntax of the *da* honorific form offers an interesting topic for the study of Japanese honorifics, I will not investigate it here for want of space.

b. Object honorifics.

HP + INF *itas-*	(see the later discussion of suppletion)
HP + INF *moosiage-*	(very polite)

Suppletive Forms

Besides the regularly formed honorifics, we have also suppletive forms, some of which are presented in (11). Suppletion may replace a whole honorific expression, as is the case with *ossyar-* in place of the expected **o-i(w)i ni nar-*, or only the infinitive part of it, as is the case with *go-ran ni nar-* in place of **o-mi ni nar-*.[9]

(11)

	SH	OH	PH
ar-u 'be'	*irassyar-u* *o-ide* (+RF)	—	*gozai-* (+RF)
i-ru 'be'	*irassyar-u* *o-ide*	—	*ori-* (+RF)
ik-u 'go'	*irassyar-u* *o-ide* *o-kosi* (+RF?)	*(ukagaw-u)*	*mairi-* (+RF)
ku-ru 'come'	*irassyar-u* *o-ide* *o-kosi* *mie-ru* *o-mie*	—	*mairi-* (+RF)
su-ru 'do'	*nasar-u* *asobas-u*	—	*itasi-* (+RF)
iw-u 'say'	*ossyar-u*	—	*moosi-* (+RF)
atae-ru 'give'			
(i) *kure-ru*	*kudasar-u*	—	(RF)
(ii) *age-ru*	(RF)	*sasiage-ru*	(RF)
moraw-u 'receive'	(RF)	*itadak-u* *tyoodai su-ru*	(RF)
mi-ru 'see, look'	*go-ran*	*haiken su-ru*	(RF)
kik-u 'hear, listen'	(RF)	*haityoo su-ru* *ukagaw-u*	(RF)
omow-u 'think'	(RF)	—	*zonzi-ru* *zonzu-ru*
sir-u	*go-zonzi*	*zonziage-ru*	*zonzi-ru*

[9]Note the alternation of *o-* and *go-*. While *mi-* is a native morpheme, its suppletive form *ran* is a Sino-Japanese morpheme.

	SH	OH	PH
'know'	(+RF?)		*zonzu-ru* (+RF)
sin-u 'die'	*o-kakure* *o-nakunari*	—	*nakunar-u* (+RF)
aw-u 'meet, see'	(RF)	*o-me ni kakar-u* (idiom)	(RF)
kaw-u 'buy'	*o-motome* (+RF)	—	*motome-ru* (+RF)
kari-ru 'borrow'	(RF)	*haisyaku su-ru*	(RF)
ki-ru 'wear'	*mes-u* *o-mesi*	—	(RF)
nom-u/tabe-ru 'drink' 'eat'	*(mesi)agar-u* (+RF)	*itadak-u*	*itadak-u* (+RF)

NOTES:
1. Suppletive forms replacing infinitives are listed in the form of honorific infinitive (e.g., *o-ide*).
2. A dash indicates that there is no form expressing the idea.
3. (RF) indicates that the idea is expressible only with regular forms; (+RF) means that regular forms exist alongside of suppletive forms.

Suppletive forms of performative honorifics may require a special comment. As already noted, performative honorifics are not conditioned by the presence of an SSS in the propositional content of a sentence. Rather, their use is dependent on a relation between the speaker and the addressee. Very roughly, we can say that one uses performative honorifics in order to talk 'politely' to the addressee, to make one's speech sound 'milder'. The suppletive performative honorific forms, expecially those shown in (11) terminated with a hyphen, are used to express the notion in a more 'polite' way than the regular forms. Thus, to the question:

(12) Sebun Sutaa *ari-mas-u ka?*
(brand of cigarettes) be
'Have you got Seven Stars?'

one may answer with either (13a) or (13b):

(13) a. *Hai, ari-mas-u.*
Yes
'Yes, we have.'
b. *Hai, gozai-mas-u.*

Example (13b) sounds more formal, more polite, more respectful to the addressee. Note that most of the suppletive performative honorific forms are not used except in front of *-mas-*: one cannot say, e.g.:

(14) **Kono mise ni wa* Sebun Sutaa *ga gozat-ta tamesi ga*
store previous case
na-i.
not be

but, rather:

(15) *Kono mise ni wa* Sebun Sutaa *ga at-ta tamesi ga na-i.*
'This store has never got Seven Stars, as far as I know.'

In Japanese there are a number of verbs that are formed with a combination of a Sino-Japanese morpheme (SJM) and the verb *su-*, e.g., *kenkyuu su-* 'study', *seikoo su-* 'succeed', *kekkon su-* 'marry', *renraku su-* 'inform, contact'. Their honorific formation involves a further complexity. Instead of the expected forms:

(16) a. Subject honorifics:
*HP + [SJM *si*] *ni nar-*, e.g., **go-kekkon si ni nar-*
b. Object honorifics:
*HP + [SJM *si*] *su-*, e.g., **go-renraku si su-*

we have the forms:

(17) a. Subject honorifics:
either HP + SJM *ni nar-*, e.g., *go-kekkon ni nar-*
or (HP) + SJM *nasar-*, e.g., *(go)-kekkon nasar-*
b. Object honorifics:
HP + SJM *su-*, e.g., *go-renraku su-*

Neutralization of Semantic Distinctions

It is interesting to note that suppletive honorifics sometimes neutralize a semantic distinction that holds between nonhonorific forms. For instance, the form *irassyar-* covers the whole range of meanings expressed by the nonhonorific words *ar-*, *i-*, *ku-*, and *ik-*. Here, the distinctions between state and motion, between coming and going, are neutralized. The situation is somewhat similar to that of the so-called 'mother-in-law' language of Dyirbal, discussed by Dixon (1971). Whether this is a mere coincidence or a systematic aspect of the honorific system is an interesting question, but I do not pursue the problem here.

3. TITLES AND PERSONAL (PRO)NOUNS

One important characteristic of the honorific style is in its special ways of naming people. A full treatment of the problem must await a far-reaching sociolinguistic investigation of contemporary Japanese. Here, I shall only describe the most rudimentary facts.

The general Japanese titles, corresponding to English 'Mr.', 'Mrs.', and 'Miss', are as follows:

(18) a. *-sama* (very polite)
-san (average)
cf. -tyan (diminutive)
b. *-kun* (used for men only)
c. *sensei* (to be explained)

The items in (18) are used for both sexes, for both married and unmarried people. They are suffixable either to a given name (e.g., *Sin-Iti-san*), a surname (e.g., *Harada-san*), or their combination (e.g., *Harada Sin-Iti-san*). The formality and politeness increase in this order. The suffix *-tyan* is phonologically related to *-san* (which is itself a weakened form of *-sama*), but is not an honorific title; hence, it is almost never suffixed to a surname.[10]

The title *sensei* has a peculiar status. Etymologically, it means a person who was 'born earlier', but contemporary usage confines it to a person who is respectable for his capabilities, mainly in intellectual work. As a common noun it means primarily 'teacher' (as in *Sensei ni nari-ta-i* 'I want to be a teacher'), but as a title it covers not only teachers or professors but also authors, movie directors, artists, medical doctors, Diet representatives, and so on. Its translation into English will, thus, vary from context to context, and I will not give a gloss for it.

Other titles are formed from words indicating institutionally defined positions. Some are listed in (19):

(19) a. In a company.
syatyoo 'president'
huku-syatyoo 'vice president'
senmu 'executive director'
butyoo 'section chief'
katyoo 'department chief'
kakarityoo 'chief clerk'
b. Academic ranks.
gakutyoo 'president'
gakubutyoo 'dean'
...
kyoozyu 'professor'

[10] I have recently encountered such an exceptional case. In the hospital attached to the Faculty of Medicine, University of Tokyo, where my daughter was born, names coined in that way are given to newborn babies, most of whom are, of course, nameless. Thus, my daughter was called 'Harada-chan' during the first week of her life.

zyokyoozyu	'associate professor'
koosi	'(full-time) lecturer'
zyosyu	'(research) assistant'
...	
hakase, hakusi	'doctor'

c. Military ranks.

taisyoo }	'general' }
tyuuzyoo } *syoogun*	'lieutenant general' } 'general'
syoosyoo }	'major general' }
taisa	'colonel'
tyuusa	'lieutenant colonel'
syoosa	'major'
taii	'captain'
tyuui	'first lieutenant'
syooi	'second lieutenant'
gunsoo	'sergeant'
...	

Note that this is not intended to be an exhaustive list of titles; these titles are presented here just for illustrative purposes. They are used either independently or as a suffix to a name, and either in address or in reference.

Instead of using names (with or without title), one can also address or refer to people by personal pronouns. In Indo-European languages, first and second persons are referred to exclusively by means of personal pronouns, though occasional deviations are, of course, possible. In Japanese, however, there are no real personal pronouns that correspond to the Indo-European personal pronouns. What is expressed in English by a personal pronoun is always expressible with a zero if the context permits. Thus, we can say, for instance:

(20) a. *Asita ki-mas-u ka? Ee, ki-mas-u.*
tomorrow Yes
'Are you coming tomorrow?' 'Yes, I will.'

b. *Ugok-u na! Ugok-u to ut -u zo!*
move don't! if-then shoot sentence particle
'Don't stir! I'll shoot you if you move.'

Note that in the second sentence of (20), the subject of the conditional clause (second person), the subject of the main clause (first person), and the object of the main clause (second person) all surface as zero, since the context provides sufficient information as to the reference of those unrealized NPs.

But this does not mean that Japanese has no word for naming the speaker, addressee, and so on. On the contrary, there are a host of such words, each with a different connotation. Syntactically they behave like nouns, more precisely, like proper nouns. Some of them are illustrated in (21):[11]

(21) a. First person.

watakusi	(very formal for men; less so for women)
watasi	(formal for men, but average for women; incidentally, this is the standard word from a prescriptive point of view)
atakusi	(rare for men; sounds snobbish for women)
atasi	(chiefly for women; colloquial)
ware	(archaic)
wasi	(dialectal, chiefly for men; regarded as characteristic of an old generation)
boku	(exclusively for men; prescriptively, not recommended when talking to an SSS)
ore	(exclusively for men; colloquial)
ora	(dialectal)

b. Second person.

anata	(standard and polite, but not used to refer to an SSS)
anta	(informal)
sotira	(polite and very formal)
sotti	(colloquial)
kimi	(chiefly used by men to refer to men of equal or lower social status)
omae	(informal and colloquial, somewhat pejorative)
kisama, temee	(derogatory and very impolite)

[11]In lists (21a), (21b), and (22), I enumerate singular forms only. Plural forms are obtained by suffixing *-tati*, *-gata*, *-ra*, *-domo*. They have different degrees of politeness and formality, and none of them goes with everything in the lists. The points to note are as follows:

1. *-gata* is an honorific plural marker suffixable only to an item ending in *-ta*.
2. *-domo* is a pejorative plural marker and is, hence, suffixable to most first-person items and some second- or third-person items.
3. *-tati* and *-ra* are the commonest suffixes, but their suffixability is governed by principles that are as yet unclear.

It is important to see, incidentally, that these suffixes are, strictly speaking, not markers of plurality but are, rather, equivalent to the English phrase '... *and the ilk*'. Cf.:

(i) *Kesa* *Hanako-tati ni at-ta.*
this morning see
'I saw Hanako and her friends (cousins, brothers, sisters, etc.) this morning.'

The third person pseudo-pronouns present complexities, for they are basically formed by a combination of a deictic category (the series *ko-*, *so-*, and *a-*) and a noun. For instance, we have *kono kata*, *sono kata*, and *ano kata*, each translatable as 'he' and yet having a different sense. Representing the deictic elements *ko-*, *so-*, and *a-* with the symbol *D*, we may show the third-person pseudo-pronouns in the following way:[12]

(22) Third person.

D-tira sama	(very polite and formal)
D-no kata	(polite)
D-no hito	(standard)
D-tira san	(somewhat colloquial)
D-tira	(colloquial)
kare	(slightly formal; for men only)
kanozyo	(formal; for women only)
yatu	('the bum', 'the guy'; very informal)
D-itu	(informal; sometimes derogatory)

4. JUSTIFICATION OF THE TRANSFORMATIONAL ANALYSIS OF HONORIFICATION

The theoretical framework of this study is that of transformational grammar. I assume, in addition, that the remotest syntactic structure of a sentence represents the aspect of meaning that serves to identify a particular state of affairs to which the sentence refers, while the aspects of meaning that relate to the classification of the pieces of information conveyed by the sentence (e.g., topic, comment, focus, presupposition) are directly associated with the structural information contained in surface structure.[13]

[12] A similar diversity is observed in kinship terms. For example, the English word *wife* is translatable into Japanese by either of the following terms, each differing in formality and speech level:

oku-sama	(referring to second or third person's wife; very polite and formal)
oku-san	(almost identical to the preceding, but less formal)
tuma	(general but not honorific; formal)
kanai	(referring to first person's wife; formal)
nyoobo (o)	(not polite, and informal)
waihu	(borrowed from English 'wife'; jargon of intellectual people)
(o)-kami-san	(colloquial and informal)
gu-sai	(condescending; formal)

[13] My theoretical standpoint is, thus, almost similar to the so-called 'interpretive theory', as advocated in Chomsky's recent works (1970, 1971). But I am inclined to limit the contribution of surface structure to semantic interpretation far more narrowly than he does.

Furthermore, I propose that propositional honorifics are not present in underlying structure but are introduced by a set of transformations, on the basis of the presence of an NP referring to an SSS in a term of grammatical relation.

Preliminary Justification

The necessity of referring to abstract levels of syntactic structure can be easily demonstrated. Compare, for instance, the following two NPs (where *PRO* stands for an unspecified NP):

(23)
a. *kuro-i boosi*
black hat
'a hat which is black'
b. *isogasi-i toki*
busy time
'the moment PRO is busy'

Superficially, they have exactly the same structure: ADJ-N. Their honorific versions differ entirely, however:

(24)
a. **o-kuro-i boosi*
b. *o-isogasi-i toki*

(25)
a. *kuro-i o-boosi*
b. **isogasi-i o-toki*

The asymmetry between the (a) and (b) forms is easily explained in our framework. Notice that (23a) and (23b), despite their identity in surface structure, have different syntactic derivations. On the one hand, the adjectives are both derived from underlying relative clauses, but with different subjects, as in:[14]

(26)
a. *boosi ga kuro-i.*
'(The) hat is black.'
b. PRO *ga (sono) toki isogasi-i.*
'PRO is busy at that moment.'

That is, in (23a), the underlying subject of the adjective is *boosi*, but in (23b), it is a pronoun (surfacing as a zero) referring to a human being. On the other hand, only (23a) can be regarded as having a deleted possessive NP, as in:

(27)
a. PRO *no ... boosi.*
b. *PRO *no ... toki.*

[14] The unspecified NP, PRO, is deleted by a late transformation.

These differences in syntactic derivation between (23a) and (23b) function crucially in explaining the contrast observed in (24) and (25), for there are independent reasons for believing that the grammar of Japanese has the following two rules for honorific formation, among others:[15]

(28) a. *A predicate receives the honorific prefix if its subject is an SSS.*

b. *A noun receives the honorific prefix if it is modified by a possessive NP that is an SSS.*

The underlying structures of (23a) and (23b) are representable as follows, respectively:[16]

(29) a. PRO *no* [*boosi*$_i$ *ga kuro-i*]$_S$ *boosi*$_i$
SSS

b. [PRO *ga (sono) toki*$_i$ *isogasi-i*]$_S$ *toki*$_i$
SSS

It is obvious, then, that (29a) satisfies the structural condition of Rule (28b) but not of (28a), and that the opposite is the case for (29b): Hence the asymmetry in (24) and (25).

However, in order for this account to be valid, it must be the case that the rules in (28) apply BEFORE the PRO elements in (29) are deleted. If we did not accept the transformational framework, that is, the possibility of recognizing abstract levels of syntactic structure, an explanation like the one just given would not be available, and the contrast between (23a) and (23b) with respect to honorific formation would be left totally unexplained.

Further Justification

Although the preceding argument shows the adequacy of the transformational framework in accounting for the behavior of honorifics, it does not show the adequacy of our specific proposal, namely, the transformational introduction of (propositional) honorifics. We can still conceive, for instance, of an alternative, 'phrase structure' analysis, in which underlying structures are assumed to contain honorific elements such as the honorific prefix, and the information as to which NP is an SSS is obtained not at the underlying level of syntactic structure but, rather, at a shallower level by means of 'interpretive rules'. According to this alternative, the underlying structures of (23) would be as follows:

(30) a. PRO *no* [*boosi*$_i$ *ga kuro-i*]$_S$ *o-boosi*$_i$

[15] For discussion, see Sections 5 and 7, in which further details are described.

[16] Identical subscripts indicate identity of reference. The notation SSS under PRO is a compromise between two radical positions imaginable: to regard SSS as a kind of syntactic feature or to regard it as a mere mnemonic device for some otherwise available linguistic information.

b. [PRO *ga (sono) toki*$_i$ *o-isogasi-i*]$_S$ *toki*$_i$

Instead of the transformations (28a) and (28b), we would have interpretive rules like:

(31) a. *If a predicate takes a subject honorific form, its subject will be marked as an SSS.*
b. *If a noun takes an honorific form, its possessive NP will be marked as an SSS.*

If we had structures like:

(32) a. PRO *no* [*boosi*$_i$ *ga o-kuro-i*]$_S$ *boosi*$_i$
b. [PRO *ga (sono) toki*$_i$ *isogasi-i*]$_S$ *o-toki*$_i$

they would be filtered out as semantically deviant, because they either do not undergo the interpretive rules [as in (b)] or create semantically deviant combinations (as in (a), in which *boosi* would be marked as an SSS).

Actually, the choice between my analysis and the alternative just mentioned does not crucially affect our discussion, for the interpretive rules are, in most cases, just inverse rules of our transformations (to be stated later). Whatever properties I may adduce to my transformations would also have to be associated with the interpretive rules that would be postulated by the alternative analysis. The reverse is not always true, however. That is, not every transformation I will propose has an interpretive rule equivalent in descriptive power. Consider the following sentence:

(33) *Yamada sensei wa Taroo ni kono hon o yom-ase ni nat-ta.*
book read cause
'Yamada *sensei* made Taro read this book.'

which is a subject honorific version of:

(34) *Yamada sensei wa Taroo ni kono hon o yom-ase-ta.*

In the standard analysis of Japanese, this sentence is derived from an underlying structure like:[17]

[17] I would like to dissociate myself from everything that is controversial in the analysis of such sentences. Diagram (35) makes the following assumptions:

1. There is no VP node in Japanese (cf. Hinds, 1973b).
2. Verbs, adjectives, and nominal adjectives form a higher class, which I call 'predicates' (cf. Nakau, 1973).
3. Case particles such as *ga*, *o*, *ni* are introduced transformationally (cf. Kuroda, 1965b).

As I indicated in the parentheses, these assumptions are all justified by previous attempts at the generative account of Japanese. They are, however, not absolutely necessary for our present purposes.

(35)

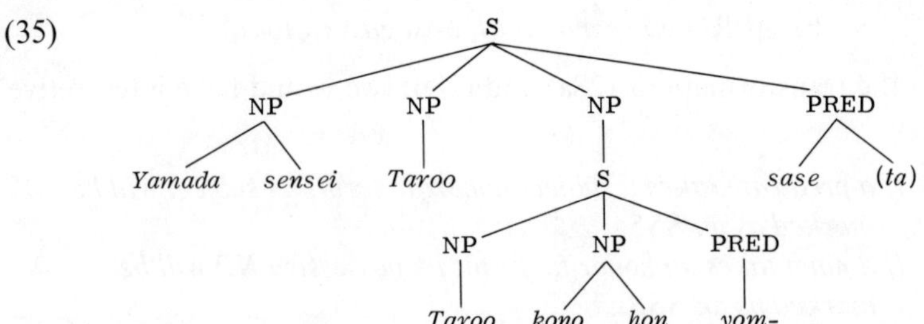

This structure is converted into the following by a couple of transformations, of which the most important to our discussion is the rule of predicate raising:[18]

(36)

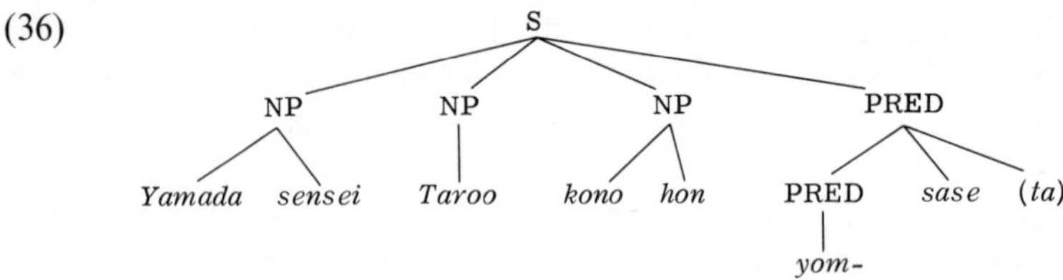

If honorific forms are introduced by transformations, all we have to say is that the rule for introducing subject honorifics applies at this stage of derivation, putting the morphemes *o* ... *ni nar-* around the derived predicate *yom-ase-*. If, however, honorific forms were regarded as existing in underlying structure, we would be forced to appeal to a complicated statement of distribution of honorific elements. Since interpretive rules are not statements about distribution of morphemes, the interpretive analysis forces us to accept an excessive apparatus for accounting for the distribution of honorific elements.

Moreover, as we shall see in Section 8, the distribution of honorific forms is subject to a constraint that is defined over two nonconsecutive stages of a derivation, which is not statable by an interpretive rule.

These considerations, then, justify our decision to adopt the transformational analysis of (propositional) honorifics.

5. SUBJECT HONORIFICATION

Rules

We shall now consider the rules of propositional honorification. In this section, let us restrict our attention to subject honorifics. In (28a), I gave,

[18] See Nakau (1973: Chapter 7) for justification of this rule in Japanese.

for expository purposes, a highly tentative formulation of subject honorification. That formulation was evidently insufficient, for it cannot account for the subject honorification of verbs, which involves, in addition to the addition of the honorific prefix, such processes as infinitivization and introduction of the elements *ni nar-*. We see, therefore, that subject honorification is statable not as a single process but, rather, as a set of rules. Rather than setting up a separate system of rules for each lexical category (which would leave unexplained the fact that some of the rules apply under the same structural conditions and even share some common structural changes), I shall set up a sequence of rules, some applying to all lexical categories but the others only to verbs. Specifically, I propose the following system of rules:

(37) a. Subject honorific marking (optional).
Mark the predicate as [Subject Honorific] if its subject is an SSS.

b. Honorific suppletion (governed).
If the predicate marked as [Subject Honorific] belongs to the class of 'suppletive verbs', substitute an appropriate suppletive form (mentioned in the lexicon) for it.

c. Honorific prefixation (obligatory).
Adjoin the honorific prefix to the predicate marked as [Subject Honorific].

d. Honorific infinitivization (obligatory).
Infinitivize a verb if it has an honorific prefix adjoined to it.

e. Honorific auxiliary attachment (obligatory).
Adjoin the honorific auxiliary **nar-** *to the right of the honorific infinitive marked as [Subject Honorific].*

f. *Ni* insertion (obligatory).
Adjoin the particle **ni** *to the right of the honorific infinitive immediately preceding* **nar-**.

g. Honorific prefix spelling (obligatory).
Spell out the honorific prefix as **o-** *or* **go-**, *the choice depending on the etymological class of the immediately following lexical item.*

These rules are assumed to apply in this order; some of them will be generalized in later sections.

Syntactic Features

The system of rules presented in (37) makes crucial use of the syntactic feature that I have tentatively named [Subject Honorific]. In consideration of the recent arguments against the use of syntactic features,[19] I feel some need to defend the employment of the feature [Subject Honorific] here. Although I agree that syntactic features often serve to state actually impossible processes as if they were impeccable linguistic rules, I see no other way to express the generalization underlying the system of honorification in Japanese. Of course, one can easily dispense with this syntactic feature [and, at the same time, Rule (37a)], at the cost of adding the structural condition 'if the subject is an SSS' to three rules, honorific suppletion, honorific prefixation, and honorific auxiliary attachment. From the point of view of simplicity, such an analysis would be no more complicated than my analysis. Notice, however, that some of my rules are subject to an obvious extension. Honorific prefixation, for example, can be generalized in such a way as to cover the prefixation in object honorifics and in NP honorifics. In terms of syntactic features, such an extension is easily achieved, simply by replacing the feature [Subject Honorific] with a more general feature, say, [+P(ropositional) H(onorific)].[20] Honorific prefixation would now be reformulated

[19]See, especially, Lakoff (1973). I see no reason, however, for not making use of syntactic features in cases in which there is no known semantic basis for syntactic discrepancy. For instance, the deletability of the complementizer *for* after verbs of desire seems to remain unaccounted for if we do not appeal to a rule feature like [+ *for* deletion]:

(i) a. *John wants* $\left\{\begin{matrix}\emptyset \\ *for\end{matrix}\right\}$ *Mary to leave.*

b. *John desires* $\left\{\begin{matrix}*\emptyset \\ for\end{matrix}\right\}$ *Mary to leave.*

Cf.:

(ii) *What John* $\left\{\begin{matrix}wants \\ desires\end{matrix}\right\}$ *is* $\left\{\begin{matrix}*\emptyset \\ for\end{matrix}\right\}$ *Mary to leave.*

[20]We here assume the following feature hierarchy:

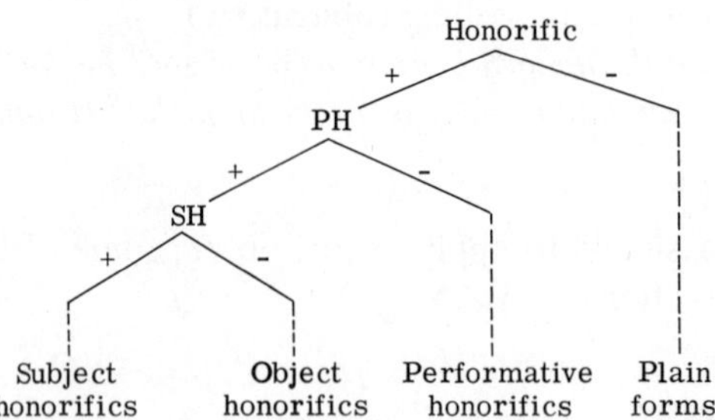

It is not obvious whether it is appropriate to use binary-valued features like [±SH]. Later in this chapter I shall use the notation [Object Honorific] to refer to the feature that would be described in the system under consideration as something like [+PH, −SH].

to refer to the feature [+PH], while rules of suppletion, for instance, would refer to the lower-level feature [±SH].

But such a general statement of the extended version of honorific prefixation is impossible in a theory that excludes syntactic features. In such a theory, the extended honorific prefixation would be nothing but a set of partially identical subrules; it would be no less accidental if we had three different prefixes for subject honorifics, object honorifics, and NP honorifics.[21] It seems, however, that the prefixation in these three cases is a unitary phenomenon. Since theories excluding the use of syntactic features do not enable us to state this generalization, we reject them as descriptively inadequate.

Furthermore, there is some possibility that the syntactic feature [Subject Honorific] (or the set of features [+PH, ± SH]) might receive an intrinsic interpretation. I have argued (in Section 4) that honorific forms are transformationally introduced and, thus, are not present in underlying structure. But clearly, honorific forms convey quite different information than nonhonorific forms, and this difference must somehow be reflected in semantic representation. We could, therefore, conceive of a set of interpretive rules, operating on shallower levels of structure and assigning a stylistic value to each sentence. If such interpretive rules are formulated, the syntactic feature(s) here proposed will provide information necessary for their operation.[22]

Derivations

Sample derivations of subject honorification are given in Table 1. The first column represents the derivation from nonverbal categories. The second represents the derivation from regular (nonsuppletive) verbs, and the third and fourth columns are sample derivations of suppletive honorific verbs. The derivations seem quite straightforward and require no special comment, except for the treatment of suppletive forms and the problem of derived structure.

Suppletive Forms

Let us first discuss the treatment of suppletive forms. As we saw in Section 2, there are two types of suppletion. In one case, the suppletive form replaces the entire honorific verb form, as in *ossyar-* instead of the expected **o-ii ni nar-*. In the other, the suppletive form replaces only the infinitival part, under-

[21] Note that this partial identity of rule environments is easily statable by using 'curly brackets'. It is instructive in this respect to recall McCawley's remark (1973b) that 'curly brackets are applicable only in cases where [we] would normally speak of "missing a generalization" [p. 297].'

[22] I might have been mistaken in calling such rules 'interpretive', but I have no idea as to the status of such a rule.

TABLE 1

(38)	*isogasi-i* Adjective 'busy'	*yom-* Verb 'read'	*ik-* Verb Suppletive: *ide-* 'go'	*iw-* Verb Suppletive: *ossyar-* 'say'
Subject honorific marking	*isogasi-i* [+SH]	*yom-* [+SH]	*ik-* [+SH]	*iw-* [+SH]
Honorific suppletion	—	—	*ide-*	*ossyar-*
Honorific prefixation	HP-*isogasi-i*	HP-*yom-*	HP-*ide-*	(does not apply)
Honorific infinitivization	—	HP-*yom + i*	HP-*ide* + ∅	—
Honorific auxiliary attachment	—	HP-*yomi nar-*	HP-*ide nar-*	—
Ni insertion	—	HP-*yomi ni nar-*	HP-*ide ni nar-*	—
Honorific prefix spelling	*o-isogasi-i*	*o-yomi ni nar-*	*o-ide ni nar-*	—

going all the other rules of honorification. Thus, the form *ide-* is substituted for *iki* in the expected form **o-iki ni nar-*. A few possibilities of the treatment of this fact immediately suggest themselves. The simplest solution, which requires no theoretical innovation, is to assign the rule feature [−Honorific Prefixation] to the part of the vocabulary that undergoes honorific suppletion. That is, predicates like *iw-* are marked as doubly exceptional in that they undergo an exceptional rule (honorific suppletion) and, moreover, fail to undergo a rule that is usually obligatory (honorific prefixation). Failure to undergo late transformations is automatically guaranteed as a result of rule ordering.

In an earlier study (Harada, 1970), I argued for another solution, in which honorific suppletion was ordered after all the other rules of honorification. Under that analysis, the suppletion rule operated on such forms as:

(39) a. *o-**ik** + **i** ni nar-*
b. ***o-iw + i ni nar-***

in which the parts in bold type are replaced by appropriate suppletive forms. I preferred that analysis to the one here proposed, on the ground that the use of rule features is an ad hoc way of describing the facts. Notice, however, that the phenomenon is itself exceptional, and there is no reason to suppose that use of an ad hoc set of suppletive rules is superior to the use of rule features. Further, under the second alternative analysis there is no a priori reason why suppletive forms do not replace the honorific infinitive part (or, for that matter, the honorific infinitive + *ni*, or just infinitive + *ni* + *nar-*, and so on). Thus, the nonexistence of such suppletive forms as **setu*, which would replace just the honorific infinitive part in (39b), giving a form like **setu ni nar-*, would be totally accidental and unexplainable under the second alternative. On the other hand, under the rule feature analysis, which I am advocating here, gaps like **setu* are fully systematic. Note that Rules (37d–g) are intrinsically dependent on the prior application of honorific prefixation: A lexical item that undergoes suppletion must be either subject to honorific prefixation or not; if it is, then it must take all the remaining decorations of subject honorifics, and if it is not, then no other change takes place.

There is an interesting fact that supports the rule feature analysis. Consider the subject honorification of verbs consisting of a Sino-Japanese morpheme and the inflection carrier *su-*, about which I summarized basic facts in Section 2. Recall that Sino-Japanese verbs manifest the following three subject honorific forms:

(40) a. HP + SJM *ni nar-*, e.g., *go-kenkyuu ni nar-*
b. SJM *nasar-*, e.g., *kenkyuu nasar-*
c. HP + SJM *nasar-*, e.g., *go-kenkyuu nasar-*

Under the analysis against which I am arguing, all of these forms must derive from a common intermediate structure like:

(41) HP + SJM *si ni nar-*, e.g., **go-kenkyuu si ni nar-*

Form (40a) is derivable from this through a rule that deletes infinitivized occurrences of *su-* in Sino-Japanese verbs under certain conditions, a rule that has an independent motivation, as can be seen from such pairs as:

(42) a. *Sono hito wa Nabaho-go o kenkyuu si ni Arizona e*
Navajo language study
it-ta.
'He went to Arizona to study the Navajo language.'
b. *Sono hito wa Nabaho-go o kenkyuu ni Arizona e it-ta.*

(43) a. *Tomonaga Hakusi wa Nooberu-syoo o zyusyoo* ***si***,
Dr. Nobel Prize be-awarded
itiyaku yuumei ni nat -ta.
on the spot famous become
'Dr. Tomonaga was awarded the Nobel Prize and instantly became famous.'

b. *Tomonaga Hakusi wa Nooberu-syoo o zyusyoo, itiyaku yuumei ni nat-ta.*

Forms (40b) and (40c), however, are not derivable without additional rules. Notice, first, that in order to derive them from structure (41) one must replace the sequence *si ni nar-* with *nasar-*, but such a suppletion is just without analog anywhere else (cf. the impossibility of a hypothetical suppletive form like **setu*, discussed earlier). In the case of form (40b), the situation is still worse, for one needs a further rule that drops the honorific prefix. But these two rules are simply ad hoc.

In the rule feature analysis, these two rules are not necessary. Note that low-level morphological processes often apply ambiguously to compound forms. Thus, in this case the feature [+ SH] can be interpreted as being associated either with its lexical head (i.e., SJM), or with the inflectable part of it (i.e., *su-*), or with both of its lexical members. In the first case, the *si* deletion rule will delete the infinitival occurrence of *si* in (41), giving form (40a). In the second, the inflectable part *si-* receives the specification [+ SH], and the suppletion rule converts it to *nasar-*. In the last case, the suppletion rule converts *si-* to *nasar-*, but honorific prefixation will also apply, giving HP to the SJM. Schematically, the three derivations can be shown as in Table 2.

TABLE 2

(44)

	kenkyuu-su-	*kenkyuu-su-*	*kenkyuu-su-*
Subject honorific marking	[+ SH]	[+ SH]	[+ SH] [+ SH]
Honorific suppletion	—	*kenkyuu-nasar-*	*kenkyuu-nasar-* [+ SH]
Honorific prefixation	HP-*kenkyuu-su-*	—	HP-*kenkyuu-nasar-*
Honorific infinitivization	HP-*kenkyuu-si*	—	—
Honorific auxiliary attachment	HP-*kenkyuu-si nar-*	—	—
Ni insertion	HP-*kenkyuu-si ni nar-*	—	—
Honorific prefix spelling	*go-kenkyuu-si ni nar-*	—	*go-kenkyuu-nasar-*
—			
Si deletion	*go-kenkyuu ni nar-*	—	—

I have, thus, demonstrated that my system of honorification rules accounts for not only the range of data with which I was initially concerned but also the data beyond them with independently motivated and natural extensions.

Derived Constituent Structure

Let us next consider the problem of derived constituent structure. Our system of rules assigns the following derived structure to a subject honorific verbal chain like *o-yomi ni nar-*:

(45)

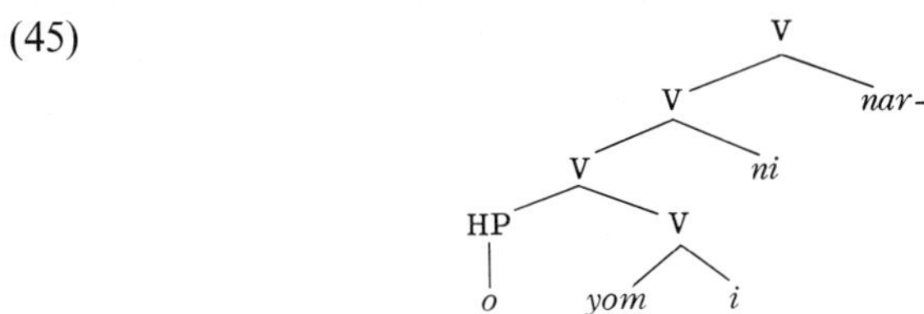

Alternatively, one might argue that the derived structure should be something like:

(46)

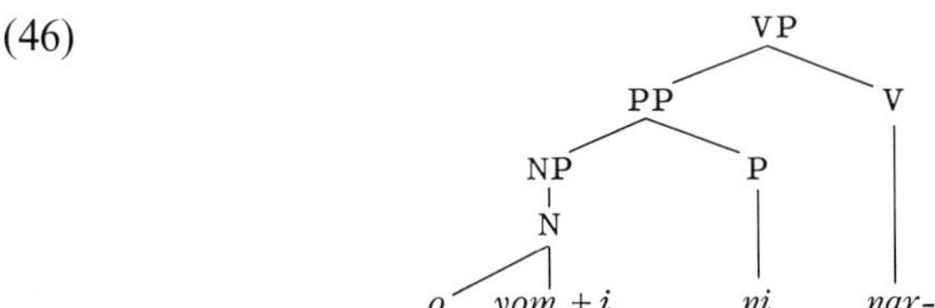

on the basis of the structural parallelism between honorific sentences and the construction of 'becoming', as in:

(47) a. *Taroo wa Hanako ga suki ni nat-ta.*
like
'Taro came to like Hanako.'

b. *Sumisu-san wa zyo -kyoozyu ni nat-ta.*
Smith Mr. associate professor
'Mr. Smith became an associate professor.'

But this second alternative does not seem plausible to me. In the first place, it is not clear how such structures as (46) could possibly be assigned. Under the assumption that honorifics are transformationally introduced, it is simply impossible to create such node labels as NP, PP, etc. Under an alternative assumption that honorifics are generated through the rules of the base component, we would now face the problem of selectional restriction. Suppose that the object of the honorific main verb (nominalized in the underlying structure, under the analysis with which we are concerned here) were introduced as a sister of the *ni*- phrase in (46), as in:

(48)

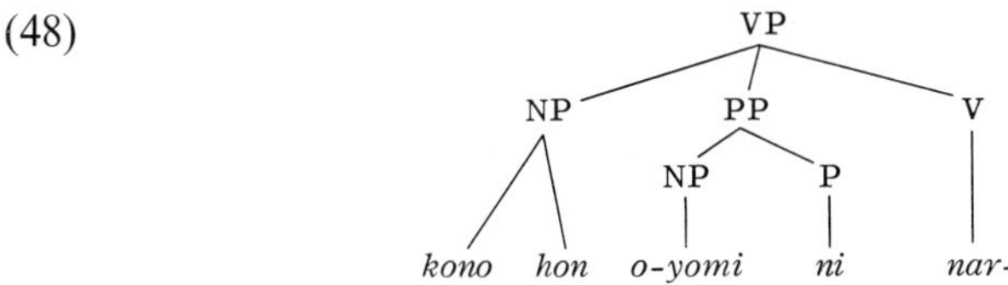

In this case, the selectional restrictions that hold in nonhonorific sentences between the main verb and its objects would now have to be restated separately for honorific sentences, but now between the head noun of the *ni*-phrase and the preceding constituents. Furthermore, the honorific auxiliary *nar-* would have a subcategorization feature of an indefinite shape, for its arguments would be all the arguments that the infinitivized main verb takes plus an extra PP. But there is no gain in explanatory power that would justify such a drastic complication of the theory of selectional restriction.

Suppose, then, that the object of the nominalized honorific main verb were introduced as a constituent of the NP, as in:

(49)

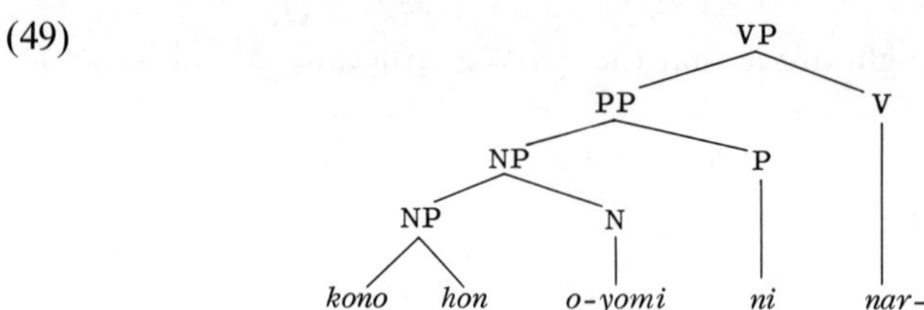

In this case, honorification would be interpreted as a kind of nominalization, like the mechanism introducing derived nominals like:

(50) a. *Kokuzei-tyoo* *no oote-syoosya no*
Tax Administration Agency large firms
tyoosa
investigation
'the investigation of large firms by Tax Administration Agency'

b. *Toyama Hakusi no unagi no ransi no kenkyuu*
Dr. eel ovum research
'Dr. Toyama's research on eel's ova'

c. *gen'yu ga ne-age -s-are-ta to no sirase*
crude oil price advance news
'the news that the price of crude oil was advanced'

But constituent structures like (49) cannot be justified. It makes the wrong prediction that the object would be marked with the particle *no*, as in (50), which is not true:

(51) *Yamada sensei wa kono hon o/*no o-yomi ni nat-ta.*
'Yamada *sensei* read this book.'

In general, it seems that the honorific infinitive cannot be identified with an NP. First, it cannot be anaphorically deleted:

(52) a. *Sumisu san wa moo zyo-kyoozyu ni nari-masi-ta ka?*
'Has Mr. Smith become an associate professor yet?'
Ee, nari-masi-ta.
'Yes, he has.'

b. *Yamada sensei wa moo kono hon o o-yomi ni nari-masi-ta ka?*
'Has Yamada *sensei* read this book yet?'
**Ee, nari-masi-ta.*
'Yes, he has.'

Second, it cannot be relativized:

(53) a. *Taroo ga nat-ta yaku wa Hamuretto da.*
role Hamlet
'The role Taro played was that of Hamlet.'

b. **Yamada sensei ga kono hon o nat-ta o-yomi wa ...*
(untranslatable)

Finally, it cannot be clefted:

(54) a. *Sumisu sensei ga kondo nat-ta no wa zyo-kyoozyu de,*
this time
koosi de wa ari-mase-n.
lecturer
'What Smith *sensei* has become is an associate professor, not a lecturer.'

b. **Yamada sensei ga kono hon o nat-ta no wa o-yomi ni de, o-kai ni de wa ari-mase-n.* (untranslatable)
buy

Thus, there is no reason at all for regarding the derived structure of a subject honorific verbal chain as something like (46).

Note, in passing, that it will not do, either, to regard *ni* and *nar-* as constituting a single constituent, as in:

(55)

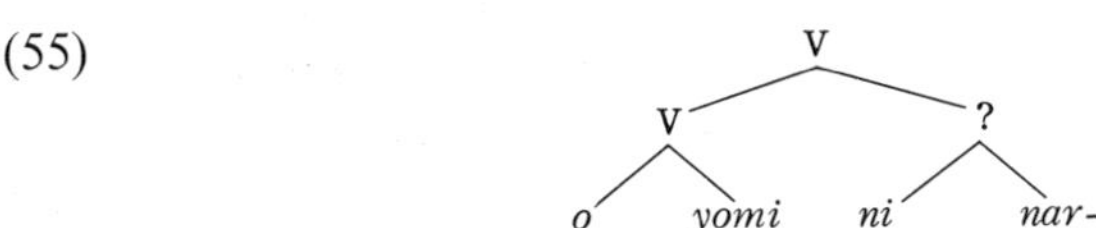

This is demonstrated by the fact that contrastive particles such as *wa* or *mo* come after *ni*, rather than before it:

(56) a. *Yamada sensei wa kono hon o o-yomi ni wa nari-mase-n desi-ta.*
'Yamada *sensei* didn't réad this book (but ...).'

b. **Yamada sensei wa kono hon o o-yomi wa ni nari-mase-n desi-ta.*

Since such particles are associated only with a single constituent and not with a set of discontinuous elements, the grammaticality judgment in (56) shows that *ni* must be grouped together with the honorific infinitive.

6. OBJECT HONORIFICATION

Let us now turn our attention to object honorification, that is, to such expressions as:

(57) a. *Watasi wa Yamada sensei ni sono koto o* ***o-tazune si****-masi-ta.*
ask
'I asked Yamada *sensei* about that matter.'

b. *De-wa, watasi ga sensei no o-nimotu o* ***o-moti si****-mas-yoo.*
then baggage bring
'OK, then, I'll bring *sensei*'s (or, your) baggage.'

c. *Bukka-zyoosyoo no gen'in ni tuki -masi-te wa, watakusi*
price advance cause concern
kara ***go-setumei moosi-age****-masu.*
from explain
'As for the price advance, let me explain its cause to you.'

d. *(Watasi wa) sensei no go-hon wa itu-mo* ***haidoku si****-te*
always read
ori-masu.
'I always read *sensei*'s (or, your) book.'

e. *Zannen-nagara, watakusi wa sono kata no koto wa* ***zonzi-age****-*
regrettably know
mase-n.
'Regrettably, I don't know anything about that person.'

Of these, (57c–e) are instances of suppletive object honorification.

The object honorifics, especially those that are formed regularly in the pattern honorific infinitive + *su-*, have a number of peculiarities that serve to distinguish them from subject honorifics. In this section we shall concern ourselves mostly with those peculiarities.

The rules for object honorification that I propose are essentially similar to those for subject honorification, except for obvious modifications (e.g., honorific auxiliary attachment must now insert *su-* instead of *nar-*, and *ni* insertion is not needed here). In particular, we need a rule marking the predicate as [+ O(bject) H(onorific)]. This rule, henceforth called object honorific marking, is subject to a number of special restrictions. We shall examine them in the following discussion.

Benefactivity

Nonsuppletive (regular) object honorification of a predicate is possible only when the predicate denotes a voluntary action. Thus, while we have such object honorifics as:

(58)	*o-ai su-*	'see, meet'
	o-hanasi su-	'talk to'
	o-kaesi su-	'return, give back'
	o-kiki su-	'ask'
	o-kotowari su-	'excuse oneself'
	o-mati su-	'wait for'
	o-negai su-	'ask, plead'
	o-sasoi su-	'invite'
	go-setumei su-	'explain'
	o-susume su-	'recommend'
	o-ukagai su-	'question; visit'

we do not have:

(59) a. **Watasi wa Yamada sensei no oi ni* ***o-atari***
nephew come under
***si**-masu.*
'I happen to be a nephew of Yamada *sensei*.'

b. **Watasi wa Kami o* ***o-sinzi si**-masu.*
God believe
'I believe in God.'

Perhaps this is inherently related to the fact that nonsuppletive object honorifics often have a benefactive interpretation. Consider, for instance, such sentences as:

(60) a. ?*Watakusi ga o-bentoo o* ***o-tabe si**-mas-yoo.*
lunch eat
'I'll eat your lunch (for you).'

b. ?*Watasi ga kawari ni Eberesuto ni* ***o-nobori si**-masu.*
instead Everest climb
'I'll climb Mt. Everest instead (of you).'

They are admittedly strange sentences, but their strangeness originates in the difficulty of finding appropriate contexts in which they could naturally be uttered. Once such contexts are given, the sentences in (60) do not appear to be unacceptable. Suppose, for example, that (60a) was uttered by a butler in charge of a millionaire's son who would be severely punished by his father if he left anything in his lunchbox. Suppose that one day the millionaire's son happened to have no appetite and asked the butler to eat up the lunch. Given such a situation, (60a) can quite naturally be interpreted in a benefactive sense, and the sentence sounds perfectly acceptable.

The fact that object honorification is possible only with predicates denoting a voluntary action might be a consequence of the fact that object honorific sentences are benefactively interpreted, because the benefactivity of an action presupposes that it is a voluntary action.[23]

Verbs versus Adjectives

There appears to be no object honorific version of an adjective or a nominal adjective. While we have subject honorific forms of an adjective or of a nominal adjective, as in:

(61) a. *Ano kata wa* ***o-utukusi -i***.
beautiful
'She is beautiful.'
b. *Syatyoo wa goruhu ga* ***o-suki da***.
golf
'The president likes playing golf.'

we do not have object honorific forms like:

(62) a. **Watasi wa Yamada sensei ga* ***o-kowa -i***.
afraid
'I am afraid of Yamada *sensei*.'
b. **Watasi wa Yamada sensei ga* ***o-suki da***.
'I like Yamada *sensei*.'

[23] Cf., in this connection, sentences like:

(i) *Watasi wa Yamamoto sensei o o-tasuke-si-ta.*
help
'I helped Yamamoto sensei out.'

The plain-style counterpart:

(ii) *Watasi wa Yamamoto sensei o tasuke-ta.*

is ambiguous between the senses 'What I did turned out to have helped Yamamoto sensei out (though I didn't intend to)' and 'I did something in order to help Yamamoto sensei out.' The object honorific version in (i) sounds unambiguous, having only the latter sense.

Sentences like (57e) pose some problems, however. Notice that predicates like 'know' do not refer to a voluntary action, or, for that matter, do not refer to an action at all. Hence, we must restrict our generalization to regularly formed object honorifics. Whether this is indicative of a fundamental deficiency of our analysis is an interesting problem, but I do not intend to pursue this matter any further here.

Presumably, this can be explained by the same principle that governs the fact discussed previously: Adjectives and nominal adjectives do not denote voluntary actions and, hence, are incapable of referring to benefactive actions.

Grammatical Function of the SSS

Though object honorification usually takes place when the object refers to an SSS, there are cases in which the object itself does not refer to an SSS:

(63) a. *O-nimotu o* ***o-moti si****-masu.*
'I'll bring your (= SSS's) baggage.'
b. *Kinoo Yamada sensei no o-taku o* ***o-tazune si****-ta.*
yesterday home visit
'Yesterday I called at Yamada *sensei*'s.'

Compare these with subject honorification, in which the subject by itself must refer to an SSS:

(64) a. **Sensei no o-nimotu ga* ***o-todoki ni nat****-ta.*
reach
'*Sensei*'s baggage has reached me.'
b. **Yamada sensei no go-hon wa yoku* ***o-ure ni nar****-u.*
well sell
'Yamada *sensei*'s book sells well.'

In the case of object honorification, the SSS that governs it may occur INSIDE the object, and need not be an object by itself.[24]

Indirect versus Direct Objects

Consider verbs that take two objects, like *hanas-* 'talk' and *syookai su-* 'introduce'. With such verbs, the governing SSS seems to have to occur in the indirect object rather than in the direct object. Thus, we do not have:

[24]Though, of course, it cannot occur indefinitely down, I know of no example in which the trigger SSS occurs in the second embedded NP, i.e.:

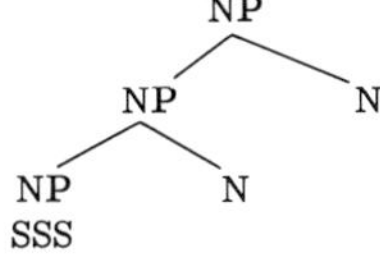

as would be the case in:

(ii) **Watasi wa Suzuki sensei no o-taku no tonari o o-tazune si-ta.*
next door
'I visited the house next door to Suzuki sensei's.'

(65) **Watasi wa otooto* ni *Yamada sensei no koto o*
younger brother
***o-hanasi si**-ta.*
'I talked about Yamada *sensei* to my (younger) brother.'

while we have:

(66) *Watasi wa Yamada sensei ni otooto no koto o* ***o-hanasi si**-ta.*
'I talked to Yamada *sensei* about my (younger) brother.'

Likewise, (67a) is unacceptable, while (67b) is not:

(67) a. **Otooto ni Yamada sensei o* ***go-syookai si**-ta.*
'I introduced Yamada *sensei* to my (younger) brother.'
b. *Yamada sensei ni otooto o* ***go-syookai si**-ta.*
'I introduced my (younger) brother to Yamada *sensei*.'

The same thing seems to hold for any ditransitive verb like *osie-* 'teach', *sirase-* 'inform', or *tutae-* 'report'. Since I have no natural explanation for this fact, it must be represented by an ad hoc condition on object honorific marking.[25]

Rule

To summarize, we can formulate the rule of object honorific marking in the following way:

(68) Object honorific marking.
Mark the predicate as [Object Honorific] when an SSS is ***included*** *in* (a) *the indirect object, if the predicate is ditransitive, or* (b) *the direct object, if the predicate is transitive.*

The asymmetry between regular and suppletive object honorifics (cf. footnote 23) is not accounted for by this formulation. Several possibilities come to mind, but I have no solid grounds to choose between them. Evidently, a more extensive study is needed to say anything definite here.

[25]If we have an independent motivation for an hierarchy like:

1. subject
2. indirect object
3. direct object
4. nonterms of grammatical relation

then we might be able to speak of a hierarchy among propositional honorification rules. That is, we could say that applicability of propositional honorification is determined exclusively by the HIGHEST occurrence of an SSS in that hierarchy. The formulation is not immediately obvious, and I do not go into this matter here.

Morphological Transformations

Before leaving the topic, let me briefly sketch the morphological transformations needed for object honorifics. They can be easily constructed after the corresponding rules for subject honorifics presented in (37):

(69) b. Honorific suppletion (governed).
Substitute an appropriate suppletive form for a predicate marked as [Object Honorific].
c. Honorific prefixation (obligatory).
Same as (37c), except that [Subject Honorific] is generalized to [Propositional Honorific].
d. Honorific infinitivization (obligatory).
Same as (37d).
e. Honorific auxiliary attachment (obligatory).
(i) *Same as (37e).*
(ii) *Adjoin the (honorific?) auxiliary* **su-** *to the right of the honorific infinitive marked as [Object Honorific].*[26]
g. Honorific prefix spelling (obligatory).
Same as (37g).

Thus, we can see that only (69e) contains the real addition to the system of rules in Section 5. The other rules are either exactly the same as the corresponding rules in Section 5, or their generalized versions.

7. HONORIFICATION IN NOUN PHRASES

We have thus far been concerned with honorification of predicate categories, that is, verbs, adjectives, and nominal adjectives. Here we shall discuss honorification of nouns and try to show that it is governed by essentially the same principles as the honorification of predicates. Before going into the discussion of honorification, some remarks are in order on the structure of an NP.

General Remarks on the Structure of NPs

A Japanese NP consists of at least a head noun, which is optionally preceded by a variety of prenominal modifiers, such as determiners, relative clauses, etc. But the kind of prenominal modifier that is of central concern to our topic is what I call a 'complement phrase'. Consider the following NPs:

[26] I put a question mark on the qualification 'honorific' in view of the fact that *su-* serves elsewhere as a general inflection carrier for uninflectable morphemes. It is possible, then, to imagine a rule of *si* deletion as proposed in Section 5. Unfortunately, there is scant evidence as yet to argue for one alternative over another.

(70) a. *Taroo no Amerika e no syuppatu*
toward start
'Taro's departure for America'
b. *Taroo no Hanako to no kenka*
quarrel
'Taro's quarrel with Hanako'
c. *Sumisu Hakase no Nabaho-go no kenkyuu*
'Dr. Smith's study of the Navajo language'

By the term COMPLEMENT PHRASE I will refer to a prenominal phrase ending in the particle *no*, such as *Taroo no*, *Amerika e no*, *Hanako to no*, *Sumisu Hakase no*, and *Nabaho-go no* in (70). In some cases a complement phrase corresponds to a genitive or an *of* phrase in English, but this is not always true. As we can see from the complement phrases *Amerika e no* and *Hanako to no*, the constituent that precedes *no* in a complement phrase does not necessarily have to be an NP but can be a postpositional phrase. In fact, it can even be an adverbial clause, as in:

(71) *sinbun o yomi-nagara no syokuzi*
newspaper while meal
'eating while reading a newspaper'

Now, notice that NPs that contain one or more complement phrases (which I call 'derived nominals' (DN), though I am not very happy about this name) are often structurally parallel to sentences. Thus, the DNs in (70) and (71) can be related to the following sentences, respectively:

(72) a. *Taroo ga Amerika e syuppatu-si-ta.*
'Taro started for America.'
b. *Taroo ga Hanako to kenka-si-ta.*
'Taro quarreled with Hanako.'
c. *Sumisu Hakase ga Nabaho-go o kenkyuu-si-ta.*
'Dr. Smith studied the Navajo language.'
d. *Sinbun o yomi-nagara syokuzi-si-ta.*
'(He) had a meal reading a newspaper.'

It is obvious, then, that such DNs as those in (70) and (71) involve the same set of grammatical relations as do the corresponding sentences. In general, it seems that we can speak of SUBJECTS or OBJECTS of a noun, just as we can speak of subjects or objects of a predicate. Thus, *Taroo* in (70a) can be said to be the subject of the noun *syuppatu*, just as *Taroo* in (72a) is the subject of the predicate *syuppatu-si-ta*.

Within linguistic theory, one can account for this either by deriving DNs from an underlying structure that contains the underlying structure of the corresponding sentence, or by generating them by base rules. In the latter analysis, the structural parallelism is accounted for by having in the lexicon a set of lexical entries that have constant contextual features but are ambiguous as regards the categorial status. The former analysis is known as the 'transformationalist analysis' and the latter as the 'lexicalist analysis'.[27] The choice between them is not crucial to our present purposes, and I will tentatively adopt the latter view here in order not to complicate our discussion, for there are cases like the following in which the sentential source is not immediately obvious:

(73) a. *yakusyo kara no tuuti*
public office from notice
'a notice from a public office'
b. *kinoo no sinbun*
'yesterday's newspaper'

Along these lines, I develop my account of the structural properties of DNs in the following way. The DNs in (70) and (71) are derived from structures like:

(74) a. *Taroo ga Amerika e syuppatu*
b. *Taroo ga Hanako to kenka*
c. *Sumisu Hakase ga Nabaho-go o kenkyuu*
d. *sinbun o yomi-nagara syokuzi*

I propose to regard the particle *no* as a mere structural marker that is obligatorily added to a sister phrase of the head noun, regardless of what category it belongs to. This *no* insertion rule, then, converts structures like those in (74) to those in (75):

(75) a. *Taroo ga no Amerika e no syuppatu*
b. *Taroo ga no Hanako to no kenka*
c. *Sumisu Hakase ga no Nabaho-go o no kenkyuu*
d. *sinbun o yomi-nagara no syokuzi*

In order to convert them to well-formed surface structures, we need a rule that drops particles *ga* and *o* in front of *no*. But notice that there is, indeed, an independently motivated rule with exactly this effect, namely, Kuroda's *ga/o* deletion transformation (see Kuroda, 1965).

Honorification of Nouns

In the preceding section, we saw that not only predicates but also nouns can have subjects and objects. From this we would naturally expect the rules of propositional honorification to apply also in NPs, affecting the head noun. This expectation is actually borne out. Consider such NPs as:

[27] See Chomsky (1970) and J. D. McCawley (1973b) for further details.

(76) a. ***Esaki Hakusi*** *no han-dootai ni-tui-te no go-kenkyuu*
semiconductor concern
'Dr. Esaki's research on semiconductors'
b. ***Yamada sensei*** *no Amerika e no go-syuppatu*
'Yamada *sensei*'s departure for America'
c. ***Sasaki Taroo-san*** *no Yosida Hanako-san to no go-kekkon*
'Mr. Taro Sasaki's marriage to Miss Hanako Yoshida'

in which the subject (shown in bold type) refers to an SSS and the head noun takes an honorific prefix. I take them to be instances of subject honorification applied in NPs. As a piece of evidence, compare (76) with the following NPs, which are ungrammatical:

(77) a. ****watasi*** *no koku -mazyutu no go-kenkyuu*
black magic
'my research on black magic'
b. ****boku no imooto*** *no Ahurika e no ga-syuppatu*
sister Africa
'my sister's departure for Africa'
c. ****watasi no musuko*** *no Tanaka-san to no go-kekkon*
son
'my son's marriage to Miss Tanaka'

Their ungrammaticality is not explained unless we take note of the fact that the subjects in (77) do not refer to SSS's. Put in another way, the ungrammaticality of the NPs in (77) is due precisely to a violation of the condition on subject honorific marking.[28]

Instances of object honorification are somewhat harder to find, but there do exist such cases. Consider sentences like:

(78) a. *Asita* ***o-denwa*** *de go-henzi-itasi-mas-u.*
phone (call) by means of reply
'I'll give you my reply tomorrow over the phone.'
b. *Watakusi no kangae wa* ***sensei e no o-tegami*** *ni nobe-te*
opinion letter describe
oi-ta toori de gozai-mas-u.
put as
'My opinion is just the same as I wrote in my letter to sensei (often = 'you').'

From the meanings of these sentences, it is clear that the honorific nouns *o-denwa* and *o-tegami* have the speaker as the subject and an SSS (= the addressee, in the most probable sense) as the indirect object. Schematically,

[28]Rules of subject honorification can easily be extended for honorification in NPs, provided that the operand is generalized to the head of a cyclic node, i.e., S or NP.

the pertinent NPs have the following structure at some point in the derivation at which honorification rules operate:

(79) $[NP_1\ NP_2\ e\ N]_{NP}$

where NP_2 contains an SSS.

We said in Section 6 that object honorification is applied only when either the indirect or the direct object contains an SSS, and that the normal case marker for the former is *ni* and that for the latter is *o*. In (79), however, NP_2 is marked with a different particle, *e*.

I argue that this fact does not run counter to my generalization about object honorification, nor to my contention that the NPs in bold type in (78) are object honorifics. Note that the particle *ni*, when it denotes a goal of movement,[29] alternates with *e*:

[29]From a transformational point of view, the various uses of the particle *ni* can be boiled down to the following four:

1. Indication of the place (or time-point) at which a non-durational activity or a state holds:

Sinzyuku-Eki ni i-ru
station
'be at the Shinjuku Station'
go-zi ni ki-ta
'(He) came at 5 o'clock.'

2. Indication of the goal of movement or of change of state:

Yokohama ni tuk -u
arrive
'arrive at Yokohama'
isya ni nar -u
M.D. become
'become a medical doctor'

3. Indication of an experiencer:

Konna hon wa boku ni wa omosiro-ku na -i.
such interesting not
'Such books aren't interesting to me.'

4. Indication of a de-ranked subject:

Taroo ni koros-are-ta.
kill
'(He) was killed by Taro.'
Ziroo ni tabe-sase-ta.
eat
'(He) made Jiro eat (it).'
kodomo ni wakari -nikui hon
child understand hard
'a book that is hard to understand for children'

It is only category (2) that alternates with particle *e*. Other cases alternate with various particles and quasi-particles, depending on the semantic role.

(80) a. *Taroo ga Honako* ***ni*** *sen en kasi-ta.*
thousand yen loan
'Taro loaned ¥1000 to Hanako.'
b. *Taroo ga Hanako* ***e*** *sen en kasi-ta.*

(81) a. *Taroo ga Toodai* ***ni*** *tootyaku-si-ta.*
University of Tokyo arrive
'Taro arrived at the University of Tokyo.'
c. *Taroo ga Toodai* ***e*** *tootyaku-si-ta.*

When such sentences are nominalized, only the versions with *e* are grammatical:

(82) a. **Taroo no Hanako* ***ni*** *no sen en no kasi*
b. *Taroo no Hanako* ***e*** *no sen en no kasi*
'Taro's loaning ¥1000 to Hanako'

(83) a. **Taroo no Toodai* ***ni*** *no tootyaku*
b. *Taroo no Toodai* ***e*** *no tootyaku*
'Taro's arrival at the University of Tokyo'

Actually, the particle *ni* never occurs before *no*. Thus, in cases like the following, in which no particle alternates with *ni*, we have no grammatical nominalizations:[30]

(84) a. *Hito-kui-zinsyu ga Ahurika ni sonzai-su-ru koto wa yoku*
man-eating-race exist well
sir -are-te i-ru.
know
'It is well known that in Africa there exist cannibal races.'
b. **Hito-kui-zinsyu ga Ahurika e sonzai-su-ru koto wa yoku sir-are-te i-ru.*

(85) **Hito-kui-zinsyu no Ahurika ni/e no sonzai wa yoku sir-are-te i-ru.*
'The existence of cannibals in Africa is well known.'

[30]Compare (85) with the following:

(i) a. *Kono wakutin ga kik -ana-i biirusu ga sonzai-su-ru koto wa yoku sir-are-te i-ru.*
vaccine efficacious not virus
'It is well known that there exists a kind of virus against which this vaccine is not efficacious.'
b. *Kono wakutin ga kik-ana-i biirusu no sonzai wa yoku sir-are-te i-ru.*
'The existence of a kind of virus against which this vaccine is not efficacious is well known.'

Our discussion up to now sufficiently demonstrates the need for the following two devices in the grammar of Japanese:

1. A transformation that optionally converts *ni* (indicating a goal of movement) into *e*.
2. A surface structure constraint that obligatorily discards any surface structure containing the particle sequence *ni no*.

Returning to the main theme, it is clear, given the grammatical devices just listed, that structure (79), which underlies the NPs in bold type in (78), is in fact derived from the following structure, in which NP_2 functions as an indirect object:

(86) $[NP_1\ NP_2\ \textit{ni}\ N]_{NP}$

We can, therefore, conclude that the NPs in bold type in (78) are instances of object honorification applied within NPs.

On the Possessive Construction

Consider, now, the so-called 'possessive' construction, an NP one of whose complement phrases denotes the possessor of the head noun,[31] e.g.:

(87) a. *Taroo no boosi* 'Taro's hat'
b. *Hanako no syasin* 'Hanako's picture'
picture
c. *boku no yuuhan* 'my supper'
supper

(88) a. *watasi no kodomo* 'my child'
child
b. *Ziroo no oyayubi* 'Jiro's thumb'
thumb
c. *sono onna-no-ko no me* 'that girl's eyes'
girl eye

(89) a. *Suzuki-san no tosi* 'the age of Mr. Suzuki'
age
b. *Yosio no kaotuki* 'the features of Yoshio'
features (of a face)

[31] More precisely, when I say that a nominal construction A *no* B is 'possessive', I assume that it is in a certain paraphrase relation with a sentence of the type A *ni* B *ga ar-u* 'A has B'. Many of the examples to be discussed in this section also have nonpossessive senses, but they are irrelevant in the present context. For example, (87b) also has a sense in which *Hanako* is the object of *syasin*, translatable as 'a picture of Hanako', i.e., a picture in which Hanako figures.

c. *Yosida-san no keireki* 'the personal history of
personal history Mr. Yoshida'

Semantically, the possessive construction has two different meanings: ALIENABLE and INALIENABLE possessions. The expressions in (87) represent alienable possession, namely, possessional relation arising a posteriori as a result of acquisition. On the other hand, the expressions in (89) represent inalienable possession, that is, a priori possessional relation. Expressions like (88) are ambiguous between these two senses, but their normal interpretation is that of inalienable possession.[32]

I know of no previous attempt at a syntactic account of the possessive construction in Japanese, but a fairly plausible analysis is obtained by extrapolation from the analyses of English possessive construction. First, a possessive phrase with the alienable sense seems to be best accounted for if we derive it from a restrictive relative clause, as in:

(90) [*Taroo ni boosi ga ar-u*]$_S$ *boosi*

Structures like this are converted to structures like (87) by the relativization transformation (which, in Japanese, is an identity deletion transformation) and a subsequent rule that replaces the sequence *ni aru* with the particle no.[33]

On the other hand, no relative clause source is imaginable for the inalienable possessive phrase. Consider, for instance, the following sentences, which would be part of the underlying structure of (89) if inalienable possessives were derived from relative clauses:

(91) a. **Suzuki-san ni tosi ga ar-u.*
'Mr. Suzuki has an age.'
b. **Yosio ni kaotuki ga ar-u.*
'Yoshio has features.'
c. **Yosida-san ni keireki ga ar-u.*
'Mr. Yoshida has a personal history.'

[32]Thus, (88a), for instance, could mean 'a child of whom I am temporally in charge' instead of the more normal meaning 'a child I gave birth to' or 'a child who is my offspring'.

[33]Alternatively, one could set up a rule that optionally deletes *aru* in some environments, and a rule that drops the particle *ni* (in the nonmotional use) before *no*. I know of no basis for choosing between these alternatives.

Note, incidentally, that the process of converting the sequence *ni aru* into *no* applies to other constructions than possessive ones, as can be seen from examples like:

(i) *tukue no ue* ***no*** *hon*
desk surface
'a book on the desk'

(ii) *tukue no ue* ***ni ar-u*** *hon*

Such sentences are quite funny, though my feeling is that they are not altogether ungrammatical.[34] In the absence of any other plausible sentential source, it is safer to assume that possessive phrases denoting inalienable possession are not derived from a sentential source at all. Thus, constructions like (89) are derived from underlying structures of the form:

(92)

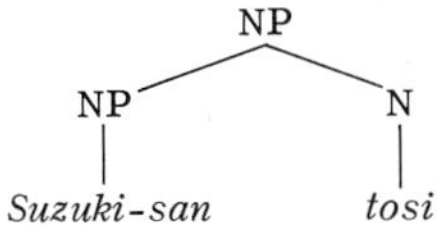

```
            NP
          /    \
        NP      N
        |       |
  Suzuki-san   tosi
```

through the *no* insertion transformation.

This somewhat lengthy discussion of the possessive construction in Japanese becomes crucial when we realize that honorification of nouns is also triggered by the occurrence of an SSS in the possessive phrase. Consider the following examples:

(93) a. *Yamada-sensei no o-boosi*
'Yamada *sensei*'s hat'
b. *sono kata no o-ko -san* 'his child'
child
c. *Suzuki-san no o-tosi* 'Mr. Suzuki's age'

It is apparent that possessive phrases, regardless of whether they denote alienable or inalienable possession, can always trigger honorification. Since our rules in the present form do not provide for such honorification, we must set up a third system of honorification rules. Let us, then, tentatively assume the following rule:

(94) Possessive honorific marking.
Mark a noun as [+*Honorific*] *when its possessive NP refers to an SSS.*

Though I have no evidence solid enough to refute the other analyses, I have some weaker evidence that tends to suggest that Rule (94) can be totally dispensed with by virtue of an extension of subject honorification

[34]Rather, the oddity seems to come mostly from the lack of informative value of the alleged source sentences. Thus, when the object noun is modified by an appropriate adjective, we often get a perfectly acceptable sentence like:

(i) *Yosida-san ni wa kawat-ta keireki ga ar-u.*
unusual
'Mr. Yoshida has an unusual personal history.'

rules.[35] Firstly, in such constructions the trigger SSS must be the possessive that is in an immediate syntactic relation to the head noun. Stated in another way, expressions like the following are not grammatical:

(95) a. **Yamada sensei no gakusei no o-boosi*
student
'Yamada *sensei*'s student's hat'
b. **sono kata no neko no o-ko-san*
cat
'his cat's babies'
c. **Suzuki-san no desi no o-tosi*
apprentice
'the age of Mr. Suzuki's apprentice'

This restriction is reminiscent of the condition on subject honorification that the trigger SSS by itself be the subject of the honorificized element (cf. Section 6). Secondly, in English and other languages, the subject of a noun occurs in the same syntactic position as a possessive NP. Thus, in English, both subjects and possessives of a noun can occur either prenominally or in an *of* phrase:

(96) a. *Pompidou's death*
b. *Mary's friends*

(97) a. *the death of Pompidou*
b. *several friends of Mary's*

And thirdly, notice that given the generalization about the occurrences of *no* in DNs made earlier, we may conceive of hypothetical particle that is associated with a possessive NP at some level of structure in the derivation

[35]If this is the case, we must regard the *ni* phrase in a possessive like the one contained in (90) as the SUBJECT of that sentence, though subjects are not usually marked with the particle *ni*. I think, however, that a fairly good case can be made for the claim that this *ni* phrase is, indeed, the subject.

Notice, first, that the *ni* phrase in a possessive sentence alternates with the normal subject marker *ga*, while the *ni* phrase in an existential sentence does not:

(i) a. *Taroo ni (wa) zaisan ga ar-u.*
property
'Taro is a man of property.'
b. *Taroo ga zaisan ga ar-u.*
'Taro is a man of property.'

(ii) a. *Tukue no ue ni hon ga ar-u.*
'There's a book on the desk.'
b. **Tukue no ue ga hon ga ar-u.*

Second, while the Japanese verb of being ordinarily shows an agreement in animateness with the subject (*ar-u* with an inanimate subject and *i-ru* with an animate one):

of such constructions. That particle must be either *ga* or *o*, for the other particles do not delete before *no*. The later possibility, however, is not plausible, and this leaves us with the possibility that a possessive phrase in general receives the particle *ga* at some intermediate level of syntactic structure.[36]

Although we have not accumulated a sufficient amount of evidence, what we have stated seems to offer a most promising line of future investigation, toward the elimination of Rule (94).

Beautificative Honorifics

There are nouns that have honorific shapes but whose appearance is not conditioned by an occurrence of an SSS in the subject, object, or possessive. Some examples follow:

(iii) a. *Sono ki no sita ni ike ga ar-u/*i-ru.*
tree under pond
'There's a pond beneath the tree.'
b. *Boku no ie no mae ni kawai-i onna-no-ko ga *ar-u/i-ru.*
house front cute girl
'There's a cute girl (standing) in front of my house.'

the agreement seems optional in possessive sentences:

(iv) a. *Watasi ni (wa) go-nin no kodomo ga ar-u.*
classifier
'I have five children.'
b. *Watasi ni (wa) go-nin no kodomo ga i-ru.*

(though the version with *i-ru* has an additional, nonpossessive sense, paraphrasable as something like 'I have five children to back me up').

Third, the *ni* phrase in a possessive sentence is capable of serving as the antecedent of *zibun*, the Japanese equivalent of the reflexive pronouns in English. As is shown by N. McCawley (this volume) or Kuno (1973), it is a privilege entertained only by a subject:

(v) *Hanako ni wa zibun o rikai-si-te kure-ru hito ga ari-mase-n.*
comprehend give not
'Hanako has nobody who would understand her.'

Fourth, and perhaps the strongest evidence as far as honorification is concerned, the *ni* phrase in a possessive sentence does in fact trigger subject honorification:

(vi) *Ano kata ni wa zaisan ga* ***o-ari ni nar****-u.*
'He is a man of property.'

[36]Actually, this is not the only possibility. We may take the deleted particle to be *ni*, in view of the alternative proposal made in footnote 33. Either way, the possessive NP in the analysis under consideration comes from the subject of an underlying sentence. If this is the case, we are obliged to recognize an extra device to convert what was originally the subject of the embedded sentence into the subject of a noun. Whether or not such reranking is plausible (or, for that matter, feasible) is beyond the scope of our present concern.

(98) a. ***O-biiru*** *ikaga?*
'Would you care for some beer?'
b. ***O-hiru*** *ni nat-ta no de,* ***o-bentoo*** *o tabe-ta.*
noon
'(We) had lunch because it was noon.'
c. *Asa wa boku wa* ***o-tya*** *sika nom -anai.*
morning tea only drink
'In the morning I only drink tea.'

Such occurrences of honorific nouns are usually referred to as 'beautificative' honorifics.

Beautificative honorifics have a nontrivial stylistic effect of making the utterance sound soft and feminine. Thus, their absence is usually taken as a token of virile speech. Their abuse is a favorite means of caricaturing a snobbish middle-class housewife who tries to boast of her education and good manners. The following exaggerated sentence may serve as an example:

(99) a. *Ee, taku no syuzin nado* ***o-syokuzi*** *no toki ni*
(my) home master for instance meal
o-biiru *o takusan itadaki-masu no de komat-te sima-u n'*
take be at a loss
zaamasu no yo.
'Yes, I have some trouble because my husband drinks (too) much beer at table.'
b. *Tugi ni* ***o-kyabetu*** *o kit-te itadaki-mas-yoo.* ***O-niku*** *wa*
next cabbage slice meat
arakazime ***o-sio*** *de* ***o-azi*** *o tuke-te itadaki-mas-u. ...*
previously salt taste put
O-nomi-mono *wa wain ga yorosi-i yoo de gozai-mas-u.*
beverage wine good seem
'Next, slice cabbage. You've got to season meat before cooking. I think wine is the best beverage suited for this dish.'

In some cases, such grammatically unconditioned occurrences of honorific nouns become fossilized. That is, etymologically honorific nouns become standard and nonhonorific, while originally nonhonorific forms become obsolete or scarce. Some examples are:

(100) *o-tya* 'tea'
(o)-kasi 'candies'
o-mi-o-tuke 'miso soup'
(o)-kane 'money'
go-han 'meal, rice'

8. HONORIFICATION IN COMPLEMENT CONSTRUCTIONS

We have seen in previous sections that honorification very often applies to predicates. In this section, we shall examine the behavior of honorification rules within complement constructions, i.e., constructions of the following sort:[37]

(101) a. *Soo i-eba, [kare ga zikan doori ni ki-ta]* ***koto*** *wa*
so say time exactly
iti-do mo nakat-ta na.
once sentence particle
'Come to think of it, he has never came here punctually, has he?'

b. *[Ano omosiro-i hito ga ko-nakat-ta]* ***no*** *wa zannen da.*
amusing regret
'I regret that that amusing person didn't come.'

c. *Boku wa [Nan-Ka-Dai ga kondo no*
University of Southern California coming
siai ni kat-u] ***to*** *omo-u.*
game win think
'I think the Trojans will win the next game.'

d. *Dore, hitotu [niwa de-mo sanpo-si-**te**] mi-ru ka.*
well garden take a walk try
'Well, I think I'll have a walk in the garden.'

e. *[Ano hito wa Nihon-go ga syaberi-]niku-i.*
Japanese speak hard
'He *has* some trouble with speaking Japanese.'

f. *Kono Doitu-go no kyoozyu wa [Doitu-go ga titto-mo*
German at all
hanas-]e -na-i.[38]
speak can
'This professor of the German language can't speak German at all.'

where [] indicate the boundaries of underlying embedded complement clauses, and the elements in bold type are 'complementizers', i.e., morphemes characteristic of complement constructions.

Examination of the behavior of honorification rules in complement constructions is important, since those constructions exhibit various modes of

[37]See Nakau (1973), Inoue (1969), Makino (1968) and Josephs (this volume), for discussion of the complement constructions in Japanese.

[38]This is a case in which the complementizer is null. Other such cases include causatives and passives, among a few others.

application of syntactic processes. Here, we shall restrict our attention to subject honorification, for subjects of complement clauses undergo more operations than objects in complement constructions.

Propositional versus Performative Honorifics

As stated in Section 1, most complement constructions in Japanese do not permit the occurrence of performative honorifics, while none of them prohibit the occurrence of propositional honorifics as far as they allow personal subjects in the complement sentence. The few complement constructions that do permit performative honorifics to occur are interpretable, without exception, as 'direct discourses', and, as such, they are all instances of *to* complement constructions:[39]

(102) a. *Taroo wa [Hanako ga ki-ta]$_S$ to it-ta.*
'Taro said, "Hanako came."'
b. *Taroo wa [Hanako ga ki-masi-ta]$_S$ to it-ta.*

(103) a. *Taroo wa [zibun no tuma ga CIA no supai da]$_S$ to sinzi*
self wife spy believe
-te i-ru.
'Taro believes that his wife is a CIA agent.'
b. **Taroo wa [zibun no tuma ga CIA no supai des-u]$_S$ to sinzi-te i-mas-u.*

(104) a. *Taroo wa [sono hikooki ga tuiraku-si-ta]$_S$ koto o*
airplane fall
sira-nakat-ta.
know not
'Taro didn't know that the airplane fell down.'
b. **Taroo wa [sono hikooki ga tuiraku-si-masi-ta]$_S$ koto o sira-nakat-ta.*

Propositional honorification can occur in any of these environments:

(105) a. *Taroo wa [Simizu sensei ga irassyat-ta]$_S$ to it-ta.*
'Taro said that Shimizu *sensei* had come.'
b. *Taroo wa [Yamada sensei ga soo ossyat-ta]$_S$ to sinzi-te i-ru.*
'Taro believes that Yamada *sensei* said so.'
c. *Taroo wa [Satoo-san ga kono tokei o kudasat-ta]$_S$ koto o*
watch give
sir-anakat-ta.
'Taro didn't know that Mr. Sato gave this watch.'

[39]See Section 9 for discussion of relative clause constructions, which offer other instances of performative honorifics occurring in embedded sentences.

Degree of Politeness

In nondirect discourse complement constructions, propositional honorification takes place independently of the structure of the matrix clause. Applicability of propositional honorification rules is determined autonomously in each clause, depending only on whether the subject (or object) of that clause refers to an SSS. Thus, corresponding to a plain-style sentence like:

(106) *Yamada sensei wa* [*Yosida sensei ga ki-ta*]$_S$ *koto o kii-ta.*
(Cf. *kii-* < *kik* + *i-*)
'Yamada *sensei* heard that Yoshida *sensei* had come.'

we have three possible propositional honorific variants:

(107) a. *Yamada sensei wa* [*Yosida sensei ga* ***o-ide ni nat****-ta*]$_S$ *koto o kii-ta.*
b. *Yamada sensei wa* [*Yosida sensei ga ki-ta*]$_S$ *koto* ***o o-kiki ni nat****-ta.*
c. *Yamada sensei wa* [*Yosida sensei ga* ***o-ide ni nat****-ta*]$_S$ *koto o* ***o-kiki ni nat****-ta.*

Of course, they are based on different presuppositions about the status of *Yamada sensei* and *Yosida sensei* relative to that of the speaker. Sentence (107a) treats *Yosida sensei* (but not *Yamada sensei*) as being superior to the speaker. Sentence (107b) exhibits the opposite treatment, and (107c) treats both of them as SSS's.

Consider, now, sentences like the following, in which the subject of the complement clause is always identical to that of the matrix clause:

(108) a. *Taroo wa* [*Karuizawa ni ik-u*]$_S$ *koto ni kime-ta.*
decide
'Taro decided to go to Karuizawa.'
b. *Taroo wa* [*"Faust" o yomi*]$_S$ *hazime-ta.*
begin
'Taro began to read *Faust*.'
c. *Ziroo wa* [*ikura de-mo sake o nomu*]
how much even alcoholic beverage
koto ga deki-ru.
can
'Jiro can drink indefinitely.'
d. *Ziroo wa* [*ikura de-mo sake o nom-*]$_S$ *e-ru.*
can
[synonymous with (108c)]

Suppose that the subject of the matrix clause refers to an SSS. Then the subject of the complement clause, too, must necessarily be an SSS. We would, thus, expect to have honorific forms on the predicates of both clauses or of neither. But this is not the case:

(109) a. *Yamada sensei wa [Karuizawa ni* ***o-ide ni nar****-u]$_S$ koto ni kime-ta.*
'Yamada *sensei* decided to go to Karuizawa.'
b. *Satoo sensei wa ["Faust" o* ***o-yomi ni nari-****]$_S$ hazime-ta.*
'Sato *sensei* began to read *Faust.*'
c. *Sasaki sensei wa [ikura de-mo sake o* ***o-nomi ni nar****-u]$_S$ koto ga deki-ru.*
'Sasaki *sensei* can drink indefinitely.'
d. *Yoshida sensei wa [ikura de-mo sake o* ***o-nomi ni nar-****]$_S$ e-ru.*
'Yoshida *sensei* can drink indefinitely.'

(110) a. *Yamada sensei wa [Karuizawa ni ik-u]$_S$ koto ni* ***o-kime ni nat****-ta.*
b. %*Satoo sensei wa ["Faust" o* ***o-yomi-****]$_S$* ***hazime ni nat****-ta.*[40]
c. *Sasaki sensei wa [ikura de-mo sake o nom-u]$_S$ koto ga* ***o-deki ni nar****-u.*
d. %*Yoshida sensei wa [ikura de-mo sake o* ***o-nom-****]$_S$* ***e ni nar****-u.*

(111) a. *Yamada sensei wa [Karuizawa ni* ***o-ide ni nar****-u]$_S$ koto ni* ***o-kime ni nat****-ta.*
b. ————
c. *Sasaki sensei wa [ikura de-mo sake ga* ***o-nomi ni nar****-u]$_S$ koto ga* ***o-deki ni nar****-u.*
d. ————

From these paradigms we see that subject honorification takes place either in the complement clause [as in (109)], or in the matrix clause [as in (110)], or in both [as in (111)].[41]

Syntactic paradigms such as those found in (109)–(111) evidently demonstrate the fact that subject honorification is an optional process. If it were an obligatory agreement, then its nonapplication in one of the clauses in sentences like (109) and (110) would result in self-contradictory, ungram-

[40]The diacritic % indicates that the acceptability of the sentence marked with it is subject to idiolect variations.

[41]The (b) and (d) sentences obligatorily undergo predicate raising, which raises the complement main verb to the matrix main verb. The fact that they do not occur in the set of sentences in (111) merely indicates that subject honorification applies after predicate raising. If the latter rule preceded the former, it would be possible to apply honorification to both complement and matrix main verb, but this would result in such ungrammatical sentences as:

(i) a. **Satoo sensei wa ["Faust" o* ***o-yomi ni nari-****]$_S$* ***o-hazime ni nat****-ta.*
b. **Yosida sensei wa [ikura de-mo sake o* ***o-nomi ni nar(i)****]$_S$* ***o-(r)e ni nar****-u.*

matical sentences, for in those sentences the subjects of the matrix and the embedded clauses are required to be identical.

The optionality of honorification suggests that its application (or nonapplication) should have some effects on the 'meaning' of the resulting sentence or, more properly, on its stylistic value.[42] I think this is really the case. I find the sentences in (110) the most natural honorific sentences, those in (109) a bit awkward and less polite, and those in (111) somewhat too polite to use in ordinary honorific contexts. The intuition about which of the three forms is the 'standard' honorific version would vary from speaker to speaker, but every speaker would agree that the three forms have different degrees of politeness associated with them, that is, (109) < (110) < (111), where A < B means that expression A has a lower degree of politeness than expression B.

Consider, now, the problem of what is the most adequate device to account for such difference in the degree of politeness and under what conditions it operates. It seems to me that we should have a set of 'interpretive rules' that apply to surface structure and measure the degree of politeness depending on the place and the number of occurrences of honorific items.[43] I propose, quite tentatively, the following rule:

(112) *Given a pair of sentences, S_1 and S_2, that contain a sequence of verbs V_1 V_2 ... V_n whose subjects are identical.*
Assign a higher degree of politeness to S_1 than to S_2 if:
(a) *S_1 contains more occurrences of honorific items than S_2.*
(b) *S_1 has an honorific item in a higher predicate than S_2.*
(c) *S_1 has a sequence of consecutive occurrences of honorific items but S_2 does not.*

The three subconditions are to be interpreted as conjunctively applied. That

[42]In general, only in cases in which the occurrence of an item is subject to the speaker's choice does the item have an effect on the stylistic value of the utterance. The point has been expressed by a number of linguists on a variety of occasions. The following is a quotation from Chomsky (1964):

> In general, it seems reasonable to regard an item as meaning-bearing just in case selection of it is subject to an optional rule (thus most lexical items are meaning-bearing, as are optional transformations and constructions given by rewriting rules, but not, e.g., phonemes). Where the grammar provides for an optional choice, it makes sense to search for the conditions under which it is appropriate to make this choice (this being one aspect of the study of meaning) [p. 68, n14].

[43]I am not quite sure whether such a rule is of the same formal nature as the so-called 'surface structure interpretation rules' proposed, e.g., in Chomsky (1971). Rule (112) may not even be a rule of grammar but, rather, a rule of performance, to be included in the 'stylistic component' envisioned by Ross (1967).

is, sentences satisfying two of these conditions receive higher degrees of politeness than those satisfying only one, and those satisfying all receive the highest degree. In the present case, (112) correctly predicts that (109) < (110) < (111). Subcondition (a) tells us that (109) < (110) and (110) < (111). Subcondition (b) tells us that (109) < (110). And finally, by Subcondition (c) we see, again, that (109) < (111) and (110) < (111). Subconditions (a) and (c) give us the same information in the present case, but I have included both in (112) because they make different predictions about cases in which more than two honorific verbs are involved.[44] My intuitions about such cases are, however, not secure enough to pursue this topic any further here.

What seems worth noting is the fact that having rules like (112) grants us a means of quantificational study of the problem. Suppose, for instance, we assign a value *n* to a sentence with *n* occurrences of honorific items, and

[44] Cf. (ii), which is a paradigm of honorific variants corresponding to the sentence:

(i) *Yamada sensei wa Karuizawa ni it-te mi-ru koto ni kime-ta.*
try
'Yamada *sensei* has decided to try visiting Karuizawa.'

(ii) *Yamada sensei wa Karuizawa ni*
a. ***o-ide ni nat****-te mi-ru koto ni kime-ta.*
b. *it-te* ***go-ran ni nar****-u koto ni kime-ta.*
c. *it-te mi-ru koto ni* ***o-kime ni nat****-ta.*
d. ***o-ide ni nat****-te* ***go-ran ni nar****-u koto ni kime-ta.*
e. ***o-ide ni nat****-te mi-ru koto ni* ***o-kime ni nat****-ta.*
f. *it-te* ***go-ran ni nar****-u koto ni* ***o-kime ni nat****-ta.*
g. ***o-ide ni nat****-te* ***go-ran ni nar****-u koto ni* ***o-kime ni nat****-ta.*

According to the quantificational rules to be proposed, these sentences would receive the following values of politeness:

(iii)

	Number of Honorifics	Values for Height of Honorifics	Occurrences of Consecutive Honorifics	Sum
a.	1	0.25	0	1.25
b.	1	0.50	0	1.50
c.	1	1.00	0	2.00
d.	2	0.75	$1\ (\times \frac{1}{2})$	3.25
e.	2	1.25	0	3.25
f.	2	1.50	$1\ (\times \frac{1}{2})$	4.00
g.	3	1.75	$2\ (\times \frac{1}{2})$	5.75

I do not know if these values could be justified by some empirical investigations, but my intuitions are quite consistent with the predictions about (c) and (f) that they are standard for my idiolect and for very formal situations, respectively. The table makes a further correct prediction that (iig) is too polite even for a very formal situation.

value $1/n$ for each occurrence of an honorific item in the predicate of the $(n-1)$th embedded clause from the top, and finally, value 1/2 for each consecutive pair of honorific items. This convention would assign a value of 1.5 to (109), 2 to (110), and 4 to (111). We might then imagine a 'cardinal point' in this scale of quantified degree of politeness that fixes the standard and preferred levels of speech for a given speaker or for a given situation. For me, for instance, the cardinal point is at value 2, and hence (110) is the standard, (109) a bit less polite and (111) hyperpolite. In contrast, at a very formal meeting like a typical wedding ceremony in Japan, the standard degree of politeness would be much higher than this; in such situations sentences like (111) are very frequent, so that we could tentatively consider value 4 to be the cardinal point for this kind of situation.

I seem to have spoken too much about the quantificational approach to the degree of politeness, which is not supported at present by empirical evidence and, hence, is merely conjectural. The adequate way to assign values of politeness, for instance, needs further examination, but the basic notions introduced in this section will, I believe, prove very useful in sharpening our understanding of the problem.

Cyclicity of Honorification

Complement constructions offer the only place to examine the cyclicity of honorification rules. In Section 4, I showed that subject honorification (or at least subject honorific marking) must apply after predicate raising in the derivation of sentences like (33). Now consider the following sentences:

(113) a. *Yamada sensei wa [hon o **o-yomi ni nari**]$_S$-hazime-ta.*
'Yamada *sensei* began to read a book.'

b. %*Yamada sensei wa [hon o **o-yomi**]$_S$**-hazime ni nat**-ta.*

c. **Yamada sensei wa [hon o **(o-) yomi (ni nari)**]$_S$ **o-hazime ni nat**-ta.*

Note that the grammaticality of (113a) indicates that subject honorification MAY apply BEFORE predicate raising, or, more precisely, before equi-NP deletion, which deletes the subject of the embedded complement clause.

The contrast between the ordering needed to derive sentence (33) in Section 4 and the one needed to derive (113a) is sufficient to demonstrate the fact that subject honorification is a cyclic operation. In the derivation of (33), subject honorification and predicate raising both apply in the matrix clause, and the former follows the latter. In the derivation of (113a), on the other hand, subject honorification applies in the complement clause but predicate raising in the matrix clause, and here the former precedes the latter. Summing up, we can conclude that:

(114) *Subject honorification is a cyclic operation that follows predicate raising in the cycle.*[45]

Constraints on Honorification

Consider, now, the derivations of the three sentences in (113). The underlying structure common to them is roughly representable in the following fashion:

(115)

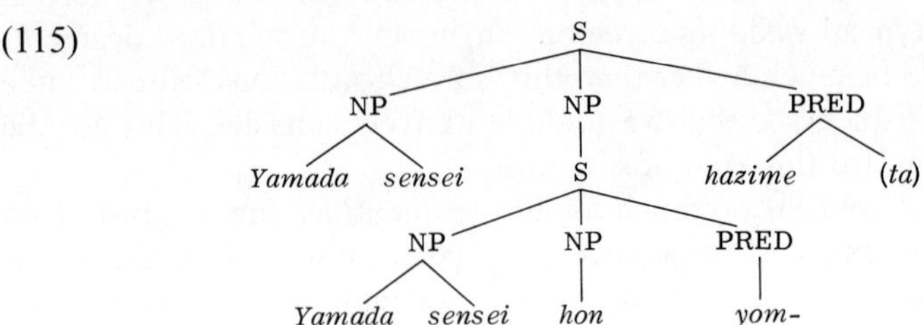

On the complement cycle, predicate raising is inapplicable, so only subject honorification may apply. If it applies, we get a structure like:

(116) *Yamada sensei* [*Yamada sensei hon* ***o-yomi ni nar-***]$_S$ *hazime-ta.*

On the matrix cycle, equi-NP deletion first applies and erases the subject of the complement clause. Since predicate raising is obligatory for such complement constructions, it is obligatorily applied. At this stage, then, we have two possible intermediate structures:

(117) a. *Yamada sensei hon* ***o-yomi ni nari****-hazime-ta.*
b. *Yamada sensei hon yomi-hazime-ta.*

Structure (117a), derived from intermediate structure (116), will no longer undergo subject honorification. The following sentences, which would result if subject honorification were applied to (117a), are both ungrammatical:

(118) a. **Yamada sensei wa hon o* ***o-yomi ni nari o-hazime ni nat****-ta.* (= 113c)
b. **Yamada sensei wa hon o* ***o-o-yomi ni nari-hazime ni nat****-ta.*

Sentence (118a) is easily filtered out by the proposed rule ordering: predicate raising before subject honorification. The ungrammaticality of (118b), however, is not readily explained in terms of the system of rules and conventions

[45] Note, in passing, that (114) does not necessarily provide a piece of evidence for the necessity of an extrinsic rule ordering. The ordering of predicate raising before subject honorification (or, in particular, before subject honorific marking) follows from the obligatory–optional principles proposed by Ringen (1972), and the rules in the block referred to as 'subject honorification' are intrinsically ordered with respect to each other.

proposed so far. We need for such cases a constraint against reapplication of subject honorification, which would be statable in the following way:

(119) *Subject honorification does not reapply to an item that contains an item that has already undergone subject honorification.*

This restriction holds not only for cases in which its violation would result in double marking with the honorific prefix (i.e., **o-o-* ...) but also for cases in which a suppletive form would have been introduced (e.g., **o-irassyari-hazime ni nar-*).

Now, consider (118b), which the application of subject honorification on the matrix cycle would convert to (113b). This sentence, however, is not accepted by prescriptive accounts of Japanese honorifics. Indeed, a lot of people do not accept such a sentence, though there are many others who find it perfectly natural. The same situation is observed in cases in which the embedded sentence originates in an underlying subject complement:[46]

(120) a. *Suzuki sensei wa sake o* ***o-nomi ni nari****-sugi-ta.*
exceed
Suzuki *sensei* has drunk too much.'
b. %*Suzuki sensei wa sake o* ***o-nomi-sugi ni nat****-ta.*

(121) a. *Tanaka san wa eigo de wa* ***o-hanasi ni nari****-niku-i*
English speak hard
soo des-u.
it is said
'I heard that Mr. Tanaka finds some difficulty in speaking English.'
b. %*Tanaka san wa eigo de wa* ***o-hanasi-niku****-i soo des-u.*

Thus, we can see that the variation cannot be attributed to casual mistakes

[46]Further examples follow:

(i) ***O-tukai-yasu****-ku nari -masi-ta.*
use easy become
'It has become easier to use.'

(ii) *Hi-denka ga watasi no yama-goya nado ni o-kosi-niku-ku nar-u to*
Her Imperial Highness cottage
sabisi -i no de, ima made kaki -hikae -te i-ta no de at-ta ga ...
feel lonely now up to write refrain
'I have kept myself from writing this for fear that it should make it hard for Her Imperial Highness Princess Michiko to pay a visit to my humble cottage, ...'

The second example, reported by Oishi (1966) to have been used by Yasunari Kawabata, is of some interest because there is no acceptable plain form like **kosi-niku-i* in the sense of 'pay a visit'. The form *kosi-* here is a suppletive infinitival form for *tazune-*.

or errors in usage of honorifics, as the prescriptive treatments often claim those expressions to be. Rather, here we have two independent subsystems in present-day Japanese, one excluding such expressions as those marked with % and the other allowing them. Let us call these two subsystems 'System I' and 'System II', respectively, for ease of reference.

System I differs from System II in having an extra mechanism that prevents subject honorification from applying on the matrix cycles in the derivations of such sentences as (113b), (110d), (120b) and (121b).

The problem now is to specify the contents of this extra device to be included in System I. I see no way to formulate it except to state it as a global constraint on the applicability of subject honorification, in the following manner:

(122) *Subject honorification is blocked on a certain cycle if:*
  (a) *the input structure is an output of predicate raising on the same cycle, and*
  (b) *subject honorification was applicable, but did not apply, on the previous cycle.*

Note that both conditions must be met if a given derivation is to be filtered out. If Condition (a) is met but (b) is not, we will obtain a grammatical sentence like (33) in Section 4. If, on the other hand, Condition (b) is met but not (a), we will again obtain grammatical sentences like (110a) or (110c).

Let us illustrate the way in which the global constraint in (122) operates, taking (121b) as an example. The underlying structure would be something like this:

(123)

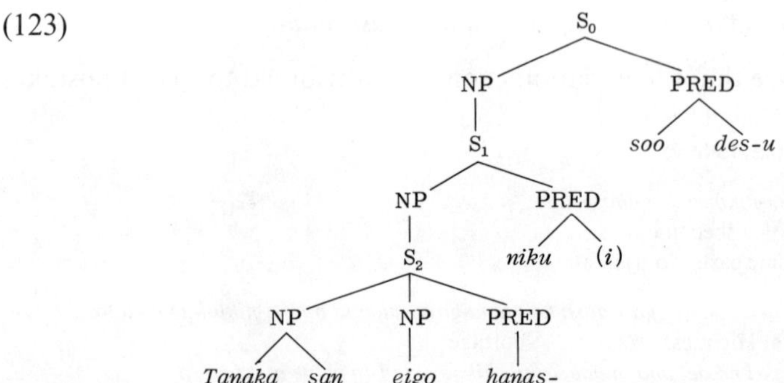

where *Tanaka san* is an SSS. Subject honorification first becomes applicable on the S_2 cycle, and its application on this cycle will result in (121a). If it does not apply, then we will get the following structure on the S_1 cycle, after predicate raising has applied:

(124)

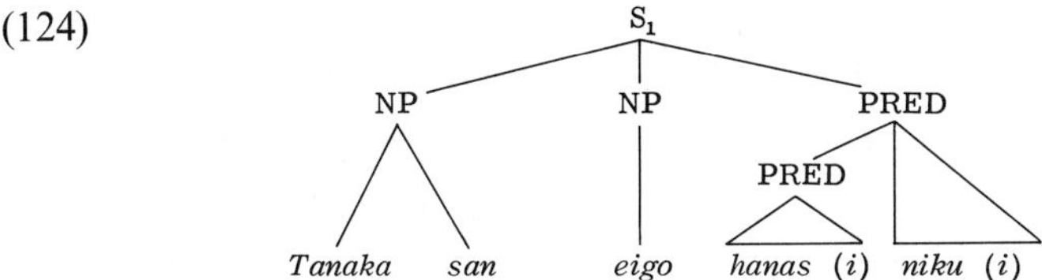

Constraint (122) blocks the application of subject honorification to this structure, for (124) is an output of predicate raising and the structure on the previous cycle [i.e., S_2 in (124)] satisfied the structural conditions of, but did not undergo the operations of, subject honorification.[47]

9. REMARKS ON PERFORMATIVE HONORIFICS

Little has been said thus far about the class of honorifics that I have called 'performative honorifics'. However, I feel it absolutely necessary to sketch the basic properties of honorifics of this class, for they are far more frequent in actual speech than propositional honorifics, and hence, it is not imaginable for anybody to master the Japanese language without knowing the principles underlying the uses of performative honorifics.

Performative Categories and Speech Levels

I have called the items *-mas-* and *des-* 'performative honorifics' because their occurrence is conditioned not by elements in the propositional content of the sentence in which they occur but, rather, by such categories as the speaker, the addressee, the situation in which the sentence is uttered, and so on, that is, by what we may call 'performative categories.'[48]

The use of performative honorifics differentiates the speech level to which the sentence belongs. Compare the following three sentences, which are basically synonymous but belong to different speech levels:

(125) a. *Koko ni hon ga ar-u.*
'Here is a book.'

[47] In this section, I have stated the existence of two subsystems of honorification as a synchronic fact, but it seems quite important to reconsider the fact from a diachronic point of view. Though there is no readily accessible statistical evidence, the intuitions of older generations appear to be in greater conformity with the prescriptive grammar than those of younger generations. If this is indeed the case, then we are attesting a historical change in progress. The change is elimination of a global constraint on the applicability of subject honorification and is, thus, a kind of grammar simplification.

[48] The notion of 'performativity' was first introduced by Austin (1962). See Ross (1970) for an important attempt to integrate this notion into current linguistic investigations.

b. *Koko ni hon ga ari-**mas**-u.*
c. *Koko ni hon ga **gozai-mas**-u.*

The speech levels represented by these sentences will henceforth be referred to as the 'plain', 'polite', and 'hyperpolite' styles, respectively.

Let us discuss the conditions under which polite-style sentences such as (125b) occur. As a first approximation, consider the following statement:

(126) *A sentence is put in the polite style only if the addressee is a person who is socially superior or equal to the speaker.*

Notice, here, that the crucial factor is the social status of the ADDRESSEE (but not of the subject nor of the object), and that it need not be superior but can be equal to that of the speaker. In these two respects, performative honorifics are different from propositional honorifics.

The basic correctness of this statement can be demonstrated by the interaction of performative and subject honorifics in a construction with a second-person subject. Consider, for instance, a plain-style sentence like:[49]

(127) *Koohii o nom-u ka?*
coffee
'Do you drink coffee?'

To put the sentence in the polite style, we can add the performative honorific auxiliary *-mas-*, convert the predicate into a subject honorific, or make both changes. Now, statement (126) predicts that if the predicate is made into a subject honorific, it must also be followed by the auxiliary *-mas-*, though the reverse need not be the case. This prediction is actually borne out:

(128) a. *Koohii o nomi-**mas**-u ka?*
b. **Koohii o **o-nomi ni nar**-u ka?*
c. *Koohii o **o-nomi ni nari-mas**-u ka?*

As predicted, (128b) is totally unacceptable in the sense under consideration, in which the subject is in the second person.[50] Statement (126), in conjunction with the condition on subject honorification, makes a further prediction that (128c) is more appropriate for cases in which the addressee is socially superior to the speaker and (128a) is more appropriate for cases in which the addressee is socially equal to the speaker. This prediction seems also to be borne out.

Consider, next, the distinction between the polite and hyperpolite styles. This distinction correlates with the difference in the degree of politeness and

[49]Sentence (127) is, of course, interpretable in other ways, but here we shall only consider the interpretation in which the unrealized subject refers to the second person.

[50]Sentence (128b) may be an acceptable sentence if its subject is a third person who is socially superior to both the speaker and the addressee.

is of the same nature as the distinction between (128a) and (128c), except that the former distinction is not reflected in the absence or presence of a subject honorific form. Rather, the hyperpolite style is characterized by the use of special suppletive forms like *gozai-*, the beautificative use of the honorific prefix on nouns (see Section 7), the appropriate choice of personal pseudo-pronouns, and so on. Cf. the contrast in:

(129)

a. { *Boku* / *Watasi* / ?*Watakusi* } *wa gakusei da.*

'I am a student.'

b. { *Boku* / *Watasi* / *Watakusi* } *wa gakusei* ***des**-u.*

c. { ?**Boku* / *Watasi* / *Watakusi* } *wa gakusei de* ***gozai-mas**-u.*

Note that most lexical items are neutral as to the speech level of the construction in which they are employed. Thus, there are no special polite-style or hyperpolite-style forms for the thematic particle *wa*, and the same form occurs at any of the three speech levels. Diagrammatically, it appears as in Table 3.

(130) **TABLE 3**

Items	Speech Levels		
	Plain	Polite	Hyperpolite
Neutral items	OK	OK	OK
Items characteristic of polite style	*	OK	OK
Items characteristic of hyperpolite style	*	*	OK

I have discussed the INTERNAL difference between the polite and the hyperpolite styles. Now, consider the EXTERNAL difference between the two categories. Here, we will discuss three points. First, in actual speech situations we often encounter occasions in which it is not immediately obvious whether the person to whom the utterance is addressed is socially superior to the speaker. In the case of propositional honorifics, if one is not certain about the social status of the person about whom he talks, he is free to use or not use propositional honorific forms. But in the case of performative honorifics, when one faces such incertitude, the general tendency is to employ the polite-style forms. Thus, when the addressee is a person one does not know, it is safer to talk to him with (125b) or (128a) rather than with (125a) or (127), unless the addressee is obviously inferior to the speaker, e.g., when the addressee is a child or a beggar. Second, the choice of speech levels is determined, to a fairly large extent, by the situation of the utterance. In general, the more formal the situation, the more politeness is expected. Suppose that there are two people who are very close friends. They would talk to each other in the plain style in normal everyday situations. But when they talk to each other on formal occasions, e.g., in a discussion at an annual meeting of an academic society, they will speak in the polite (or even hyperpolite) style. Third, there is an imbalance in the expected degree of politeness of speech between male and female speakers. Briefly, female speakers are expected to speak at a more polite speech level than male speakers. Thus, while a male speaker can talk to his friend in the plain style, a female speaker is expected to talk to her friend in the polite speech, unless they are very close friends. Where a male speaker is expected to speak in the average polite style, a female speaker is expected to speak in the hyperpolite style. This seems to be an influence of the Confucianist tradition and is diminishing in present-day Japanese. On the one hand, female speakers tend to use less polite expressions, and on the other hand, male speakers tend to use more polite expressions. It seems that it would not need a long time to arrive at the stage at which the distinction is totally leveled.

Performative Honorifics and Sentence Embedding

I have stated several times in this chapter that performative honorifics are excluded from some embedding constructions. This statement, though correct, is not sufficiently precise to give an insight into the nature of performative honorifics. Here, I shall discuss the problem in some detail to reveal the peculiarities of honorifics of this class. Embedding constructions are, in general, classifiable into three categories: complements, relative clauses, and conjunctions or adverbial clauses. These categories will be discussed in that order.

Complements

I have already noted (in Section 8) that performative honorifics are excluded from most of the complement constructions. The only exceptions that were mentioned are direct discourse *to* complements. It seems, however, that nondirect discourse complements may contain performative honorifics if they are factive complements. Compare (131) and (132):

(131) a. *Hon-zitu kaku mo oozei no kata-gata ni go-sankai itadaki-*
this day so many people come receive

masi-*ta koto wa, makoto ni ari-gata-i koto de gozai-mas-u.*
truly be hard
'I do appreciate it that so many people have gathered here today.'

b. *Yamada kun ga kono tabi Nooberu-syoo o zyuyo-sare-*
this time Nobel-prize give
masi-*ta koto wa mina-sama go-zonzi to omoi-mas-u.*
all know
'I think you all know that Mr. Yamada was given the Nobel Prize lately.'

(132) a. **Ano kata wa hon-zitu wa go-kesseki* ***des***-*u to omoi-mas-u.*
absent
'I think that he is absent today.'

b. **Suzuki san ga o-ide ni nat-te i-****mas***-*u ka doo ka go-zonzi des-u ka?*
'Do you know whether Mr. Suzuki is here?'

Relative Clauses

Performative honorifics may also occur in relative clauses, though apparently only in the hyperpolite style:

(133) a. *(Watasi ga) sono toki kaki-****masi***-*ta hon wa mattaku ur-e-*
at all sell
mase-n desi-ta.
not
'The book I wrote at that time didn't sell at all.'

b. *Sensei ga o-ai ni nari-****masi***-*ta kata to iu no wa donata*
see who
des-yoo ka?
'Who is it that you saw?'

c. *Atira ni mie-****mas***-*u yama ga Huzi-san de gozai-mas-u.*
there be seen mountain Mt. Fuji
'You can see Mt. Fuji over there.'

This seems possible, however, only in cases in which the NP to which the relative clause is adjoined has a specific referent. In the preceding examples, the environments give sufficient information about the specificity of the NPs in question. Cf. examples like:

(134) *Watasi wa mizu- tama- moyoo no ari-****mas***-*u kami ga hosi-i to*
water-circle-design paper want
omoi-mas-u.
'I want the paper with polka dots.'

This sentence is not ambiguous, though its nonhonorific version is:

(135) *Watasi wa mizu-tama-moyoo no ar-u kami ga hosi-i to omo-u.*
'I want (the) paper with polka dots.'

Sentence (134) does not have the interpretation in which the pertinent NP is understood as nonspecific, i.e., in the sense that any sheet of paper is OK if it has polka dots on it. Rather, the sentence means that of the sheets of paper (which the speaker has presumably been shown), only the one with polka dots satisfies his desire.

CONJUNCTIONS AND ADVERBIAL CLAUSES

In Japanese, both conjunctions and adverbial clauses occur in the following configuration:

(136)

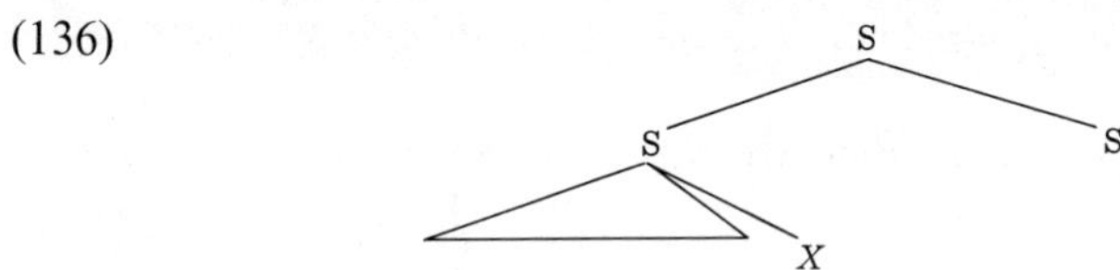

where *X* is an element characteristic of the construction. In conjunction constructions, *X* may be *si* (e.g., in *kai-ta si*), *-te* (e.g., in *kai-te*), or the infinitival ending (e.g., in *kaki*). In adverbial clauses, *X* is realized as a 'conjunctive particle', which corresponds to a 'conjunction' in English (e.g., *though*, *because*, etc.).

These constructions all allow performative honorifics to occur in the subordinate position.[51] Consider:

(137) a. *Kesa wa ame ga huri-**masi**-ta si, samu-i tenki desi-ta.*
this morning rain fall cold weather
'This morning, it rained, and it was cold, too.'

b. *Kesa Ueno Doobutu-en ni iki-**masi**-te sukosi sanpo o si-te mairi-masi-ta.*
zoological garden a little take a walk
'This morning I went to the Ueno Zoo and took a short walk.'

c. *Ii tenki **desi**-ta keredo, sukosi atu-sugi-ta no de, nodo ga kawaki-masi-ta.*
though hot throat become dry
'It was a fine day, but it was a bit too warm and I got thirsty.'

[51]Except the infinitival construction. I do not know how this should be accounted for.

d. *Hima* ***desi****-ta kara Ginza ni iki-masi-ta.*
free
'I went over to the Ginza Street because I had nothing to do.'

SUMMARY

We have seen that performative honorifics may appear in an embedded sentence, provided that it is one of the following constructions:

1. direct discourse complement
2. factive complement
3. nonrestrictive relative clause
4. conjunct clause
5. adverbial subordinate clause

The basic feature shared by all these constructions seems to be that they are more or less independent from the main clause. How this independence should be reflected in the grammatical account of such constructions is not entirely transparent, but it is quite interesting to note that for each of them one can argue for an underlying configuration in which the superficially embedded clause is quasi-conjoined, as in the diagram in (136). This is surely a very plausible way to explain the asymmetry in the distribution of performative honorifics, but I think it is still premature to draw any definitive conclusion here, for we do not yet know what the alternative accounts might look like.[52]

Performative Honorifics and the Performative Analysis

A linguistically sophisticated reader might suspect that I would try to account for the occurrences of performative honorifics in terms of the 'performative analysis', proposed by Ross (1970), according to which almost all the sentences are derived from underlying structures that contain such superordinate clauses as *I say to you* ..., *I request it of you* ..., and *I request it of you that you tell me* ..., which are obligatorily deleted in the course of the derivation.

If one subscribes to that analysis, he will naturally arrive at the conclusion that there actually is no such separate grammatical processes as 'performative honorification', for this would be but a special instance of object (propositional) honorification, this time applied to the superordinate performative clause. Consider, for instance, the following sentence:

[52]See Tagashira (1973) for an interesting attempt to account for this fact.

(138) *Taroo ga sini-masi-ta.*
die
'Taro's dead.'

The performative analysis demands that its underlying structure be something like as follows:

(139)

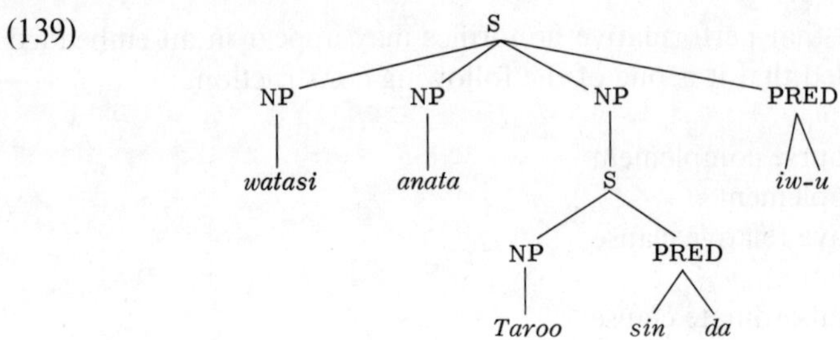

When the indirect object, which is in the second person, is an SSS, the topmost predicate is made into an object honorific. At the stage of the derivation in which the topmost clause is wiped out by the transformation called 'performative deletion', the extra information about object honorificness remains, and is finally realized by the auxiliary *mas*.

Though the line of argument just sketched is quite attractive, it does not seem persuasive to me. This is primarily because the conditions on performative honorifics are slightly, though significantly, different from those on object honorifics. For one example, note that in the former the addressee may be equal to the speaker in social status, though in the latter the object NP cannot be socially equal to the speaker (cf. the discussion at the beginning of Section 9).

If we have an independent piece of evidence for the performative analysis, we can, of course, use this as evidence for treating performative honorifics in that fashion, but the reverse is not the case. In brief, the properties of performative honorifics are not of primary relevance to arguments for the performative analysis.

10. FINAL REMARKS

I do not pretend that this chapter has covered everything that has to be said about the complex system of Japanese honorification. My purpose here has been simply to give the reader the first clue to what it is all about. If I am successful in so doing, you must have seen that at least propositional honorifications in Japanese are basically quite mechanical and automatic. Various topics remain untouched in the present chapter. The most important ones are (1) subject honorification by means of *rare*-suffixation and (2) the syntax of giving and receiving verbs, which play an important role in the formation of request sentences.

I have also avoided reference to earlier transformational accounts of Japanese honorification, namely, Prideaux (1970) and Makino (1970). This omission was rather intentional. In the first place, my analysis of Japanese honorification was shaped quite independently of either of these works. Second, neither of these works has proven to be useful in revising my original 1970 analysis. The failure of these works seems to me to stem from the fact that both of them try to incorporate the evaluation of politeness into the grammatical account of honorifics. Prideaux (1970), for example, assigns inherent politeness features to each noun in the sentence, and treats the honorification processes on predicates essentially as agreement rules. As I argued in Section 8 of this chapter, however, the grammatical aspect of honorification is independent of the evaluation of politeness, though the latter is partly dependent on the former. I have therefore tried to separate these two aspects of honorification, with emphasis on the grammatical aspect. The need for much deeper studies is obvious, and I hope that the present chapter will be of some help to future studies on the same topic.

ACKNOWLEDGMENTS

This chapter is a revised and simplified version of my B.A. thesis, "A study of Japanese honorification," University of Tokyo, 1970. I am grateful to Osamu Fujimura for his constant advice and encouragement as my thesis supervisor. My gratitude is also due to Masayoshi Shibatani, who invited me to write this chapter. Kazuko I. Harada has assisted me both as a typist and as a colleague, and I am deeply indebted to her for her patient assistance and encouragement. The errors that will probably be found in this chapter are entirely my own.

BIBLIOGRAPHY

Akatsuka, Noriko (McCawley). NP movement in Japanese. M.A. thesis, University of Illinois, Urbana, Ill., 1969.

Akatsuka, Noriko (McCawley). Psych movement in Japanese and some crucially related syntactic phenomena. *Working Papers in Linguistics*. Ohio State University, 1971, **10**; 8–34.

Akatsuka, Noriko (McCawley). Emotive verbs in English and Japanese. In G. Green (Ed.), *Studies in Linguistic Sciences*. Vol. 2 Urbana, Ill.: University of Illinois, 1972. pp. 1–15.

Alfonso, Anthony. *Japanese language patterns: A structural approach*. Tokyo: Sophia University, 1966.

Alfonso, Anthony. On the "adversative" passive. *Journal-Newsletter of the Association of Teachers of Japanese*, 1971, **7**, 1–7.

Anderson, Stephen. West Scandinavian vowel systems and ordering of phonological rules. Ph.D. dissertation, MIT, Cambridge, Mass., 1970.

Anderson, Stephen, and Kiparsky, Paul. *Festschrift for Morris Halle*. New York: Holt, 1973.

Arnauld, Antoine, and Nicole, P. *The art of thinking: Port-Royal logic*. [1662] Trans. James Dickoff and Patricia James. Indianapolis: Bobbs-Merrill, 1964.

Austin, John L. *How to do things with words*. Cambridge, Mass.: Harvard University Press, 1962.

Baker, C. L. Double negatives. *Linguistic Inquiry*, 1970, **1**, 169–186.

Berko, Jean. The child's learning of English morphology. *Word*, 1958, **14**, 2–3, 150–177.

Berman, Arlene. Adjectives and adjective complement constructions in English. Ph.D. dissertation, Harvard University, Cambridge, Mass., 1973.

Berman, Arlene, and Szamosi, Michael. Observations on sentential stress. *Language*, 1972, **48**, 304–327.

Bloch, Bernard. Studies in colloquial Japanese. III: Derivation of inflected words. *Journal of the American Oriental Society*, 1946, **66**, 304–315.

Bloomfield, Leonard. *Language*. New York: Holt, 1933.

Borkin, Ann. Polarity items in question. In D. Adams, M. A. Cambell, V. Cohen, J. Lovins, E. Maxwell, C. Nygren, and J. Reighard (Eds.), *Papers from the Seventh Regional Meeting of the Chicago Linguistic Society*. Chicago: University of Chicago Department of Linguistics, 1971. Pp. 53–62.

Brown, R. and Ford, M. Address in American English. In D. H. Hymes, (Ed.), *Language in culture and society*. New York: Harper, 1961. Pp. 234–244.

Brown, R. and Gilman, W. A. The pronouns of power and solidarity. In T. A. Sebeok (Ed.), *Style and language*. New York: Wiley, 1960. Pp. 253–276.

Chomsky, Noam. *Current issues in linguistics*. The Hague: Mouton, 1964.

Chomsky, Noam. *Aspects of the theory of syntax*. Cambridge, Mass.: MIT Press, 1965.

Chomsky, Noam. *Cartesian linguistics*. New York: Harper, 1966.

Chomsky, Noam. *Language and mind.* New York: Harcourt, 1968.

Chomsky, Noam. Remarks on nominalization. In R. Jacobs and P. Rosenbaum (Eds.), *Readings in English transformational grammar*. Waltham, Mass.: Ginn, 1970. Pp. 184–221.

Chomsky, Noam. Deep structure, surface structure, and semantic interpretation. In R. Jakobson and S. Kawamoto (Eds.), *Studies in general and oriental linguistics*. Tokyo: TEC Co., 1971. Pp. 52–91.

Chomsky, Noam. Conditions on transformations. In S. Anderson, and P. Kiparsky (Eds.), *Festschrift for Morris Halle*. New York: Holt, 1973. Pp. 232–286.

Dixon, R. M. W. A method of semantic description. In D. Steinberg, and L. Jakobovits (Eds.), *Semantics: An interdisciplinary reader in philosophy, linguistics, and psychology*. New York: Cambridge University Press, 1971. Pp. 436–471.

Dunn, C. J., and Yanada, S. *Teach yourself Japanese*. London: English University Press, 1958.

Elisseeff, E., Reischauer, E. O., and Yoshihashi, T. *Elementary Japanese for college students*. Part II. Cambridge, Mass.: Harvard University Press, 1944.

Elliot, Dale. The grammar of emotive and exclamatory sentences in English. *Working Papers in Linguistics*, Ohio State University, 1971, **8**, 1–110.

Emonds, Joseph. Root and structure-preserving transformations. Ph.D. dissertation, MIT, Cambridge, Mass., 1970.

Fillmore, Charles J. The case for case. In E. Bach and R. Harms (Eds.), *Universals in linguistic theory*. New York: Holt, 1968. Pp. 1–89.

Fillmore, Charles J. Types of lexical information. In D. Steinberg, and L. Jakobovits (Eds.), *Semantics: An interdisciplinary reader in philosophy, linguistics, and psychology*. New York: Cambridge University Press, 1971. Pp. 370–392. (a)

Fillmore, Charles J. Space. Notes from lectures at the Summer Program in Linguistics, University of California, Santa Cruz, 1971. (b)

Fillmore, Charles J. Time. Notes from lectures at the Summer Program in Linguistics, University of California, Santa Cruz, 1971. (c)

Fodor, Jerry A. Three reasons for not deriving "kill" from "cause to die." *Linguistic Inquiry*, 1970, **1**, 429–438.

Geach, Peter T. Subject and predicate. *Mind*, 1950, **LIX**, 461–482.

Geer, Sandra, Gleitman, Henry, and Gleitman, Lila. Paraphrasing and remembering compound words. *Journal of Verbal Learning and Verbal Behavior*, 1972, **11**, 348–355.

Geis, Michael L., and Zwicky, Arnold M. On invited inferences. *Linguistic Inquiry*, 1971, **2**, 561–566.

Gleason, Henry A. *An introduction to descriptive linguistics*. New York: Holt, 1956.

Gleitman, Lila, and Berheim, Rebecca. The recall of compound nouns. Eastern Pennsylvania Psychiatric Institute, 1967.

Gleitman, Lila, and Gleitman, Henry. *Phrase and paraphrase: Some innovative uses of language*. New York: W. W. Norton, 1970.

Greenberg, Joseph. Some universals of grammar with particular reference to the order of meaningful elements. In J. Greenberg (Ed.), *Universals of Language*. Cambridge, Mass.: MIT Press, 1963. Pp. 73–113.

Gruber, Jeffrey S. Studies in lexical relations. Ph.D. dissertation, MIT, Cambridge, Mass., 1965.

Harada, S. I. A study of Japanese honorification, BA thesis, University of Tokyo, 1970.

Harada, S. I. An ordering paradox involving psych-movement in Japanese. Duplicated, University of Tokyo, 1971.

Harada, S. I. Counter Equi NP Deletion. *Annual Bulletin*, Research Institute of Logopedics and Phoniatrics, University of Tokyo, 1973, **7**, 113–147.

Haraguchi, Shosuke. Remarks on dislocation in Japanese. Unpublished paper, MIT, Cambridge, Mass., 1973.

Hasegawa, Kinsuke. Nihongo bunpoo siron (A sketch of Japanese grammar). *Gengobunka*, 1964, **1**, 3–46.

Hasegawa, Kinsuke. The passive construction in English. *Language*, 1968, **44**, 224–243.

Hashimoto, Shinkichi. *Kokugohoo Kenkyuu*. Tokyo: Iwanami, 1948.

Hayashi, Shiro, and Minami, Fujio (Eds.). *Keigo no Taikei* [*The system of honorifics*]. *Keigo Kooza 1*. Tokyo: Meiji Shoin, 1974. (a)

Hayashi, Shiro, and Minami, Fujio (Eds.). *Sekai no Keigo* [*Honorifics in the world*]. *Keigo Kooza 8*. Tokyo: Meiji Shoin, 1974. (b)

Helke, M. The grammar of English reflexives. Ph.D. dissertation, MIT, Cambridge, Mass., 1971.

Higgins, Francis R. The pseudo-cleft construction in English. Ph.D. dissertation, MIT, Cambridge, Mass., 1973.

Hinds, John V. Some remarks on *soo su-*. *Papers in Japanese Linguistics*, 1973, **2**, 18–30. (a)

Hinds, John V. On the status of the VP node in Japanese. *Language Research*, 1973, **9.2**, 44–57. (b)

Horn, Lawrence R. On the semantic properties of logical operators in English. Ph.D. dissertation, University of California, Los Angeles, 1972.

Householder, Fred W. Review of *The grammar of English nominalizations* by Robert B. Lees. *Word*, 1962, **18**, 326–353.

Householder, Fred W., and Cheng, Robert L. Universe-scope relations in Chinese and Japanese. Mimeographed. Indiana University 1971.

Howard, Irwin. The so-called Japanese passive. Mimeographed. Honolulu: Education Research and Development Center, University of Hawaii, 1968.

Howard, Irwin. A semantic–syntactic analysis of the Japanese passive. *Journal-Newsletter of the Association of Teachers of Japanese*, 1969, **6**, 40–46.

Howard, Irwin, and Niyekawa-Howard, Agnes M. On "picture nouns" in Japanese. *Gengo Kenkyu*, in press.

Howard, Irwin, and Niyekawa-Howard, Agnes M. Semantics of the Japanese passive. Forthcoming. (a)

Howard, Irwin, and Niyekawa-Howard, Agnes M. On the passivization transformation in Japanese. Forthcoming. (b)

Inoue, Kazuko. *A study of Japanese syntax*. The Hague: Mouton, 1969.

Inoue, Kazuko. Henkei bunpoo to nihon-go [Transformational grammar and the Japanese language]. *Eigo Kyoiku*, 1971–1973.

Inoue, Kazuko. The role of the "Case" in a generative grammar. *Studies in Descriptive and Applied Linguistics*, International Christian University, 1972, **V**. Pp. 238–256. (a)

Inoue, Kazuko. *Agent* and *source* in Japanese. *Papers in Japanese Linguistics*, 1972, **1**, 195–217. (b)

Inoue, Kazuko. Self-controllability and self-changeability. *Studies in Descriptive and Applied Linguistics*, International Christian University, 1973, **VI**. Pp. 23–57. (a)

Inoue, Kazuko. Perception verbs and related matters. *Eigobungaku Sekai* [*World of English Literature*], 1973, September number. (b)

Inoue, Kazuko. Experiencer. *Studies in Descriptive and Applied Linguistics*, International Christian University, 1974. Pp. 139–162. (a)

Inoue, Kazuko. Japanese relative clauses. Unpublished. International Christian University 1974. (b)

Iwakura, Kunihiro. A generative–transformational study of negation: A contrastive analysis of Japanese and English. Ph.D. dissertation, Michigan State University, East Lansing, 1973.

Izui, Hisanosuke. *Gengo no Koozoo*. Tokyo: Kinokuniya, 1967.

Jackendoff, Ray S. *Semantic interpretation in generative grammar*. Cambridge, Mass.: MIT Press, 1972.

Jacobs, Roderick A., and Rosenbaum, Peter S. (Eds.). *Readings in English transformational grammar*. Waltham, Mass.: Ginn, 1970.

Jorden, E. H. *Beginning Japanese*. Part II. New Haven, Conn.: Yale University Press, 1963.

Josephs, Lewis S. Selected problems in the analysis of embedded sentences in Japanese. Ph.D. dissertation, Harvard University, Cambridge, Mass., 1972. (a)

Josephs, Lewis S. Phenomena of tense and aspect in Japanese relative clauses. *Language*, 1972, **48**, 109–133. (b)

Kachru, Yamuna. *An introduction to Hindi syntax*. Urbana, Ill.: University of Illinois Linguistics Department, 1966.

Kachru, Yamuna. On the semantics of the causative constructions in Hindi-Urdu. In M. Shibatani (Ed.), *Syntax and semantics: The grammar of causative constructions*. Vol. 6. New York: Academic Press, 1975.

Kajita, Masaru. Problems of relative clauses in a transformational grammar. *Eigokyoiku* [*English Teacher's Journal*], 1968, June and July. (a)

Kajita, Masaru. A generative transformational study of semiauxiliaries in present-day American English. Tokyo: Sanseido, 1968. (b)

Karttunen, Lauri. The logic of English predicate complement constructions. Duplicated. University of Texas 1970. (a)

Karttunen, Lauri. On the semantics of complement sentences. In M. A. Campbell, J. Lindholm, A. Davidson, W. Fisher, L. Furbee, J. Lovins, E. Maxwell, J. Reighard, and S. Straight (Eds.), *Papers from the Sixth Regional Meeting of the Chicago Linguistic Society*. Chicago: University of Chicago Department of Linguistics, 1970. Pp. 328–339. (b)

Kimball, John (Ed.). *Syntax and semantics*. Vol. 1. New York: Seminar Press, 1972.

Kieda, Masuichi. *Kootoo Kokubunpoo Sinkoo* [*New Course in Advanced Japanese Grammar*]. Tokyo: Toyotosho, 1937.

Kindaichi, Haruhiko. Huhenka zyodoosi no honsitu (Essence of uninflected auxiliary verbs). *Gengo Kenkyu*, 1952, **15**, 48–63.

Kiparsky, Paul, and Kiparsky, Carol. Fact. In D. Steinberg and L. Jakobovits (Eds.), *Semantics: An interdisciplinary reader in philosophy, linguistics, and psychology*. New York: Cambridge University Press, 1971. Pp. 345–369.

Kitagawa, Chisato. Expressions of purpose, emotive response, and contrariness to expectation—A study of Japanese *No Ni* constructions. Ph.D. dissertation, University of Michigan, Ann Arbor, 1972.

Kitagawa, Chisato. Case marking and causativization. *Papers in Japanese Linguistics*, 1974, **3**.

Klima, Edward S. Negation in English. In Katz and Fodor (Eds.), *The structures of language*. Englewood Cliffs, N.J.: Prentice-Hall, 1964. Pp. 246–323.

Kneale, William, and Kneale, Martha. *The development of logic*. New York: Oxford University Press (Clarendon), 1962.

Kokuritsu Kokugo Kenkyujo. *Keigo to Keigo-isiki* [*Honorifics and the consciousness of them (by the speaker)*]. Tokyo: Shuei Shuppan, 1957.

Kokuritsu Kokugo Kenkyujo. *Taiguu-hyoogen no Zittai* [*Actual usage of expressions of personal treatment*]. Tokyo: Shuei Shuppan, 1971.

Kuno, Susumu. Notes on Japanese grammar. Mathematical linguistics and automatic translation, Report No. NSF-27. The computation laboratory of Harvard University, Cambridge, Mass., 1970. (= Kuno, 1973)

Kuno, Susumu. The position of locatives in existential sentences. *Linguistic Inquiry*, 1971, **2**, 333–378.

Kuno, Susumu. Pronominalization, reflexivization, and direct discourse. *Linguistic Inquiry*, 1972, **3**, 161–195.

Kuno, Susumu. *The structure of the Japanese Language*. Cambridge, Mass.: MIT Press, 1973.

Kuno, Susumu. The position of relative clauses and conjunctions. *Linguistic Inquiry*, 1974, **4**, 117–136. (a)

Kuno, Susumu. A note on subject raising. *Linguistic Inquiry*, 1974, **5**, 137–144. (b)

Kuno, Susumu. Natural explanation of some linguistic universals. *Linguistic Inquiry*, 1974. (c)

Kuroda, S. -Y. Causative forms in Japanese. *Foundations of Language*, 1965, **1**, 30–50. (a)

Kuroda, S. -Y. Generative grammatical studies in the Japanese language. Ph.D. dissertation, MIT, Cambridge, Mass., 1965. (b)

Kuroda, S. -Y. *Ga*, *O*, oyobi *Ni* ni tuite [Concerning *Ga*, *O*, and *Ni*]. *Kokugogaku*, 1965, **63**, 75–85. (c)

Kuroda, S. -Y. Remarks on the notion of subject with reference to words like *also*, *even*, or *only*. Part 1. *Annual Bulletin*, Institute of Logopedics and Phoniatrics, University of Tokyo, 1969, **3**, 111–129. (a)

Kuroda, S. -Y. Some historical remarks on what might be taken, etc. Mimeographed, University of California, San Diego, 1969. (b)

Kuroda, S. -Y. The categorical and the thetic judgement: Evidence from Japanese syntax. *Foundations of Language*, 1972, **9**, 153–185.

Kuroda, S. -Y. Where epistemology, style, and grammar meet. In S. Anderson and P. Kiparsky (Eds.), *Festschrift for Morris Halle*. New York: Holt, 1973. (a)

Kuroda, S. -Y. On Kuno's direct discourse analysis of the Japanese reflexive *zibun*. *Papers in Japanese Linguistics*, 1973, **2**, 136–147. (b)

Kusanagi, Yutaka. Time focus within the Japanese tense system. *Papers in Japanese Linguistics*, 1972, **1**, 52–68.

Lakoff, George. *On the nature of syntactic irregularity*. Report No. NSF-16. Cambridge, Mass.: Harvard University Computation Lab. [=Lakoff, George (1970a)]

Lakoff, George. *Irregularity in syntax*. New York: Holt, 1970. (a)

Lakoff, George. Linguistics and natural logic. *Synthese*, 1970, **22**, 151–271. (b)

Lakoff, George. Arbitrary basis of transformational grammar. *Language*, 1973, **48**, 76–87.

Lakoff, George. Pragmatic constraints on lexical items. Paper delivered at the University of Southern California Causative Festival, Los Angeles, May 4, 1974.

Lakoff, George, and Ross, John R. A note on anaphoric islands and causatives. *Linguistic Inquiry*, 1972, **3**, 121–125.

Lakoff, George, Perlmutter, David, and Ross, John R. Why are negatives like factive predicates? Unpublished manuscript. MIT, 1970.

Lakoff, Robin T. A syntactic argument for negative transportation. In R. I. Binnick, A. Davison, G. M. Green, and J. L. Morgan (Eds.), *Papers from the Fifth Regional Meeting of the Chicago Linguistic Society*. Chicago: University of Chicago Department of Linguistics, 1969. Pp. 140–147. (a)

Lakoff, Robin T. Some reasons why there can't be any *some–any* rule. *Language*, 1969, **45**, 608–615. (b)

Lalande, André. *Vocabulaire Technique et Critique de la Philosophie*. Paris: Presses Universitaires de France, 1968.

Lancelot, Claude, and Arnauld, A. *Grammaire Générale et Raisonnée*. 1660. 2d ed. 1664. (Available in photostatic reprint, Scolar Press, 1967.)

Langacker, Ronald W. On pronominalization and the chain of command. In D. A. Reibel and S. A. Schane (Eds.), *Modern studies in English*. Englewood Cliffs, N.J.: Prentice-Hall, 1969. Pp. 160–186.

Leech, Geoffrey N. *Meaning and the English verb*. London: Longman, 1971.

Lee, Gregory. Subjects and agents: II. *Working Papers in Linguistics*, Ohio State University, 1971, **7**, L1–L118. (a)

Lee, Gregory. Notes in defense of case grammar. In D. Adams, M. A. Campbell, V. Cohen, J. Lovins, E. Maxwell, C. Nygren, and J. Reighard (Eds.), *Papers from the Seventh Regional Meeting of the Chicago Linguistic Society*. Chicago: University of Chicago Department of Linguistics, 1971. Pp. 174–180. (b)

Lees, Robert B. *The grammar of English nominalizations*. The Hague: Mouton, 1960.

Lees, Robert B. Problems in the grammatical analysis of English nominal compounds. In M. Bierwisch and K. Heidolph (Eds.), *Progress in linguistics*. The Hague: Mouton, 1970. Pp. 17–186.

Lees, Robert B., and Klima, Edward S. Rules for English pronominalization, *Language*, 1963 (Jan.–Mar.).

Lyons, John. *Introduction to theoretical linguistics*. New York: Cambridge University Press, 1968.

Makino, Seiichi. Some aspects of Japanese nominalizations. Ph.D. dissertation, University of Illinois, Urbana, 1968. (Published by, Tokyo: Tokai Daigaku Press, 1970.)

Makino, Seiichi. Two proposals about Japanese polite expressions. In J. M. Sadock and A. L. Vanek (Eds.), *Studies presented to Robert B. Lees by his students*. Edmonton, Canada: Linguistic Research, Inc., 1970. Pp. 163–187.

Makino, Seiichi. Adverbial scope and the passive construction in Japanese. *Papers in Linguistics*, 1972, **5**, 73–98.

Makino, Seiichi. The passive construction in Japanese. In B. B. Kachru, R. B. Lees, Y. Malkiel, A. Pietrangel, and S. Saporta (Eds.), *Papers in linguistics in honor of Henry and Renee Kahane*. Urbana, Ill.: University of Illinois Press, 1973. Pp. 588–605.

Makiuchi, Masaru. A study of some auxiliary verbs in Japanese. Ph.D. dissertation, University of Illinois, Urbana, 1972.

Marchand, Hans. Review of *Affixal negation in English and other languages* by Karl E. Zimmer. *Language*, 1966, **42**, 134–142.

Martin, Samuel E. *Essential Japanese*. (3rd ed.) Tokyo: Tuttle, 1962.

Matsushita, Daizaburo. *Hyoozyun Nihon Koogohoo* [*Standard Japanese Colloquial Usage*]. Tokyo: Hakuteisha, 1930.

McCawley, James D. The role of semantics in a grammar. In E. Bach and R. Harms (Eds.), *Universals in linguistic theory*. New York: Holt, 1968. Pp. 124–169. (a)

McCawley, James D. Lexical insertion in a transformational grammar without deep structure. In B. J. Darden, C-J. N. Bailey, and A. Davidson (Eds.), *Papers from the Fourth Regional Meeting of the Chicago Linguistic Society*. Chicago: University of Chicago Department of Linguistics, 1968. Pp. 71–80. (b)

McCawley, James D. On the deep structure of negative clauses. *Eigo kyoiku*, 1970, **19.6**, 72–75.

McCawley, James D. Prelexical syntax. In R. O'Brien (Ed.), *Monograph series on linguistics: 22nd Annual Round Tab e*. Washington D.C.: Georgetown University, 1971. Pp. 19–33. (a)

McCawley, James D. Tense and time reference in English. In C. J. Fillmore and D. T. Langendoen (Eds.), *Studies in linguistic semantics*. New York: Holt, 1971. Pp. 96–113, (b)

McCawley, James D. Kac and Shibatani on the grammar of killing. In J. Kimball (Ed.), *Syntax and semantics*. Vol. 1. New York: Seminar Press, 1972. Pp. 139–149. (a)

McCawley, James D. An argument for a cycle in Japanese. *Papers in Japanese Linguistics*, 1972, **1**, 69–73. (b)

McCawley, James D. External NPs versus annotated deep structures. *Linguistic Inquiry*, 1973, **4**, 221–240. (a)

McCawley, James D. *Grammar and meaning*. Tokyo: Taishukan, 1973. (b)

McCawley, James D. Syntactic and logical arguments for semantic structures. In O. Fujimura (Ed.), *Three dimensions of linguistic theory* Tokyo: TEC Co., 1973. Pp. 261–376. (c)

McCawley, Noriko Akatsuka. A study of Japanese reflexivization. Ph.D. dissertation, University of Illinois, Urbana, 1972. (a)

McCawley, Noriko Akatsuka. On the treatment of Japanese passives. In P. M. Peranteau, J. N. Levi, and G. C. Phares (Eds.), *Papers from the Eighth Regional Meeting of the Chicago Linguistic Society*. Chicago: University of Chicago Department of Linguistics, 1972. Pp. 256–270. (b)

Mikami, Akira. *Zoo wa hana ga nagai*. Tokyo: Kuroshio, 1960.

Mikami, Akira. *Gendai gohoo zyosetu*. Tokyo: Kuroshio, 1972.

Muraki, Masatake. Presupposition, pseudo-clefting and thematization. Ph.D. dissertation, University of Texas, Austin, 1970.

Nakau, Minoru. *Sentential complementation in Japanese*. Tokyo: Kaitakusha, 1973.

Niyekawa (-Howard), Agnes M. A study of second language learning: The influence of first language on perception, cognition and second language learning—a test of the Whorfian hypothesis. Mimeographed. Honolulu: Education Research and Development Center, University of Hawaii, 1968. (a)

Niyekawa (-Howard), Agnes M. A psycholinguistic study of the Whorfian hypothesis based on the Japanese passive. Mimeographed. Honolulu: Education Research and Development Center, University of Hawaii, 1968. (b)

Oishi, Hatsutaro. *Tadashii Keigo* [*Correct use of honorifics*]. Tokyo: Oizumi Shoten, 1966.

Ota, Akira. Comparison of English and Japanese, with special reference to tense and aspect. *Working Papers in Linguistics*, University of Hawaii, 1971, **3.4**, 121–164. Also in *Studies in English Linguistics*, 1972, **1**, 30–70.

Ota, Akira. Tense correlations in English and Japanese. *Studies in English Linguistics*, 1973, **2**, 108–121.

Oyakawa, Takatsugu. Japanese reflexivization, 1. *Papers in Japanese Linguistics*, 1973, **2**, 49–135.

Oyakawa, Takatsugu. Japanese reflexivization, 2. *Papers in Japanese Linguistics*, 1974, **3**.

Perlmutter, David. *Deep and surface structure constraints in syntax*. New York: Holt, 1971.

Perlmutter, David. Evidence for the cycle in Japanese. *Annual Bulletin*, Research Institute of Logopedics and Phoniatrics, University of Tokyo, 1973, **7**, 187–210.

Pope, Emily. Questions and answers in English. Ph.D. dissertation, MIT, Cambridge, Mass., 1972.

Postal, Paul M. *Cross-over phenomena*. New York: Holt, 1970. (a)

Postal, Paul M. On the surface verb *remind*. *Linguistic Inquiry*, 1970, **1**, 37–120. (b)

Postal, Paul M. *On raising*. Cambridge, Mass.: MIT Press, 1974.

Prideaux, Gary D. *The syntax of Japanese honorifics*. The Hague: Mouton, 1970.

Reibel, David A., and Schane, Sanford A. (Eds.). *Modern studies in English*. Englewood Cliffs, N.J.: Prentice-Hall, 1969.

Ringen, Catherine. On arguments for rule ordering. *Foundations of Language*, 1972, **8**, 266–278.

Rosenbaum, Peter. The grammar of English predicate complement constructions. Cambridge, Mass.: MIT Press, 1967.

Ross, John R. Constraints on variables in syntax. Ph.D. dissertation, MIT, Cambridge, Mass., 1967.

Ross, John R. A proposed rule of tree-pruning. In D. A. Reibel and S. A. Schane (Eds.), *Modern studies in English*. Englewood Cliffs, N.J.: Prentice-Hall, 1969. Pp. 288–299.

Ross, John R. On declarative sentences. In R. A. Jacobs and P. S. Rosenbaum (Eds.), *Readings in English transformational grammar*. Waltham, Mass.: Ginn, 1970. Pp. 222–272.

Ross, John R. Primacy. MIT, in press.

Schachter, Paul. Review of *The grammar of English nominalizations* by Robert B. Lees. *International Journal of American Linguistics*, 1962, **28**, 134–145.

Shibatani, Masayoshi. Three reasons for not deriving "kill" from "cause to die" in Japanese. In J. Kimball (Ed.), *Syntax and semantics*. Vol. 1. New York: Seminar Press, 1972. Pp. 125–138. (a)

Shibatani, Masayoshi. Remarks on the controversy over the Japanese passive. *Papers in Japanese Linguistics*, 1972, **1**, 145–166. (b)

Shibatani, Masayoshi. Lakoff and Ross on the anaphoric island constraint. Paper read before the Annual Meeting of the Linguistic Society of America, Atlanta, Ga., 1972. (c)

Shibatani, Masayoshi. Semantics of Japanese causativization. *Foundations of Language*, 1973, **9**, 327–373. (a)

Shibatani, Masayoshi. Where morphology and syntax clash: A case in Japanese aspectual verbs. *Gengo kenkyu*, 1973, **64**, 65–96. (b)

Shibatani, Masayoshi. Lexical versus periphrastic causatives in Korean. *Journal of Linguistics*, 1973, **9**, 209–383. (c)

Shibatani, Masayoshi. A linguistic study of causative constructions. Ph.D. dissertation, University of California, Berkeley, 1973. (d)

Shibatani, Masayoshi. The grammar of causative constructions: A conspectus. In M. Shibatani (Ed.), *Syntax and semantics: The grammar of causative constructions*. Vol. 6. New York: Academic Press, 1975. (a)

Shibatani, Masayoshi (Ed.). *Syntax and semantics: The grammar of causative constructions*. Vol. 6. New York: Academic Press, 1975. (b)

Smith, Carlota. Determiners and relative clauses in generative grammar of English. *Language*, 1964, **40**, 37–52.

Smith, Donald L. A study of Japanese sentence complement constructions. Ph.D. dissertation, University of Michigan, Ann Arbor, 1970.

Smith, Steven B. Meaning and negation. Ph.D. dissertation, University of California, Los Angeles, 1970.

Soga, Matsuo. Some syntactic rules of modern colloquial Japanese. Ph.D. dissertation, Indiana University, Bloomington, 1966.

Soga, Matsuo. Similarities between Japanese and English verb derivations. *Lingua*, 1970, **25**, 268–397.

Soga, Matsuo. Negative transportation and cross-linguistic negative evidence. *Papers in Japanese Linguistics*, 1972, **1**, 103–119.

Steinberg, Danny, and Jakobovits, Leon (Eds.). *Semantics: An interdisciplinary reader in philosophy, linguistics, and psychology*. New York: Cambridge University Press, 1971.

Strawson, P. *Introduction to logical theory*. London: Metheun, 1964.

Tagashira, Yoshiko. Polite forms in Japanese. In C. Corum, T. C. Smith-Stark, and A. Weiser (Eds.), *You take the high node and I'll take the low node*. Chicago: Chicago Linguistic Society, 1973. Pp. 121–134.

Taylor, Harvey M. *Case in Japanese*. South Orange, N.J.: Seton Hall University Press, 1971.

Teramura, Hideo. The syntax of noun modification in Japanese. *Journal-Newsletter of the Association of Teachers of Japanese*, 1971, 64–74. (a)

Teramura, Hideo. *-Ta* no imi to kinoo—*aspect, tense, mood* no koobunteki itizuke [The aspectual, temporal, and modal functions of *-ta*]. *Gengogaku to Nihongo-mondai* [*Linguistics and the problems of Japanese, in memory of Professor T. Iwakura's retirement*] Tokyo: Kuroshio, 1971. Pp. 24–89. (b)

Uyeno, Tazuko. A study of Japanese modality: A performative analysis of sentence particles. Ph.D. Dissertation, University of Michigan, Ann Arbor, 1971.

Vendler, Zeno. *Linguistics in philosophy*. Ithaca, N.Y.: Cornell University Press, 1967.

Watanabe, K. Japanese complementizers. In G. Bedell (Ed.), *Studies in East Asian syntax: UCLA Papers in Syntax* No. 3, 1972, 87–133.

Weinberg, Harry L. *Levels of knowing and existing*. New York: Harper, 1959.

Weinreich, Uriel. On the semantic structure of language. In J. Greenberg (Ed.), *Universals of language*. Cambridge, Mass.: MIT Press, 1963.

Yang, In-Seok. *Korean syntax*. Seoul: Paek Hap Sa, 1972.

Zimmer, Karl E. Some general observations about nominal compounds. *Working Papers on Language Universals*, Stanford University, 1971, **5**, 1–21.

Zimmer, Karl E. Appropriateness conditions for nominal compounds. *Working Papers on Language Universals*, Stanford University, 1972, **8**, 4–20.

INDEX

F

G

H

I

J

K

L

M

N

O

P

Q

R

S

T

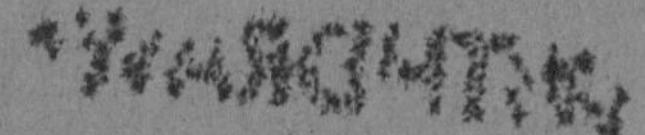